Homicidal Ecologies

Why has violence spiked in Latin America's contemporary democracies? What explains its temporal and spatial variation? Analyzing the region's uneven homicide levels, this book maps out a theoretical agenda focusing on three intersecting factors: the changing geography of transnational illicit political economies, the varied capacity and complicity of state institutions tasked with providing law and order, and organizational competition to control illicit territorial enclaves. These three factors inform the emergence of "homicidal ecologies" (subnational regions most susceptible to violence) in Latin America. After focusing on the contemporary causes of homicidal violence, the book analyzes the comparative historical origins of the state's weak and complicit public security forces and the rare moments in which successful institutional reform takes place. The evaluation of regional trends in Latin America is followed by the presentation of original case studies from Central America, which claims among the highest homicide rates in the world.

Deborah J. Yashar is Professor of Politics & International Affairs at Princeton University. She is lead editor of *World Politics*, co-chair of SSRC's Anxieties of Democracy project, and a series editor for Cambridge Studies in Contentious Politics. She is the author of *Demanding Democracy* (1997) and *Contesting Citizenship* (2005), as well as co-editor of *Parties, Movements, and Democracy in the Developing World* with Nancy Bermeo (2016) and *States in the Developing World* with Miguel Centeno and Atul Kohli (2017), both with Cambridge University Press. She is the recipient of Fulbright, USIP, and other awards.

Cambridge Studies in Comparative Politics

General Editors
Kathleen Thelen *Massachusetts Institute of Technology*
Erik Wibbels *Duke University*

Associate Editors
Catherine Boone *London School of Economics*
Thad Dunning *University of California, Berkeley*
Anna Grzymala-Busse *Stanford University*
Torben Iversen *Harvard University*
Stathis Kalyvas *Yale University*
Margaret Levi *Stanford University*
Helen Milner *Princeton University*
Frances Rosenbluth *Yale University*
Susan Stokes *Yale University*
Tariq Thachil *Vanderbilt University*

Series Founder
Peter Lange *Duke University*

Other Books in the Series
Christopher Adolph, *Bankers, Bureaucrats, and Central Bank Politics: The Myth of Neutrality*
Michael Albertus, *Autocracy and Redistribution: The Politics of Land Reform*
Santiago Anria, *When Movements Become Parties: The Bolivian MAS in Comparative Perspective*
Ben W. Ansell, *From the Ballot to the Blackboard: The Redistributive Political Economy of Education*
Ben W. Ansell, David J. Samuels, *Inequality and Democratization: An Elite-Competition Approach*
Ana Arjona, *Rebolocracy*

Homicidal Ecologies

*Illicit Economies and Complicit States
in Latin America*

DEBORAH J. YASHAR
Princeton University

CAMBRIDGE
UNIVERSITY PRESS

University Printing House, Cambridge CB2 8BS, United Kingdom

One Liberty Plaza, 20th Floor, New York, NY 10006, USA

477 Williamstown Road, Port Melbourne, VIC 3207, Australia

314–321, 3rd Floor, Plot 3, Splendor Forum, Jasola District Centre,
New Delhi – 110025, India

79 Anson Road, #06–04/06, Singapore 079906

Cambridge University Press is part of the University of Cambridge.

It furthers the University's mission by disseminating knowledge in the pursuit of education, learning, and research at the highest international levels of excellence.

www.cambridge.org
Information on this title: http://www.cambridge.org/9781107178472
DOI: 10.1017/9781316823705

© Deborah J. Yashar 2018

This publication is in copyright. Subject to statutory exception and to the provisions of relevant collective licensing agreements, no reproduction of any part may take place without the written permission of Cambridge University Press.

First published 2018

Printed in the United States of America by Sheridan Books, Inc.

A catalogue record for this publication is available from the British Library.

Library of Congress Cataloging-in-Publication Data
NAMES: Yashar, Deborah J., 1963– author.
TITLE: Homicidal ecologies : violence after war and dictatorship in Latin America / Deborah Yashar, Princeton University.
OTHER TITLES: Violence after war and dictatorship in Latin America
DESCRIPTION: Cambridge ; New York, NY : Cambridge University Press, [2018] | Series: Cambridge studies in comparative politics | Includes bibliographical references and index.
IDENTIFIERS: LCCN 2018017040 | ISBN 9781107178472 (alk. paper)
SUBJECTS: LCSH: Violence – Central America. | Violence – Political aspects – Central America. | Civil war – Social aspects – Central America. | Crime – Economic aspects – Central America. | Central America – Social conditions. | Democratization – Latin America. | Democracy – Latin America.
CLASSIFICATION: LCC HN125.2.V5 Y37 2018 | DDC 303.6098–dc23
LC record available at https://lccn.loc.gov/2018017040

ISBN 978-1-107-17847-2 Hardback
ISBN 978-1-316-62965-9 Paperback

Cambridge University Press has no responsibility for the persistence or accuracy of URLs for external or third-party internet websites referred to in this publication and does not guarantee that any content on such websites is, or will remain, accurate or appropriate.

For Sarah and Rebecca

Contents

List of Figures and Tables	*page* x
Acknowledgments	xiii

PART I INTRODUCTION — 1

1 Violence in Third Wave Democracies — 3
    Violence: Empirical Trends — 5
    Research Design — 15
    The Argument and Book Outline — 18
    Appendix: Homicide Rates in the Americas, 1995–2014 — 22

2 Engaging the Theoretical Debate and Alternative Arguments — 24
    Political Transitions: Civil Wars and Democratization — 25
    Sociological Arguments — 36
    Economic Incentives and Violence — 44
    Historical Institutional Legacies of State Formation — 55
    Conclusion — 59
    Appendix: Homicide Rates and Gini Coefficients in Latin America — 61

PART II THE ARGUMENT ABOUT HOMICIDAL ECOLOGIES — 63

3 Illicit Economies and Territorial Enclaves: The Transnational Context and Domestic Footprint — 65
    Forefronting and Conceptualizing the Illicit — 66
    Latin America's Illicit Economies and Organizations: Drugs, Organized Crime, and Gangs — 72
    Conclusion — 98

4	State Capacity and Organizational Competition: Strategic Calculations about Territory and Violence	100
	States and State Capacity: Shaping Calculations about Illicit Geographies	101
	Organizational Territorial Competition: The Micro-Mechanisms of Violence	119
	Conclusion	131
	Appendix: Alternative State Capacity Data for Rule of Law and Corruption	133

PART III DIVERGENT TRAJECTORIES: THREE POST-CIVIL WAR CASES — 145

5	High Violence in Post-Civil War Guatemala	149
	Violence Patterns	152
	State Capacity: Weak Law and Order	155
	Illicit Actors, Political Economies, and Organizational Territorial Competition	176
	Conclusion	199
	Appendix: Newspaper Violence Database: Guatemalan Patterns	201
6	High Violence in Post-Civil War El Salvador	208
	State Capacity: Weak Law and Order	212
	Illicit Actors, Organizational Territorial Competition, and Violence	235
	Conclusion	273
	Appendix: Newspaper Violence Database: Salvadoran Patterns	275
7	Circumscribing Violence in Post-Civil War Nicaragua	279
	Forging a More Capacious Set of Law-and-Order Institutions	282
	Violence and the Illicit in Nicaragua	312
	Coda	334
	Appendix: Homicide Rates by Nicaraguan Department	338

	PART IV LOOKING BACKWARD AND FORWARD	339
8	Concluding with States	341
	Revisiting States and Violence	343
	Territories Big and Small: Policing National Boundaries and Subnational Enclaves	357
	Policy Implications and Future Research	362
	Conclusion	368
Bibliography		371
Index		399

Figures and Tables

FIGURES

1.1	Homicide rates in the Americas per 100,000 (1995–2014, per WHO/PAHO)	page 9
1.2	Homicide rates in the Americas per 100,000 (2000–2012, per UNODC)	10
1.3	Homicide rates in Latin America per 100,000 (2010, per WHO PAHO and UNODC)	11
1.4	Central America's homicide rates by subnational area	17
1.5	The argument	20
2.1	Map of Guatemala: departmental homicide rates (2004)	31
2.2	Social investment in young people in Latin America (2012)	40
2.3	Average wage and unemployment in Latin American countries in the 2000s	41
2.4	Homicide rates and Gini coefficients in Latin America, five-year averages (1997–2013)	50
2.5	Homicide rates and Gini coefficients in Latin America, annual patterns (1999–2013)	61
3.1	Cocaine seizures in Central America, the Caribbean, and Mexico	82
3.2	Main global cocaine flows (2008)	84
4.1	Number of primary cocaine movements destined for or interdicted in selected Central American countries and Mexico (2000–2011)	105
4.2	Stylized calculation by drug trafficking organizations	107
4.3	Conviction rates by country for adult citizens in Central America and Mexico (2003–2013, rate per 100,000 for all crimes)	113
4.4	Perceptions of police (2000 and 2011)	115
4.5	Belief that police are involved in crime (2004–2014)	116

4.6	The argument	132
4.7	Rule of law in Latin America (2009)	135
4.8	Distrust of police (1996–2016)	138
4.9	Indicators of corruption (2009)	142
5.1	Homicide rates in the Americas (1995–2014)	151
5.2	Homicide rates in northern Central America (2000–2012)	151
5.3	Guatemala: regional homicide levels, per 100,000 (1994, 1998, 2002, 2004)	153
5.4	Comparing geographies in Guatemala: homicide rates, organized crime groups, and prime drug trade routes	179
6.1	Homicide rates in El Salvador (1999–2015, rate per 100,000 population)	210
6.2	Homicide rates in Salvadoran departments (1999–2013, rate per 100,000)	211
6.3	Trust in Salvadoran institutions (2012 and 2004–2016)	225
6.4	Perceptions of insecurity in the Americas (2012 and 2004–2016)	226
6.5	Comparative homicide data by Salvadoran department (1965–2013)	242
6.6	Map of El Salvador's cocaine trafficking routes	260
6.7	El Salvador's subnational per capita homicide rates (2006)	268
7.1	Social indicators in Central America (early 2000s)	280
7.2	What is the most important issue facing your country in 2010?	281
7.3	Belief in Latin America that police are involved in crime (2004–2014)	308
7.4	Criminal cases filed and solved by Nicaraguan police (1997–2014)	311
7.5	Homicide rates in Nicaragua (1997–2013, per 100,000)	312
7.6	Nicaraguan police data on homicides (2000–2014, rates per 100,000)	314
7.7	Percentage identifying crime as the most important problem (2004–2014, Central America and other high-violence cases in Latin America, excluding Colombia)	316
7.8	Gangs in Central America (early 2000s)	318
7.9	Interdiction of cocaine in Nicaragua, reported by Nicaraguan police	326
7.10	Trade trafficking routes in Nicaragua, according to Nicaraguan police	328
7.11	Homicide rates in Nicaraguan departments (1998–2014, rate per 100,000 population)	333

TABLES

1.1	National homicide trajectories: stability and levels (1995–2014, based on WHO data)	12
1.2	Homicide rates in the Americas (1995–2014, per 100,000 inhabitants)	22
2.1	National homicide trajectories: stability, levels, and varied experiences with recent civil war (1995–2012)	29
2.2	Firearms owned by civilians in Central America (2007)	30
2.3	Income inequality in Latin American countries (1990–2012)	48
2.4	Inequality and violence rates (combining Tables 1.1 and 2.3)	49
3.1	Conceptualizing ideal-type institutions	71
3.2	Gang members per 100,000 in Central America	92
4.1	Reliability of police services in Latin America	139
4.2	Transnational Institute (TNI) Corruption Perceptions Index, Latin America (1998–2010)	141
4.3	Weak relationship between TNI rankings and levels of violence: a few examples	143
5.1	Firearms owned by civilians in Central America (2007)	204
5.2	Reported homicide patterns in *Prensa Libre,* Guatemala	205
6.1	El Salvador's subnational per capita homicide rates (1999–2006)	267
6.2	Homicide rates in Salvadoran departments (1965–2013, rates per 100,000 population)	270
6.3	Percentage of homicides in El Salvador reported in *La Prensa Gráfica* (2000–2010, newspaper violence database)	275
6.4	Percentage of homicides reported in El Salvador by department in *La Prensa Gráfica* (2000–2010, newspaper violence database)	276
6.5	Homicide characteristics for El Salvador reported in newspaper violence database, *La Prensa Gráfica* (2000, 2010, 2015)	277
7.1	Reliability of police services in Latin America	309
7.2	Perceptions of Central American security and safety (2010)	310
7.3	Technologies of violence reported by press for homicides in Nicaragua (2000, 2005, 2010)	315
7.4	Comparative table of Nicaraguan gangs (*pandillas*)	319
7.5	Homicide rates by Nicaraguan department (1998–2014)	338

Acknowledgments

This project was unexpected. I traveled to Central America over a decade ago to start a new research project about civil wars and the third wave of democratization. I left the field with a sense of urgency about a different topic: the violence that was taking place not before but *after* the democratic transition. Everyone I interviewed politely entertained questions about the past, but they wanted to talk about the violence that was occurring at that moment, in the aftermath of civil wars and military rule. People felt unsafe. They recounted witnessing homicides on street corners, uniformly noted how unsafe it was to take buses, and cautioned against the seeming randomness of violence in poor as well as wealthy urban neighborhoods. Political affiliations no longer seemed like a good predictor of who would become the next target of violence. Homicides were becoming commonplace. The question was why homicides had become so widespread in this period of civilian rule and why homicides were reaching epidemic proportions in some places and not others. There was an urgency to the discussions with colleagues, friends, and acquaintances. I left Central America certain that there was an academic and normative imperative to analyze the violence *after* civil war and dictatorship.

Over the course of the next decade, I worked on this project, hoping that the problem would subside. It did not. While homicide rates saw some variation in Central America, a key comparison remained: violence was rampant in the northern triangle, while it was much more contained in the southern part of the isthmus. Violence rates, moreover, were high or becoming higher in other parts of the region as well – Mexico and Venezuela, in particular. Brazil's homicide rates were always notoriously high and remained quite alarming, particularly once subnational variation was taken into account. Thus, the project started with a focus on Central America but necessarily placed these cases in comparative perspective.

Given the scope of the project, I was fortunate to have a wonderful team of colleagues and research assistants (RAs). A few people were pivotal in helping me plan subsequent forays into the field. I am deeply grateful for the early advice provided by Consuelo Cruz, David Holiday, Rachel Sieder, Elisabeth Wood, and Loly de Zúniga. They helped me identify my first round of interviews, especially when I first started to work on El Salvador and Nicaragua. Loly de Zúniga provided invaluable logistical support in El Salvador, and I thank her for her wonderful assistance so many years ago.

I was invited to participate in two collaborative projects, in which I was able to advance my own thinking about citizenship. I thank Mario Sznajder and Luis Roniger for inviting me as a 2009 fellow in the "Contesting Liberal Citizenship" working group at the Institute for Advanced Studies, Hebrew University. The four-month hiatus provided a stimulating, deliberative environment, culminating in "Institutions and Citizenship: Reflections on the Illicit," Mario Sznajder, Luis Roniger, and Carlos A. Forment, eds., *Shifting Frontiers of Citizenship: The Latin American Experience*, Leiden: Brill, 2012. I also thank Steven Levitsky and Kenneth Roberts for inviting me to take part in the volume workshops that culminated in "The Left and Citizenship in Latin America," Kenneth Roberts and Steven Levitsky, eds., *The Resurgence of the Latin American Left*, (2011). While I had previously worked on citizenship and ethnic politics, I updated my own thinking about citizenship in light of concerns for violence and security – ideas that were subsequently incorporated into this book.

This volume also benefited from collaborations on three other projects. I am particularly grateful to Miguel Centeno and Atul Kohli, with whom I coedited the book *States in the Developing World*; Nancy Bermeo, with whom I coedited *Parties, Movements, and Democracy in the Developing World*; and Peter Kingstone, with whom I coedited the *Handbook of Latin American Politics*. These three very different projects provided a stimulating theoretical backdrop to the issues raised in this book, and I thank my coeditors for their terrific insights, collaboration, and friendship. I am sure they will see the footprint of these edited volumes in the pages of this book. I thank in particular Miguel Centeno, who offered more than once to comment on my manuscript and gave me outstanding advice to sharpen the argument, prose, and theoretical punch line.

Many other colleagues also influenced this project in direct and indirect ways: inviting me to give talks, commenting at conferences, and/or giving general feedback on the project. For their constructive comments and collegiality, I thank Tani Adams, Peter Andreas, Desmond Arias, Mark Beissinger, Sheri Berman, Rogers Brubaker, David Collier, Ruth Collier, José Miguel Cruz, Consuelo Cruz, Diane Davis, Alberto Diaz-Cayeros, Kent Eaton, Tulia Faletti, David Holiday, James Holston, Amaney Jamal, Ira Katznelson, Atul Kohli, Steve Levitsky, Beatriz Magaloni, Shannan Mattiace, Maria Victoria Murillo, Grigore Pop-Eleches, Ken Roberts, José Luis Rocha, Luis Roniger, Victoria Sanford, Rachel Sieder, Dan Slater, Rich Snyder, Susan Stokes, Mario Sznajder, Kathy Thelen, Guillermo Trejo, Andreas Wimmer, and Elisabeth Wood. In turn, I thank the following universities, where I shared my work at various stages of conception, including Brown University; Columbia University; Facultad Latinoamericana de Ciencias Sociales, Ecuador; Harvard University; Hebrew University; New York University; Northwestern University; Oxford University, Social Science Research Council; University of California, Berkeley; University of California, Los Angeles; University of Chicago; University of Notre Dame; University of Oklahoma; University of Pennsylvania; and Yale University. I am also grateful to colleagues who attended conference sessions where I presented this work at APSA, Canadian Association for Latin America and Caribbean Studies, Latin American Studies Association, and Southeastern Council of Latin American Studies.

The project also relied on an outstanding group of RAs. Vinay Jawahar worked with me at the earliest stages of this project, and I thank him for gathering the first round of homicide data, creating GIS coded maps, and conducting an early round of interviews in El Salvador. Alisha Holland also helped by gathering bibliographic information at the start of the project. I am particularly indebted to Yanilda González and Bethany Park for the role they played when constructing and evaluating the newspaper violence database for this project. They helped oversee a team of RAs that heroically read and coded the most gruesome of articles; thanks to Sergio Gálaz García, Marcus Johnson, Nathalie Kitroeff, and Alexander Slaski for coding these entries. González and Park also played a critical role in analyzing this database and the collection of articles. Finally, I extend a special thanks to Daniela Barba-Sánchez for helping me in the final stages of this project; she meticulously reviewed the manuscript; updated tables, maps, and figures; recreated camera-ready images; and polished the bibliography. I was fortunate to work with this extraordinary team of RAs, who showed great commitment, skill, and good humor as we worked on this difficult topic.

This project would not have happened without the generous funding opportunities provided by Princeton University. I thank the Woodrow Wilson School for the research support to travel and hire RAs. An intellectually stimulating 2008 conference on Violence and Citizenship in Post-Authoritarian Latin America provided an initial space to engage with colleagues and was sponsored by the Project on Democracy and Development, with support from the Princeton Institute for Regional Studies and the Program in Latin American Studies (PLAS). PLAS also generously subsidized the photograph for the book cover. I recognize my great fortune to have access to these resources and thank my home institution for this support.

At Cambridge University Press, Robert Dreesen was a terrific editor – providing sage advice about the book's content, title, and cover. I am grateful for his insight, humor, creativity, and great stories. In addition, I am indebted to the three outstanding reviewers. The deeply insightful reviews sharpened my argument in more ways than I could have imagined; indeed, one of the reviewers inspired the term "homicidal ecologies." The project manager, Samantha Town, skillfully oversaw the project, and Lois Tardío took on the unenviable task of copyediting this book. As I searched for the final book image, my colleague and friend María Gabriela Nouzeilles generously took the time to send me images by innovative artists addressing the issue of violence; she thus shared her brilliant insight into their work. In this way, I learned about Fernando Brito, the phenomenal photojournalist whose powerful photograph graces the cover of this book. I am grateful to him for granting the use of this image, from his series "Tus pasos se perdieron con el paisaje."

As I complete the project, I continue to be outraged at the ongoing violence in the Latin American region and the implications for the next generation of children. While they are victims of the homicidal ecologies in which they were born, they are also victims of a torturous escape route and an unwelcoming and cruel response by many North Americans. I despair at their disadvantage and hope that this book contributes, if only in some small way, to a better understanding of their plight and a more informed and compassionate response to their plea for a better life in the Americas (both in their sending and receiving countries).

My daughters, Sarah and Rebecca Yashar-Gershman, have accompanied me on this journey – although they had little to say in the matter. They put up with my long hours, embraced our travel to difficult places, showered me with laughter, and moved me with their compassion and curiosity. They were young when this project began; they are now young women. My hope is that they never have to endure the violence that this book addresses. This book is dedicated to them.

PART I

INTRODUCTION

I

Violence in Third Wave Democracies

Violence invokes images of military regimes, wars, and revolution, and with good reason. The twentieth century has been marked by devastating patterns of violence tied to each of these political episodes. The third wave of democratization was heralded, therefore, not only as a turn to electoral rule but also as a reversal of the violence that marked some of the darkest days in Latin America, Europe, Africa, and Asia. With the transition from authoritarian rule, many forms of violence declined significantly: the military largely returned to the barracks, human rights abuses declined in these new regimes, and the demobilization of (para)military and guerilla forces signaled the end of political violence in many parts of Latin America and Africa. Revolutionary movements (so rare to begin with) receded in this contemporary era.

Yet violence remains prevalent in Latin America's third wave of democracy. From statistical evidence to political conversation, violence is part of daily life. Homicide rates are among the highest in the world, and national surveys convey prevailing concerns about rising violence. The media commonly reports on violent crimes – with some cities reporting multiple homicides a day and others (also) riddled with concerns about kidnapping and femicide. In editorials, reports, and ethnographic studies, citizens reacting to the violence express concern about taking public transportation, walking the streets, and staying out late at night. They fear getting caught in the crossfire. In these circumstances, citizens are not only mourning the loss of loved ones but are also anticipating and strategizing to avoid further harm. The recent waves of undocumented Central Americans (including children) risking their lives to travel to the United States exemplify the noxious impact of this violence on Latin American families. Governments, nongovernmental organizations, and international institutions, in turn, are launching security reforms to address the crisis of violence – with many countries implementing harsh security measures to deter and punish violent offenders. In short, violence remains very much a part of contemporary Latin America.

This book sets out to explain why homicidal violence has reached such high levels in the contemporary democratic period. It does so by analyzing Latin America, the world region that was among the earliest movers in the third wave of democratization (following Spain and Portugal in southern Europe) and yet has arguably become home to the most violent of third wave democracies in the contemporary period. Why has violence emerged as a pandemic phenomenon in third wave, Latin American democracies, and how do we explain its categorical, temporal, and spatial variation?

The goal of this book is to explain varied homicide levels in contemporary democracies and to chart out a theoretical agenda that focuses on violence at the intersection of three factors: the geography of illicit political economies, the capacity of state security forces, and organizational competition over territorial enclaves. These three factors interact within and across borders, explaining much of the categorical variation in violence across the region. They help explain "homicidal ecologies" (subnational regions most susceptible to violence) and associated mechanisms (to explain when and why violence spikes). Taken in reverse order, I argue in particular that organizational competition to control subnational, illicit, territorial enclaves drives the high violence patterns in the region; this competition occurs between illicit actors and/or with the state. However, the violence-inducing, competitive mechanisms are playing out in specific homicidal ecologies: geographically, violence-prone subnational enclaves are emerging most clearly along prized illicit trade and transit routes, where security forces are weak and/or corrupt (although this situation has also arisen in capital cities). While some isolated cases of violent struggle might be politically motivated (to take state power and/or influence policy), most are not. In this regard, the violence of the contemporary period is distinct – less ideological, more dispersed, more fragmented, and arguably harder to control.

Alongside these analytic and theoretical ambitions, normative concerns also motivate this book. The violence in the region is widespread, endemic, and impactful. It is affecting daily life for citizens, and yet the English-language social science literature has until recently turned a blind eye to this phenomenon. Recognizing the methodological challenges of working systematically on the illicit, this book has ventured forth nonetheless to discuss this phenomenon that has so deeply scarred many people who had hoped democracy would usher in a brighter future – at the very least one relatively free from violence. Yet, democracy has *not* done so for so many.

To understand why, we must look beyond formal institutions and national boundaries to explore the interaction of the illicit, the state, and organizational competition. The rest of this chapter introduces the phenomenon and the methods used in this book.

VIOLENCE: EMPIRICAL TRENDS

Latin America has a long history of violence, often surpassing that found in other regions.[1] In recent decades, however, the face of violence in Latin America has changed dramatically. Although the data are poor, the trends are clear. In the 1960s and 1970s, Latin America was defined by authoritarian regimes marked by widespread political violence. Political assassinations, disappearances, lack of habeas corpus, and/or involuntary military recruitment were commonplace in many countries – particularly El Salvador, Guatemala, Argentina, Brazil, and Chile. With transitions away from authoritarian rule, there was a sharp decline in human rights abuses, with some recent and notable exceptions.[2] While state violence is not entirely a thing of the past, its scope and intensity are markedly different than that of the prior authoritarian period. The power of militaries to subvert civilian control, engage in widespread human rights abuses, and act with impunity has been seriously weakened. In this context, Latin America's third wave democracies have promoted deeper and more meaningful patterns of citizenship, with citizens gaining basic political and civil rights that were coercively denied them in earlier decades.[3]

Despite these advances in civil and political rights, there has been a startling rise in homicide levels in several Latin American countries. These can no longer be analyzed solely as the product of military regimes and/or civil wars (with Colombia's civil war offering the obvious exception). To the contrary, non-civil-war-related homicide rates have reached startling levels in much of the region. Based on these contemporary trends, Latin America consistently stands out in the new millennia as one of the

---

[1] Homicide levels have outpaced those in Europe and Asia by five to eight times, according to time series data (using a three-year moving average) dating from 1955 to 2012. That said, this data averages only five countries for Latin America, three for Asia/Oceania, and fifteen for Europe (UNODC 2014b: 12).
[2] As I complete this book, human rights abuses and political violence have risen in Venezuela (whose democratic origins predate the third wave of democracy and whose democratic future is currently uncertain).
[3] Not all third wave democratic countries have achieved equal levels of political and civil rights; Guatemala ranks far below Chile, for example. However, all third wave democracies have improved political and civil rights relative to those of the authoritarian period.

most violent regions in the world – especially when compared with non–civil war cases. The 2012 global average homicide rate was estimated at 6.2 per 100,000 people. Latin America (with just 8% of the global population) was responsible for the highest percentage (36%) of the 437,000 homicides reported in that year (UNODC 2014b: 11–12). Moreover, Central America (along with Southern Africa) claimed the dubious distinction of being the most violent subregion in the world, with an estimated homicide rate of four times the global average (UNODC 2014b: 12).[4] El Salvador has often been singled out, in particular, for its exceedingly high homicide rates, but other countries (e.g., Guatemala and Honduras) have also been standouts in this regard. Comaroff and Comaroff (2006a: 219) have cautioned against the reification of these kinds of data since "police statistics everywhere are erected on an edifice of indeterminacies and impossibilities." Yet even while recognizing the imprecision of homicide statistics, Latin America appears to be in a category all by itself *and* also to encompass a great deal of variation therein.

This book focuses on one particularly egregious and definitive form of violence: homicides. Recognizing that other types of violence (kidnapping, armed robbery, rape, battery, etc.) are not inconsequential, I choose to focus on homicides for both normative and methodological reasons. Normatively, homicide rates are of particular concern. Homicide is arguably the most extreme form of violence: it is not necessarily the most brutal form (we can imagine horrible forms of torture that do not take one's life, just as we can imagine a quick form of homicide), but the taking of a life is the final form. This ultimate disregard for life drives this project. What leads to this kind of violent behavior? Why do people kill others in such high numbers – especially since the numbers do not necessarily correlate with those of other patterns of violence?[5] Alongside these normative

---

[4] Homicide data are often difficult to gather and compare because definitions and measure of homicide vary across countries and even across national institutions within the same country. Even recognizing this problem, UNODC (2007: 53) notes as follows: most data indicate that Guatemala and El Salvador are among the most violent places in the world (alongside Jamaica, Colombia, and South Africa/Swaziland); Costa Rica, Panama, and Nicaragua are considerably less violent; data on Honduras are incomplete, but existing evidence suggests that it is closer to Guatemala and El Salvador than to the other Central American cases. For a map of homicide rates by country or territory (2012 or latest year), see UNODC (2014b: 23).

[5] High homicide rates do not necessarily equal high rates of other crimes. Armed robbery victimization in 2008, for example, was reportedly highest in Ecuador (15.6%), Venezuela (13.3%), Haiti (12.1%), and Argentina (12.0%) in 2008, followed by Guatemala (11.4%), El Salvador (10.6%), and Chile (8.6%). Honduras comes in twelfth on the list, after the prior countries and Colombia, Brazil, Peru, and Bolivia (World Bank 2010, volume 2: 4, based on LAPOP surveys of percentage of adults victimized by armed robbery

concerns, the motivation to focus on homicides is also methodological. It is difficult to count violence. Most of it goes unreported, and most states in the region have uneven records for the wide range of violence that takes place – e.g., rape, kidnapping, and assault. Not only have state agencies demonstrated limited capacity to keep systematic and comparable records on these forms of violence, but people also hesitate to report violent acts given limited confidence in state institutions. In this context, homicides are more reliably compared than many other forms of violence. It is not that state homicide records are excellent; it is that they are the best existing records of violent acts at this point. In this book, "homicides" refer to the intentional and unlawful taking of another life, a definition that draws from and coincides with the UN's definition (see UNODC 2011: 15). Thus, ethical and methodological reasons combine and drive the decision to focus on homicides as the basis for identifying violence trends and rates across the region.

While homicide data represent the best comparable violence statistics that we have, it is important to underscore that the data are estimates. It is a challenge to measure and compare homicide data, not only because this assumes intentionality and not only because different states use different legal definitions, but also because developing states often lack the capacity and incentive to collect, systematize, and share statistics (although, notably, reported homicide rates are highest in cases with very low state capacity). Moreover, criminal records and health records often diverge for the same country (although datasets using one or the other tend to be broadly compatible when it comes to ranking countries). For this book, I started off using the collection of health records in the World Health Organization's classic and oft-cited study on homicides; however, I also rely on the United Nations Office on Drugs and Crime (UNODC) dataset, which includes criminal records reported by national police and other rule-of-law institutions (which tend to report higher numbers, on average). Were that one could say with

---

in past twelve months). House burglary victimization rates, based on LAPOP surveys, suggest a list led by Uruguay, Peru, Bolivia, Haiti, Chile, Paraguay, Brazil, Ecuador, the Dominican Republic, Venezuela, Costa Rica, Nicaragua, Guatemala, El Salvador, Colombia, Panama, Mexico, Jamaica, and then Honduras. Note that the high homicide rate cases are in the bottom half of the house burglary list (World Bank 2010, volume 2: 3–4).

confidence that one set of records was always best.[6] Because this is not possible, I use both datasets to evaluate, rank, and triangulate data across countries.

Given the decision to focus on homicides, it is also important to emphasize what this book does and does not do. This book sets out to explain different categorical levels of homicidal violence: comparatively very high, medium, and low.[7] It does not explain individual acts of homicide. It also does not explain slight ordinal variations. Nor does it presume that homicide levels vary with other forms of violence, which they do not. I self-consciously restrict my argument to explaining a tripartite categorization in homicide levels. When referring to violence from this point on, I am referring only to homicides, unless otherwise stated. Thus, I cautiously but explicitly take some poetic license by interchangeably using the terms "violence" and "homicides" – even though the former is a more capacious term than the latter and violent trends across violent categories do not always coincide.

Two figures convey the cross-national trends in homicides. Figure 1.1 provides the figures reported by WHO (in collaboration with its regional counterpart, the Pan American Health Organization) on homicide rates in the Americas. The dataset begins in 1995, earlier than the UNODC dataset, but reports lower and more-discontinuous figures. Given the lack of time trend data for Bolivia, Haiti, Honduras, and Jamaica, these cases are excluded from the first graph.[8] Figures 1.2 and 1.3 provide UNODC figures, which start later (2000) but include more-continuous data. Notably, UNODC figures are often higher than WHO figures – especially for Honduras.

---

[6] See Ribeiro, Borges, and Cano (2015) for an overview of different data sources and their strengths and weaknesses. Import discrepancies exist in datasets using criminal records versus health records. Databases (such as those of WHO and PAHO, the Pan American Health Organization) that use health records/death certificates tend to use specific protocols (which can lead to greater reliability but also an underestimation of homicides – especially if they are not certain about how and why the death occurred). Databases that use criminal records (such as UNODC) tend to report higher homicide levels than those based on death certificates but can suffer from other problems, including differences in if/how they record intentionality – i.e., killings by police officers and/or civilians engaging in self-defense.

[7] As noted later, "medium" is a relative category for the region. By other regional standards, medium could be considered exceptionally high.

[8] These figures are the most comprehensive and commonly cited comparative figures for the region (although, as we will see in future chapters, the figures arguably underreport homicide levels – particularly for Guatemala and Mexico – and fail to report for Honduras up to 2007).

Violence in Third Wave Democracies

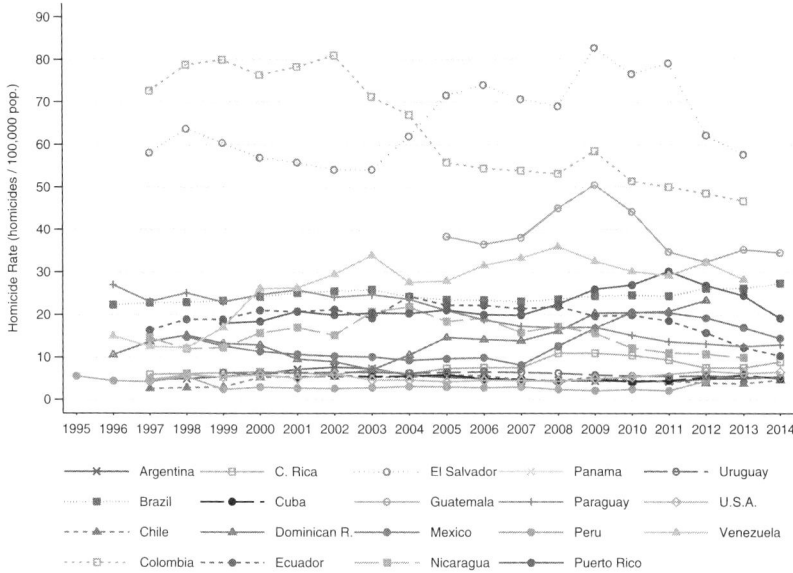

FIGURE 1.1 Homicide rates in the Americas per 100,000 (1995–2014, per WHO/PAHO)
Figure created for this project by Daniela Barba-Sánchez using Stata.
Sources: Panel dataset published online by Pan American Health Organization and World Health Organization. *Health Information Platform for the Americas (PLISA).* Washington DC, 2016. Available at http://phip.paho.org/views/Pro_Reg_Fin_Nca_Pub_Anu_Tab_Ing_IBS_homicides/Table?:embed=yes&:comments=no&:display_count=no&:showVizHome=no. Last visited in September 2017.
Data for Figure 1.1 are reported in the Appendix in Table 1.2. Figures marked with * in Table 1.2 are from the panel dataset published online by Pan American Health Organization, Health Surveillance and Disease Management Area, Health Statistics and Analysis Unit. *PAHO Regional Mortality Database.* Washington DC, 2010. Available at www.paho.org/Spanish/SHA/coredata/tabulator/newTabulator.htm.
Data for Peru come from the panel dataset published online by the Pan American Health Organization, Health Information and Analysis Unit. *Regional Core Health Data Initiative.* Washington DC, 2014. Available at www1.paho.org/English/SHA/coredata/tabulator/newTabulator.htm. Last visited in July 2015. Corrected mortality rates are based on observed mortality data, applying a correction for mortality under-registration and ill-defined deaths.
Notes: Figures for Honduras are excluded from this figure since they are *significantly* lower than the data reported in UNDP 2013 Informe Regional de Desarrollo Humano 2013–2014 Seguridad Ciudadana con Rostro Humano: Anexo Estadístico-Metodológico. New York, NY, p. 65 (37 for 2005, 46.2 for 2006, 49.9 for 2007, 57.9 for 2008, 66.8 for 2009, 77.5 for 2010, and 86.5 for 2011).

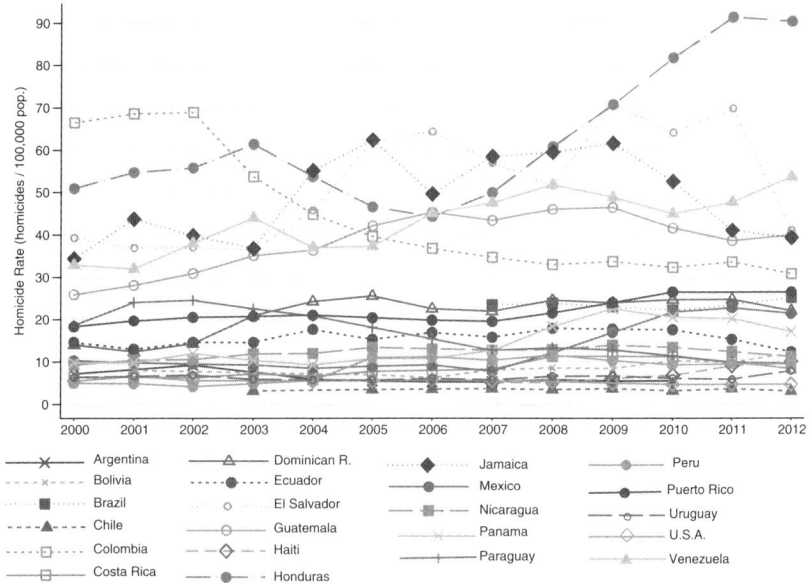

FIGURE 1.2 Homicide rates in the Americas per 100,000 (2000–2012, per UNODC)
Graph created for this project by Daniela Barba-Sánchez in June 2016 using Stata.
Source: UNODC 2014b. See www.unodc.org/gsh/data.html.

CAPTION FOR FIGURE 1.1 (cont.)

Figures for Guatemala (1995–2004) were originally reported in the PAHO 2010 report. They were, however, dropped in the 2016 report, and thus I do not include them in this figure, although they are reported in the Appendix.

Figures for El Salvador and Guatemala are sometimes reported elsewhere as considerably higher than the figures reported in this table. See, for example, Inter-American Development Bank 2000 Report. Reprinted in Hugo Acero Velásquez. 2002. "Salud, violencia y seguridad." *Ciudad y políticas públicas de seguridad y convivencia.* www.suivd.gov.co/ciudad/MexicoMarzohacero.doc. Even these comparatively lower estimates, however, place these cases at the upper tier of per capita homicide rates in the region.

Violence in Third Wave Democracies

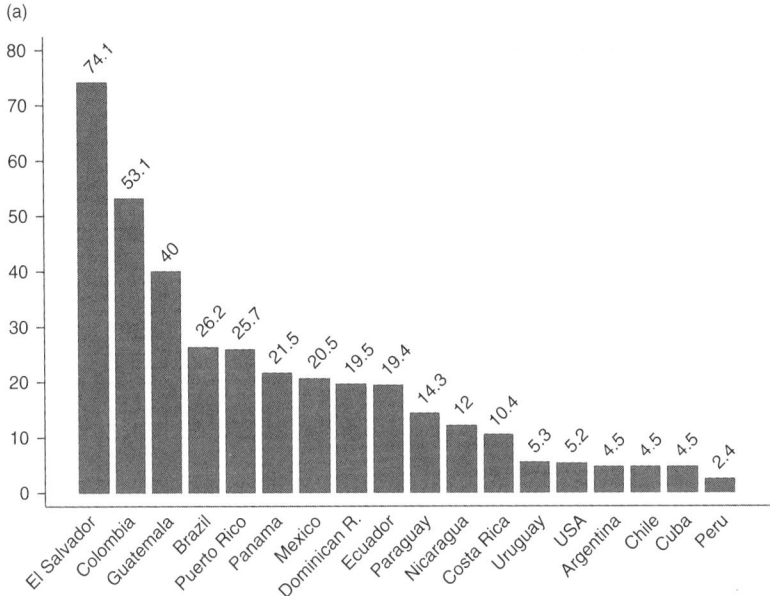

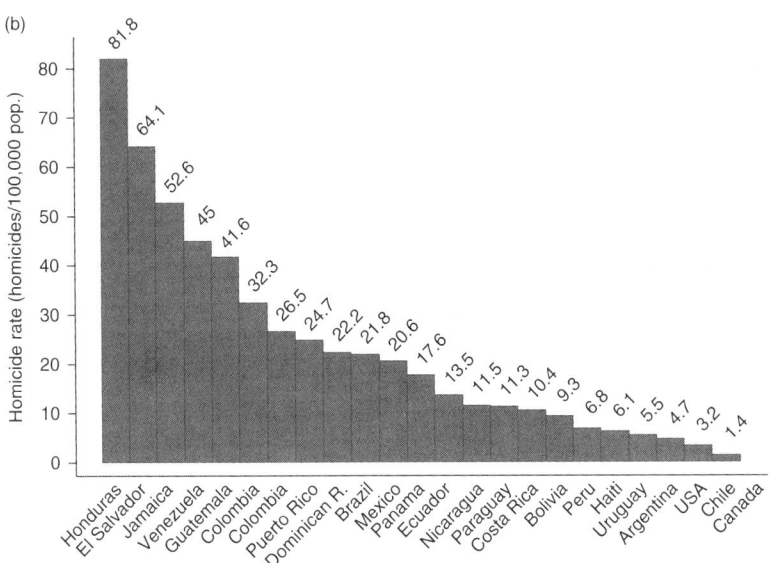

FIGURE 1.3 Homicide rates in Latin America per 100,000 (2010, per WHO/PAHO and UNODC)
Source: First figure (a) based on WHO/PAHO 2014. Second figure (b) based on UNODC (2014b).

TABLE 1.1 *National homicide trajectories: stability and levels (1995–2014, based on WHO data)*

	"Low" levels (< 10 annual homicides per 100,000 per capita)	"Intermediate" levels (10–39 annual homicides, per 100,000 per capita)		Extremely high levels (> 40 annual homicides per 100,000 per capita)
		Lower band (10–19 per 100,000)	Upper band (20–39 per 100,000)	
Relative stability of homicide rates	Argentina, Chile, Costa Rica,[*] Cuba, United States, Peru, Uruguay	Dominican Republic, Ecuador, Nicaragua, Panama, Paraguay	Brazil, Puerto Rico	
Relative instability of homicide rates		Mexico	Venezuela[**]	Colombia, El Salvador, Guatemala[**]

[*] Costa Rica's rate is between 10 and 11 per 100,000 in 2008, 2009, and 2010.
[**] UNODC data would place Honduras, Venezuela, and Jamaica in the bottom right cell.

The WHO/PAHO data allow us to discern the range both in levels of homicide rates and temporal trends. Table 1.1 compiles and distills these indicators – levels and temporal (in)stability – to give a snapshot of the patterns in the region. On the first dimension (levels of homicide), we know that the region as a whole has sustained globally high levels. But within the region, homicide levels vary. From a regional perspective, relatively low levels of homicides (less than 10 per 100,000 annual homicides per capita) are found in Argentina, Chile, Costa Rica, Cuba, Peru, and Uruguay – maintaining levels comparable to (and in some cases lower than) those of the United States. Also from a regional perspective, intermediate levels of violence (10–39 per 100,000 annual homicides per capita) are found in several countries, with Brazil and Venezuela in the upper band of this residual category and with Mexico moving up within this category after 2007. Notably, these intermediate levels are still very high and particularly so when compared against global averages; in Table 1.1, I break down this category into lower and upper intermediate bands.[9] Finally, extremely high levels of homicide (higher than 40 per 100,000 annual homicides per capita) have been found in El Salvador, Guatemala, Honduras, and Colombia.

Temporal trends also reveal a great deal of variation in terms of the (in)stability of homicide rates. Using a blunt instrument, where a country's homicide rate varies less than ten points across the seventeen-year period covered in the WHO data,[10] there is deemed to be *relative* stability. This applies to thirteen Latin American countries (see Table 1.1). Conversely, there is relative instability in six countries – with a notable decline in Colombia and a notable fluctuation and/or overall dramatic increase in El Salvador, Guatemala, Mexico, and Venezuela. Were we to use the UNODC figures (rather than the WHO data), the ranking in Table 1.1 would remain essentially the same.[11]

Viewed together, one can identify a few trends in these data.

1. Low homicide rates appear relatively stable. No country that starts with low homicide rates moves definitively into a higher category during the nineteen-year period covered in the data. Costa Rica momentarily crosses the threshold of 10 between 2008 and 2010 (10.9, 10.9, 10.4) but then dips below it again. This observation suggests that facilitating conditions that might explain violence are (and thus far remain) low in these countries. These countries also do not appear to have the underlying conditions that give rise to high levels of homicides.

2. High homicide rates appear to be inherently unstable. Countries that fall in this category experience great fluctuation in their homicide rates. This observation logically suggests either (a) that a change in facilitating conditions takes place in these countries, (b) that micro-mechanisms/catalysts vary over time even if the facilitating conditions remain constant, or (c) that both facilitating conditions and micro-mechanisms change over time. This book argues that these countries possess structural or

---

[9] This intermediate range for the region still includes countries with violence levels that are very high by global standards. "Intermediate" is thus a residual category between the two extremes of violence.

[10] No countries maintain perfectly stable patterns. And indeed, any increase/decrease is notable. But given that this book is looking at categorical differences, and given that statistics have a high margin of error, I use 10 percent as the cutoff point for relative stability versus instability – both to mark important changes *and* to minimize the possibility that these changes are simply better record keeping in one year versus another.

[11] Were we to include UNODC data, we would find some slight variations. Costa Rica (2008–2011) and Peru (2005–2009) go slightly over the threshold of 10 before dropping below it again. Honduras, Jamaica, and Venezuela (included in UNODC data) would all fall in the bottom right corner.

facilitating conditions that create "homicidal ecologies" (macro-conditions that more readily give rise to high homicide rates). However, high homicide rates do not occur in the absence of micro-mechanisms that are responsible for generating high and volatile homicide rates.

3. **The highest homicide rates tend to emerge in small countries,** especially in Central America (including El Salvador and Guatemala),[12] where certain cities and provinces drive the data, affecting the per capita rates more dramatically than in large countries (where the range of homicide rates across large territories can be obscured once per capita averages are taken into account). Colombia is an exception to this observation, although it is also the only country in this period that experiences an ongoing civil war (and for this reason is excluded from the subsequent study of post-civil war democratic cases). Venezuela's record is perhaps the other exception, as its national data (according to UNODC rather than WHO/PAHO data) suggest a steeply rising homicide rate in the final years covered.

4. **National homicide rates (and the stability thereof) belie subnational variation.** In particular, countries with high homicide rates have significant variation across cities and provinces. Countries with intermediate homicide rates, moreover, include an enormous range within each country – with some provinces reaching very high levels while others remain comparatively low, as in the cases of Brazil and Mexico. The stability of national rates is sometimes at odds with the instability at subnational levels. There is, for example, a stable national rate that places Brazil in the intermediate category; yet there is subnational variation, with some regions and cities reaching extraordinarily high and fluctuating homicide rates. This is shown in the declining rates in Rio de Janeiro (29 percent) and Sao Paulo (11 percent) between 2007 and 2011 and in the increasing rates in these same years of almost 150 percent in Paraiba and around 50 percent in Bahia (see UNODC 2014b: 26). Mexico suffers from the same fate, with some provincial states exhibiting enormously high rates that are obscured by the national per capita figures.

These four overall observations highlight the need to pursue a *multilevel* study that analyzes regional, temporal, and subnational variation. In writing this book, I have set out to strike a balance between

---

[12] Importantly, the WHO data on Honduras is lacking for 1995–2007 and provides per capita homicide estimates that fall far below what other sources would indicate. See the book's conclusion for a discussion of this case.

explaining one of the world's most egregious contemporary patterns of homicidal violence, while also advancing our theoretical understanding of why different homicidal levels emerge (with some places more likely than others to suffer from high homicide rates). In doing so, I highlight the interplay between formal national institutions and illicit activity occurring within and across borders. In particular, I analyze three core features across the region: the changing geography of illicit trade and transit, variation in state capacity, and subnational territorial competition among armed organizations (including illicit groups and the state). While the first two factors are critical in shaping homicidal ecologies (territories prone to more violence), the last factor constitutes the most proximate mechanism for explaining where and why violence surges in these subnational spaces.

RESEARCH DESIGN

The research design for this book aims to address these questions: Why has homicidal violence become so prevalent during the third wave, and why is it so high in some places and not others? The goal of this project is not to explain *all* violence but rather to explain why homicidal violence has reached such dramatically high levels in Latin America's third wave of democracy and why we find variation therein. In this regard, the project explains different relative levels of homicidal violence (comparatively low, moderate, and high) rather than specific homicide rates in particular.

Violence encompasses many possible forms. This study narrows its focus to homicides, in particular, as noted at the start of the book. Homicide rates are the most readily compared – not only because they can be counted, but also because we have the best cross-national records for them. In most cases, I have used government-reported data on homicides, from both criminal and public health records, where available. I also use victimization surveys and public opinion surveys to triangulate with the homicide data. Finally, it is important to reiterate that there are many disturbing patterns of violent homicides that are taking place – particularly violence against women, extrajudicial community lynchings and killings, and dismemberment. While these patterns of violence are alarming, they are not generalized across all the cases of high violence but instead appear to be localized (at least at the time of this writing) in a few cases such as Guatemala and parts of Mexico. Hence, I will not claim to explain the *particular* forms of violence that are taking place across the high-violence cases but, rather, will look exclusively at homicides.

To explain varied levels of homicide, I deploy various strategies. To start, I evaluate longitudinal data for the region as a whole. As explained earlier, national quantitative data are available through WHO and UNDP (United Nations Development Programme) studies; I supplement these commonly used studies with new subnational longitudinal datasets for several critical cases. Excellent research assistants worked with me to gather these data; the task of creating the subnational datasets and displaying them in tabular and map form was first undertaken by Vinay Jawahar. These cross-national and subnational datasets provide the basis for clarifying overall patterns of homicidal violence in post-authoritarian regimes, for initially evaluating the competing theoretical arguments discussed in the next chapter, and for proposing plausible arguments about violence facilitating conditions and mechanisms that vary across the region. The homicide data are supplemented by victimization surveys and other survey data. Yanilda González assisted me in gathering and evaluating the survey data from LAPOP and Latinobarometer. These data were updated in the final development of this book with the assistance of Daniela Barba-Sánchez.

Second, I pursue a small-N comparative study to probe the mechanisms explaining varied levels of violence. The heart of this small-N study focuses on Central America – a region marked not only with the highest violence rates in the Americas but also one with significant variation over time, across countries, and within countries. The region is thus ripe for comparative analysis, using a "most similar" and "most different" system design to probe these patterns. This part of the analysis focuses on Central America's three post-civil war cases: Guatemala and El Salvador (high homicide rates) and Nicaragua (lower band of intermediate homicide rates). They are the most similar cases in the region (histories of civil war, inequality, authoritarian rule) and yet exhibit strikingly divergent patterns of homicidal violence in the contemporary period.[13] Part III of this book probes these cross-national variations, while also probing subnational and temporal variation within the two high-violence cases of El Salvador and Guatemala. Figures 1.1, 1.2, and 1.3 (included at the start of the chapter) show how high the homicide rates are for El Salvador and Guatemala, relative to the rest of Latin America. Figure 1.4 maps subnational homicide rates in Central America in particular.

---

[13] The conclusion to the book will discuss other cases, including how this argument applies to Honduras – a non–civil war case (although it was implicated in the civil wars of its neighbors), which has had among the highest homicide rates in the region.

Violence in Third Wave Democracies 17

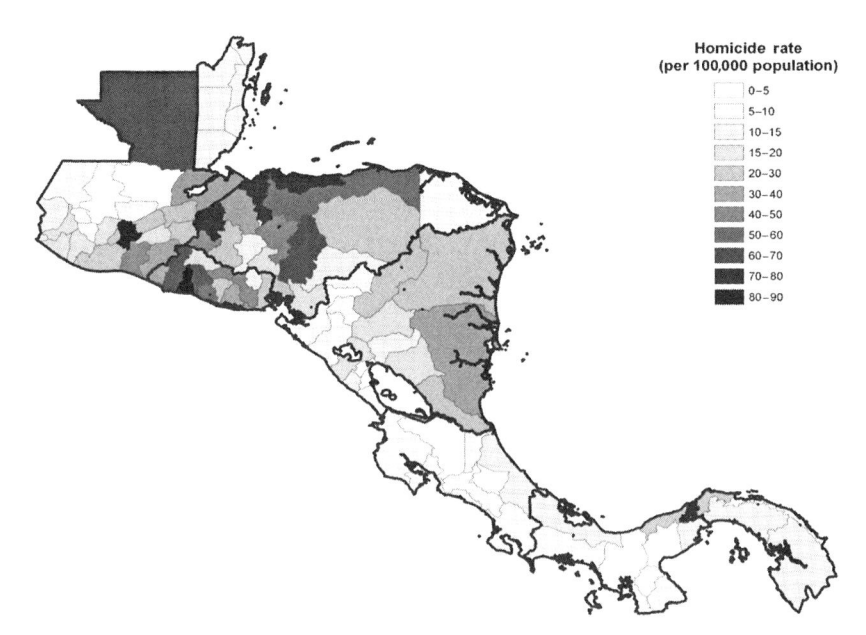

FIGURE 1.4 Central America's homicide rates by subnational area
Source: World Bank. 2011. Crime and Violence in Central America: A Development Challenge – Main Report. World Bank. © World Bank. https://openknowledge.worldbank.org/handle/10986/2744 License: CC BY 3.0 IGO. p. 3.
Notes: This map can also be found in World Bank (2010, volume 2, iv and 4) as well as Demombynes (2011: 5). In all cases, the publications cite Cuevas and Demombynes (2009) as the original source. Demombynes (2011: 3) indicates that these subnational data are from 2006. The accompanying text for the 2010 publication indicates that they used homicide data from national authorities for the most recent data available prior to publication.

In the comparative analysis of Guatemala, El Salvador, and Nicaragua, I complement the quantitative cross-national and subnational data with case-specific research strategies. Original interviews were conducted in each country with a range of relevant actors in government, international organizations, academia, and nongovernmental organizations; the names are listed in the bibliography. Moreover, I compiled an original newspaper database (referred to in the text as the "newspaper violence database") to unpack the dynamics of violence in these same three countries. The task was completed by a team of outstanding research assistants. Yanilda González collaborated with me to create the database template; González and Bethany Park then helped coordinate a team to generate these data for El Salvador, Guatemala, and Nicaragua for three newspaper years (reading and coding all relevant newspaper articles for one national newspaper in each country in 2000, 2005, and 2010). This team included González and Park as well as Sergio Gálaz García, Marcus Johnson, Nathalie Kitroeff, and Alexander Slaski. González and Park then helped compile the data and write memos for 2000, 2005, and 2010 for El Salvador, Guatemala, and Nicaragua. I am grateful to this team for working with me on this time-consuming project and for coding the gruesome details that comprise the database.[14]

Viewed as a whole, this book relies on a multilevel analysis to place Latin America in a global context, explaining variation across cases and over time. The heart of the book relies on a small-N comparison of highly divergent cases, discussed in Part III. Parts I and II frame these case studies in light of broader comparative trends and theoretical debates.

THE ARGUMENT AND BOOK OUTLINE

Previewing Approach and Argument

The main theoretical approaches have tended to focus both on *national* and *formal* patterns: e.g., national political legacies (civil wars and democratization), national economic structures (inequality), national sociological factors (civil society, demographics, and cleavages), and national institutions (state formation). This book evaluates these theoretical alternatives in subsequent chapters but develops a different point of departure. It assumes that violent crime is not simply an individual response to national and formal patterns. Therefore, this book develops an argument that analyzes formal and illicit patterns and features the role of organizations; it does so at multiple levels of analysis.

In particular, this book emphasizes three factors and situates them geographically: the transnational illicit economy, state capacity, and territorial competition among organizations. The skeletal argument unfolds as follows. First, I contend that the development of a transnational illicit economy and illicit criminal organizations set the stage for the high levels

---

[14] I thank, in particular, Vinay Jawahar and Yanilda González for their excellent research assistance throughout the project. Vinay Jawahar played a critical role in tracking down and cleaning up national and subnational homicide data and in pursuing the laborious process of generating the maps used in this book. Yanilda González played a critical role in stratifying and analyzing the LAPOP survey data and in generating the original newspaper dataset used in this book.

of violence that we now see in Latin America. In particular, the development of high value-added illicit trade and transit has created high-stakes incentives for illicit organizations to control lucrative territories/transit routes; these are the areas most susceptible to high violence since there are strong economic motives to assert control and no legal channels to institutionalize hegemonic domains and adjudicate conflicts. Second, I argue that illicit trade and transit is likely to take hold where illicit actors find weak and/or complicit state institutions (particularly law-and-order institutions such as the police and courts). In this context, illicit organizations are moving into areas where they are unmonitored (and thus have a greater likelihood of assuming control over territorial enclaves to support the trade and transit of illicit goods) and/or where they are able to strike deals with state actors and thus create a situation of collusion.[15] Third, and finally, I find that the highest levels of violence are emerging particularly where illicit organizations encounter organizational competition (either from other illicit organizations or the state or both) to control previously hegemonic territorial enclaves. This means that where organizations are hegemonic, the use of violence will be low. Where organizations compete to assert control over common territories, violence will be high.[16] No single factor determines the outcome. The combination of factors, however, can be deadly.

These factors are introduced analytically, separately and sequentially, in Part II. Part III then analyzes the case studies, which reveal an endogenous process that unfolds across the three factors. This tripartite argument is depicted in Figure 1.5.

The tripartite argument moves from the macro to the micro, from transnational to local levels, and between the formal and the illicit. The following chapters introduce alternative arguments (Chapter 2), develop this book's argument theoretically and cross-nationally (Chapters 3 and 4), probe the mechanisms in a small-n analysis – both of national cases and subnational patterns (Chapters 5–7) – and then revisit the scope conditions and theoretical implications of this book

---

[15] Labor markets might affect entry into the illicit economy. As such, it is possible that this factor might also help explain the growth of illicit actors (which would multiply the possible number of at-risk offenders). However, as far as I know, the comparative data on subnational labor markets is weak. As such, I do not currently have access to data on local-level labor markets to be able to make the claim that this is (or is not) so.

[16] The third factor draws on Gambetta's (1996) classic argument about the Italian mafia and parallels more recent work by Snyder and Durán-Martínez (2009). It also has its parallel in the civil war literature (see Kalyvas 2006).

Argument

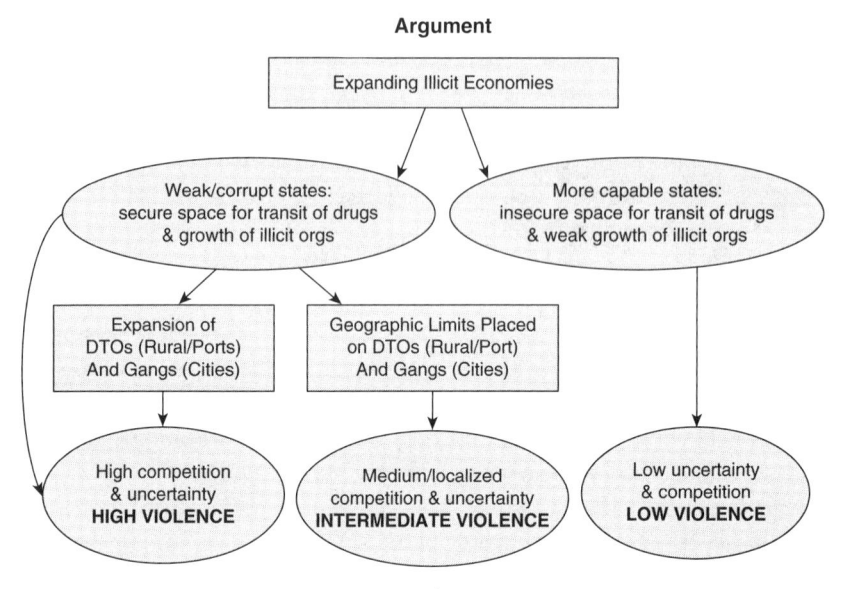

```
                    Expanding Illicit Economies
                    /                          \
    Weak/corrupt states:                    More capable states:
    secure space for transit of drugs       insecure space for transit of drugs
    & growth of illicit orgs                & weak growth of illicit orgs
           |                    |                        |
    Expansion of          Geographic Limits Placed
    DTOs (Rural/Ports)    on DTOs (Rural/Port)
    And Gangs (Cities)    And Gangs (Cities)
           |                    |                        |
    High competition      Medium/localized          Low uncertainty
    & uncertainty         competition & uncertainty  & competition
    HIGH VIOLENCE         INTERMEDIATE VIOLENCE     LOW VIOLENCE
```

FIGURE 1.5 The argument

(Chapter 8). While grounded in three case studies, the theoretical argument speaks to other non–civil war cases – including Brazil, Mexico, Venezuela, and Honduras.

Ultimately, the tripartite argument developed in this book opened up a second set of historical institutional questions and arguments about why otherwise similarly situated countries emerge with such divergent state capacity (making them more susceptible to illicit trade and transit, organizational competition, and ultimately violence). Chapter 7 pursues this question empirically in the relatively lower-intermediate-violence case of Nicaragua, which developed an impressive police force (unparalleled by its neighbors and uniquely capable when compared to other parts of the Nicaraguan state). Chapter 8 revisits the comparative question of state capacity and engages with the comparative historical debates about when and why otherwise sticky state institutions are successfully reformed – not only changing institutional design but also affecting corresponding organizational and societal behavior.

In closing, I have several aspirations in writing this book. I hope that this manuscript increases our understanding of why violence is occurring at such high levels in Latin America and why it assumes varied levels across time and space. I hope that the project will highlight the need to precise the interactions between the illicit and licit world (to focus in on territorially rooted organizations, rather than individuals, that seek to dominate illicit economic enclaves in a context of weak and complicit states) and to precise the interactions between the formal and informal spaces that define the lives of so many citizens. Finally, I hope that this book will lead to a more focused and informed discussion of the needs of citizens living in the context of this violence and the need to better understand when and why coercive institutions can and do defend/betray the population they are reputedly designed to serve. That said, my bold goals are tempered by an underlying humility about how much we know and how far we still have to go. I thus ultimately hope and expect that this book will not be the last word. Rather, I wrote this book to motivate further discussion of this question – to collect better data; to collaborate further; and to share our results not only to advance theoretical debates but also to inform alternatives for securing deeper, stronger, and more democratic security.

Chapter 1

Appendix

TABLE 1.2 *Homicide rates in the Americas (1995–2014, per 100,000 inhabitants)*

	1995	1996	1997	1998	1999	2000	2001	2002	2003	2004	2005	2006	2007	2008	2009	2010	2011	2012	2013	2014
Argentina	4.2*	4.7*	4.7	4.9	5.4	6.0	7.1	7.6	7.3	5.8	5.2	5.0	4.4	4.5	4.4	4.4	4.3	4.9	5.0	5.4
Bolivia	0.6	0.5	0.8	0.3	0.4	0.6	0.3	0.2	1.2	NA	NA	NA	NA	NA	NA	NA	NA	NA	NA	NA
Brazil	25.7	22.3	22.8	22.9	23.3	24.2	25.1	25.5	25.9	24.2	23.5	23.4	23.1	23.6	24.4	24.6	24.4	26.2	26.2	27.4
Chile	3.2*	3*	2.6	2.8	3.0	5.2	5.4	5.4	5.3	5.3	5.8	5.6	4.7	4.5	5.3	4.5	4.4	3.9	3.8	4.6
Colombia	76.6	80.1*	72.6	78.8	80.0	76.4	78.3	81.0	71.2	67.0	55.8	54.4	53.9	53.2	58.5	51.4	50.0	48.5	46.7	NA
Costa Rica	5.2	5.5	5.9	6.1	6.3	6.5	6.3	5.9	7.0	6.1	7.3	7.5	7.5	10.9	10.9	10.4	9.3	7.5	7.5	8.9
Cuba	7.8*	6.7	6.8*	7.9*	5.9*	5.8*	5.2	5.6	5.4	5.5	5.8	4.9	4.8	4.2	4.8	4.2	4.5	5.2	5.7	5.0
Dominican Rep.	9.8	10.6	13.7	15.2	13.3	12.9	9.5	8.9	7.0	10.5	14.6	14.1	13.8	16.1	20.4	20.5	20.8	23.4	NA	NA
Ecuador	13.4	16.1	16.4	18.9	18.9	21.0	20.7	21.2	19.2	24.3	22.2	22.2	21.4	21.9	19.7	19.9	18.5	15.7	12.2	10.3
El Salvador	51.2	52.3	58.1	63.7	60.4	56.9	55.8	54.1	54.1	61.9	71.5	74.0	70.7	69.0	82.8	76.6	79.1	62.2	57.7	NA
Guatemala	19.7*	21.2*	28.7	26.2*	18*	19.3*	20*	23.7	27.8*	27.5*	38.3	36.5	38.1	45.0	50.5	44.2	34.8	32.4	35.3	34.6
Haiti	NA	NA	0.0	NA	12.6	NA	16.0	20.2	19.2	17.7	NA	NA	NA	NA	NA	NA	NA	NA	NA	NA
Honduras	NA	NA	NA	NA	NA	NA	NA	NA	NA	NA	NA	NA	NA	NA	7.3	6.9	8.4	8.2	13.3	NA
Jamaica	NA	NA	NA	0.5	0.5	1.0	1.1	0.5	0.6	0.4	61.4	0.7	NA	NA	55.7	1.6	32.9	NA	NA	NA
Mexico	18.4	17*	15.8*	14.8	12.7	11.3	10.6	10.2	10.0	9.2	9.6	9.8	8.1	12.6	16.8	20.6	20.5	19.2	16.9	14.4
Nicaragua	NA	11.7	14.6	12.0	12.3	15.7	17.0	15.2	20.7	21.8	18.4	19.2	15.8	17.2	15.6	12.1	11.0	10.7	9.9	NA
Panama	NA	9.4	12.2	10.6	9.8	11.1	12.2	14.4	13.3	12.9	13.4	12.5	15.2	19.2	23.0	21.4	20.9	19.4	18.9	17.0
Paraguay	NA	27.0	23.1	25.1	23.0	24.7	25.8	24.1	24.7	23.6	21.0	18.8	17.3	17.0	17.0	15.1	13.6	13.1	12.5	12.9
Peru**	5.5	4.4	4.2*	5.4*	2.4	2.9	2.7	2.6	2.8	3.1	3	2.8	3	2.4	2.1	2.4	2.1	4.4	NA	NA
Puerto Rico	25.1	24.9	23.4	21.3*	18.0	18.4	20.8	19.9	20.4	20.3	21.1	20.0	19.9	22.5	26.0	27.0	30.2	26.9	24.5	19.1
USA	8.3	7.6*	7.1	6.4*	6.3	6.1	6.3	6.4	6.4	6.2	6.4	6.5	6.4	6.2	5.8	5.6	5.5	5.6	5.3	5.2
Uruguay	4.7	4.4	4.7	5.8	5.3	5.8	5.0	5.9	4.6	4.6	4.2	4.5	4.5	4.3	4.9	5.3	NA	6.7	6.2	6.5
Venezuela	NA	15.0	12.6	12.2	17.0	26.1	26.3	29.5	33.9	27.6	27.9	31.6	33.3	36.0	32.6	30.2	29.2	32.3	28.3	NA

Table created for this project by Daniela Barba-Sánchez and used to create Figure 1.1.
Sources: Panel dataset published online by Pan American Health Organization and World Health Organization. *Health Information Platform for the Americas (PLISA)*. Washington DC, 2016. Available at http://phip.paho.org/views/Pro_Reg_Fin_Nca_Pub_Anu_Tab_Ing_IBS_homicides/Table?:embed=yes&:comments=no&:display_count=no&:showVizHome=no. Last visited in September 2017.
Notes: Figures marked with * are from the panel dataset published online by Pan American Health Organization, Health Surveillance and Disease Management Area, Health Statistics and Analysis Unit. *PAHO Regional Mortality Database*. Washington DC, 2010. Available at www.paho.org/Spanish/SHA/coredata/tabulator/newTabulator.htm. We did not include these 2010 data in the figures and graphs created for this chapter (since they were subsequently dropped from the 2016 PAHO report) but include them here for readers' reference.
Data for Peru (marked with **) come from the panel dataset published online by the Pan American Health Organization, Health Information and Analysis Unit. *Regional Core Health Data Initiative*. Washington DC, 2014. Available at www1.paho.org/English/SHA/coredata/tabulator/newTabulator.htm. Last visited in July 2015. Corrected mortality rates are based on observed mortality data, applying a correction for mortality under-registration and ill-defined deaths.
NA means that the data for that year/country are not available.
Figures for Honduras are significantly lower than the data reported in UNDP 2013 Informe Regional de Desarrollo Humano 2013–2014 Seguridad Ciudadana con Rostro Humano: Anexo Estadístico-Metodológico. New York, NY, p. 65. (37 for 2005, 46.2 for 2006, 49.9 for 2007, 57.9 for 2008, 66.8 for 2009, 77.5 for 2010, and 86.5 for 2011). Thus, we did not include them in this table. The book's conclusion revisits the case of Honduras.
Figures for El Salvador and Guatemala are sometimes reported as considerably higher than the figures reported in this table. See, for example, Inter-American Development Bank 2000 Report, reprinted in Hugo Acero Velásquez. 2002. "Salud, violencia y seguridad." In *Ciudad y políticas públicas de seguridad y convivencia*. www.suivd.gov.co/ciudad/MexicoMarzohacero.doc. Even the lower estimates, however, place these cases at the upper tier of per capita homicide rates in the region.

2

Engaging the Theoretical Debate and Alternative Arguments

Why would homicide levels spike in third wave democracies? How do we explain why some countries emerged from war with extreme homicide rates and others with relatively low rates? This book features an argument about the types of illicit political economies that underpin homicidal ecologies – one that tracks the tripartite interaction between weak states, transnational and local illicit trade and transit, and organizational competition over subnational enclaves. In this way, the argument is self-consciously attentive to political-institutional conditions that facilitate violent crime, political economy factors that define core material interests (which depend on territorial control), and the organizations that act in homicidal ways. Thus, in its focus on why, when, and where actors will kill, my argument privileges the role of *organizations* rather than individuals. These organizations privilege territorial control as a sine qua non for short-term and long-term survival and material gain; they maneuver within and across borders, operate between licit and illicit spaces, and assume both state and parastatal forms. This book unpacks its general argument in Part II (Chapters 3 and 4), before analyzing the particular cases in Part III.

A vast literature on violence exists. This chapter evaluates the literature about violence in democratic, non–civil war settings. As discussed later, there is much to glean from this literature. I analyze four different, alternative approaches to explaining violence, discussing them on their own terms as well as highlighting where they do (or do not) provide a compelling explanation of Latin America's contemporary patterns of homicidal violence. These four types of arguments contend that (1) political transitions (following civil wars and/or as part of democratization) create institutional uncertainty and insecurity gaps that can result in higher violence, (2) sociologically fractured civil societies (including weak social capital) offer up anomic individuals both prone to violent behavior and unregulated by their environments, (3) harsh economic conditions (i.e., inequality and/or neoliberal reforms) generate individual grievances that increase the risk of violent behavior, and (4) historical legacies of state formation privilege certain actors who resort to coercion to defend their privilege. The first three approaches, as a whole, aim to explain why *individuals* are compelled to violence to address a range of poor political and economic conditions. The final approach highlights class and state actors. I contend that these four approaches begin with the wrong point of departure, since organizations and organizational dynamics – not particular individuals or classes – will prove key to explaining high-homicide-level cases in contemporary Latin America. In some cases, organizational actors will react against poor conditions as a survival strategy. In others, they will take advantage of new illicit "opportunities," seeking to reap huge advantages. Organizations are consequential to this argument, particularly when they form part of the illicit economy and are seeking to control subnational territorial enclaves; they are able to do so in the context of weak states (which are a legacy best explained by the fourth approach outlined earlier).

Thus, before this book develops its tripartite argument featuring how organizations navigate the transnational illicit economy, weak states, and territorial competition, the current chapter first sketches out the broader theoretical debates addressing violence in democracy. It introduces and evaluates four sets of alternative arguments, which privilege different assumptions about the core actors and their propensity to commit violent crimes. Readers interested in jumping straight to this book's core argument can turn to Chapters 3 and 4.

POLITICAL TRANSITIONS: CIVIL WARS AND DEMOCRATIZATION

A first set of arguments about violence privileges political context in general, and political transitions in particular, following civil wars and/ or during a period of democratization. The overarching argument in this line of thought is that some political environments are more propitious than others for violence – especially where public security gaps are filled by actors who were adversely affected by the outgoing regime and/or disadvantaged by political transitions. This dynamic is tied to poor institutional environments, whether because the state is absent, complicit, changing, and/or corrupt. In this regard, institutions are not fully instantiated, societies are in flux, and violence is therefore less contained. Individuals of various backgrounds accordingly resort to higher crime and violence. Two significant versions of this argument start with this premise and trace out why homicide rates have skyrocketed in the new democracies. One emphasizes the impact of civil war transitions in particular, while the other focuses on democratic transitions in general.

Civil War Legacies

Civil wars are credited with leaving a legacy of violence. They are moments of extreme polarization and uncertainty – during the fighting and often in its aftermath. Thus, the end of civil wars can leave societies with institutional vacuums that are prone to post–civil war violence – including crime and homicides. The reasons offered are manifold, and the outcome is arguably overdetermined in countries that were wracked by years of political violence and political polarization. Arguments focused on *post–civil war transitions* highlight some combination of the following four factors:

1. *Demobilization and arms*: With the end of civil wars, demobilized paramilitaries, insurgencies, and armies left many without jobs, and elevated levels of arms made their way into society. The democratic effort to promote peace in fact multiplied the agents and arms that were subsequently used by now-unemployed or disengaged former soldiers and combatants – some of whom themselves had been involved in the illicit economy.
2. *Destroyed families*: As families were torn apart by civil wars, generations of children were left without families and networks. Gangs and organized crime provided a space for displaced youth seeking community and support. Over time, these gangs socialized and compelled people to engage in violence.
3. *Habits and tolerance for political violence:* High levels of political violence from the authoritarian period translate into generalized social violence during the democratic period.
4. *Militarized states*: Civil wars reinforced militarized states that foster violence and benefit from it. This multitiered argument incorporates various dimensions – all of which are informed by the civil war, its end, and the transition away from military rule – that foster various forms of violence.

Charles T. Call (2003) deftly makes these kinds of arguments and was among the first to analyze post–civil violence rates in El Salvador. It is worth quoting his discussion at length:

The end of civil war and the political transition fuelled a dramatic rise in crime for several reasons. First, the vast majority of combatants were demobilised in an extremely brief period following the end of the war. Within one year, 12,362 guerillas, some 20,000 soldiers and around 30,000 civil defence guards were left unemployed. Leaving a *public security gap*, the number of people circulating under arms decreased from 60,000 (including combatants on both sides) to only about 6,000 National Police officers, as all armed forces personnel were confined to quarters during the demobilisation process in early 1992. The peace processes in both El Salvador and Nicaragua left thousands of weapons in civilian hands. In 2000, the Defence Ministry reported 165,186 firearms registered for personal or commercial use, with an estimated 200,000 additional unregistered. Social habituation to using violence as a means of resolving conflicts also contributed to the crime wave.

The transaction costs of security reform also abetted growing crime. Disruption of the internal security system took its toll. The eventual turnover of almost the entire investigative units meant that networks of informants had to be reconstructed. A large number of former combatants were also implicated in criminal activity, sometimes working together in gangs. A 1999 survey sample of the country's prison inmates found that 22 per cent of them had been members of the armed forces or the old security forces, and 6 per cent were ex-guerillas. Of prisoners between 26 and 40 years of age, 44 per cent were ex-combatants, even though only 6 per cent of the general population had served in the war. Furthermore, while the retention of relatively few former police helped vacate a prior institutional culture of impunity and military-style policing, it also left fewer experienced police on the force. *In sum, the combination of peace and regime change opened the door both to reforms and diffuse violence.* (Call 2003: 843; emphasis added)

Rising violent crime, it would seem, is overdetermined by the end of civil wars, especially where a public security gap emerges because of ready access to arms, the disruption of security institutions capable of securing law and order, and unemployed former members of armed forces and ex-guerillas. These kinds of civil war–oriented arguments have been particularly revealing and prevalent in discussions of Central America, particularly those analyzing Guatemala and El Salvador.[1] Call brought our attention to many of these dynamics that played out so vividly in the context of El Salvador, in particular.

Yet, despite their initial plausibility, civil war transition arguments, when taken as the core causal variable, do not easily explain the comparative causes, timing, and geographic scope of violence in the region as a whole – not least because they do not correlate with the cases that experience high and low homicidal violence. While Call's argument

---

[1] See, for example, Call (2003) and Levenson (2013).

(based on impressive and original fieldwork) does provide important insight into high-homicide, post–civil war cases in Central America (El Salvador and Guatemala among them), it does not *explain* subnational patterns. Nor does it clearly travel beyond these national cases. Intermediate, high, and rising homicide rates also occur in non–civil war cases (for example, Honduras, Brazil, Mexico, and Venezuela). Moreover, parallel patterns of violence have not occurred in all civil war cases, as in Nicaragua (which experienced a civil war and rapid demobilization, although its security forces remained relatively stable, as discussed in Part III of this book).[2] In other words, there seems to be no necessary or direct relationship between the homicidal ecologies/geographies and historic transitions and legacies of national civil wars/transitions in the region. If we revisit Table 1.1 (presented in Chapter 1) and this time demarcate which cases experienced recent civil wars (Table 2.1), we see that civil war is a blunt (and arguably misleading) instrument for explaining regional variation.

Indeed, even a discussion of firearm rates (a partial legacy of the war) provides much too blunt an instrument for explaining if, why, and how firearms are deployed. Not only does the subnational geography of civil war violence fail to map onto the subnational geography of contemporary violence, but, moreover, arguments about residual firearms increasing violence do not explain the varied cross-national patterns that we see. While it is reported that firearms (licensed and unlicensed) are responsible for 65–70 percent of reported homicides in the region (World Bank 2010, volume 2: 73), this does not mean that firearm levels primarily cause or explain this outcome.[3] The World Bank 2010 study, for example, suggests that availability of firearms might be part of the explanation; yet the data that it provides question that tentative assertion. As Table 2.2's final column highlights, very high and intermediate homicide rates correlate with comparable estimated per capita gun rates. Thus, while high levels of gun ownership increase the capacity to kill, they do not explain the

---

[2] Civil war human rights violators, moreover, are not necessarily confined to national borders: for example, according to reports that some former military men such as the Guatemalan Kaibiles (an elite Guatemalan counterinsurgency unit that committed some of the worst human rights violations during Guatemala's civil war) moved to (and were arrested in) Mexico to take part in organized crime (UNODC 2007: 37). UNODC (2007: 37) cites 2005 LatinNews.com security reports for developments in the Mexican Gulf Cartel, which actively recruited the Kaibiles (some of whom have provided security to local drug bosses).

[3] World Bank 2010 (volume 2: 75), further on in the report, states that this rate is 80 percent of killings for El Salvador (2006) and approximately the same for Guatemala.

TABLE 2.1 *National homicide trajectories: stability, levels, and varied experiences with recent civil war (1995–2012)*

| | "Low" levels (< 10 annual homicides per 100,000 per capita) | "Intermediate" levels (10–39 annual homicides, per 100,000 per capita) || Extremely high levels (> 40 annual homicides per 100,000 per capita) |
		Lower band (10–19 per 100,000)	Upper band (20–39 per 100,000)	
Relative stability of homicide rates	Argentina, Chile, Costa Rica,* Cuba, United States, PERU, Uruguay	Dominican Republic, Ecuador, NICARAGUA, Panama, Paraguay	Brazil, Puerto Rico	
Relative instability of homicide rates		Mexico	Venezuela**	COLOMBIA, EL SALVADOR, GUATEMALA**

Note: Modification of Table 1.1: countries with recent civil war in bold type and capitalized.
*Costa Rica's rate is between 10 and 11 per 100,000 in 2008, 2009, and 2010. Of note, Costa Rica experienced a civil war prior to its transition in 1949. However, it is not highlighted in this table because that period significantly precedes the contemporary third wave of democratization.
**UNODC data would also place Honduras, Venezuela, and Jamaica in the bottom right cell.

circumstances under which firearms are deployed. As with deterrence theory and theories of war, we must *also* ascertain the motives for restraining versus deploying weapons of destruction. Therefore, we must turn to other core factors.

Central American arms imports over time (2000–2006) also do not suggest a powerful explanation of levels of homicide (World Bank 2010, volume 2: figure 5.1: 75). El Salvador has had the highest rate of per capita homicide, and yet its firearm rate is significantly below that of Guatemala and also that of Honduras for most of these years. Guatemala's firearm rates skyrocket in these same years (which corresponds with rising homicide rates), but the question is why violence is not even higher in Guatemala than in the other countries listed. By contrast, Costa Rica's and Nicaragua's firearm rates sometimes surpass El Salvador's, despite the fact that the former two countries have significantly lower homicide rates.

TABLE 2.2 *Firearms owned by civilians in Central America (2007)*

Country	Registered	Estimated	Guns per 100 people	Homicide levels
Costa Rica	43,241	115,000	2.8	Low
El Salvador*	198,000	450,000	7.0	Very high
Guatemala	147,581	1,950,000	15.8	Very high
Honduras	133,185	450,000	6.2	Very high
Nicaragua	NA	385,000	7.0	Intermediate
Panama	96.600	525,000	5.4	Intermediate

*Hume (2004: 16), citing work from Cruz and Beltrán (2000: 9), indicates that of the 400,000–450,000 firearms held by civilians, less than 36 percent are held legally. Importantly, they indicate, "this translates into 2 firearms for every ten adults," which is significantly higher than the figure cited in the table.

Source: World Bank (2010, volume 1: 20 and volume 2: 75), based on Karp 2008 and Arias Foundation 2005.

Notes: Final column inserted by author based on Table 1.1. Rocha (2007: 23) notes that in 2000, Nicaragua did have relatively low levels of legal guns. He cites similar numbers for registered guns, with some differences: Nicaragua (52,390), Costa Rica (43,241, same as cited here), El Salvador (170,000, lower than cited here), Guatemala (147,581, same as cited here), and Panama (96,614, lower than cited here). While recognizing that there is likely to be a significant number of unregistered arms, he maintains that the overall level is lower in Nicaragua than in the "northern triangle" of Central America. His data come from Gonick, Muggah, and Waszink (2003), *Balas perdidas: el impacto del mal uso de armas pequeñas en Centroamérica*. Published jointly with the Small Arms Survey and the Norway initiative on the transference of small arms.

In short, guns kill. And gun control is essential. But the availability and imports of guns are both likely to be endogenous to some other factor and begs the question of why rates diverge, why there are different markets for arms, and why people choose to deploy them more often in some places than in others.

Finally, even were we to restrict our gaze to post–civil war cases with high national homicide rates, the analytical/geographical reach of this civil war legacy argument must be probed further – especially since *contemporary subnational patterns of violence are not duplicating the subnational terrain of the civil war*. Indeed, high homicide rates are not occurring in the Salvadoran and Guatemalan regions where war was most severe. Taking Guatemala as an example, we know that contemporary homicide rates have been geographically highest in the Petén (with 60–70 homicides per 100,000), the eastern states (Jutiapa, Santa Rosa, Zacapa, Chiquimula, Izabal – with the ranking among them shifting across years), and the department of Guatemala (see Figure 2.1).

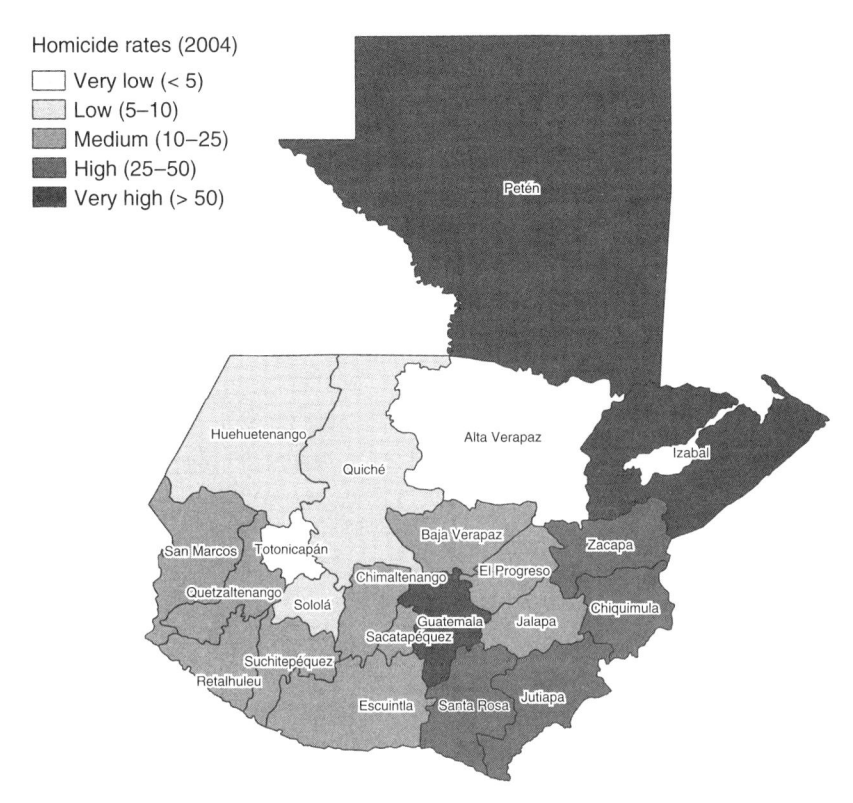

Engaging the Theoretical Debate and Alternative Arguments 31

FIGURE 2.1 Map of Guatemala: departmental homicide rates (2004)
Map (2004) created by Vinay Jawahar and reformatted by Daniela Barba-Sánchez.
Source: Homicide data obtained from Carlos Mendoza, Instituto Nacional de Estadística (Guatemala). 2005. *CD-ROM de homicidios 1986–2004*, Guatemala: INE, Departamento de Estadísticas Vitales. Estimates for 2000–2004: Instituto Nacional de Estadística (Guatemala). 2001. *Guatemala, proyecciones de población a nivel departamental y municipal por año calendario: período 2000–2005*. Guatemala: INE.
Note: Homicides are defined according to the World Health Organization standard classification E960–E969 in the *International Classification of Diseases*, 9th rev. (ICD-9), or X85–Y09 in the *International Statistical Classification of Diseases and Related Health Problems*, 10th rev. (ICD-10). Homicide rates are defined as the number of homicides per 100,000 population and calculated using homicide data and population estimates.

The 2004 map in the figure highlights this geographic variation (although using a different scale than the one used for most of the book). While the civil war did eventually move into the Petén, it was largely fought in the western highlands, where homicide rates are considerably lower than in the rest of the country. Thus, the main violence in Guatemala neither occurs where the civil war was largely fought nor is it necessarily perpetrated by actors (on either side) that took the lead in fighting the civil war. More research is needed to identify the collective actors and the motives of those who take up arms to kill their fellow citizens.

If we zoom in even further to analyze municipal data, two violent departmental capitals stand out: Guatemala City, Guatemala, has experienced high homicide rates, reaching as high as 100-plus murders per 100,000 inhabitants in 2002 and even higher in subsequent years; Cuilapa, Santa Rosa, experienced homicide rates as unfathomably high as 200 in the mid-1990s and wavering in the high/low 100s in years after that (falling below 100 in 2003 and 2004). Of course, given the size of the cities (Cuilapa is much smaller than Guatemala City), the absolute numbers are much higher in Guatemala City and environs, but the violence has been proportionally higher or equal in Cuilapa. These departmental (and municipal) data indicate that the highest homicide rates are *not* occurring in the departments where the civil war was largely fought (the western side/highland region of the country, with some fighting in the Petén), but rather in the eastern and northern parts of the country (for reasons explored in later chapters).[4] Therefore, today's homicide rates in Latin America's highest homicide-rate countries (Guatemala and El Salvador) do not map onto the subnational geography of what is understood to be the area of heaviest civil war violence. A similar analysis for El Salvador (which is undertaken in Part III of the book) also shows that the area of violence is not duplicating the terrain of the civil war.

Hence, civil wars can be the primary explanation of *neither* region-wide *nor* subnational trends in violence. Civil war transition/legacy is too specific a variable to explain the geographic scope of violence in the Americas, which extends beyond civil war cases (and is not duplicated in all post–civil war cases). If we are to understand these regional trends, we need to consider what these post–civil war countries share with their

---

[4] Also see World Bank (2010). That report notes that while civil wars have at times increased the availability of arms, a possible causal connection to violence is plausible but not entirely clear.

non–civil war counterparts (as well as what explains the variation *among* post–civil war cases). In this regard, Call's work, in particular, provides an important analytic cue about which state institutions matter. As discussed later, we *do* need to analyze rule of law and security institutions in countries that face high homicide rates; weak/corrupt security apparatuses can emerge in post–civil war cases, but they can also be present in non–civil war cases. Thus, while civil wars have certainly affected contemporary security institutions, civil wars alone do not provide a compelling comparative explanation of which contemporary security institutions across Latin America impact or deter high violence rates in this third wave of democracy. Importantly, then, although civil war transitions do increase uncertainty, and civil war legacies *might* plausibly explain *repertoires of violent acts* (i.e., *how* people kill) and even *tolerance levels* for risk and security, the civil war transitions explanation (and the various mechanisms noted at the start of this chapter) does not explain where and why homicidal crime skyrockets in contemporary Latin America. To answer this question, we must complement the political opportunity/constraints reasoning posed in this type of argument with a focus on who is driving the high homicide rates and why.

Regime Change/Democratization

A second subset of political transitions focuses less on the inherited institutions of the state and more on the changes that accompany democratization. Democratization arguments include those about transitional moments (Lafree and Tseloni 2006), politicized actors defending national identities and elite interests (Snyder 2000; Mansfield and Snyder 2002), and permissive security institutions (Cruz 2011b). To some degree, all of the cited works pinpoint democratic transitions as generating the uncertainty that often leads to greater violence (of varying sorts).

Lafree and Tseloni (2006) probe the relationship between market-based democratization and violence. Their statistical analysis aims to adjudicate between different and contradictory claims in the literature about whether the spread of democracy and/or markets/inequality (which are presumed to go together) generate more or less violent crime.[5] Their statistical analysis of the World Health Organization (WHO) dataset

---

[5] Unfortunately, Lafree and Tseloni (2006) conflate the terms *democratization, development*, and *market-based democratization* in much of their text. This inhibits their ability to distinguish analytically between regime changes and economic reforms.

leads them to support a Durkheimian interpretation that democratization's rapid transformation predicts greater violent crime (as opposed to the argument that democratization necessarily decreases it or that democratic *markets* induce the kind of inequality that leads to greater violence). According to Lafree and Tseloni (2006), violence seems to peak during the transitional phase of democratization – although violence *also* appears to be affected by the percentage of the population between the ages of 15 and 24, prosperity (measured by the Gini index and GDP), and regional effects. They also note that over the long term, crime will increase in full democracies but not in transitional ones. This study, while suggestive, is unpersuasive. Not only is the concept of transitional democracy underspecified (and too readily equated with markets, for which it has an elective affinity), but the exact relationship between crime peaking in transitional democracies but ultimately increasing over time in full but not transitional democracies is vague and unspecified. The authors identify a general statistical relationship but neither explain nor substantiate the link, leaving little analytical traction for evaluating if and how democratization affects violence.

More to the point, the variation in violence levels in Latin America's new democracies remains unexplained by this statistical study, which Lafree and Tseloni (2006) readily admit is based on incomplete information and biased toward trends in advanced industrial countries, given data-reporting problems in the WHO sample. Almost the entire Latin American region transitioned from authoritarian to democratic rule (and almost all subsequently increased the marketization of their economies), and yet violence levels do not affect this region equally. What this suggests is that the democratization variable used by Lafree and Tseloni is poorly specified *and* too general to explain the variation in trends that we see in the Latin American region, in particular.

Mansfield and Snyder (2002) also analyze the link between regime change and violence and find a positive relationship. Transitional regimes are the ones most prone to violence, they argue. Violent nationalist wars and interstate wars are most likely in regimes transitioning from autocracy to democracy – particularly where institutions are weak, power is not concentrated in the hands of public officials, and elites feel threatened by the transition.[6] In this study, the authors are careful to define their terms;

---

[6] The Mansfield and Snyder (2002) article, "Democratic Transitions, Institutional Strength, and War," *International Organization*, elaborates on arguments made in earlier versions of their work.

they use a precise and institutional measure of democracy.[7] But the particular focus of their study is on violent nationalist wars and interstate wars, which do not echo the empirical pattern in Latin America. Therefore, Mansfield and Snyder's argument does not travel to the Latin American context and provides little direct analytical traction to the question posed by this book.

Turning to Central America in particular, Cruz (2011a and 2011b) argues for a link between criminal violence and democratization. He contends that the terms of different public security reforms impacted the state's ability to manage violence in three high-homicide cases (El Salvador, Guatemala, and Honduras), in striking contrast with one relatively low-homicide case (Nicaragua). Not only did violent entrepreneurs continue to operate in the post-authoritarian security institutions, but they also sustained relations with governing elites – all of which provided a permissive political environment for violence in Central America's northern triangle (again in contrast to Nicaragua). My work approximates that of Cruz. Like Cruz (and Call), I analyze the kinds of security institutions that emerged from transitions (although not necessarily democratic transitions). And like Cruz, I find that they provided a permissive political environment. This is a critical and shared observation. However, permissive environments are only one part of the analytic, as I argue that we must also identify the most likely perpetrators and why and under what conditions they drive the high homicide rates. Thus, I find Cruz's argument compelling as an initial building block. However, I do not feature democratization, per se, as the core variable defining subsequent paths. Rather, when focusing on political institutions, I privilege the role of state security institutions (the police in particular) whose origins are not solely reducible to the democratic transition moment.

In short, political transition arguments (whether focused on civil war transitions and/or democratization) cannot fully explain the violence that we see in contemporary Latin America. They provide leverage for thinking about opportunities but not for analyzing the collective actors that emerge and deploy violence in this context. Yet the literature, particularly work by Call (2003) and Cruz (2011b), does importantly and usefully spotlight

---

[7] Also see Snyder (2000), where he argues that nationalist violence can be particularly rife at moments of democratization. While ethnic violence is conceptually distinct from violent crime, the common argument is that democratization can provide the political opportunity for actors to use violence.

the importance of state institutions and features the ones that might matter most – namely those responsible for maintaining law and order, such as the military, the police, and the courts. This last point will prove crucial in this book, and thus I explore it at the end of the chapter in light both of arguments about historical institutional legacies of state formation – an approach that might allow us to analyze the varied reach of the state and the circumstances under which we find weak and complicit security forces.

SOCIOLOGICAL ARGUMENTS

A second set of arguments shifts the analytic frame to feature the societies that experience high levels of violence. The claim is that sociological factors are key in explaining the constraints that actors face. While the point of departure is distinct, these sociological arguments tend to analyze how society conditions *individual* actors to (dis)engage in violent crime. Strikingly, these approaches – which ironically look at the organization of society as it facilitates or impedes violence – largely neglect to analyze the collective actors responsible for committing the violence.

Civil Societies

A prevalent sociological approach privileges the role of civil societies (drawing on the now-abundant literature on civil society and social capital).[8] It advances the claim that the *density* of civil society might explain patterns of violence. In particular, where communities are densely organized (especially if they bridge and bond across different cleavages), organizations and the people therein are able to prevent individual youth from turning to a life of crime and, hence, violence. For example, initial quantitative studies by Moser and McIlwaine (2004 and 2006) and a three-volume University of Central America (UCA) study (UCA 2004)[9] suggest that stronger civil societies work to make violence less possible – not only because they work against youth joining gangs (since they have other places to join), but also because they can provide

---

[8] "Dilulio argues that the prevalence of high crime rates in U.S. cities is related to the depletion of what social scientists call social capital" (Fajnzylber, Lederman, and Loayza 2000: 231). Of course, crime does not equal violence, but the argument parallels the one found in some of the literature on Latin America.

[9] *Maras y pandillas en Centroamérica*. Volumes I–III. 2004. Managua, Nicaragua: Universidad Centroamericana.

community checks (via community policing strategies and communication). In the cases of Central America, for example, one could hypothesize that whereas civil wars destroyed urban networks in El Salvador and Guatemala, leaving youth open to mobilization, the Sandinistas in Nicaragua left in place strong community networks that were subsequently used to channel youth into activities and to place checks on their engagement with groups that deployed violence.

A civil society argument resonates with some anecdotal narratives found in the UCA (2004) study, although that early study is self-consciously exploratory rather than definitive, given the difficulty of studying communities in which violent crime is high and the corresponding methodological challenges. Mo Hume (2004: 24) introduces a variant of this argument (as part of her broader analysis of poverty and violence in El Salvador) when noting that the massive movement of people (not only those leaving the country but also massive urbanization patterns) inserted an element of mistrust in a context of a civil war that perhaps had already weakened social capital in urban centers. She notes that San Salvador's population increased by over 400 percent between 1950 and 1992, fostering a climate of mistrust in a context of already-mistrustful relations fostered by the presence of intelligence structures. A vicious cycle has ensued in post-war El Salvador, she argues, wherein high violence further exacerbates mistrust, thereby weakening the very social capital that might otherwise place (some) check on the individual actors and by extension the ensuing violence.

Yet, broader critiques of civil society arguments have shown that dense social networks can be normatively neutral – captured and deployed for a variety of ends. If there are examples where community organizing prevented individual youth from turning to violent crime, there are also examples where criminal organizations were able to capture civil society organizations toward other ends. In his study of local communities in Rio de Janeiro, Brazil, for example, Arias (2006a, 2006b) highlights the ways in which civil society networks were captured to perpetrate corruption and the domination of organized crime. Indeed, for all the euphoria that emerged around civil society and social capital organizations, what has also become clear is that there can be a "dark side" to these organizations.[10] Thus, the important analytical question about social capital and civil society networks is not simply their presence (and how

---

[10] See Sheri Berman (1997), James Putzel (1997), and Amaney Jamal (2007) for examples.

individuals respond) but *who* structures and uses these social ties (or captures them) and how organizations can martial them for different ends.

Another set of civil society arguments do not look at *density* (and its impact on individuals) but rather the *types* of organizations that can monitor violence: horizontal versus vertical (Putnam 1993), intra- versus inter-communal ties, and quotidian versus associational interactions (Varshney 2002), as well as bridging and/or bonding (World Bank studies such as Woolcock and Narayan 2000). While this approach might hold more promise than a focus on the density and vibrancy of civil society per se, there is little evidence at present to argue one way or another about the types of social organizations that constrain the rise in violence in the region. Indeed, a focus on civil society networks (whether looking at density or quality) begs the question as to why those networks are present (i.e., whether they are endogenous to, for example, national liberation movements, state policy, inequality, etc.), why the violence *rises* in countries whose civil societies took form long before the homicide spikes, and *who the actors are that are engaging in higher levels of violence*. In these studies, social capital and civil society usually serve as breaks in, not drivers of, violence. Therefore, they fall short of explaining when and *why* collective actors turn to violence. Accordingly, civil society arguments might play a mediating role, but absent analysis of the political parties and states within which civil societies are embedded, these arguments are incomplete and arguably endogenous to other factors (as argued by Berman 1997 and Jamal 2007).

Demographic Variables

An alternative sociological approach assesses prevailing demographic patterns in society. In particular, this approach analyzes risk factors such as the number of youth as a percentage of the (urban) population, single-headed households, unemployment rates especially for male youth (related to the labor market discussion under "Arguments about Violence and Economic Incentives"), education levels (or patterns of school attendance), patterns of domestic and societal violence (which arguably socialize youth to engage in further violence), or social spending on youth. WHO especially argues that these kinds of factors help discern the types of individuals that are at risk.

One of the prevailing demographic-type arguments is that higher percentages of youth in a given population (especially male youth or urban youth) increase the odds of violence. These types of arguments are commonly mentioned in Latin America, but the data do not seem to support a simple causal relationship. There are minimal differences in youth rates across countries, with the highest youth rates coinciding with a wide range of homicide rates. By 2012, young people as a percentage of the total population ranged from a low of 20.4 in Cuba to a high of 30.2 in Nicaragua, with most Latin American countries reporting rates in the mid-20s and most of Central America's cases, excepting that of Panama, reporting on the higher end of that range (Economic Commission for Latin America and the Caribbean [ECLAC] 2014: 53). If one analyzes social investment figures in youth (by percentage of social spending or by GDP), one also fails to predict the tripartite categorization of homicide rates outlined in Chapter 1 (see Figure 2.2).

One might in turn hypothesize that the youth are among the poorest and thus most amenable to criminal and violent behavior. While poverty is higher among Latin America youth compared to older citizens (i.e., those over 55) (ECLAC 2014: 69), and while unemployment data are difficult to capture and compare, these data do not predict which countries are likely to exhibit higher homicide levels. National unemployment rates among those ages 15–24 do not go far toward explaining the highest violence rates (in El Salvador, Guatemala, and Honduras – excluding Colombia as a civil war) (see Figure 2.3).

Thus, a demographic approach (often deployed in medical/clinical fields) might reveal risk factors, but it begs the analytical question of who the perpetrators are likely to be (are they in fact largely youth?) and when and why these perpetrators would choose to kill. Moreover, the cross-national data provide limited purchase on cross-national, cross-temporal, or cross-sectional variation on homicide rates. While one can infer why unemployed youth might engage in a life of crime, it is not clear why they would *kill* absent other causes. Moreover, even if high rates of unemployed urban youth correlate in some cases with high violence (e.g., in Honduras), the same does not hold for all cases (e.g., Nicaragua). And there are examples of an increase in violence in the years when urban youth percentages decline (as in Mexico). Importantly, the WHO outlines many risk factors in thinking about violence, and it reports that the numerous risk factors are neither causes nor elements necessary for explaining violence when and where it emerges. Risk factors are not causal. For this study, therefore, I privilege an analysis of the conditions, the likely actors, and the motives leading to violent crime rather than beginning with a demographic approach that implicitly, if

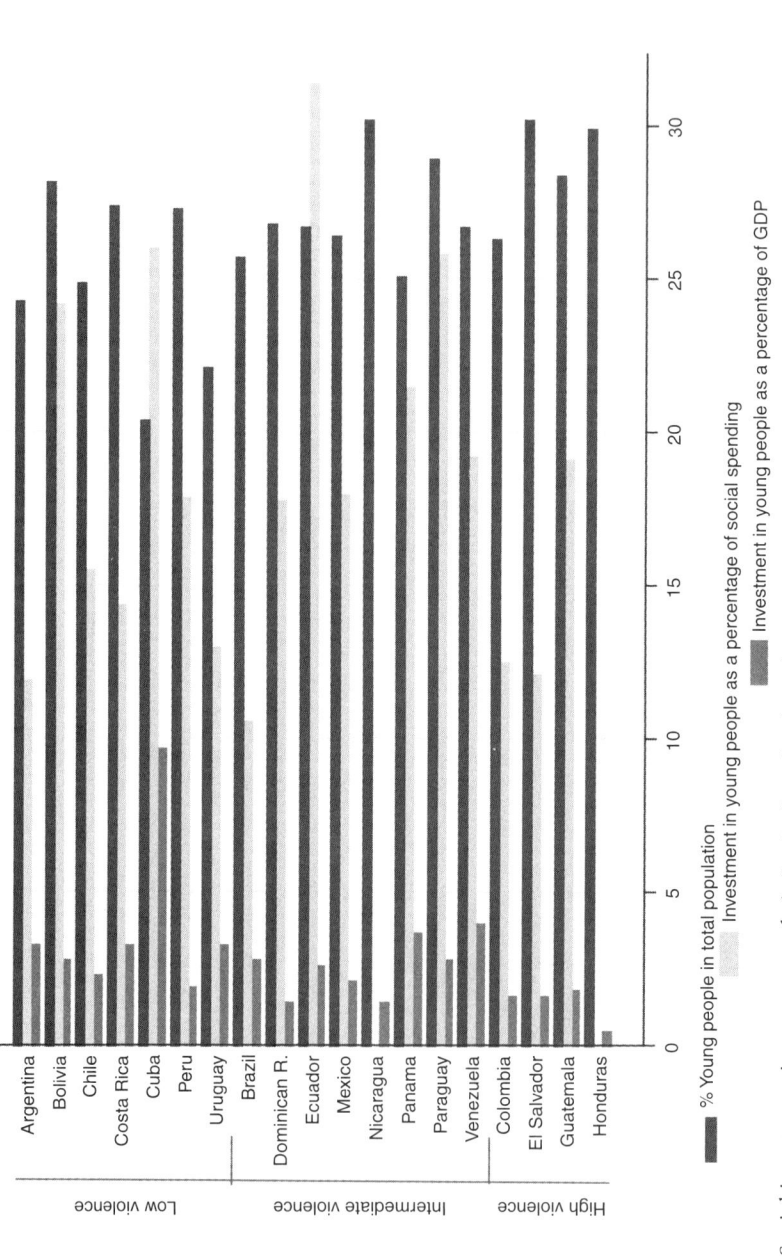

FIGURE 2.2 Social investment in young people in Latin America (2012)
Graph created for this project by Daniela Barba-Sánchez using Stata.
Source: Data from ECLAC. 2014. *Social Panorama of Latin America 2014*. Santiago, Chile, p. 268.
NB: "Economic Commission for Latin America and the Caribbean (ECLAC), social expenditure database and calculations on the basis of conditional cash transfer programmes and data provided by the UNESCO Institute of Statistics, World Health Organization and Inter-American Development Bank (IDB)."

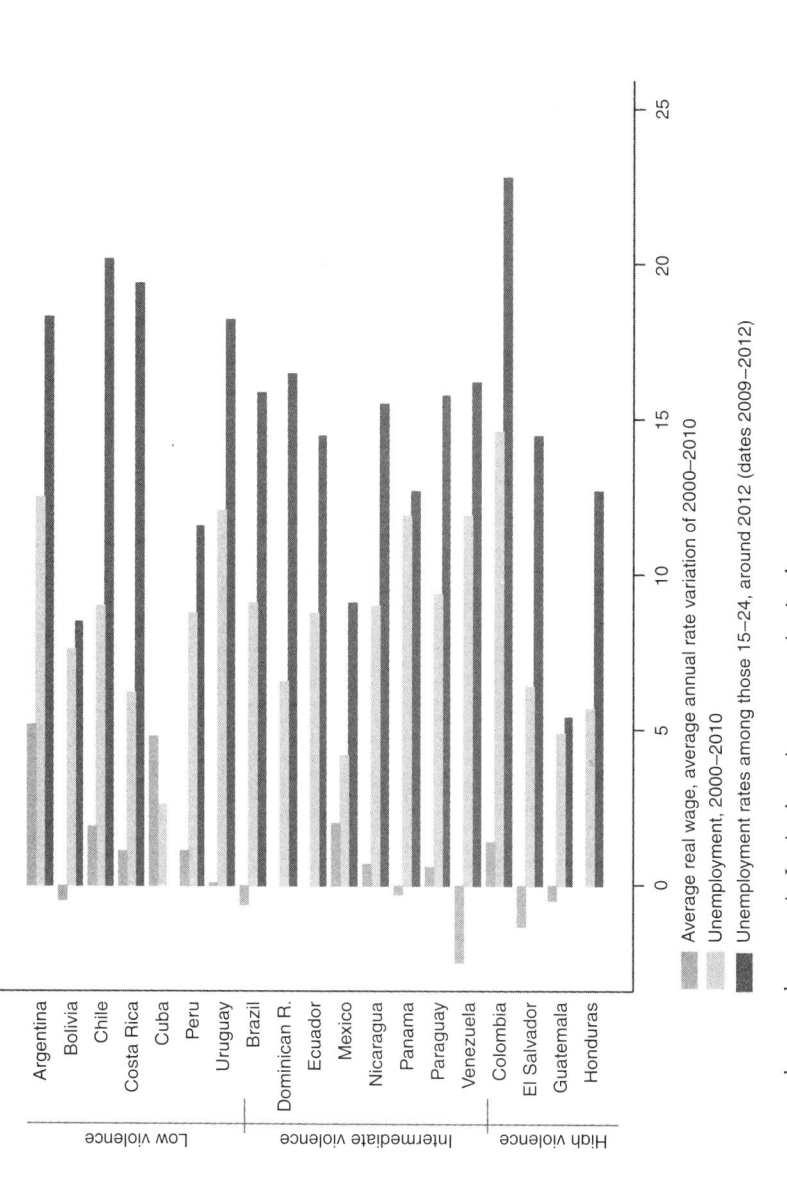

FIGURE 2.3 Average wage and unemployment in Latin American countries in the 2000s
Source: Data from ECLAC. 2014. *Social Panorama of Latin America 2014*. Santiago, Chile, pp. 60–62 (reformatted as bar graph).
NB: ECLAC (2014: 60–62) reports data for average real wage and average unemployment. The Guatemala data for 2000–2010 include statistics for 2002–2004 and 2010. Honduras data refer to 2001 onward. Peru's unemployment figures are for Lima (city) only.
ECLAC (2014: 28) reports data for unemployment rate among those aged 15–24, around 2012, on the basis of special tabulations of data from household surveys conducted in Latin American countries. For Caribbean countries: Mónica Parra-Torrado, "Youth Unemployment in the Caribbean," Working Paper, Caribbean Knowledge Series. Washington, DC, World Bank, 2014.

unintentionally, demonizes the youth and the poor, with limited empirical evidence to back it up.

Ethnic Cleavages

A sociological approach might look beyond civil society (prevention) and/or risk (demographics) to focus on particular types of cleavages (motivation). The social science literature, for example, often poses the question of whether ethnic diversity, ethnically strong cleavages, and reinforcing ethnic and class cleavages are particularly prone to violence. Yet across the region there is also little evidence to suggest that ethnic cleavages are driving the violence in Latin America.[11] There are no visible signs (platforms, discourse, actions) that suggest that the perpetrators or victims are defined by ethnic cleavages or motivated by ethnic concerns. Nor does the violence correlate systematically with countries with the most ethnically diverse or polarized situations. The Andean countries of Bolivia, Ecuador, and Peru have amongst the most diverse ethnic populations in the region (and increasingly politicized ethnic cleavages); however, they exhibit relatively low violence levels in the third wave of democracy. Guatemala is the one case that does exhibit great ethnic diversity and high violence; however, I find no causal link between the two, as I discuss in Chapter 5. Ethnic demography is constant, and violence has been rising; more importantly, post-civil war homicides do not appear to have an ethnic or racial cast for the subjects or objects of the violence. Indeed, the UNODC (2007: 55) indicates (citing UNDP 2005: 395 data) that in 2004, violence in Guatemala was lowest in the regions with the highest indigenous populations. There is no visible relationship between ethnic composition and regions with the highest murder rates (also see Regina Bateson, n.d.); the lowest contemporary homicide rates are precisely where the greatest ethnic diversity exists (the western highlands), and

---

[11] The ethnic politics literature has long noted that ethnic cleavages are politically weaker in Latin America that other parts of the world. In recent years, these cleavages have become politicized – with the emergence of significant indigenous movements (Yashar 2005), indigenous parties (Van Cott 2005), and Afro-Latin movements (Hanchard 1998, Nobles 2000). However, these cleavages have rarely coincided with conflict. Bolivia has witnessed some violence during the 2000s but it is notable that Bolivia is not in the high violence category and, therefore, ethnic politics offer a weak explanation of violence patterns across the region.

the highest homicide rates often coincide with the regions (eastern lowlands) that are overwhelmingly mestizo/ladino (of mixed heritage, arguably the second-largest ethnic category in the country). Although it is possible that ethnic cleavages might shape the kinds of homicides that take place in some regions (i.e., how killings take place – lynching, whipping, etc.), I do not find evidence that ethnic cleavages are largely determining the *levels* of violence across the region.[12] Nor does it seem that electoral competition stokes ethnic violence, as some literature might suggest (Chandra 2004; Wilkinson 2004).[13]

Some interesting, new subnational work explores whether some indigenous communities might contribute to the violence – containing it in some Mexican regions while exacerbating it in some regions of Guatemala.[14] These promising studies reveal a great deal about subnational variation and dynamics, but at their core, their arguments are less about indigeneity or indigenous conflict and more about how the subject communities are differentially organized. Some of Mexico's indigenous communities are placing a check on the penetration of violent organizations, according to Ley, Mattiace, and Trejo (2016), while the legacy of civil defense patrols exacerbates local violence in what is today a relatively low-homicide region of Guatemala, according to Bateson (n.d.). Thus, it is important to disentangle ethnicity from organizational dynamics, which might not be derivative of or reducible to ethnicity per se.[15]

If ethnic cleavages are not driving the violent trends, do other cleavages or organizations matter? Might there be organizational forms and divides that are motivating the violence that we see? The next chapters take up this question and find that *organizations do matter*, but not as expressions of old institutions and/or old cleavages. Chapter 4 will discuss this argument in light of the illicit economies and state organizations that shape the homicidal ecologies in much of Latin America.

---

[12] Indeed, UNODC (referencing and perhaps romanticizing a civil society type of argument) hypothesizes that "it may be that predominantly indigenous provinces have greater levels of social cohesion, and this serves as a point of resilience to crime." United Nations Office on Drugs and Crime (UNODC). *Crime and Development in Central America: Caught in the Crossfire.* United Nations Publication, 2007, p. 55.

[13] While I am confident that the high violence in the region is not explained by electoral cycles stoking ethnic violence, it would be interesting to explore what impact electoral cycles might have on violence patterns as a whole.

[14] See the Ley, Mattiace, and Trejo (2016) paper on Mexico, presented at Brown University conference. Also see Regina Bateson book manuscript, n.d.

[15] See Chandra (2006) for a thoughtful conceptualization of ethnicity.

ECONOMIC INCENTIVES AND VIOLENCE

Economic arguments are also marshaled to explain contemporary violence. This approach often focuses on individuals and their motives for becoming criminals or engaging in criminal acts. Nobel laureate Gary Becker (1974), for example, whose arguments I refer to in this section, theorized the calculations taken by a would-be perpetrator – not only the economic incentives of engaging in a life of crime but also which policies are most/least likely to serve as a deterrent.

The perpetrator-focused explanation has led many scholars to focus on economic motivations (poverty and inequality chief among them) and the corresponding evaluation of costs and benefits. These arguments tend to be grievance based and make rationalist assumptions. These classic arguments understandably focus on individual actor motivations, and the literature is better at theorizing theft than homicide. Moreover, by focusing on individual motivations rather than organizational incentives and strategies, it cannot explain Latin America's extraordinarily high homicide rates relative to other regions. A brief foray into arguments about inequality and neoliberalism exemplify these analytic strengths and limitations.

Inequality

Inequality is often singled out as a cause of violent crime. Economists influenced by Becker have empirically analyzed inequality's relationship to crime – assuming a rationalist cost/benefit calculation on the part of individuals who evaluate the benefit of crime (related to socioeconomic gaps or inequality) relative to the cost (the likelihood of being apprehended and the degree of likely punishment). Econometric studies of global violence (measured as homicide rates), for example, have tested the inequality proposition by assessing homicide rates against the Gini index. These econometric studies suggest that the relationship is quite strong.[16] Gartner (1990) evaluates this relationship in the advanced industrial countries. Fajnzylber, Lederman, and Loayza (2000) observe that crime rates in the second half of the twentieth century increased all over the world and set out to explain the underlying patterns by analyzing

---

[16] See WHO report (2002: ch. 2, p. 37), which refers to studies by Gartner (1990); Unnithan and Whitt (1992); and Fajnzylber, Lederman, and Loayza (1999).

forty-five advanced industrial and developing countries.[17] (In this regard, one might argue that Latin America is part of a global trend.) They report that "crime rates in industrialized countries have increased by 300 to 400 percent since the late 1960s. From the early 1980s to the mid 1990s, the rate of intentional homicides increased by 50 percent in Latin America and sub-Saharan Africa and by more than 100 percent in Eastern Europe and Central Asia" (Fajnzylber, Lederman, and Loayza 2000: 220). Their econometric study of forty-five countries (covering the period of 1970–1994) finds that negative GDP growth rates, high inequality rates (measured by the Gini index), and lagged crime rates are all associated with national crime rates – in particular for homicides and robbery (Fajnzylber, Lederman, and Loayza 2000: 244 and passim).[18] Regarding GDP, they see a counter-cyclical effect. Economic decline is tied to an increase in violent crimes, both for robbery and homicides. They argue that increasing job opportunities and rising wages in the legal job market reduce the chances that actors will turn to criminal labor markets, and in turn engage in violent crime. Homicide rates might be explained in significant part, they suggest, "from economically motivated crimes that become violent" (Fajnzylber, Lederman and Loayza 2000: 246).

The estimated coefficients for the growth rate are not only statistically significant, but they are also economically important in magnitude. For homicides, the estimated growth coefficient implies that a one percentage point increase in the GDP growth rate is associated with a 2.4 percent decline in the homicide rate in the short run. In the case of robberies, a similar increase in the GDP growth rate leads to a short-run fall of 13.7 percent in the robbery rate. Thus, economic activity, using the GDP growth rate as a proxy, has a larger impact on typically economic crimes, such as robberies, than on more violent crimes, such as homicides. (Fajnzylber, Lederman and Loayza 2000: 247)

---

[17] Also see Fajnzylber, Lederman, and Loayza (2002a and 2002b), which make similar arguments to the 2000 article cited in text. For a critique of Fajnzylber, Lederman, and Loayza (2000), see the comments that follow this article by Peter Reuter and John Roman (2000: 279–288), who question the paucity, inconsistency, and conceptually distinct meanings of the data and therefore the reliability of cross-national statistical findings; also see Gaviria (2000: 288–295), who uses a different estimation technique (OLS) and finds much higher standard errors for GDP growth rates and inequality – leading him to question the significance of the overall results. The Reuter and Roman responses are printed without titles.

[18] Importantly, the Fajnzylber, Lederman, and Loayza 2000 study had a restricted sample and was largely based on UN World Crime Survey data from sixteen advanced industrial countries and none from sub-Saharan Africa; the authors tested for robustness with forty-five cases reported in the WHO mortality statistics datasets.

Regarding income inequality, they also find a significant and independent effect on violent crime rates, including both homicides and robberies.

> According to our point estimates, a 1 percentage point increase in the Gini coefficient is associated with a 1.5 increase in the homicide rate and a 2.6 percent rise in the robbery rate. These are the impact effects. If the increase in the Gini index represents a permanent worsening of income inequality, the permanent effects are 3.7 and 4.3 times larger for homicide and robbery rates, respectively. (Fajnzylber, Lederman, and Loayza 2000: 248)

When regional dummies are included in this first economic model, the results are still robust (also see the authors' 2002b article). "In particular, the Latin America dummy showed no statistical significance when the proposed economic determinants of crime rates were included in the econometric analysis" (Fajnzylber, Lederman, and Loayza 2000: 248).[19]

But do these studies explain Latin American patterns? The 2002a study reports that Latin America has higher crime rates than inequality models would predict and that statistical significance in Latin America, where it exists, *is important for robbery but not necessarily for homicide*. The ensuing question is why this should be so. Using a different estimation technique (ordinary least squares, OLS, rather than generalized method of moments, GMM), Gaviria (2000: 290–291) reevaluates the core findings, suggesting a significant and substantial relationship between inequality and homicide rates. However, once a Latin American dummy is included, the relationship is not only much weaker but "loses its significance completely."[20] Indeed, both Gaviria (2000) and Reuter and Roman (2000) note that Fajnzylber, Lederman, and Loayza (2000) posit several

---

[19] Although in Fajnzylber et al. (2002a: 1347) the authors argue that the GDP growth rate remains important but "it lost its significance when the death penalty, the fraction of young males, and the regional dummies were included." In this article, they also argue that inequality and GDP growth rates are significant across several models (using the same technique as that used in their 2000 model). They suggest (1349): "These variables – economic growth, inequality, and past crime rates – worked well for homicides and remarkably well for robbery rates. Their sign and statistical significance survive the addition of other explanatory variables, including measures of crime deterrence, illicit drug activities, demographic characteristics, and cultural traits." See Pablo Fajnzylber, Daniel Lederman, and Norman Loayza (2002a). "What Causes Violent Crime." *European Economic Review* 46, pp. 1323–1357.

[20] Gaviria observes: "If the empirical association between the Gini and the homicide rates is mainly driven by the differences between Latin America and the rest of the world, the causal link between these two variables becomes very difficult to defend, as one can think of many circumstances surrounding the history and institutions of Latin America that can explain both its high inequality and its high crime rates. The authors explain some of these circumstances but many others remain to be studied" (Gaviria 2000: 290–291).

mechanisms by which inequality might impact violent crime but in fact do not substantiate their claims. This exchange highlights the need for further research – including regional analyses alongside small-N research to identify, probe, and evaluate mechanisms. The relationship between economic factors (whether analyzing GDP, labor markets, or inequality) and violence rates is far from clear.

Notably, inequality also does not provide much analytic purchase when analyzing variation *within* the Latin American region. For the previously cited econometric arguments to hold up in the context of contemporary violence rates in Latin America, one would expect violent crime to emerge as a particular problem in countries experiencing either (a) severe levels of inequality and/or (b) increasing inequality (as relative deprivation theorists might suggest).[21] Yet the income inequality data do not support either hypothesis. Table 2.3 reports the Gini index on income distribution in Latin American countries during 1990–2012 using data reported by ECLAC. Table 2.4 combines these ECLAC data with those of Table 1.1, which catalogues homicide in terms of levels and stability over time based on WHO data (see Chapter 1). Figure 2.4 plots the five-year average Gini

---

[21] Relative deprivation theories argue that people are likely to mobilize for change when their circumstances are *relatively* worse – relative to expectations, relative to past living conditions, and/or relative to others. Hence, even if one lives better today than yesterday, the question is one of relative position (and associated expectations) and whether it can lead to violence. Gurr (1970) used this type of argument to explain the psychological impulse that can result in *political* violence and rebellion. Brenneman (2011) adopts a similar logic in his anthropological study depicting how socioeconomic conditions generate the kind of chronic shame that leads youth to join Central American gangs, organizations that provide solidarity alongside violent crime. His work significantly focuses on youth in gangs, based on interviews with sixty-three former gang members in Central America and an analysis of the social structural causes of chronic shame. While this argument compels scholars to consider the emotional draw of violent organizations and violent behavior, its *comparative* argument about socioeconomic conditions is less compelling since the reported HDI rank, per capita GDP, population living on less than $2/day, and Gini Index do not clearly predict patterns among the Central American homicide rates. The human development index and per capita GDP would lead one to hypothesize that violence would be lowest in Mexico and highest in Nicaragua. However, Nicaragua's violence levels are considerably closer to those of Costa Rica than to those of the other cases, and Mexico's violence levels are both increasing and regionally diverse. For the population living on less than $2/day, Nicaragua is lower than Guatemala and Honduras but higher than El Salvador – again raising questions as to why El Salvador's violence level is so much higher than that of Nicaragua. The Gini index would lead one to presume comparable violence levels across Mexico, Costa Rica, and El Salvador, which is not the case. Brenneman's anthropological work leaves us with a powerful sense that shame *might* be pervasive and perhaps even a proximate explanation. However, the economic foundations of this comparative argument are not clear. See, in particular, Brenneman (2011: 104, table 3).

TABLE 2.3 *Income inequality in Latin American countries (1990–2012)*

Stratification of Countries According to the Gini Coefficient of Income Distribution, 1990 - 2012
(includes income equal to zero)

Level of inequality	1990	1994	1997	1999	2002	2006	2009	2012
Very high 0.5800 - 1	0.627 Brazil 0.615 Colombia 0.582 Guatemala*	0.621 Brazil* 0.601 Bolivia 0.582 Nicaragua*	0.638 Brazil* 0.595 Bolivia 0.584	0.640 Brazil 0.586 Argentina* b/ Honduras	0.634 Brazil 0.590 Honduras 0.588 Guatemala Dom. Rep.	0.605 0.605 0.585 0.583	0.576 Brazil 0.574 Colombia f/ 0.554 0.553 0.526 0.524	0.567 0.536
High 0.5200 - 0.5799	0.554 Honduras 0.545 Chile 0.538 Mexico 0.536 Panama b/ 0.531	0.560 Colombia 0.552 Chile* 0.539 Guatemala* 0.537 Honduras Panama b/ Mexico* Peru Argentina a/	0.569 Colombia 0.560 Honduras 0.560 Chile* 0.558 Paraguay b/ 0.543 Dom. Rep. 0.539 Peru 0.532 Mexico* 0.530 Argentina c/ Ecuador b/	0.572 Nicaragua* 0.564 Colombia f/ 0.559 Panama 0.558 Bolivia* b/ 0.554 Chile* 0.545 Guatemala 0.542 Dom. Rep. 0.539 El Salvador* 0.521 Peru*	0.579 Panama 0.567 Argentina d/ 0.567 Ecuador 0.554 Chile 0.550 0.542 0.537 0.525 0.525	0.540 Brazil 0.549 Dom. Rep. 0.527 Honduras 0.522 Colombia f/ Panamá Chile		
Intermediate 0.4700 - 0.5199	0.501 Argentina a/ 0.492 Uruguay b/ Venezuela	0.501 Argentina* c/ 0.492 Bolivia e/ 0.471 Paraguay b/ El Salvador* Venezuela Ecuador b/	0.515 El Salvador 0.514 Venezuela 0.511 Paraguay* b/ 0.507 0.486 0.479	0.510 El Salvador 0.507 Panama b/ 0.493 Venezuela Costa Rica	0.518 Mexico 0.499 Ecuador b/ 0.498 Paraguay* b/ 0.473 Venezuela*	0.514 Mexico 0.513 Costa Rica 0.511 Venezuela 0.500	0.506 Paraguay 0.482 Argentina d/ 0.447 Bolivia Costa Rica Ecuador El Salvador Nicaragua	0.512 Dom. Rep. 0.510 Costa Rica 0.508 Paraguay 0.501 Mexico 0.500 Argentina d/ 0.478 Peru 0.478 El Salvador 0.437
Low 0 - 0.4699	0.461 Ecuador b/ 0.447 Paraguay g/ 0.438 Costa Rica	0.461 Costa Rica 0.447 Uruguay b/	0.461 Ecuador b/ 0.423 Costa Rica Uruguay b/ 0.450 0.430	0.469 Uruguay b/	0.440 Uruguay b/	0.455	0.469 Venezuela 0.433 Uruguay 0.416	0.517 0.504 0.502 0.492 0.475 0.449 0.405 0.379

SOURCES: Observations marked with * come from Economic Commission on Latin America and the Caribbean (ECLAC). 2005. Social Panorama of Latin America, 2004. Santiago, Chile: United Nations, page 23 (Table 1: Stratification of Countries According to the Gini Coefficient of Income Distribution, 1990-2002). Information based on survey data.
The rest of the data comes from Economic Commission for Latin America and the Caribbean (ECLAC): Statistics Division. Social Statistics Unit. Based on special tabulations of household interviews in each of the countries. Retrieved August 9th,, 2015 from http://interwp.cepal.org/sisgen/ConsultaIntegradaFlashProc_HTML.asp
a/ Greater Buenos Aires
b/ Urban areas.
c/ Twenty urban settlements.
d/ Thirty one urban settlements.
e/ Eight main cities plus El Alto.
f/ From 2002, income figures are not comparable with those of previous years, given that the Colombian Department of Statistics and Planning applied new methodological criteria.
g/ Asunción metropolitan area.

TABLE 2.4 *Inequality and violence rates (combining Tables 1.1 and 2.3)*

	Low inequality	Intermediate inequality	High inequality	Very high inequality
Low and stable violence	Costa Rica 1990, 1994, 1997; Uruguay 1994, 1997, 1999, 2002, 2009, 2012; Peru 2009	Argentina 1990, 1994, 2009, 2012; Uruguay 1990; Costa Rica 1999, 2006, 2009, 2012; Peru 2012	Chile 1990, 1994, 1997, 1999, 2002, 2006, 2009; Peru 1997, 1999, 2002; Argentina 1997, 1999, 2006	Argentina 2002
Intermediate and stable violence	Ecuador 1990, 1997; Paraguay 1990	Ecuador 1994, 2002, 2009; Paraguay 1997, 2002, 2009, 2012; Panama 1999; Nicaragua 2009	Panama, 1990, 1994, 1997, 2002, 2006, 2009; Paraguay 1999; Ecuador 1999, 2006; Nicaragua 2002; Brazil 2009, 2012	Brazil 1990, 1994, 1997, 1999, 2002, 2006; Nicaragua 1994, 1997
Intermediate and unstable violence	Venezuela 2009, 2012	Venezuela 1990, 1994, 1999, 2002, 2006; Mexico 2002, 2006, 2012	Mexico 1990, 1994, 1997, 1999	
High and unstable violence		El Salvador 1994, 1997, 1999, 2009, 2012	Colombia 1990, 1997, 2002, 2009, 2012; Honduras 1994, 1997, 1999, 2009; Guatemala 1997, 2002; El Salvador 2002	Honduras 1990, 2002, 2006; Colombia 1994; Guatemala 2006

Note: Weak relationship between patterns of income inequality reported by ECLAC (1990–2012) and overall homicide patterns reported by WHO (1995–2014).

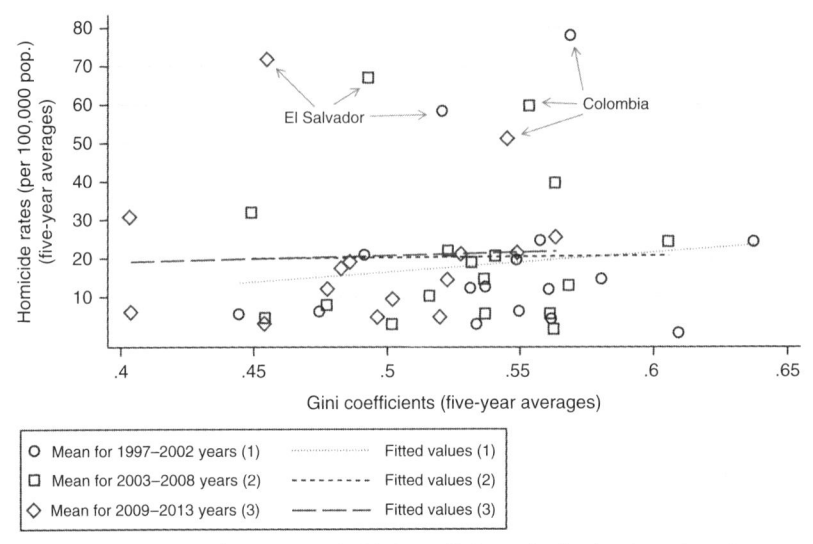

FIGURE 2.4 Homicide rates and Gini coefficients in Latin America, five-year averages (1997–2013)
Source: Homicide rates from WHO/PAHO 2016. Inequality data from ECLAC 2015.

coefficients and the five-year average homicide rates for every country in the region, with each shape representing a different time period. Regression lines for each period are shown (also see Figure 2.5 in Appendix).

These tables and figures on inequality reveal no simple relationship between levels of inequality and violence. High-violence cases (El Salvador, Honduras, Guatemala, Colombia, Brazil, and Venezuela, for example) fall into the very high category, high category, and medium categories of inequality. El Salvador claims among the highest violence rates in the world and yet falls into the intermediate category for inequality for most years. Venezuela has experienced rising violence for years, but inequality falls into the lowest category in the 2009 and 2012 data (although some might question the veracity of this data). And low-violence cases also bridge the very high to low categories of inequality. Again, Nicaragua is at times at the highest level of inequality, and yet violence is comparatively moderate to low in this case; Chile has had among the highest inequality rates in the region, and yet violence is, again, comparatively much lower in this country than in others. Figure 2.4 analyzes five-year averages of both homicide rates and Gini coefficients (1997–2002, 2003–2008, 2009–2013) and again finds no relationship with this measure for the three, five-year measures analyzed. In the appendix, additional figures report inequality and homicide rates in the region on an annual basis; here too the regression lines are relatively flat, and in 2000 and 2006 the regression line flipped ever so slightly in the direction opposite to what was theoretically expected. Therefore, inequality (and/or changing patterns of inequality) has a less certain relationship to high and rising levels of violence than generally asserted. At the very least, there is not a mono-causal relationship here.

However, there appears to be one notable exception to this statement. Cases that have low inequality (0–0.4699 on the Gini scale) nearly all experience comparatively low levels of violence; these cases include Costa Rica, Ecuador, and Uruguay – with Venezuela serving as the exception (with rising violence rates coinciding with inequality rates reportedly falling). This snapshot suggests (perhaps unsurprisingly) that there is likely a threshold rather than a linear relationship between inequality and violence. Below a certain level of inequality, violence will probably be low (perhaps even stable, as we observed earlier), although this observation begs the question as to what drives varying patterns of violence above that threshold. Using 1990s data, Gaviria (2000: 293) uses a simple regression to track a log of homicide rates with the Gini coefficient and also finds almost no relationship between the two variables. Even Fajnzylber, Lederman, and Loayza (2000: 274), writing before violence rates skyrocketed in several cases, find that whereas inequality, economic crises, and poor growth performance contribute to violence and crime, further explanation is needed to explain cases with extremely high violence rates. Since Latin America claims a disproportionate number of these extreme cases (and since these numbers continue to go up in several core cases in the following years), further explanation is clearly needed.[22]

Recognizing the limitations of the Gini index, ECLAC has complemented it with other measures, including the Wolfson index of income polarization (to analyze concentration around the extremes rather than around the mean of income distribution). Yet these figures also reveal no clear pattern.[23]

Thus, inequality is a blunt instrument for explaining the rise in homicides and the extremes of violence. Very low levels of inequality appear to

---

[22] Fajnzylber, Lederman, and Loayza (2000) recommend that we look more carefully at the production of illicit drugs and/or higher rates of drug possession, although they do not take up this task. Later I will return to the question of the drug economy, although I will focus less on production and consumption and more on trade, transit, and competition.
[23] ECLAC, Social Panorama of Latin America, 2014 (LC/G.2635-P), Santiago, Chile, p. 23 (for description of index) and 102 (for relevant table). Accessed August 10, 2015, http://repositorio.cepal.org/bitstream/handle/11362/37627/S1420728_en.pdf?sequence=4.

moderate the structural impulse to turn to violent crime. It seems to work against homicidal ecologies. However, once one moves out of the lowest level of inequality, this economic structural condition provides little explanation as to where high violence levels are likely to emerge and rise. It is possible that we need (a) more local-level data and/or (b) to look at inequality as mediated by access to local job markets, public goods provision, inflation rates, etc. But since these data are not currently available, we are left thus far with limited empirical support for the relationship between inequality and very high and rising homicide levels in Latin America's third wave democracies.

Neoliberal Reforms

A complementary explanation features policy-induced economic despair, with a focus on neoliberal reforms,[24] globalization,[25] and neoliberal reforms in the context of globalization[26] as they impact rising inequality and/or poverty. Like the earlier arguments, the presumption is that poor economic conditions motivate individual actors to engage in crime but that these patterns are endogenous to policy. This argument has been analyzed by many scholars of Latin America, in particular, in light of the region's 1980s debt crisis, the adoption of neoliberal reforms, and the integration into increasingly integrated globalized markets.

Portes and Roberts (2005) have analyzed, for example, the impact of neoliberal reforms on Latin American cities. They argue that neoliberalism has adversely affected social service delivery, labor markets, and urbanization patterns. They find that these changes have correlated with a rise in urban crime. Arias and Goldstein (2010), Gay (2010), and Bobea (2010) echo these arguments. They have highlighted powerful and suggestive correlations; however, the precise mechanisms by which these macro processes translate into crime are left unexplored in their research – particularly crime's impact on violence and homicides. Indeed, the highest levels of violence are now *not* in the countries that had the most consequential neoliberal reforms. Violence is generally highest in Central America, although neoliberal reforms were generally weaker in these countries because the state sectors were also weaker to begin with. Neoliberal reforms went very far in Mexico and Argentina, by contrast,

---

[24] See Portes and Roberts (2005), Portes and Hoffman (2003), Wacquant (2006), and Snodgrass Godoy (2006).
[25] Naím (2005). [26] See Arias and Goldstein (2010), Bobea (2010), and Gay (2010).

and yet these countries initially exhibited much lower *national* homicide levels than did many other cases – with Mexico's recent rise in violence following many years *after* its neoliberal reforms. Moreover, it is not clear how neoliberal reforms would affect the subnational patterns of homicide (patterns that vary a great deal within any given country, as discussed in Part III of this book). In short, the precise mechanisms and comparative patterns are far from clear.

Neoliberalism, however, has not only negatively affected citizens but has also weakened the state, as pointed out by another set of scholars. In particular, Bobea's (2010) study of the Dominican Republic argues that globalization and neoliberalism (among many other factors) have not only limited the provisions of services to underprivileged areas but also hollowed out the *state*, leaving vacuums in authority and state capacity. Bobea writes as follows:

> The recent surge in criminal violence in the Dominican Republic is associated with various factors, including globalization and neoliberalism. In societies such as the Dominican Republic, the diminished administrative capacities of the neoliberal state created vacuums that have been gradually filled by nonstate actors and autonomous bureaucratic elements able to capitalize on these conditions ... The unforeseen effects of political and economic liberalization have promoted a ferocious competition among bureaucratic units, as well as the perverse decentralization of security forces and their autonomization from state control [Davis 2006].
>
> In this context of institutional weakness, the actual increase of criminal activity, as well as a perception of insecurity by middle- and upper-class sectors have allowed security forces to exercise excessive and extralegal power, diminishing the rule of law and the possibility of reinforcing democratic institutions. (Bobea 2010: 166–167)

This institutional weakness, according to Bobea, has provided circumstances propitious for violent individuals and organizations (within and outside the state) to assume greater prominence and impact. Arguably, recalling Becker's earlier argument, neoliberalism's deleterious consequences for the security forces have lowered the costs/constraints on possible criminals, thereby increasing the incentives for actors to pursue a life of crime. Yet, as with the arguments by Portes and Hoffman, Bobea's argument about neoliberalism (in combination with other factors) cannot explain *varied* levels of violence across and within countries. Indeed, Gay (2010: 202), writing in the same edited volume, rightly cautions that while this general context is important, the impact is not direct. Economic factors might matter, but neoliberalism (or globalization) as a broad causal force needs to be disaggregated to focus on specific policies and institutions and their impacts.[27] Indeed, the argument developed in this book focuses on some aspects of the illicit global market and institutional weakness; but I do not find or presume that neoliberalism and globalization are their cause.

Labor Markets

Finally, labor markets might also theoretically serve as an explanation of homicide levels. Economic incentives might propel individuals to engage in crime where labor markets are weak and job prospects (perhaps also in the informal market) are low. The argument still invokes the idea that a life of crime pays. This argument is intuitively plausible (as with the inequality argument). However, the data on labor markets are poor – especially at the subnational level. This factor creates obstacles to conducting serious comparative analysis of this particular variable. But even if the data were excellent, the labor market variable tells us little about why individuals would choose crime rather than enter the informal market and/or migrate. Moreover, even for those who enter a life of crime, it tells us little about *why* or *when* actors would choose to kill. One would expect robbery to increase significantly, but it is not immediately apparent why homicides would jump so dramatically and why they would do so in some markets and not others. Thus, poor labor markets might prime individuals to a life of crime, but they provide little explanation for why homicidal violence would increase significantly.

In short, economic arguments about inequality, neoliberal reforms, and labor markets are marshaled to explain the individual motivation to turn to a life of crime. These arguments often presume that individuals are acting out of desperation. Whether informed by cost-benefit calculations or psychological impulse, the reasoning is that individuals are responding to economic marginalization (inequality and poverty) sometimes amplified by political opportunity (limited punishment regimes or diminished state capacity). This might explain some anomic crimes. However, these factors do not explain the extreme patterns that we see in the high-homicide-rate countries of Latin America. To understand these patterns, one must make several analytical moves: move past the

---

[27] Levitt (2004) observes that economic recovery cannot explain drop in violent crime. The recovery might have an impact on crime, but it cannot explain the changing recourse to violence.

formal markets that most of these studies analyze to probe certain types of *illicit economies*, analyze not only individuals but the *organizations* that forge and define the illicit markets, analyze weak capacity and complicity in state security forces (not just punitive policy and/or generalized state capacity), and finally analyze the subnational territorial enclaves within which actors are maneuvering to gain control. These challenges are pursued in Chapters 3 and 4, which will analyze the interaction between particular kinds of illicit economies, weak states, and organizational competition.

HISTORICAL INSTITUTIONAL LEGACIES OF STATE FORMATION

A fourth approach explicitly privileges the historically informed role of institutions.[28] While all of the prior approaches make *some* reference to institutions, these generally are not the core point of departure. By contrast, historical institutionalists (whether inspired by Charles Tilly or Douglas North) begin with the explicit argument that institutions, and the state in particular, can shape the incentives and constraints of a wide range of actors – including public officials (elected and appointed), powerful collective actors (including economic elites and organized sectors), and individual citizens. *The state can try to impose order on a polity, and the first overall question is in whose interests does it do so?* Is the state an autonomous actor that can rise above private interests, acting to serve the "public" and provide "public goods"? Does it act at the service of a despot? Is it perhaps captured by groups of rent-seeking politicians and/or powerful economic elites? *The second overall question is whether the state in fact has the capacity to achieve its ends.* Does it have the

---

[28] For economists (such as North 1990), institutions are contractual commitments that outline credible commitments and generate information about future behavior, and thus can lead to predictable and systematized patterns (for both formal and informal institutions). For historical institutionalists, they are the sticky byproduct of critical junctures and path dependence. See Kathleen Thelen and Sven Steinmo (1992). "Historical Institutionalism in Comparative Politics," in Steinmo, Thelen, and Longstreth, *Structuring Politics: Historical Institutionalism in Comparative Perspective*, Cambridge University Press, 1–32; Peter A. Hall and Rosemary R. Taylor (1996). "Political Science and the Three New Institutionalisms," *Political Studies* XLIV, 936–957; Kathleen Thelen (1999). "Historical Institutionalism in Comparative Politics," *Annual Review of Political Science* 2, 369–404; Paul Pierson (2000). "Increasing Returns, Path Dependence, and the Study of Politics," *American Political Science Review* 94: 2, 251–267; James Mahoney and Kathleen Thelen, "A Theory of Gradual Institutional Change," in James Mahoney and Kathleen Thelen (eds.) (2010), *Explaining Institutional Change: Ambiguity, Agency, and Power*, Cambridge University Press, 1–37.

organizational and bureaucratic capacity to achieve governing ends – including necessary resources, territorial reach, professional staff, and institutional coherence (Centeno, Kohli, and Yashar 2017: chapter 1)? Theoretically, where state capacity is weak, there should be fewer checks on violent entrepreneurs within the state and society. The theoretical claim, at its most general, is a macro one. Violence is most likely in countries that inherit states that either (a) lack institutional capacity to regulate, (b) use violence as a means of governance (to impose order on unruly citizens and/or gain the upper hand over other states), and/or (c) are complicit in actions taken by those non-state actors who engage in violence. This theoretical approach echoes somewhat the civil war and democratization literature but is distinct from them – encompassing them without being reduced to a particular political event (civil war legacies or democratization) and focusing instead on the institutions in place at that particular moment (some of which might result from deep historical processes of state formation and others reshaped by contemporary state reforms). In this case, institutions hypothetically shape the incentives and behaviors of actors disproportionately responsible for driving the homicide rates in some countries and not others. State institutions involved in coercion and/or rule of law, in particular, are the site of analysis.[29]

Diane Davis's important historical institutional work (2006a, 2006b, 2017) explains contemporary violence in Latin America by analyzing the legacies of state formation, providing insight into where and why violence

---

[29] Scholars have naturally analyzed the role of the military to explain war violence during Latin America's authoritarian periods. In one particularly interesting study, Pereira (2005) analyzed how distinct institutional configurations between the military *and* courts in Argentina, Brazil, and Chile privileged or deterred violence during the authoritarian period and later the pursuit of truth commissions in the post-authoritarian period. He finds that where the military and courts were tightly integrated, violence was high during the authoritarian period and the subsequent pursuit of truth commissions was difficult. However, where militaries and courts were more autonomous, violence was checked during the authoritarian period and the pursuit of truth commissions was more tenable. This focus on institutional relations of power and accountability are theoretically suggestive for thinking about contemporary violence in democracies. Pereira does not directly take up the question of why violence is so high in contemporary democracies. Focusing on human rights abuses, he focuses on state-directed violence rather than the contemporary violence in the third wave of democracy. It is therefore reasonable to ask what lessons, if any, one can draw from this work. Historical processes and relations among institutions are key. Coercive forces can be bound (or empowered) by rule-of-law institutions. Thus, even if the precise hypotheses do not travel, the theoretical questions posed do hint at the particular state institutions (and the relationship among them) that shape political opportunities for widespread violence while leaving open how this occurs in democracies, who is responsible, and what their primary goals are.

has become so prevalent. In her extensive original research on Mexico (analyzed in comparative perspective), she argues that one can only understand Latin America's security forces (military and police) vis-à-vis their deployment to control unruly crowds in the context of rapid urbanization, import substitution industrialization, and capitalist development. The resulting legacy of this situation was a form of pact making between security forces and political officials – one that alternated between corruption and coercion – with the police force developing, in the process, locally corrupt and collusive ties with criminal organizations. Today's violence, Davis argues, has a particularly urban cast, springing from the rise of informal and also criminal markets in the wake of long-term developmental policies that increased urbanization, followed by declining job opportunities and limited welfare policies to support those battered by contemporary waves of deindustrialization: "That most of the violence plaguing Latin America unfolds in urban locations owes to the spatial legacies of developmental-state actions" (Davis 2017: 63), with informal areas developing beyond the reach of the rule of law and yet deeply imbricated in collusive patterns with the police (also see Arias 2006a and 2006b, and Arias and Goldstein 2010). In the wake of patterns of deindustrialized globalization, these areas have given way to competing or fragmented territorial sovereignties (with various public and private actors vying for control and citizens unclear about who will protect them from harm); declining state developmental capacities (a consequence of late development and attending patterns of urbanization) is the cause, Davis argues (2017: 66). Her argument in this later work echoes parts of the globalization arguments discussed earlier (insofar as the current conditions have exacerbated life for economically marginalized people, while hollowing out the state not only in terms of public goods provision but also for the state's coercive institution). But Davis's work is more historically informed, insofar as it centrally focuses on how long-term developmental patterns created the very states and spatial configurations that shape where crime has become most prevalent and state corruption is most severe in Mexico.[30]

Davis's work is theoretically original and provocative. We learn a great deal about Mexico's coercive history (especially the role of the police) – one that has been downplayed in most studies of state formation in general and Mexican politics in particular. For the purposes of the current

---

[30] Also see Giraudy and Luna (2017) for a discussion of fragmented states and their uneven territorial reach. See Arias (2017) for a discussion of how historical institutional patterns shape criminal governance.

book, however, this macro-analytic work of historical institutionalism leaves unanswered core questions: (1) why violence has become so prevalent in urban *and* nonurban areas – indeed, the most violent regions in Mexico and Central America are in nonurban regions; (2) why *homicide* levels vary so considerably over time; and (3) why use violence and to what end. Indeed, the self-consciously historical and endogenous process that Davis highlights makes it hard to disentangle cause from argument, although it is rich with theoretically and intuitively plausible arguments. The following chapters set out to distinguish state capacity from illicit markets and the organizations that vie to control specific territorial spaces. Thus, I set out to analyze specific geographies where violence is high and analyze what kinds of states are present, to whom they are beholden, and the degree to which they have capacity.

In short, institutional legacies surely matter – affecting the propensity for violence in certain political geographies. But on their own they cannot explain why and when violence breaks out. Davis's work does not fully explain the varied levels and patterns of violence in contemporary democracies, although her pathbreaking work does pose important insights that are pursued further in Chapters 3 and 4. First, we will see that varied state institutions *do* help explain *where* violence is most likely to develop (although it does not explain *why* violence breaks out and when it will reach high levels). Second, a focus on the police (in interaction with the military and courts) is key insofar as it sheds light on corruption and complicity (factors that can contribute to the violence that we see on the streets). Third, where the police (again in interaction with the military and courts) have weak state capacity, we can infer that they play little deterrent role for those who are likely to engage in violent crimes. Fourth, state capacity has subnational variation – a point that Mann theorized in his work on infrastructural power and has been analyzed by many scholars since.[31] We revisit these points in the chapters that follow, especially in Chapter 4, which focuses on the role of the state.

---

[31] There is a substantial literature on state capacity and its varied penetration – drawing on Mann's idea of infrastructural power. For a summary of some of this literature, see Giraudy and Luna (2017 – especially footnote 10 on page 95), which includes scholarship featuring subnational state capacity and its link to violence. I return to this particular literature in Chapter 4, when discussing the state.

CONCLUSION

This chapter has introduced and surveyed a rich social science literature that aims to explain violence in the third wave of democracy.[32] It has reviewed four general approaches to violence in (new) democracies. The first set of arguments focused on the political uncertainty associated with political transitions and the untethered actors that maneuver therein. The second set focused on societal constraints and conflicts. The third set focused on economic grievances associated with economic structures and/or economic policies. The fourth privileged historical processes of state formation that advantaged powerful and/or corrupt security forces, which often collude with non-state actors. Each approach raises plausible hypotheses, but they appear to provide partial analytic advantage when explaining contemporary Latin American violence. If we want to explain the temporal and spatial patterns in homicidal violence, we cannot focus solely on formal and informal institutions as they shape either individual economic grievances or socio-political opportunities/constraints. Analyzing the illicit political economy (as it manifests subnationally and transnationally) must be front and center. Nor can we privilege micro-level or macro-level explanations at the expense of analyzing the organizations that mediate between them. Finally, we need to develop a territorially grounded understanding of where the violence is taking place and why. It is not happening equally across the region; nor is it happening evenly across national territories. Violence rates are skyrocketing in particular subnational enclaves at particular times.

Thus, without tying my hat to one approach alone, I draw on the combined questions posed in this chapter to consider the political institutional conditions that attract and nurture violent organizations, the political economy that creates material incentives to dominate certain

---

[32] This chapter has not discussed the broader literature about violence during authoritarian periods, which includes important scholarship on the move to take up arms for revolutionary causes; the onset of civil wars as well as the (non)discriminatory killing of noncombatants; the coercive politics of authoritarian regimes, including coup making and human rights abuses; among other topics. This literature has analyzed political violence against or by the state, or casualties that occur in the context of authoritarian or civil war contexts. As a whole, it presumes to know who the perpetrators are, although it debates when/why they use arms (to rebel, kill, and/or overthrow/defend governments). It assumes that the key actors are political (although they might not always pursue political ends). And it assumes a nondemocratic context. None of these assumptions can be made when explaining high homicide rates in Latin America's third wave – rates that assume their highest form in post-military regimes that have transitioned to some form of democratic rule.

territories, and the organizational dynamics that lead actors to take up arms to defend those territories, even if it entails killing one's competitors. As this book argues, probing these questions requires one to move beyond formal institutions, national boundaries, and violent individuals to consider the interactions between *illicit transnational economies, weak and complicit states, and organizational competition* over specific territories. Considering their interaction provides a more powerful analytic optic for considering what is often assumed in the studies cited in this chapter: *Who* are the actors/perpetrators, and *what* are their motives? *Why* do they cluster in some places and not others? And *under what conditions* are actors more/less likely to kill and thus contribute to higher versus lower homicidal ecologies? I take up these questions in the subsequent chapters.

CHAPTER 2
Appendix

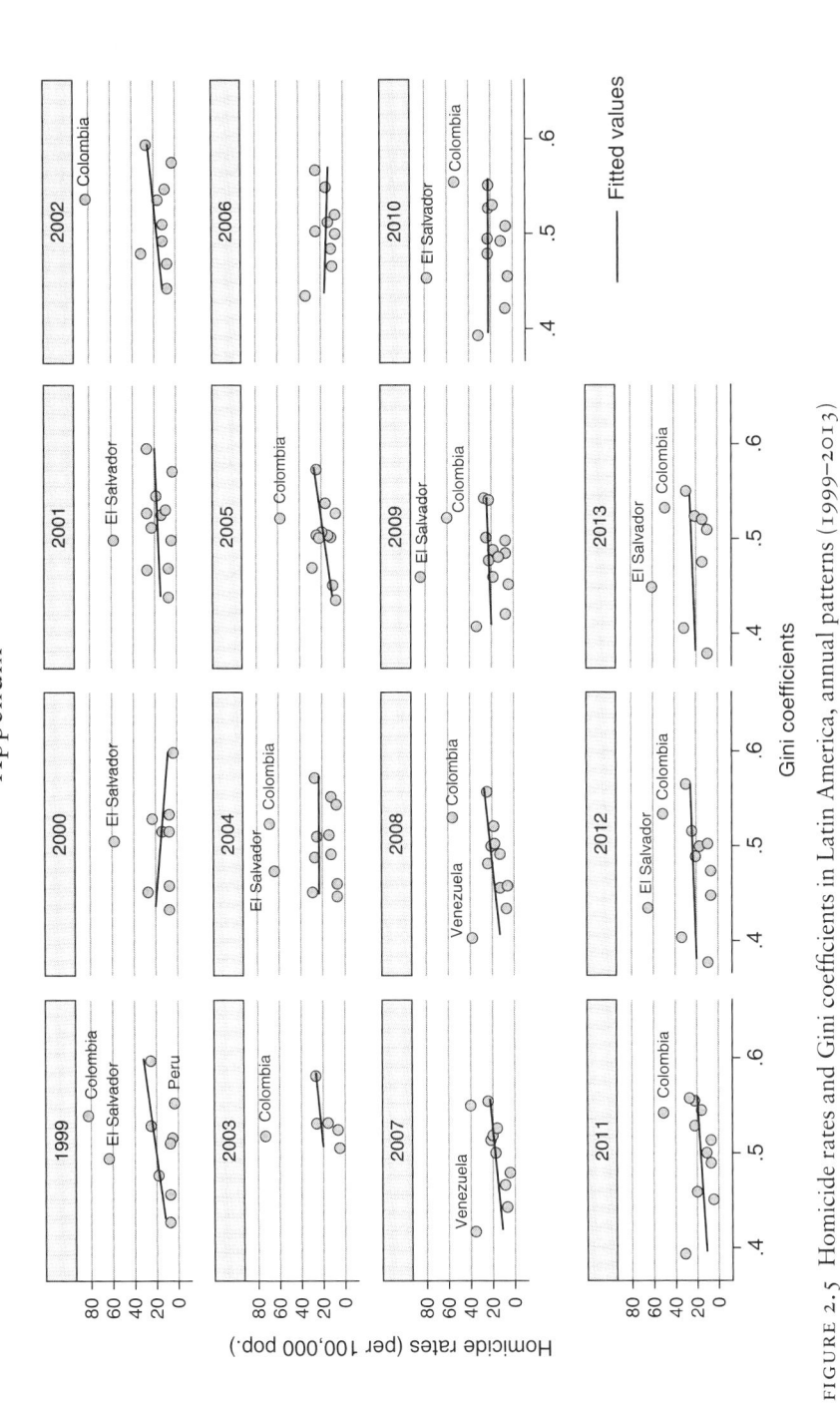

FIGURE 2.5 Homicide rates and Gini coefficients in Latin America, annual patterns (1999–2013)
Source: Homicide rates from WHO/PAHO 2016. Inequality data from ECLAC 2015.
Note: Plotted country/years for which both inequality and homicide data are available.

PART II

THE ARGUMENT ABOUT HOMICIDAL ECOLOGIES

3

Illicit Economies and Territorial Enclaves

The Transnational Context and Domestic Footprint

To explain violence in Latin American democracies, this book proposes an argument featuring the role of competitive organizations operating in the context of illicit economies and weak state capacity. Astronomically high homicide rates are not the result of hordes of individual thieves or anomic individuals committing crimes that somehow include death; nor is it simply a function of individual actors taking advantage of the uncertainty of democratic transitions; nor can it be analyzed by only taking into account formal political, economic, and social factors. Rather, high levels of violence in the third wave of democracy are being orchestrated by organizations that pursue certain goals (usually profit, order, and/or territorial hegemony), use violence toward that end, and operate in particular geographies. While certainly individuals are engaging in crime (as they do everywhere) and robbery is likely to correspond with economic downturns, the comparatively highest national and subnational homicide rates are, this book argues, the result of organizational dynamics in the illicit economy, within which individuals are pursuing broader ends. These individuals will not appear in an index of civil or political society. These organizations are not bound by national boundaries. Rather, they take root in particular subnational geographies where state capacity is weak and illicit economies are forged.

This book therefore develops the argument that *organizational competition to control illicit territorial enclaves* is driving the very high violence patterns in the region; these enclaves are emerging most clearly where law-and-order state institutions are weak and corrupt. A range of illicit and state organizations deploy violence in higher measure to control (or develop) lucrative territorial enclaves within and across national boundaries. To explain why this violence has occurred in the contemporary period, this book first introduces changing patterns in the illicit political economy, then the states that foster this or allow it to occur, and finally the organizational actors that have emerged therein to stake out and defend illicit subnational enclaves in the region. These three core factors (transnational illicit economies, weak state capacity, and organizational competition over subnational territory) together help explain the high rates and varied geography of homicides in the region. Chapters 3 and 4 develop this argument by tackling each of these variables sequentially. Chapter 3 discusses the illicit – conceptualizing the term, empirically introducing Latin America's transnational illicit economies, and highlighting the high-stakes incentives to dominate certain territorial enclaves. Chapter 4 then addresses how varied state capacity explains where illicit economies are most likely to develop and how organizational competition therein has driven much of the highest homicidal violence in the region; homicides, in particular, have become a means (or currency) to defend and expand the territorial reach of these illicit territorial enclaves. This pair of chapters sets up the conceptual and theoretical framework for the empirical studies in Part III, which probe the sequenced (and at times endogenous) relationship of the three factors as they shape varied homicidal ecologies in Central America, Latin America's most violent and varied region.

Before embarking on this empirical and conceptual argument, some humility is in order. It is impossible to make absolute claims about the illicit. I am not a member of this world. I cannot claim to have engaged in ethnographic work, participant observation, or a systematic random study of all such groups and their contexts. Therefore, it would be a fool's errand to talk about definitive conclusions. Rather, what I can do and have done is put forth a conceptual framework followed by plausible claims; these are based on the observable evidence we have in official documents, reports, media, and interviews. My argument about illicit economies and violence (in particular, homicidal ecologies) takes inspiration from the types of claims made by the late Charles Tilly (2003, *The Politics of Collective Violence*) and Stathis Kalyvas (2006: 10, *The Logic of Violence in Civil War*). While using very different methodologies, both books start their respective work on violence by emphasizing the plausibility of their claims rather than the absolute validity of their findings. This book follows suit. It aims to make a credible argument about the importance and impact of illicit economies on violence.

FOREFRONTING AND CONCEPTUALIZING THE ILLICIT

This book looks beyond formal political economy factors to analyze the world of the illicit, since violent organizations are often embedded at the intersection of formal and illicit interactions. While Chapter 2 critically reviewed economic arguments focusing on individuals responding to formal inequality and labor markets, this chapter redirects that economic gaze to focus on the organizations that are tied to the burgeoning and illicit drug trade and extortion rackets. In this regard, it joins an important round of newer scholarship focusing on the drug economies – especially those that have prospered in Mexico, Colombia, and Brazil.[1] These are critical, even foundational, studies that have elucidated the growth and consequences of the drug economy on societies, economies, and polities. They have demonstrated the consequences of competitive drug markets and state crackdowns on the homicide rates in these three countries (among others). I complement these studies by comparing high- and low-violence cases in the Americas, by conceptualizing the illicit (and its relationship to formal and informal institutions) and by placing the illicit political economy in its transnational context.[2]

Indeed, in contemporary Latin America, illicit institutions have been rife. Some of them have put down deep roots; some have expanded over time. While the social science literature has primarily and often single-mindedly focused on the formal (and at times informal) aspects of the contemporary period in Latin America, the illicit has become a visible and integral part of the political, social, and economic landscape – a point made emphatically by scholarship on drugs and smuggling.[3] It has fundamentally impinged on governance, social service delivery, and citizens' daily lives in many Latin American cities and regions. Politically, we know well the types (if not the actual patterns) of illicit activity that often take place – including vote fraud, coups, and corruption, among others. Certainly, acts of corruption and embezzlement remain part and parcel of national political debate. All of these illicit acts curtail the practice of citizenship (whether votes cast are counted, whether elected presidents can complete their terms, and whether state resources designated for social services are embezzled – to give but a few examples). But something

---

[1] Important examples of recent works on the illicit drug economy in Latin America include Reuter (1985, 2009); Andreas (2004, 2011); Naím (2005); van Schendel and Abraham (2005); Arias (2006a, 2006b, 2011, 2017); Gootenberg (2008); Naylor (2009); Snyder and Durán-Martínez (2009); Calderón et al. (2015); Durán-Martínez (2015, 2018); Lessing (2015); Magaloni, Franco, and Melo (2015); and Osorio (2015).
[2] This conceptual section draws on Yashar (2013).
[3] See Reuter (1985, 2009); Andreas (2004, 2011); Naím (2005); van Schendel and Abraham (2005); Arias (2006a, 2006b, 2011, 2017); Gootenberg (2008); Naylor (2009); Snyder and Durán-Martínez (2009); Calderón et al. (2015); Durán-Martínez (2015, 2018); Lessing (2015); Magaloni, Franco, and Melo (2015); and Osorio (2015).

equally fundamental is taking place in the broader economy as illicit trade expands and shifts locations. In particular, I argue that two types of illicit political economies (transnational routes regulated by organized crime and urban local spaces dominated by urban gangs) have created high stakes that often coincide with the geographically concentrated high violence patterns found in contemporary Latin America. This chapter introduces core aspects of this illicit economy, focusing in particular on its high profits, territoriality, and shifting geography.

But what is the illicit?[4] The illicit is not an inherent property of goods or behaviors; it is a political construct. Just as Polanyi (1944) undermined the idea of markets as natural constructs and noted that markets are forged by states, so too the illicit is the byproduct of the state role in forging legal boundaries. The illicit exists only where states define, regulate, and uphold formal laws, beyond which informal and illicit practices take place. If "the informal" refers to areas beyond state regulation, "the illicit" refers to behaviors and transactions prohibited by state law, including what cannot be practiced, produced, traded, taxed, and/or consumed.[5] Laws

---

[4] See Moisés Naím (2005). Naím was among the first to discuss the illicit economy at length, although he does not aim to engage with debates about formal and informal institutions, or to explain violence, per se, as the outcome. My use of the illicit as a category separate from the informal does not entirely accord with Centeno and Portes (2006), who also conceptualize these institutions vis-à-vis the state. They focus, however, explicitly on the economy, while I suggest that this distinction also applies to the political and social realms. Centeno and Portes (2006: 27), drawing on Portes and Castells (1989: 14), distinguish between the licit and illicit but use this to distinguish practices within and between the formal, informal, and criminal. For them, formal institutions entail licit processes of production/distribution and licit final products; criminal institutions entail illicit processes of production/distribution and illicit final products; and the informal moves from illicit processes to licit products. In this process, they note the relationships among the types of economies as well as the central role played by the state (with varied impacts, depending on the degree of regulation and capacity to enforce the economy). Other studies have also empirically analyzed the illicit in the region – including Andreas (2004), Arias (2006a and 2006b), Caldeira (2000), Dammert (2006), Davis (2006a), and Frühling (2003) – but more systematic conceptual and theoretical work is still required.

[5] Portes (and his subsequent collaborators) argued that much of the economy operates "beyond" state regulation, leading him to distinguish between the formal and informal economy. The informal economy refers to "transactions where the state neither provides protection nor receives a 'cut'" (Centeno and Portes 2006: 26). This describes a significant part of the economy in Latin America, affecting both those who cannot be absorbed by the formal labor market and those who might maneuver to avoid it. It includes street vendors, shoeshine boys, maids, and security guards, among others, who might constitute a significant economic sector but work beyond state regulation. Centeno and Portes argue that it is not just that the state does not regulate these areas but also that entrepreneurs find ways to escape state regulation. "The relationship between the state and the informal economy is thus cyclically causal and negatively correlated. In general, the

(rather than certain inherent properties of goods and firms) define the illicit. Sometimes these laws are domestic; sometimes they have the force of international law (and pressure). But in all cases, the illicit refers to those spaces that disobey legal rules. Consequently, illicit activity is an unintentional byproduct of any contemporary state, economy, or society. In the economy, in particular, once goods are formally defined as illicit, it is likely that actors will try to forge black markets to provide them (at a higher cost). As states define the boundaries of what is legal, actors often find ways to supply and access those illegal goods at a profit. The creation of illicit categories, therefore, creates the incentives for some subset of actors to subvert these regulations if doing so can lead to material gain (and/or the promise of increased political power, social status, etc.), which in turn is partially predicated on state capacity to implement the law. Otherwise stated, prohibition creates incentives for actors (collective and individual) to take advantage of, and make profit from, these prohibitions. The illicit economy can grow in this context around drugs, human smuggling, extortion, and even licit goods (such as music) if they are traded illegally. Indeed, state efforts to criminalize goods can create negative externalities that were unforeseen – providing the very incentives for organized crime that the law was intended to constrain. As Keefer notes, when discussing the drug trade,

weaker the state, the greater the likelihood of an economy being able to escape its gaps. The more ambitious the scope of state regulation, the more cause for escape" (Centeno and Portes 2006: 29). Indeed, many states tolerate the informal economy, Portes argued, because it can be functional to the maintenance of capitalist systems; this systemic economic accommodation, however, can create political distortions by providing short-term remedies for citizens that in the long term minimize their ability to formally demand and protect their rights. See Helmke and Levitsky (2004: 727), who also argue that formal studies alone miss much of the causal action, since informal institutions are often so critical to the political process. They write that informal institutions are "socially shared rules, usually unwritten, that are created, communicated and enforced outside of officially sanctioned channels" (Helmke and Levitsky 2004: 725–726). These informal political institutions (much like informal economic institutions) are not formally recognized by the state. They are not a priori illegal or normatively problematic.; they simply constitute the area that falls outside of legally regulated practices. Some of these practices might try to subvert formal politics, some might grease the wheels to defend it, and others might in fact try to enhance it. As Centeno and Portes (2006), North (1990), and Helmke and Levitsky (2004) highlight, these institutions can complement and accommodate state institutions where the latter formal institutions are effective, and they can substitute for and compete with state institutions where the latter are ineffective and/or corrupt. Therefore, informal institutions can shape the practice and/or shore up the meaning of formal processes. They are neither inherently progressive nor reactive; they are neither inherently legal nor illegal.

Arguably the most harmful of the unintended consequences of the criminalization of the drug trade are organized crime and the political instability they can unleash. The existence of a potentially large drug market means that there are large rents to be collected by producers and/or distributors. But since the market operates illegally, organized groups have a comparative advantage in setting up distribution network and the associated enforcement of distribution contracts. These groups substitute for both the state and other market institutions that would otherwise provide these services. However, the organized-crime enforcement of contracts entails violence, and violence is also used to raise entry barriers for potential competitors. (Keefer et al. 2008: 6)

Hence, state actions define what is formal, informal, and illicit. While variations in state *regulations* determine the (in)formality of institutions, variations in state *prohibition* codify what is illicit; the latter point is definitional (rather than causal or normative). Using these two dimensions – regulation (by state) and prohibition (by law) – we find ideal typical conceptual distinctions between these institutions (see Table 3.1). Accordingly, *formal* institutions refer to what is regulated by the state and lawful. *Informal* institutions refer to what is beyond state regulation but not necessarily illegal.[6] *Illicit* institutions refer to what the state has defined as unlawful, regardless of whether the state plays an active role in regulating it; indeed, minimal state regulation (alongside state corruption) can prove a boon to illicit economies.

The actors involved in illicit activity might occupy legal positions (in the state and/or civil society), but their actions and activities defy the law. Indeed, in some cases formal institutions are deeply embedded in (or compromised by) illicit institutions – including members of the military, the police, the courts, ministries, and elected officials (Reno 2000; Naím 2005; Arias 2006a and 2006b; Cruz 2010). In practice, informal and illicit institutions are often intertwined, with social norms concerning what is criminal activity varying across countries.[7]

Accordingly, the illicit is not coterminous with immorality (van Schendel and Abraham 2005: 4).[8] While the examples presented

---

[6] Helmke and Levitsky (2004: 725) note that this might entail activities that are not "officially sanctioned."

[7] I thank Mario Sznajder for raising this point.

[8] Van Schendel and Abraham (2005) highlight that illegality is not necessarily immoral or socially unaccepted behavior; they therefore distinguish between illegal (defined by law) and illicit (defined by social norms and perceptions). While agreeing with their overall point that (a) we should not assume that legality is neutral or moral, (b) states are constituted by power relations and therefore the law is a reflection of these power relations, and (c) law and society do not necessarily share the same norms, I do not sustain the semantic distinction that van Schendel and Abraham make between illegal and illicit

TABLE 3.1 *Conceptualizing ideal-type institutions*

		State prohibition	
		Yes	No
State regulation	Yes	Illicit Institutions	Formal* Institutions
	No	Illicit Institutions	Informal Institutions

*Illicit activities can and do take place within formal/legal institutions.

throughout this book largely draw on illicit goods and institutions that are morally charged, it is important to emphasize that (a) not all state laws have morality on their side (consider slavery, apartheid, discriminatory gender and sexuality laws, and immigration bans, for example); (b) some illicit activity can lead to morally progressive outcomes (e.g., overthrowing authoritarian regimes in favor of democracy or fighting for equal freedoms) and/or have a Robin Hood effect (stealing from the rich to give to the poor); and (c) some illicit goods have become licit (e.g., alcohol and now marijuana, both with varying degrees of restriction).

With these conceptual distinctions in mind, political economy scholarship would benefit from complementing studies of the formal and informal with studies of the illicit. Otherwise, we are likely to miss a great deal: who the critical actors are, what power they wield, what their goals and incentives might be, how they interact across spheres, and when they engage in violent behavior. While scholars have increasingly paid considerable attention to illicit politics (corruption and coups in particular), they have not labeled it as such. Parallel interest is emerging in the discussion of illicit economies, which has recently gained scholarly traction.[9] Drawing on this latter literature, I turn next

---

(the latter term they argue can refer both to law and social norms). Rather, I choose to follow common practice and use these terms interchangeably.

[9] See, for example, Reuter (1985, 2009); Andreas (2004, 2011); Naím (2005); van Schendel and Abraham (2005); Arias (2006a, 2006b, 2011, 2017); Gootenberg (2008); Naylor (2009); Snyder and Durán-Martínez (2009); Calderón et al. (2015); Durán-Martínez (2015, 2018); Lessing (2015); Magaloni, Franco, and Melo (2015); and Osorio (2015).

to describe a pair of core illicit markets and organizations that have come to dominate certain geographies in which homicidal violence is particularly high. As future chapters illustrate, these illicit markets have created high-stakes organizational incentives to defend some territorial enclaves. They are critical to understanding where homicide rates are high. They are not, however, independent of the state, because they are defined by state rules and, moreover, emerge where states are weak and/or complicit. In this way, illicit markets are very much part of Latin America's political economy.

LATIN AMERICA'S ILLICIT ECONOMIES AND ORGANIZATIONS: DRUGS, ORGANIZED CRIME, AND GANGS

Latin America's illicit economies have thrived. They have occupied both high-profit and low-profit markets and have generated enormous revenues. But of greatest import for this book are the ones that have assumed a territorial dimension – the ones that require organizations to control highly valued territories to sustain their livelihood and turn a profit; this is because the dramatic rise in contemporary violence is spatially tied to the changing geography of illicit economies[10] and the presence, in particular, of illicit groups competing to control these territories.[11] Organized crime

---

[10] This focus on the illicit production of illicit goods differs from the more expansive discussion by Schneider, Buhn, and Montenegro (2010: 444), who focus on "all market-based legal production of goods and services that are deliberately concealed from public authorities" to avoid various payments, legal obligations, restrictions, and/or accountability. In this book, goods that are both legal and illegal might be part of an illicit market, although I focus primarily on the illicit goods associated with the drug trafficking economy – highlighting the earlier and broader point that the illicit economy is a political construct (Yashar 2013). It is a by-product of state laws that determine what can be produced, traded, taxed, and/or consumed. It is the definition of these laws (rather than certain inherent properties of goods) that makes illicit certain goods and the economies that develop around them. Once goods are made illicit, it is likely that black markets emerge in which prices are higher and transactions are harder to regulate. Moreover, creating an illicit market (particularly in drugs) has served to distort the markets, not only limiting the profits accrued by farmers but also concentrating them further down the chain, in the hands of intermediary organizations (which will be discussed later in the text) that oversee the trade and transit of the goods. Indeed, criminalization of goods can lead to a transfer of rents from farmers to drug traffickers, according to Keefer et al. (Keefer et al. 2008: 5).

[11] This argument is supported by several reports written by international organizations, all read after the initial argument was originally conceived – for example, the UNODC (2007: 9 and passim) report, which also argues that Central America is at increased risk of violence because of its geographic position between producers and consumers of cocaine. In particular, the reports highlight trafficking routes. The World Bank study

and gangs (alongside corrupt states) are important actors in Latin America's political economy – in some countries increasingly so. These organizations do not seek to overthrow or defend the national state. Rather, they seek to assert control over subnational territorial enclaves, especially (but not exclusively) in search of economic profit. These parastatal groups operate outside of legal norms (although they often do so in conjunction with state actors). Strikingly, both organized crime and gangs deploy a territorial strategy; their illicit activities are thus geographically stamped and demarcated, as is the context in which violence is deployed.

The rest of this chapter therefore focuses on illicit organizations, paying particular attention to organized crime's role in the trade and transit of illicit drugs (with a briefer discussion of gangs and their control over specific neighborhoods and urban spaces). As argued further on, the national geography of the trade and transit of illicit drugs explains which countries are most likely to have higher levels of violence. Organized criminal actors associated with illicit economies seek to assert monopoly control of specific territories. When they do so, homicidal levels are often relatively low; however, when they are competing with other organized crime groups and/or the state, they will more readily deploy violence to assert hegemony and defend and extend local control. Thus, illicit does not equal violence. But illicit spaces (especially where there is competition over core subnational spaces such as ports, highways, airstrips, and borders) have a greater propensity than licit spaces to experience high homicide levels. Logically, where trade routes shift, one should also likely see attending changes in the geographic patterns of violence. Tracing the geography of illicit economies is thus a key first step to understanding homicidal ecologies.

An expansion of urban gangs has occurred in tandem with the expanding drug trade – with gangs also seeking to demarcate territories within which they establish illicit forms of extraction. Gangs have been involved in extortion rackets and selling drugs; this starts on a local scale, although over time there is some evidence of organized crime's efforts to incorporate them into the trade and transit of illicit drugs moving north. As with organized crime, gangs have become particularly prevalent and powerful

---

(2010, volumes 1 and 2) argues as well that drug trafficking is the strongest single explanation of high rates in the region: "Controlling for other factors, areas with intense levels of drug trafficking in Central America have homicide rates 65 percent higher than other areas in the same country" (World Bank 2010, volume 2: i). The Organization of American States (OAS 2013: 75) makes a similar claim.

where the state has either demonstrated weak capacity in regulating urban spaces or complicity in profiting from gang activities or both.

Viewed together, drug trafficking organizations and youth gangs have redefined the contemporary shape of Latin American illicit economies. This chapter outlines the contours of this burgeoning illicit economy and then explains how at first blush it correlates broadly with high-violence geographies. Chapter 4 analyzes this illicit economy in interaction with state capacity and organizational competition.

Illicit Economies: Background on the Rising Drug Trade

Organized crime has particularly flourished in Latin America's drug economy. While the illicit infiltrates many economic domains – from money laundering to the smuggling of people, human organs, weapons, and drugs – this book focuses on organized crime's role in the market of illicit drugs. The illicit drug economy has arguably been the most geographically expansive – with high yields, high profits, high competition, and high violence – generating strong incentives to join and intense competition to dominate sectors and territories. Latin America produces many different kinds of illicit drugs (marijuana, cocaine, heroin, and other kinds of chemical substances, such as methamphetamine).[12] In the Americas, cocaine has been the most profitable (per kilo) illicit drug produced; heroin (produced from opium) joins cocaine as a lucrative and important illicit drug for transnational traffickers (see UNODC 2010). Coca growing has a long history in the region, but the market for processed cocaine started to take off in the 1960s and 1970s, with the strongest growth in the 1980s (see Gootenberg 2008 and UNODC 2010: 65).[13] Organized crime

---

[12] Cannabis/marijuana has the highest levels of use, with an estimated 3.5–4 percent of the population using the drug at least once a year between the late 1990s and 2004/2005 (UNODC 2006: 35; also see UNODC 2010 executive summary, especially p. 25). That said, marijuana is neither the most lucrative nor the most violence producing part of the economy; and increasingly it is produced nationally (rather than forming a significant part of a transnational market). Opium is largely produced elsewhere (Afghanistan, Laos, and Myanmar), although Colombia and Mexico have also increasingly undertaken its production: "Since 2003, Mexico has been the world's third largest source of opium" (UNODC 2010: 20). As the writing of this book came to a close, marijuana's status as an illicit drug was undergoing significant changes – with Uruguay legalizing the drug and certain US cities doing the same. The consequences are currently unclear; this book would predict, however, that violence associated with the supply chain for this drug should decline dramatically as the illicit economy becomes formal (regulated).

[13] For a fascinating history of cocaine, see Paul Gootenberg. 2008.

has been drawn to cocaine, in particular, for many reasons. From a consumption perspective, it has higher addictive properties than many other drugs; thus its consumers will generally want more. From a business perspective, its profit yield is much higher per ton than marijuana. Indeed, cocaine has been the highest-value illicit drug. By way of example, one UN report from the early twenty-first century observed that "South America produces an estimated 900 tons of cocaine annually, most of which is shipped to 10 million users in the United States and Europe, a market worth some US$60 billion in 2003. The value of the drug flow rivals that of the legitimate economies of the nations through which it passes" (UNODC 2007: 15).

In the twentieth and twenty-first century, Latin America became a world producer of cocaine (and increasingly produced heroin as well). While the cocaine market has fluctuated some over time,[14] the cocaine *production* market (which remains largely in the Americas) has been a particularly lucrative illicit one in recent decades. Accordingly, world seizures of cocaine have also increased significantly in this time frame.[15] There is of course subregional variation, since the locus of production has shifted over time. Cocaine was primarily produced in Peru and Bolivia and later surpassed in quantity by Colombia, with levels varying across these three cases since that point. Together, these three countries have dominated the cocaine production market. According to the *World Drug Report 2008* (UNODC 2008), global cocaine production in Colombia, Peru, and Bolivia varied between nearly 800 and 1,000 metric tons from 1990 to 2007, reaching 1,000 metric tons in 2004 and staying around that level in 2005, 2006, and 2007. Colombia assumed the greatest share of production in these years, followed by Peru and then Bolivia (UNODC 2008: 13, 14); indeed, a 2008 UNODC report indicated that Colombia produced 55 percent of the global total. The Obama administration

---

[14] Some argue that cocaine consumption has leveled off and perhaps even declined in the United States, while increasing in South America; moreover, cocaine markets have increased in Europe and West Africa (UNODC 2008: 13).

[15] One must use seizures data cautiously. While some cite these to reflect production levels, they might also reflect changes in policy and/or capacity. Cocaine world seizures fluctuated between 300 and 400 metric tons from 1996 to 2002; they went up significantly and steadily between 2002 and 2005 (increasing by almost 100 metric tons each year and reaching more than 700 metric tons in 2005) and then declined to just less than 700 metric tons in 2006 (UNODC 2008: 27).

estimated that the 2015 combined production potential for these three countries was 1,130 metric tons.[16]

Organized crime has aggressively pursued strategies to dominate the trade and transit associated with this market.[17] While the cocaine market is difficult to measure and by some estimates has declined in value in recent years (making competition among illicit actors even more fierce), it is still large and consequential. The UNODC calculates that "the retail value of the US cocaine market declined by about two thirds in the 1990s, and by about another quarter in the last decade" (UNODC 2010: 76). Yet the market has remained sizable.

The global cocaine retail sales were equivalent to 0.15% of global GDP in 2008, down from 0.4% of global GDP in 1995. *Even with this drop, the value of global cocaine retail sales in 2008 were still higher than the gross domestic product (GDP) of 123 out of 184 countries for which the World Bank provided estimates for the years of 2007 or 2008.* (UNODC 2010: 69; emphasis added)

The destination markets in 2008 were largely North America (6.2 million people) and Europe (4–5 million people), with emerging markets in South America, Central America, and the Caribbean (totaling an estimated 2.7 million people) (UNODC 2010: 70). Thus, the cocaine market has been a high economic draw for organized crime and other actors seeking high-yield (and high-risk) gains. With price elasticity and declining prices, the imperative to control trade routes and sales is critical to high-end profits. And with the logistical demands and political

---

[16] The Obama administration brief on drug production in Colombia, Peru, and Bolivia (2008–2015) and US policy is online: https://obamawhitehouse.archives.gov/ondcp/targeting-cocaine-at-the-Source.

[17] Profit margins, while high, have varied. In these years of increased production, the inflation-adjusted US$ wholesale price remained low in the United States (although it went up significantly in 2006) and remained flat in Europe in inflation-adjusted euros (*World Drug Report*, UNODC 2008: 260). Despite the drug wars (which should have lowered the supply relative to the demand), cocaine prices continued to fall and purity levels remained high, according to a 2008 report issued by the Obama administration's Office of National Drug Control Policy (Walsh 2009: 2–3). The Obama administration's data supplement to their 2016 Drug Control Strategy reports, moreover, that the price per pure gram of cocaine (2012 $) dropped dramatically in the 1980s (from a high of $753 to a low of $238) and then continued to drop steadily until about 2006 (fluctuating between a high of $287 and a low of $120). In turn, purity went up until about 2006 (with the lowest price per pure gram – 2012 $), after which it started to decline again (https://obamawhitehouse.archives.gov/sites/default/files/ondcp/policy-and-research/2016_ndcs_data_supplement_20170110.pdf, p. 83). Also see John Walsh (2009: 4), Keefer et al. (2008: 7), and UNODC (2010: 170–172).

challenges of moving the product north and west, organized crime has played a critical role in coordinating this high-risk venture.

Transnational Illicit Trade and Transit

This geographically expansive commodity stream is high stakes for organized crime – especially given the threat that the state will eradicate crops, locate processing plants, seize the product, and imprison sellers and consumers. It is perhaps not surprising that violence accompanies this illicit market. However, violence does not occur in equal measure everywhere; it is geographically concentrated, as I will demonstrate, along trade and transit routes (rather than production sites). Indeed, drug production is not the core comparative factor explaining homicidal violence throughout the region. Undoubtedly, drug production has been important in the Andes (Colombia, Bolivia, and Peru) and increasingly so in Mexico. Yet, homicide rates are not equally visible across these drug-producing cases. Homicide rates have been very high in Colombia (hard to disentangle from the civil war)[18] and relatively low in Bolivia and Peru (see Chapter 1 figures). Moreover, violence is high in several countries that are not (at least to date) major drug producers (Guatemala, El Salvador, Honduras, and increasingly Venezuela). These data suggest that production is not the primary explanation as to where and why violence has become so high across the region.[19] Indeed, drug production's profit margins (while high compared to those of other, legal crops) are not particularly high compared to those of trade and transit. Nor does drug consumption explain the spike and variation in regional homicide rates.[20]

---

[18] Colombia is not included in this study precisely because this book focuses on democracies and Colombia has until very recently experienced civil war. Thus, we would expect homicide levels to be high in this country. Moreover, the fact that Colombia's drug economy became entangled in the country's civil war in its later years makes this case a particularly thorny one from which to generalize.

[19] Gay (2010), in his study of Rio de Janeiro, Brazil, also argues that increased trafficking (both internationally and domestically) is more important than production in explaining violence. He contends that the increase in global drug trafficking has also increased violence in the context of the economic conditions delivered by neoliberal reforms. The latter does not cause violence directly, but it provides the context within which drug trafficking does. That said, Gay suggests that the drug markets' impact on violence is particularly significant because of domestic retail (the habits and addictions that fueled profits) even more so than transshipment (see 202 and 217–218, in particular).

[20] In analyzing "drug-related deaths" (a term that varies across member states but includes categories such as fatal drug overdoses and drug-related trauma) and mortality rates per million persons aged 15–64, UNODC (2014a: 3–4) reported that Latin America has

Competition over trade and transit (rather than production per se) are driving much of the violence in the region; this is the first empirical leg of the tripartite argument in this book.[21] The profit margin is the highest – and, arguably, the stakes are the most dramatic – when we look at transit routes (rather than production sites). Scholars of the drug trade have emphasized the supply chain along which the profit, risks, and returns are quite distinct. Disproportionate economic returns occur between production and consumption of certain goods – particularly coca/cocaine in the Americas and opium/heroin in Asia (Keefer et al. 2008; Williams 2009; Reuter 2014). In particular, high-level drug-trafficking organizations (DTOs) seeking to move drugs northward are relatively small in number. They invest strategically to dominate certain routes that can move goods transnationally from poor production zones to advanced industrial markets – by dominating certain ports, borders, roadways, or landing strips. The DTOs that oversee this process often invest to secure these spaces; they do so with the purchase of transit vehicles (submersibles, boats, trucks, planes) and/or by buying off communities through which they travel.

The return on investment is very high – as is the risk of seizure. Thus, they have incentives to occupy/dominate certain trade routes (and to prevent their competitors from doing the same, while also avoiding law enforcement) so that they can gain greater market share and be price setters along the route. Reuter (2014: 361, citing Paoli, Greenfield, and Reuter 2009: 201–234) has described this chain of supply as an hourglass, characterized at one end by millions of agricultural coca producers in the Andes (poppy in Myanmar and Afghanistan) who receive a very small percentage of total drug revenues (Reuter estimates 1 percent) and are price takers in this process; at the other end, there are hundreds of thousands of retailers in advanced markets who collectively make a great deal, although very few who make a great fortune; and in the middle, there are a small number of smugglers and drug traffickers who receive the greatest return on their investment (Reuter 2014: 364–365).

---

the lowest estimated rate (15.1) compared to a global average of 40. Indeed, while cocaine use is high in Latin America (especially in South America), use rates are low for all other illicit substances, save ATS (UNODC 2014a: 15).

[21] A related hypothesis might be that drug consumption has increased, thereby increasing the recourse to violence – in some cases to purchase drugs, in others responding with disproportionate violence when taking drugs. This might be true, but at present I have no evidence to make this case.

Thus, the organizations that control trade and transit are relatively few in number and competing to control a limited number of highly lucrative trade routes. Accordingly, the concentration of profits/returns is incurred along trade and transit routes, although the highest price per kilo occurs the closer the goods get to market. For example, one kilo of pure cocaine in the mid-1990s assumes the following price structure – jumping from $370 per kilo in Peru to $148,000 for final retail in Chicago (a 400-fold jump) (Keefer at al. 2008: 15, citing Peter Smith 2005). Keefer reports the price structure as follows: coca leaf (farm gate in Peru – $370); export of finished product (Colombia – $1,200); import of finished product (Miami – $20,500); wholesale by kilo (Chicago – $31,000); wholesale in one-ounce packets (Chicago – $62,000); and final retail value (Chicago – $148,000) (Keefer et al. 2008: 15 citing Peter Smith 2005). The striking jump in prices occurs between Colombia and Miami, where the price increases by an estimated 1,700 percent, or seventeen times, although absolute numbers skyrocket between wholesale and retail value in Chicago alone (Keefer et al. 2008: 5–6). Hence the profit incentives and stakes are particularly high when it comes to trade and transit routes throughout the Americas.[22] The UNODC *World Drug Report* (WDR) (2010: 18, 77–78) also estimates that the many local farmers producing coca in Andean countries make a pittance (1.5 percent of profits) when compared to the few international traffickers, who claim about 13 percent of the profits along the supply chain. And while the greatest share of overall profits goes to the mid-level wholesalers and dealers in the United States, this is a very large group distributing the profit across a wide network.

Looking at international markets, other estimates suggest that a kilo of cocaine can increase 500-fold along the value chain (from production to sale), with most of the profit accruing at the end of the commodity chain.[23] Most of these sales are in North America (about 47 percent), followed by West and Central Europe (about 39 percent) (OAS 2013: 57). Thus, high profits are found from the transit and sale of drugs toward (and in) advanced industrial markets, with sales in Latin American markets as a second-priority strategy, at best. As Reuter (2014) notes, however, since a large number of actors produce and sell but only a small number

---

[22] In a relative sense, it would be possible to argue that small farmers have the most to gain/lose since they often live on the economic margins and depend on this livelihood.
[23] OAS (2013: 54) calculations, based on UNODC and US Department of Justice's National Drug Intelligence Center.

of organized actors oversee the trade and transit, the concentration of profits accrues to those who manage the process of moving the drugs internationally to market.

Prohibition also affects the generation and distribution of profits along the production and distribution chain of the illegal drug. The organized criminal network required for trafficking the good (because of the illegality of its production, distribution and consumption) leads to funneling gains from farmers and farm-gate traders, upstream, and from consumers, downstream, to those criminal organizations. Because of the high barriers to entry into these links in the distribution chain – barriers imposed by violence and official corruption – these organizations can command high prices from consumers and offer lower prices to producers or farm-gate traders than they would receive if repressive policies were relaxed. (Keefer et al. 2008: 5–6)

Clearly, state prohibition of these drugs in advanced industrial markets concentrates profits upstream (Keefer et al. 2008: 5–6). Since the drug market is neither confined by national borders nor contained by state efforts to control it, these illicit markets have developed transnationally through trade and transit routes in borderlands, waterways, and airspace.

With such high returns on trade and transit, the cocaine market has experienced a dynamic playing field of highly aggressive and powerful criminal organizations seeking to gain control over territories through which drugs (and other goods) must pass to reach large consumer markets (namely, the United States and Europe). In some cases, these organizations have been transnational in scope – as with the infamous Medellín and Cali "cartels"[24] from Colombia or the multiple Mexican criminal organizations that have assumed increasing dominance of this trade in the late 2000s – including but not limited to the Tijuana/Arellano Felix organization, Sinaloa, Gulf, Juarez/ Vicente Carillo Fuentes organization, Familia Michoacana, Zetas, and Beltrán Leyva.[25] In others cases, they are more nationally oriented, as elaborated in the ensuing chapters on El Salvador and Guatemala. In still others they take a more local form – as with the gangs that have come to dominate many urban landscapes (more focused on trade than transit per se). The point is that *these organizations need to control territories – especially for organized crime, which seeks to move*

---

[24] Of course, these are not cartels in their classic definitional sense. I refer to them here as "cartels" given that this is the most commonly noted nomenclature associated with these particular criminal organizations.

[25] For a recent report on the Mexican DTOs, see June S. Beittel. 2017. "Mexico: Organized Crime and Drug Trafficking Organizations." *Congressional Research Service*. https://fas.org/sgp/crs/row/R41576.pdf.

(and sell) the product as the illicit goods move northward and upstream. This is particularly the case for high-profit illicit drugs such as cocaine (produced in South America but traveling through Central America and Mexico).[26]

Because the absolute volume and patterns of illicit trade are hard to track, the drug-monitoring community knows much more about production and consumption than about trade, the "middle link of this chain" (UNODC 2006: 1). Given these difficulties, the UN tends to track trade through seizures. Although this is a highly imperfect measure (arguably telling us more about state policy and capacity than about flows per se), it provides one way to track trade flows. This proxy tells us that cocaine is largely intercepted in the Americas – with some estimates of 45 percent intercepted in South America, 33 percent in North America, and 8 percent in Central America and the Caribbean (UNODC 2006: 87). The following figures highlight cocaine seizures along a range of dimensions. Over time, seizures increase in Central America relative to the Caribbean and Mexico (see Figure 3.1).

Trade and Transit and Violence

Strikingly, the cocaine trade passes through countries with the highest levels of homicidal violence. Indeed, the trade and transit of illicit goods appears to be significantly correlated with the violence in the region – whether we look over time or cross-nationally. The Caribbean was once the central portal though which cocaine passed before heading to advanced industrial markets. Colombian drugs largely passed through the Caribbean (which in turn also experienced very high levels of violence). "The Colombian Cali and Medellin 'drug cartels' preferred the Caribbean corridor and used it from the late 1970s. In the 1980s, most of

---

[26] Reuter (1985) emphasizes that not all illicit goods and drugs produce the same incentives for illicit actors. The demands of production and risks of illicit organizations can vary by goods. Reuter (2014) pursues this theme in other work, where he highlights the difference between cocaine and poppy (both produced in poor agricultural countries with long chains between producer and consumer) versus cannabis and methamphetamine. In the context of Latin America, cocaine is not the only illicit good. Other drugs also pass through Mexico, such as cannabis, heroin, and methamphetamine. However, cannabis can be produced domestically and thus has a shorter supply chain than cocaine. Methamphetamine is not necessarily produced in agricultural countries with low labor costs, as with cocaine, and requires a different technology to produce this synthetic drug. As such, both cannabis and methamphetamines are likely to produce different incentives and returns on investment than cocaine, with its high-yield profits (Reuter 2014: 361–366).

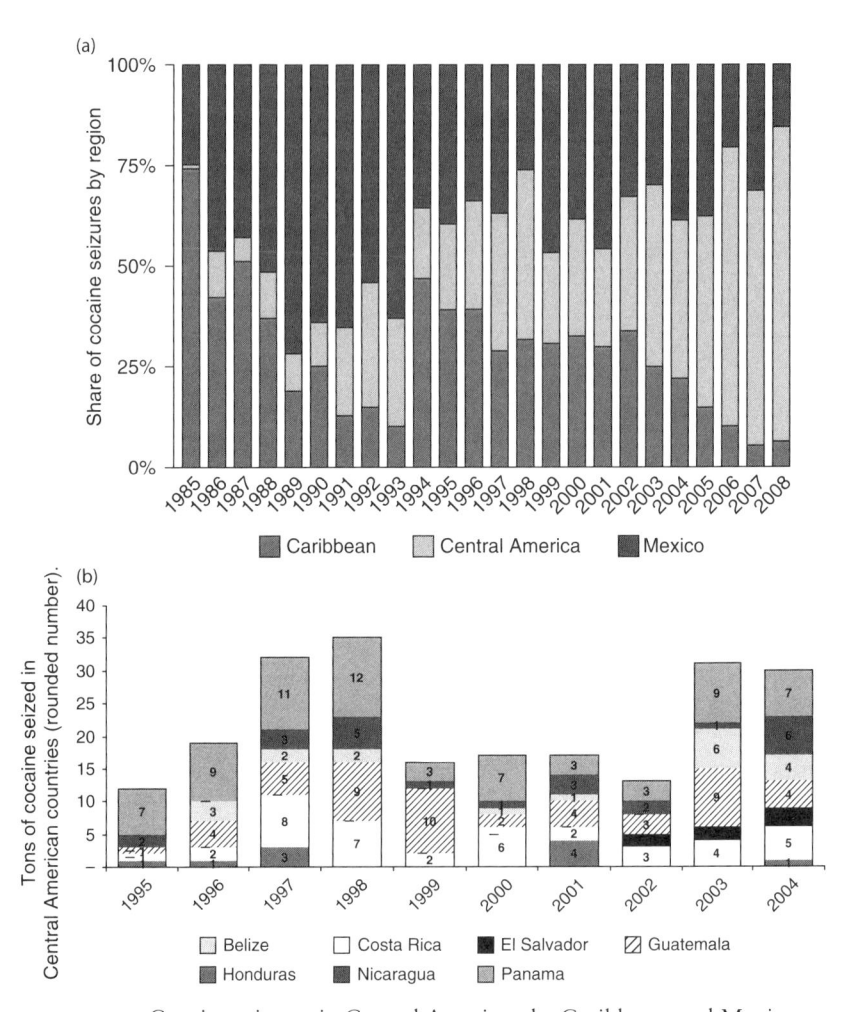

82   *Part II The Argument about Homicidal Ecologies*

FIGURE 3.1 Cocaine seizures in Central America, the Caribbean, and Mexico
Figure a: Distribution of cocaine seizures in Central America, the Caribbean and Mexico, 1985–2008. *Source:* UNODC *World Drug Report* 2010:74.
Figure b: Tons of Cocaine seized in Central American countries (rounded). *Source:* UNODC 2007:47.

the cocaine entering the United States came through the Caribbean into South Florida. But the interdiction successes caused the traffickers to reassess their routes" (Astorga 1999; UNODC 2007: 15, 46). Homicide rates in the Caribbean were remarkably high in these years when it was a main trade and transit route.

Since the late 1990s, however, the trade and transit of drugs has shifted – due to US interdiction efforts in the Caribbean (and

Colombian/US efforts to crackdown on Colombian cartels). Interdiction did not prevent global drug flows; it simply induced a change in the geography of illicit trade and transit. The majority of Latin American drugs started to pass by alternative sea routes, staying close to the Central American coast and crossing over the Mexican border (UNODC 2007: 15, 46). Indeed, from the late 1990s on, the majority and increasing share of US-destined cocaine has gone through Central America as illustrated in figures from USDIC/UNODC.[27] Thus, in the wake of a crackdown/regulation both on the Colombian cartels and the interdiction/prohibition of goods along the Caribbean waters, DTOs responded strategically to less-regulated spaces.[28] Central America, in particular, subsequently became a central geographic corridor for the movement of drugs. UNODC (2007: 12, 17, 46, 47) reports that 88 percent of the cocaine going to the United States passes through Central America in some way, with most of the cocaine taking a maritime route and the overwhelming majority (75 percent according to a US embassy official speaking anonymously in 2005) passing through Guatemala in particular.[29] OAS (2013: 47) reports that around 80 percent of cocaine headed for the United States passed through Central America and Mexico. Some earlier estimates are even higher. See Figure 3.2.

Although the Caribbean was a major transshipment route for cocaine until the mid-1990s, today 80 percent of U.S.-bound cocaine moves through Central America and Mexico. It flows primarily from Colombia via the Caribbean and Pacific coasts. In the Pacific, cocaine moves north from Colombia and lands in Central America or in Mexico. Another route passes through Ecuador and heads west to

---

[27] UNODC (2007: 25–26) reports that the drug trade started to move through Central America during the civil wars – although it is clear that the volume of trade increased subsequently. See maps of cocaine trafficking at UNODC *World Drug Report 2010*, p. 70, and UNODC *World Drug Report 2007*, p. 46.

[28] See Kenny (2007) for a discussion of the strategic or competitive adaptation that takes place within the drug trade.

[29] Lee (1999: 17–18) reports that in fact the organization and logistics of Colombian drug organizations started changing in the 1980s as demand increased in the United States, seeking greater economies of scale. "Production and transport were revolutionized. The 'mule' system was superseded by fleets of light aircraft that could carry loads of 500 to 1,000 kilograms of cocaine. By the 1990s, traffickers were using merchants' shipping, cargo jet aircraft, and semisubmersible vessels to export multi-ton loads of cocaine to foreign markets. Export routes, developed with extreme care, required the complex coordination of many activities: air, sea, and overhead transport; aircraft refueling and maintenance; loading and unloading and storage of drugs; delivery of bribes to appropriate officials in transit countries; and – in recent years – intensive collaboration with trafficking organizations in these countries."

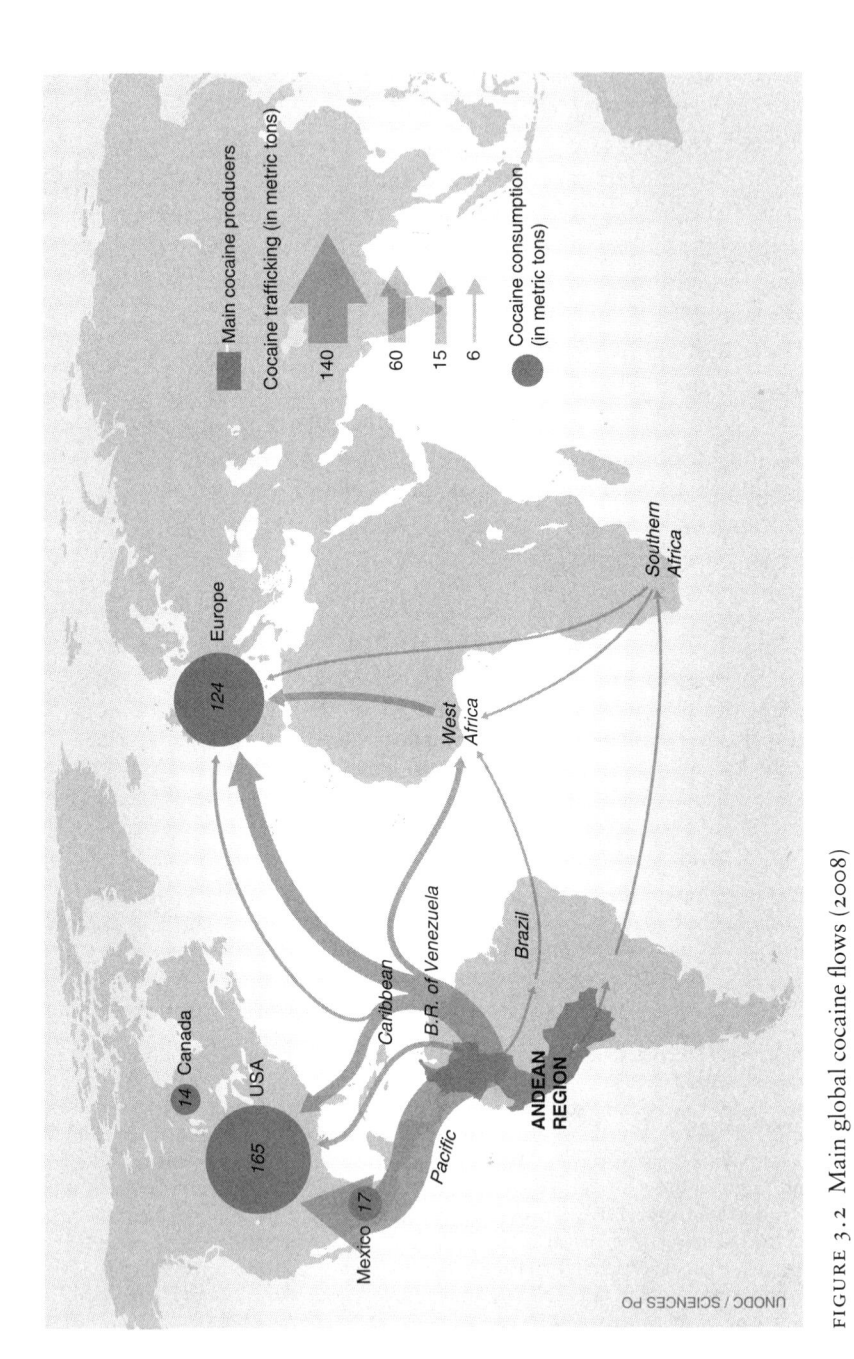

FIGURE 3.2 Main global cocaine flows (2008)
Source: UNODC *World Drug Report* 2010: p. 70. Accessed May 12, 2015 at www.unodc.org/documents/wdr/WDR_2010/1.3_The_globa_cocaine_market.pdf/
Note: For a more detailed map of 2005 trafficking in cocaine, see UNODC *World Drug Report* 2007: 46.

the Galápagos, from where it heads north to rendezvous with vessels on the high seas that take the cocaine ashore in Mexico or Central America. With increasing use of semi-submersible cocaine transporters or submarines, it has become less clear what amount of cocaine still goes far west into the Pacific before turning north. (OAS 2013: 47)

Part III of this book elaborates on the trade and transit of cocaine in Central America and its relationship to the geography of high violence patterns. Here I explore the fit of the trade/transit/high violence pattern in Mexico. The country has produced illicit drugs for quite some time – although there was relatively little violence emerging around the production of the relatively lower-profit goods (marijuana and heroin). And while the market did expand over the years, what seems to have driven the violence is less the expansion of drug production and more the competition to control the trafficking of these and other illicit goods (namely cocaine).[30] While cocaine is produced in the Andes, Mexico (like Central America) has become a core geographic node of Mexican organized crime for moving the drugs northward. With a more heavily patrolled Caribbean/Floridian port of entry, and later in the 1990s with the decline of the Colombian drug organizations (Medellín and Cali), Mexican organized crime expanded into trafficking as it confronted a particularly propitious business opportunity to assume control of distribution routes. Given the history of complicity by various Mexican officials (discussed in Chapter 4), trafficking expanded in Mexico.[31] Writing in the mid-2000s, Meyer et al. (2007: 2) noted: "According to the U.S. State Department, about 90% of all cocaine consumed in the United States passes through Mexico." UNODC (2007: 47) also reports on the increasing dominance of Mexican organized crime, which evolved from simply transporting the drugs to controlling other parts of trade and transit, at times competing for markets in the United States. While Colombian drug

---

[30] There are competing and plausible explanations that this violence also coincides with the changing jurisdictions that shattered longstanding alliances between illicit actors and the state (see Snyder and Durán-Martínez 2009) and electoral and partisan politics (see Dell 2015).

[31] In earlier periods, domestic organized crime in Sinaloa primarily focused on national production of lower-profit drugs (marijuana and heroin, primarily). At the present time, marijuana and poppies are still produced in four departments (Sonora, Chihuahua, Sinaloa, and Durango), but this has also spread to Michoacán and Guerrero. Moreover, methamphetamine production takes place in Jalisco, Sinaloa, Michoacán, Sonora, and Baja California, sharply increasing after 2003 (Meyer et al. 2007: 2, 4, 6). Information in this paragraph comes from Astorga (1999: 183–191). Also see Maurer (2012).

organizations and their Dominican partners dominated the US Northeast, Mexican DTOs started to compete elsewhere (UNODC 2007: 47; also see Lee (1999: 30).[32] In this context, several authors have noted changing cocaine routes and their increasing prevalence in Central America and Mexico (with the latter experiencing a particular rise in DTOs assuming control of those territories) (Meyer et al. 2007: 2; UNODC 2010: 74).[33]

Cocaine is typically transported from Colombia to Mexico or Central America by sea (usually by Colombian traffickers) and then onwards by land to the United States and Canada (usually by Mexican traffickers). The US authorities estimate that close to 90% of the cocaine entering the country crosses the US/Mexico land border, most of it entering the state of Texas and, to a lesser extent, California and Arizona, through [sic] the relative importance of Arizona seems to be increasing. According to US estimates, some 70% of the cocaine leaves Colombia via the Pacific, 20% via the Atlantic and 10% via the Bolivarian Republic of Venezuela and the Caribbean. The routes have changed over the years. (UNODC 2010: 74)

In this context, Mexican organized crime flourished in several regions, particularly in Sinaloa (home to the Guadalajara, Tijuana, Juárez, and Beltrán Leyva DTOs) and the Gulf of Mexico (home to the Gulf Cartel DTO and later the Zetas) but also in Michoacán and Guerrero (Grillo 2016: 251–252ff). Some of these organizations were previously involved in the marijuana and heroin trade but grew in power and wealth once the cocaine trade moved into Mexico (Grillo 2016: 252–253). Violence, including homicides, has increased in the wake of this growing

---

[32] Changing trade routes are partially a function of the success of US interdiction efforts in Florida and the Caribbean – a point developed by both UNODC (2007) and Kenney's (2007) book on competitive adaptation. Because Mexican organized crime groups apparently charge much more (50 percent of each shipment) than those of the Dominican Republic and Puerto Rico (20 percent), the UNODC text leads one to wonder whether it is only a matter of time before the Colombians try to move back to the Caribbean as the primary site of transport.

[33] "Small-time drug smugglers in Mexico then blossomed into more sophisticated drug trafficking organizations with increasing power to corrupt officials and police, eventually becoming the modern syndicates that control key corridors for the flow of drugs into the United States. Although many drug trafficking organizations operate in the country, the trade is currently dominated by what are commonly termed the Gulf, Sinaloa/Federation, and Tijuana 'cartels,' named for their places of origin. It is estimated that at least 20% of all drugs that enter the United States pass through the hands of at least one of these organizations. They control the flow of drugs within Mexico, as well as the transport of cocaine from South America, mainly produced in Colombia, through Mexico's Pacific ports and coastline, the Atlantic port cities of Cancún and Veracruz, and overland traffic through Mexico's southern states from Guatemala. Their man ports of entry into the United States are the border towns of Matamoros, Nuevo Laredo, Juárez, Agua Prieta, Nogales, Mexicali, and Tijuana" (Meyer et al. 2007: 2).

competitive trade, particularly in the context of the weak/corrupt rule of law that prevailed (as discussed in Chapter 4): "The government lost the ability to be the arbitrator that could control organized crime. Instead, gangsters disputed power themselves under strength of arms. Amid this bloodshed, the mobsters turned from traffickers into warlords. And rather than the police ordering gangsters about, gangster fought over who could control police forces" (Grillo 2016: 255). While not reducing all homicides to drug wars, there is no doubt that the competitive terrain associated with the increasing trade and transit of illicit drugs has been associated with the rise in homicidal violence. Mexico and Central America (and the Caribbean before that), thus, have proven key to trade and transit because of their proximity to the US market; these are cases with extraordinarily high homicide rates.

To date, the United States remains the largest global market for cocaine consumption, although the market has declined over the same time as it has increased in Western Europe. Accordingly, trade routes have also expanded westward toward Europe. Indeed, over time, Europe has become an increasingly important destination market. UNODC (2010: 26) reports that Venezuela and Ecuador served as major transit points for over half of the maritime shipments to Western Europe between 2006 and 2008; the Caribbean and Brazil both sent about 10 percent of the shipments to Western Europe, according to UNODC.[34] Significant trade routes also go through Brazil – destined, in particular, for Europe (UNODC 2010: 75). Reports about 2010 and 2011 activity show transit from Venezuela through the Caribbean and West Africa, with entry via the Iberian Peninsula, among other routes, noted particularly (OAS 2013: 48). Moreover, the 2016 EU Drug Market (issued by the European Monitoring Centre for Drugs and Drug Addiction and Europol) states that Venezuela, alongside Brazil, and Colombia have become important points of departure for drugs moving to Europe.[35] Organized crime overseeing the trade and transit toward Europe has included groups from Colombia and the Caribbean (Dominicans, Jamaicans, and Antilleans), among others (including some from West Africa) (UNODC 2010: 88, 90).

These treetop observations about Latin American illicit economies, as a whole, reveal a correlation between the countries that have the highest

---

[34] See UNODC (2010: 83–92) for a more extended discussion of the European market.
[35] See "New Report Offers Details on Cocaine Traffic to Europe," *InSight Crime*, by Mimi Yagoub, June 2, 2016, www.insightcrime.org/news-analysis/cocaine-trafficking-to-europe-explained-by-new-report.

homicide rates (Central America and Mexico, but also Venezuela and Brazil) and the regions/countries through which the most profitable illicit goods are moving (trade and transit). Homicide rates were in turn very high in the Caribbean when drugs primarily flowed through these islands. Homicide rates increased in Central America, moreover, when drugs started to flow primarily through this region.[36]

Future chapters will address why drug flow moves through certain countries/regions and not others (speaking to endogeneity concerns about what explains where the illicit economy flourishes) and why violence occurs where it does (speaking to the mechanisms by which violence unfolds). This chapter, by contrast, has focused on developing the plausibility of the claim that the geography of illicit trade/transit corresponds with high-violence cases. In short, there are incredibly high returns on cocaine's illicit supply chain; Latin America, in general, and Central America and Mexico, in particular, are key geographic nodes in this commodity stream, with organized crime pursuing high-stakes economic profits associated with the trade and transit of this good. Notably, the Central American region claims the highest homicide rates in the world (see UNODC 2007, passim, especially 24 and 45).[37] Thus, there is a plausible relationship between illicit trade and transit on the one hand and violence levels on the other – a relationship probed further in the empirical chapters that follow.

Observable Implication: A Word about Transit Points

An observable implication of this argument is that illicit trade routes should correspond subnationally to places with the corresponding infrastructure needed to move the goods: ports, roads, frontiers, unmonitored spaces (where landing strips can be built and planes can land and refuel). The following chapters will explore and substantiate the claim, particularly for the Central American cases, that illicit trade and transit (and homicide rates) are higher in these subnational spaces. Homicide rates reported in 2007, for example, are highest in the provinces with major

---

[36] Increased trade and transit of illicit goods through Venezuela also coincides with rising homicide rates in that country, although at the time of this writing, political violence has also increased as the state cracks down on street protests.

[37] "The flow of cocaine from South America to the United States is one of the highest value illicit commodity streams in the world" (UNODC 2007: 25); "Central America suffers from being the conduit for the highest-value flow of drugs in the world" (UNODC 2007: 45).

Illicit Economies and Territorial Enclaves 89

ports (e.g., La Libertad and Sonsonate in El Salvador and Escuintla and Izabal in Guatemala) and ports with "airport graveyards" where DTOs leave their transport behind (e.g., the Petén in Guatemala).[38] Stated otherwise, the highest violence in El Salvador and Guatemala corresponds not to the largest urban areas or those where the civil war was fought but rather to the places with the infrastructure to move illicit drugs northward. In Mexico, well-defined subnational geographies also highlight a link between trade/transit regions and violence.[39] In particular, we see a link between border towns/regions and violence (although violence is not limited to these areas).[40]

Similarly, in Brazil, drug trafficking and violence have been particularly high in the cities with the largest ports: Rio de Janeiro, São Paulo, and Vitória (Arias 2006b: chapter 6). Rio has the second-largest port in Brazil and the fourth largest in South America; it has been a major site of drug transshipment and increasingly an important consumer market (Arias 2006b: 31, 53, 186, 187).[41]

---

[38] UNODC. *Crime and Development in Central America*, pp. 45, 54–55.
[39] Also see Snyder and Durán-Martínez (2009), Dell (2015), and Maurer (2012).
[40] As Williams (2009) noted, "in Mexico it has been largely about the control of what might be termed strategic warehousing on the northern border and the major routes into the United States. After being shipped in bulk from Colombia, cocaine is broken down into smaller loads and moved to the northern border where it is re-aggregated into larger shipments. This is why border cities such as Nuevo Laredo, Cuidad [sic] Juarez, and Tijuana have been the focus of intense fighting. In 2008, according to one report, the number of drug-related killings in Cuidad [sic] Juarez was at least 1,400. The high level of violence among trafficking organizations also stems partly from personal animosity, which results in and is perpetuated by the killing of family members in rival organizations. An additional factor is that Mexico has become a consumer as well as transshipment state and has witnessed the development of local drug markets. Some of the violence in places like Acapulco reflects a struggle for control of these retail markets" (Williams 2009: p. 11, online version).
[41] Arias (2006b) also observes in case studies that infrastructure and secure spaces such as seaports and airports, as well as control of specific territories, can be important for the trade and transit of drugs: "drug transshipment requires access to a quality port and airport facilities in close proximity to relatively secure, short-term storage facilities. Thus, Kingston, Jamaica, and Rio de Janeiro, with their large tourism and export trades located near nodes of urban poverty, provide ideal locations to store drugs in underserved communities as they wait for shipments to consumer markets in Europe and North America" (Arias 2006b: 53). In addition, "Rio, São Paulo, and Vitória all display the characteristics of areas involved in the transshipment of drugs. In these cases, criminals need control of secure locations to store drugs prior to shipment. This entails proximity to good port facilities and an ability to hide or defend the product prior to putting it on a plane or ship" (Arias 2006b: 187).

To revisit the arc of the argument thus far, state prohibition of certain goods results in illicit markets where the trade and transit of goods are highly prized. This has particularly been the case for the high-value-added drug cocaine and has been particularly consequential in the trade and transit between production and consumption. While US interdiction might shut down certain avenues, it does not foreclose relocation to other geographies – whether with regard to supply (from the Caribbean to Central America/ Mexico) or demand (with European markets joining the United States). Regardless of why illicit economies emerge, once in place, they generate incentives to control certain lucrative transit territories – a situation within which competition can lead to increased violence. Illicit organizations have responded strategically to formal prohibitions and regulations by inserting themselves into, and taking advantage of, this illicit market; this entails taking control of particular territories. And, strikingly, these territories (national and subnational) often seem to correspond with high homicide rates. In this regard, these spaces often coincide with homicidal ecologies; they do not determine violence, but they certainly seem to have an elective affinity with it.

Local Gangs, Illicit Economies

Gangs have also become an important part of Latin America's illicit economy. While they do not compare with organized crime in terms of their yield, profits, or transnational networks, they have come to dominate certain urban spaces (illicit microeconomies) and in some countries have started to develop broader territorial control. Like organized crime, gangs have become increasingly important illicit actors that share a desire to control territory for profit. Extortion, in particular, has become the currency of control.[42] While DTOs and gangs are not the only illicit actors operating in the region, they are strikingly similar in their territorial dimensions and have increasingly shaped territorial spaces within which violence is taking hold.

Gangs are partially defined by their age cohort.[43] Their members and leaders are largely youth (ages 15–24), and their members are often from

---

[42] Gangs are multivalent organizations. They are more than economic organizations – with many scholars noting their social and psychological dimensions. I do not deny this. However, to draw out the parallel with organized crime, I discuss them here in terms of their shared economic motives.

[43] Gangs are classically not defined as organized crime. For the purposes of this essay, I respect this colloquial distinction between organized crime and gangs. However,

poor neighborhoods. This does not mean that youth and poverty equal violence. However, poor males are disproportionately implicated in contemporary gang activity and violence: "In the end, this population group – marginalised urban males between the ages of 15 and 24 – are responsible for a large share of the violence in any given society, whether or not it has a gang problem" (UNODC 2007: 61).[44] Of course one should not assume that all poor youth are gang members or that all gang members are poor youth – although it has been common to demonize today's contemporary youth, as Levenson (2013) observes in her powerful study of Guatemalan gangs.

Like organized crime, gangs vary. They do not exist everywhere in equal measure. They have become a particularly visible and active part of the urban landscape in Central America (the empirical focus of this book) and in Mexico and Brazil. News reports have highlighted the rising prominence of these actors. And while attention has particularly focused on El Salvador, the reach of gangs is wider than that. Honduras stands out for the largest number of gang members and highest estimated per capita gang membership. El Salvador stands out for the lowest number of centralized gangs (resulting in the largest per-organization membership). Guatemala claims more gang members than El Salvador, but the per capita ratio is lower, with a more dispersed organized gang structure. Table 3.2 provides estimates of gangs from the early 2000s, although they should be read with caution, given the difficulty of gathering this data.

Many of these gangs have their roots in urban slums (favelas, shantytowns, *pueblos jóvenes*, etc.), but their presence has become more geographically widespread. In the Central American countries (notably, Guatemala, El Salvador, and Honduras), these gangs started off as neighborhood youth associations – often composed of impoverished youth (in some Central American cases initially appealing to youth whose families had suffered during the prior civil wars). It was common to portray these gangs (or *pandillas*, as they are known in Spanish) as unattached and marginalized youth who were in search of community, family, trust, respite, and identity; early academic studies highlighted the relatively nonviolent characteristics of some of these organizations, which provided

---

analytically speaking, I see gangs as one form of organized crime – all the more so if gangs turn to extortion, drug sales, and other forms of illicit organized activity.
[44] According to one estimate, "in 1996, 29% of all reported homicides in Latin America were committed by youth who ranged in age between 10 and 19 years old, and more than 34% were committed by youth between 20 and 29 years of age" (Rocha 2007: 11).

TABLE 3.2 *Gang members per 100,000 in Central America*

	Gang members per 100,000 population	Number of gangs	Total membership	Average number of members per gang
Panama	43	94	1,385	15
Nicaragua	81	268	4,500	17
Guatemala	111	434	14,000	32
Belize	36	2	100	50
Honduras	500	112	36,000*	321
Costa Rica	62	6	2,660	443
El Salvador	152	4	10,500	2,625
Total			69,145	

Source: UNODC (2007: 60), figure 50, and table 4. Information was calculated and adapted from S. Hernández (2005).
Notes: Also see USAID (2006), "Central America and Mexico Gang Assessment," www.usaid.gov/locations/latin_america_caribbean/democracy/gangs_assessment.pdf.
* According to UNODC (2007: 94), Delgado reports higher figures (40,000) for Honduras. See Jorge Delgado, "La criminalización de la juventud centroamericana: el predominio de las políticas públicas represivas." Paper submitted at Cartagena de Indias, Colombia, 2005. As quoted in Fundación Arias para la Paz, *La cara de la violencia urbana en América Central*. San José: Fundación Arias para la Paz, 2006.

youth an organizational home after years of military violence that had torn apart families and homes (Levenson 1988). Rocha's work (2007) on Nicaraguan gangs also highlights the search for community that these gangs can offer – providing cultural, social, and even drug-induced experiences that tie them together. Brenneman's anthropological work (2011) argues that chronic shame leads youth to join gangs – organizations that provide solidarity alongside violent crime.

Yet these youth gangs have taken different routes, with some becoming exceptionally violent organizations – in some cases responding to state efforts to crack down on them in the United States and in their home countries. While they started off as somewhat limited territorial groups that engaged in petty crime including "mugging, pickpocketing, shoplifting, brawling and other rather low-level felonies," by the end of the century (late 1990s), their criminal offenses became more serious and included "murders, rapes, assaults, and robberies; some of the cliques started to collaborate systematically with drug trafficking cartels, began to

Illicit Economies and Territorial Enclaves 93

consume hard drugs and got involved in the firearm trade more regularly" (Cruz 2012b). Several gangs became more expansive, professional, and territorial (and violent in some cases). Many of these organizations in Guatemala, El Salvador, Honduras, and Brazil have transformed from "youth neighborhood associations" into youth organizations that violently dominate certain territorial spaces within which they have come to assert their authority. In these spaces, gangs extract taxes, execute justice, wield violence, and at times provide physical security (when they are not challenged by competing gangs or the state).

Notably, many have argued that the deportation from the United States (Los Angeles in particular) of Central American gang members contributed to this process,[45] just as the crackdown on gangs in places like El

---

[45] Following a crackdown on undocumented residents, the United States sent many former Central American gang members from Los Angeles back to their country of birth (even though many had grown up in the United States). This pattern disproportionately affected countries in the northern triangle (El Salvador, Guatemala, and Honduras) rather than Nicaragua; perhaps not coincidentally, those who fled Guatemala and El Salvador did so in the context of military rule and civil wars, while those who fled Nicaragua did so because of their opposition to the Sandinista regime and civil war.

The number of Central Americans deported from the United States was calculated by Rocha (2007: 22) by drawing from the Statistical Yearbook of the Immigration and Naturalization Service. He found a dramatic increase (sometimes over tenfold) when comparing the numbers of Central Americans deported from 1992–1996 to those of 1998–2004: for El Salvador, they rose from 9,767 to 87,013; for Guatemala, from 7,267 to 64,312; for Honduras, from 9,497 to 106,826; and for Nicaragua, from 1,585 to 7,745. Nicaragua clearly experienced a much lower absolute starting point and a lower percentage increase.

Some would argue that this explains the disproportionately high violence in El Salvador and Guatemala (versus Nicaragua). Many Salvadoran youth, in particular, became active members of LA gangs, while Nicaraguan youth did not (most of these migrated to Costa Rica or Miami, per Rocha 2007: 20–12). There is something to this argument. Clearly, these transnational processes had an impact – exile or deportation, alongside cultural and violence practices. However, this argument seems more descriptive of one case (El Salvador) than explanatory of the region as a whole. For El Salvador, it remains unclear how deported gang members were integrated (if at all) into prior gangs and if/how/why old gangs embraced them. Relatedly, it begs the question as to why/how gangs evolved in the various countries – Honduras, in particular. Moreover, it leaves open why youth from Nicaragua and Guatemala did not become as actively involved in US gangs as their Salvadoran and Mexican counterparts. Indeed, even if there were more Salvadorans and Hondurans in LA than Nicaraguans, there were still nearly 30,000 Nicaraguans in residence. Moreover, of the deportees across these cases, the numbers tell us nothing about the participation in violent gangs on either side of the deportation process. Even if none of the Nicaraguan deportees were gang members and all the rest were, this set of numbers does not help explain how and why deported gang members were integrated into preexisting gangs in Central America. Thus, US deportation polices certainly raised ethical questions about the process of deporting young people to their home country –

Salvador (via policies such as *mano dura* and *super mano dura*) led them to become more professionalized organizations[46] – points that will be elaborated in the following chapters. Much remains to be learned about how much domestic versus international factors shaped the violent turn of some of these organizations, often referred to as *maras*.[47]

---

especially with little advance warning or information to the receiving countries. But this in and of itself cannot explain if and why deported gang members were welcomed into gangs or if/when/why they would kill. Part III of this book analyzes the gangs in the context of three Central American cases to explain why they deploy varying levels of violence.

[46] Cruz highlights the perverse incentives provided by El Salvador's *mano dura* policies (discussed later), with imprisoned leaders now operating from prisons and engaging in a more-organized and orchestrated form of crime. In turn, with the increasing penetration of Colombian and Mexican DTOs, they turned to gang members as hit men. "According to a survey conducted among gang members in Salvadoran prisons as early as 2006, 27 percent of gang members who had collaborated with drug cartels have worked as hit men, 21 percent have smuggled arms into the country, and 17 percent have participated in car hijacks" (Cruz 2012b).

[47] Why have gangs emerged in some places and not others? There is an unsettled debate about the role of US deportation policy, hardline domestic policies in Central America, civil war legacies, inequality, tight labor markets, drug economies, among other factors. That said, weak state capacity to govern impoverished areas coupled with poor employment prospects (a stagnant labor market characterized by limited formal and informal employment opportunities and low wages) likely provide increased incentives for otherwise trapped youth to join gangs. "Latin American youth of today are more severely affected than other groups by a series of troubling paradoxes, such as the combination of *greater access to education with fewer employment opportunities* ... In addition, the young people of today possess higher levels of productive skills but yet are largely excluded from the production process," according to ECLAC (2005: 15–16). The informal sector accounts for over 50 percent of unemployment in Central America, excluding Costa Rica (UNODC 2007: 21). Countries with stagnant labor markets in the context of growing illicit economies arguably provide incentives for youth and existing gangs to seek (and be more open to) alternative economic opportunities. For those that do not (or cannot fully) move into the formal economy, the options are limited. Some have joined the informal economy, some have joined the illicit market, and still others have migrated ("Over 20 million Latin Americans and Caribbeans reside outside the country of their birth," ECLAC 2005 report, 32). Thus the question of labor markets cannot be divorced from patterns of informality and migration. Overall, then, it is not that the economy forces a life of violent crime; however, tight labor markets do arguably increase the probability that youth will be increasingly attracted to mobilization by illicit organizations. Another point of view might consider labor markets in light of the percentage of youth relative to the total population. Strikingly, the youth population in Latin America is declining due to falling fertility rates and rising life expectancy. US Census data suggests, moreover, that the number of youth per capita in the population does not distinguish the Central American cases from one another, with all cases projected to fall between 9 percent (Panama), 10 percent (El Salvador and Costa Rica) and 11 percent (Guatemala, Belize, Honduras, and Nicaragua) (UNODC 2007: 26, based on US Census International Data Base). High-

Gangs thus have come to form part of *urban illicit economies*. Over time, they have become increasingly powerful urban actors and organizations that compete for control not only over turf but also over micro-level illicit economies – including widespread extortion (especially over transportation routes) and occasional drug sales. The central importance of territoriality is noted in Demoscopía's (2007) empirical work on Central American gangs, which highlights the fact that gangs seek to dominate a given territory and even seek to expand their control over larger spaces, taking them away from other gang members.

> An important aspect of pandilla organization is territoriality... In these spaces gang members engage in recreational and delinquent (and lucrative) activities ... The present study reveals a strong struggle between gangs to control and dominate territories, whose dynamic of control and reunion is not hidden; to the contrary, maras or gangs try to appropriate open and visible spaces from those who live in them. This visibility forms part of the control that they want to show and certainly have acquired over the territory and its inhabitants ... [T]he first relevant aspect regarding mara and pandilla organization [two forms of gangs] is to conquer and defend a territory at a local level and this is tied to identity construction for those youth who are involved. This territoriality is, at the same time, simultaneous with the establishment of a basic hierarchical structure. (Demoscopía 2007: 15–16)

Territoriality's centrality means that gangs in many Central American, Mexican, and Brazilian countries have developed social and economic incentives to control urban enclaves. They have assumed a parastatal role where the rule of law is weak. In this regard, gangs have occupied urban spaces over which they develop social identities, project authority, demand obeisance, and secure profits. They have been able to do so by force and/or by extracting rents in exchange for security – security that others will not steal their cars, violate their homes, rape their daughters, and kill their neighbors. While the need for security might in fact be a product of the gangs themselves, once ensconced in areas, gangs provide a parastatal way of resolving the problem when in fact the police and

---

and low-violence cases fall across this range. Finally, it is often argued that unemployment, poverty, and inequality are determinants of juvenile crime: "Juvenile crime is positively associated with local unemployment and poverty, and decreases with family income and education" (*World Drug Report*, UNODC 2007: 177); "Criminologists generally agree that inequality is a major 'structural' determinant of delinquency, especially of practices such as theft and robbery aimed at the illegal acquisition of property (Londoño 1996; Bourguignon 1999; Arriagada and Godoy 2000)" (see Portes and Roberts 2005: 67). Yet if this relationship holds, the presence of criminal groups does *not* explain where they are likely to kill more versus less often. As noted in Chapter 2, an explanation of criminal behavior cannot be equated with an explanation of homicide.

courts do not do so (more on this later). This is not just a question of the informal economy; it is often about an illicit one.

In this regard, gangs have created protection rackets (recalling Tilly's 1985 discussion of the state as organized crime). If states use the threat of violence to uphold their hegemony over territories, the same is true of gangs (and organized crime, more generally). Indeed, violence has become an important part of gang culture and practice. Gangs use violence to defend local territories, for which they charge protection (in theory, gangs do not commit crimes in their own backyards but rather commit them in other territories), although with the rising importance of domestic drug sales, this is perhaps no longer as true as it once was (Demoscopía 2007: 51–53). They use violence strategically to assert power within their organizations and over territory.[48] Violence is most likely in contested spaces and areas where no authority is hegemonic; that is to say, in places where neither the state nor rival gangs have assumed dominance, as discussed in Chapter 4, it is the competition over these spaces that often results in violence. In this context, uncontrolled public spaces – including bus routes, intersections with traffic lights, streets without nighttime illumination, and the like – are potentially lucrative ones over which to assert control. While the high rates of urban homicide cannot be explained solely by gang activity, it is quite evident that the rise of gang activity (and in particular competition between and among gangs) is responsible for some of the crime (and homicidal violence) that we see in parts of Guatemala, Honduras, El Salvador, Venezuela, and Brazil.[49]

The rise in gangs has therefore shaped the daily lives and political economies of families living in these communities. While citizens might feel free to vote for whomever they like, they are not free to ambulate around their communities at will; nor do they expect the state to protect them or meet their needs. To the contrary, the gangs often set the terms of order and violence on the streets. Accordingly, citizen rights are restricted – especially for youth, who are sometimes compelled to choose sides in those communities afflicted by gang violence.[50] The rise in gangs

---

[48] For parallels with the United States, see Levitt and Venkatesh (2000a, 2000b) as well as Klein and Maxson (2006).
[49] The relationship between gangs and the larger organized crime groups in Central America is open to interpretation and debates. We know that they are not linked organically and have historically operated independently from one another. Some contend, however, that over time gangs have connected to drug trafficking (see debate in the pages of Demoscopía 2007 and Grillo 2016 for examples). Both Demoscopía and Grillo note that competition to control territory drives much of the violence.
[50] Indeed, the territorial claims and violent actions of gangs (and illicit actors and markets in general) have implications for citizens who inhabit these local spaces; violence and fear

and criminal activity has led to a marked rise in citizen fears about criminality and victimization – as highlighted in multiple surveys by Latinobarometer and LAPOP. People are afraid to take public transit, to flag a taxi on the street, to go out at night, to stop their cars at certain traffic lights, and to visit certain neighborhoods that once were open to them. The rise in gang activity has resulted in increased efforts to demand state regulation (through ballot box calculations),[51] a turn to the marketplace for security (a pattern evidenced by the rise in private security firms over the past few years; Arias and Ungar 2009),[52] and increased citizen efforts to take matters into their own hands (including *extrajudicial actions*[53] and *citizen security*[54]).

are high. Holston and Caldeira's (1999) exemplary work highlights the many ways in which citizens have come to fear urban spaces (particularly in Brazil), as well as how citizens (including gang members and prisoners) have come to use talk of rights to assert their claims (Holston 2008).

[51] See Chevigny (2003a), Holland (2013), and Cruz (2010). The feared rise in gang activity in particular and organized crime in general has translated in the 1990s and 2000s into ballot box calculations in El Salvador and Honduras, where presidents who advocated draconian *mano dura* policies were elected into office. These policies seriously restricted the rights of suspected criminals – in particular those who were presumed to be gang members. In other words, the fear of gangs led politicians to enact policies that restricted the rights of citizens not only to associate freely but also to have a fair trial. Many of these policies were found to be unsuccessful in containing gang activity (in some cases leading gangs to become even more professional, hierarchical, and violent than previously). Moreover, some have charged that these policies were unconstitutional because of the restrictions on civil rights.

[52] I thank Mario Snjajder for making this observation during a 2009 conference at Hebrew University's Institute for Advanced Studies. He noted that security is increasingly seen as a commodity that should be bought rather than publicly guaranteed and provided. It is a point that is compatible with the data on rising security firms and the anthropological work by Caldeira (2000).

[53] Citizens have also responded by engaging in *extrajudicial actions* – particularly in Brazil and Guatemala. Paulo Sergio Pinheiro (2007) has written about the social cleansing campaigns that ordinary citizens and policeman have initiated against street children and gang members. Similar stories have appeared in Guatemala and El Salvador, where citizens have taken matters into their own hands; ironically, their fear of crime and distrust of the integrity and capacity of judicial institutions has encouraged actors to engage in extrajudicial actions against suspected criminals. Angelina Snodgrass Godoy's (2006) fascinating work on popular (in)justice highlights that in fact extrajudicial responses have been more widespread than those to gang activity. In the highlands, they provide a means for taking action in a context where communities have a profound distrust of the state and its ability to provide and uphold the rule of law.

[54] There is a significant literature on citizen security, with particularly important and extensive scholarship by Lucía Dammert (e.g., 2006) and Hugo Frühling (e.g., 2003), among others.

Notably, these gangs (in contrast to the organized crime organizations discussed earlier) have operated on a more microeconomic scale. They have not been important players in the trade and transit of illicit drugs, although that has arguably started to change recently. Nor has the sale of drugs been a major component of what they do. UNODC (2007, *World Drug Report*, passim, 17, 62–63, 180 in particular) notes that current estimates suggest that there is a relatively small local/domestic market for drugs; cocaine trafficking is largely maritime, while gangs are not; the percentage of estimated drug users is lower than the number of gang members; and gang members are more likely to use drugs than the population at large (except in Panama, where cocaine use has been the highest in the region and far outpaces the size of gangs, which is reported as the second smallest per 100,000). "So while gang members surely deal drugs, as they do everywhere in the world, there are simply too many of them and not enough of a market for this to become a basis of support for the majority of the membership" (UNODC 2007: 63). The report goes on to say that "in fact, while drug trafficking organization from a number of Central American countries are mentioned in the 2007 National Drug Threat Assessment, the maras [the most violent form of gangs] are not" (UNODC 2007: 64). In short, gangs have historically not been major actors in the drug trade. Rather, they started off as youth groups seeking to control territorial enclaves and have increasingly become involved in illicit microeconomies that include extortion in neighborhoods, on bus routes, and among other clearly defined territorial spaces.

CONCLUSION

Illicit economies are the expected underbelly of any economy and state regulation. This is because entrepreneurs (large and small) will always emerge to try to profit by what is made illicit, making it available and trying to secure a dominant market share over it. The success of illicit actors in this world rests on their ability to control territorial enclaves. For the drug organizations, it is about trade and transit – moving the drugs transnationally. For the gangs, it is about asserting control over specific urban territories, in which they oversee extortion and illicit sales. In each case, economic livelihood depends on territorial hegemony. While these organizations include many other characteristics (including strong identities, social behaviors, among other features), this chapter emphasizes their insertion into the illicit economy, their territoriality, and their associated economic motives to assert hegemonic control over lucrative spaces.

These illicit territorial enclaves, in turn, have a high propensity to generate high levels of violence; thus they constitute homicidal ecologies. That said, violence is neither inherent nor inevitable to illicit economies per se (Naylor 2009; Williams 2009; Reuter 2009 and 2014). Indeed, despite the sensationalism around organized crime and gangs, the emergence of these organizations does not in and of itself explain the rising recourse to violence and/or why they would wield violence for profit.

In strict theory, violence in illicit market activity could take any or all of these forms; but it could just as well take none at all. There is actually nothing in the inherent logic of production, marketing, income distribution or wealth redistribution in illegal markets that suggests inevitability of violence. True, given the fact that illegal markets have no access to the mechanisms of peaceful dispute resolution that are normal for legal ones, there might be a temptation to resort to crude force. But on-going illegal market activity likely relies more on trust between peers or extended family members, and the threat of excommunication for future deals, than hiring a biker with a baseball bat to settle disagreements. Yet clearly such violence does occur from time to time, a function partly of the nature of the market (is it prone to attack by upstarts or already dominated by existing underground entrepreneurs?), and partly of the nature of the commodity (selling crack cocaine is more likely to be associated with violence than peddling counterfeit Louis Vuitton handbags). Therefore it is necessary to ask further if there is potentially something in the nature of particular illegal markets, rather than illegal markets per se that is conducive to violence. (Naylor 2009: p. 5 of online version)

In Chapter 4, I argue that violence is not simply a product of the presence of these illicit organizations and illicit territorial enclaves. If anything, the actors have an incentive to assert hegemonic control (or pacted alliances), which would arguably decrease violence in their enclaves. But instead, violence proliferates where organizational competition ensues, to control these territories. As elaborated in future chapters, the empirical link between the presence of a significant illicit economy based on trade and transit and medium-to-high violence seems rather robust, although it begs the question as to why some countries become part of that trade route and others do not (a point addressed next). Other factors also play a part; crucial among them are *state capacity* and *organizational competition*, as discussed in Chapter 4.

4

State Capacity and Organizational Competition

Strategic Calculations about Territory and Violence

Illicit political economies map onto particular territories. In Latin America, many of these spaces have given rise to the highest contemporary homicide rates in the world. This pattern plays out both along trade and transit drug routes dominated by organized crime and, to a lesser degree, in some urban spaces dominated by *mara*-type gangs. This argument was presented in Chapter 3 and is developed at length in the empirical case studies that follow in Part III.

This chapter advances the argument presented in Chapter 3 by introducing two corollary questions related to illicit groups and territoriality. Why do illicit groups choose to set up illicit activity in some countries (and subnational spaces) and not others? Under what circumstances do these illicit groups deploy violence in these territories? Both questions speak to strategic calculations about territoriality on the part of illicit organizations. While the first question focuses on antecedent macro-strategic calculations about *where illicit groups set up shop*, the second question addresses the subsequent strategic calculations about *when violence is likely to be used in those spaces*.

State capacity critically addresses the first question. It shapes decisions about where illicit organizations choose to establish their business (and where they flourish). I argue that this factor fundamentally shapes geographies of illicit activity. Since state capacity is a multi-institutional and multivalent variable, however, I focus in particular on the state institutions functionally responsible for maintaining order and upholding the rule of law – namely the police (in interaction with the military and courts). As argued further on (and empirically discussed in later case studies), illicit actors are likely to avoid territories that have the greatest monitoring and accountability. Thus, the organizational performance of the police (courts and military) is critical for transnational and national illicit organizations deciding on trade and transit routes as well as gangs deciding on the boundaries of their urban domain. State capacity, thus, is analytically prior to the emergence of large illicit economies (although in practice state capacity and illicit economies have an endogenous relationship). This is the first argument developed here.

This chapter complements the meso-political argument about geographies of illicit political economy with a micro-argument about when illicit actors will deploy violence. As scholars have long recognized, violence is costly. Illicit actors strategically prefer to avoid violence when there are other options. They will deploy violence, however, to defend their territorial control – whether challenged by other illicit organizations or by the state – or to extend their territorial reach. I therefore argue that *organizational competition* explains the emergence of high-stakes and high homicide rate violence within these economies. Interorganizational territorial competition, in this regard, provides a core mechanism explaining the prevalence of high violence patterns within illicit territories. It is not the only cause of homicides, but it is a major cause of the turn to extreme levels of violence within illicit political economies.[1]

The rest of this chapter discusses strategic calculations by illicit actors in light of these two variables: state capacity and interorganizational territorial competition. These variables help explain where and why violence becomes particularly prevalent.

STATES AND STATE CAPACITY: SHAPING CALCULATIONS ABOUT ILLICIT GEOGRAPHIES

If we start with the assumption that drug trafficking organizations and youth gangs seek to maximize profit, then one must consider how these illicit actors decide on economic geographies – including, trade routes and byways.[2] In the process of "jurisdiction shopping," how do they determine where to set up shop, move the goods (drugs, people, merchandise,

---

[1] This argument about organizational competition over territory was inspired a decade ago by reading Gambetta (1996), Tilly (2003), and Kalyvas (2006). Despite their diverse theoretical orientations and empirical foci, they all revealed that hegemonic violent organizations do not wield violence if they can use other means. Rather, violence escalates where there is organizational competition over territory. Snyder and Durán-Martínez (2009) arrived at a similar conclusion. The argument echoes more-recent work – for example, in the special issue "Drug Violence in Mexico" in the *Journal of Conflict Resolution* (59, no. 8, December 2015).

[2] See Lee (1999) for the argument that drug organizations act like both "traditional economic elites," businessmen, and "entrepreneurs" (passim, see esp. 4, 18, and 19). They act to maximize profit and also seek to shape politics to that end.

money, etc.), and export?[3] Since organized crime is a business – one that is concerned with its investment and return – illicit actors (if they are going to survive and prosper) need to figure out how the state will structure the situation to their (dis)advantage. Corrupt states with poor rule of law can be bad for the overall economy but good for illicit businesses that are seeking to buy off officials and spaces to move their goods. Thus, businesspersons tied to the illicit economy often develop trade routes in geographically advantageous countries where state monitoring and accountability are perceived to be low. Similarly, youth organizations are most likely to set up shop and seek to expand in those urban areas where the state's administrative reach is weakest. This basic observation manifests in two ways.

Obviously, business must address the strategic question of maximizing geographic advantage. Classically, studies have considered economic advantage in terms of access to natural resources including land, cheap and/or skilled labor, capital, and taxes, among other formal economic issues. However, geographic advantage is also a function of physical proximity to market and politically favorably states. Thus, when considering transnational business, (illicit) organizations must consider supply chains and target destinations. The United States and Europe are prime destination markets for narcotraffickers, in particular, as discussed in Chapter 3. Therefore, the primary drug-producing states (Colombia, Peru, and Bolivia) have an incentive to identify geographically proximate countries (to their north and to their east) to move their illicit product to northern markets. Geographically speaking, landlocked countries (Paraguay) and countries to the south and/or west (Chile and Argentina) would not be ideal places for trade and transit routes. Conversely, countries to the north (e.g., Venezuela, the Caribbean, Central America, and Mexico) would appear as prime locations for movement northward to the United States just as countries located on the Atlantic Coast would be prime targets to move illicit goods eastward to Europe. They provide the most direct line between (drug-) producing and (drug-) consuming markets and thus are geographically auspicious locations. While geography does not predetermine fate, it has (until perhaps more recently) provided critical incentives for developing trade and transit routes in some places (and not others).

Within these physical geographic incentives and constraints, illicit actors deciding on geographies of trade and transit must consider the political opportunity costs of state (and interstate) monitoring. As they

[3] I thank Stephanie Golub for introducing the term "jurisdiction shopping."

seek to avoid monitoring by the strongest states, illicit organizations simultaneously seek to situate their trade where state monitoring is the weakest. Drug trafficking organizations, for example, seek to avoid state actions that can result in capture (either of goods or of persons); captures would obviously result in a decline of profits as well as a decline in personal freedoms. Indeed, it is estimated that a significant portion of cocaine is interdicted in transit – an estimated 42 percent in 2007–2008 and about 24 percent a decade earlier (UNODC 2010: 67). Figures and tables in the prior chapter highlight the varied patterns of interdiction across the region and over time.

Hence, DTOs have a clear motive: illicit organizations seek to avoid geographies with strong state capacity to monitor them and therefore relocate when they cannot outmaneuver or coordinate with the state.[4] In practice, state monitoring happens at two levels: the international level and the domestic level. Regarding the first, the United States has played a critical role in monitoring international trade and transit. Accordingly, illicit organizations have played a cat-and-mouse game with the US Drug Enforcement Agency (DEA), responding with increasingly sophisticated means of transport (Kenney 2007). When the DEA started to crack down on drug production in Colombia and on trade in the Caribbean, Colombian drug organizations had to regroup. They did so in various ways, including by moving operations to Mexico and Central America, as noted earlier. Thus, trade and transit routes often shift in response to state actions – both on international and national fronts.

These shifts [declining demand for cocaine in the United States and rising demand for cocaine in Europe], combined with interdiction efforts, have also affected trafficking patterns. As the Colombian government has taken greater control of its territory, traffickers are making more use of transit countries in the region, including the Bolivarian Republic of Venezuela and Ecuador. Mexican drug cartels emerged over the last 10 to 15 years as the primary organizers for shipments of cocaine into the United States, largely replacing the previously dominant Colombian groups. In response to Mexican enforcement efforts, Central American countries are increasingly being used as transit countries. West Africa started to be used as a way station to Europe around 2004. The situation remains fluid, and the impact on transit countries can be devastating. (UNODC *World Drug Report* 2010: 16)[5]

---

[4] See Kenney (2007). The OAS (2013: 82) arrives at a similar conclusion about the lack of state presence (discussed as impunity and a culture of disregard for the state) and the entrepreneurial motivations and calculations of drug traffickers.

[5] UNODC (2010), *World Drug Report 2010*, New York, NY.

If DTOs respond to international state monitoring, so too they respond to domestic crackdowns. Colombian drug trafficking organizations, such as the infamous Medellín and Cali DTOs/cartels, once dominated the trade and transit of cocaine in the Americas. With the crackdown on Colombian DTOs, these two dominant organizations were severely hampered (replaced by a wide range of organizations). This organizational disarray left open spaces for other DTOs to grab hold of trade and transit routes. Mexican entrepreneurs did exactly that by increasing their role in the trading and transit of drugs in Mexico (UNODC 2012: 31). However, starting in 2006, when the Mexican government adopted a more draconian policy against drug traffickers operating in the national territory, Mexican DTOs responded by further penetrating and increasing use of the Central American landmass (UNODC 2012: 31); in turn, interdiction in the Central American isthmus increased in the following years (see Figure 4.1).[6] Thus, strong state monitoring (including by international forces) can force illicit organizations to shift geographies and set up alternative trade routes (or urban geographies in the case of gangs).

This push factor (illicit organizations seeking to avoid strong state monitoring) is complemented by a pull factor (illicit organizations seeking to identify geographies with the weakest state capacity to monitor and crack down on illicit activity).[7] Hence, in deciding to shift locales from the Caribbean to Mexico and Central America, DTOs still needed to decide *which* countries (or subnational regions) were most propitious for that activity. This is not just a question of identifying ports, borders, and landing strips, as noted in Chapter 3; it is also fundamentally a question of identifying which ports, borders, and byways are the least monitored – i.e., which states either have weak professional capacity (ill-defined organizational mandates, poor accountability mechanisms, and weak

---

[6] The Mexican government cracked down starting in 2006, through increased extradition, going after kingpins, sending in troops, increasing cocaine seizures, and making it harder to move drugs through Mexican territory (UNODC 2012: 11, 18). See special issue of *Journal of Conflict Resolution* (59, no. 8, December 2015), particularly chapters by Shirk and Wallman (2015), Calderón et al. (2015), Durán-Martínez (2015), Osorio (2015), and Lessing (2015).

[7] Thoumi (1999: 137) argues that the drug trade flourished in Colombia largely because of a weak national regime. Maingot (1999: 144) also identifies the following conditions as propitious for the growth of illicit economies: geography, corruption, laundering possibilities, and increasingly open economies. He argues that these factors made Venezuela and Brazil attractive locations for major international drug organizations.

State Capacity and Organizational Competition

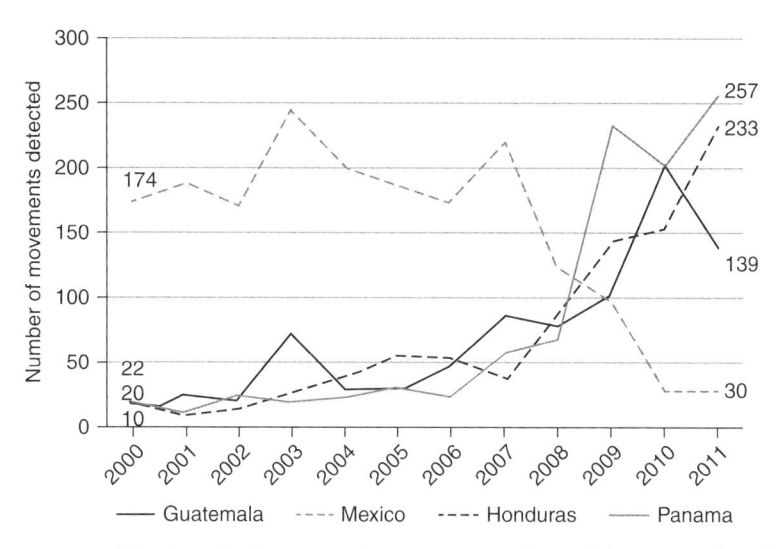

FIGURE 4.1 Number of primary cocaine movements destined for or interdicted in selected Central American countries and Mexico (2000–2011)
Source: UNODC (2012: 20)

resources, including training and infrastructure) and/or are perceived as highly corrupt/complicit in illicit activities.[8]

Thus, state capacity is critical to these calculations – particularly the rule-of-law institutions responsible for imposing and upholding domestic order. The state institutions most responsible for tracking illicit organizations include rule-of-law/public security institutions (police, attorney general's office, and courts). Obviously, the police (sometimes supplemented with military support) are the ones tasked with monitoring public spaces (streets, parks, neighborhoods, etc.). They are the ones that would theoretically make it harder for illicit organizations to form and flourish, they

---

[8] In one striking example, following the 2009 Honduran coup against President Zelaya, UNODC speculated that political uncertainty led to the increasing use of Honduras for transit (UNODC 2012: 12, 19). Given that cocaine seizures nearly tripled in two years and then stabilized, UNODC inferred a significant rise in the transit of cocaine through the region, a conclusion also reached by the US government (UNODC 2012: 19): "The share of all detected 'flow events' whose first destination or point of seizures were in Central America (rather than in Mexico or the Caribbean) shot from a quarter in 2000 to 85% in 2011. Detected direct shipments to Mexico dropped from 174 in 2000 to 30 in 2011, while those in Panama, Costa Rica, Guatemala, and Honduras rocketed upwards, most markedly after 2006. Honduras went from 20 incidents in 2000 to 233 in 2011" (UNODC 2012: 20).

hold primary responsibility for regulating these spaces, and they are the most visible part of the state. Lipsky (1980) refers to the police as street-level bureaucrats, given their proximity to everyday citizens. The attorney general's office and the courts are the second institutional layer tasked with upholding the rule of law, by investigating and prosecuting suspected criminals (although the boundaries of investigation vary by country, with different responsibilities designated across the police, the attorney general's office, and the courts).[9]

These rule-of-law institutions generally have a poor record and reputation in Latin America. It is commonly noted that they have limited resources, weak training, limited accountability (i.e., high levels of impunity), and high levels of corruption. Thus, the region as a whole seems to be conducive for illicit activity. But the more interesting question is relative: Which countries are weakest along these dimensions and therefore most conducive to the illicit trade and transit of drugs? As discussed later, the drug trade is most pervasive in those Central American countries on the isthmus (Guatemala, El Salvador, and Honduras) with particularly weak rule-of-law institutions. In parallel fashion, in the countries where state institutions (particularly rule-of-law institutions) are comparatively strongest (Chile, Uruguay, and Costa Rica), the drug trade is the weakest. Of course, there are many states that are weak and do not have a significant drug trade; thus, to state the obvious, weak states are necessary/critical but not sufficient for the drug trade to flourish in a particular region.

The types of strategic calculations made by illicit organizations are noted in Figure 4.2, identifying prime geographies in order to maximize international physical location (pull), avoid international monitoring (push), and take advantage of weak domestic rule-of-law institutions (push and pull). Although these decisions do not always occur in this temporal order (and while illicit actors can further weaken and corrupt host states), Figure 4.2 provides a useful heuristic for identifying initial constraints (push factors) and incentives (pull factors) operating at the international and domestic levels.

While the relationship between illicit organizations and weak states is conceptually logical and geographically correlated, demonstrating this link is a tall order – especially when analyzing the capacity of public security agencies to check illicit organizations, their violence, and

---

[9] Theoretically, coast guards would also be important, although we have very little information on this state institution.

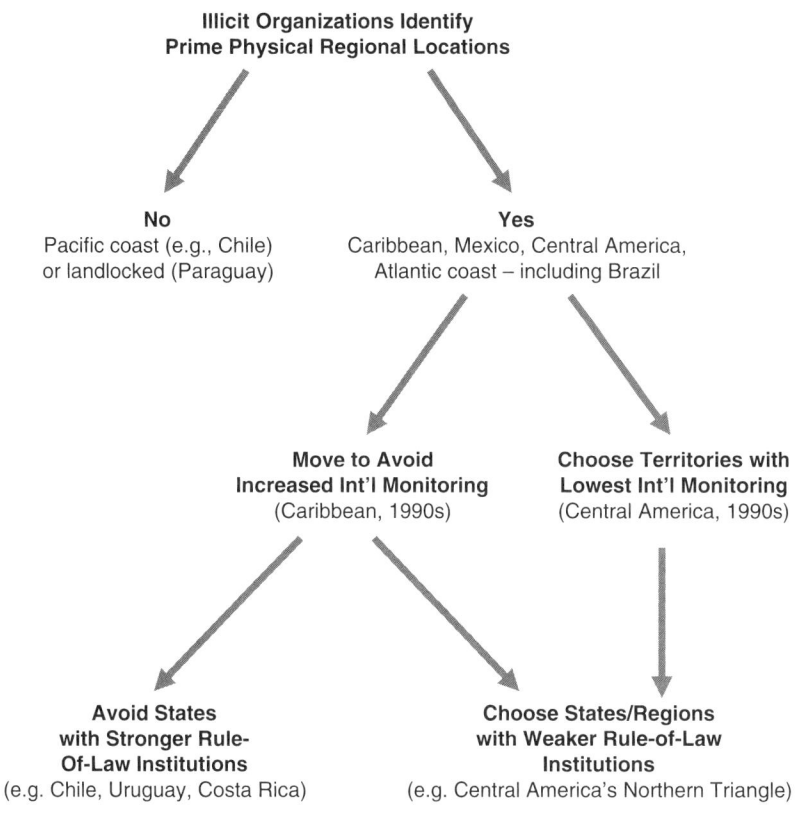

```
                  Illicit Organizations Identify
                  Prime Physical Regional Locations
                      ↙                  ↘
            No                                Yes
   Pacific coast (e.g., Chile)      Caribbean, Mexico, Central America,
   or landlocked (Paraguay)         Atlantic coast – including Brazil
                                         ↙              ↘
                            Move to Avoid         Choose Territories with
                        Increased Int'l Monitoring  Lowest Int'l Monitoring
                           (Caribbean, 1990s)       (Central America, 1990s)
                              ↙         ↘                    ↓
                  Avoid States            Choose States/Regions
               with Stronger Rule-         with Weaker Rule-of-Law
                Of-Law Institutions              Institutions
          (e.g. Chile, Uruguay, Costa Rica)  (e.g. Central America's Northern Triangle)
```

FIGURE 4.2 Stylized calculation by drug trafficking organizations

corrupting influence. "The central problem is that the quality of data on state weakness is negatively affected by the very weakness it tries to measure: the more corrupt or criminalized a state, the worse [i.e., less reliable] its measures of corruption and criminality will be" (Wilkinson 2004: 72).[10]

Therefore, there is a circular process by which weak states provide promising territories for illicit actors, which in turn can further corrupt these weak states. Because of this, the weakest states are often the ones

---

[10] Wilkinson (2004) develops an electoral logic for when politicians do or do not use security forces to control ethic violence (once it has started). This logic does not explain the homicidal levels found in Latin America, although the security forces do prove key for playing a deterrent or complicit role, as elaborated in this chapter and the case studies.

that are also the most susceptible to corruption by illicit actors (often becoming involved in the very activities they are supposed to monitor). Indeed, illicit actors operate not only where the state is weak but also where the state is complicit (Arias 2006a and 2006b; Cruz 2010).[11] In practice, then, the illicit rubs up against the formal in unexpected ways – sometimes in tension, sometimes in collaboration.

While recognizing the paucity of data and endogeneity challenges, I next provide a brief conceptual definition of state capacity, followed by a review of how various quantitative and qualitative indicators reveal why certain state institutions are more/less relevant to illicit actors making strategic calculations about geographies of illicit political economy. For a discussion of indicators reviewed but not used, see the appendix to this chapter.

Defining State Capacity

State capacity is a notoriously contested concept and one for which it is challenging to disentangle cause and consequence.[12] Along with my colleagues Miguel Centeno and Atul Kohli, I take "state capacity" to refer to the organizational ability to implement governing projects – separate from the political will to deploy it.[13] In this sense, it is a term of potential utilization; it is normatively neutral, as it can be used for good and for ill. As a multidimensional variable, it is based on territorial reach, resources, human expertise, and organizational coherence (including clear hierarchies, mandates, information, accountability, and ability to juggle multiple/competing mandates). Since states, moreover, are composed of multiple agencies, analysis should specify the institution responsible for those outcomes and ascertain the capacity thereof; certainly, different state institutions and associated capacities are required, for example, to promote economic growth and social inclusion versus security and order (Centeno et al. 2017).

---

[11] In this sense, the range of organized crime and gang activity is in part a product of the kind of state that is present, which in turns determines, as Helmke and Levitsky (2004) would hypothesize, whether gangs compete, undermine, accommodate, and/or complement the state that is present.
[12] See Gallie (1956); Wilkinson (2004); Kurtz and Schrank (2007); and Centeno, Kohli, and Yashar (2017).
[13] This discussion of state capacity draws on Centeno, Kohli, and Yashar (2017, chapters 1 and 15).

To explain homicidal violence, I zero in on a particular set of state institutions (law-and-order institutions that include the police and courts) and a particular set of indicators of state capacity (organizational coherence and territorial reach).[14] It should be readily apparent why one would look at law-and-order institutions, in particular. Various law-and-order states have the ability to squeeze or leave open spaces for illicit activity. And indeed some studies conclude that the strength of rule-of-law institutions in particular is correlated with homicide rates. For example, the UNODC assessed the relationship between rule of law (using 1996/1998 and 2009 data from the World Bank) and homicide rates (using UNODC 2010 data).[15] They found various positive correlations. First, countries that experienced an increase in homicides tended to coincide with countries that had comparatively lower levels of rule of law. Second, countries that had experienced an improvement in the rule of law also tended to experience a decline in homicides (and vice versa). However, this is a rather broad brushstroke conclusion, which leaves open which state institutions matter and how. Thus, we need better datasets and more disaggregated measures, as we discuss further on.

Indeed, since the state is not a homogenous unit where all institutions take responsibility equally for holding illicit actors to account – preventing, monitoring, judging, rehabilitating, and/or punishing those suspected of illicit activity – I focus in particular on the police (and other coercive state institutions such as militaries), which is the first line of "defense" in all these domains.[16] In turn, the courts (and attorney general's offices) are the institutions responsible for holding criminals to account and determining responsibility and judgment. In Latin America, these are the agencies

---

[14] Durán-Martínez (2015) analyzes state cohesion and competition in her analysis of types of violence in Mexico and Colombia. There are some parallels in our arguments, although she analyzes states' "cohesion" to explain the *visibility* of the violence that occurs, whereas I analyze state capacity to explain where DTOs are likely to set up shop. We agree that competition can increase the intensity of the violence that occurs.

[15] See UNODC (2011: 33–34, including fig. 2.3 on p. 33).

[16] Frühling (2009: 24–25) highlights, for example, the different organizational structures of police across the hemisphere. While Guatemala, El Salvador, and Peru, for example, have centralized police forces, this is not true everywhere; Chile has had multiple centralized police forces, and federal countries have more than one police force, although with varied degrees of fragmentation (in some cases, such as Mexico, they might have many coterminous forces that report to different levels of government). As Frühling notes, fragmented police forces confront considerable coordination problems. Moreover, despite demilitarization efforts, some police still fall under the military or defense departments (and/or coordinate with the military for basic policing functions).

on the frontline (at times with the military and the prison system also assuming a role).

To measure state capacity for law-and-order institutions in Latin America, I analyze the *organizational coherence* and *territorial reach* alongside other behavioral measures (how [in]efficacious they are in holding criminals to account) – elaborated later and discussed at greater length in the case studies.[17] Where law-and-order institutions lack organizational coherence (i.e., they have poor role specification, limited internal accountability, and marginal esprit de corps), territorial reach (i.e., deployment of police officers throughout the territory), and efficaciousness (i.e., poor homicide clearance rates), it is difficult to hold other licit and illicit actors to account (both illicit actors outside of the institutions and public officials in associated state institutions). Weak state capacity can facilitate (and reflect) complicity and corruption on the part of the very institutions designed to reign in these behaviors.[18] It provides fertile ground for the growth of illicit activity (as well as possible state incompetence and/or complicity). The rest of this section unpacks this point, with reference to the relevant (albeit limited) cross-national data. See chapter 4 Appendix for a discussion of various additional datasets that speak to rule-of-law questions.

Identifying Institutional Patterns of Efficaciousness and Impunity (Lack of Accountability)

Latin American law-and-order institutions are generally weak – with some notable exceptions (in the cases that have had the longest, albeit not uninterrupted, history of democratic rule). Indeed, despite concerted efforts at institutional reform, change has been slow and uneven – as

---

[17] One approach (the most straightforward one) is to evaluate standard numerical measures of resources (budgets and salaries) or personnel (police offices, judges, or lawyers). Logically, there must be a resource/personnel baseline below which a country cannot fall and still accomplish basic governing tasks. However, empirically, these particular measures of state capacity reveal little about what that baseline would be since there is no clear linear relationship between resources and the violence patterns that emerge. Despite low resources, Nicaragua's police force is generally described as competent and capable – relative to other Nicaraguan state institutions and relative to other Central American police forces. As a result, Nicaragua's homicide rates are relatively low for the region (see UNODC 2007: 30 and Cruz 2012a). I explore how and why this is the case in Chapter 7.

[18] Of course, the uses of state capacity depend in part on political decisions (about whether, if, and how to deploy it), alongside societal reactions (whether society abides by and/or resist it). See Centeno, Kohli, and Yashar (2017).

evidenced by disappointing reform efforts to demilitarize and professionalize these forces (WOLA 2009: 2–3). Even in cases where police forces have been restructured, their organizational capacity remains generally quite low, while their reputation for corruption and complicity remains quite high.

Police efficaciousness entails many features, but at a minimum it requires organizational coherence. Role specification provides one way of evaluating organizational coherence; it requires that the police force know its mandate and that the boundaries of the job are clearly defined. Unfortunately, police functions in Latin American countries are neither clearly defined vis-à-vis the military (Withers, Santos, and Isaacson 2010) nor with relation to the attorney general's office (in terms of investigative responsibilities, for example). Withers, Santos, and Isaacson (2010) identify this poor role specification when they observe that (a) governments (including US aid programs) have not historically built up Latin American police forces, which have taken a back seat to the military as a coercive institution[19] and (b) there is no bright line to demarcate military and police functions in all cases, save in Argentina and Chile and to a lesser degree in Uruguay.[20] Therefore the military has assumed (to varying degrees) many police functions in Mexico, Central America, the Andes, and Brazil.[21] The institutional blurring of roles (coupled with poor

---

[19] Withers, Santos, and Isaacson (2010) also note that US laws and practice have benefited Latin American militaries over the police (not only during the Cold War but also in its aftermath) – with more aid and support flowing to the latter over the former, even when it comes to addressing domestic issues.

[20] Costa Rica does not officially have a military force, which was abolished after the 1948 civil war.

[21] Within this general panorama, Withers, Santos, and Isaacson (2010, passim) highlight the following variation in police/military boundaries: Constitutional provisions demarcate separate roles for the police and military in Argentina and Uruguay, with the military assuming the traditional external role (being called in only by the executive in cases of emergency). Differing roles are also assigned in Brazil, although the constitution does not prohibit the military from engaging in internal functions (e.g., in response to crime). Differing roles are also assigned in Central America (El Salvador, Honduras, Nicaragua, and Guatemala), although there are conditions under which the military can intervene in domestic affairs, such as natural disasters. With rising crime, the military in Central America has also assumed a more active role in response to rising violence, illicit trade, and illicit social actors. While Mexico has a more professional military than its Central American counterparts, it too has increasingly intervened to combat high violence/narco-trafficking and legally has the ability to intervene for a range of reasons, including public works, natural disasters, and public need. Finally, the military assumes a more encompassing role in the Andes (Bolivia, Colombia, Ecuador, Peru, and Venezuela), with military involvement in external security, business, development, and law enforcement. In short, the police have a poorly defined terrain of activity in many countries in the region

training and resources for the police) has created police forces that are poorly positioned to achieve successful law enforcement. This is true even though countries throughout the region (especially Central America, following their civil wars) made a concerted effort to reform the police. This point is elaborated in Part III's case studies, where role specification is blurred in two cases (Guatemala and El Salvador) but more clearly demarcated in the third (Nicaragua). Poor role specification coincides with poor accountability practices, in marked contrast to the Nicaraguan case, where the police has a clearer mandate and clarity in institutional accountability; this functional clarity corresponds, moreover, with a greater esprit de corps in the Nicaraguan police.

Alongside role specification, another key indicator of state capacity is effectiveness in fighting crime. The homicide clearance rate (the percentage of recorded crimes for which a suspect is identified), in particular, reveals interesting intra-regional differences (see Figure 4.3). The data is scattered, albeit telling. Taking a look at Central America alone, one finds very high homicide clearance rates reported by UNODC (2007: 31–32) in Nicaragua (81 percent) and Costa Rica (82 percent), a significantly lower rate in El Salvador (44 percent), and a very low rate in Guatemala (7 percent, although in the year prior it was higher, at 16 percent). Actual conviction rates are presumably even lower (UNODC 2007: 31–31). Indeed, UNODC reported on the percentage of a country's citizens who were convicted of *any* crimes, revealing quite a notable variation in conviction rates across Central America and Mexico. While data for Nicaragua and Honduras was lacking (only one data point each), the strikingly low rates in Guatemala and El Salvador contrasted significantly with those of Costa Rica and Panama.

Another UNODC report (2014b: 18, 92) does not disaggregate the country-level data but notes considerable regional disparities when looking at 2007–2008 and 2011–2012 data, with Latin America (based on 11–14 countries) having an estimated homicide clearance rate of around 50 percent (conviction rate of 24 per 100 victims) – the lowest in the world – compared to Europe's homicide clearance rate of around 85 percent (conviction rate estimated at 80 per 100 homicides) and an estimated global average homicide clearance rate of 60 percent (based on 41–60 countries with a conviction rate of about 43 perpetrators per 100 victims). These reported homicide clearance rates are noteworthy. They highlight quite clearly that Latin American police capacity is distinct compared to

and have had weak training, poor resource allocation, and limited success in law enforcement.

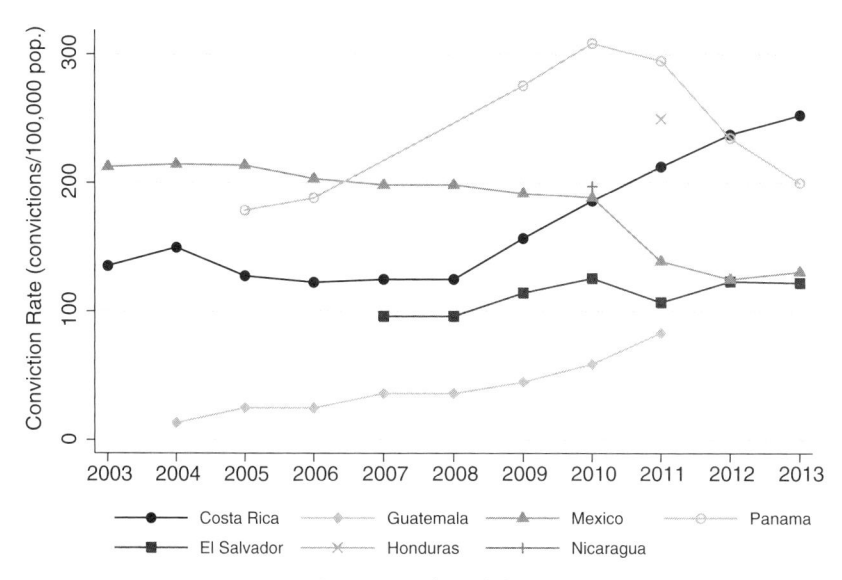

FIGURE 4.3 Conviction rates by country for adult citizens in Central America and Mexico (2003–2013, rate per 100,000 for all crimes)
Graph created by Daniela Barba-Sánchez using Stata. Data available at www.unodc.org/unodc/en/data-and-analysis/statistics/crime.html (accessed September 17, 2014).
Notes: "Persons convicted" means persons found guilty by any legal body authorized to pronounce a conviction under national criminal law, whether or not the conviction was later upheld. The total number of persons convicted should also include persons convicted of serious special law offenses but exclude persons convicted of minor road traffic and other petty offenses. Changes in definitions and/or counting rules are reported by Panama, resulting in a break in the time series.

that of Europe and Asia, and provide some suggestive data on differences even within the Central American isthmus. These indicators provide a powerful indication of the incentives faced by illicit actors who are trying to decide which states provide a more propitious political geography for setting up shop and acting with impunity.[22]

[22] "El Salvador secuestrado," *La Prensa Gráfica* (El Salvador), reports that kidnapping clearance rates are also very low in El Salvador. In the first semester of 1999, the Salvadoran national police received 89 reports of kidnapping (not including all the kidnappings that went unreported). The police made 61 arrests, 12 of these cases went to trial, and 7 people were convicted. "La relación entre las denuncias y las condenadas es de 12 a 1. Es decir, en el 89 por ciento de los casos investigados por la Policía no hay suficientes pruebas para procesar a los sospechosos, o las víctimas prefieren callar para evitar represalias" (August 23, 1999, accessed on *La Prensa Gráfica* website).

A discussion of institutional behavior (e.g., homicide clearance rates) is more telling than a focus on societal perceptions of efficaciousness, in general. Figure 4.4, for example, asks people how efficient they believe the police are in fighting crime. Notably, this question does not tell us (a) efficient for what kinds of crime and for whom, (b) efficient in what sense (upholding the rule of law, engaging in extrajudicial actions, or something else), and (c) whether perceptions coincide with performance. As a result, we see some inexplicable national juxtapositions, with Nicaragua having among the highest homicide clearance rates and yet among the lowest perceptions of efficiency in fighting crime (Figure 4.4). Similarly, El Salvador has among the lowest homicide clearance rates and yet has among the highest perceptions of efficiency in fighting crime. The survey question was only fielded in 2000 thus it was not possible to compare the responses over time. However, a 2011 question on satisfaction with police work reveals an altogether different ranking. Given these disparities, I prioritize the (reported) *institutional performance* of how the police address homicides (over societal perceptions thereof); from this I infer some key (dis)incentives to commit homicide. Identifying where the police are least likely to hold killers to account provides a strong indication of where illicit actors might conclude that they are most likely to operate with relative impunity, should they choose to set up shop and should they choose to use violence to defend their turf.

Complementing the two previously mentioned dimensions of state capacity (poor role specification, poor homicide clearance rates) with imputed patterns of police complicity provides additional leverage to analyze the deterrent effect of national police forces. It is commonplace to observe that the Latin American police are complicit in many kinds of crimes, including in countries where homicide rates are relatively low but police complicity has been reported (see Auyero 2006 and 2007 for an example about Argentina). See Figure 4.5.

All cases of high violence tend to also exhibit high societal perceptions of police complicity, although many cases with lower homicide rates also fall on this high end of perceived police complicity (suggesting that it is not a sufficient variable, although weak state capacity might be necessary as part of the explanation). Looking at the other end of the spectrum (and excluding the civil war case of Colombia), one notes that no high homicide rate cases coincide with low perceptions of police complicity. Indeed, when we zero in on imputed complicity, Nicaragua's placement on the right side of this chart is striking – distinguishing it from other post-civil war cases in Central America and marking it as an "island of excellence"

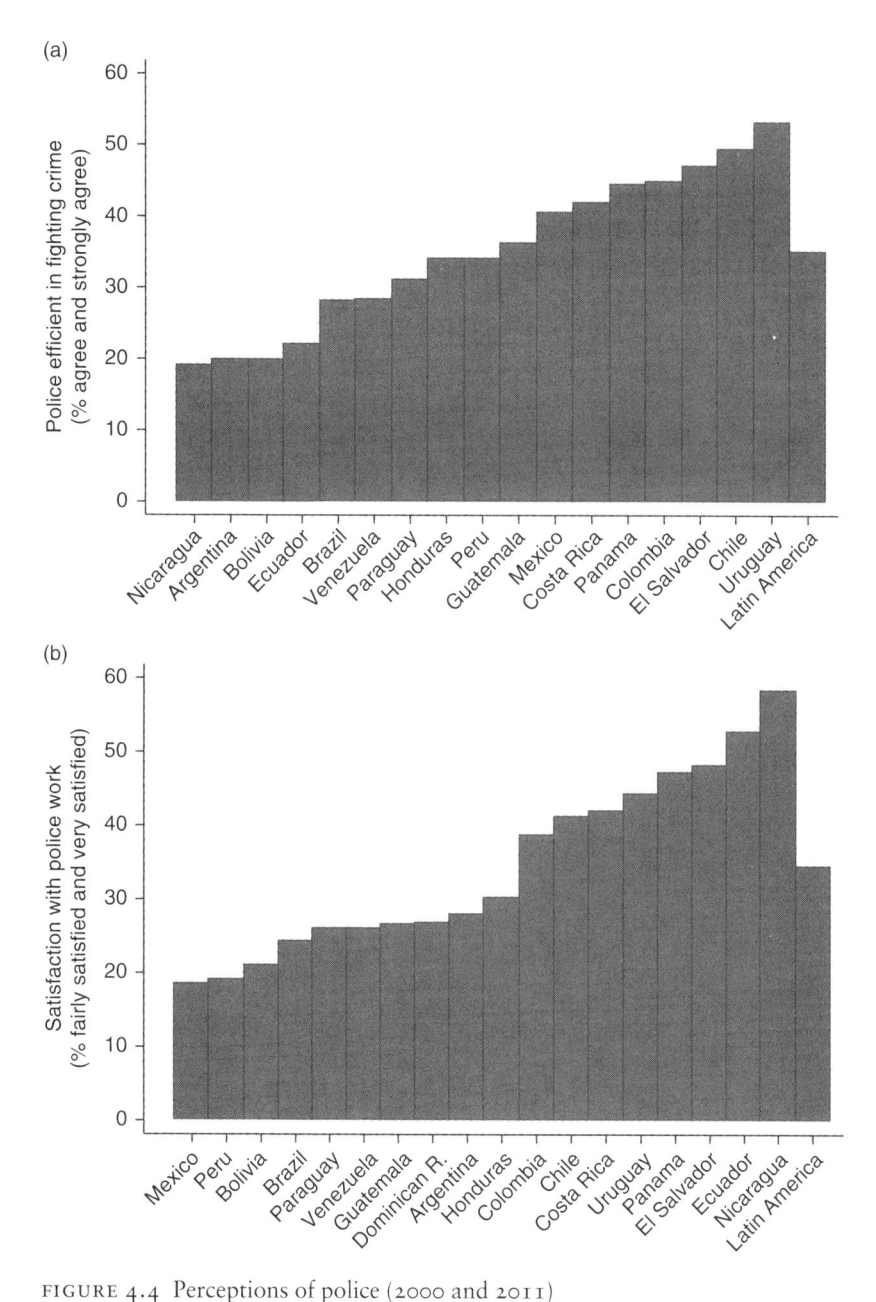

FIGURE 4.4 Perceptions of police (2000 and 2011)
Figure 4.4a: Police efficient in fighting crime (2000)
Figure 4.4b: Satisfied with police work (2011)
Source: Latinobarometer (2000) and (2011).

(notes/survey questions continue on next page)

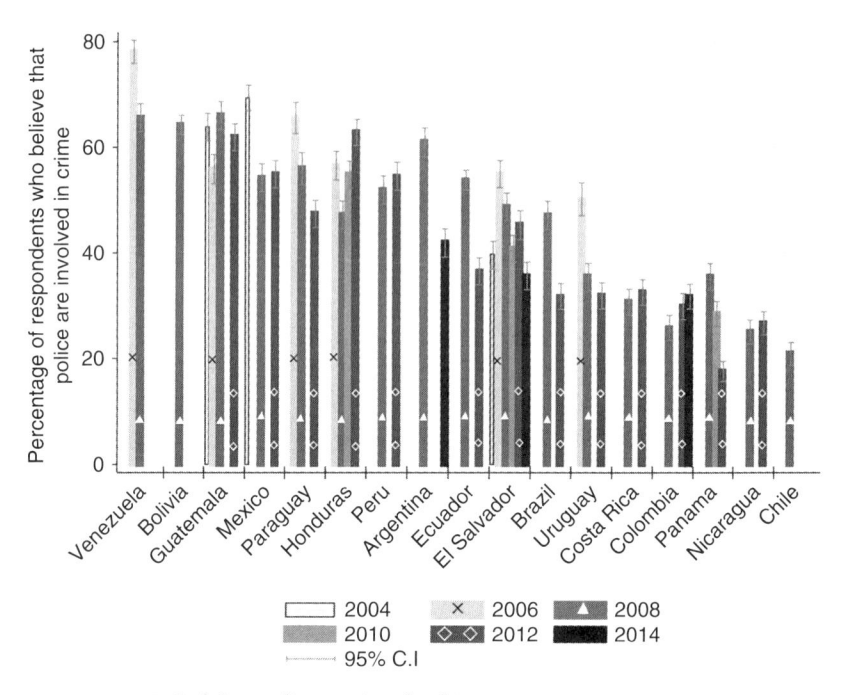

FIGURE 4.5 Belief that police are involved in crime (2004–2014)
Research by Yanilda González and Daniela Barba-Sánchez. Graph prepared by Daniela Barba-Sánchez using Stata.
Source: LAPOP Data 2004–2014 Core Data. Specific country data for years 2010 and 2014.
Notes: Question AOJ18 in LAPOP (AmericasBarometer) 2004–2012 Codebook (Merged Datasets): "Some people say that the police in this community (town, village) protect people from criminals, while others say that the police are involved in the criminal activity. What do you think? (1) Police protect people from crime or (2) Police are involved in crime (3) [Don't Read] Doesn't protect, but is not involved in crime or protects and is involved in crime (8) DK/DR."
The data for 2014 comes from the specific country questionnaires for Argentina and El Salvador, and from the 2013 questionnaire for Colombia, given that the survey question was not included in the core questionnaire in 2014. The wording of the question was consistent across questionnaires.

FIGURE 4.4 (cont.)

Notes: The survey question for Figure 4.4a is "Following with the crime problem, do you think that the police is sufficiently efficient in the fight against crime (in your country)? Do you strongly agree, agree, disagree, or strongly disagree with this view?" The survey question for Figure 4.4b is "Would you say that you are very satisfied (1), fairly satisfied (2), not very satisfied (3) or not at all satisfied (4), with the way the police works?"

in a state otherwise known for high corruption. As we will discuss in Part III, by the mid-1990s, the Nicaraguan police and military had developed a reputation in Central America for being the first or second leading professional (nonpartisan) police organization in the region[23] – even if there are of course street-level bribes. UNODC (2007: 30) reaches a similar conclusion.

> Statistics indicate that Nicaragua is arguably the second safest country in Central America and it also has the least law enforcement capacity, at least in terms of raw numbers. But Nicaragua's police and prisons system are regarded by some experts as the best in the region, suggesting there is more to government capacity than simply gross expenditure. (UNODC 2007: 30)

These cases are discussed at greater length in future chapters. The point to emphasize here is that varying police capacity (role specification, homicide clearance rates, accountability) plays a differential deterrent role for illicit organizations seeking territories in which to set up shop. This is important not just for the Becker hypothesis about individual-level crime but also for the organizational decisions made by illicit organizations such as DTOs and youth gangs.

In short, while data on state capacity and state corruption is universally poor, both the quantitative and qualitative records indicate that state security forces are at the crux of the matter – both as ineffective and complicit institutions. In both circumstances, I infer that these deficiencies in state capacity affect the decision-making process of organizations that are trying to decide the geography of their trade: for drug organizations, they are trying to decide where to move the goods (all the more so after the crackdown on the Caribbean coast); for urban gangs, they are trying to figure out not only which territories they can dominate (at first blush a function of urban residence) but also which routes are lucrative (e.g., bus routes) and where they can buy off or avoid police monitoring.

Finally, state capacity can also be defined by territorial reach. As Michael Mann (1984) theorized and many others have noted, the actual infrastructural power of the state varies considerably within states' respective territories, a point highlighted in O'Donnell's 1993 discussion of brown areas in Latin America and further conceptualized and studied

---

[23] March 2007 interviews in Nicaragua with General Cuadra (former head of the military), General Halleslevens (former head of the military, 2005–2010), Comisionado Cordero (former head of the national police) Comisionada Aminta Granera (head of the national police), and Antonio Lacayo (former chief of staff to former president Violeta Chamorro). Nicaragua's police are discussed in Chapter 7.

by a new wave of important scholarship (Soifer and Vom Hau 2008, Soifer 2015, and Giraudy and Luna 2017, among others). Certainly, illicit actors will turn to countries with weak overall states. However, within those countries, they are most likely to privilege spaces where the police are minimally present – either physically absent (as in some border areas), functionally inactive (i.e., not pursuing their roles), and/or complicit. In these cases, illicit actors can evade the state due to its uneven territorial reach. While it is relatively easy to note where the police are not present, identifying its poor performance and/or complicity is, as stated at the outset, much more difficult.

Combined, these indicators of state capacity (role specification, homicide clearance rates, perceptions of complicity/accountability, and uneven territorial reach) suggest that it makes sense for illicit organizations to move into the Central American isthmus and, in particular, into Guatemala, El Salvador, and Honduras. Not only is there precedence for buying off state officials where necessary, but even where one is unable to do so in advance, it is highly unlikely that one will be held accountable for illicit activity, including murder.

Hence, what deters legal business investments can incentivize the growth of illicit ones. This is particularly so for drug organizations that have the transnational field of vision to decide where they are going to move the goods. While gangs are not as transnational in scope and operation, it is clear that they have flourished and grown precisely where the state is incapable of controlling them *and* where local police officers are themselves complicit. Weak state capacity (understood as an inability to monitor or hold to account either complicit state officials or illicit actors or both) provides an attractive field of investment for organized crime seeking to prosper via trade and the transit of illicit goods and for gangs engaged in extortion and other forms of criminal delinquency.[24] State capacity, accordingly, creates a push/pull factor (or incentives and constraints) for illicit actors, who must decide where to establish their territorial bases. Therefore, weak capacity contributes to a homicidal ecology; on its own, it does not determine the outcome, but in tandem with other factors, it can increase the risk that violence will occur.

---

[24] As future case studies reveal, sometimes these entrepreneurs assume a parastatal role (de facto and/or de jure), sometimes they are aided by the state, sometimes they become competitors with the state, and sometimes they simply coexist with the state.

ORGANIZATIONAL TERRITORIAL COMPETITION: THE MICRO-MECHANISMS OF VIOLENCE

Competition and Uncertainty

Thus far I have highlighted macro-level structures and processes that shape the incentives and constraints for illicit organizations: why they would enter into the illicit drug trade (Chapter 3) and why they would set up shop in some states rather than others (Chapter 4). My argument,[25] however, has thus far been silent on when and why these illicit organizations would use violence. This last question also requires an explanation, especially since the presence of illicit organizations alone does not explain violence. While illicit organizations might be more likely than licit ones to engage in violence, violence is rarely a first response. Indeed, homicidal violence is costly; it not only can lead to more deaths, but in the short term it can also harm profits. Thus, the preferred strategy for illicit organizations should be to establish hegemonic control over a given territory – whether hegemony is defined in terms of monopoly over territory, markets, government, information, or social interaction. Many scholars have highlighted that where armed groups establish territorial monopoly, violence is low – be it organized crime, bandits, the mafia, drug trafficking organizations, or even civil war combatants (Gambetta 1996, Tilly 2003, Kalyvas 2006, and Snyder and Durán-Martínez 2009, among others). Where armed groups are able to establish governing structures absent competition from either other illicit organizations or the state, they try to impose order, not chaos. Violence is always threatened; the order is coercive. But it can exist without recourse to high levels of homicide. And where illicit groups can govern absent the recourse to high levels of killing, they are likely to do so. Territorial hegemony, therefore, is a clear goal that clears the way for high profits, among other benefits.

Yet drug organizations and gangs cannot always establish or maintain hegemony. Given the lure of high profits, there is often an incentive for other organizations to try to hone in and capture profits, to try to discipline internal divisions, and to assert hegemony when under threat.

---

[25] While UNODC (2011: chapter 3) makes an argument similar to the one developed here, these arguments were developed independently.

Indeed, the illicit world – and the drug trafficking world in particular – is generally one of high competition and uncertainty. Where security and profit stakes are high, competition is present, and uncertainty is generalized, illicit groups are increasingly likely to resort to violence – perhaps at no time more likely than when organizational territorial competition intensifies. Violence is wielded more often in the context of organizational competition and uncertainty to establish precedent and power – including to stake out turf (taxes, sales, etc.), scare/increase membership, undercut competitors, and enforce the illicit rules of the game. In short, organizational competition to control territorial space significantly motivates illicit actors to turn to homicidal violence. In these circumstances, violence demonstrates a kind of "credible antagonism" (i.e., that one is willing and able to wield violence now and in the future) to defend (or acquire) territorial spaces where illicit actors can maneuver and grow their businesses. While violence occurs for many reasons, this book contends that organizational competition to control certain territories is, in particular, driving the extraordinarily high homicide rates that have emerged in the region.

This argument about organizational territorial competition was initially and primarily informed by the literature on the mafia, gangs, and protection rackets (Tilly 1985, 1990, 2003; Gambetta 1996; Levitt and Venkatesh 2000a and 2000b; Volkov 2002). Throughout the course of the research for this book, the initial argument found echo in the burgeoning literature on the drug war, especially in Mexico (Snyder and Durán-Martínez 2009; Calderón et al. 2015; Durán-Martínez 2015; Lessing 2015; Osorio 2015). Yet it extends beyond these cases to the rest of the region (and arguably beyond that). In all these situations, "competition" refers to efforts by more than one organization to control territory (including the parastatal authority to determine the passage of people and goods, to extract taxes, and even to command silence). In this book, the term does not refer to electoral competition: while electoral competition has proven important in the Mexican case[26] as well as in discussions of ethnic violence in India,[27] electoral competition does not

---

[26] Dell (2015) argues that electoral competition affects post-2007 drug trade violence in Mexico (especially where the PAN wins after close elections). Trejo and Ley (2016) analyze electoral incentives and partisan strategies for policing criminal violence and find that criminal violence was more intense in municipalities in states ruled by opposition parties (leaving areas governed by the opposition/Left less protected than areas governed by copartisans).

[27] See Wilkinson (2004) and Chandra (2004).

appear to provide general explanatory weight for homicide rates across the Americas, where violence rates do not (yet) appear systematically tied to electoral politics. Rather, in this book, competition refers to organizational efforts to assert territorial control, including efforts by illicit organizations and/or the state to (re)assert and defend primary control over a given turf.

This argument about organizational territorial competition also finds some striking, but limited, parallels with the civil wars literature. Notably, illicit organizations encompass both DTOs and insurgents. Both types of organization assume a territorial dimension, are armed, and fight to control specific geographies. The competitive imperative to fight can lead to higher violence. This competitive territorial dynamic is shared, especially where information is limited and credible commitments are uncertain.[28] However, the neat parallels with the civil war literature stop there – even if some microdynamics are shared (see Lessing 2015 and Kalyvas 2015). DTOs and gangs do not generally have political motives to assume state control (with Pablo Escobar as a partial exception, given his personal political motives), although they might collude with the state in important cases. And Latin American insurgencies have not generally and primarily pursued economic profit motives (again, with Colombia and Peru at the end of their wars as partial exceptions) – unlike examples in the now-famous literature on greed and civil wars.[29] Thus, the primary motives for asserting territorial control and the underlying ways they might do so vary significantly between insurgents and organized crime. Also, much of the civil war literature has focused on explaining violence against noncombatants; yet in the contemporary context, there is no reason to assume that high homicide rates in Latin America are the result of civil war collateral damage, especially since Latin American civil wars ended prior to the dramatic rise of violence in the region. One might reasonably wonder if the civil war argument about (in)discriminate violence against noncombatants travels, nonetheless. At its most general level, one can answer affirmatively since territoriality, competition, and uncertainty are critical to both the civil war literature and the

---

[28] See Fearon on information and credible commitments; Fearon and Laitin (1996) on information, uncertainty, and conflict; and Tilly (2003) and Kalyvas (2006 and 2015) on competition.
[29] See Collier and Hoeffler (2004) and Weinstein (2007) for examples.

argument outlined in this book; in turn, organizational actors are making strategic decisions that are not only about defending/securing territory but also about how other actors will respond (maintaining organizational unity, limiting retaliation, and minimizing local opposition). However, the specific mechanisms leading to violence in times of civil war are different, particularly when referring to indiscriminate violence, as elaborated in the associated footnote.[30] Weinstein's important principal-agent argument about varied organizational qualities (tied to different resource endowments) does not readily help identify which illicit organizations are most/least likely to kill in a context of DTOs and gangs vying to control a given territory. And Kalyvas's brilliant (2006) argument about the relative balance of military control across five zones does not necessarily explain where and why homicidal violence will spike in times of "peace." Indeed Kalyvas (2015) reminds us of these differences while encouraging scholars to think less about precise parallels across the civil wars and drug war literatures and more about the micro-mechanisms that might be shared.

[30] Kalyvas (2015) argues that indiscriminate violence is very costly and can be counterproductive (because of the increased likelihood of retaliation and loss of local support). In what might be called an Arendtian logic, it can destroy power but cannot create it. It might occur in cases where there is an imbalance of power (e.g., insurgents might be weak and cannot offer protection), information is low, rivals control a given territory, and an armed group therefore might target a given area indiscriminately in an effort to generate a changed equilibrium. But by doing so, these actors might lose whatever support they had and invite retaliation; thus, it is a very costly strategy. This situation might parallel what the state has done in some cases, as in Mexico, and might set off a high-violence spiral; however, this is not a common strategy, for the reasons noted by Kalyvas (2015). More common than indiscriminate violence are cases of discriminate violence against noncombatants. Discriminate violence occurs against specific targets and, according to Kalyvas, is jointly produced (with local collaboration to share information with armed groups). It is most likely in cases where the armed group has predominant but not total control of a given area and where citizens expect protection in exchange for information. Violence is meted out against those identified as traitors and snitches, and, strikingly, patterns of violence against noncombatants thus vary by the territorial balance of power. Where one group is hegemonic, discriminate violence by hegemonic groups will be low (no one to denounce, no one to target) and indiscriminate violence by opposing group is possible but costly. Where the balance of power favors one side but the area remains contested, discriminate violence will be highest. Where the territory is the site of highest contestation and competition, violence against noncombatants will be low although violence against combatants will presumably be the highest. In all these scenarios, armed groups will seek to advance the war effort based on information, logic, and control but depend on citizens for access to information; the latter will collaborate and denounce co-citizens, often based on emotional concerns (rather than on a master ethnic or ideological cleavage) in cases where the armed group can offer some level of protection.

In this spirit, rather than directly borrow from the civil war literature's explanations about violence against noncombatants, the mechanism developed here is pitched at an arguably higher level of abstraction: highlighting organizational competition to control a given territory. Where different DTOs, gangs, and/or state actors vie to control a given territory, violence is likely to surge. This is most likely to occur, as argued earlier, in certain homicidal ecologies: in lucrative illicit drug trade and transit routes and/or areas where extraction has been high – both of which develop in places where the state has historically been weak and/or complicit. In this regard, my argument dovetails most clearly with the older and newer literatures on organized crime, state formation, and gangs.

Thus, violence should appear most intense in those cases and years where there is *competition* – competition between illicit groups and/or with the state – to establish geographic hegemony over transit, trade, and distribution routes and/or urban enclaves.[31] This heightened competition occurs in three parallel ways: among drug trafficking organizations (or narcotraffickers) seeking to establish control over trade and transit routes, among gang members seeking to defend or acquire control of urban territory, and ultimately if and when states intervene to seek to reassert control. I briefly discuss them in turn.

Drug Trafficking Organizations (DTOs)

Drug trafficking organizations illustrate this pattern of organizational territorial competition and high violence. DTOs are not new actors, although they have become increasingly visible and often powerful, especially with the rising prevalence of cocaine sales. They oversee the movement of drugs from production to consumption and thus, as noted earlier, their "business" exists across countries and in particular territorial locations. Since the business is illicit, however, they cannot rely on legal contracts or formally depend on the state to establish, regulate, and defend their transactions. The illicit nature

---

[31] UNODC (2011: 49) includes a graph indicating that gang/organized crime–related homicides are higher in Latin America (around 26 percent) than in Asia (around 7 percent) and Europe (around 4 percent). However, the confidence intervals are large, with Latin America's range moving from about 10–37 percent, Asia from about 4–21 percent, and Europe from about 2–11 percent. Thus, Latin America's lowest range overlaps with Europe's highest. I have not included this in the main text, although it is a suggestive figure.

of the business means, therefore, that authority and transactions are underwritten with the threat of force. The most lucrative situation is for DTOs to assert their hegemony over critical territorial areas without actually deploying homicidal violence. However, in a context of uncertainty and heightened competition, we know that they resort to high levels of violence to define territories and settle scores.

[S]ince the [drug] market operates illegally, organized groups have a comparative advantage in setting up distribution networks and the associated enforcement of distribution contracts. These groups substitute for both the state and other market institutions that would otherwise provide these services. However, the organized-crime enforcement of contracts entails violence, and violence is also used to raise entry barriers for potential competitors. (Keefer et al. 2008: 6)

This economic incentive has been heightened with the rising prevalence of cocaine as a trading commodity. And given the enormous profits (even relative to other drugs) to be had and the high level of risk, DTOs had incentives not only to control particular areas and carve out new markets but also to "eliminate smaller competitors" (Smith 1999: 200).[32] With the rising interorganizational competition over trade and transit territories (in part a consequence of high profits), followed in turn by increasing confrontations with law enforcement, we have seen a rise in violence among these actors.

A ... consequence of drug trafficking, especially the movement of cocaine, has been the escalation of violence. Much of this reflects tension and rivalry between opposing gangs: throughout the early 1990s, for instance, the Tijuana and Sinaloa groups were locked in a bitter struggle for control of the Pacific corridor. The increase in violence might also result from expansion in the economic stakes involved, as the dollar volume of Mexico's drug trade swelled rapidly in the late 1980s and early 1990s. It may in addition demonstrate the influence of Colombians, especially former associates of the rough-and-tumble Medellín cartel, which unleashed a civil war in their own country for several excruciating years. Further, the rise in violence may represent a response by traffickers to heightened law enforcement, which has multiplied the number of clashes and raids. (Smith 1999: 205)

---

[32] Cocaine markets incur a high level of risk, even relative to other illicit drug markets. Smith (1999: 200) observes that this has implications for small-scale operators, who are at a disadvantage in high-profit/high-risk illicit markets such as those of cocaine: "Where levels of risk are lower and rates of return are more modest, as in the case of methamphetamine and marijuana, there is more room for the small-scale operators who cluster at the industry's bottom rung."

Thus, where rates of return are very high, illicit organizations are more likely to try to carve out core territories that they will acquire and defend with violent means. For organized crime, this calculus is particularly salient in port towns, frontiers, and unmonitored territories (where airplanes can refuel). For gangs, we would expect it to be particularly important in cities (in shantytowns, near ports, and on main roads).

The available evidence corroborates this intuition. Where competition is limited, the violence has also been more moderate. However, where there is heightened competition for control, reports suggest that violence has also risen. The experience of Colombian drug organizations vying for power and control along their various trade routes is an infamous example. The competition between the Medellín and Cali cartels resulted in many deaths as these DTOs set out to control the lucrative cocaine markets. This is becoming increasingly commonplace in the west and northern regions of Mexico, where various DTOs compete for monopoly over trade routes and sales. And it is precisely in this region where we see the highest homicide rates in Mexico – first among drug organizations and increasingly in 2007 and 2008 against police officers sent in by the Calderón administration (Maurer 2012; Calderón et al. 2015; Durán-Martínez 2015; Lessing 2015; Osorio 2015). There are striking parallels in the region's highest homicide rate cases discussed later in this book. These violent examples have fed images of violence-hungry DTOs. And certainly the DTOs have unleashed astonishing levels of violence, often coupled with disturbing methods of harming and disposing of their victims. Tragic examples abound, and there are certainly cases where they have spiraled, seemingly out of control. However, logic suggests that the core, long-term economic incentives for DTOs is not to wield violence for violence sake but to use violence strategically to undercut competitors and establish territorial hegemony. Over time, hegemony should lead DTOs to kill less; and if the state formation literature is right, it might lead them to provide services and resources to secure the neutrality, support, and/or allegiance of those residing in their territorial domain (Tilly 1985; Olson 2000).

Thus, violence should rise not where DTOs are hegemonic but where there is organizational territorial competition between DTOs over domestic routes or between DTOs and a state seeking to undercut them (see Lessing 2015). The violence is wielded to wipe out competitors but also might serve as an example of credible antagonism to establish a monopoly on power, resources, and allegiances.

In the following chapters, we will chart out this dynamic in the context of Central America.

Gangs

We see a parallel "organizational territorial competition → violence" mechanism among youth gangs in Latin America (as well as in the United States).[33] Gangs have a long history in the Americas. They have historically been described as groups of boys looking for community in a context of displacement and bleak futures. These youth organizations are historically portrayed as deeply tied to particular territories or turfs that define their origins and identity.

The sharply violent turn among gangs in Latin America is relatively recent, occurring at the end of the twentieth century and the start of the twenty-first – precisely as they became more "professionalized" and more embedded in illicit activities (including extraction and drug sales). Reports show that the violence has increased particularly *between* gangs to establish precedent and power. Where gang authority is unchallenged, violence is considerably lower than in places where it is contested. Unsurprisingly, therefore, gang-on-gang violence increased significantly in El Salvador and Guatemala (the two high-violence cases analyzed later in this book) as well as Honduras. In El Salvador, for example, IUDOP-based surveys show that gang-on-gang violence was more significant than gang violence against the population as a whole – consistent with the argument about competition and uncertainty (see Santacruz Giralt, Concha-Eastman, and Cruz 2001). They reported that in 2001, the targets of gang violence in El Salvador included a rival gang (63.2 percent of total violence), people on the street (19.4 percent of total violence), community members (9 percent of total violence), the police (3.6 percent of total violence), "not involved in violence" (2.8 percent of total violence), and other responses (1.9 percent of total violence).[34] The Washington Office on Latin America (WOLA, 2006) estimates that gang violence in El Salvador has been responsible for about 30 percent of homicides.

---

[33] Gangs are classically not defined as organized crime. For the purposes of this book, I respect this colloquial distinction between organized crime and gangs. However, analytically speaking, I see gangs as one form of organized crime – all the more so as gangs increase their involvement in extortion, drug sales, etc.

[34] Santacruz Giralt, Concha-Eastman, and Cruz (2001).

Gay (2010: 206, 208) portrays a territorial competition dynamic in discussing violence patterns in Rio de Janeiro, Brazil (where the gangs are sometimes likened to DTOs in other cases): "It is this competition for market share and for the millions of dollars in drug-related spoils that, more than anything, have transformed not just a select few neighborhoods but an entire city into a war zone" (Gay 2010: 206). Moreover, "the emergence of *rival* drug gangs and drug-gang *factions* in Rio constitutes by far the most significant factor in the recent increase in violence, not only because drug-gang factions exist in an almost constant state of war but also because of the violent nature of the response that their presence and operations have elicited from the police" (Gay 2010: 208; emphasis added by author).

It is not that gangs are new (they are not) but that they have transformed into organizations that compete not only for control over turf but also over micro-level illicit economies, including extortion and drug sales. While much has been made of the transnationalization of gangs in Central America, what appears most striking for an explanation of violence is the local-level organizational competition to control turf, a point emphasized by Demoscopía (2007; as discussed in Chapter 3) and also highlighted by Dowdney's (2005: 45) comparative ethnographic volume on armed youth groups in Brazil, Colombia, El Salvador, Ecuador, Honduras, Jamaica, Philippines, South Africa, Nigeria, Northern Ireland, and the United States.

Participation in informal and illicit economies is a defining factor of all armed groups investigated by this study. The notion of *territory* as a base for economic gain was also shared by all groups investigated. Thus, in addition to the symbolic importance of *territory* as self-definition, and the practical and social importance of *territory* for protection and population control, *territories* are also economically important as defensible spaces where money can be made ... involvement in illicit economic activities such as drug dealing has led to a number of armed groups becoming increasingly *territorial* and *more violent in the defence or expansion of their territory*. (Dowdney, 2005: 45; emphasis added)

Dowdney's report (2005: 46) finds in his multi-country comparison that armed youth have been involved in a wide range of illicit activities (including, and primarily, armed robberies, other robberies, car theft, and kidnapping, and only secondarily in drug dealing); the use of violence, however, varies. He finds that armed violence is used largely to settle *territorial* disputes with rival groups – largely for economic gain ("related to controlling locally based illicit markets or resources") or symbolic import ("related to self-definition, e.g. ethnic" or rival groups infringing on their territory). "The most common economic reason for territorial disputes is competition between groups for the control of drug dealing ... The domination of defendable spaces for the control of drug sales is common to groups in nine of the ten countries covered by the study" (2005: 49). The last observation coincides with this book's emphasis on the mechanism of organizational competition over territory.

Where gangs are hegemonic, homicides are lower than where competition occurs. When I started this research, it was commonplace to say that it is better to have a gang in your neighborhood than not – a refrain heard many times when doing the initial fieldwork for this book (especially in Guatemala). While unsettling, the logic is that where gangs are in control, they provide a parastatal form of security; while extortion is the price, relative security on the streets is the promised outcome. However, where turf is up for grabs, gangs can and do engage in violence (particularly against other gangs) to establish control and hegemony. Of course, others are caught in the crossfire. This micro-level violence is visible particularly in poor neighborhoods in high-crime cities.

But gangs can also be mobile, moving to control not only neighborhood turf (a historic characteristic of gangs) but also more dispersed but potentially lucrative geographies (selling drugs, taxing bus routes, etc.). Violence has followed in turn where competition emerges to control these more mobile (and potentially lucrative) territorial spaces, as discussed in Chapters 5 and 6.

Hence, homicide rates have increased where illicit organized groups (including organized crime and gangs) compete for territorial control with other illicit organized groups and/or the state (in some cases competing for survival, in others to assert control).[35] Illicit groups also flaunt their presence in some cases by wielding violence to stake out territorial claims, to punish defectors, and to beat out competitors. Indeed, Part III of the book emphasizes that this violence is particularly intense along the trade and transit routes (much more so than it is in the sites of production and

---

[35] In this context, surveys also show an increase in uncertainty and fear about crime (Caldeira 2000; Chevigny 2003a).

consumption).[36] These patterns of violence are particularly in evidence in western Mexico, northern Central America (northern triangle), and Brazil; they have become increasingly visible in Venezuela. Where these markets are not legally regulated, economic obligations are underwritten with the threat of force. In this context, where actors confront uncertainty and heightened competition, they are increasingly likely to use violence to define territories and settle scores. This is as true of transnational organized crime in the drug economy as it is of local gangs – even though the scope and method deployed are often different across these organizations.

Bringing the "State and Society Back In?"

The first wave of violence is hypothesized to be a result of this interorganizational competition (both between drug organizations and between gangs) over territory. However, violence is not static. In the context of heightened competition, violence can beget more violence, creating a generalized security gap. Over time, that violence is not limited to organized crime alone but can draw in other elements of the state and society that start to respond with violence as well. As gang and organized crime–related violence increases, police might be drawn into the conflict – in some cases because officers are actually on the take, using violence in the same ways that gang and drug organization members would to establish authority, power, and profit. In these cases, the same state officers that are expected to prevent and control illicit activities are in fact complicit in that same criminal activity and violence. In other cases, police officers (both those on and off duty) are reported to engage in extrajudicial violence to penalize those seen as the sources of the violence and "disorder" – for example, in Brazil against street children, in Guatemala in what is referred to as "social cleansing."

---

[36] While drug production has been important in the Andes (Colombia, Bolivia, and Peru) and also increasingly so in Mexico, the patterns of high violence are not equally visible across these cases. National homicide rates have been very high in Colombia (where a civil war made it hard to disaggregate what percentage of the violence was a function of war versus the illicit economy), moderately so in Mexico (although much higher along the western route than these national figures would suggest and showing a marked spike in 2007), and relatively low in Bolivia and Peru. These data suggest that production is *not* the primary issue; trade and transit are.

Alongside complicit and extrajudicial actions, the state has in some cases also adopted formal policies (some of which include extrajudicial actions) to undercut DTOs and (re)assert territorial control. These actions have also generated higher violence (at least in the short term). The war on drugs is one such example. This is a form of organizational territorial competition between the state and the illicit to assert control over specific geographies and establish hegemonic control. It can lead to state attacks on particular geographies and DTO responses in turn – both against the state and against rival DTOs. In Lessing's (2015 and 2017) work on Brazil, Colombia, and Mexico, he analyzes the strategic interaction between the state and DTOs, with a focus on when state policies induce more/less violence by DTOs. Lessing argues that when states pursue an unconditional crackdown (i.e., regardless of DTO actions, they are equally likely to be the target of state repression), this can generate a spiral of violence, as DTOs have no incentives to moderate competitive violence. By contrast, where the state targets its actions, DTOs might moderate violence so as to minimize the likelihood of being the object of a state-led attack. Other scholars have noted that Mexico's kingpin strategy of cracking down on the leadership of all Mexican DTOs initiated a spiral of violence in particular geographies that explains the dramatic rise in homicides starting in 2007 (see Calderón et al. 2015). And recent reporting has noted that these drug wars have generated not only higher homicide rates but, unfortunately, corresponding human rights abuses – as noted by Human Rights Watch (2007 and 2017) reports for Brazil and Mexico. In short, organizational territorial competition can occur between illicit organizations, but it can also include competition with the state (as it pursues licit and illicit avenues to regain territorial control).

I end this section by noting an additional normative concern. In this world of increasing competition, uncertainty, and violence, we also increasingly hear examples of communities engaging in extrajudicial violence. The violence, in this sense, has spilled over into other realms. This *escalation* of violence, therefore, ultimately parallels arguments by Fearon and Laitin (1996) in their work on ethnic conflict as well as arguments in a broader literature on cascades. For where there is uncertainty about who is on their side and what they can do, people might turn to violence – sometimes aggressively, sometimes preemptively. Uncertainty can lead to preemptive and redemptive acts of violence, even among those who were not initially participating in the competition for turf, authority, and money.[37] The uncertainty is literally killing people. The real-world implications of these violence cascades are daunting.

CONCLUSION

Before concluding Part II and turning to the empirical chapters in Part III, this conclusion pulls together and restates the tripartite argument developed in Chapters 3 and 4. I have identified three core factors that help explain the geography, location, and motivation behind Latin America's extraordinarily high and yet uneven patterns of homicidal violence: (1) the changing geography of transnational illicit trade and transit; (2) varied patterns of state capacity; and (3) varied patterns of organizational territorial competition. Combined, they have shaped the region. I reinsert the figure originally introduced in Chapter 1 to summarize the analytic ground covered and to lay the foundation for what follows (Figure 4.6).

Stepping back from this argument, a few broader points should be emphasized. Although the violence in Latin America's new democracies has a very real national and urban character, I have argued that the deep macro-causes are tied to a broader transnationalized economy of illicit trade. Transnational illicit economies, however, do not take root in (or pass through) all countries in the same way. They do so where public security forces are particularly weak and corrupt (a reinforcing dynamic) and where they can draw on a reserve of domestic actors to move goods through. This is the story of organized crime in the contemporary world. However, the penetration of a transnational illicit economy (particularly the drug economy) has found a parallel in gangs, which have transformed into increasingly violent organizations in search of greater authority and more money (sometimes tied to the sale of drugs but commonly also tied to extortion and other kinds of crime). This changed national landscape has created a great deal of organizational competition and uncertainty that, I argue, has fed the rise in homicidal violence (by drug organizations, gangs, and the police) and filtered down into the actions of petty criminals and ultimately, although in smaller measure, of extrajudicial community actions.

---

[37] This is not just theoretical. Examples of such behavior were shared with me during anonymous interviews in Guatemala City (summer 2007).

Argument

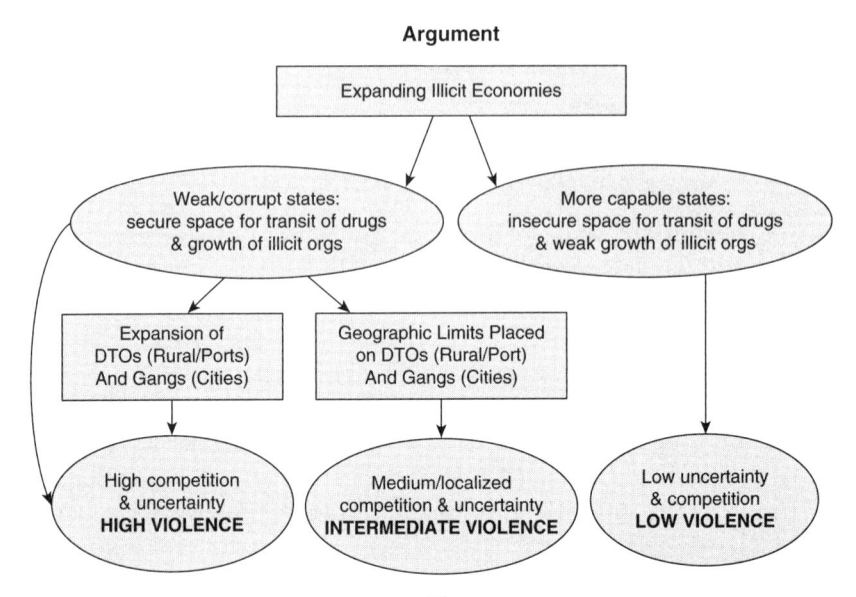

```
                    ┌─────────────────────────────┐
                    │  Expanding Illicit Economies │
                    └─────────────────────────────┘
                         ↙                    ↘
        ╭─────────────────────────╮    ╭─────────────────────────╮
        │   Weak/corrupt states:  │    │   More capable states:  │
        │ secure space for transit│    │insecure space for transit│
        │  of drugs & growth of   │    │  of drugs & weak growth │
        │      illicit orgs       │    │    of illicit orgs      │
        ╰─────────────────────────╯    ╰─────────────────────────╯
                ↓                   ↓                    ↓
      ┌──────────────────┐  ┌──────────────────┐
      │   Expansion of   │  │Geographic Limits │
      │ DTOs (Rural/Ports)│  │Placed on DTOs    │
      │ And Gangs (Cities)│  │(Rural/Port) And  │
      │                  │  │  Gangs (Cities)  │
      └──────────────────┘  └──────────────────┘
                ↓                   ↓                    ↓
        ╭──────────────╮   ╭─────────────────╮   ╭──────────────╮
        │High competition│  │ Medium/localized│   │Low uncertainty│
        │ & uncertainty  │  │ competition &   │   │ & competition │
        │ HIGH VIOLENCE  │  │   uncertainty   │   │ LOW VIOLENCE  │
        ╰──────────────╯   │INTERMEDIATE VIOL.│   ╰──────────────╯
                           ╰─────────────────╯
```

FIGURE 4.6 The argument

The tripartite argument about these homicidal ecologies was presented sequentially in Part II of this book. This was a heuristic choice designed to feature the temporal order in which things likely unfolded. Logically, transnational illicit economies developed most clearly where states were weak, and violence skyrocketed where illicit organizations competed (with other illicit organizations and the state) over particular territorial routes. This heuristic allows us to identify and temporize the motives, geography, and timing of high violence. Insofar as it allows for clarity of presentation, it is a powerful tool.

However, once we dig deeper into the case material, it becomes increasingly evident that there is an endogenous process in play, particularly as we analyze the empirical relationship between illicit economies and weak states. Illicit economies flourish in weak states because organizations choose to set up shop in these locations, but illicit economies can in turn also weaken/corrupt states once they are in place. Weak states can then spawn (further development of) illicit economies. Thus, the process is not simply linear but unfolds endogenously over time. Part III addresses this tripartite argument and probes these endogenous dynamics across high- and low-violence cases.

CHAPTER 4

Appendix

ALTERNATIVE STATE CAPACITY DATA FOR RULE OF LAW AND CORRUPTION

For this project, I gathered and analyzed several different indicators of state capacity, particularly focusing on corruption and rule-of-law indicators. In this appendix, I discuss these alternative measures as well as why they were not used in the main body of the text. Although these alternative measures of state capacity were interesting, the analytical payoff proved low for this project. This was so for several reasons.

First, these studies most clearly reveal what we already know. Whether looking at rule-of-law or corruption data, one finds a generally weak assessment of state institutions in Latin America. Strong state capacity has been largely elusive in the region for all but Chile, Uruguay, and Costa Rica. This is not news, although it does confirm (or perhaps simply report back) widely held perceptions about the region.

Second, World Bank indicators (introduced further on) provide us with shaky grounds for distinguishing among the countries that remain. While the indicators provide some hint as to how to rank the countries, the confidence intervals often overlap considerably among many of the countries – even when we modify the presentation of data to include 95 percent confidence levels.

Third, World Bank indicators, in particular, seem highly driven by political evaluations of a given political administration; hence, those countries with leftist presidents are the ones where evaluations are the lowest. While it is evident that some leftist/populist measures in Venezuela, Ecuador, Bolivia, and Nicaragua are negatively evaluated by business, it is not clear that this should necessarily affect the scores in question for the rule of law and corruption – although in each case it *seems* that they do, and in each case, there are charges of corruption. Indeed, when we juxtapose the World Bank figures with the Latinobarometer surveys and World Economic Forum data on trust for the police, the result suggests that we need additional information to adjudicate among these scores and to discern if and how these institutions are shaping illicit trade flows and decisions related to them.

Fourth, the quantitative studies are largely based on *perceptions* of the police rather than a more explicit analysis of institutional constraints (or opportunities) and institutional performance. While perceptions *do* matter for business calculations, so do actions – arguably more so. Thus, the main body of the text in Chapter 4 focuses on organizational characteristics and performance rather than on perceptions of these factors. That said, the rest of this appendix provides a quick sweep of this data for the reader's reference.

Rule of Law

Rule-of-law indicators can be found in studies by the World Bank and LAPOP and Latinobarometer surveys, which are each briefly discussed here (see Figure 4.7). Quantitative rule-of-law data are largely based on perceptions. World Bank data define rule of law as "capturing perceptions of the extent to which agents have confidence in and abide by the rules of society, and in particular the quality of contract enforcement, property rights, the police, and the courts, as well as the likelihood of crime and violence." In these data, we find the usual suspects topping the list. Chile assumes top rank, followed by Uruguay and Costa Rica (with a 90 percent confidence interval). One can therefore conclude with some confidence that relatively strong scores in these three countries make them less propitious for illicit activity. It is not that illicit activity does not occur in these countries; it is simply that these will not be the primary sites chosen by transnational illicit organizational actors or the sites where this activity is likely to flourish *relative* to other countries.

In contrast to these strong rule-of-law cases, one can infer that states with weak rule-of-law patterns provide a propitious context/opportunity structure for the growth of illicit organizations (which can therefore operate illicitly with relative impunity).[38] The World Bank indicators reveal challenges in Venezuela, Ecuador, Bolivia, Guatemala, Paraguay, Honduras, Nicaragua, and El Salvador. Theoretically, while weak rule of law is a negative for licit economies, it can have the obverse effect on illicit ones. Where there is a deficit in public security and the rule of law, as indicated in this second set of countries, illicit organizations and activity can develop *beyond the reach of the state* and/or in some cases *with state*

---

[38] See Gambetta's (1996) classic study of the Italian mafia, for an example. Also see Lee (1999: 22–25) for a discussion of the ways in which organized crime benefits from weak states: e.g., corruption, collusion, and tolerance.

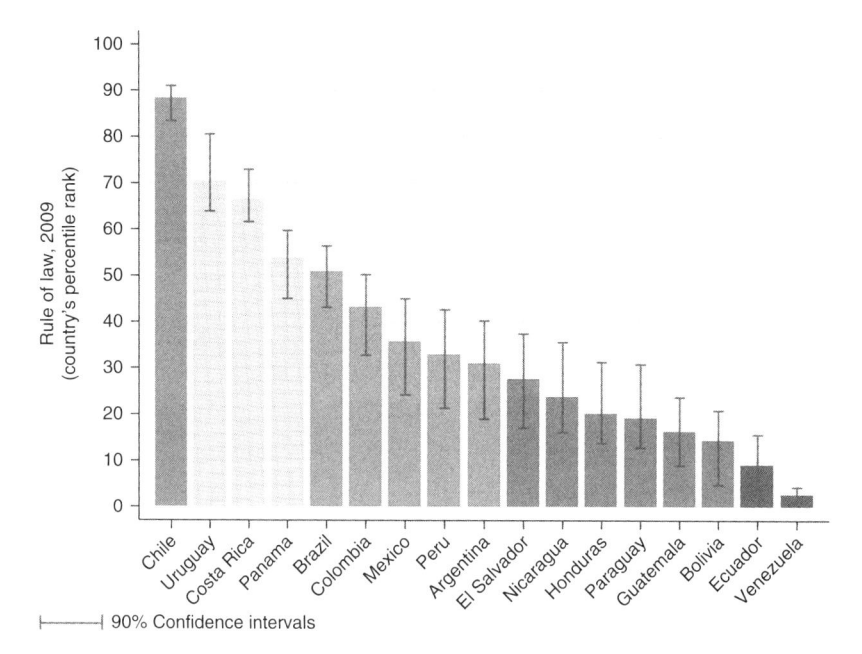

FIGURE 4.7 Rule of law in Latin America (2009)
Source: Downloaded February 8, 2018 from World Bank Governance Indicators website. Data is publicly available: http://info.worldbank.org/governance/wgi/index.aspx#home. The Worldwide Governance Indicators, 2017 Update, www.govindicators.org, September 22, 2017. Also see D. Kaufmann, A. Kraay, and M. Mastruzzi (2010). "The Worldwide Governance Indicators: Methodology and Analytical Issues."
Note: The Worldwide Governance Indicators (WGI) are a research dataset summarizing the views on the quality of governance provided by a large number of enterprise, citizen, and expert survey respondents in industrial and developing countries. These data are gathered from a number of survey institutes, think tanks, nongovernmental organizations, international organizations, and private sector firms. The WGI do not reflect the official views of the World Bank, its executive directors, or the countries it represents. The WGI are not used by the World Bank Group to allocate resources.

complicity. Accordingly, in poor rule-of-law situations, organized crime can more readily make use of landing strips, ports, weakly monitored roads, banks, and other infrastructure needed to move goods.[39] For gangs, it means that they can occupy neighborhoods with minimal concern that

---

[39] This point raises the question of whether countries must have a minimum basic infrastructure to be attractive to organized crime.

the state will or can crack down on them (and in some cases encourages expectations that the gangs can buy off relevant state actors).[40]

Yet, when we consider rule-of-law indicators and the violence patterns of interest in this study, the relationship appears weak. Outside of the top tier (Chile, Uruguay, and Costa Rica), we find medium-to-high violence across the other general, perceptual indicators of "rule of law." This uneven pattern suggests that this indicator of state capacity is either not relevant, insufficient, not necessary, or measured inadequately or all of the above (e.g., aggregated at too high a level, too perceptual, perhaps political – points raised in the introduction to this appendix). Although one might therefore be tempted to conclude that the rule of law is unimportant, this book draws a different conclusion. It moves from the study of perceptions to the study of particular institutions (focusing on particular state institutions and their behavior – particularly homicide clearance rates, as discussed in the text of Chapter 4).

LAPOP and Latinobarometer surveys provide data on perceptions of specific institutions. These surveys reveal low levels of trust and confidence in rule-of-law institutions across the high-violence/low-capacity states – both in the police and courts. Surveys on trust and confidence in the police reveal the following patterns: distrust is relatively high across these cases. Figure 4.8a includes Central American cases plus a subset of cases with high homicide rates; Mexico and Guatemala emerge over time with particularly high levels of distrust (Mexico starts and ends high; Guatemala rises and stays relatively high); Venezuela starts high, fluctuates considerably, and then rises dramatically starting in 2013; distrust levels in Nicaragua spike in 2000 but then steadily decline over time, ranking the lowest in 2007 (and then fluctuating at the bottom and middle of the pack); the remaining cases also fluctuate within this band. Subsequent reports by Latinobarometer continue to reveal low institutional trust in the very institutions that are

---

[40] Indeed, in a comparative study of children and youth in organized armed violence in seven countries, Dowdney finds that the state was directly or indirectly involved in each case – a suggestive finding that merits further comparative investigation. In his comparison of three favelas in Rio de Janeiro, Arias (2006) also identified where criminal organizations develop in coordination with state officials (particularly police), politicians, and civic associations/leaders. Bobea (2010: 165), analyzing the Dominican Republic, argues similarly: "The dilemma originates in the extreme weakness of states and their attendant inability to implement institutional reforms that guarantee citizens the social and security services they require" (Bobea 2010: 165).

designed to uphold the rule of law.[41] For readability, Figure 4.8a does not include all Latin American cases, and Figure 4.8b includes a wider range of cases. Chile stands out for the lowest levels of distrust, fluctuating between 30 and 50 percent, ending in 2016 with 40 percent. Uruguay is also at the bottom of the band, and Argentina exhibits relatively high distrust (between 60 and 80 percent) in its own police, as do other cases.

Confronted with the violence in the streets, people are hesitant to turn to the police – presuming incompetence, complicity, or extrajudicial involvement. Indeed, there is reason to hold these views: a number of studies argue that police officials (and in some cases political party officials) are deeply implicated in the very violence that is taking place – directing, profiting, and/or ignoring the violence in play.[42] Accordingly, rather than controlling the violence, many police officers are implicated in it – in some cases profiting from the violence (kickbacks/forms of corruption) and in others actually carrying it out (e.g., as off-duty hit men and/or as members of private security forces).[43] The state in this case is not a Hobbesian answer to the problem but constitutes part of the very problem to be addressed. If weak/corrupt security forces provide added incentives for illicit trade to move in, then it is also likely that once illicit economies take hold, the latter will further corrupt state institutions.

Trust on the part of the population is thus one indicator of weak state capacity; however, by definition, this perceptual component does not necessarily equal institutional behavior (complicity, corruption, and/or incompetence); nor does trust reveal how institutions shape the behavior of state actors. Indeed, trust levels fluctuate quite a bit, and even the most "reliable rule-of-law countries" can have high levels of distrust in their police. Costa Rica, for example, receives strong rule-of-law scores from the World Bank, and yet Latinobarometer surveys reveal rising distrust,

---

[41] A 1998 opinion poll in El Salvador indicated, moreover, that the national civilian police (PNC) is the second most likely to violate human rights (45 percent), exceeded only by "criminals" (Call 2000: 35).

[42] See, for example, Arias (2006a, 2006b), Auyero (2006), and Davis (2006a, 2006b).

[43] "Social cleansing" refers to extrajudicial police actions to murder "unwanted" societal groups – including gang members (in the case of Central America) and street children (in the case of Brazil). At this point, there is plausible deniability that social cleansing is state policy, although it seems equally plausible that subordinate state officials are taking matters into their own hands for a price. In what has become the ultimate irony, we find some citizens supporting these extrajudicial actions (and in some cases supporting *mano dura* policies) so as to control the violence on the streets. Alongside these actions, we have witnessed lynchings carried out by communities taking "justice" into their own hands.

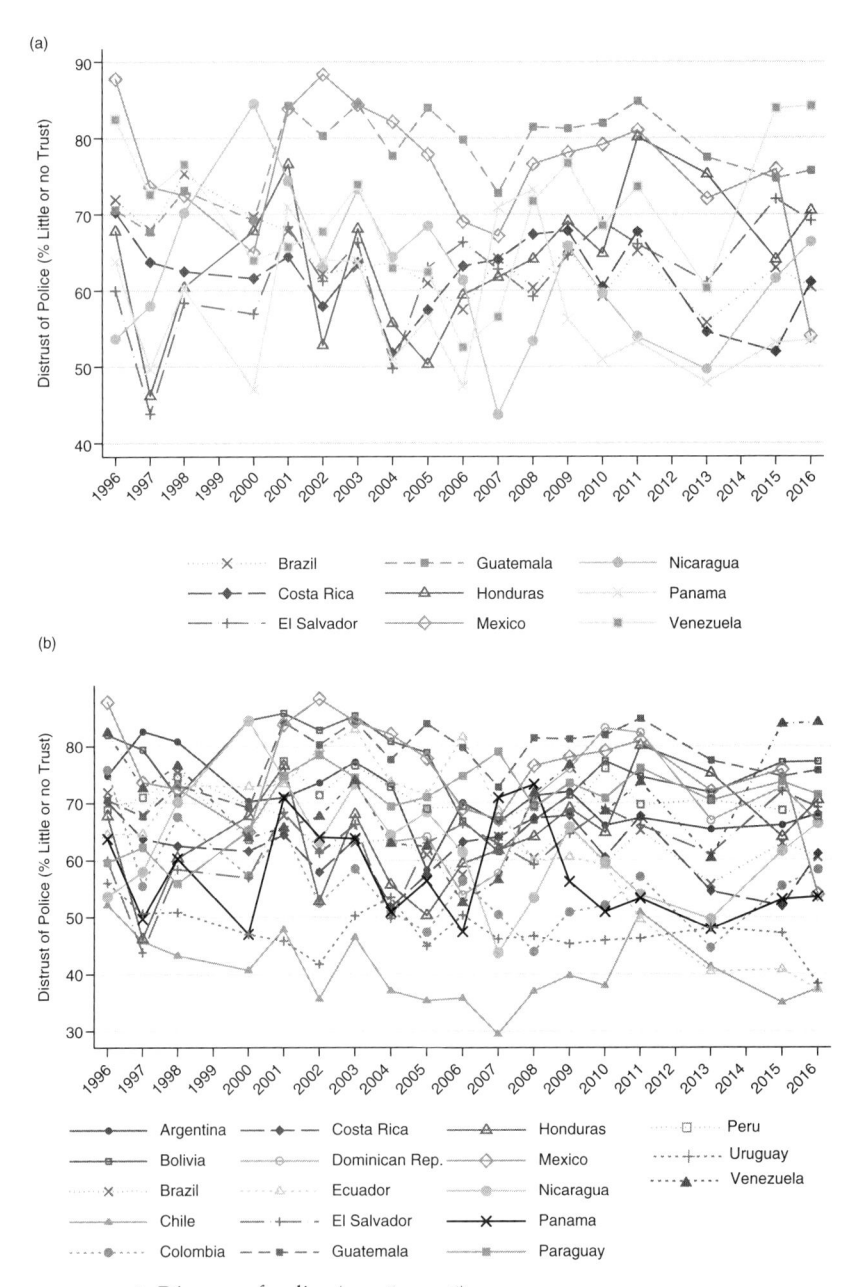

FIGURE 4.8 Distrust of police (1996–2016)
Figure 4.8a: Central America and subset of cases with high homicide rates
Figure 4.8b: Latin American comparison
Source: Latinobarometer Surveys (1996– 2016). Average responses. Responses in Likert scale.
Note: Question: "Please look at this card and tell me how much confidence you have in each of the following groups, institutions or persons mentioned on the list; a lot, some, a little or no confidence?" (Shown here: percentage indicating little or no confidence/trust in the police).

with Costa Rica appearing worse than Brazil and El Salvador in 2008 (which does not correlate with objective patterns of violence, although it does reveal a heightened concern). Thus, perceptions give us a good sense of the depth of the concern but not necessarily a strong understanding of the performance of the institutions themselves.

World Economic Forum data (2013, part II, Country Economic Profiles) echo some of the patterns found in Latinobarometer. The former measures twelve pillars of global competitiveness, one of which is institutions. Within this category, the seventeenth component measures the reliability of police services (see Table 4.1). Chile and Costa Rica continue to score high – relative to the 144 cases included in the dataset and relative to the Latin American region. Nicaragua also ranks relatively high (as does Brazil), compared to its Central America, Andean, and North American counterparts. These data

TABLE 4.1 *Reliability of police services in Latin America (ranking of Latin American cases out of 144 cases studied worldwide)*

Country	Rank	Value
Chile	14	16
Costa Rica	46	4.8
Panama	52	4.7
Brazil	60	4.4
Uruguay	71	4.2
Colombia	74	4.2
Nicaragua	94	3.8
Ecuador	116	3.2
El Salvador	118	3.1
Bolivia	122	3.0
Honduras	125	3.0
Peru	128	3.0
Argentina	131	2.9
Mexico	134	2.8
Guatemala	137	2.6
Venezuela	142	2.1

Source: World Economic Forum (2013: 91, 111, 117, 137, 141, 143, 157, 161, 183, 191, 257, 277, 287, 291, 361, 363, 365).

align most clearly with the outcome of interest in this book. However, since the data reported are from 2013 (late in the process), it is problematic to use these to explain prior events – i.e., the incentives of illicit organizations to set up shop or the violent events that precede it.

Corruption

A parallel way to study state capacity is to look at corruption indices. Transparency International (TNI) surveys, for example, are based on business surveys tracking perceptions of corrsuption. The world as a whole, beyond Latin America specifically, looks fairly ripe for illicit activity, except for the advanced industrial world (United States, Canada, Western Europe, and Australia) and small pockets in Latin America and the developing world (including Chile, Uruguay, and Costa Rica in Latin America). Trust in the police is low throughout the Latin American region, and police corruption is rampant in most cases. TNI data for 2006 (Table 4.2) show that Latin Americans are twice as likely to pay bribes to the police than they are to bribe other state institutions. Indeed, according to TNI, only Africa surpassed Latin America in terms of bribing the police.

Although Latin America scores high for corruption relative to the advanced industrial world, TNI maps tell us little about significant variation among the scores (or even about variation across the developing world).[44] They provide limited analytic purchase for explaining where and why drug organizations and gangs would decide to set up shop; we need more-precise measures.[45] Once we look at TNI's intra–Latin America data, variation exists across the corruption indicators – in the numerical scores reported by both TNI and the World Bank.

The TNI data (see Table 4.2 and Figure 4.9) suggest the following: (a) as expected, that Chile, Uruguay, and Costa Rica have categorically lower levels of corruption than the rest of the region and that they have among the lowest levels of violence as well; (b) less compellingly, that high- and medium-level

---

[44] For a Transparency International Map of the International Corruption Perceptions Index, 2007, see www.transparency.org/policy_research/surveys_indices/cpi/2007.

[45] Seligson (2006) suggests that the patterns in corruption do not correlate in any direct way with patterns of/trends in violence. He argues that, in fact, we should not rely on perceptual data alone since experiential data is likely to be more reliable. However, given the scope of Transparency International and World Bank data, we might still need to use their datasets for comparative work on these issues. His work consistently finds that corruption in El Salvador is not as high as in countries where violence is reported to be much lower – e.g., Nicaragua, Bolivia, and Paraguay.

TABLE 4.2 *Transnational Institute (TNI) Corruption Perceptions Index, Latin America (1998–2010)*

	1998	1999	2000	2001	2002	2003	2004	2005	2006	2007	2008	2009	2010
Argentina	3.0	3.0	3.5	3.5	2.8	2.5	2.5	2.8	2.9	2.9	2.9	2.9	2.9
Bolivia	2.8	2.5	2.7	2.0	2.2	2.3	2.2	2.5	2.7	2.9	3.0	2.7	2.8
Brazil[++]	4.0	4.1	3.9	4.0	4.0	3.9	3.9	3.7	3.3	3.5	3.5	3.7	3.7
Chile	6.8	6.9	7.4	7.5	7.5	7.4	7.4	7.3	7.3	7.0	6.9	6.7	7.2
Colombia[+++]	2.2	2.9	3.2	3.6	3.6	3.7	3.8	4.0	3.9	3.8	3.8	3.7	3.5
Costa Rica	5.6	5.1	5.4	4.5	4.5	4.3	4.9	4.2	4.1	5.0	5.1	5.3	5.3
Ecuador[+]	2.3	2.4	2.6	2.3	2.2	2.2	2.4	2.5	2.3	2.1	2.0	2.2	2.5
El Salvador[* +++]	3.6	3.9	4.1	3.6	3.4	3.7	4.2	4.2	4.0	4.0	3.9	3.4	3.6
Guatemala[* +++]	3.1	3.2		2.9	2.5	2.4	2.2	2.5	2.6	2.8	3.1	3.4	3.2
Honduras	1.7	1.8		2.7	2.7	2.3	2.3	2.6	2.5	2.5	2.6	2.5	2.4
Mexico[+]	3.3	3.4	3.3	3.7	3.6	3.6	3.6	3.5	3.3	3.5	3.6	3.3	3.1
Nicaragua[* +]	3.0	3.1		2.4	2.6	2.6	2.7	2.6	2.6	2.6	2.5	2.5	2.5
Panama[+]				3.7	3.0		3.7	3.5	3.1	3.2	3.4	3.4	3.6
Paraguay[+]	1.5	2.0			1.7	1.6	1.9	2.1	2.6	2.4	2.4	2.1	2.2
Peru[*]	4.5	4.5		4.1	4.0	3.7	3.5	3.5	3.3	3.5	3.6	3.7	3.5
Uruguay	4.3	4.4		5.1	5.1	5.5	6.2	5.9	6.4	6.7	6.9	6.7	6.9
Venezuela[++]	2.3	2.6	2.7	2.8	2.5	2.4	2.3	2.3	2.3	2.0	1.9	1.9	2

Source: compiled from TNI website (www.transparency.org/policy_research/surveys_indices/cpi); accessed on March 17, 2011.

Note 1: TNI scores are ranked from 1 to 10. The higher the score, the lower the corruption perceived. The scores are compiled from several sources, including expert assessments and opinion surveys (particularly from business).

Note 2: Drawing on Tables 1.1 and 2.1 (based on WHO data), [*] denotes post-civil war countries, including El Salvador, Guatemala, Nicaragua, and Peru (but excluding Colombia, given its ongoing civil war); [+++] denotes cases with extremely high levels of per capita homicide rates during this period, including Colombia, El Salvador, and Guatemala; [++] denotes cases with upper-band intermediate levels of violence, including Brazil and Venezuela; and [+] denotes cases with lower-band intermediate levels of violence, including Ecuador, Nicaragua, Panama, Paraguay, and Mexico. NB: Had we used UNODC rather than WHO data, Honduras and Venezuela would have fallen in the [+++] category.

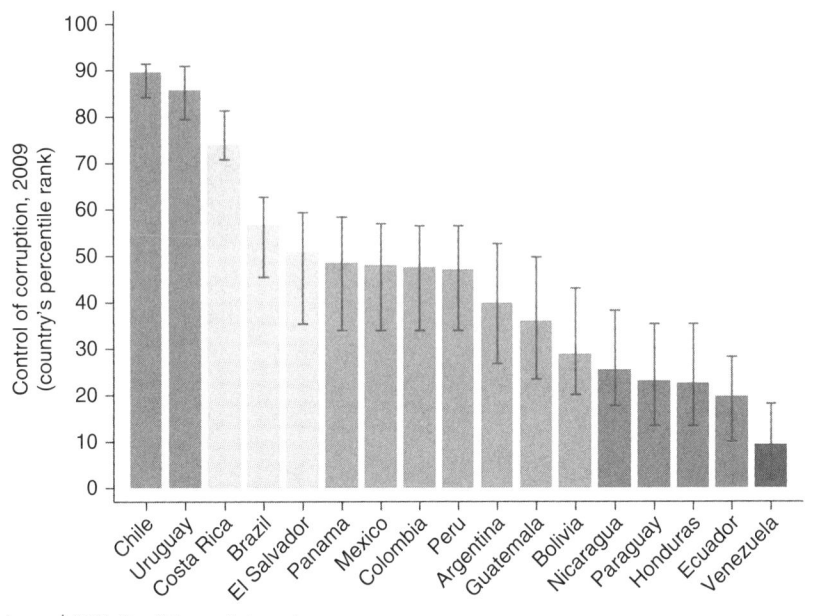

[Bar chart: Control of corruption, 2009 (country's percentile rank) with 90% confidence intervals, showing countries from highest to lowest: Chile (~89), Uruguay (~86), Costa Rica (~74), Brazil (~56), El Salvador (~50), Panama (~49), Mexico (~48), Colombia (~48), Peru (~47), Argentina (~40), Guatemala (~36), Bolivia (~29), Nicaragua (~26), Paraguay (~23), Honduras (~23), Ecuador (~20), Venezuela (~10).]

FIGURE 4.9 Indicators of corruption (2009)
Source: Downloaded February 8, 2018 from World Bank Governance Indicators website. Data is publicly available: http://info.worldbank.org/governance/wgi/index.aspx#home. The Worldwide Governance Indicators, 2017 Update, www.govindicators.org, September 22, 2017. Also see D. Kaufmann, A. Kraay, and M. Mastruzzi (2010). "The Worldwide Governance Indicators: Methodology and Analytical Issues."
Note: The Worldwide Governance Indicators (WGI) are a research dataset summarizing the views on the quality of governance provided by a large number of enterprise, citizen, and expert survey respondents in industrial and developing countries. These data are gathered from a number of survey institutes, think tanks, nongovernmental organizations, international organizations, and private sector firms. The WGI do not reflect the official views of the World Bank, its executive directors, or the countries it represents. The WGI are not used by the World Bank Group to allocate resources.

cases of violence tend to coincide with a wide range of TNI scores; and (c) that there are many more cases with scores lower than 4 than there are cases with high levels of violence (see Table 4.3). Thus, this measure provides little analytical purchase for considering if and how corruption shapes violence outcomes. Of note, moreover, the country rankings shift when compared to the data presented by the World Economic Forum.

TABLE 4.3 *Weak relationship between TNI rankings and levels of violence: a few examples*

Ranked by TNI Estimated Control of Corruption (2009) TNI Data	Country	2009 Homicide rate according to Pan American Health Organization (2014)	2010 Homicide rate according to UNDP (2013)	Homicide rank based on 2010 homicide rates (UNDP 2013). Lowest number corresponds with highest homicide rate.
High (4th quartile)				
	Chile	5.3	2	14
	Uruguay	4.9	6.1	13
Moderate (3rd quartile)				
	Costa Rica	10.9	11	9
	Brazil	26	22.2	7
	El Salvador	80	64.4	2
Low (2nd quartile)				
	Panama	23.3	21.2	8
	Mexico	16.4	23.8	6
	Colombia	60.4	34	5
	Peru	2.1	9	12
	Argentina	4.5	n/a	n/a
	Guatemala	45.6	41	4
	Bolivia	n/a	n/a	n/a
Very low (1st quartile)				
	Nicaragua	15.1	13	10
	Paraguay	15.9	10.7	11
	Honduras		77.5	1
	Ecuador	19.2		n/a
	Venezuela	33.9	45.1	3

In short, there are many quantitative indicators one might use to evaluate state capacity. As outlined in this appendix, they have their limitations. Therefore, for the main analysis in this book, I chose to focus on organizational characteristics and performance of specific state institutions – particularly those responsible for law and order (as discussed in Chapter 4). Although I reference perceptions/surveys, they play a secondary role in the analysis of state capacity.

PART III

DIVERGENT TRAJECTORIES
Three Post-Civil War Cases

Central American children surged across the United States border in 2014. They largely emigrated from the northern triangle of Guatemala, El Salvador, and Honduras. While US politicians debated what to do with the unforeseen numbers of undocumented – and often unaccompanied – boys and girls, no one doubted that this surge was in part related to the high levels of violence occurring in the countries of origin. The conditions in the northern triangle have become so unbearable that children (and parents) are open to traveling along a highly violent and uncertain set of roads, railways, and forests to reach the US border – a path sometimes chosen by people seeking economic livelihood, a path once chosen by refugees of the civil wars that racked the region, and one now chosen even in the aftermath of civil wars as individuals flee the violence that continues to rack the region. The violence, however, is not just a product of 2014 (and migration is not just an issue of that same year). Violence has become a staple in the region, even in the aftermath of democratic transitions. Indeed, while homicide rates decreased for Latin America as a whole from 1995 to 2004, there was a significant increase in Central America's regional homicide rates from 2007 to 2012 (UNODC 2014b: 33).[1]

The region's extraordinarily high levels of violence, thus, are more than legacies of the past. The homicidal ecologies are explained by the combination of the three core factors introduced in Parts I and II: changing geographies of illicit trade and transit, weak state capacity (especially for law-and-order institutions), and organizational territorial competition. Part II of this book probed the plausibility of this comparative argument

---

[1] In Latin America, the number of male victims in the 15–29 age group is four times higher than the global average. Strikingly, Central America's male homicide rate is highest among those in the 30–44 age group (UNODC 2014b: 28–30).

in light of regional trends. Part III probes this argument through case studies of Central America, one of the two most violent regions in the world (with southern Africa being the other).[2]

Chapters 5–7 of this book compare high- and low-violence cases in the region. Chapters 5 and 6 focus, in particular, on the causes of these high-violence patterns in Guatemala and El Salvador.[3] Nicaragua's comparatively low violence is the focus of Chapter 7. These three cases pose a striking comparison, given a shared history of colonialism, civil war, high inequality, geographic proximity, low levels of development, and yet significantly varied levels of violence. Thus, Central America provides a normatively and methodologically important site for comparative research on the topic of homicidal violence.

The two core high-violence cases, El Salvador and Guatemala, have had a checkered political record. Throughout much of their post-colonial history, these countries have experienced authoritarian rule, civil wars, and repressive military practices.[4] In this context, peace accords signed in the 1990s were landmark events, raising hopes that the formal transition to democratic rule in the 1980s would have substantive meaning for citizens of each country. Both countries experienced significant declines in human rights abuses and regular alternation of power, although political violence still occurs, especially in the case of Guatemala. In this third wave of democracy, therefore, cautious hopes were raised that violence would recede. And political violence has declined significantly in both countries. Yet the post-accord phase has witnessed rising violence in each case, leading both countries to arrive at markedly high (and yet distinct) patterns of violence. Guatemala became one of the major transit routes for cocaine in the 2000s, just a decade after the peace accords. El Salvador emerged from the late 1990s on as one of the major sites of gang violence.

---

[2] Economist Intelligence Unit. "El Salvador." April 14, 2014. Accessed July 14, 2014. EUI reports UNODC figures, highlighting that if Latin America is the most violent region in the world, Central America is the most violent subregion (although Southern Africa's number is actually slightly higher). In 2012, the global average was 6.2 homicides per 100,000 people, with 25 for Latin America and 26 for Central America (and Southern Africa at 30).

[3] Honduras also exhibits very high levels of violence. However, it is not part of this paired comparison because that country does not share a history of civil war, although it played a satellite role since the United States used Honduran bases. The Honduran case, alongside others, will be discussed in the concluding chapter, Chapter 8.

[4] For comparative analyses of Central American political trajectories, see Woodward (1999), Dunkerley (1989), Booth and Walker (1993), Paige (1998), Yashar (1997), Mahoney (2001), and Cruz (2005).

These two Central American cases represent parallel trajectories by which violence has surged in the region. While these trajectories ultimately converge (with significant spillover effects), they are discussed separately.

Chapters 5 and 6 trace the two routes by which violence has spiraled upward. Organized crime is particularly prevalent in Guatemala (as in the Caribbean, Mexico, and Venezuela), while gangs are particularly prevalent in El Salvador (as in Honduras).[5] It is important to note up front that these two categories (gangs versus organized crime) are not hermetically sealed: gangs are arguably a form of organized crime, and gangs and more traditional organized crime increasingly interact over time. Moreover, organized crime and gangs exist in *all* these cases. Nonetheless, while different sets of actors take the lead in initiating spikes in violence, violence trajectories in all cases spike when illicit organizations (gangs, organized crime, paramilitaries) deploy violence to control territory or trade routes. The key players are illicit actors fighting to control particular territorial spaces (although the exact organizational form diverges across cases), sometimes fighting other illicit organizations, sometimes fighting the state.[6]

Guatemala (Chapter 5) and El Salvador (Chapter 6) are compared to Nicaragua (Chapter 7), where homicidal ecologies are much more circumscribed. These empirical chapters explore this variation by analyzing the three variables mentioned earlier (and throughout this book): the geography of illicit economy and organizations, state capacity, and organizational competition over territory. While these variables are introduced separately, the cases also reveal their endogeneity because they are at times mutually constitutive. Across these three cases, varied state capacity (in terms of law-and-order institutions) shaped the space for the (varied) proliferation of illicit geographies of gangs and organized crime (which in turn took advantage of weak states and in some cases provided further incentives for state corruption and complicity). The presence of these illicit organizations alone does not explain homicide rates, however; rather it is the territorial competition between these organizations and/or with the state that generates the peaks in violence that we have seen in much of the

---

[5] Moran (2009: 8) also argues that although violence is high in Guatemala and El Salvador, drug trafficking has been higher in the former while gangs have been more prevalent in the latter.

[6] As discussed further later on, state actors also contribute actively to the violence levels once they compete to control illicit organizations and extend their command over specific territories.

region and in El Salvador and Guatemala (alongside Honduras) in particular, in marked contrast to Nicaragua.[7]

Thus, Part III features two parallel trajectories by which violence takes off in Guatemala and El Salvador, and one divergent trajectory where violence occurs at a considerably lower level (although with a few subnational exceptions noted further on).[8] Notably, this analytical focus implies the need to move beyond nation-centric case studies (all the more since homicides are localized, not generalized, and since the causes are operating at multiple levels), international changes in illicit economies, national patterns of state capacity, and local patterns of competition. If we only presume national cases as the denominator and national-level factors as the causes, then we miss the territoriality that proves so critical to understanding and explaining these outcomes, including those geographic pockets within Nicaragua, where violence significantly exceeds the national average. Hence, I analyze these cases at both the national and subnational level, probing the argument for temporal and geographic variation.

Part III draws on primary documents, an original newspaper database, and original interviews in Guatemala, El Salvador, and Nicaragua.[9]

---

[7] UNODC (2012) also makes a similar point, arguing that it is not the cocaine or the illicit trade alone that generates violence but rather competition between groups (or a changing balance of power) that does.

[8] UNODC (2012) makes an important distinction between territory-bound organized crime groups, which are prevalent in Guatemala, and trafficking groups, which are prevalent in El Salvador. I do not use this precise language, since the distinction between the two categories loses its edge across time. Rather, I seek to emphasize a point in common, which is that we should look at a range of illicit organizations and the competition that emerges to control spaces in which trade and transit take place.

[9] The research included the creation of a newspaper database that drew on three years (2000, 2005, and 2010) of reporting in three newspapers: *Prensa Libre* in Guatemala, *La Prensa Gráfica* in El Salvador, and *La Prensa* in Nicaragua. The database itself included two components: (1) coding reports on specific homicides (2000, 2005, and 2010), for which there was a terrific team of research assistants (names listed in the acknowledgments), coordinated by Yanilda González and Bethany Park; (2) reading the more general articles about violence. Yanilda González and Bethany Park wrote thematic memos for 2000, 2005, and 2010 that analyzed each of these years. I thank González and Park for these outstanding memos, which provided the basis for the newspapers cited, summarized, and discussed in Chapters 5–7. Of course, all errors are mine.

5

High Violence in Post-Civil War Guatemala

Si uno no mata, lo matan, pues uno tiene que defenderse de los sicarios, agentes policiales y de las bandas rivales. Por esa razón, siempre están armados... Uno no sabe ni el lugar ni la hora en que pueden matarlo.
Prensa Libre, July 13, 2005
"Si uno no mata, lo matan"
Anonymous member of Guatemalan gang

Creo que es muy difícil enfrentar los temas violentos con el clima de narcotráfico y pandillas. Venimos de 36 años de violencia, y encontramos todas las instituciones infiltradas y corruptas.
Guatemalan President Oscar Berger
Reported in Prensa Libre, January 10, 2005
"La violencia me decepciona mucho"

In the end, the presence of gangs alone is not enough to explain high murder rates. Nor is the presence of drug trafficking. Rather, violence is occurring in areas where substate groups have been brought into conflict with one another, presently because of flux in the cocaine markets. These conflicts appear to span borders, and the frontier between Guatemala and Honduras is one of the most dangerous strips in the world.
UNODC (2012: 69–70)

Guatemala is no stranger to violence. Military dictatorship, civil war, paramilitaries, and human rights abuses have defined much of the postcolonial period in Guatemala. Indeed, during the Cold War, Guatemala's military engaged in genocide and political assassinations, killing some 200,000 people, creating model villages to control its population, torturing countless more, and leaving the country with some 150,000–200,000 orphans and 40,000–80,000 widows,[10] with many arms circulating around the country. The peace accords of 1996 were therefore cautiously celebrated.

Yet, Guatemala's post-civil war accord record has been anything but pacific. Violence has remained a common part of daily life (although its form has changed). Newspapers report daily killings that make Guatemala yet again one of the most violent countries in the world. The national homicide rate rose steadily and tragically following the peace accords (with a peak in 2009). By 2008, the WHO reported that Guatemala had reached a homicide rate of 40.7, although some estimates placed that figure even higher.[11] In 2009, it increased to 45.6 and then returned to 40 in 2010 (after which it declined in 2011 and 2012). Given the end of the civil war, it was tragic to hear former Guatemalan President Oscar Berger, and other top officials, talk about the "Colombianization" of Guatemala due to rampant money laundering, violence in the streets, kidnapping, and narcotrafficker control of territories of which the government had lost sovereignty.[12]

Guatemala is not alone. Alongside El Salvador and Honduras, Guatemala has emerged with astoundingly high violence rates – with the latter two surpassing Guatemala, according to World Bank and UNODC reports (Figures 5.1 and 5.2).

This chapter explores how Guatemala's weak state capacity provided especially propitious territory for illicit actors to assume control of particular territorial enclaves. Homicidal violence has reached extremeley high rates in this case, where illicit actors have competed to establish territorial control and/or the state has stepped in to do the same. Thus, illicit economies, weak state capacity, and organizational territorial competition have been three interactive factors that provide a lens for understanding where homicidal violence has been particularly prevalent. This

---

[10] There are many important books and articles about Guatemala's violence. For example, see Handy (1984), Carmack (1988), Manz (1988), Jonas (1991), and Schirmer (1999).

[11] Organización Panamericana de la Salud, Unidad de Análisis de Salud y Estadísticas, Iniciativa Regional de Datos Básicos en Salud; Sistema de Información Técnica en Salud, Washington, DC, 2010, www.paho.org/Spanish/SHA/coredata/tabulator/newTabulator.htm. The raw data is from Pan American Health Organization, Health Surveillance and Disease Management Area, Health Statistics and Analysis Unit, PAHO Regional Mortality Database. Rates based on World Population Prospects 2006, revised 2008. Figures for El Salvador and Guatemala are sometimes reported as much higher than those found in the WHO reports – e.g., 150 for each country in 2000. See, for example, Inter-American Development Bank (2000) report, reprinted in Hugo Acero Velásquez. 2002. "Salud, violencia y seguridad." *Ciudad y políticas públicas de seguridad y convivencia.*

[12] *Prensa Libre* 6.19.2005 Colombianización copa el país.

High Violence in Post-Civil War Guatemala

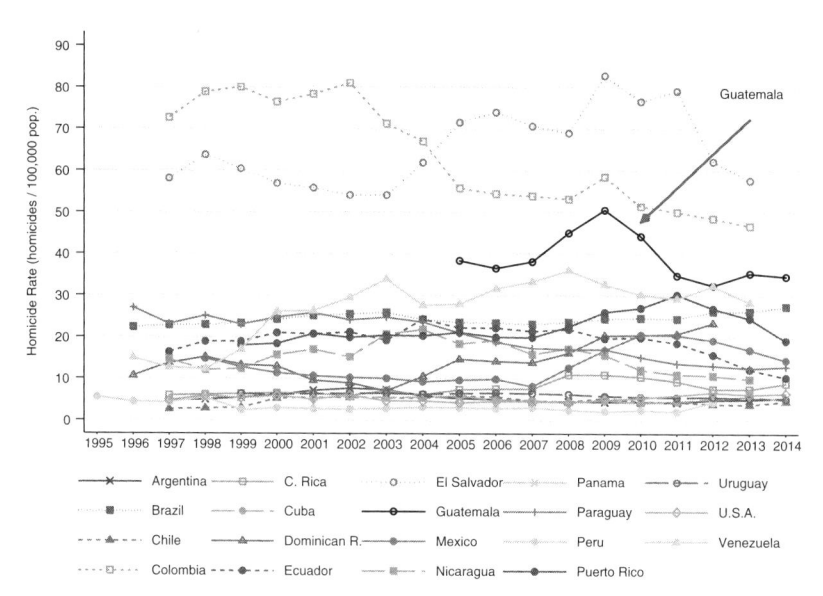

FIGURE 5.1 Homicide rates in the Americas (1995–2014)
Graph created by Daniela Barba-Sánchez using Stata.
Source: PAHO 2014 (or 2010 when 2014 revised data were not available).

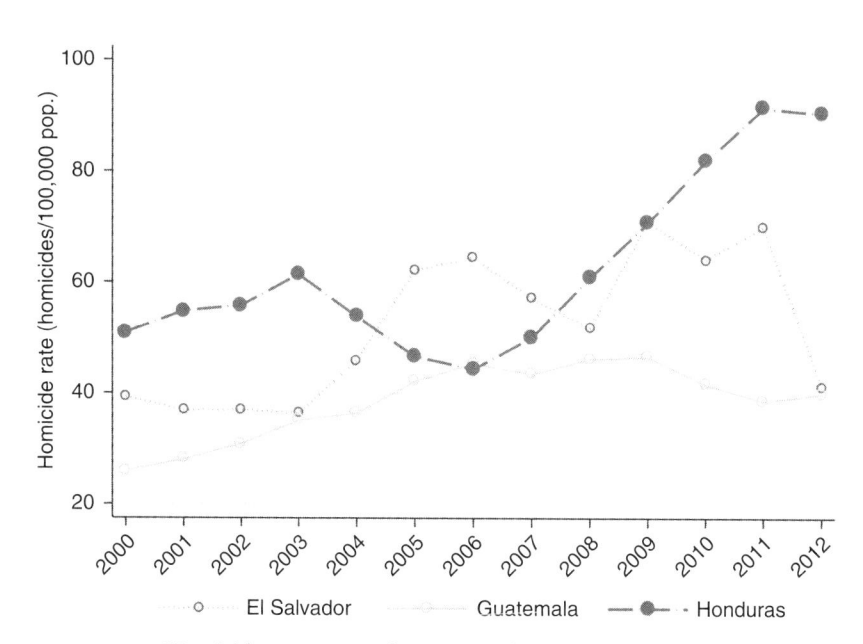

FIGURE 5.2 Homicide rates in northern Central America (2000–2012)
Source: UNODC (2012: 16)

chapter is organized in three parts. After first elaborating on violence patterns in Guatemala, I provide a depiction of Guatemala's law-and-order institutions, followed by a third section on illicit organizations and territorial competition. The conclusion zooms back to place the Guatemalan case in comparative perspective.

VIOLENCE PATTERNS

In the aftermath of the civil war, Guatemala's official homicide rates continue to be the highest in the northern and eastern parts of the country, in addition to the capital. The Petén, on the northern border with Mexico, has consistently reached very high levels (often the highest) for the period 1986–2004, which covers years before and after peace accords – never dipping below 39 per 100,000 homicides and often reaching much higher (see Appendix to this chapter as well as GIS maps in Figure 5.3). Other contenders have included the eastern regional departments (states) of Izabal, Jutiapa, Chiquimula, Santa Rosa, and the metropolitan capital of Guatemala. The following data and maps depict this variation. Figure 5.3 includes four examples of GIS maps of the subnational violence by regional departments for 1994–2004. While the absolute homicide rates vary somewhat across these years, the geographic location of the highest (high and very high) homicide rates is geographically consistent. Notably, they do not mirror where the civil war violence was highest – namely the western highlands.[13] While there are some high-visibility cases of lynching in the

---

[13] It is common to explain this contemporary violence as a legacy of the country's civil war. In fact, Benson, Fischer, and Thomas (2008) caution against those that minimize the legacies of state violence and attending conditions of economic and social inequality. Yet the geographical and temporal patterns of post-civil war homicidal violence do not simply replicate or extend earlier patterns. This chapter argues that the civil war is *not* the root of the contemporary problem. While tolerance for violence, the brutality, and even the weaponry used to commit the violence might find some of its origins in the civil war, the levels reached by contemporary violence is not simply a reflection of the past. Civil wars are neither necessary nor sufficient for violence (as illustrated by high violence in non–civil war Honduras and low violence in post-civil war Nicaragua). While the worst civil war atrocities occurred in the indigenous highlands (in the western and northwestern parts of the country), these regions include among the lowest homicide rates in the country. Data accuracy should obviously be questioned for the civil war years (which might have underreported homicides in the western highlands during these years).

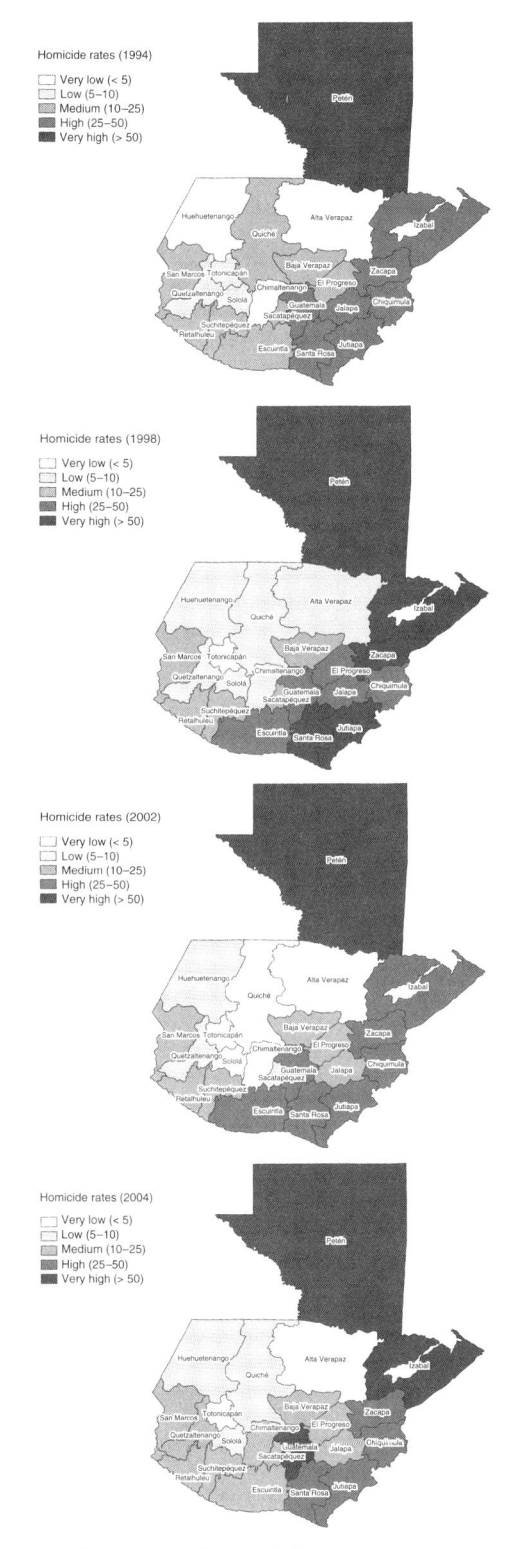

FIGURE 5.3 Guatemala: regional homicide levels, per 100,000 (1994, 1998, 2002, 2004)

highlands, they constitute a minority of the homicides that have taken place in recent years.[14]

By 2010, the government reported that the worst violence was taking place in the department of Guatemala (57.7 percent), with three-quarters

---

FIGURE 5.3 (cont.)

Map created by Vinay Jawahar and reformatted by Daniela Barba-Sánchez.
Note: Homicides are defined according to the World Health Organization standard classification E960–E969 in the *International Classification of Diseases*, 9th rev. (ICD-9), or X85–Y09 in the *International Statistical Classification of Diseases and Related Health Problems*, 10th rev. (ICD-10). Homicide rates are defined as the number of homicides per 100,000 population and calculated using homicide data and population estimates.
Source: Homicide data obtained from Carlos Mendoza, Instituto Nacional de Estadística (Guatemala). 2005. *CD-ROM de homicidios 1986–2003*, Guatemala: INE, Departamento de Estadísticas Vitales. Population estimates for 1986–1990: Instituto Nacional de Estadística (Guatemala). 1989. *Guatemala: población urbana y rural estimada por departamento y municipios, 1985–90*. Publicaciones Estadísticas temáticas, 2.11.4. Guatemala: INE. Estimates for 1991–1995: Instituto Nacional de Estadística (Guatemala). 1991. *Guatemala: población urbana y rural estimada por departamento y municipio, 1990-95*. Publicaciones Estadísticas temáticas, 2.11.4. Guatemala: INE. Estimates for 2000–2004: Instituto Nacional de Estadística (Guatemala). 2001. *Guatemala, proyecciones de población a nivel departamental y municipal por año calendario: período 2000–2005*. Guatemala: INE. Estimates for 1996–1999: calculated by linear interpolation using 1995 and 2000 data.

---

[14] There have been some high-visibility lynching cases in Guatemala's highlands (see Vilas 1992, Mendoza 2006, Snodgrass Godoy 2006, and Bateson n.d.). The press has reported on these as well and has highlighted the effort to understand why mobs have occasionally formed to attack tourists (often for fear that children were being abducted), redress crimes within their own communities, and attack police stations. Some of these cases have resulted in deaths, with an increasing number over the decade of 2000–2010 (UNODC 2012: 71). Yet even recognizing these events, homicide rates in these communities are often among the lowest in the country, making it illogical to pin the high homicide rates on these isolated, if dramatic, events. Thus, this book does not focus on them in particular. (For examples of reporting, see *Prensa Libre* 12.19.2000 Cincuenta años a linchador; 12.21.2000 Amenazan a jueces; 7.19.2000 Nuevo intento de linchamiento; 9.3.2000 Foro Maya: rechazan violencia). Lynching continued throughout the period of this study, although these high-profile events seem isolated: *Prensa Libre* 5.24.2005 Breves; 5.23.2005 Quiché: seis linchados en menos de 10 días; 11.6.2005 Intentan linchar a policías en Antigua Guatemala.

of those murders taking place in Guatemala City. Escuintla on the Pacific coast (which has a significant port) followed with 12.5 percent of the murders.[15]

These numbers are striking but do not capture the types of homicides that are taking place. To gather a fuller understanding of the homicide patterns, a team of research assistants coded the Guatemalan newspaper *Prensa Libre* for three years (2000, 2005, and 2010) and compared the data against newspaper reporting of violence in El Salvador and Nicaragua (see the Appendix to this chapter). Media reporting suggests that while homicide rates are high in both El Salvador and Guatemala, rates are highest in the former and the incidence of grotesque brutality appears highest in the latter. As hypothesized in the opening chapters, homicide rates are particularly high in capital cities and near transit points such as ports, borders, and highways. It is in these regions that we find the emergence of illicit actors as well as the trade and transit of illicit substances. It is also in these regions that we have increasingly found competition to control territorial enclaves.

To explain these patterns, we first analyze Guatemala's state before analyzing illicit actors and their efforts to control prime territorial space.

STATE CAPACITY: WEAK LAW AND ORDER

High violence rates are tied to Guatemala's state capacity. It is common to presume state strength given the militarization of the country and the brutal violence unleashed against its own population.[16] Many of these human rights abuses are documented in recently discovered police archives,[17] but scholars and human rights agencies have amply documented these abuses as well. Vividly commenting on the impact of

---

[15] *Prensa Libre* 12.27. 2010 Más de seis mil muertes se reportan en el 2010.
The Ministry of the Interior (Gobernación) reported more than 6,000 murders in 2010. "La espiral de violencia que afecta al país ha llevado a que este año se cierre con más de seis mil homicidios, mayor crueldad en los crímenes al localizarse más de 20 cuerpos desmembrados y una amplia área de operaciones del crimen organizado por la incapacidad de las autoridades para combatirlo." The ministry observed that up to 60 percent of the murders might be tied to organized crime, and the other 25 percent to gangs struggling over territory. Other news reporting about the ministry questioned its command of basic facts about who had committed the reported murders (see newspaper violence database).

[16] During the civil war, Guatemala's military government ruled the country with an iron fist, creating a military presence throughout much of the country, setting up model villages in much of the highlands, and engaging in devastatingly high levels of repression.

[17] See the digital archives of the of Guatemalan National Police Historical Archive (https://ahpn.lib.utexas.edu/).

Guatemala's state violence against its own citizenry, Iduvina Hernández stated that the aggression was so constant, the levels so high, and the torture so extreme that people started to lose their identity and self-worth; they lost the capacity to be surprised, and they developed incredibly high levels of tolerance for state violence and human rights abuses.[18]

It might seem counterintuitive, therefore, to refer to Guatemala as having a weak state capacity. However, once we consider basic organizational and bureaucratic ability to implement democratic rule-of-law projects, even Guatemala's coercive state branches appear quite weak, as do its judicial and penal ones.[19] When looking at the military and the police, weak state capacity is indicated by poor role specification, limited internal and external accountability, paltry homicide clearance rates, low professional training and commitment, limited resources, uneven territorial reach, widespread corruption, and complicity. This kind of weak state capacity provides facilitating or permissive conditions that are conducive to the growth of illicit actors and activity. Indeed, with the crackdown in the Caribbean, it made Guatemala an attractive alternative for DTOs seeking to adapt and move drugs northward.

The 1996 peace accords, despite mandated reforms designed to democratize and professionalize Guatemala's rule-of-law institutions, did not fundamentally change this situation. Guatemala's military has maintained its reputation for human rights abuses, impunity, and corruption. Its courts and prison system have also been severely hampered in their efforts to uphold the rule of law. But it is the police that is perhaps least understood in this process and arguably at the frontlines of monitoring domestic territorial space.

The Police

The Guatemalan police force has historically been an agent of violence, unpredictability, and corruption; it was subordinate to a military that engineered systematic human rights abuses. This history contrasts sharply with what we theoretically expect of the police – arguably the state agency closest to the people: street-level bureaucrats armed with guns who are

---

[18] Interview with Iduvina Hernández, cofounder and director of SEDEM, July 2006.
[19] See Chapter 4 for a discussion of states in the developing world, as well as Centeno, Kohli, and Yashar (2017), including a conceptual first chapter about state capacity, state formation, and state performance.

supposed to prevent the "unrule of law" and track down those who break the law.[20]

There was no major overhaul to replace underlying police institutions and personnel, despite institutional reforms following the 1996 peace accords, including removing the Guatemalan police from military control and new educational requirements.[21] Thus the institutional and behavioral weight of the past remained – with a legacy of nondemocratic institutions, lack of accountability to civilians, and recycling of agents from one coercive branch to another. There was no effort to dismiss prior police officers, many of whom had been involved in the most atrocious human rights activities during the military period. Interestingly, the Spanish civil guard (not the UN, as in El Salvador) assumed the role of training and advising the new force (Moran 2009: 47). By 1999, some 73 percent of the Guatemalan police were filled with members of the former national police (Moran 2009: 49). Indeed, several deficiencies in the police were noted in a 1999 study that was jointly conducted by Guatemala's Ministry of the Interior (Ministerio de Gobernación), the UN Mission (Misión de Naciones Unidas para Guatemala, MINUGUA), and the Danish Center for Human Rights (Centro Danés para los Derechos Humanos) and reported in a March 2000 *Prensa Libre* article: "The principal problems confronted by the PNC include, deficiencies to combat organized crime, the population's lack of trust, and a precarious administration."[22] In terms of fighting organized criminal groups, "the principal problem that the PNC faces in fighting organized crime is the Investigation Department (Academia de Investigaciones), which has little

---

[20] See Michael Lipsky (1980) for a discussion of street-level bureaucrats; also see Yanilda González's 2014 dissertation for a discussion of Latin American police as an example of street-level bureaucracy.

[21] See Ruhl (2005) on the peace accords and their impact on the military. Also, Moran (2009) and Stanley (1996) have argued that the strength of organizations coming into the peace accord affected the depth of the reform agenda. El Salvador's opposing sides had strong associations (FMLN was the guerrilla front that also had a corresponding strong party, and the right had ARENA), while Guatemala did not (the URNG was weak by the time the accords were negotiated, the right had strong chamber associations but no serious political party, and the military emerged as an important player before and after the accords). Moran indicates that this affected the depth of the reforms and the weak reforms that followed in Guatemala.

[22] *Prensa Libre* 3.20.2000 PNC acepta debilidades: "Deficiencia para combatir el crimen organizado, falta de confianza de la población y precaria administración, son los principales problemas que afronta la PNC."

capacity."[23] The weight of the past was also observed when talking about problems in civil intelligence, observed to have ongoing connections to the old military intelligence.[24]

The press has reported on the police's low capacity – including insufficient police agents and resources to meet the demand,[25] a lack of "special forces" police, insufficient technology, insufficient data, lack of inter- and intradepartmental coordination, lack of helicopters in the Department of Antinarcotics Operations (DOAN), and lack of antiriot technology.[26] In 2000, *Prensa Libre* reported that the "PNC is impotent in fighting crime," a statement supported by quotes from the PNC director, Rudio Lecasan – e.g., "We haven't been able to consolidate a PNC capable of resolving security problems."[27] Academics have also commented on this weak capacity, including an interview with security expert Gabriel Aguilera Peralta, who noted a decade after the peace accord that the PNC had low capacity as indicated by low levels of entry, low academic training, and limited resources – alongside a state penetrated by organized crime.[28]

Indeed, the police are often considered among the most corrupt sectors of society, including by United Nations agencies and NGOs working on Latin America.[29] In a comparative study of Central American police, WOLA (2009) found that Guatemala's police force was severely lacking

---

[23] *Prensa Libre* 3.20.2000 PNC acepta debilidades: "el principal problema que afronta la PNC para combatir el crimen organizado es que la Academia de Investigaciones cuenta con poca capacidad."

[24] *Prensa Libre* 3.20.2000 PNC acepta debilidades.

[25] In Escuintla, one article reports on the insufficient number of investigators to cover the rise in violence. See *Prensa Libre* 2.17.2000 Clima de inseguridad agobia a escuintlecos. In San Marcos, the PNC also complained of insufficient agents per capita: *Prensa Libre* 12.14.2000 Disminuye seguridad.

[26] The institutional weight of the past has arguably provided obstacles to achieving the police mandate. Birgit Gerstenberg, head of the Proyecto de la Academia de la Policía Nacional Civil (the PNC), as part of the Misión de Naciones Unidas para Guatemala (MINUGUA) noted that the peace accords required a "recycling" of security personnel, without which there would have been 12,000 unemployed police officers. Nonetheless, the old security forces that remained were not unencumbered but rather impeded those who might have wanted to achieve reform. As Julio Arango Escobar (head of the PDH) put it, "La intromisión de las fuerzas militares perdura, y por ello las autoridades deben ponerle fin al problema, pues nos hace retroceder en la justa aplicación de la justicia." See *Prensa Libre* 4.6.2000 PNC se encuentra dividida.

[27] *Prensa Libre* 7.11.2000 PNC impotente en combate del crimen.

[28] Interview with Gabriel Aguilera Peralta, July 28, 2006.

[29] See UNODC (2007: 30, citing 2005 Transparency International's Global Corruption Barometer) and WOLA (2009).

(as were the forces in El Salvador and Honduras) and penetrated by organized crime, lacking in internal discipline and accountability, among other indicators. While initially modeled after the Spanish Civil Guard (from which most funding emanated), the police disciplinary model was reformed in 2003 (with help from MINUGUA, international aid agencies, and members of civil society). Yet even with these changes, WOLA found that the police were still penetrated (or influenced) by organized crime, riven by corruption, and engaging in serious human rights abuses: "The inability to monitor and control the police is due in large part to the weakness of internal control mechanisms and the lack of real support from police leadership" (WOLA 2009: 22). Police records (which presumably underreport the level of the problem) indicate that in 2003 there were almost 1,600 complaints of serious criminal activity and/or infractions by the police, ostensibly affecting some 12 percent of the Guatemalan police force; of these complaints, 33 percent were not investigated and 55 percent were investigated but found inconclusive, leaving just 12 percent remaining (WOLA 2009: 22).

All these observations underscore the high levels of distrust, a lack of serious investigation, and thus a climate of perceived impunity. Whereas the Office of Professional Responsibility saw its staff reduced by almost one-half between 2004 and 2006, there has been a practice of transferring police to other units rather than pursuing investigations of them; and when cases are sent to the Ministry of the Interior, the courts rarely prosecute them (WOLA 2009: 22–23).

The questionable role of the police was infamously placed in sharp relief in a high-profile 2007 incident. In that year, police officers were not only implicated in gunning down three Salvadoran politicians (suspected of involvement in the drug trade) traveling by car on the Pan-American Highway, but then the same police officers were detained and gunned down a few days later in a Guatemalan maximum-security prison, where they were awaiting investigation.[30] This scandal led to a round of resignations and police reforms. Some 3,000 officers were dismissed within the next year; efforts were made to improve discipline, but WOLA (2009: 23) notes that officers have rarely been subject to criminal investigation – with dismissal serving as the more likely penalty. While dismissal can act as a deterrent for some, it is not a particularly harsh measure. Some concluded that the incident of the Salvadoran politicians lay bare the evident

---

[30] This incident was reported in all the papers. For a succinct overview, see WOLA (2009: 23).

ties between top state officials in the police and Ministerio de Gobernación, a pattern that was not new to the country (Ranum 2011: 76).

Overall, some minor institutional reforms did occur following the peace accords, but there is no doubt that throughout the 1990s and 2000s, police capacity and integrity have been ongoing issues and challenges.

> Guatemala has had numerous chilling cases of police involvement, including at the highest levels in corruption, assassinations, and criminal activities. These have exposed an alarming degree of infiltration by organized criminal networks into the Guatemalan police and other state institutions. (WOLA 2009: 30)

Moreover, the police force is far from being a professional organization. While its Nicaraguan counterpart (discussed in Chapter 8) was developing an increasingly professional and autonomous police force in the 1980s, 1990s, and 2000s (and engaging communities in preventative policies), Guatemala's police force remained hampered by unprofessionalism. In the study of four Central American police forces (Guatemala, El Salvador, Honduras, and Nicaragua), Guatemala's stood out as the only one without a formal police career law (WOLA 2009: 17–18). While this institutional mechanism cannot be blamed for high violence (after all, other high-violence cases do have this mechanism in place), in practice it illustrates the lack of a basic infrastructure to socialize and sustain institutional professionalism. "Corruption, political interference, and nepotism" has plagued the nominations and promotion process, there has been a shortage of mid- and high-level career officers, and there has been continual change in the high command, according to WOLA (2009: 17–18). Turnover rates are a serious issue, moreover: during the presidency of Alfonso Portillo (2000–2004), there were eight police directors and three interior ministers; during the presidency of Oscar Bérger (2004–2008), there were three police directors and three interior ministers; and during the presidency of Alvaro Colom (2008–2012), the pattern continued (WOLA 2009: 18).

Police brutality and criminality are also an issue. In the context of calls to purge the PNC, the country's human rights prosecutor (Procurador de los Derechos Humanos, PDH) stated that "53.44% of the violations of fundamental rights were committed by actors (elementos) in the PNC in 1999."[31] Off-duty police officers are also reportedly engaging in violent

---

[31] *Prensa Libre* 3.23.2000 Piden depuración de PNC.

crimes: a series of 2,000 newspaper articles reported on police involvement in attacking armored trucks (Santa Rosa), hold-ups (Petén), extortion (Petén), and carrying pistols even off duty.[32] Over the years, many articles have highlighted other cases of police complicity.[33]

Police crime and corruption, thus, is widespread and has sparked complaints lodged with the PDH and occasional purges (a pattern also found in the military) for crimes that included corruption, extortion, kidnapping, assault, drug trafficking, homicides, and rape.[34] Police involvement in crime, in fact, has been so pervasive that the national police created a unit (Unidad Multidisciplinaria) in 2005 to investigate these issues, with the director stating (aware of at least three "bandas" operating within the PNC) that "it is not anything new, and we know that we have to combat it."[35] Acknowledging the depth of the problem, then-chief of police Erwin Sperisen (the PNC director) indicated that 20 percent of PNC officers were involved in crime, leading to the dismissal of 500 agents in that year alone (reported in August 2005).[36] Disciplinary orders, problematic mindsets, and poor resources were also problems identified by the police chief.[37] Sperisen starkly noted the overall inability of the police to do its job. Low homicide clearance rates highlight the severity of the problem.

Let me give you but one clear example: in the United States, bank security experts tell banks that if they come to assault you, don't put up a fight, because there is a 98 percent change that the criminal group will be caught.

Here what they say is that you should not let them enter and that you should defend yourself in any way you can, because we are not going to catch them ... why? Because we do not have the tools, we are a police without resources. Tools don't only include people but also technology, legislation, and investment.[38]

---

[32] *Prensa Libre* 11.26.2000 Policías de día, pillos de noche. Also see the following *Prensa Libre* articles for reporting on similar sorts of incidents: 1.26.2000 Depurarán la PNC; 3.23.2000 Piden depuración de PNC; 4.15.2000 Siguen abusos de policías; 9.9.2000 Sindican a PNC en hechos criminales; 5.18.2000 Policía descarta "limpieza social."

[33] See, for example, www.prensalibre.com/pnc-esta-calada-por-criminalidad, August 17, 2015.

[34] See, for example, *Prensa Libre* 1.6.2005 Destituyen a 542 policías; 8.12.2005 Delinque el 20% de agentes de la PNC.

[35] *Prensa Libre* 7.11.2005 Siguen abusos de PNC en la capital; 7.26.2005 Investigan a policías por hechos delictivos; 7.24.2005 Capturan a banda de policías.

[36] *Prensa Libre* 8.12.2005 Delinque el 20% de agentes de la PNC.

[37] *Prensa Libre* 7.16.2005 Policía en democracia; 4.17.2005 Erwin Sperissen: "Una policía sin recursos."

[38] *Prensa Libre* 4.17.2005 Erwin Sperissen: "Una policía sin recursos." The Spanish quotation is: "Sólo le pongo un ejemplo claro: en Estados Unidos, los expertos en seguridad

Chief of Police Sperisen's comments are striking, given his own sordid trajectory. Appointed in 2004, Sperisen fled in 2007 to Switzerland, where he has dual citizenship. He in turn was arrested in Switzerland in 2012 for violent criminal acts, based on investigations by the UN-backed Comisión Internacional Contra la Impunidad en Guatemala (CICIG). He was charged with involvement in overseeing the 2006 extrajudicial killing of prisoners at El Pavón prison by security forces – reportedly to take the prison back from the gangs. However, CICIG also suggests that he was part of a criminal organization, along with former minister of the interior Carlos Vielman. Former prison service director Alejandro Giammattei was also implicated.[39]

The accused "formed part of a criminal organisation based in the interior ministry and civil police that was dedicated to extrajudicial executions of people detained in prisons," CICIG said in a statement. The group was also involved in other crimes including "murder, drug trafficking, money-laundering, kidnapping, extortion and the theft of drugs," it further alleged. Among the accused are the former interior minister Carlos Vielman and former prison service director Alejandro Giammattei – a losing candidate in the 2007 presidential election. The international commission against impunity in Guatemala was set up by the UN in 2006 to help Guatemala reform its justice system and confront organised criminal gangs that have infiltrated the state.[40]

In 2014, Sperisen was sentenced in Switzerland to life in prison for the extrajudicial killing of seven prisoners at El Pavón, although the CICIG report suspected high-level criminal activities across the board.[41]

The Guatemalan state, in short, has a police force that has proven incapable of policing itself and the territory that it is supposed to protect.

bancaria les dicen a los bancos que si llegan a asaltarlos no se opongan, pues hay un 98 por ciento de posibilidades de que se atrape a la banda. Aquí lo que les dicen es que no los dejen entrar y que se defiendan con lo que haga falta, porque no los vamos a agarrar ... ¿por qué?, porque no tenemos las herramientas, somos una Policía sin recursos. Las herramientas no sólo son personas, es la tecnología, la legislación, la inversión."

[39] BBC News, Latin America and Caribbean. "Switzerland Arrests Guatemala Ex-Police Chief Sperisen." www.bbc.co.uk/news/world-latin-america-19445049. Accessed August 18, 2013. Also see *El Periódico* 04.15.2013 Declaran testigos en caso contra Sperisen, Vielmann y Figueroa, www.elperiodico.com.gt/es/20130415/investigacion/226941/, accessed August 18, 2013, and *Prensa Libre* 6.12.2011 Cierran proceso contra el exministro Carlos Vielman, www.prensalibre.com/noticias/Cierran-proceso_0_604139597.html, accessed August 18, 2013.

[40] BBC News, Latin America and Caribbean. "Switzerland Arrests Guatemala Ex-Police Chief Sperisen." www.bbc.co.uk/news/world-latin-america-19445049. Accessed August 18, 2013.

[41] www.bbc.com, "Guatemala Ex-Police Chief Jailed for Life by Swiss Court." June 6, 2014. Accessed online February 19, 2015.

A senior Guatemalan official acknowledged the police force's problem with state weakness when the Ministerio de Gobernación identified fifty-eight municipalities as "ungovernable" or "without police presence" (UNODC 2012: 67, quotes in UNODC text). In short, while Guatemala's police force wields arms, it lacks the kind of organizational competence, territorial reach, professionalism, and integrity to maintain law and order across the country. While it polices in a post-military period, it has not developed the kind of democratic policing and capacity that one would have hoped with the transition to electoral rule and subsequent peace accords. Therefore, there has been latitude for illicit activity within its own ranks and among entrepreneurial actors eager to take advantage of illicit markets.

Indeed, illicit actors have little reason to believe that they will be held accountable for their violent actions. Guatemala's homicide clearance rate is shockingly low. Guatemala comes in at 7 percent compared to El Salvador's 44 percent, Nicaragua's 81 percent, and Costa Rica's 82 percent (UNODC 2007: 31–31). Actual conviction rates are presumably even lower, a point illustrated by UNODC (2012: 77) reporting, based on the UNODC Crime Trends Survey. Here we see strikingly low conviction rates in Guatemala (6 percent in 2009) and El Salvador (2 percent in 2006) compared to Costa Rica (46 percent in 2006) – calculated as convictions as a share of all cases brought before the court (UNODC 2012: 77).[42]

Low homicide clearance rates and poor investigation have also been noted with respect to concerns of femicide. In 2005, the Grupo Guatemalteco de Mujeres conducted a study of 160 murder cases against women and discovered incomplete recording of the crime and the victim, inadequate forensic work, and no suspects identified in nearly three-quarters of the cases studied.[43] The brutality of some of these murders against women is striking, as noted by an Amnesty International representative: "In addition to the death itself, the body of the victims show

---

[42] Interview with anonymous source from US embassy, August 4, 2006. This source also estimated that the prosecution rate is less than 3 percent (i.e., that less than 3 percent of 225,000 cases reach the public prosecutor's office/*ministerio público*); the source elaborated that less than 3 percent file formal complaints, and of these less than 1 percent are prosecuted. It was estimated that homicides have a resolution rate of less than 5 percent. While these numbers are not corroborated, they feed into the generalized sense among experts working in this area that the homicide clearance rate, the prosecution rate, and resolution are paltry.

[43] *Prensa Libre* 2.17.2005 Suspenden licencias para armas ofensivas.

signs of having been raped, tortured, mutilated and even quartered, which is inadmissible." Furthermore, the press reported that the state seems to have little interest in resolving these crimes, in some cases blaming the victims and their families.[44] In this context, there is little reason to believe that the police can/will deter illicit activity and/or hold the actors to account.

Iduvina Hernández of SEDEM cautions against blaming all problems on weak state capacity. She notes that the state sends the message that violence is tolerated, that there is no pursuit of criminal justice, and that there is no justice, but she observes that there is also, or primarily, a lack of will to change things. As an activist playing a lead role in promoting democratic security, she reminds us that there are opportunities to try to redress poor state capacity and turn things around – a point discussed in the conclusion of this book.[45]

Military and Police: Unclear Boundaries

The police's poor record is troubled, moreover, by poor role specification vis-à-vis the military. Formally, since the peace accords, the military and police are institutionally separate: military officers cannot command police units, and the police is not subordinate to the military institutional structure (Ruhl 2005: 74–75). In practice, however, the boundaries between these institutions are not always clear – not least since the military has ultimate authority to maintain Guatemala's internal security and military intelligence trains the police's criminal investigation service (Ruhl 2005: 74–75). According to WOLA, the police/military divide is often merged and the military has been brought in to redress citizen security issues – generally seen as a domestic situation that forms part of the police mandate – particularly since the police have proven incompetent. In March 2000, for example, then-president Portillo announced that the army would join the PNC in public security "due to the PNC's incapacity to confront organized crime and delinquency."[46] In response to concerns raised by civil society organizations, Portillo justified military involvement by pointing to the prevalence of international crime

---

[44] *Prensa Libre* 6.10.2005 Ni protección ni justicia. As if recalling Keck and Sikkink, the failure to solve some 580 cases of femicide led Amnesty International activists to protest in front of Guatemalan embassies across Europe: *Prensa Libre* 11.24.2005 Campaña contra feminicidio.
[45] Interview with Iduvina Hernández, July 2006.
[46] *Prensa Libre* 5.27.2000 Seguridad: preocupa a diputados participación militar.

organizations and drug trafficking: "Now it is not only a question of organized crime that is present in [se vive en] the country, but there is also international crime such as drug trafficking."[47] In June 2000, the press reported that the military had in fact been deployed, alongside the national police, the PNC, while the military's public relations department (Departamento de Divulgación del Ejército, DIDE) stated, in line with the defense minister's announcement, that it could deploy between 33 and 45 percent of each command to engage in patrolling. The PNC spokesperson explained that this was taking place in marginal areas in response to the gangs (referred to as *pandillas* in the article).[48]

The incorporation of the military is fraught – not least because the military itself is Janus faced when it comes to state capacity. Strikingly, while the military entered the democratic period with a powerfully coercive branch with a long history of human rights abuses,[49] the peace accords set out to reform the military and police in line with the demands of a democratic society.[50] Yet both institutions have been roundly criticized. Human rights abuses are still an issue, and impunity largely reigns.

---

[47] *Prensa Libre* 5.25.2000 Ejército dará seguridad ciudadana.
[48] *Prensa Libre* 6.18.2000 Seguridad: pobre inicio.
[49] The Guatemalan military governed (often very coercively) for most of the 1954–1985 period. It formally relinquished power in 1985 when President Vinicio Cerezo was elected. However, no one doubted that it maintained significant autonomy and authority over this very weak civilian president; human rights abuses continued, as did the civil war. The 1996 peace accords provided another formal change that reduced and constrained the military's power as it also ended the civil war that had raged for decades. Following the peace accords, institutional changes took place, although many former human rights abusers remained in office and/or maintained influence. Ruhl (2005: 68–69) recounts that President Portillo (the second president following the peace accords) reportedly was counseled by former military officers who had been identified with past human rights abuses (president of legislature General Ríos Montt and General Ortega Mendado) and alleged collaboration with the Moreno gang's criminal activities (General Ortega Menaldo, Colonel Jacobo Esdras Salán, and Major Napoleón Rojas – all of whom had been dismissed by the prior president for their alleged activities).
[50] For example, President Arzú asserted civilian control over the military as he took office and during the peace accords (in part because of a discredited military and increasing elite autonomy from it). Of the reforms implemented, reductions in military size and budget decreased by an estimated one-third, with the Congress gaining control over defense spending (Ruhl 2005: 60–61). Four military zones and thirty-five garrisons were closed (Ruhl 2005: 61), decreasing their bases in the countryside, and the president tried to decrease military jurisdiction by holding military men accountable in civilian courts – although the courts had not convicted any military officers of serious crimes before Ruhl's report was published (Ruhl 2005: 61, citing Spence 1998). However, many other substantive reforms did not take place, with the military still playing a key role in gathering domestic intelligence (as opposed to developing the primacy of a civilian intelligence agency) and keeping some military institutions intact (e.g., EMP). No civilian was

Charges of corruption, complicity, and incompetence, moreover, are pervasive. However, the military (including both active duty and retired military personnel) has remained largely immune from prosecution and has not been held accountable to the rule of law (Ruhl 2005: 77–78). Thus, while its brute force signaled strength, its conduct signified a riddled institution open to capture and profit seeking. Reports and purges highlight the pervasiveness of the corruption issues during this time (a possible legacy of the military period itself).[51] Discipline, accountability, and honesty have been severely lacking in the military. According to Ruhl (2005: 65, 79), the institution has been subordinated to civilian rule and yet sustains significant autonomies and immunities – including limited civilian involvement in, or supervision of, military affairs and lack of fiscal clarity or accountability (Ruhl 2005: 65). The administration of Oscar Berger, faced with this problematic situation, forced early retirement on 500 military officers and significantly reduced the size of the force to 15,500 (Ruhl 2005: 79–80). Even so, the military's integrity has consistently been called into question with charges of complicity and corruption.

Given this checkered history, it is striking that presidents have continued to rely on the military for domestic "security." It is not just that the military has consistently violated and stood above the rule of law but that it is also not trained to address domestic policing. Accordingly, some military officers stated that the military was not prepared to fight organized crime or delinquency and that they preferred to leave this responsibility to the police (Ruhl 2005: 67): "Most officers recognized that the army was untrained to combat either organized crime or common delinquency and viewed internal security work as a difficult and thankless task better left to the police."[52] Nonetheless, subsequent Guatemalan presidents have relied on the military to aid the police in the fight against organized crime and delinquency. Rather than restricting the military's role, in some cases presidents increased it; President Portillo, for example, expanded missions and increased the military budget beyond previously

---

named as defense minister, and human rights impunity remained an issue (see Ruhl 2005: 60–61, 79).

[51] Some suggest that this pattern of corruption predates the democratic period (Peacock and Beltrán 2003; Moran 2009: 9). Moran (2009: 9) argues: "During the period of internal conflict, the military regime in Guatemala relied more than the Salvadoran military on drugs and illicit activity to fund counterinsurgency activities."

[52] Ruhl (2005: 67), citing interviews with General Julio Balconi, former minister of national defense; General Marco Tulio Espinosa, former minister of national defense; and scholar Guillermo Pacheco. Also see Sieder et al. (2002: 41).

agreed-upon limits and at the expense of the military and other social agencies (Ruhl 2005: 71–72).

They [President Portillo and the FRG-dominated Congress] maintained all existing military missions and added many new ones. With crime levels still high, the president easily won congressional approval to keep the army in the streets to aid the new PNC. The PNC itself was removed from the control of ex-military officers only when Portillo replaced Interior Minister Arévalo Lacs with a civilian in July 2002, in response to wide criticisms of the ministry's militarization. In addition, Decree no. 40-2000 explicitly enlisted the armed forces' help to fight illegal trafficking in narcotics and arms and to protect Guatemala's forests and historic sites. The Portillo administration also used the military instead of less reliable civilian agencies to guard prison perimeters, deliver fertilizer and library books, vaccinate children, and improve school nutrition (MINUGUA 2002, 26–27), even though many officers found these duties unappealing. Retired minister of national defense Julio Balconi stressed that the armed forces never asked for any of these additional duties (*Prensa Libre* 2002e). Indeed, Portillo's ability to force unwanted civic action missions on the military was an indicator of how much the Guatemalan military had been subordinated to civilian political control. (Ruhl 2005: 71)

Thus, Guatemala's military started to patrol civilian tasks – a job generally seen as the professional responsibility of the police. President Berger, in fact, announced that the police patrols would be joined by an increased number of army personnel – with priority given to Guatemala City, Petén, Izabal, Zacapa, Santa Lucía Cotzumalguapa, San Marcos, and the borders – to guard against abuses. He noted that the human rights prosecutor's office, the PDH, would accompany the patrols.[53] As discussed in Chapter 6, this blurring of military-police lines also occurred in El Salvador as the government devised its strategy to deal with increased violence.

Even with increased military presence alongside the police, rule of law remains weak. Many urban areas, for example, are rife with crime, with many businesses and business owners (including vendors, taxis, restaurants, merchants, businesspeople, delivery services, etc.) indicating that they will no longer operate in those areas for fear of robbery, extortion, and even death. They fear that their collectors will be held up, and they also no longer extend credit to people living in certain *colonias* (city neighborhoods).[54]

---

[53] *Prensa Libre* 7.26.2005 Presentan nuevo plan de seguridad; 7.24.2005 Elaboran plan para combatir el crimen; 7.18.2005 Medidas contra la inseguridad.
[54] *Prensa Libre* 1.6.2000 Marginados por falta de seguridad; 8.28.2000 Inseguridad afecta servicios a domicilio: "En otros casos, los pilotos de las unidades se ven obligados a pagar 'impuesto' a maras para salir o entrar sin problemas a determinadas colonias."

The Judicial System

Weak police capacity also finds echo in a weak judicial system. While numbers increased for judges and courts (the number of judges doubled between 1994 and 1995, and over 100 new courts were created after the peace accords), institutional capacity remained compromised: insufficient budgets, low salaries, and incomplete training were all obstacles, as was minimal judicial independence and charges of complicity (Kitroeff 2011: 53, drawing on Sieder). Moreover, it is commonly recognized that the courts have been severely compromised by the inability of the state to protect judges, prosecutors, and witnesses (a point made by Ruhl 2005: 78 specifically when noting how difficult it has been to prosecute military men charged with past human rights abuses).

CICIG also documented the lack of state response to violent crimes: "Of some 50,000 crimes reported per month in 2010 only 429 were solved, resulting in an astonishing impunity rate of over 99 percent" (Kitroeff 2011: 7). These data coincide with a widespread perception that impunity remains high.[55] US Assistant Secretary of State for the Western Hemisphere Affairs Otto J. Reich testified before a congressional committee and indicated the following:

> there were increased signs of the participation of clandestine groups in illegal activities linked to employees of the Public Ministry, military intelligence, justice system, and police. These groups appear to act with relative autonomy, and while there was no evidence that they were part of government policy, they did operate with impunity. (quoted in Peacock and Beltrán 2003: 8)

The courts have also exhibited poor performance. One study finds a 10 percent response rate (of any kind) to cases reported to the judicial system in 2002 and hearings occurring in only 1 percent of cases of "crimes against life" in 2005.[56] Another estimate suggests that of 5,338 reported cases, only 115 successful murder prosecutions took place, which is just over 2 percent of cases. Researchers concluded: "In such a climate, the deterrent effect of the law is minimal" (UNODC 2007: 31). Even with the creation of a prosecutor's office for homicides (Fiscalía de Delitos contra la Vida) to address murders in the department of Guatemala (not including Mixco, Villa Nueva, San Juan Sacatepéquez,

---

[55] There are innumerable examples of concerns about impunity. For example, see *Prensa Libre* 1.6.2005 "Crímenes en la impunidad" and 5.18.2005 "Muertes, sin castigo."

[56] Levenson 2013: 49, citing S. Ramírez and Claudia Paz. 2002. *Diagnóstica de conflictividad local en la pos-guerra*. Guatemala City: Instituto de Estudios Comparados en Ciencias Penales de Guatemala.

and Amatitlán), there remained a paltry record; by mid-2005, charges were brought in less than 2 percent of the homicide cases in the department of Guatemala (40 out of 2,397, since the creation of the office), according to newspaper reporting.[57] With no capacity to protect witnesses, people would not testify, according to the prosecutor. "Let God be the one to judge, since I don't want to lose more children," said one victim's mother.[58] With such low performance rates, the courts and prosecutors were hardly serving justice or playing a deterrent role.

Other state and professional agencies have also commented on the prevalence of impunity in the court system. The human rights prosecutor, Sergio Morales, stated that only 1 percent of crimes were resolved (of the 64,000 crimes that were committed each year).[59] Of those crimes that were resolved, some complained that judges let the criminals go free.[60] The International Commission of Jurists (Comisión Internacional de Juristas, CIJ) also reported that the justice system was riddled with problems, including the lack of investigation, lack of process for appointing judges to cases, threats to judges, impunity, and near absence of sentencing (only 3 percent of complaints presented to the Ministerio Público, the public prosecutor's office, were taken as far as sentencing).[61]

Victoria Sanford's (2008) ethnographic work has highlighted how weak and complicit the judiciary is, providing virtual impunity for those who might be involved in crimes. Former Guatemalan president Portillo also commented on the weakness of the courts, their susceptibility to outside pressures, and the power of organized crime to constitute the primary threat to Guatemala's rule of law.[62] It is not just that there is intimidation

---

[57] *Prensa Libre* 5.18.2005 Muertes, sin castigo.
[58] *Prensa Libre* 5.18.2005 Muertes, sin castigo. Also see 10.14.2005 "Antejuicio por no investigar muertes" for a discussion of the lack of murder investigations and the formal complaint filed against the attorney general by longtime human rights activist Amílcar Méndez.
[59] *Prensa Libre* 8.14.2005 Sergio Morales: "Violencia es una amenaza." In this article, the reporter remarked, "Hay una percepción de la población de que la PDH defiende delincuentes," and the procurador replied that that is an understandable impression to have.
[60] *Prensa Libre* 2.15.2005 Preocupa libertad de delincuentes.
[61] *Prensa Libre* 8.6.2005 Justicia está en crisis. This point was also cited in an interview with an anonymous source from the US embassy, August 4, 2006.
[62] Portillo is reported to have said, "The application of justice ... has an intimate relationship with the processes for transformation of the state. Criminal organization, be it political or common, represents a parallel power to that of the state, and constitutes the principal threat of consolidating the democratic Rule of Law" (Peacock and Beltrán 2003: 41–43, quoting President Portillo in his January 14, 2000, inaugural address).

of the members of the courts; it is that they are bought off, as these quotes from Peacock and Beltrán (2003: 43) illustrate:

> After a visit to Guatemala, Param Cumaraswamy, the UN Special Rapporteur on the Independence of Judges and Lawyers, concluded that corruption, influence-peddling and their associated ills remain widespread, fed by the political factors which continued to influence the tenure, appointment and dismissal of judges. (Peacock and Beltrán 2003: 43)

> In March 2003, after an official visit to Guatemala, the InterAmerican Commission on Human Rights of the OAS noted that: "In Guatemala, the attacks on and threats to judicial officers, the existence of unlawful pressures and influences on judges, the insufficiency of resources, the lack of serious and timely investigation by the Public Ministry, in particular in cases of special importance ... are factors that contribute, among other things, to the widespread impunity that seriously affects the rule of law." (Peacock and Beltrán 2003: 43)

The legal process, moreover, is riddled with delays, poor judgment, and inefficiencies, and incapacity in one institutional domain affects others. After the police captured the head of drug trafficking operations for the Luciano Cartel (Sergio Arrivillaga Tánchez, alias Lencho) and confiscated 994 kilos of cocaine, for example, the courts let him go: "Escuintla's Attorney General did not present evidence, so the judge ordered that he be absolved."[63]

The scope of judicial incapacity is also highlighted by the difficulty of protecting judges and finding judges willing to serve in high-conflict areas. Judges are themselves victims of homicide, creating obvious challenges for those judges remaining on the bench or those asked to serve. Not only do many judges fear for their lives, but those overseeing high-profile cases find it difficult to issue rulings and sentences.[64] This has been a problem particularly in places holding trials for drug trafficking. In May 2005, for example, the assassination of a high court judge in Chiquimula made it

---

Portillo, in turn, was extradited in New York for taking bribes from Taiwan and attempting to launder the money through US banks. See BBC News. "Alfonso Portillo Jailed in US." May 22, 2014. Accessed online February 19,2015. Also "Guatemala: Ex-President sentenced," by Benjamin Weiser, *New York Times*, May 22, 2014. Accessed online February 19, 2015.

[63] See *Prensa Libre* 2.20.2000 Nuevas rutas de la droga and 8.27.2000 Guatemala es un buzón de drogas: "la Fiscalía de Escuintla no presentó las pruebas, por lo que el juez ordenó absolverlo."

[64] See, for example, articles in 2005 about murders in San Marcos and Chiquimula, respectively: *Prensa Libre* 4.27.2005 Jueces solicitan seguridad; 5.25.2005 Temor a ser juez en Chiquimula. Also see 5.19.2005 Jueces y fiscales ven mensaje en últimos atentados and 6.29.2005 Conocen amenazas de maras contra jueces.

difficult to fill the post, with four lawyers declining the request to serve.[65] A newspaper article highlighted how consequential and challenging this post, in particular, was given that it tries many high-profile cases (including drug trafficking charges) from the departments of Zacapa, Petén, and Izabal.[66] In light of the foregoing homicide data, we can see that these are also the departments with the highest death rates – demonstrating both high demand but also potentially high risk. This is illustrated further by the following quotes from judicial officials. The president of the Tribunal de Alto Impacto (court for serious crimes), Carlos Guillermo Sosa, remarked, "We give thanks because they have not captured the leaders of the drug cartels, because I doubt that anyone could protect us."[67] Solving cases and issuing sentences is thus more than a procedural act of justice; sometimes prosecutors and judges have themselves become victims in this process, and the police's low homicide clearance rate echoes the courts' limited ability to judge. Had we also looked at the Ministerio Público, interviews conducted in 2005 and 2006 suggest that we would have also found a situation of overworked and under-resourced staff, incompetence, and/or corruption.[68] As Mayra Alarcón, from the renowned Myrna Mack Foundation, stated regarding the state in general, "[T]here is no institutionalization ... No institutionality ... the message is that there is a lack of certainty regarding the value of the rule of law. There is a subliminal message of total, extrajudicial insecurity."[69] In this context, we should perhaps not be surprised by Celvin Galindo's declaration that "people in the Ministerio Público are afraid to talk."[70]

Prisons

Finally, the prison system is also notoriously weak, poorly managed, degrading, and corrupt. It also has among the most overcrowded prisons in the region, at nearly three times official capacity.[71] The infamous case of the Guatemalan police officers who not only killed the Salvadoran

---

[65] *Prensa Libre* 5.25.2005 Temor a ser juez en Chiquimula.
[66] *Prensa Libre* 5.25.2005 Temor a ser juez en Chiquimula.
[67] *Prensa Libre* 5.19.2005 Jueces y fiscales ven mensaje en últimos atentados.
[68] Interview with anonymous source from the US embassy, August 4, 2006.
[69] Interview with Mayra Alarcón, Myrna Mack Foundation, August 3, 2006.
[70] Interview with Celvin Galindo, Fiscal Jefe de la Fiscalía, August 2006.
[71] "Guatemala Prison Programs Rehabilitate 70% of Minors: Report," July 18, 2016, David Gagne, www.insightcrime.org/news-briefs/guatemala-prison-programs-rehabilitate-70-of-minors-report, citing work by the Institute for Criminal Policy Research and World Prison Brief: www.prisonstudies.org/country/guatemala

public officials traveling along the Pan-American Highway, but who were then themselves killed in the prison shortly after being placed there, highlights the weakness of state institutions and raises a host of unanswered questions about impunity, complicity, corruption, and crime.[72]

Stories of prison escapes, moreover, suggest the complicity of prison guards in illicit activity.[73] In one example, a high-security prison in Escuintla experienced a massive breakout in October 2005, with the escape of seventeen prisoners (most found guilty of homicide and kidnapping), according to *Prensa Libre* reporting. Following this breakout, the PDH attorney, Sergio Morales, said: "If before the justice system was on its knees, now, after the [prison] flight, it is on the ground."[74] He speculated that the police and military probably had prior knowledge of the escape plans.[75] Strikingly, even the prison guards' union called for the investigation of prison directors for illicit activity and escapes within prison walls: "[I]n many cases, they are the ones who approve the entry of arms, drugs and persons into the prisons, and they collaborate in the escapes."[76]

In addition, inmates often govern spaces within prison walls and reportedly can affect criminal behavior on the outside, through coordination of homicides, extortions, and kidnappings.[77] One of the most visible examples was reported in 2005, when the gang Mara Salvatrucha (MS) held forty-one prison guards hostage for six hours in El Boquerón prison; during this standoff, gang leaders made a number of demands, all of which were reportedly met by prison authorities – including the removal of a rival gang (Mara 18), new amenities (e.g., televisions and fans), and family and conjugal visits, among others.[78] Another high-profile violent incident at El Pavón prison led to over twenty-five injured and at least twelve dead – including Byron Lima, an ex-army captain convicted of

---

[72] See Levenson (2013: 123) for a version of these events within the prison system.
[73] *Prensa Libre* 1.12.2000 reports on a prison escape of eleven inmates (some very high profile) in El Preventivo prison, in Zone 18. *Prensa Libre* reports other incidents in 2005.
[74] *Prensa Libre* 10.26.2005 Piden seguridad para jueces y magistrados; 2005.10.25 Víctimas están atemorizadas. The quote read, "Si antes el sistema de justicia estaba de rodillas, ahora, después de la fuga, está por el suelo."
[75] *Prensa Libre* 10.26.2005 Piden seguridad para jueces y magistrados; 2005.10.25 Víctimas están atemorizadas.
[76] *Prensa Libre* 2.23.2000 Vigilarán penales.
[77] *Prensa Libre* 2.11.2000 Amenazas de reos provocan renuncia. In another article, there are reports that the banda Los Pasaco planned kidnappings from inside the prison; 2.11.2000 Amenazas de reos provocan renuncia.
[78] *Prensa Libre* 10.29.2005 Salvatruchas con el control.

killing Bishop Juan Gerardi (following the release of a report highlighting government human rights abuses). Notable here, not only was this violent incident an example of poor state control of the prison system, but it also revealed that Byron Lima was presumed to command great power within the prison system itself. This power included command over gang members, drug traffickers, and other criminals, and Lima was believed to recruit some criminals into his army while also providing services to others. He maintained important ties to top government officials and those operating the prison system and also wielded control over prison economies, extorted goods from jailed drug traffickers, and apparently controlled freedom of movement and protection (e.g., there were reported cases of prisoners partying in Guatemala City).[79]

In short, Guatemala's prison system demonstrates not only low capacity but also low performance. Rather than contain and deter crime, it seems to provide a space for gangs and others to operate. Examples of drug lords and gang leaders controlling prisons – even forming "committees of order and discipline," sometimes with the apparent collaboration of prison guards, is reported in Levenson (2013: chapter 4, especially pages 112–113).

Revisiting State Complicity and Corruption

In short, weak state capacity in law-and-order institutions such as the police, the military, the courts, and prisons has created a propitious context for the growth of illicit actors and their activity. This includes illicit action within the state. We know that former and current military officials have themselves become involved in illicit activity. During the civil war, military officers, among others, not only became vested in the formal economy (the military had its own bank, which was subsequently absorbed by the Banco del Crédito Hipotecario Nacional in the early 2000s) but also started to engage in organized crime – including arms, human, and car trafficking (Peacock and Beltrán 2003; and Kitroeff 2011: 49).

A weak police force and court system has provided ample grounds for the military to become involved in organized crime. MINUGUA human rights reports, WOLA publications (various, including those of Peacock and Beltrán), and the Myrna Mack foundation have all reported on this

---

[79] The 2016 uprising was reported by Steven Dudley. "'King' of Guatemala Inmates, Byron Lima is Killed in Prison." *InSight Crime*. July 18, 2016. www.insightcrime.org/news-analysis/king-of-guatemala-inmates-capt-byran-lima-is-killed-in-prison.

problem. Peacock and Beltrán (2003: 1 and passim) called this phenomenon "hidden powers," which "refers to an informal, amorphous network of powerful individuals in Guatemala who use their positions and contacts in the public and private sectors to enrich themselves from illegal activities.[80] Moreover, these hidden powers (not all of which are in the state) actually call the shots and have done so for decades ... "[81] They note, in addition, that counterinsurgent groups from earlier periods merged with organized crime; this reporting draws on a 2002 Hemisphere Initiatives report (Peacock and Beltrán 2003: 35). They state that General Luis Francisco Ortega Menaldo (who worked in the Public Finance Ministry for military intelligence and later was subdirector and then director of army intelligence and was head of the presidential general staff, EMP, in the early 1990s) was involved in drug trafficking along with his peers. While the US Drug Enforcement Agency had worked with him, the US government later revoked his visa for having allowed or conspired in drug trafficking (Peacock and Beltrán 2003: 16–17). Ortega's associate Colonel Jacobo Esdras Salán Sánchez was also reported, when he was involved in counternarcotic operations, to have goods that had been confiscated from drug traffickers; he was later investigated for involvement with organized crime (Peacock and Beltrán 2003: 37–38).

The depth of organized crime penetration of the state is further highlighted by Central American scholar Ralph Lee Woodward's observation that during the administration of Colom, there were listening devices found in the president's office:

Government efforts to reduce the high rates of violent crime were hampered by the degree to which organized crime and drug traffickers had infiltrated law enforcement. In September, Colom fired his security chief after discovering seven unauthorized listening devices and cameras in the presidential office and residence; the surveillance presumably had been engineered by organized crime."[82]

---

[80] One of these corrupt networks has historical roots and was developed in the 1970s by Alfredo Moreno Molina: "Over time he built and oversaw an illegal network involving personnel at different border crossing points. He developed a contraband operation that implicated the courts, the national police, the treasury police, the Public Ministry, the army, and the Public Finance Ministry, according to Peacock and Beltrán (2003: 29). Court records show that this group thought that it could act with impunity; indeed, it has (Peacock and Beltrán 2003: 29–32).

[81] While the book lacks systematic evidence to substantiate links between particular officers and illicit crime, the general phenomenon is recognized to exist by both UN agencies and local human rights organizations.

[82] Cited in *Encyclopedia Britannica* (2008). "Guatemala: Year in Review." Accessed online at www.britannica.com/EBchecked/topic/1493276/Guatemala-Year-In-Review-2008?anchor=ref1014352 August 8, 2013.

US officials have also expressed concerns about the rising prevalence of drug trafficking (either with ties to the government and/or limited state efforts to combat it).[83] For example, concerns were raised by Paul E. Simons (Acting Assistant Secretary of the Bureau of International Narcotics and Law Enforcement Affairs), Dan Fisk (State Department Deputy Assistant Secretary for Western Hemisphere Affairs, and President George W. Bush in 2003 (Peacock and Beltrán 2003: 65–67). Simons, for example, stated the following in 2002 before the Subcommittee on the Western Hemisphere of the House International Relations Committee of the US Congress:

Narcotics trafficking ... money laundering and organized crime are on the increase in Guatemala. Some of the leaders of these activities have very close ties to the president and regularly influence his decisions, especially with respect to personnel nominations in the military and ministry of government. (Peacock and Beltrán 2003: 65)

In short, state weakness and complicity have been endemic in Guatemala's law-and-order institutions – as well as among the highest elected offices – and have continued, even with the transition to electoral politics. As Karin Wagner from the research think tank ASIES noted when talking about law and order in Guatemala, "There is no respect for institutions."[84]

In this context of weak rule of law, communities have occasionally assumed the mandate to restore "order" and mete out "justice." Reports and studies refer to extrajudicial killings as one response.[85] The formation of community-based security organizations is another response.[86] By 2000, newspaper reporting on neighborhood watches and citizen security committees increased. But assessments remained mixed. Some of these community organizations seemed to be forged with the state, others independently by the community. Reporting in 2005 of these community responses continued, with some communities and organizations praising their impact in lowering crime and others concerned about possible (or actual) abuses. These groups were suspected of several

---

[83] Interview with anonymous source from US embassy, August 4, 2006.
[84] Interview with researcher, Karin Wagner, ASIES, August 3, 2006.
[85] Angelina Snodgrass Godoy. *Popular Injustice: Violence, Community, and Law in Latin America*. Stanford University Press, 2006.
[86] *Prensa Libre* 5.16.2000 Comités de seguridad crean temor entre indígenas; 5.29.2000 Juntas de seguridad en Quiché. The latter article reports that the police-organized *comités de seguridad* in Zacualpa, Quiché, and Rabinal, Baja Verapaz, led to indigenous group protests for fear of the much-maligned civil defense patrols (*patrullas de autodefensa civil*, PACs) of the past – community-organized Juntas Locales de Seguridad (JLS) in Quiché.

extrajudicial actions, including killing suspects, forcing young people to strip in order to show their tattoos, making tattooed persons wash graffiti off of walls, and charging residents who did not participate in the security committees.[87] In some cases, community members patrolling the streets were armed and wore ski masks, raising concerns about accountability.[88] In this regard, community policing has not been a substitute for an effective police force.[89]

ILLICIT ACTORS, POLITICAL ECONOMIES, AND ORGANIZATIONAL TERRITORIAL COMPETITION

Given Guatemala's weak state capacity, it is no surprise that state and non-state actors would take advantage of these permissive conditions to pursue profit and power in the illicit economy. During the third wave of democracy, two patterns have emerged, each contributing to the spike in violence that has occurred. As discussed next, Guatemala has provided auspicious territory both for the expansion of the trade and transit of illicit goods (especially drugs) and for gang activity (partially based on extortion). I discuss each in turn.

Trade and Transit of Drugs

Illicit activity is pervasive in Guatemala's political economy. Guatemala has emerged as a key hub of the trade and transit of drugs, with illicit activity especially along its borders and at its ports. "When it comes to Central American cocaine trafficking, all roads lead to Guatemala" (UNODC 2012: 39). As discussed in earlier chapters, and addressed by

---

[87] *Prensa Libre* 7.28.2005 Medidas preventivas.
[88] For example, of 2005 reporting on these neighborhood organizations, see *Prensa Libre* 7.27.2005 Rechaza patrullaje; 2.14.2005 Vecinos se unen a PNC para evitar robos; 6.28.2005 Capitalinos se unen contra la delincuencia; 3.17.2005 Noticias en corto; 3.3.2005 Quetzaltecos patrullan calles ante inseguridad; 4.28.2005 Vecinos se encapuchan; 7.8.2005 Rondas de vecinos reduce violencia; 4.10.2005 Buscan imitar plan de seguridad ciudadana; 6.25.2005 Maras accionan en Antigua Guatemala; 6.24.2005 Vecinos forman su propia policía; 11.15.2005 Alianza por la seguridad; 3.16.2005 Crearán policía comunitaria; 6.3.2005 Inseguridad une a vecinos; 8.13.2005 Propuestas para mejorar seguridad; 9.24.2005 Vecinos contra el crimen; 7.27.2005 Piden a PNC que no los deje solos; 10.29.2005 Policías de confianza; 7.7.2005 Municipios sin protección; 7.28.2005 Medidas preventivas; 7.17.2005 Delincuencia divide a los vecinos; 7.26.2005 Abusos de Junta de Seguridad; 7.27.2005 Dar seguridad no es función de vecinos.
[89] See Yanilda González, PhD dissertation (2014), for more information about different forms of policing and community participation.

other scholars, drug trafficking became particularly salient following the crackdown in Caribbean routes (which had been dominated by Colombian DTOs). At that point, DTOs needed to find new geographic routes to move drugs northward toward the United States market. DTOs diverted drug shipments from the Caribbean to Central America. In that process, Guatemala became particularly important – not only because of geographic proximity but also because weak state capacity provided permissive conditions for DTOs to move their product with minimal state intervention, state complicity, and/or impunity. Mexican organizations, in particular, took advantage of this situation to dominate transit corridors in Guatemala. Extant organizations assumed increasingly active roles in helping move drugs northward following the switch from the Caribbean to Central America, while Mexican DTOs increasingly turned south as the Mexican government cracked down on the dominant kingpins.[90] By 2012, the Cartel del Pacífico (an alliance between the Sinaloa federation and the Gulf Cartel),[91] in competition with the Zetas (originally the armed wing of the Gulf Cartel, before it broke off), was increasingly visible in Guatemala (López 2012; UNODC 2012: 22–23).[92] One intrepid Salvadoran reporter reports one version of how and why the Zetas ended up in Guatemala, arguing that their presence "shattered criminal stability in Guatemala":

There was a time when Guatemalan drug traffickers lived under a pact of mutual respect. A time when you could still count on one hand the number of black sheep who would break that pact. One of these black sheep proposed that a drug family contact a hit man from a Mexican cartel expanding control throughout the country.

---

[90] Some 50,000, organized crime–related deaths in Mexico were recorded from December 2006 to October 2011 (Guerrero 2012).

[91] The Sinaloa "cartel" has a longstanding role in drug production and trafficking – including cannabis, heroin, and methamphetamine. It's involvement in trafficking cocaine came later. Since Sinaloa does not border the United States, it had to create alliances with other DTOs to move the drugs north – leading to the Cartel del Pacífico in the mid- to late 2000s (UNODC 2012: 22–23).

[92] Honduras's role has also increased, especially for smuggling by air (with some three quarters of all planes smuggling cocaine out of South America first landing in Honduras, according to *Latin News*, June 2014, Honduras "In Vicious Cycle," accessed July 11, 2014). This same report cites the US State Department's 2014 International Narcotics Control Strategy Report (INCSR), which is quoted as saying, "'The Caribbean coastal region of Honduras is a primary landing zone for drug-carrying flights and maritime traffic. The region is vulnerable to narcotics trafficking due to its remoteness, limited infrastructure, lack of government presence and weak law enforcement institutions. Drug trans-shipment to points north from the Caribbean coastal region is facilitated by subsequent flights north as well as by maritime and riverine traffic and land movement on the Pan American Highway,' notes the INCSR" (*Latin News*, June 2014, Honduras "In Vicious Cycle," accessed July 11, 2014).

Intelligence officers, soldiers, workers inside the world of narcotrafficking, as well as a controversial declaration of a state of emergency, all point to the single factor that shattered criminal stability in Guatemala: los Zetas. (Martínez 2016: 43)

In these initial years organized crime tended to lay claim to distinct geographic spaces. According to Martínez (2016: 46), old families had been engaging in lower levels of trafficking since the 1970s. However, as hypothesized in Part I of this book, high violence emerged precisely where organizations competed for territorial control, which arguably occurred most intensely in prized areas along the coasts and borders, as well as in capitals. Indeed, a UNODC 2012 report comes to similar conclusions. I first lay out the UNODC findings, followed by newspaper reports gathered as part of the newspaper database collected for this book.

UNODC found that drug trafficking organizations could be found in many parts of the country – as noted in the quote and figures (Figure 5.4) that follow – but that violence peaked along borders, at ports, and on roadways, where competition to control drug trafficking areas has been the most intense (UNODC 2012: 39, 66–67).

[T]he country has been divided cleanly between supply routes to the Cartel del Pacífico, which remains close to the Pacific coast and depart the country primarily from San Marcos, and those that supply the other groups, which skirt the north of the country and leave through Petén. (UNODC 2012: 39)

Broad swathes of land in the southwest of the country (where the *Cartel del Pacífico* and their allies, the Chamales, operate) and in the interior provinces of Alta and Baja Verapaz (area of influence of the Zetas) have very little violence. The most troubled areas in Guatemala appear to be along the borders with Honduras and El Salvador, areas that could be contested by *Cartel del Pacífico* ally *Los Mendozas* and Zetas ally *Los Lorenzanas*. (UNODC 2012: 66–67)

If we compare the GIS homicide rate maps generated for this book with the UNODC maps showing areas where illicit territorial groups operate, the correspondence is suggestive (see Figure 5.4).

Over time, however, these distinctly controlled geographies became increasingly contested, not least as Mexican DTOs sought to extend control and undermine competing trafficking presence in prime territory, including border areas. Indeed, with the influx of cocaine, one finds the realignment of Mexican DTOs (which affected the alliances within Guatemala as well) and the increasing presence of the Zetas in trying to control part of the route from the Honduran border to Mexico (through

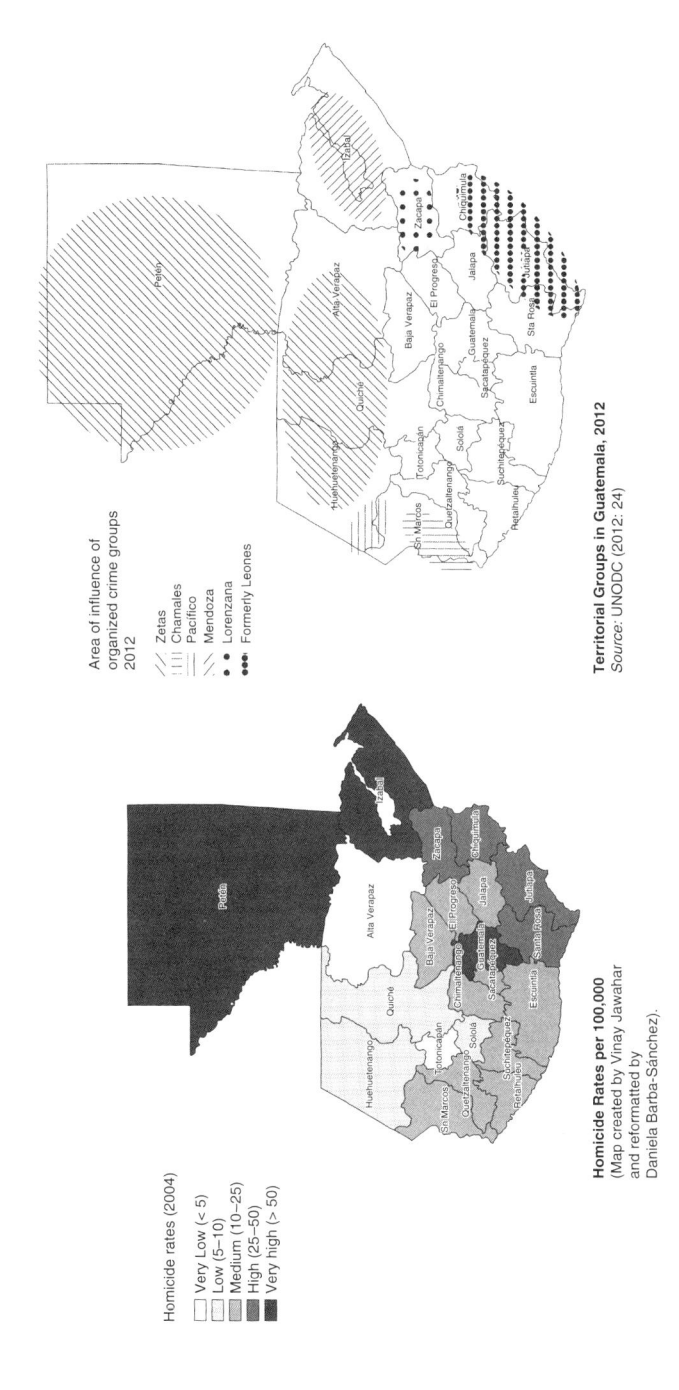

FIGURE 5.4 Comparing geographies in Guatemala: homicide rates, organized crime groups, and prime drug trade routes
Map 1: Guatemala's regional homicide rates, 2004 (Source: see Figure 5.3)
Map 2: Territoriality of organized crime groups in Guatemala (Source: UNODC 2012:24)
Map 3: Cocaine trafficking routes in Guatemala (Source: UNODC 2012:38) (see next page).

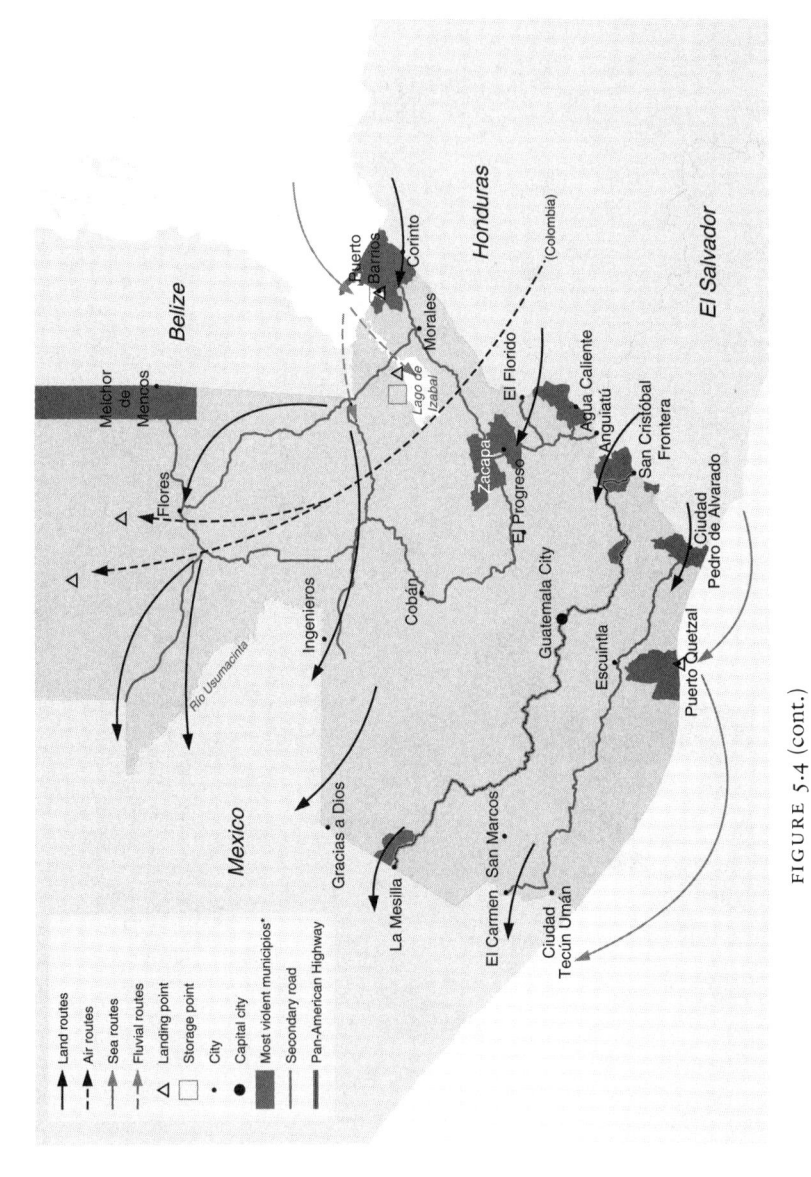

FIGURE 5.4 (cont.)
Map 3: Cocaine trafficking routes in Guatemala
Source: (UNODC (2012: 38)

Cobán)[93] and perhaps later the east coast as well (UNODC 2012: 39). "The Zetas and Sinaloa cartel in particular have linked up with domestic illegal security groups to infiltrate security and judicial bodies at both the local and national levels. They are estimated to have assumed control of over 30,000 acres in the northern departments of Petén, Izabal, and Chiquimula" (Kitroeff 2011: 57, drawing on Brands 2010).

In 2012, Guatemala had "at least four major borderland territory-bound organized crime groups" that were staking out particular geographies (UNODC 2012: 23). I will now summarize these UN findings (which are corroborated in some cases by Mendoza 2016).

First, the Mendoza family reportedly operates in the northeast, in the Izabal Province, on the border with Honduras. This is prime geography since one of Guatemala's most important ports (Puerto Barrios) is located on this coast (where one could receive/send maritime shipments). Moreover, the most direct line from Honduras to Mexico (via the Petén) goes through this region. The Mendoza family's presence predates the cocaine boom through Central America, as they have been cattle ranchers with sizable landholdings and reportedly oversee an interplay of licit and illicit businesses (UNODC 2012: 23–25; Martínez 2016: 48). There were, moreover, shifting alliances with the Mexican DTOs, with the Mendozas and the Mexican Gulf Cartel becoming allies in the illicit trade and transit of cocaine.

The Mendozas had been traditional allies of the Gulf Cartel, transporting cocaine northward to the east coast of Mexico, the Gulf's area of influence, while groups allied with the former "Sinaloa Cartel" were trafficking along the west coast. After the Zetas split from the Gulf Cartel, the Mendozas, became their enemy, and the Zetas formed an alliance with the Lorenzanas. As the Gulf began to lose its influence further south, the Mendozas allied with the "Federation." (UNODC 2012: 24)

The Zetas are also reported to have created their operational base in the Alta Verapaz region, which borders Izabal and Petén – both states along the corridor to Mexico – thus positioning them to control traffic to the Petén. This was reported to have also been the center of Central American operations (Martínez 2016: 50): "Alta Verapaz is the bottleneck on the way to Petén ... Alta Verapaz has also traditionally been the main trafficking hub for both weapons and drugs. It's almost impossible to reach Petén without passing through Alta Verapaz, which is only a three-hour drive from

---

[93] The route from Honduras to Petén (which borders Mexico) can only pass through one of two cities: Cobán, Alta Verapaz, or near Morales, Izabal) (UNODC 2012: 39).

Guatemala City" (Martinez 2016: 50). UNODC maps the Zetas's presence as extending beyond Alta Verapaz (see Figure 5.4, Map 2).

Second, in the east, in the department of Zacapa (south of Izabal), a second group operates: the Lorenzanas. They have been involved in longstanding trafficking of illicit goods since the 1990s and have some interest in the Verapaces – both Baja (low) and Alta (high) – as well as the Petén (UNODC 2012: 23, 25; Martínez 2016: 48). As noted in the previous quote, they have had alliances with the Zetas.

Third, along the Salvadoran border zone, Los Leones were involved in trafficking. However, they were less successful and turned to robbing other cocaine shipments (an activity referred to as *tumbador*). Los Leones originally had an alliance with the Gulf Cartel in cocaine trafficking, but at the time of this writing, the alliance has ceased to exist, with the Zetas filling the resulting vacuum in this southern region (UNODC 2012: 24).

Fourth, in the southeast corner, the Chamales operate in the province of San Marcos. This is also prime geography, as it borders the Pacific coast and Mexico, and the Chamales have long been involved in "smuggling people, foodstuffs, subsidized Mexican petrol, and other goods" (UNODC 2012: 24). However, the Chamales have since moved into other kinds of drug trafficking. Reportedly, there is virtually no police presence or other active opposition to them (UNODC 2012: 25). UNODC (2012) highlights how tricky it is to map a fixed geography – not least because there have been shifting alliances – both between groups and within Mexican DTOs. The Zetas, for example, had been the coercive branch of the Gulf Cartel but broke off from the latter in 2010. So too the Gulf Cartel has allied with the Sinaloan Federation (forming the Cartel del Pacífico), some would argue as a counterweight to the growing prevalence of the Zetas. While foreign DTOs have tended to work by proxy, it seems that the Zetas have a physical presence in the Guatemalan territory, as reported by UNODC (2012: chapter 2) and Martínez (2016: chapter 3) and as depicted in the second map reproduced in Figure 5.4.[94] Indeed,

---

[94] Martínez (2016: chapter 3) narrates that the Zetas were initially invited in 2008 by two drug families (the Lorenzanas and the Mendozas) that wanted to settle a score with a thieving Guatemalan who was stealing drugs, even though he reportedly worked for the Lorenzanas. Martínez concludes that this gave the Zetas an entrée into Guatemala, and with their recent break from the Gulf Cartel, they were primed to look for new opportunities to stay. With a prior reputation for violence, the Zetas's presence is reported to have broken the fragile pact between the families. Like the other drug families, the Zetas are known to have developed strong ties with local politicians and police in Alta Verapaz,

some former members of the Kaibiles (perhaps the most coercive military group during Guatemala's military period) were reportedly recruited to Mexico when the group first started off.

The UNODC's overview of DTOs and territorial strongholds echoes reporting in the Guatemalan newspaper *Prensa Libre*. In one such case, an article notes "cartels" in Sayaxché (Petén), the Golfo in Izabal and Zacapa, the cartel "Luciano" in the south, and a narcomilitary cartel in the center of the country.[95] A public prosecutor for drug activity in the southwestern part of the country (Fiscal de Narcoactividad del Suroccidente del País), Felipe Pérez Santos, stated in a 2005 interview that "Guatemala has converted itself into a mailbox (buzón) for drugs."[96] News reporting on the prevalence of crimes (including drug trafficking, traffic of women, carjacking, and kidnapping), observed that drug trafficking was particularly prominent to the north and east of Guatemala City.[97] Organized crime has become so prevalent that it was reportedly earning around 10 percent of Guatemala's gross domestic product, a figure that included drug trafficking, kidnapping, extortion, and vehicle theft, according to reports in a UNDP analysis.[98]

El Petén is geographically critical because it borders Mexico. It is here that the factors highlighted in this book are arguably most apparent. It is also here that homicide rates are critically high, despite the fact that the region has low density and is forested. The drug families and DTOs just outlined arguably all have a stake and presence in this region – smuggling drugs, and other goods, northward. The state presence is low and corrupt, and state efforts to contain drug flows target the weakest link (rather than the most significant actors in the business), according to Martínez (2016: 61, chapter 4). Indeed, some of the controlling families reportedly own large landholdings and use the protected lands for drug operations

in a state that is otherwise lacking state presence: "Alta Verapaz had been so abandoned that even the state-owned runway was left to Los Zetas. There was no air traffic controller, no scheduled flights and no record of who would pilot which plane at what time. Sometimes Los Zetas even used the runway for their monster car shows, their horse races and parties. For all practical purposes, the runway was theirs to use as they pleased" (Martínez 2016: 56–57).

[95] See *Prensa Libre* 2.20.2000 Nuevas rutas de la droga; 8.27.2000 Guatemala es un buzón de drogas.
[96] *Prensa Libre* 8.27.2000 Guatemala es un buzón de drogas.
[97] *Prensa Libre* 7.7.2005 Municipios sin protección. Also see *Prensa Libre* 3.11.2005 "Escuintlecos demandan seguridad," in which three mayors in Escuintla identify drug trafficking, kidnapping, and assaults on trucks as significant issues in the department.
[98] *Prensa Libre* 1.28.2010 Ganancias del crimen equivalen al 10% del PIB en Guatemala.

(Martínez 2016: 69–71, discussing the 2011 report *Power Brokers in Petén: Territory, Politics and Business*, which the author corroborated by analyzing publicly registered cadastres and other official and international reports, alongside interviews and testimonies). "Narco land reaches all the way to the Mexican border, to the Usumacinta River. 'Each property,' according to the report, 'is equipped with armed guards'" (Martínez 2016: 71).

Petén has become a sort of condominium for the big families of organized crime. The Mendozas aren't the only ones in the limelight. The Leóns, originally from Zacapa, a state bordering Honduras, own 316 caballerías in Petén that are nestled, so the report explains, "in strategic places along the drug route." The Lorenzanas, also from Zacapa, own four ranches within the nationally protected park of Laguna del Tigre. One of these ranches – proof of the broken system – was openly registered under the name of the family patriarch, Waldemar Lorenzana, who in 2011 was extradited to the United States for drug-trafficking charges.

The report concludes that the property linked to organized crime groups reaches a four-digit figure: 1,179 caballerías. (Martínez 2016: 71–71)

Drug trafficking was able to expand in Petén and elsewhere because the police had low capacity (from low resources, to complicity, to corruption). Residents often noted the low ratio of police in the region (although, given Nicaragua's low police presence, numbers cannot be the whole story); they also remarked on state complicity in numerous newspaper accounts. Reporting on Escuintla included quotes from anonymous residents and civil society organizations that emphasized that crime was taking place "under the shadow (bajo la sombra) of the police – in some cases with the police arriving to receive their cut."[99] The paper included various reports of police and military complicity in crimes, including those related to drug trafficking.[100] Three major drug dealers who were extradited to the United States between 2012 and 2014 (Walter Overdick in 2012, Waldemar Lorenzana in 2014, and Juan Alberto Ortiz López in 2014) did not even have a record in Guatemala at the time they left the country (Martínez 2016: 158), highlighting the impunity with which they operated in Guatemala. Reporting on the corruption and blind eye of the police and elected officials, Martínez (2016: chapter

---

[99] *Prensa Libre* 3.11.2005 Escuintlecos demandan seguridad. Also see 4.12.2005 "Escalada de violencia en Escuintla," for reporting of a slow police response to a man's death, even though it took place in a store across the street from the station.

[100] For example, see *Prensa Libre* 8.24.2005 Muertes por venganza de narcos; 11.21.2005 Nexos entre militares y narcotraficantes.

9, esp. 162) reports that the police has largely only moved on DTO leaders when pressed by the United States and/or when these leaders overstepped certain boundaries with the police (e.g., a massacre of police officers); otherwise, impunity has been the norm. And when these DTO heads have been targeted, the businesses remain – often with more atomized organizations in place.

The presence of illicit activity creates fertile ground for violence but on its own does not explain the high homicidal violence that has occurred. As discussed in Chapter 3, violence is costly and usually a last resort. That said, drug trafficking is particularly prone to violence because the high profits tend to generate competition and ambition to expand geographies of control. Citing Cuevas and Demombynes's 2009 econometric study, the World Bank reports: "Drug trafficking is an important driver of homicide rates. Within any one country, controlling for other factors, drug-trafficking hot spots have murder rates more than double those in areas of low trafficking intensity; in this case hot spots refers to locations with high levels of confiscation" (World Bank 2010, volume 1: 21).[101] Similarly, UNODC (2012: 37) notes that with Honduras serving as the "single most popular point of entry for cocaine headed northward into Guatemala, the border between these two countries is particularly dangerous."

Some of the most dangerous places in Central America lie in a swath running between the northwestern coast of Honduras and southwestern coast of Guatemala. There are hundreds of informal border crossing points between the two countries, but, due to corruption and complicity, it appears that most cocaine crosses at the official checkpoints, such as Copán Ruinas/El Florido (CA-11). Municipalities on both sides of the border are afflicted with very high murder rates, which is peculiar given that these are mostly rural areas. Given the competition between groups allied with the Zetas and the *Cartel del Pacífico*, it is highly likely that these deaths are attributable to disputes over contraband and trafficking routes. (UNODC 2012: 37)

Violence has escalated particularly where there has been competition to control these territorial regions.

---

[101] Importantly, this measure conflates high-level drug flows with state confiscation. This book suggests that if the former occurs without the latter and without other forms of competition, homicidal violence is in fact likely to be low, all things being equal. This is because it is the *competition* to control the drug routes that ultimately drives actors to resort to the extraordinary high levels of violence.

Gangs

The geography of violence has been significantly shaped by the presence and competition of organized crime. DTOs, in particular, have clearly contributed to the high-violence patterns. Yet they do not operate alone. They have penetrated the state, which is sometimes a partner in crime. In turn, gangs have emerged as the urban and youth counterpart to this violent pattern in Guatemala. As noted by Ranum (2011: 71), the gangs are thus not the cause of all violence but are part of a complex and broader dynamic of weak state institutions and pervasive crime problems; the contemporary gangs have developed in a context of "institutional weakness, inequality, and an uncertain separation between the legal and illegal spheres."

Gangs are not new to the country, although their current form certainly is.[102] Minor youth gangs are reported as early as the 1940s or 1950s; boys and young men occasionally committed petty crimes and took part in gang brawls, but they were not violent, territorial organizations known for killing and dominating neighborhoods (Ranum 2011: 72; Levenson 2013: 32). Little is reported on gangs during the long civil war in Guatemala; the youth were often portrayed as taking part in other kinds of movements, including student associations, trade unions, and other social and revolutionary movements (Levenson 2013: 32 and passim). They became more visible in the mid-1980s as associations that gathered youth, although it was not clear at that point that they would become violent collective actors dominating certain urban spaces and deploying violence to defend their turf against rival gangs. This section outlines this move from youth gangs in the mid-1980s to violent *maras*.

In 1985, gangs emerged publicly when they protested the rise in bus fare, alongside other students, but at this point they were not violent organizations known for killing (Levenson 2013: 3, 34). While the youth gangs of the 1980s were often portrayed by the state and the media alike as threats, Levenson (2013: introduction and chapters 1–2) emphasizes that these early youth groups were often composed of young boys and girls who were seeking community and support at a time of great political upheaval (also see Ranum 2011). In the context of the violent civil war that killed and tortured so many, Guatemala City became home to many more families, widows, and orphans, some of whom had

---

[102] Levenson (2013) and interview with anonymous source in the US embassy (August 4, 2006).

migrated from the countryside and had experienced unimaginable atrocities. The gang members that Levenson interviewed in the mid-1980s were often articulate and seeking a social community/family but also defended their thieving as justified in a context of great economic injustice. She reminds the reader that the youth were born into violence, but one in which the military was gaining the upper hand in the civil war and the social and revolutionary movements were declining in strength. The violent context included a politically violent civil war, a weak economy (which would be wracked by neoliberal policies), a weak justice system, a corrupt and vicious state, and a declining but memorable social justice framework. Youth sought community and belonging through friends, support, fun such as breakdancing, and refuge. Some sixty youth gangs existed by 1987, with a range of different names (Levenson 2013: 56).[103] Levenson's earlier 1987 work with AVANCSO in the 1980s and her 2013 book found that these same young people were seeking family, acceptance, affirmation, community, empowerment, self-esteem, and fun, among other things; they had a certain group consciousness that still used class-based language to justify some of their actions (Levenson 2013: chapter 2). Over time, these young people came to dominate and defend certain territories, especially in Guatemala City, which fueled gang rivalries – although these were not particularly violent in these early years (Ranum 2011: 73). These early gangs "were rich in life, ambiguities, creativities, and contradictions, and they had the possibility of developing in different directions, for better or worse" (Levenson 2013: 75). The youth groups became known as *pandillas*.

The *pandillas*, or gangs, did not remain the groups just described. They transformed into *maras*, which are more structured, extractive, and violent organizations that have come to dominate certain geographies (particularly urban ones). The older *pandillas* were commonly described as tied to the community, even protecting it. During my early research, I was often told that it was better to have a gang than not, since gangs had been in the business of protecting local communities (tied as they were to the neighborhoods from which they came) whereas the absence of gangs invited these organizations to compete violently to control that territorial turf. As *pandillas* merged into or

---

[103] These young people were described as similar to others in the city, although they seemed to be better educated and stole more – according to a government study that interviewed two rounds of gang members (40 in 1987 and 290 in 1998) (Levenson 2013: 59–60).

were replaced by *maras*, there was an increasing association of *maras* with violent urban crimes.[104]

Local gangs were joined by two US gangs that came to assume a dominant role both organizationally and culturally: Mara Salvatrucha (MS) and Calle 18 (Ranum 2011: 72). Some of the violent actors in MS and Calle 18 were part of the US deportation of undocumented people convicted of crimes – a point commonly noted in studies of gangs. Some of the newspaper reporting also spoke of the transnational dimension of these gangs – either noting the influence of Salvadoran and Honduran gang members or the impact of US deportation or both.[105] And the Guatemalan police, PNC, claimed that US deportations contributed to the gang problem in Guatemala, with deportees reportedly including 50 percent gang members, 20 percent criminals, and others having a propensity to join gangs if they could not find work.[106]

However, it seems problematic to reduce Guatemala's gang problem to deportation or international influence alone, since many of the deportees had no links to the country prior to their return and could not simply impose a structure there; notably, there was no tabula rasa, but there was a prior local structure that received them and incorporated the violent rituals associated with their counterparts in Los Angeles (also see Levenson 2013: 9, 41). Indeed, most gang members are *not* deportees, and MS and Calle 18 were in fact already present in Guatemala by the late 1980s, prior to the mass deportations (Ranum 2011: 73, 82). According to a US embassy source, while MS-13 was the strongest, Calle 18 was the oldest.[107] The Guatemalan state institutions did little to incorporate those who later arrived from the United States or otherwise address these deportees or other gang members (foreign or domestic born). As powerfully noted by Levenson (2013: 9, 41), Guatemala's violent context conditioned the process, generating the exodus of youth who were subsequently returned to a country defined by a long history of violence, a weak and corrupt state, a weak economy, and poor social

---

[104] See, for example, *Prensa Libre* 2.28.2000 "Vigilancia es insuficiente" for a discussion of robberies that took place in the Zone 4 market La Terminal: "La Policía Nacional Civil, PNC, señala que no se trata de bandas organizadas dedicadas al robo, sino 'mareros' que asaltan a transeúntes en las cercanías del mercado, para luego vender los objetos y comprar estupefacientes o licor."

[105] See *Prensa Libre* 4.28.2005 Pandilleros reclutan a niños y jóvenes; 4.4.2005 Alcaldes demandan mayor seguridad; 3.4.2005 Miles de deportados son mareros.

[106] *Prensa Libre* 3.4.2005 Miles de deportados son mareros.

[107] Interview with anonymous source from the US embassy (August 4, 2006).

services (especially given neoliberal policies), among other factors. These elements characterize El Salvador and Honduras as well as Guatemala – in striking contrast to Nicaragua (on both the sending and receiving sides of this process). Interestingly, one source in the US embassy noted that gang migration to Guatemala also came from El Salvador and Honduras, following the policy crackdown known as *mano dura*.[108]

Regardless of their origins, violent gangs started to form and flourish in Guatemala (and even more so in El Salvador and Honduras). Guatemala's weak state provided auspicious conditions for deported youth to introduce MS-13 and M-18 to Central America and to "absorb" and "reorganize" Guatemalan *maras* in the process (Levenson 2012: 42–43).

What started as a trickle of INS deportations in the early 1990s turned into a flood that included incarcerated gang members by 1996. Taken from prisons and flown home in shackles, these deportees brought with them MS-13 and M-18, as well as whatever slogans, clothing styles, hand signals, and vocabulary had not already traveled to Central America through the media and immigration. MS-13 and M-18 absorbed and reorganized local Maras in Guatemala City into *clikas* with names such as "Los Locos," which then formed the base of the MS-13 or M-18 pyramids. Each clika was under the supervision of a *veterano*; *veteranos* designated *palabras* (words) who communicated between the *clikas*. (Levenson 2013: 42–43)

While overall gang numbers are estimates only, UNODC (2012: 29), concluded that as of 2012, Guatemala had some 22,000 gang members (17,000 M-18 and 5,000 MS-13), El Salvador some 20,000 (12,000 MS-13, 8,000 M-18), and Honduras 22,000 (7,000 MS-13, 5,000 M-18)[109] – although as Moran (2009) notes, we know much more about Salvadoran gangs (and MS-13 in particular) than we do about Guatemalan gangs (which are fewer in number and probably emerged as such later in the game). Images of these gangs are daunting and fear inducing. Levenson

---

[108] Interview with anonymous source from the US embassy (August 4, 2006).
[109] The press used many different words to refer to crime groups. Alongside the gangs, there seem to be other kinds of smaller crime groups that are not necessarily transnational cartels or youth gangs per se. *Bandas* is commonly used to refer to an organized group (but also appears often to be used to refer to organized groups within gangs and organized crime). The press particularly highlighted in 2000 that *bandas* were implicated in rural crimes, including highway attacks, kidnappings, bank robberies, and murder for hire. In one such report in 2000, a group of hit men (*banda de sicarios*) located in Izabal (although often traveling to the capital) was said to have killed over 100 people in several Guatemalan departments, particularly the Petén, Zacapa, and Chiquimula, according to Byron Barrientos, second Minister of the Interior. *Prensa Libre* 8.19.2000 Suman cien asesinatos.

(2013) reminds us that Guatemalan youth were not always imagined as so violent and predatory but rather were once celebrated as the future of the country. Youth were in fact historically portrayed, both by late nineteenth-century statesmen and mid-twentieth-century revolutionaries, as heroes who could forge the nation. By the 1990s, this aspirational imagery had changed dramatically: youth were often identified with violence. While not all youth were gang members and not all gang members were killers, the gangs themselves had changed in orientation and practice.

Too many gang members in Guatemala City have become the victimizers that they were once falsely accused of being ... Although without a doubt still accused of far more crimes than they commit, as the Mexican scholar Rossana Reguillo Cruz points out, the Maras also "unfortunately actively participate in the propagation of their own legend." Invented and real, they huddle together around violent identities and practices ... (Levenson 2013: 4)

Death has become the daily context within which the gangs live and power is asserted. Devoid of any political project to redress society's injustices, in a context where the peace accords remain unfulfilled and social movements and revolutionary imaginaries have declined in strength, killing and being killed has become commonplace and a source of power. Contemporary gangs might not have "political" aims, but they are the product of a political moment: "the Maras have come out of a political crucible, and politicians have found political uses for them" (Levenson 2013: 8; also see introduction and chapter 1).

In the city, the postwar mareros control life through their power to take it away ... I am suggesting that within the mareros' social imaginary, in Charles Taylor's sense of that "common understanding which makes possible common practice," violent death controls the management of life, short as that may be. The average marero is murdered by the time he or she is twenty-two. Perhaps even worse: one's own early demise is part of the marero imaginary, and the average gang member *expects* to die by that age. (Levenson 2013: 6)

As in Chicago, El Salvador, and Brazil, gangs have been the target of crackdowns and imprisonment in Guatemala (especially 2003–2004 with Plan Escoba/Broom), although not as well orchestrated as in El Salvador. As in these other cases, imprisonment has arguably strengthened gangs rather than debilitated them, with "closer gang cohesion, stronger internal organization, and more powerful leaders. The repression also forced the gangs to adopt more sophisticated methods, to increase their use of violence, and to engage in new activities that generate more income," even leading to claims that nonimprisoned gang members implemented plans that were hatched within prison walls (Ranum 2011: 81).

The increasing presence of violent gangs has been covered by the media. Gang control of one neighborhood is described vividly, if anecdotally, in the following newspaper excerpt:

"El Gallito" is located in zone 3 in Guatemala [City]. It is known that Kevin is the chief captain [capo mayor]. In each building one finds flags – spies – with radio communication and binoculars so as to control entrance and departure into the zone. Everyone is heavily armed with automatic long-range weapons. The only ones who leave alive are the buyers. Delinquency has become so prevalent that the Police cannot enter. There are people in the streets who are supposedly selling hotdogs, but they are spies and inform the "capo" about who is entering and leaving. They make 100 quetzales a turn (a turno), apart from their "line" of pure cocaine for consumption. Most striking is the recognition that people in Guatemala know that "El Gallito" is an impenetrable zone. Those who enter this place perhaps don't know or aren't afraid of death, according to a nearby neighbor. Firefighters have a free pass to come and take those who have been injured or to put out fires, as do funeral homes to take out the dead. Vehicles who enter the zone must do so with their windows down and must identify themselves.[110]

In a conversation with a female taxi driver (name withheld) on July 21, 2006, she used similar language to describe El Gallito. She remarked that organized groups had closed off the streets (literally placing cement blockades at almost every street entrance) to monitor movement in and outside of the zone. She also noted that when driving in, one should have nontinted glass and rolled-down windows, so that the gangs could identify the people inside. While the state had apparently made efforts to recapture control of the area, she concluded both that it was not working *and* that people did not trust the police, which was often complicit. When we drove by, the area literally looked like an occupied zone, featuring both the gangs' coercive control of this territorial area and the state's inability to govern it. Academics and activists interviewed in mid-2005 and 2006 agreed with this concern, one anonymously noting that this area was a site of drug dealing and distribution. Concerns about El Gallito as an illicit territorial enclave remained a source of concern in the press even a decade later.[111]

---

[110] *Nuevo Diario*, Managua, Nicaragua, May 16, 2006. Three anonymous interviewees (a taxi driver, a researcher, and a US embassy worker, summer 2006) all described the zone in similar ways. In one interview, the person noted that drug sales were particularly relevant here compared to many other gang areas, where drug sales were less prevalent.

[111] www.prensalibre.com/guatemala/justicia/asedio-de-narcos-esta-de-vuelta-en-el-gallito, August 30, 2016.

Newspaper coverage of gangs in 2005 increasingly noted the presence of Mara Salvatrucha (MS or MS-13) and M-18. Compared to the 2000 reporting, the gangs appeared more organized, active, and menacing. Gangs were most active, according to *Prensa Libre*, in the departments of Huehuetenango, Escuintla, Chimaltenango, Alta Verapaz, and Guatemala. While often described as an urban phenomenon, the press noted that the gangs were no longer limited to the capital city alone but had spread throughout the territory – although apparently no gang-related violence was reported in Chiquimula or Santa Rosa. One such report noted, in particular, that while significant youth gangs (*pandillas juveniles*) were operating in the highlands (38 in Quetzaltenango, 35 in Huehuetenango, 19 in Sololá, 12 in Quiché, and 15 in Chimaltenango), sixty-six *maras* (the more violent and hierarchical gangs) were operating "with total impunity" in the Pacific coast departments of Escuintla, Retalhuleu, and Suchitepéquez, and thirty-nine *pandillas* were also noted in the northeastern departments of Petén, Izabal, and Alta Verapaz.[112]

Guatemala City and environs (Villa Nueva, Mixco, Palín, and Amatítlan) have been deeply affected by gang competition. MS-13 and M-18 chronically fight to control different turf and mete out revenge, especially in the poorer neighborhoods (Levenson 2013: 83). They have been known to use violence to do so, and over time one sees a discourse whereby gang youth presume that they kill or will be killed. "The internal life of the Maras has shifted away from dancing or the possession of expensive consumer goods to a focus on drugs, painful rites of loyalty, and annihilating the other gang" (Levenson 2013: 91). And with the increasing incarceration of gang members, and their concentration in certain prisons, the prisons have joined (arguably replaced) the neighborhood as a site of gang organization, socialization, control, and even violent competition (Ranum 2011: 79–81; Levenson 2013: chapter 4).

Gang activities, when illicit, are almost by definition difficult to track. Given weak police and court state capacity, we are left to infer types of gang activities and patterns.[113] Newspapers, however, provide some

---

[112] *Prensa Libre* 2.6.2005 Pandillas copan el territorio nacional.
[113] While gang violence is real, the proportion of gang-related homicides is unclear (World Bank 2010, volumes 1 and 2). While one study drawing on police figures reports that 14 percent of violence is attributed to gangs (with more violence attributed to organized crime and drug trafficking), another using the data from the Attorney General's Office for Human Rights claims that one-third of homicides was tied to gangs (World Bank 2010, volume1: 16). World Bank (2010) *Crime and Violence in Central America*. Volume 1. Washington, DC. World Bank Sustainable Development Department and

insight, even if incomplete and biased. *Prensa Libre* reporting suggests that gangs have been actively involved in drug consumption and distribution as well as extortion (of merchants, residents, and especially bus drivers). PNC statistics reported in *Prensa Libre* highlight the consumption and distribution of drugs (23 percent), robbery (20 percent), and homicides (2 percent) as the main illicit activities of the gangs, although it is unclear how they calculated these percentages (reported crime, convictions, and/or estimates).[114] A life of violence, thus, was integral to much gang life, particularly when trying to dominate new spaces. As emphasized in a 2005 interview with a gang member, while his gang engaged in drug sales (in prisons/*centros carcelarios*) and extortion, they did not historically extort or kill in their own neighborhood (*barrio*).[115] The uncertainty associated with inter-gang (and even intra-gang) rivalries, as well as the uncertainty of state reactions to them, has certainly fueled this situation.

If one does not kill, one is killed, since one must defend oneself from assassins, police agents, and rival bands. For this reason, they are always armed. He explained: One knows neither the place nor the hour in which they can kill you.[116]

The anonymous gang member observed that he had been desensitized to killing, had in fact killed others, and that once in the gang, it was difficult to leave.[117] Gangs are, after all, coercive organizations with a leadership, structure, and sanctioning mechanism. In the process of extorting, they have threatened and used violence.

Every youth gang (pandilla) is directed by a "gran líder," who is in charge of two groups: one that is responsible for collecting traffic and war tax, and the other whose job is to physically eliminate those businesspeople and drivers who oppose this extortion. They are also used to kill the members of rival *maras*.[118]

Poverty Reduction and Economic Management Unit Latin America and the Caribbean Region (July). Also see volume 2: 64.

[114] *Prensa Libre* 1.21.2005 Pandillas copan la capital.

[115] *Prensa Libre* 7.13.2005 "Si uno no mata, lo matan."

[116] Anonymous member of Guatemalan gang, *Prensa Libre* 7.13.2005: "Si uno no mata, lo matan, pues uno tiene que defenderse de los sicarios, agentes policiales y de las bandas rivales. Por esa razón, siempre están armados. Explicó: Uno no sabe ni el lugar ni la hora en que pueden matarlo."

[117] *Prensa Libre* 7.13.2005 "Si uno no mata, lo matan." Also repeated in anonymous interview, August 2005.

[118] *Prensa Libre* 3.10.2005 Policía identifica a 500 líderes de pandilleros: "Cada pandilla juvenil es dirigida por un 'gran líder', quien tiene a su cargo a dos grupos: uno que se encarga de cobrar el impuesto de circulación y de guerra, y otro cuya labor es eliminar físicamente a los comerciantes o pilotos que se oponen a las extorsiones. También son utilizados para matar a los integrantes de maras rivales."

Extortion has been a primary activity for Guatemalan gangs. Comparing newspaper reports from 2000 to 2005, one sees increasing coverage and concern about extortion, particularly of bus drivers, who have come to fear that gangs (seeking extortion) will hold them up and perhaps use violence in the process. With reports of some 200 daily attacks, bus companies found it increasingly hard to hire drivers,[119] who in turn frequently went on strike to protest both extortion by gangs and the limited corresponding police response. In one such case, bus drivers explicitly pinpointed the M-18 and indicated that each driver was being charged 150 quetzales per week.[120] In this generalized context of violence and uncertainty, residents have been confronted with deciding between two unpalatable choices when taking public transportation: "whether to place oneself in the hands of known gang members or to go with unknown people who the gang members will assault."[121] Arguably, where gangs have been able to establish hegemonic control over a given area, it was sometimes safer than where territories and routes were being contested – thus recalling a comment commonly voiced in interviews when I first started this research: "Better to have a gang than not."

In short, the *maras* (MS-13 and M-18) commonly target "drivers, security officers, and passengers on public transport. Extortion is the primary source of income for the *maras*, and public transport is one of their favorite targets" (UNODC 2012: 67). Importantly however, UNODC notes that extortion alone is not the cause of violence, since high violence is prevalent only in two areas where these attacks are high (and where the Ministry of Interior deemed the cities ungovernable): Guatemala City and Villa Nueva (the two largest cities in the country). UNODC also concludes that gangs are likely to be driving less of the violence in Guatemala than in El Salvador (UNODC 2012: 69). This book agrees and contends that violence spikes not where illicit actors are

---

[119] *Prensa Libre* 6.15.2005 Prevención del delito.
[120] See *Prensa Libre* 2.8.2005 Usuarios sin buses por maras; for coverage of another bus strike, see 11.17.2005 Suspenden servicio de buses por violencia. For discussion of bus drivers refusing to pay extortion fees, see 10.24.2005 De pacífico a violento; 7.23.2005 Maras exigen impuesto. Levenson also observes the very difficult situation faced by transportation workers confronted with a "circulation tax" and the increased killing of municipal bus drivers and their assistants – over 500 killed between 2006 and 2008 and almost 200 killed in 2008 alone (Levenson (2013): 86–87).
[121] *Prensa Libre* 6.1.2005 Prevención del delito: "si ir en manos de conocidos de pandilleros o desconocidos a los que los pandilleros asalten." For a discussion of proposals to deal with the attacks on bus routes, see 7.12.2005 Plan para evitar asaltos a buses.

present alone but where there is *competition* to assert and defend control of these territorial spaces and routes.

The newspaper database supports the plausibility of these claims about gangs. While the data do not cover the universe of homicide cases, they do highlight the importance of roadways and transportation routes. Correspondingly, a major theme in *Prensa Libre*'s 2000 reporting was the attacks on commercial trucks traveling the highways. A series of articles highlights the depth of the problem. When asked in 2000 which routes were the most dangerous, the president of the Central American Federation of Transport (Federación Centroamericana de Transportes, Fecatrans) responded, "Everything that is the natural corridor. From the moment one leaves Tecún Umán, just two blocks from the people, they are already robbing the trucks. From Escuintla until the border Pedro de Alvarado. And yes, in the Atlantic, one of the most critical places is Río Hondo, Zacapa …"[122] The titles of newspaper articles is telling: "The interminable wave of attacks on highways" and "The wave of assaults worsens" – with the latter reporting some seven daily attacks between Ciudad Tecún Umán, San Marcos y Coatepeque, and Quetzaltenango.[123] These attacks were sometimes quite violent, using military-grade weapons, attacking commercial vehicles, and targeting security guards.[124]

---

[122] The original quote is "Todo lo que es el corredor natural. Desde que se sale de Tecún Umán, a las dos cuadras del pueblo ya se han robado los camiones. De Escuintla hasta la frontera Pedro de Alvarado. Y si es en el Atlántico, uno de los lugares más críticos es Río Hondo, Zacapa," *Prensa Libre* 6.26.2000 Interminable ola de atracos en carreteras. The interview continues as follows:
PL: ¿Qué características tienen estas bandas?
Juárez: El tipo es la mayor parte de aspecto militar o guerrilleros. Regularmente, andan en picops grandes o camionetas con vidrios polarizados; se les describe como de pelo corto entre los 30 y 45 años. Actúan entre seis y nueve personas en más de un carro. Usan armas largas; M-16, AR-15 y AK-47 son las más utilizadas. Para nosotros, gran parte de lo que nos afecta son los efectos de la posguerra, por tanta gente que quedó desplazada.
PL: ¿Qué porcentaje de asaltos se denuncia a la Policía?
Juárez: Tal vez 10%, porque la gente tiene miedo.
PL: ¿Han identificado algunas bandas?
Juárez: No. Nosotros no conocemos a nadie. Tenemos sospechas de que gran parte de los asaltos podría ser autoasaltos. Que el mismo importador mande a asaltar el vehículo, para no pagar impuestos, cobrar el seguro y quedarse con la mercancía.

[123] *Prensa Libre* 6.26.2000 Interminable ola de atracos en carreteras; 9.11.2000 Recrudece ola de asaltos.

[124] See *Prensa Libre* 2.10.2000 Agentes mueren en atracos; 11.5.2000 Repunte de asaltos; 3.17.2000 Preocupa la inseguridad; 4.20.2000 Asedian Palín; 7.4.2000 Urge seguridad. For other press reporting, see 7.27.2005 Rechaza patrullaje; 01.14.2000 Crímenes imborrables en la mente de niños; 2.12.2005 Vecinos, a merced de las maras; 2.21.2005 Sitiados por la violencia; 5.27.2005 Clamor por seguridad; 3.1.2005

A particularly vivid article portrays the risk and violence that organized armed groups of about twenty men unleash on bus and truck drivers traveling between La Libertad and Sayaxché, Petén;[125] there are an estimated three daily assaults, with more than 800 victims (including a dozen assassinations), reported – although the police have noted that people do not always formally denounce these attacks given the disincentives to do so. The report speculated, based on the weapons used, that the different groups (*bandas*) included army deserters and/or former insurgents.[126]

UNODC also reports on public transportation attacks, including a map of municipal rates of attack in 2011 based on data from Guatemala's prosecutor for human rights (UNODC 2012: 69). Given these extortionary practices along roadways, businesses paid increasing security costs to protect their vehicles and products, as noted by a representative of Guatemala's historically powerful agricultural association (the Comité Coordinador de Asociaciones Agrícolas, Comerciales, Industriales y Financieras, CACIF).[127]

Alongside bus drivers, businesses and residents were also frequent victims of extortion, according to newspaper reporting, with threats to harm a family member if they did not pay a tax.[128] Viewed as a whole, the complex of weak state capacity (and complicity) alongside the increasing prevalence of illicit actors placed Guatemala in the unenviable ranking of 4 out of 54 countries polled by the World Bank about business accruing losses due to crime and first in terms of concerns about corruption (UNODC 2007: 28, reporting from a 2005 World Development Report). Businesses express low trust in Guatemala's rule-of-law institutions. Drawing on Enterprise Surveys, UNODC highlights that Guatemala, along with El Salvador, exhibits enormously high concerns about crime and corruption – in marked contrast to Nicaragua, a point also observed

---

Mareros acechan negocios; 5.23.2005 Vecinos se organizan para combatir asaltos; 2.26.2005 Temor en Jutiapa por inseguridad; 7.1.2005 Crímenes provocan sicosis; 10.9.2005 ¿Por qué somos violentos?

[125] *Prensa Libre* 11.6.2000 Tres asaltos diarios. Also see 2.10.2000 "Agentes mueren en atracos," for another example.

[126] *Prensa Libre* 11.6.2000 Tres asaltos diarios. Also see 2.10.2000 "Agentes mueren en atracos," for another example.

[127] *Prensa Libre* 5.26.2000 Empresarios demandan seguridad. The CACIF representative, Augusto García Noriego, claimed that business was at that point paying approximately 1,500 million quetzales annually for protection – a figure that he noted was likely to rise.

[128] See, for example, *Prensa Libre* 3.19.2005 Unidos contra las pandillas; 4.25.2005 Extorsiones de maras; 1.21.2005 Pandillas copan la capital; 6.24.2005 Pandillas extorsionan por electrodomésticos.

by UNODC (2012: 73), drawing on Enterprise Surveys reporting that the "share of firms in Central America who said crime was their primary barrier to investment in 2010 was 21% each in El Salvador and Guatemala, 11% in Honduras and 7% in Nicaragua."[129] "To bring investment to Guatemala is like going toward a place where one hears gunshots," quipped César García following a Latin American Business Chronicle report singling out Guatemala, El Salvador, and Honduras as the most dangerous places for executives and multinationals.[130]

That said, one should not presume that gangs are the main or only source of violence. As noted earlier, the greatest homicide rates occur in the east and the north, places where organized crime, not gangs, are most visible and consequential (a point also noted by Ranum 2011: 83). And it is worth noting that extrajudicial killings of gang members are not necessarily restricted to inter-gang rivalry, as state officials, DTOs, and even citizens have been known to target gangs as well (Ranum 2011: 85 and numerous confidential interviews). In short, there is an endogenous process that has unfolded whereby gangs have gained, penetrated, and controlled certain territorial spaces (e.g., cities and transportation routes) in a context of a weak and historically (and ongoing) violent state.

Gangs have not only competed to control neighborhood territories and transportation routes, but when incarcerated, they have also competed (sometimes violently) to control space within prison walls. Weak prison capacity (characterized also by poor conditions), alongside prison complicity, facilitates the ability of gang inmates to gain control over spaces, operate with some autonomy, and continue to operate their illicit businesses. If anything, the complicity/incapacity of the state is visible and palpable (as in the bold assassination within prison walls of the imprisoned police officers who themselves had murdered the Salvadoran parliamentarians). Strikingly, what we see (in Guatemala as well as El Salvador and Brazil) is a prison system in which gang members exert considerable control.

In this context, gangs have engaged in turf wars and competed over territory, with violent consequences on either side of prison walls. Some very high-visibility incidents were reported in the 2005 press, including gang attacks that resulted in numerous deaths, gruesome and gratuitous

---

[129] Newspaper reporting also indicated rising business concerns about violence. See, for example: *Prensa Libre* 3.4.2010 Cámaras de ocho países claman contra violencia; 11.16.2010 Empresarios amenazan con tomar acciones ante inseguridad.

[130] *Prensa Libre* 11.16.2010 Empresarios amenazan con tomar acciones ante inseguridad.

acts of violence, and prison searches that revealed weapons and drugs in various prisons.[131] When asked to explain why the turf wars had become so vicious, one convalescing gang member explained that there was intergang rivalry and they needed to assert their dominance: "we had to teach them who is in charge in this center." The fighting occurred with guns and grenades that gang members were able to smuggle into the prison (which the PNC concluded was possible because prison guards permitted some gang members to leave for the weekend). Armed with these weapons, one M-18 gang member highlighted the deep and abiding commitment to control territory, even if violence is the only mechanism for doing so: "This fight will not end until all the members of one of the two *bandas* dies."[132] Thus, we see organizational territorial competition occurring clearly and violently not only in prime geographic locations but also within prison walls.

***

In this chapter, I have largely discussed organized crime and gangs as if they were two hermetically sealed sets of illicit actors – differentiated by age, activity, and geography. They do have different origins, as noted earlier. However, with time, and as gangs have become larger, more hierarchical, and more professional, there has been speculation that their trajectories have crossed. Prisons have provided one such space, with some cases of drug lords not only dominating spaces but also using gang members to do their bidding, as noted by Levenson (2013: chapter 4). Writing of the rising and gruesome trends in 2010, *Prensa Libre* speculated about the interactions between organized crime and gangs. And scholarship on the *maras* observes that in Guatemala, gangs are often used by organized crime and can be "a scapegoat" and "cannon fodder" in the process – something that is also present in Honduras but less so in El Salvador, where organized crime is less prevalent (Bruneau 2011: 1–2). According to José Miguel Insulza, secretary general of the OAS, "Five years ago, one spoke separately about drug trafficking; about maras, bandas and pandillas; of kidnappers; of

---

[131] *Prensa Libre* 5.5.2005 Critican a los mareros; 5.21.2005 Crimen se reorganiza dentro de las cárceles; 8.16.2005 Murieron 30 reos en trifulcas en 4 cárceles; 8.17.2005 Autoridades temen ola de venganzas de maras; www.prensalibre.com/noticias/Salvatr uchas-Boqueron_0_112789599.html; 8.18.2005 Intentarán frenar venganza de maras; 8.24.2005 Temen auge de maras en Cuilapa; 8.19.2005 Paralizan servicio; 8.23.2005 Informe: 16% de reos son mareros; 8.1.2005 Cada año hay más reos; 9.22.2005 Localizan guarida de la M18; 9.21.2005 Fue venganza de la MS. Also see Ranum (2011: 81–82).

[132] *Prensa Libre* 9.21.2005 Fue venganza de la MS.

smugglers or human traffickers; now all these forms of violence appear to be converging in sui generis criminal organizations."[133] While perhaps overly dramatic, Insulza is right to note that the line is less clear – not only because there are examples of collaboration but also because gangs have arguably become a form of organized crime. In turn, these illicit organizations have also colluded with members of the state. One anonymous source in the US embassy noted that in addition to organized crime penetrating the state, gangs have penetrated legitimate businesses (like banks) and parts of the state (including police, courts, and the public prosecutor's office/*ministerio público*).[134]

CONCLUSION

Guatemala's history of violence is not new. However, the surge in homicides during the third wave has changed the geography of violence. The high homicide rates do not echo the subnational patterns of the civil war; they have emerged in border areas, port towns, roadways, and capital cities (rather than the highlands, where the civil war was largely fought). I have argued that these highly violent areas are tied to the proliferation of illicit actors seeking to control specific territorial enclaves that are considered lucrative spaces to promote the trade and transit of drugs (e.g., organized crime) and engage in extortion (e.g., by gangs). These spaces have proven most violent not because illicit economies emerge (after all violence is not equally high all along the border) but *where* actors compete to *control* them. Organizational territorial competition is the most proximate argument made in the book.

This chapter seeks to explain why Guatemala has been home to these kinds of activities. I argue that territorial enclaves have taken form and flourished because of an "advantageous" political context – one where law-and-order institutions have not only demonstrated weak state capacity but are themselves often complicit in the very activities they are supposed to prevent. In this context, Guatemala has remained a propitious country for the emergence and spread of illicit organizations, which often compete with one another and the state to control territory. For organized crime, this pattern surged following the crackdowns first in the Caribbean and then Mexico; for gangs it developed over time, especially in urban locales. In both cases, competition among illicit actors and with the state has

---

[133] *Prensa Libre* 12.29.2010 La violencia creció en 2010 en América Latina y se hızo más cruel y ritual.
[134] Anonymous source from the US embassy, August 4, 2006.

resulted in geographically concentrated areas (homicidal ecologies) in which high homicide rates have emerged – a situation that has found an even louder echo in El Salvador and Honduras, which have vied for the highest homicide rates in the Western Hemisphere.

In closing, the comparative historical record leaves one with little optimism about security in the region and much to lament. CICIG's record of exposing abuses has been laudable, and politicians have occasionally responded with preventative declarations.[135] More commonly, however, we have witnessed relative impunity coupled with hardline rhetoric, as with former president and former general Otto Pérez Molina. Yet Pérez Molina's policy stance reveals Guatemala's deep and underlying challenges. For while he first campaigned on *mano dura* policies, he subsequently joined other Latin American leaders in the notable effort to spark discussions about the decriminalization or legalization of parts of the drug trade. Pérez Molina's ability to pursue such a track was undermined by his own corruption. In 2015 he submitted his resignation following rising protests and inquiries by the UN-backed CICIG (in English, International Commission against Impunity in Guatemala) into his leadership role in a multimillion-dollar customs fraud scheme. While CICIG's historic role is striking, so too is the level of state corruption. Pérez Molina's now infamous downfall stands alongside that of former president Portillo, who was extradited to the United States for his role in money laundering.[136]

With leaders like these, and law-and-order institutions with such a paltry record, it is no surprise that Guatemala has thus far seemed like a good bet for DTOs seeking to move illicit goods northward, or that gangs would have the ability to thrive in certain regions. In their wake, new illicit economies have flourished. And where actors compete to control these illicit spaces, violence and insecurity have become an everyday occurrence. It is this dynamic that has defined a lethal homicidal ecology – one that has helped to propel the homicidal violence patterns in Guatemala and elsewhere in the region.

---

[135] The press reports that previous Guatemalan presidents did occasionally also call for some degree of prevention. See *Prensa Libre* 5.31.2005 Ex pandilleros comparten su experiencia; 5.27.2005 Clamor por seguridad; 7.8.2005 Deporte en lugar de maras; 6.20.2005 Educación física y extraescolar para prevenir maras; 6.15.2005 Prevención del delito; 6.23.2005 Prevención y no mano dura.

[136] Benjamin Weiser. "Ex-President of Guatemala Faces Judge in Manhattan." *New York Times*, May 28, 2013, and Azam Ahmed and Elisabeth Malkin. "Otto Pérez Molina of Guatemala Is Jailed Hours after Resigning Presidency." *New York Times*, September 3, 2015.

CHAPTER 5
Appendix

NEWSPAPER VIOLENCE DATABASE: GUATEMALAN PATTERNS DERIVED FROM NEWSPAPER CODING

To gain insight into patterns of violence, a newspaper database was constructed, with the assistance of the many graduate students listed in the acknowledgments. The resulting newspaper violence database includes coverage of three Central American countries (Guatemala, El Salvador, and Nicaragua) for three years (2000, 2005, and 2010). This database highlights how media portrays violence in the region but also reveals some of the micro-dynamics of violence. As with all the datasets of violence reported in newspapers, the database captures only a fraction of the total number of official homicides recorded.

In Guatemala, while the 2000 data capture only 7.6 percent of total homicides (violent deaths as a percentage of official homicide figures), 2005 and 2010 capture a minimum of 37–38 percent (although we have another subset of uncounted ambiguous cases). It is worth noting that although the reporting improves, the volume of cases in fact doubles from 2,904 (in 2000) to 5,338 (in 2005) to 5,960 (in 2010). As the volume increases, the reporting volume does as well. Reporting covers high and low-violence regional departments. In fact, the departments with the highest percentages of reported cases span the higher- and lower-violence departments – probably more a function of significant cities than of violence levels per se. If anything, we have lower reporting rates in the high-violence (and most remote) cases of the department of El Petén. While imperfect, these data provide some insight into micro-dynamics and local patterns that we would not otherwise see if we looked at official homicide data alone; based on newspaper underreporting, it is hard to generalize with confidence.

Although we constructed the newspaper violence database with the hope that we would gain access to the micro-dynamics of violence – particularly the agents and impetus – this proved unsatisfying. Ultimately, those decisions are not made by reporters but in courts of law; and since courts of law are notoriously lacking in Central America, this reporting was far from complete. The data did reveal, however, other notable patterns about geography, technologies, and the aggressiveness of violence. I will focus on these three factors in this final section.

First, most reported homicides occurred in urban settings – whether one looks at where the homicide was recorded as taking place or where the body was found. Urban-based homicides were committed in 64 percent of reported cases in 2000 (although 74 percent of the bodies were found in urban settings), 57.21 percent of reported cases in 2005 (although 66.78 percent of the bodies were found in urban settings), and 80.43 percent in 2010 (although 82.67 percent of bodies were found in urban settings). These numbers, unsurprisingly, suggest either that homicides are primarily an urban phenomenon – although not all cities share equal homicide levels – or that the database has an urban bias that needs to be kept in check when interpreting the data that follow. The latter is almost certainly true. That said, if we look at official homicide rates by city, we see that they are often driven by urban (*cabecera*) violence and that urban violence is often higher in the northeast, southeast, and metropolitan Guatemala.

Notably, the data (and general reporting – not captured in these numbers) also highlighted that homicides are significantly associated with roadsides and transportation routes. In addition to coding urban/rural spaces, we coded spaces in the following way: commercial establishment, private home, roadside, isolated space, transportation, and prison. This coding revealed some striking patterns. Of our reported cases, most homicides were committed on roadsides (19.75–41.95 percent) or in areas associated with transportation (between 11.3 and 28.56 percent); bodies, in turn, were found on roadsides (some 30–43 percent of reported cases) and in cases associated with transportation (some 10–16 percent). As previously discussed, these roadside/transportation patterns are plausibly tied to the effort to control trade and transit routes – both for gangs seeking to extort in capital cities and in areas where organized crime is seeking to control the movement of illicit goods. Notably, UNDP speculates that criminal groups were extorting public transport drivers (an estimated 800) in addition to many other sectors.[137]

Second, if we turn to technologies of violence, we see that most homicides were committed with a gun (in contrast to Nicaragua, where knives or

---

[137] *Prensa Libre* 12.29.2010 La violencia creció en 2010 en América Latina y se hizo más cruel y ritual.

machetes were most significant). The use of guns points to the availability of these weapons and the likelihood that there is a significant illicit arms market and/or guns that remained in private hands after demobilization. Indeed, Guatemala is estimated to have some 15.8 guns per 100 people, according to the World Bank (2010, volume 1: 20 and volume 2: 75, based on Karp 2008 and Arias Foundation 2005). This figure is significantly higher than in any other Central American case, making it hard to argue that gun ownership alone explains violence patterns (since Honduras and El Salvador have exceeded Guatemala's post–civil war violence patterns in most years). Moreover, arguments about residual firearms increasing violence do not neatly explain the varied cross-national patterns that we see. While it is reported that firearms (licensed and unlicensed) are responsible for 65–70 percent of reported homicides in the region (World Bank 2010: volume 2: 73), this does not mean that firearm *levels* cause or explain variations in homicide rates (see Table 5.1 for figures).[138]

Third, the newspaper violence database table reveals the variation in types of homicides. A clean shot is not the same as other forms of torture. And here the data are notably disturbing with regard to the level of mutilation associated with Guatemalan homicides. An estimated

---

[138] World Bank 2010 (volume 2: 75) later reports that this rate is 80 percent of killings for El Salvador (2006) and Guatemala (approximately). Although the World Bank study highlights that the availability of firearms might be part of the explanation, the data that they provide question that tentative assertion. As the final column of Table 5.1 (which I added to their table) highlights, very high and moderate levels of violence have comparable estimated per capita gun rates. Hence, we can infer that while high levels of gun ownership increase the capacity to kill, they do not explain the circumstances under which they are deployed. As with deterrence theory and theories of war, we must ascertain the motives for restraining versus deploying weapons of destruction. Indeed, the World Bank study (volume 2: figure 5.1: 75) shows Central American arms imports over time (2000–2006). These figures do not provide a powerful explanation of levels of violence. El Salvador has had the highest rate of per capita violence, and yet its firearm rate is not the highest – significantly lower than that of Guatemala and also of Honduras for most of these years. Guatemala's firearm rates skyrocket in these years (which corresponds with rising homicide rates), but the question is why violence is not much higher in Guatemala than in the other countries listed. And the firearm rates of Costa Rica and Nicaragua sometimes surpass those of El Salvador, despite the fact that the former two countries have significantly lower homicide rates. In short, guns kill, but the availability and imports of guns are both likely to be endogenous to some other factor and beg the question about why rates diverge, why there are different markets for arms, and why people choose to deploy them.

TABLE 5.1 *Firearms owned by civilians in Central America (2007)*

Country	Registered	Total estimated	Guns per 100 people	Violence levels
Costa Rica	43,241	115,000	2.8	Low
El Salvador*	198,000	450,000	7.0	Very high
Guatemala	147,581	1,950,000	15.8	Very high
Honduras	133,185	450,000	6.2	Very high
Nicaragua**	NA	385,000	7.0	Moderate
Panama	96.600	525,000	5.4	Moderate

Source: World Bank (2010, volume 1: 20 and volume 2: 75), based on Karp 2008 and Arias Foundation 2005.

* Hume (2004: 16), citing work from Cruz and Beltrán (2000: 9), indicate that of the 400,000–450,000 firearms held by civilians in El Salvador, less than 36 percent are held legally. NB: They indicate: "this translates into 2 firearms for every ten adults." This is significantly higher than the figure cited in the chart here.

** Rocha (2007: 23) notes that in 2000, Nicaragua did have relatively low levels of legal guns. He cites similar numbers, with some differences: Nicaragua (52,390), Costa Rica (43,241, same as cited here); El Salvador (170,000, lower than cited here); Guatemala (147,581, same as cited here), and Panama (96,614). While recognizing that there is likely to be a significant number of unregistered arms, he maintains that the overall level is lower in Nicaragua than in the northern triangle of Central America. His data comes from W. Gonick, R. Muggah, and C. Waszink (2003), *Balas perdidas: el impacto del mal uso de armas pequeñas en Centroamérica*. Published jointly with the Small arms survey and the Norway initiative on the transference of small arms.

45.3 percent of bodies were mutilated – including burns, rape, riddled/ mowed down (*acribillado*), dismemberment, and torture.[139] Only a small percentage of all reported homicides are associated with the home – taking place or being found in the home (6.7–8 percent).[140] It is important to note the rising concern about "femicide" (as noted by human rights organizations and reported in the paper *La Prensa*) not just because more women are targeted, but also because of the brutality of those murders.[141] The percentage of mutilation cases reported declined

---

[139] For discussions of brutality (torture, mutilation, and/or messages being left on bodies) see, for example, *Prensa Libre* 6.14.2005 Van tres mil 597 muertes; and 2.15.2005 Investigan crimen. The newspaper violence database codes torture, where reported.

[140] Moreover, the number of reported homicide-related robberies went from a high in 2000 of just over 20 percent (most in Guatemala) to a considerable drop of 5 percent in 2005 and 2 percent in 2010 (newspaper violence database).

[141] *Prensa Libre* 1.27.2005 Alarma por violencia; also see 2.6.2005 Son utilizadas por narcos; and 2.22.2005 Cada vez más muertes.

considerably in 2005 and 2010 but was still over 16 percent and 10 percent, respectively. Simultaneously, the number of robbery-related homicides reported also declined, although these two data points do not necessarily, or even logically, go together.

The form and number of cases of mutilation in homicidal violence suggests that there is something more here than random acts of violence. Angélica Durán-Martínez has analyzed the visibility of violence – including mutilation – and emphasizes that torture is not just to inflict horrific pain on the victim but also to send a message to the broader community.[142]

In sum, an analysis of *Prensa Libre* reveals the following pattern. Since the civil war, Guatemala's violence patterns have increased over time, have been particularly high and geographically concentrated in urban areas and the northern and eastern parts of the country (bordering the coasts, Mexico, and Honduras), and have exhibited disturbing examples of mutilation. The examples of torture are higher than in other cases in the region (including El Salvador), although reminiscent of patterns emerging anecdotally in Mexico. For some of the composite findings emerging from the newspaper violence database, see Table 5.2.

TABLE 5.2 *Reported homicide patterns in* Prensa Libre, *Guatemala*

Category	2000 Percent of total homicide events reported (%)	2005 Percent of total homicide events reported (%)	2010 Percent of total homicide events reported (%)
Technology of Violence			
Automatic weapon	4.7	1.27	0.31
Human contact	9.3	5.67 (6.18)	3.73 (3.83)
Knife	5.3	5.92 (6.38)	1.99 (2.25)
Military-grade weapon	2.0	0.81	1.18 (1.23)
Regular gun	60.7	55.90 (57.67)	69.39 (69.44)
Other*	4.0		1.89 (4.24)
Stoning	3.3	1.06 (1.16)	0.51 (0.56)
Mutilation involved**	45.3	16.20 (18.08)	10.42 (11.29)

(continued)

---

[142] Angélica Durán-Martínez (2013 and 2015).

TABLE 5.2 *(continued)*

Category	2000 Percent of total homicide events reported (%)	2005 Percent of total homicide events reported (%)	2010 Percent of total homicide events reported (%)
Geographic location where body was found			
Nonurban, border area	4.0	1.16 (1.22)	0.92 (0.97)
Nonurban, outskirts of city	5.3	1.82 (1.97)	0.92 (0.97)
Nonurban, countryside	10.0	5.62 (6.58)	7.41 (8.18)
Urban, capital city	49.3	32.76 (35.39)	44.25 (47.42)
Urban, other large city	22.7	28.76 (31.80)	33.16 (35.21)
Urban, other small city	2.0	5.32 (6.13)	5.26 (5.52)
Geographic Location Where Crime Was Committed			
Nonurban, border area	3.3	1.27 (1.32)	0.97 (1.02)
Nonurban, outskirts of city	4.0	1.42 (1.47)	0.72 (0.77)
Nonurban, countryside	9.3	6.48 (7.19)	7.26 (8.02)
Urban, capital city	44.7	29.16 (30.48)	43.33 (46.30)
Urban, other large city	18.0	23.75 (25.01)	31.99 (33.73)
Urban, other small city	1.3	4.30 (4.66)	5.11 (5.37)
Type of Space Where Body Was Found			
Commercial establishment	13.3	5.77 (5.82)	7.36 (7.46)
Private home	6.7	0.56 (0.81)	4.19 (4.45)
Roadside	32.0	29.67 (32.35)	42.92 (46.09)
Isolated space	10.0	4.81 (6.13)	5.21 (6.34)
Transportation	12.7	9.97 (10.08)	15.89 (16.30)
Prison	0.7	0.71 (0.76)	0.56 (0.66)
Type of Space Where Crime Was Committed			
Commercial establishment	14.0	5.77 (5.82)	7.51 (7.61)
Private home	8.0	5.22 (5.52)	4.19 (4.45)

(continued)

TABLE 5.2 *(continued)*

Category	2000 Percent of total homicide events reported (%)	2005 Percent of total homicide events reported (%)	2010 Percent of total homicide events reported (%)
Roadside	29.3	19.75 (20.76)	41.95 (44.97)
Isolated space	7.3	4.96 (5.27)	5.31 (6.23)
Transportation	11.3	28.56 (28.61)	16.25 (16.56)
Prison	1.3	0.76 (0.81)	0.51 (0.61)

[*] "Other" technologies of violence included hanging (2), fire (2), and dragged to death (1).
[**] Includes burns, rape, *acribillado*, dismemberment, torture.
NB: The higher parenthetical numbers refer to number if one includes ambiguous cases in the reporting.

6

High Violence in Post-Civil War El Salvador

El Salvador is no stranger to violence. The country experienced military rule for much of the twentieth century and a civil war in the 1980s. An estimated 70,000 people were killed during the war, and the country infamously gained notoriety for the assassination of Archbishop Romero, the brutal rape and murder of four churchwomen, and massacres in places such as El Mozote, among other tragedies. The 1992 peace accords therefore promised a turning point. They were widely lauded for ending the hostilities between the country's armed forces and the insurgency. Following the major guerilla offensive on San Salvador, both sides realized that neither side would win militarily. The accords marked a dramatic end to the war and delineated a wide range of reforms designed to usher in a new period of democratic peace.

In the aftermath of El Salvador's peace accords, aspirations were high. However, they were quickly dashed. Violence spiked in the 1990s and remained high throughout the 2000s, with El Salvador maintaining an unenviable lead in Latin American per capita homicide levels during much of this time.[1] Indeed, El Salvador had the third-highest violent mortality rates in the 1990s (42.3 per 100,000), surpassed only by Colombia (83.2) and the Russian Federation (42.9).[2] Following the

---

[1] Homicide data reporting changed in Honduras in 2003, and in El Salvador in 2005. In El Salvador, three agencies (the national police, the medical forensics institute, and the attorney general's office) integrated the process of reporting homicide levels (World Bank 2010, volume 2: 2). "The costs of crime to business are also higher in El Salvador than in any other Latin American country and among the highest in the world," according to a survey of World Bank data. Data compiled by *Latin Business Chronicle* (Arnson and Drolet 2011: 2, referring to "Crime Cost: El Salvador Worst," *Latin American Business Chronicle*, August 10, 2010).

[2] Carcach (2008: 18), drawing on WHO data.

civil war, homicide rates even surpassed those reached during the civil war.[3] In the next decade, they continued to maintain extremely high levels. Between 2002 and 2007, homicide rates rose to 48.9 per 100,000 (Carcach 2008: 19), and average daily homicide rates fluctuated around 6.9 from January 2002 to March 2004 and increased to a daily average of ten daily homicides between January 2005 and February 2008. Lest one think that this is driven by a few spikes, it is worth noting that the range included a low of about seven homicides a day (May 2008) and a high of over twelve a day (September 2006; Carcach 2008: 9) – extraordinarily high numbers for a country of just over 6 million. With this violent record, El Salvador arguably achieved the highest overall per capita homicide rate in the region.[4] Yet homicide rates have increased since this point, excluding 2012 and 2013 (see Figure 6.1). In 2015, El Salvador reached a homicide rate of 104 per 100,000; it dropped by one-fifth to 81.2 per 100,000 in 2016.[5] These rates make El Salvador among the most violent places in the world.

So, too, this violence has had a distinct geographic dimension.[6] Data reveal that while there was a significant geographic spread prior to 2001 and after 2012, the spread amplifies significantly in the interim decade – resulting in skyrocketing rates in Sonsonate, La Libertad, San Salvador, and Santa Ana, in particular, while rates were considerably lower in regions such as Morazón, Chalatenango, and La Paz (see Figure 6.2). There is a spike in violence in 2014 and 2015 (see Figure 6.1) that is not captured by the departmental data in Figure 6.2, since we only had access to data up to 2013.

---

[3] See WHO figures from 1960s and 1970s and discussions in Cruz and Beltrán 2000; Hume 2004: 16; Hume 2007: 740. Some argue that El Salvador's violence was distinctively and comparatively high even prior to the civil war: a homicide rate of about 30 per 100,000, which is well above the global average.

[4] Date collection changed after 2002, when the PNC started to provide municipal data to the UNDP for their Human Development Report (Carcach 2008: 45). Also see World Bank data (2010, volume 2: 2). IHRC (2007: 73–74) notes that it seems that violence also increases prior to elections.

[5] Also see Kevin Lui. "EL Salvador Reports Its First Full Day without Homicides in Two Years." *Time*. January 12, 2017. http://time.com/4634058/el-salvador-crime-gangs-murder-homicide/; Alan Gomez. "El Salvador: World's New Murder Capital." *USA Today*. January 7, 2016. www.usatoday.com/story/news/world/2016/01/07/el-salvador-homicide-rate-honduras-guatemala-illegal-immigration-to-united-states/78358042/.

[6] As part of this project, we mapped the violence – using both official data and GIS technology and drawing on parallel work done by others (including Carcach 2008).

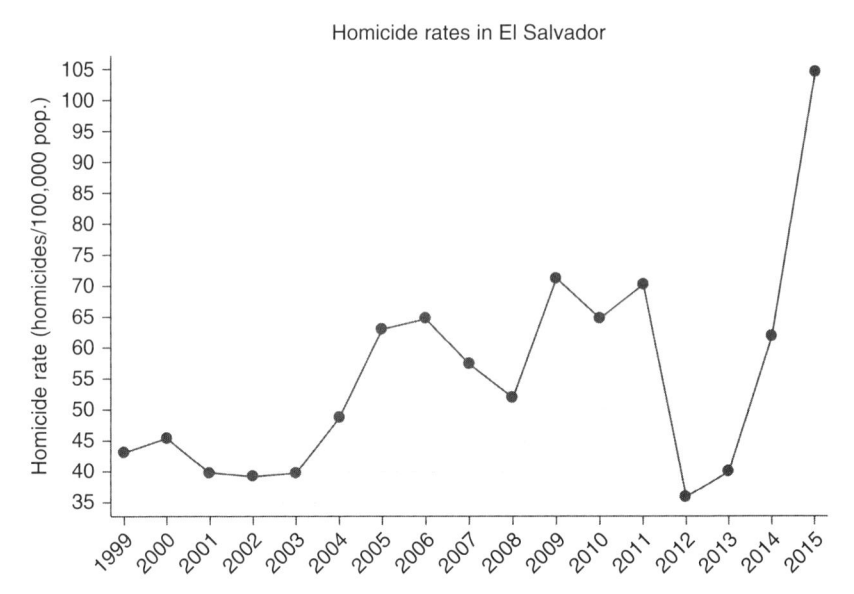

210   *Part III Divergent Trajectories: Three Post-Civil War Cases*

FIGURE 6.1 Homicide rates in El Salvador (1999–2015, rate per 100,000 population)
Graph created by Daniela Barba-Sánchez using Stata.
Source: The 1999 and 2000 absolute homicide numbers come from El Salvador's Institute of Legal Medicine (IML)'s reports *Defunciones por homicidios y suicidios en El Salvador. Años 2000 y 2001*. Available at www.csj.gob.sv/IML2013/PDFS/anuariohomic2000.pdf and www.csj.gob.sv/IML2013/PDFS/anuariohomic1999.pdf. The 2001–2008 absolute homicide figures come from IML (2009), *Epidemiología de los homicidios en El Salvador período 2001-2008*. Available at www.csj.gob.sv/comunicaciones/Estad%C3%ADsticas/IML/periodos/anuario_final_homicidios_%202001_2008.swf. The 2009 absolute homicide numbers come from IML, reported in Fundaungo (2014), "Evolución de los homicidios en El Salvador, 2009–2013" (1). Available at http://fundaungo.org.sv/pdf/2014/Aportes_final.pdf. The 2010–2015 absolute homicide figures come from www.transparencia.oj.gob.sv/portal/transparencia.php?opcion=1&texto=homicidios&categoria=0. Estimated population figures come from p. 77 in DIGESTYC, UNFPA, and CELADE (2010), *Proyecciones Nacionales 1950–2050*. Available at http://herramientas.egob.sv/estadisticas/images/docs/Proyecciones_Nacionales_1950_2050.pdf.

To address the high and yet geographically varied homicide rates in El Salvador, this chapter examines the country's homicidal ecology, which includes permissive political conditions (weak law-and-order institutions), the growth of illicit organizations (gangs, in particular), and certain mechanisms (organizational territorial competition). In this context, a range of illicit organizational actors expanded their activities and violently competed to

High Violence in Post-Civil War El Salvador

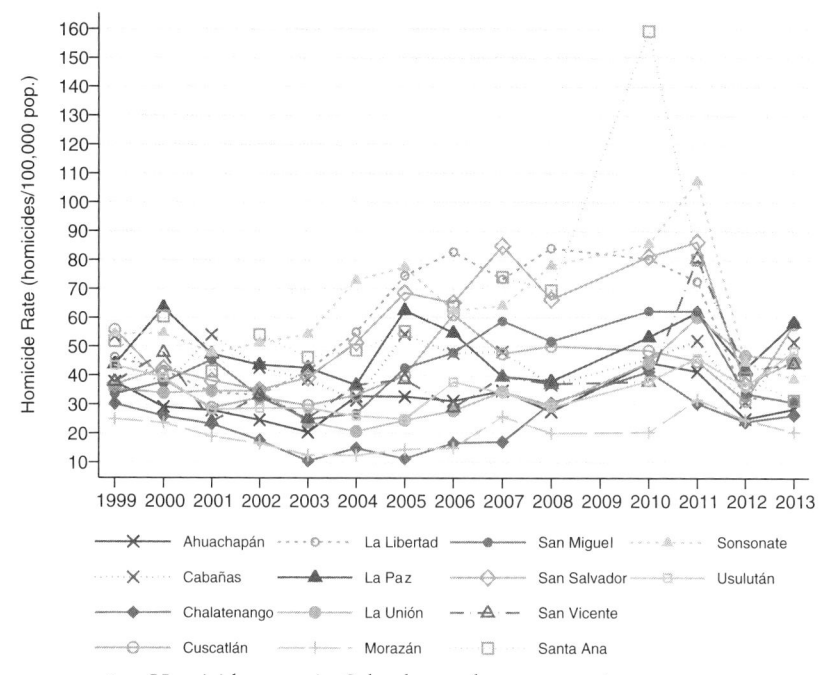

FIGURE 6.2 Homicide rates in Salvadoran departments (1999–2013, rate per 100,000)
Graph constructed by Daniela Barba-Sánchez using Stata.
Sources: Data on homicide frequencies for years 1999, 2000, and 2010–2013 come from Fabio Molina Vaquerano (2002), *Estudio de mortalidad de El Salvador*. San Salvador: IML, p. 48, available at www.csj.gob.sv/comunicaciones /Estad%C3%ADsticas/IML/periodos/1999.html; Fabio Molina Vaquerano (2003), *Defunciones por homicidios y suicidios en El Salvador 2000*. San Salvador: IML, p. 182, available at www.csj.gob.sv/comunicaciones/Estad%C3 %ADsticas/IML/periodos/2000.html; and IML homicide reports, various years, available at www.transparencia.oj.gob.sv/portal/transparencia.php? opcion=1&texto=homicidios&categoria=0.
Data on population by department for years 1999 and 2000 come from DIGESTYC, UNFPA, and Centro Latinoamericano de Demografía (1996), *Proyección de la población de El Salvador 1995–2025*. San Salvador, p. 144.
Data on population by department for years 2010–2013 come from IML reports, several years. Available at www.digestyc.gob.sv/index.php/temas/des/ehpm/publi caciones-ehpm.html.
Data on homicide rates for years 2001–2008 come from Fabio Molina Vaquerano (2009), Unidad de Estadísticas Forenses. Instituto de Medicina Legal (El Salvador). *Epidemiología de los homicidios en El Salvador período 2001–2008*, p. 113. Available at www.csj.gob.sv/comunicaciones/Estad%C3%ADsticas/IML/ periodos/imagenes_IML/hasta_2009/ANUARIO_FINAL_HOMICIDIOS_%202 001_2008.swf (accessed on September 17, 2015).

control specific territorial spaces. After discussing El Salvador's weak state capacity, I outline the rise of illicit actors and behaviors to gain insight into the geographic and temporal patterns of violence in this small country of just over 6 million – more urban and densely populated than Guatemala. With the analytic leverage provided by El Salvador's gang truce in 2012–2014 (which took place after my core argument was developed and while the book was being written), I further probe the plausibility of the book's core argument: that organizational competition to control illicit spaces is driving the high and uneven violence patterns that we see.

STATE CAPACITY: WEAK LAW AND ORDER

Despite the reforms announced with the peace accords, El Salvador's law-and-order institutions remained relatively weak, providing a permissive political environment for illicit activity. For despite widely celebrated institutional reforms, the police and courts remained ineffective and even complicit in the illicit political economy. This section develops this main theme.

The Chapultepec Peace Accords, signed in 1992, signaled an important political change in El Salvador. With the recognition that neither side could win militarily, the Salvadoran military and guerilla insurgency, the FMLN (Farabundo Martí de Liberación Nacional), signed the accords, which ended the civil war and promised a new era of democratic reforms – one that included significant reforms to a highly militarized state. Prior to the end of the civil war, all internal security fell under the constitutional domain of the defense ministry, which oversaw not just the military but also El Salvador's three police forces: the urban National Police, the rural National Guard, and the Treasury Police (Call 2003: 832).[7] The Salvadoran military and police were renowned for death squads, massacres, and torture; corruption also seemed to be endemic. As in Guatemala, the Salvadoran coercive forces had developed

---

[7] "Before and during the war, internal security was wholly militarised and no police reforms occurred except to enhance the security forces' capacity to carry out counter-insurgency. The Defence Ministry had constitutional responsibility for internal security and controlled the three main police forces: the urban National Police, the rural National Guard, and the Treasury Police. The military and police forces relied mainly on recruits drafted into service and professional career standards were minimal. Death squads operated especially out of the police forces and military intelligence although mainline army units also committed massacres and torture during the war" (Call 2003: 832).

a pattern of human rights abuses against its own population (although the level of torture was arguably an order of magnitude higher in Guatemala). Thus, El Salvador faced the imperative of dismantling repressive state institutions, including the military and police, as part of the democratization process. There were also calls to reform the judiciary (which had been a "highly politicized" institution during the authoritarian period, granting military impunity throughout the authoritarian period), including the ouster of judges and prosecutors who were "corrupt" or "unprofessional" or "threatened or killed," all for "low salaries" (Call 2003: 832).

In contrast to the more modest peace accord reforms in Guatemala, the Salvadoran accords were at first widely celebrated for providing a bright line for the reform of these state institutions and the promise of improved state capacity. Initially, the police in particular emerged as a model of civil war success, leading those in policy circles to emphasize the successes of the reforms.

However, the takeaway message from this section is that these reforms *did not* create an institutional break, and the "reformed" institutions continued to perpetuate many of the historically debilitating institutional weaknesses of the past – with the continuing participation of poorly trained, politicized, and/or corrupt state officials (police officers, judges, defenders, military officers, etc.) instead of the establishment of meaningful internal accountability. Thus, the post-civil war institutions were not equipped or committed to pursuing the rule of law. Indeed, they provided permissive conditions for the development of illicit activity in the country, providing fertile ground for the growth of gangs and a virtual invitation for drug trafficking organizations to move product northward through the territory. Thus, despite official celebrations, the police did not live up to the promise hailed by early advocates – marshaling neither the necessary human resources, infrastructure, integrity, nor performance. There was no bright line, and lots of impunity. Accordingly, El Salvador's law-and-order institutions have remained highly uneven in the years following the reforms. Limited resources (budgetary and human), poor performance, corruption, and low public confidence highlight weak state capacity in the aftermath of the accords. This is a position shared by most, if not all, subsequent research on El Salvador's police, judicial system, and prisons. Harvard's International Human Rights Clinic wrote, for example, "The weaknesses of these institutions have nurtured the conditions of violence, insecurity, and lawlessness that permeate public life in El Salvador today" (IHRC 2007: 7).[8]

The poor state of Salvadoran political institutions was raised by Senator Leahy of Vermont in a September 2013 press statement about the Second Millennium Challenge Compact. Highlighting the poor progress made in redressing corruption, criminal penetration, political autonomy, and professionalism in rule-of-law institutions, he identified the persistence of several issues within the attorney general's office, the courts, and the police. It is worth quoting at length:

While El Salvador can point to some success compared to its neighbors Honduras and Guatemala, it remains a country of weak democratic institutions where the independence of the judiciary has been attacked, corruption is widespread, and transnational criminal organizations have flourished. Money laundering is a multi-billion dollar scourge in El Salvador and other Central American countries, and impunity is the norm. The national police is discredited, infiltrated by organized crime and distrusted by the public ...

First is to significantly strengthen the capacity of the Attorney General's office and the police to combat money laundering, which is a growing problem and is driving legitimate businesses out of business. President Funes recently announced the creation of a special police unit for this purpose and I commend him for doing so, but it remains to be seen whether such a unit receives the necessary resources to be effective, and is not corrupted by the very criminals it is responsible for investigating and bringing to justice.

Second is to respect the independence of the Constitutional Oversight Court of the Supreme Court, or the Sala de lo Constitucional as it is known in Spanish, which is the chamber of the Supreme Court that rules on constitutional issues. For the first time since the Peace Accords El Salvador has an independent judicial body of magistrates who are widely recognized for being honest, who do not show fear or favor, and who have consistently ruled in an independent manner. Because their rulings have at times gone against the interests of the FMLN governing party and at other times against the interests of the opposition ARENA party, there have been efforts to replace them with individuals who can be manipulated.

Third is the concern I have raised about some public officials in positions of authority who have promoted individuals within the police and security forces who have no business being in public office because of their involvement in illegal activities.[9]

---

[8] Popkin notes, for example: "Many of the elements considered necessary to guarantee judicial independence – a guaranteed percentage of the national budget, changes in the judicial appointments and disciplinary system, and improved judicial training – were included in the Salvadoran peace accords. However, the reforms agreed to were not based on a broad national consensus or involvement of the justice sector in the discussion and implementation encountered many obstacles" (Popkin 2000: 251).

[9] Statement of Senator Patrick Leahy on a Second Millennium Challenge Compact for El Salvador, September 12, 2013 (accessed by author on July 16, 2014), www.leahy.senate

This section on weak state capacity, in general, and weak law-and-order institutions, in particular, unpacks these institutional weaknesses, with a primary focus on the police, followed by much briefer discussions of the judiciary and the prisons.[10] As this section reveals, El Salvador's complex of law-and-order institutions provides a permissive environment for illicit activity.[11]

The Police

The Chapultepec Accords created a new national civilian police force (the PNC) that included several institutional changes. First, the accords removed policing from the domain of the military (particularly the defense ministry). Second, the PNC was designed as a unified policing structure, dissolving the three police forces that had existed previously. Unification ostensibly allowed for clearer command structures, coordination, and accountability. Third, the accords were designed to civilianize and humanize the force, placing it under civilian leadership and incorporating human rights concerns (Call 2003: 833, 837); indeed, the new police consisted of 60 percent new civilian recruits and 20 percent each from the former national police and the guerilla front FMLN. Fourth, the reforms set out to professionalize the institution, creating a new police academy and raising educational requirements, including a new entrance exam (Call and Stanley 2001; Call 2003: 833; Moran 2009: 38). Thus, the new Salvadoran national police was supposed to be a new beginning following the peace accords (Costa 1999; Stanley 1999 and 2000; Call 2003).

Despite pronounced institutional and personnel overhauls, the police did not live up to its promise,[12] nor did it forge a clean institutional

---

.gov/press/statement-of-senator-patrick-leahy-on-a-second-millennium-challenge-compact-for-el-salvador. Also referenced in Silva Ávalos (2014: 29–30).

[10] While significant reforms also took place in the military and secondarily in the judiciary, I focus on the police for two reasons. First, it is the most proximate face of state capacity vis-à-vis the illicit sector; second, it is the most striking point of comparison both with Guatemala (which also shares poor performance) and with Nicaragua (which emerges with a comparatively capable and competent police force). After briefly discussing the peace accords' uneven impact, I turn to various indicators of weak police capacity and widespread perceptions of complicity.

[11] State complicity, corruption, and infiltration by organized crime were noted in interviews with Benita Lara, August 19, 2008, and Juan Daniel Alemán, August 27, 2008.

[12] See Popkin (2000: 175) and passim, Call (2003), IDHUCA (2006), and Jeannette Aguilar. "La mano dura y las políticas de seguridad." *Estudios Centroamericanos* 667. Elecciones y Medios de Comunicación: No. Monográfico 441–443 (Universidad Centroamericana

break, define a clear policing mandate, or inherit (or create) a corporatist commitment to the institution – all factors that were present in the Nicaraguan case. For even with efforts to demilitarize, unify, civilianize, and professionalize the police, serious obstacles remained to meeting these goals. The military, for one, provided obstacles in the creation of the police academy (ANSP), and the new police still included two problematic police units that had been part of the former national police – the special investigative unit (SIU) and the anti-narcotics nit (Call 2003: 838; Moran 2009: 39).[13]

Moreover, units that should have been disbanded were not; members of the old security forces remained in positions of leadership, beyond the number allowed for by the peace accords (IHRC 2007: 10); and the executive anti–drug trafficking unit (UEA) was incorporated directly into the PNC, albeit with limited accountability and oversight (Popkin 2000: 183–184). As an unintended consequence, demilitarization, where it occurred, was not well planned, leaving many without a job, on the streets, and arguably primed to engage in illicit activity:[14] "the vast majority of combatants were demobilised in an extremely brief period following the end of the war. Within one year, 12,362 guerrillas, some 20,000 soldiers and around 30,000 civil defence guards were left unemployed" – all this with a smaller police force than previously and many registered and unregistered arms on the street (Call 2003: 843).

Given the continuing role of prior institutions and actors, there was no "clean break" from the past or "integrated professional" training going forward. Silva Ávalos (2014: 5–6) reports that the PNC failed on various dimensions: in creating a new culture of legality, professional conduct, training, and the possibility for internal reform. "Like its predecessors, the PNC specialized in obstructing justice and guaranteeing impunity for those with sufficient influence or money" (Silva Ávalos 2014: 6). There was also poor coordination between police, the courts,

---

José Simeón Cañas Central American University, May 2004). Also interviews with Benito Lara, August 19, 2008, and David Morales, August 26, 2008.

[13] As discussed later, the ANU would later be charged with corruption.
[14] In an interview with Edgardo Amaya (August 5, 2008), he noted that criminal bands were comprised of ex-combatants in the years immediately following demobilization. Call (2003: 843) also notes that many ex-combatants engaged in crime and were sometimes associated with gangs. Citing a 1999 survey of prison inmates, he found a high percentage of inmates who were former members of the armed forces/security forces (22 percent) and former insurgents (6 percent). Zeroing in on the prisoner population between 26 and 40, he reports that 44 percent were former combatants.

and the attorney general's office. The latter had assumed increased responsibilities for pursuing criminal investigations, but the post-reform period did not see a corresponding increase in the budget, nor was there sufficient coordination across institutions (Popkin 2000: 217). Moreover, there were severe institutional limits to internal discipline and coordination.

There was no effective coordination among the three internal disciplinary units within the PNC, much less with other state entities such as the National Counsel of the Defense of Human Rights and the Attorney General's office. ONUSAL deplored the "failure to observe the requisite rigor which ought to accompany internal disciplinary procedures in the police's early stages of existence." (Popkin 2000: 177)

While measures were announced to address these problems in the ensuing years, the core institutional problems remained.

For example, although corruption declined at first, it later worsened – with the discovery of police officers taking part in kidnappings and other protection rackets, lack of citizen trust in the police, and ongoing concerns about violations of civil and political rights (Call 2003: 844–846). Thus, in the aftermath of the accords, further reforms were announced,[15] although their impact was also questionable, cementing societal concerns about police capacity, integrity, and commitment. Indeed, while scandals gave way to reforms, societal perceptions of the police remained "lukewarm or negative" (Call 2003: 848).

An abbreviated list of police "incapacities" in the post-accord period includes the following.

First, as a basic constraint on state capacity, the police force has had limited resources and a weak infrastructure. While resource constraints are not determinative, neither are they inconsequential.[16] When constructing the newspaper database on violence, numerous articles highlighted limited resources and correspondingly poor institutional capacity,

---

[15] For example, according to Hunt's (2008) 2007 interview with Astor Escalante Saravia, vice minister of public safety and justice, there were reforms to the ministry of governance, which resulted in the creation of a separate ministry of public safety.

[16] José Miguel Cruz presentation at Brown University workshop, "Drug Wars in the Americas: Looking Back and Thinking Ahead," at the Watson Institute, April 2–13, 2012. Cruz convincingly highlighted that the Nicaraguan police force suffers from poor resources and yet is able to defend the rule of law with greater success. Thus, poor resources can certainly be a constraint, but it is not determinative.

with PNC and Fiscalía (prosecutor's office) officials commenting on this challenge – including budgets, technology, equipment, and knowledge deficits. These comments were made not only about the police and prosecutor's office in general, but also of particular divisions responsible for the investigation of crime, such as the División de Investigaciones de Homicidios (DIHO) and the Instituto de Medicina Legal.[17]

The lack of resources was identified, unsurprisingly, as the source of many ills – not just in the capital but particularly in the interior of the country. News stories identified the inability to pay for new recruits, tattered uniforms, and police stations without clean water or funds to pay rent or utilities, among others issues.[18] "Underfunded," "poorly resourced," and "incapable of meeting organizational demands" were common refrains in these types of newspaper reports. The interior minister vividly summarized the depth of the problem: "The police lack gloves, lack tape to isolate the scene of the crime ... even [lack] bags to get rid of the cadaver."[19]

Weak infrastructure (related to poor resources, including human capital) was another indicator of weak state capacity. The basic unevenness of police presence was highlighted in a telling interview with Walter Knut (then president of the Accreditation Commission in El Salvador and a social science academic). He stated that policing of public spaces was sorely lacking (Hunt 2008: 10).[20] Not only was police presence scarce, but the numerous private security forces that *were* present had limited their tasks to guarding physical property and/ or individuals.

If you walk around San Salvador today, you will see very, I think very little police presence. You will see police cars and police trucks, but it is very unusual to see police officers walking their beat. That is one of the things that has been

---

[17] *La Prensa Gráfica* 8.24.2005 Investigación de homicidios sin recursos.
[18] For example, see *La Prensa Gráfica* 1.17.1999 PNC no abrirá más puestos en 1999; and 3.4.1999 PNC carece de todo ... hasta de uniformes; 3.25.2000 Cierran puestos policiales en tres colonias.
[19] *La Prensa Gráfica* 5.4.2005. Impune 50% muertes: "Las policías están escasos de guantes, están escasos de cintas para aislar la escena del delito ... hasta de bolsas para echar el cadáver."
[20] According to LAPOP data, confidence in the police can vary with perceptions of community involvement (reaching out to youth, attending meetings, speaking to community members), thus making Knut's observations about low police presence doubly consequential both for preventing crime and for instilling trust. Surprisingly, participation in preventative programs did not appear to have a statistically significant relationship to trust in the police in 2012 (Córdova, Cruz, and Seligson 2013: 216–217).

criticized, the fact that the police don't move and they don't mix with the people, they don't provide, if they can, on site protection in public areas. (Hunt 2008: 10)

Second, there is a yawning gap between mandate and performance. Weak performance, especially investigations (i.e., collecting evidence and investigating crimes scenes) and identifying suspects, are commonly noted by academics, journalists, and police officers alike.[21] Police did not have the training or knowledge to appropriately address crime scenes, for example. Deysi de Rodríguez, a sub-chief in the Fiscalía, remarked, "What happens in the street following a homicide? The person who arrives first is from public security; the police from public security do not have the basic knowledge regarding the collection and preservation of evidence."[22]

The police, thus, do not have a strong reputation for conducting investigations or solving serious crimes. According to a 1995 UN (ONUSAL) review, investigations have been unlikely to occur (undertaken in just over one-fifth of cases reported to the police) or undertaken with limited steps once initiated. Low state capacity to pursue investigations has coincided with turning a blind eye or even thwarting investigations entailing police and military engagement in criminal activities. The police reportedly only issued about one-fifth of judicial warrants for arrest and focused on petty rather than serious crime (Popkin 2000: 183–186). "A study released by FUSADES (the Salvadoran Foundation for Economic and Social Development) in April 1999, found that suspects were arrested in only 6 to 8 percent of murder cases" (Popkin 2000: 240).[23] Yet even public officials have noted uncertainty about prosecution figures. The attorney general of El Salvador, Félix Garrid Safie, said in December 2006 that he did not know how many of the

---

[21] In particular, see Popkin (2000: 191) for a summary of problems, including lack of professional skills, minimal equipment and training, limited oversight, problems with anti-crime strategy, etc. "With a few important exceptions, in the years immediately following the peace accords Salvadoran criminal justice continued to be characterized by inadequate – or nonexistent– criminal investigations" (Popkin 2000: 178). Importantly, investigations are not the prerogative of the police alone, as responsibilities are distributed across the police, the attorney general's office, and the courts.

[22] *La Prensa Gráfica* 1.20.2005 PNC sin acceso a datos sobre armas: "¿Qué sucede en la calle con un homicidio? La persona que primero llega es seguridad pública; los policías de seguridad pública no tienen los conocimientos básicos acerca del levantamiento y la preservación de evidencias."

[23] In one related figure, arrest rates for homicide cases were less than 2 percent in 1997 (280 arrests out of 3,926 homicides reported; Popkin 2000: 190).

approximately 3,700 homicides committed each year were prosecuted, though he suggested that it would probably not be a "praiseworthy figure."[24] Juvenile Court Judge Aída Luz Santos Mejía de Escobar noted, moreover, the lack of coordination between the attorney general's office (FGR), which is supposed to direct investigations, and the PNC, which is not always willing to share information gathered during its own investigations.[25] Accordingly, she cited a 2007 Instituto de Medicina Legal (IML) report stating that of the homicides committed between January and October 2007, a suspect was identified in only 17.9 percent.[26]

The newspaper violence database (covering 2000, 2005, and 2010) paints a similar picture; in 2005, for example, most violent crimes committed remained unsolved. One article reported that only 3–4 percent of homicide cases were brought to trial (presumably conviction rates were even lower).[27] Another 2005 article noted that of the 3,897 homicides committed in 2004, half were still "sobreaveriguar," with no known motive or suspect; in nearly a quarter of these cases (1,056), the state had identified a suspect, but they had not uncovered enough evidence to convict. Less than 3 percent of homicide cases made it to court within a year.[28]

As for actually making it to trial (an outcome that entails police, attorney general, and judicial capacities), the results are limited. Referring to data from as early as 1996 and 1997, Hume (2004: 15, drawing on work by Cóbar and Palmieri 2000) reports that just over 6 percent and 8 percent, respectively, of murder cases made it to trial. For those cases that did so, homicide investigations and trials were often stymied by the inability to secure eyewitness testimony, especially since many witnesses had been killed prior to trial.[29] Courts were therefore in a

---

[24] IHRC (2007, footnote 303). IHRC cites information from Ernesto Mejía and Gabriel Trillos. *La Prensa Gráfica* 12.4.2006 "2007 va a ser el año de la mejora en la investigación."
[25] Edgardo Amaya also noted the poor coordination between the FRG and PNC in pursuing investigations (interview August 15, 2008).
[26] Interview with Judge Aída Luz Santos Mejía de Escobar, August 14, 2008.
[27] *La Prensa Gráfica* 1.6.2005. El Ejecutivo apuesta por restringir control de armas.
[28] Newspaper violence database – 2005 General Violence Memo for El Salvador. Also see *La Prensa Gráfica* 5.4.2005 Impune 50% muertes; 5.4.2005 Heredamos de la guerra el irrespeto a la vida.
[29] *La Prensa Gráfica* 6.22.2005 Desaparece testigo de masacre en taxi. Also see 7.21.2005 Muerte de testigo clave aplaza juicio; 8.25.2005 Niño asesinado estaba bajo régimen protección; 6.22.2005 Desaparece testigo de masacre en taxi. Thirty-two people (who

quandary, often left without technical evidence *and* without eyewitness testimony. Judges have noted that "the majority of cases have to be 'proven' only with testimonies, and when they do not appear, they are almost always lost."[30]

Estimates of homicide *conviction rates* (alongside investigation and prosecution rates) are also very low (and open to interpretation), as a study of the police and attorney general data reveal.

The rates of investigation and prosecution of homicides in El Salvador remain extremely low. Precise statistics on the number of homicide cases that are prosecuted are very difficult to obtain. Researchers at FESPAD compared homicide statistics and homicide conviction totals from the PNC and the Fiscalía General de la República (Attorney General's Office ["FGR"]) for 2004. Because the PNC and FGR used differing homicide figures for that year, the conviction rates differed slightly, but both were extremely low: 7.4% based on the FGR's homicide figures and 10.4% based on the PNC's homicide figures. (IHRC 2007: 64–65)

Looking at performance in dealing with homicides and crime as a whole, the Tutela Legal del Arzobispado (Salvadoran archbishop's office; 2007) critically analyzes a whole range of deficiencies regarding the rule of law. These include the lack of a real crime policy; the lack of prevention and social policies; the largely unscientific investigatory practices and poor investigatory relations between the police and the attorney general's office; police corruption and impunity; human rights abuses; punitive approach, often with disregard for civil rights; and weak judicial oversight over police and attorney general practices (2007: 93–94). The police's (in)actions amount to a "grave breach of state obligations."[31]

In short, police capacity to address homicide is wanting. As a result, homicides are rarely investigated or prosecuted. While these state responsibilities do not only fall on the police, as discussed further in this section,

---

had been called as witnesses) were killed by June of 2005 for the period covering 2004 to mid-2005.

[30] *La Prensa Gráfica* 1.20.2005 PNC sin acceso a datos sobre armas: "La mayoría de casos tratan de ser 'probados' sólo con testimonios, y cuando no se presentan, casi siempre se pierden."

[31] Quote from source: "La persecución policial generalizada y arbitraria, en el contexto de una notoria deficiencia en la investigación de los delitos (lo que incluye responsabilidad fiscal) y de ausencia de estrategias preventivas y políticas de readaptación de los infractores, supone un estado de grave incumplimiento a las obligaciones estatales emanadas de su *deber de garantía* de la vigencia de los derechos humanos" (Tutela Legal del Arzobispado 2007: 93).

they do provide insight into poor performance. If the police cannot fulfill its most basic job, then it is hard to think about the police playing a deterrent role when considering serious crimes, as Becker (1974) might have argued. These are, by definition, permissive conditions for the growth of illicit activity.

Third, corruption and malfeasance emerged as an endemic problem in the police, serving as both causes and consequences of weak state capacity.[32] These occurred at the highest ranks. At times, they involved carry-overs from the previous police, including personnel and units that were incorporated into the new PNC. "The head of the Antinarcotics Unit, who had been appointed Deputy Chief of the new PNC, was forced to resign under suspicion of involvement in illicit activities. According to UN investigators, thirteen of the roughly hundred prior SIU agents were implicated in political murders or their cover-up *after* the ceasefire" (Call 2003: 838; also see Moran 2009: 39).[33]

Indeed, Silva Ávalos (2014: 2, 6–8) refers to former military men who had worked with criminal groups and remained in the new police as an "original sin" that left in place a corrupt PNC and one that provided an advantageous environment for the maintenance and development of criminal organizations; high-level corruption remains in the PNC, with reports of the former director interacting socially with criminals at the highest level.

Archival and field research presented here demonstrates that the PNC has been plagued by its own "original sin": the inclusion of former soldiers that worked with criminal groups and preserved a closed power structure that prevented any authority from investigating them for over two decades. This original sin has allowed criminal bands formed in the 1980s as weapon or drug smugglers to forge connections with the PNC and to develop into sophisticated drug trafficking organizations (DTOs). These new DTOs are now involved in money laundering, have secured pacts with major criminal players in the region – such as Mexican and Colombian cartels – and have learned how to use the formal economy and financial system. These "entrepreneurs" of crime, long tolerated and nurtured by law enforcement officials and politicians in El Salvador, are now major regional players themselves. (Silva Ávalos 2014: 2)

---

[32] Corruption and malfeasance are arguably part of performance. However, the prior section was written "as if" intentions were good even if outcomes were poor. This third indicator looks at actions that reveal problematic intentions.

[33] Call notes the surprising ability of ex-FMLN and military men to work alongside each other and speculates that this probably provided "security guarantees for the peace process and internal checks on police partisanship" (Call 2003: 839).

High Violence in Post-Civil War El Salvador 223

The newspaper violence database also uncovered frequent malfeasance by the police – ranging from misdemeanors and drunken behavior to homicides and involvement in criminal activity[34] – and occasional state efforts to rectify the problem with arrests, purges, and the creation of internal affairs units.[35] Purges were not uncommon. A significant purge took place in 2000, with the firing of as many as 1,200 officers, including three high-ranking officials, chiefs of regional offices.[36] A 2005 report highlighted the ongoing problem: some 4,000 policemen dismissed in the previous two years, and 1,500 more slated for dismissal for corruption.[37] Reporting of police (and military) corruption and complicity appeared even more prevalent in 2010 (compared to 2000–2005). These articles noted involvement in all kinds of crimes, 274 cases of police officer incarceration in 2010, and 2,032 complaints of police misconduct.[38] A few of these instances referenced police involvement in organized crime and gang activity.[39]

At the time of this writing, these issues have not disappeared. Shady appointments and accusations of criminal ties in the PNC (alongside criminal conviction rates of less than 55 percent in the court system) were noted in Ribando Seelke's CRS report (2014: 10–11) written for the US Congress. The same conditions were found in the military; the Salvadoran chief prosecutor, Luis Martínez, announced that the

---

[34] See, for example, *La Prensa Gráfica* 5.19.1999 Más de 400 policías detenidos desde 1998; 12.6.1999 Condenan a 8 miembros del 121; 6.28.2000 ¿Crimen organizado en la PNC? – una muestra.

[35] *La Prensa Gráfica* 6.8.1999 460 malos policías; 1.31.2000 Más de mil denuncias contra policías en 1999. See *La Prensa Gráfica* articles, including 6.1.2000 Comisión depuradora PNC se reúne por primera vez; 6.8.2000 Acuerdan reformas ley PNC; 7.26.2000 Civiles retomarán depuración policial; 7.27.2000 Estudian reformas para crear tribunales civiles PNC; 10.12.2000 PNC destituye a tres jefes policiales.

[36] See *La Prensa Gráfica* articles, including 6.1.2000 Comisión depuradora PNC se reúne por primera vez; 6.8.2000 Acuerdan reformas ley PNC; 7.26.2000 Civiles retomarán depuración policial; 7.27.2000 Estudian reformas para crear tribunales civiles PNC; 10.12.2000 PNC destituye a tres jefes policiales.

[37] *La Prensa Gráfica* 12.7.2005 Destituirán a 1 mil 500 agentes de la Policía por actos de corrupción. Also see 7.26.2005 Policía a juicio por homicidio.

[38] *La Prensa Gráfica* 5.23.2010 93 Policías detenidos en cuatro meses de 2010. Of these complaints, 503 resulted in charges dropped, 554 resulted in sanctions for serious or very serious crimes, and 411 agents received light sanctions for less serious crimes (12.22.2010 PNC reporta 274 policías detenidos durante 2010).

[39] *La Prensa Gráfica* 10.2.2010 FGR investiga casos de sicariato en San Miguel; 12.1.2010 Funes insta a evitar caer en un narco-Estado; 12.21.2010 Capturan a tres policías, presuntos miembros de banda de asaltantes; 1.21.2010 Pandillas quisieron infiltrar Fuerza Armada.

Salvadoran state had initiated investigations into whether the defense minister, David Munguía Payés, along with other high-ranking military officers, had been involved in illegal arms trafficking.[40] In this context, the police remain a highly corrupt institution.[41]

Fourth, El Salvador experienced a pervasive lack of trust in the police and parallel lack of security. When citizens were asked to gauge their trust in political institutions, rule-of-law institutions fell near the bottom among national institutions (although higher than political parties and the national assembly, for which trust was excruciatingly low; see Figure 6.3). Only 54 percent of the population expressed trust in the police in 2012 – higher than in 2008 and 2010 (when the rating fell below 50 percent) although lower than 2004 (when it was about 65 percent; Córdova, Cruz, and Seligson 2013: 156–157). Lest one think that this is a generalized distrust in the coercive forces, it is notable that the armed forces top the list at 67.4 percent (higher than the Catholic Church).

Low trust in the police coincides with perceptions of low levels of security, with El Salvador near the top of the regional charts (Córdova, Cruz, and Seligson 2013: 105–113). LAPOP AmericasBarometer public opinion surveys reveal clear patterns (see Figure 6.4).

Newspaper reporting further highlighted anxiety about crime and the underlying impression that citizens could not (or should not) trust the police (some of whom seemed to share information with extortionists), in some cases for fear of retribution.[42] More than 50 percent of victim's families declined to go to police, according to a newspaper survey analyzing behaviors in the preceding three months.[43]

Fifth, other armed institutions have been brought in to play a subsidiary policing role. In what is perhaps the clearest sign of weak police state capacity in providing the rule of law, it appears that the police cannot do this on its own. The Salvadoran state (as in Guatemala) has come to rely on military support to address public security, with 11,500 military troops

---

[40] *LatinNews*. Latin American Security & Strategic Review. June (2014). "Pointers: El Salvador: Defence Minister in Gunrunning Inquiry." Accessed online on July 11, 2014.

[41] While *perception* of corruption is high in absolute terms, comparatively speaking, it falls on the lower end of the regional range – whether looking at perceptions of corruption or victimization surveys for general crime (Córdova, Cruz, and Seligson 2013: 104–106).

[42] See, for example, *La Prensa Gráfica* 2.20.2005 El triángulo del miedo y el silencio; 11.10.2005 Maras acosan a microbuseros; 9.23.2005 Población acosada por extorsiones de mareros; 5.4.2005 Usulután, homicidios y seguridad.

[43] *La Prensa Gráfica* 9.2.2005 La mayoría no denuncia.

(a)

[Bar chart showing average trust in 2012 (0–100 scale):
Armed forces 67.4, Catholic church 62.2, Mass media 61.9, Municipality 60.9, Human rights attorney 59.6, National government 58.2, Elections 54.1, National civil police 54.0, Supreme electoral tribunal 53.2, Supreme court of justice 51.3, Justice system 50.1, Legislative assembly 49.3, Political parties 34.4]

(b)

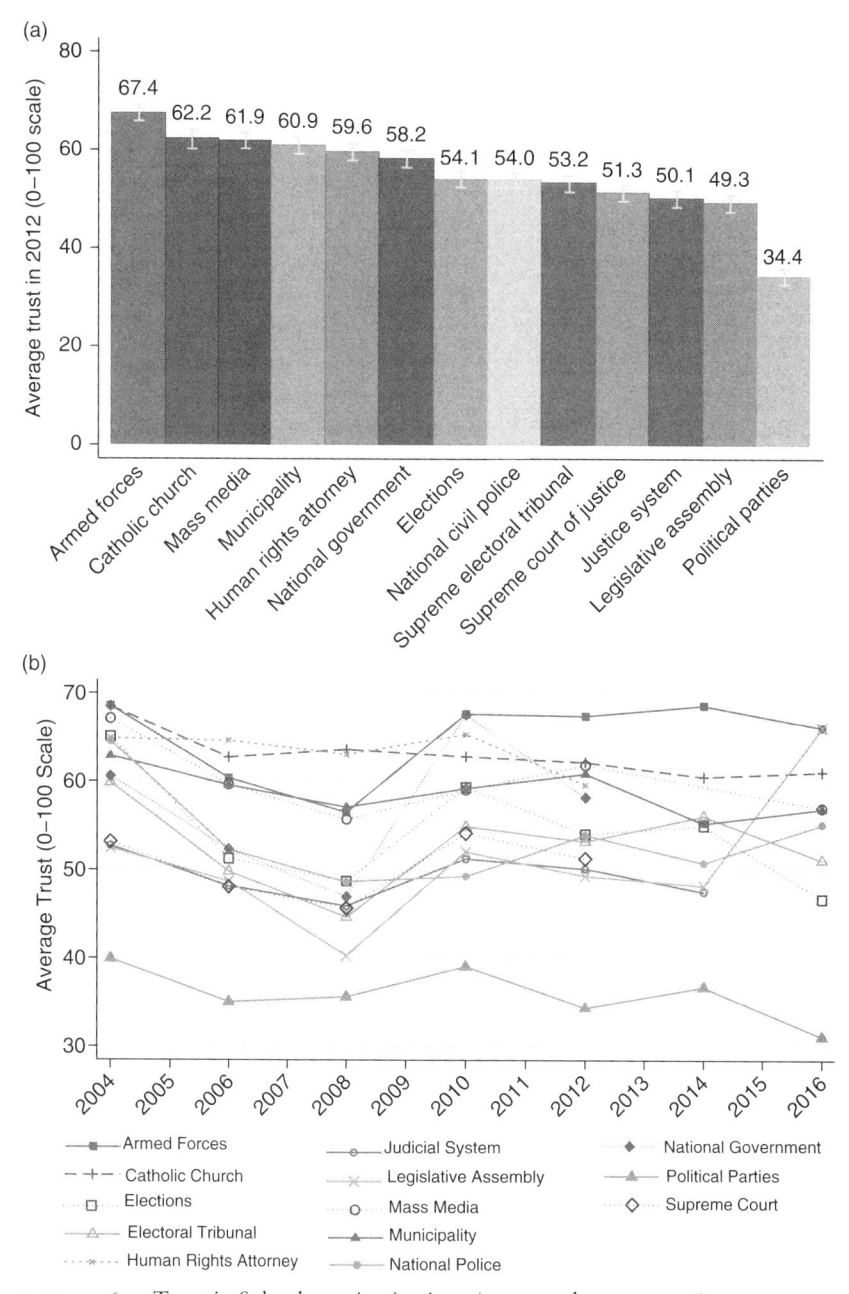

[Line chart showing Average Trust (0–100 Scale) from 2004 to 2016 for: Armed Forces, Judicial System, National Government, Catholic Church, Legislative Assembly, Political Parties, Elections, Mass Media, Supreme Court, Electoral Tribunal, Municipality, Human Rights Attorney, National Police]

FIGURE 6.3 Trust in Salvadoran institutions (2012 and 2004–2016)
Sources and Notes: Figure (a) adapted from Córdova, Cruz, and Seligson 2013: 156, figure V.22. Calculated from LAPOP 2012. Average responses. Responses in Likert scale rescaled to 0–100. Confidence intervals are located at the top of each bar, with means also reported for each institution.
Figure (b) calculated from LAPOP, various years. Responses in Likert scale rescaled to 0–100.

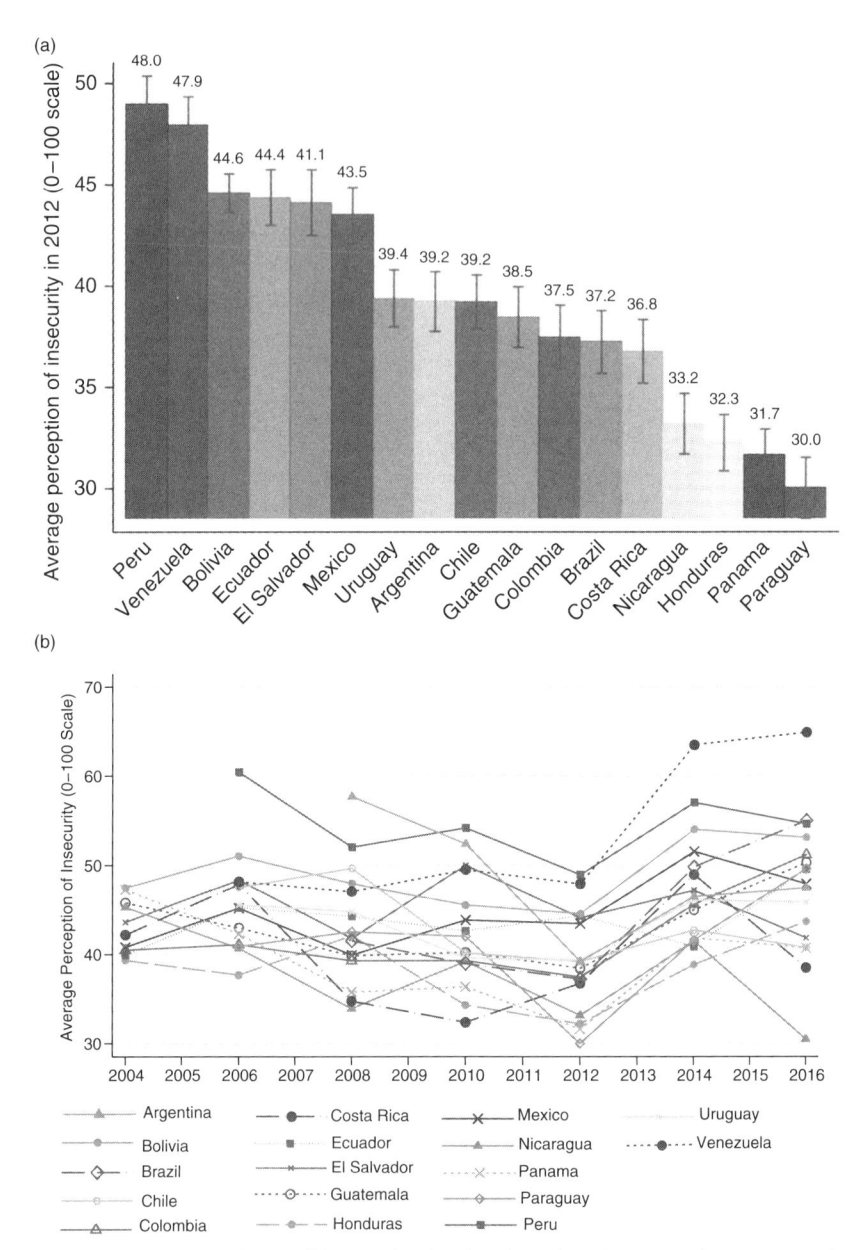

226   Part III   Divergent Trajectories: Three Post-Civil War Cases

FIGURE 6.4 Perceptions of insecurity in the Americas (2012 and 2004–2016) *Sources and Notes*: Figure (a) calculated from LAPOP 2012 (www.LapopSurveys .org). Average perceptions of insecurity in own neighborhood. Responses in Likert scale rescaled to 0–100 scale. Confidence intervals are located at the top of each bar, with means also reported for each country. Figure (b) calculated from LAPOP 2012

working with the police as of April 2014 (Ribando Seelke 2014: 11).[44] In turn, the private security sector has boomed. By 2013, there were arguably more private security guards (28,600) than PNC police (roughly 22,000) (Ribando Seelke 2014: 9).

According to the PNC's strategic plan for 2009–2014, the challenges it sought to overcome during the Funes government included "a lack of incentives and a career path for officers, deficient training, and infrastructure, and a lack of intelligence capacities, among others." Corruption, weak investigatory capacity, and an inability to prosecute officers accused of corruption and human rights abuses remain additional barriers to improved police performance. (Ribando Seelke 2014: 10)

Yet the military (like other law enforcement agencies) has also been subject to charges of gang infiltration. In January 2010, Minister of Defense David Munguía Payés reported that ten members of FAES were discharged for gang membership and that there were most likely more: "There are more cases, in almost all the military units, it is something that is taking place daily." The minister indicated that there was a premeditated plan by gangs to infiltrate the army. He also noted that soldiers had been offered up to $900 to sell their rifles to criminals.[45]

FIGURE 6.4 (cont.)

and LAPOP 2014–2016 (www.LapopSurveys.org). Average responses. Responses in Likert scale rescaled to 0–100.
In both figures, the question posed measured neighborhood insecurity by asking about the likelihood of being a victim of assault or robbery (LAPOP survey question AOJ11): Hablando del lugar o el barrio/la colonia donde usted vive y pensando en la posibilidad de ser víctima de un asalto o robo, ¿usted se siente muy seguro(a), algo seguro(a), algo inseguro(a) o muy inseguro(a)? (1) Muy seguro(a) (2) Algo seguro(a) (3) Algo inseguro(a) (4) Muy inseguro(a) (88) NS (98) NR. Coding followed AmericasBarometer standards and were recodified on a 0–100 scale (with greater insecurity corresponding with a higher number). See www.vanderbilt.edu/lapop/es/El_Salvador_Country_Report_2012_Cover_W.pdf.

---

[44] Interview with David Morales, August 28, 2008. Morales noted that the military was incorporated into joint patrols with the PNC, primarily in rural areas, by 1994. Interview with Oscar Bonilla, August 20, 2008; he also commented that operationally the police and military engage in joint patrols, largely based in rural areas.

[45] *La Prensa Gráfica* 1.21.2010 Pandillas quisieron infiltrar Fuerza Armada: "Son más casos, en casi todas las unidades militares, es algo que se está dando cotidianamente."

Finally, impunity has been the default. H. E. Hugo Martínez, El Salvador's minister of foreign relations, "argued that El Salvador's long-standing issues of impunity have facilitated the operation of criminal networks, often with the direct participation of state officials" (reported in and worded by Arnson and Drolet 2011: 3). Most would agree that the process is endogenous, with poor state capacity facilitating (even advancing) illicit activity and, in turn, illicit actors capturing and coordinating with the police. José Miguel Cruz emphasizes this point when arguing that it is not lack of state presence that fuels organized crime, but rather co-optation. According to Cruz, "these [organized crime] groups are co-opting geographical areas, recreating patronage networks instrumental to organized crime activities, and partnering with existing political and community leaders, as has been done historically" (as summarized and worded by Arnson and Drolet 2011: 7).

In this context, the PNC lacked autonomy, and interviews highlight the political uses of the institution (a common refrain in interviews). Judge Aída Luz Santos Mejía de Escobar noted that "the biggest problem of the PNC is that it is politically compromised and responds to political pressure from the executive branch. It should be an autonomous, apolitical institution, but instead the leadership proselytizes on behalf of ARENA, which makes it impossible for the institution to perform its tasks objectively."[46] Carlos López (then coordinator of the Centro de Monitoreo de la Violencia) claimed: "Despite the fact that the peace accords intended to create a completely apolitical police, ARENA has had control of the institution since its founding, and the higher ranks are full of members of the armed forces."[47] Edgardo Amaya (then Asesor del Despacho de la Procuraduría para la Defensa de los Derechos Humanos) noted that despite the fact that the PNC was born out of a compromise during the peace accords, "unfortunately, this pluralism does not extend to the police leadership; the military and ARENA-led government has steadily purged the leadership of non-loyalists, with the result that it is almost entirely led by former military personnel."[48] Agreeing that police leadership had been highly partisan, Jeanette Aguilar (director of El Instituto Universitario de Opinión Pública, IUDOP) stated that the main reason that the police has been unable to deal with crime is that "the PNC has been unable to become a professional

---

[46] Interview with Judge Aída Luz Santos Mejía de Escobar (Juzgado Primero de Ejecución de Medidas al Menor de San Salvador), August 14, 2008.
[47] Interview with Carlos López, August 11, 2008.
[48] Interview with Edgardo Amaya, August 15, 2008.

corps, in large part because of the political involvement in the institution ... The police have served political interests, concretely the ARENA party which in some ways has biased and affected its work."[49] As discussed further on, ARENA politicians seeking a political edge passed a punitive anti-crime measure (*mano dura*) that relied on the police to pursue measures deemed unconstitutional by the Supreme Court.[50]

Judicial System

The police operate in a broader context of rule-of-law institutions among which the judiciary is chief. If the police entered the post-accord period with weak institutions, so too did the Salvadoran judicial system. According to Popkin's in-depth analysis, El Salvador has historically lacked an "independent, efficient, accessible, and impartial justice system" (Popkin 2000: 97).[51]

Through the war years and before, international bodies had decried the weaknesses of the Salvadoran judicial system – particularly its inability to confront grave human rights violations ... [T]he peace negotiations represented a unique opportunity to introduce far-reaching reforms in Salvadoran institutions and constitution or, in the words of some of those involved in the negotiations, to "jumpstart" the judicial system ... In reality however, the Salvadoran justice system was in need of more than getting back on track: it had not simply been stalled or derailed by the exigencies of war. An independent, efficient, accessible, and impartial justice system had never existed in El Salvador. A profound transformation was called for, not simply the correction of certain aspects of the system. (Popkin 2000: 97)

Before highlighting the many weaknesses in the judicial system, it is important to note that rule-of-law reforms did take place – including a

---

[49] Interview with Jeanette Aguilar, August 13, 2008.
[50] Interview with Judge Aída Luz Santos Mejía de Escobar, August 14, 2008. Also see Holland (2013) for a discussion of *mano dura* as a political tool in El Salvador and González (2014) for a comparative discussion of the police, politics, and the difficulty of police reform in Latin America.
[51] Popkin (2000), a lawyer who spent many years working in and on El Salvador, has written a comprehensive overview of the Salvadoran legal system. She notes that the United States oversaw various judicial reform programs during the civil war, often viewed as part of a counterinsurgency effort that tended to focus on more technical/efficiency issues rather than the broader question of how the system was organized and the power relations in which it was embedded. Moreover, when it came time to reform the judicial system as part of the civil war peace accords, the guerilla insurgency also had limited training and foresight about what to do in this domain.

move away from the inquisitorial system, a new process for choosing judges, and greater autonomy, among other reforms (Popkin 2000: 101–102).[52] A new supreme court was selected following the war and reportedly was "more professional, more politically plural, and less partisan" – although Call underscores that the courts were pluralized but not depoliticized, with an apparent disinclination to discipline lower courts (Call 2003: 853). Reforms were also made to the attorney general's office (Call 2003: 854–855). Prior to the peace accords, El Salvador followed the continental judicial system whereby judges directed investigations. Following the 1992 accords, reforms were made to the attorney general's office to allow it to take the lead in investigations (Call 2003: 854). Moreover, the system moved toward an adversarial process, following 1998 reforms to the criminal procedure code.[53]

Despite these reforms, the challenges to overhaul and rebuild were significant – including the need for rapid increases in size, personnel, human capital, and budgeting. Call (2003) finds that the accords did not adequately address these issues, and Popkin, who anticipated these

---

[52] Popkin outlines the judicial reforms, which "changed the formula for electing judges at all levels; increased the independence of the National Judiciary Council and gave it additional responsibilities for the nomination of judges and magistrates as well as the Judicial training School; increased the budget of the judiciary; prohibited judges from serving as notaries; required a two-thirds legislative majority for the election of Supreme Court justices, the attorney general, and the state counsel; established a new human rights ombudsman; gave the attorney general greater responsibility for directing criminal investigations; and ended military court jurisdiction over civilians accused of subversive activities when constitutional guarantees are suspended. Additional political agreements set forth guidelines designed to restructure the National Judiciary Council 'to guarantee its independence from the organs of State and from political parties' and to include in the councilpersons not directly related to the administration of justice. These agreements also called for transforming the Judicial Training School and reforming the careers judicial service law. Although the Mexico Accords noted that 'the set of political agreements on the judicial system envisaged by the Parties in the Caracas Agenda has still to be negotiated,' further agreements were never negotiated" (Popkin 2000: 101). "The final Chapultepec agreement included a one-page chapter on the judicial system that reiterated the prior agreement on the National Judiciary Council and the Judicial Training School, emphasizing the need to ensure its academic independence and openness to various schools of legal thought" (Popkin 2000: 101–102).

[53] Call observes: "Oral testimony become more prevalent, and prosecutorial discretion (including the introduction of a form of plea bargaining) was introduced. Important limits on police and judicial abuses were adopted as well as procedural guarantees, including eliminating the admissibility of confessions taken without the presence of a lawyer presence [sic], limiting the time for different phases of the judicial process, capping the length of pre-trial detention, and requiring immediate appointment of defence counsel" (Call 2003: 855). Also see Popkin (2000, passim).

concerns, highlights that the FMLN did not have a clear view of what was needed (Popkin 2000: 97).[54]

As with the police, the attorney general's office needed to grow quickly, improve personnel, and retain some expertise despite having a large number of underqualified personnel. The peace accords provided for none of these exigencies. One-third of prosecutors in 1997 were not attorneys. The budget of the public ministry and its size were inadequate for assuming many tasks formerly carried out by police and judges. The UN Development Programme and bilateral donors supported projects to train prosecutors and bolster their ability (and confidence) to take control of investigations from the police. Like the PNC, the attorney general's office grew at such a high rate that quality control was sacrificed. At the end of 2000, over half the prosecutors had been in post for fewer than three years. With the enhanced role of the prosecutor, the corresponding role of defence attorneys also gained importance, but training and funding for these offices remained lower, putting poor defendants in greater jeopardy. (Call 2003: 855)[55]

The courts have been marred by institutional incapacity and politicization in the judiciary, the prosecutor's office, and the prison system – a point made in many reports (e.g., see IHRC 2007: 7–9; Farah 2011: 26–27).

Consequently, even where significant reforms were undertaken, they did not reverse longstanding behaviors associated with limited professional training, uneven vetting of judicial appointments, corruption and inefficiency, weak expectations, and norms resulting from a historically weak legal system (akin to the situation in Guatemala and Haiti; Popkin 2000: 252 and chapter 6, passim). Notably, capacity here cannot be reduced to the number or salaries of judges (which compared favorably to those of other Central American countries (Popkin 2000: 216). Rather, weak capacity arguably grew out of poor training, poor institutional oversight, and the difficulty of changing expectations and norms associated with the courts.

---

[54] The United States supported judicial reforms during the civil war, and while the Truth Commission also made suggestions, judicial reforms have had uneven consequences (Call 2003).

[55] In another powerful quote, Popkin reports: "Inadequate preparation of the terrain for reform as well as a highly formalistic legal system; institutional resistance; poorly trained police, judges, prosecutors, and defense attorneys; and a lack of societal commitment to reform led to problems in implementing the few reforms approved before 1996 and resistance to enacting others" (Popkin 2000: 233).

This deeply problematic institution was in evidence when numerous judges were dismissed in May 1997, with "inexcusable ignorance, incapacity, and negligence" cited as the most common cause.[56]

International experts working with ONUSAL were appalled by the professional level of judges in general. They found many judges unable to analyze cases and apply relevant law, unfamiliar with human rights norms and, to their dismay, provisions of the Salvadoran constitution. In this regard, the situation in El Salvador seemed far worse than in many other Latin American countries where legal education and traditions had been stronger. (Popkin 2000: 214)

Domestic polls and international indices also point to an unfavorable image of the Salvadoran judicial system – as noted previously in the cited LAPOP data about trust and institutions. Figure 6.3 highlights that reported trust in the supreme courts and rule of law is just over 50 percent, even below that of the police. Data from the 1990s also reveal negative perceptions of the country's justice system: By 1996, "four times as many people thought the country's justice system was 'corrupt' as thought it 'honest'" (Call 2003: 858). Indeed, in 2008 citizens were twice as likely to blame judges rather than the police for the troubling crime rates, according to an IUDOP poll (Call 2003: 858–859). World Bank Governance Indicators also reveal how comparatively weak El Salvador's "rule of law indicators" are relative to those in the rest of the world. At just under the 20th-percentile rank in 1996, El Salvador goes up ever so slightly over the next few years and then completes 2009 at just over 20 percent. While the confidence interval is 20 points (at 90 percent confidence), the bottom line is that El Salvador ranks among the lowest in the world, since "percentile ranks indicate the percentage of countries worldwide that rate below the selected country."[57]

The courts are also weakened by the weakness of the attorney general's office. Admitting to inadequate capacity, officials in the Fiscalía complained of the inability to address the rising caseload.[58] In a particularly striking comment from the attorney general's office in 2010, the head

---

[56] Popkin 2000: 213, citing article by J. Michael Dodson and Donald W. Jackson, "Re-Inventing the Rule of Law: Human Rights in El Salvador," *Democratization* 4 (Winter 1997): 110, 122.

[57] Information and quotation come from the World Bank Country Data Report for El Salvador, 1996–2009, which can be accessed online at www.govindicators.org. It is striking that the UNODC (2007: 30) report indicates that El Salvador ranks among the lowest in Latin America vis-à-vis the perceived ability to bribe the police or the courts.

[58] See, for example, *La Prensa Gráfica* 5.4.2005 Impune 50% muertes; 2.22.2005 Saca asocia maras con el terrorismo.

prosecutor of the Unidad Especializada Antihomicidios, Óscar Torres, stated: "It would be a lie were I to say that we have the capacity to investigate 4,000 homicides ... we cannot handle it, it is overwhelming."[59]

Thus, even were the police fully capable of fulfilling its job as a first line of defense, the courts started off as wholly incapable of meeting their judicial obligations. This pattern persisted even in the aftermath of the peace accords. Consequently, the judicial system has hardly been a deterrent to violent crime. As noted earlier when discussing the police, the capacity to investigate, prosecute, and convict has been wholly lacking in El Salvador. This combined police-court incapacity has provided permissive conditions for illicit activity and the violence that has accompanied it in El Salvador. It is perhaps striking, then, that the government would later turn to the police and the courts to crack down on gangs (through a series of policies discussed further on), only to have this plan backfire. While a 2004 supreme court ruling found this policy unconstitutional, President Antonio Saca's government proceeded nonetheless. In this context, it is clear that the courts are hamstrung. Reflecting on this situation, Judge Santos Mejía de Escobar observed that the policy and its aftermath created conflict between the courts, the police, and the executive, "which in turn leads to further institutional weakening."[60]

The Prison System

Weak state capacity is also manifest in the prison system, which forms the punitive leg of the law-and-order institutional triad. The prison guards do not control the very grounds that they are supposed to secure. The disorder that broke out several times in 2010 provides one example, among many, of this lack of control.[61] At the most dramatic point in this case, some nine or ten prisons were in rebellion; it took the authorities three weeks to control the outbreak. With

---

[59] *La Prensa Gráfica* 1.2.2010 4,300 asesinatos y capacidad puesta a prueba: "Sería mentirle si le dijera que se tiene la capacidad para investigar 4,000 homicidios ... Ya no lo manejamos, se ha desbordado."
[60] Interview with Judge Aída Luz Santos Mejía de Escobar, August 14, 2008.
[61] *La Prensa Gráfica* 11.18.2010 Extorsiones no paran de salir de centros penales; 4.22.2010 Crímenes desde las prisiones "es la regla"; 5.16.2010 Vendedores se enfrentan a "lotería de extorsiones"; 4.14.2010 Penal de Cojutepeque se suma a protesta; 4.28.2010 Refriega en centros penales causa dos muertos y 21 heridos.

charges of widespread corruption among prison staff, even the national prison director, Moreno, indicated that he could not trust his own staff.[62] And even though there were deaths to be investigated in one such incident, the Fiscalía reportedly could not enter the prison.[63] Otherwise stated, the 2010 uprisings indicated a basic inability of the prison system to control its own territorial spaces within the prison walls.[64] As one journalist reported, "authorities from the PNC [national police], FGR [Fiscal General de la República – attorney general's office], and PDDH [Procuraduría para la Defensa de los Derechos Humanos – human rights defense attorney] recognized at this moment that the prisoners had control of the compound and were not allowing the entry of authorities."[65]

Concern about prison conditions was also expressed by the United Nations. The UN statement focused on overcrowding and the scores of people awaiting trial. Prison officials indicated in 2010 that prisons are at nearly three times their capacity (23,000 inmates in facilities designed to hold 8,000). Not all of these have been convicted, since many have been waiting as much as twenty-four months to be tried. In one estimate, some 8,200 fell into this category.[66] Viewed as a whole, the prison system is unambiguously riddled with poor capacity and poor performance.

***

The police, the courts, and the prisons should uphold and defend the rule of law. In El Salvador they have not done so. They have provided permissive conditions for the growth of illicit activity (even with *mano dura* policies that harshly and yet ineffectively cracked down on gangs). Call (2003) was among the first to note that while the peace accords ushered in notable institutional reforms, the post-accord period experienced a significant rise in violent crime – homicide, robberies,

---

[62] *La Prensa Gráfica* 5.3.2010 Depuración masiva en centros penales.
[63] *La Prensa Gráfica* 5.4.2010 Nueve penales siguen en rebeldía, dice la PDDH.
[64] *La Prensa Gráfica* 4.28.2010 Refriega en centros penales causa dos muertos y 21 heridos.
[65] *La Prensa Gráfica* 5.4.2010 Nueve penales siguen en rebeldía, dice la PDDH: "las autoridades de PNC, FGR y PDDH reconocieron en ese momento que los reos tienen el control de los recintos y no permiten el ingreso de las autoridades."
[66] *La Prensa Gráfica* 11.17.2010 Hacinamiento penal preocupa a la ONU.

and kidnappings – especially in the early years.[67] Call (2003: 841) notes, in particular, that there were three phases:

> Overall violent crime seemed to conform to three stages. In 1991–95, during demobilisation, ceasefire and the replacement of the old security forces, crime skyrocketed. Between 1996 and 2000, crime stayed at high levels, with kidnappings and robberies dipping then surging once more. Finally, from 2000 until the end of 2002, all major crime categories showed a notable decline. Kidnappings dropped from 114 in 2000 to 49 in 2001, and all reported crimes declined by 14 percent between 2000 and 2001. Victimisation surveys – often considered the best indicator of crime trends – show that overall crime declined slightly after 1994, and diminished at an even higher rate in the late 1990s. (Call 2003: 841)

Yet homicides spiked again in the 2000s, despite a dip in early 2000. While this pattern was unanticipated by those focused on "democratization" per se, this criminal pattern *might* have been anticipated by those focusing on police reform and the courts. The UN created a "Joint Group for the Investigation of Politically Motivated Illegal Armed Groups," which reported in 1993 that organized crime (sometimes in collaboration with state actors in the PNC, the armed forces, the judicial system, and the governing party) was using violence to pursue a range of illicit ends. The report also noted other illicit practices, including money laundering, various kinds of theft and fraud, and weapons trafficking; it concluded that this illicit political economy flourished in the context of the complicity/collaboration and impunity that reigned (Popkin 2000: 187). It is to the emergence and the types of illicit actors that we turn to next.

ILLICIT ACTORS, ORGANIZATIONAL TERRITORIAL COMPETITION, AND VIOLENCE

El Salvador's third wave democracy experienced a change in the organizational landscape, which included illicit actors. Armed political organizations of the left and right turned into viable political parties, with ARENA and FMLN competing in elections and assuming strong electoral positions in that process. But although some armed groups of the past became legal electoral parties, other groups remained in the realm of the illicit, with no

---

[67] Reporting of kidnapping also increased in 2010 – including kidnappings perpetrated by suspected gang members; *La Prensa Gráfica* 1.21.2010 Empresarios orientes agobiados por crimen; 9.26.2010 Pandillas participan en mayoría de secuestros.

explicit formal political ambitions but quite powerful social and economic ones. Youth gangs expanded exponentially, and trafficking organizations flourished.

Weak rule-of-law institutions provided permissive conditions for the evolution and growth of these illicit organizations – as well as for illicit actions by licit organizations. As the Salvadoran archbishop's office notes, crime is not just random or social but is in fact systemic (including impunity and incompetence), with participation from a wide range of organized groups, including gangs, and various forms of violence: extrajudicial killings by the police, death squads (some of which might have police involvement), and violence by other actors (most of which were found to be indeterminate in this study).[68]

Violent homicides, which in 2006 generated 3,928 murders (almost 10 people per day) reflected systematic criminal patterns, which illustrated the participation of organized crime in repeatedly perpetrating these types of acts and making clear the unacceptable levels of impunity and inefficiency of the country's law and order (police and public prosecutor) system to pursue criminal investigations.[69]

In this section, I focus on two such organizations that have competed for territorial control, greatly contributing to the spike in homicidal violence that has occurred in El Salvador. First, the changing morphology of gangs increasingly led to the rising use of violence to control their territories and increase their profits. Over time, however, this was

---

[68] The Salvadoran archbishop's office analyzed a subset of 233 cases in 2006 – a year in which they report that 1,938 homicides took place (about ten a day). Their selection of cases is admittedly not representative. As they note, they were particularly interested in cases of extrajudicial killings (110). They found that 24.46 percent of the 233 cases they investigated appeared to be gang related, while 59.66 percent appeared to be non–gang related but extrajudicial killings (not attributed to gangs nor exhibiting violence commonly associated with gang murders but tied to PNC, politically motivated, engaged in social cleansing, engaged in collective terror, or case unknown). Of the cases studied, they suggest that 22.5 percent were executions motivated by political ends, social cleansing, or collective terror; of the 139 cases of extrajudicial killings studied, 36.9 percent are categorized as "ejecuciones arbitrarios de móvil aún no esclarecido." This revealing study is footnoted rather than appearing in the main text since the numbers are not representative, although the patterns are chilling nonetheless (Tutela Legal del Arzobispado 2007: 7, 11–12, 112, and passim). The report includes examples of cases that fit each category.

[69] "La violencia homicida, que en 2006 provocó 3,928 muertes (casi 10 personal por día) reflejó patrones criminales sistemáticos, lo que evidencia la participación de grupos organizados que perpetran recurrentemente este tipo de hechos y pone de manifiesto los inaceptables niveles de impunidad e ineficacia del sistema policial-fiscal del país en materia de investigación criminal" (Tutela Legal del Arzobispado 2007: 111).

complemented by the increasing importance of other organized criminal groups. Neither alone determines the high violence; nor do they together explain all the violence. But they do explain important geographic patterns and spikes. While political crackdowns affected Salvadoran gangs and organized crime in myriad ways (gangs were affected by the 1996 US crackdown on undocumented Salvadoran youth and the 2003–2004 *mano dura* policies; organized crime was affected by the international crackdown on Caribbean and later Mexican drug trafficking), this chapter highlights how they provided new incentives for illicit actors to organize and generated competition to control territory (leading to higher violence). The resulting organizational territorial *competition* fueled much of the violence. By contrast, the gang truce of 2012 highlights how the effort to control organizational competition drove homicides down (until the truce was broken and homicides skyrocketed once again).

Gangs

Gangs have increased in numbers, geographic scope, and recourse to violence since the 1990s. While gangs are not new to El Salvador, many have noted that these organizations were deeply affected by the US 1996 immigration reform law as a result of which, between 1998 and 2004, the United States deported more than 33,000 Salvadorans residing in the United States. Of these, some were reported to have been members of the now infamous Los Angeles–based gangs Mara 18 ("18th street gang") and Mara Salvatrucha ("MS-13");[70] while the former was originally a Mexican gang, the latter was formed by Salvadoran youth in the United States (IHRC 2007: 21–22; WOLA 2006).[71] According to US Homeland Security statistics, over 40,000 ex-convicts were deported

---

[70] Farah (2012: 55–56) recounts this oft-repeated origin story beginning in Los Angeles with the deportation of thousands of Salvadorans following the 1996 immigration law. Farah reports that the number of Salvadorans in prison increased following the 1992 riots in Los Angeles, when hundreds of Latino gang members were sent to prison on felony charges after being charged and prosecuted as adults (rather than minors). Since the 1996 immigration law allowed for the repatriation of imprisoned noncitizens sentenced to more than one year in jail, this created a pool of Salvadorans who could be deported.

[71] The United States enacted new immigration laws in 1996 (The Illegal Immigration Reform and Immigrant Responsibility Act and the Antiterrorism and Effective Death Penalty Act) that expanded the ability to deport unlawful residents and lawful permanent residents – especially those charged with crimes (IHRC 2007: 21–22).

to El Salvador between 2001 and 2010.[72] Some put the figures even higher:

> From 2000 to 2004, some 20,000 young Central American criminals were deported from the United States to their homelands. The trend further accelerated from 2008 to 2010 with another 63,000 criminals deported to El Salvador alone. In total, some 300,000 criminals, mostly gang members, have been deported to the Northern Triangle countries over the past decade. (Farah and Lum 2013: 12)[73]

Many scholars have debated if and how the influx of deported gang members reshaped Salvadoran gangs.[74] Some would argue that the

---

[72] Cited in Dudley (2013: 9) based on United States Department of Homeland Security, Office of Immigration Statistics, "2010 Yearbook of Immigration Statistics," August 2011, pp. 97–101, www.dhs.gov/xlibrary/assets/statistics/yearbook/2010/oil_yb_2010.pdf.

[73] Also published in Farah (2012: 56).

[74] The debate on the origins of the Salvadoran gangs and the impact of US deportation requires further systematic work. Drawing on work by Santacruz Giralt, Concha-Eastman, and Cruz (2001), IHRC (2007: 22) notes that the deported gang members introduced new cultures into Salvadoran gang life: "particularly the practice of staking out territory to be defended against encroachment by rival gangs." Similarly, Dudley (2013: 9) argues that they capitalized on their presumed international cache, "usurping local gangs' power." Farah (2012: 56) also notes that the deportees replicated gang structures as a means to gain social acceptance, safety, and survival. They created alliances with demobilized combatants from both sides of El Salvador's civil war (Farah 2012: 56). Indeed, Farah and Lum (2013: 11) have noted that with time, the MS-13 authority structure has apparently moved from the United States to El Salvador: "The leadership structure of the MS-13 is undergoing a shift away from its 'historic' base in Los Angeles to leadership concentrated in San Salvador, and specifically within the prisons of Ciudad Barrios and Zacatecoluca. While some of the gang leaders in Los Angeles retain leadership positions, most of the leaders now reside in El Salvador, and a portion of the money from illicit gains in the United States is funneled south via Western Union and other money transfer services" (Farah and Lum 2013: 11). Others, however, downplay the impact of deported youth on the rise of gang violence in El Salvador – noting that gangs predate deportation and that the latter fed into, but did not create, the violent spiral that took place in the country; from this perspective, the legacies of the civil war, weak institutions, government neoliberal policies, a weak urban labor market, increasing urban migration, and an overdependence on remittance all decreased opportunities for the youth (IHRC 2007: 23–24). Santacruz Giralt et al. (2001: 13–14) also note that 83 percent of gang members have poor families, nearly 73 percent live in female-headed single-family homes, parental involvement is low, and family violence is high. Moreover, youth (15–24 years old) are overwhelmingly the victims of the violence; in 1998, men 20–24 were the biggest group of victims, with 14–19-year-olds taking fifth place (Santacruz Giralt et al. 2001: 20, 24). UNODC (2007: 39–44) notes, moreover, that deportations have been significant but that the offenses of those deported are rarely for violent crime; also, there is no record of those deported assuming leadership positions or engaging in violence upon their return to Central America or the Caribbean.

deportees changed culture, ambitions, coordination, and discipline.[75] Others would argue that the links are overdrawn and are a convenient political explanation for those seeking to minimize responsibility and ask for more resources.[76] Regardless of how one comes down on this debate, it is clear that weak state capacity in El Salvador allowed these gangs (emboldened by an expanded membership) to take hold and become an important feature in the Salvadoran urban landscape. Over time, the MS-13 and M-18 gangs have become formidable forces in the northern triangle, with MS-13 gaining particular strength in El Salvador. Jointly, they are estimated to have 27,500 members, according to El Salvador's national police anti-gang unit (Farah 2012: 58).

While gangs were once rather dispersed and fragmented organizations, the late 1990s and 2000s witnessed the consolidation of the two major rival gangs, MS-13 and Mara 18. Both have maintained, developed, and consolidated a territorial base of organization and operation (Santacruz Giralt and Concha-Eastman 2001: 33, citing Cruz 1999; IHRC 2007: 25–27). Several authors emphasize that hierarchy coincides with the autonomy of subunits (Farah 2012: 58; Farah and Lum 2013: 6; Peña and Gibb 2013). Although there are various levels – *clicas* (with neighborhood leaders), *programas* (larger blocs of *clicas*), *palabreros* (several *clicas* with midlevel leaders among them), *ranfleros* (leaders who are often in prison), and then *jefes nacionales* (national leaders with authority to decide overarching issues affecting gang structure) – researchers still see the local structures as having a significant amount of autonomy to decide how to make money and distribute it, as well as with whom they want to work, including transnational criminal organizations (Farah and Lum 2013: 6; Peña and Gibb 2013). Peña and Gibb note that the national leadership cannot necessarily control the local ranks, including with regard to the 2012 truce discussed further on.[77]

---

[75] Santacruz Giralt et al. (2001: 37–38) highlight obedience, loyalty, exclusive involvement with one gang, specific initiation rituals, use of specific symbols, and no criminal harm against the community from which the gang comes.

[76] Marlon Carranza, for example, observes that the LA origin story coincides with claims made by the PNC and the US government but that it does not ring true. While there is of course communication, he claims, it is not as "Machiavellian" as some claim. Interview August 22, 2008.

[77] "The national leadership, which negotiated the truce, emerged largely as a result of crowding also many clica leaders together in jail. But they do not exercise military style

Once organic and territorially bound, El Salvador's gangs are developing more complex vertical structures, defined member roles, and consolidated chains of command. The organizational structures of both the MS-13 and Mara 18 involve local sub-groups within the gangs, or clikas, whose members typically include young people from a common neighborhood or sub-neighborhood. A 2002 police study indicated that approximately 200 *clikas* were operating in El Salvador. In the past several years, these clikas have become increasingly organized and effective at communicating and coordinating with one another. The leadership roles within the hierarchy of each gang have become specific and defined, and each gang increasingly operates according to internal rules and values. (IHRC 2007: 25)

Over time, territory has not only become a space for social identification but increasingly has also become a basis for generating wealth and power.[78] Territories form the basis not only for recruiting new members but also for generating rents through organized extortion.[79] Extortion has been widespread, reportedly even extending to schools and transportation routes, such as bus lines (IHRC 2007: 28–29; Peña and Gibb 2013; and the newspaper violence database).[80] As illustrated next, violence is particularly high along these transit routes. "The maras get most of their money from extortion of local businesses, particularly buses. In 2009, the Salvadoran transport union estimated payments of 18 million dollars ... The extortion has been enforced by murdering bus drivers and torching buses, on one occasion with passengers still inside" (Peña and Gibb 2013). The Harvard-based IHRC study provides a vivid description:

One illustration of this new dynamic is the increasingly widespread practice of extortion carried out against businesses and individuals, commonly referred to as "collecting *renta*." While gangs have engaged in asking for money on the streets for years, the phenomenon of organized extortion is relatively new, and has become a notable problem only during the last three

---

command and control. Even decisions in the jail appear to be by consensus" (Peña and Gibb 2013).

[78] Interview with Jeanette Aguilar, August 13, 2008.

[79] Extortion appeared mostly in connection with the transportation sector, but other businessmen and private citizens reported being victims. For example, a resident of a *colonia* in the south of San Salvador reported that gang members had begun charging residents $0.25 in order to leave the neighborhood (to go to work, shopping, etc. – whether by car or on foot). *La Prensa Gráfica* 11.22.2005 PNC: 20% de los transportistas bajo extorsión.

[80] *La Prensa Gráfica* 11.18.2005 Maestros sufren extorsiones de los pandilleros.

years. Such extortion has been a particular problem in the transportation sector.[81] A former gang member told our researchers about one such system of charging bus operators a daily fee of $1 per vehicle: "We would charge the owners or the drivers." His gang also exacted *renta* from others in its territory: "We would charge stores and taxi drivers a dollar a day. Every day." This practice appears to be very structured, mandated and overseen by gang leadership. A female gang member told us that her gang targeted area stores in particular for collecting *renta*. Our researchers in El Salvador also spoke to residents of various neighborhoods who told us that their families were charged *renta* simply because they happened to live in a sub-neighborhood controlled by a particular *clika*. (IHRC 2007: 28–29)

One of the most frightening features of the gang's recent extortion practices is that the gangs now possess enhanced capacity to fulfill their death threats against those who do not comply with their requests. In 2005, for example, more than 2,000 non-public transportation operators reported being subjected to extortion, and over 100 were killed that year. (IHRC 2007: 29)[82]

Gangs and Overall Violence Levels

While gangs are not responsible for all violence in El Salvador (sensationalist reporting and political posturing notwithstanding), there is no doubt that Salvadoran gangs have significantly contributed to high levels of violence in the country. Notably, the rising homicide rates seemed to have a significant impact on youth, in particular. Reportedly, homicide rates rose faster for youth (88.1 percent for minors) than for the population at large (37.3 percent) between 2008 and 2009,[83] and youth/minors have also been detained in high

---

[81] IHRC bases these claims on interviews and reporting in *El Diario de Hoy*, October 2, 2006. The rising prevalence of extortion in neighborhoods and on transportation routes was independently observed in the newspaper violence database created for this book, which analyzed articles in *La Prensa Gráfica* (2000, 2005, 2010); reports of extortion increased significantly in 2005.

[82] IHRC (2007) cites IDHUCA, Balance de los derechos humanos del 2005 8 (2006). Also see Farah (2012: 57), who identifies "petty crime, such as purse snatching, robbery, taxing bus drivers and small stores in their neighborhoods, as well as small-scale drug distribution in certain parts of the cities in order to keep themselves economically afloat. This quickly led to an escalation in homicide rates, as gang members fought each other over the most economically advantageous territory and sought to expand their geographic influence."

[83] *La Prensa Gráfica* 2.8.2010 Asesinatos de niños se han duplicado 4,367 total oficial de homicidios 2009. Youth were also targeted as perpetrators of homicide, extortion, drug possession, and illicit gatherings (*agrupaciones ilícitas*), among other things. See, for example, *La Prensa Gráfica* 4.13.2010 179 arrestos de menores en la capital en 3 meses; 5.10.2010 PNC: 10,074 menores han sido detenidos en los últimos 16 meses; 5.10.2010 Participación en homicidios en alza.

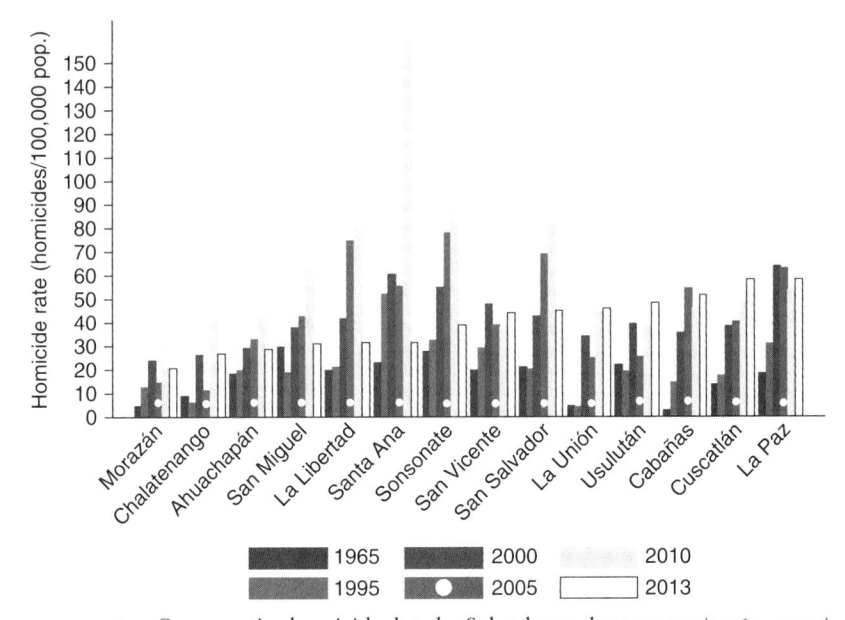

FIGURE 6.5 Comparative homicide data by Salvadoran department (1965–2013)
Source: Washington, DC, 2010, www.paho.org/Spanish/SHA/coredata/tabulator/newTabulator.html.
Notes: Raw data are from Pan American Health Organization, Health Surveillance and Disease Management Area, Health Statistics and Analysis Unit, PAHO Regional Mortality Database. Rates based on World Population Prospects 2006, revised 2008. Data reported in Table 6.2 of this chapter (also see Carcach 2008: 56).

numbers. One such report stated that an average of twenty-two youth per day (averaged over a sixteen-month period) were detained.[84] Much of the violence has taken place in the metropole, where the gangs have had the greatest growth, whether one looks at homicide or victimization data. Figure 6.5 shows departmental homicide rates over time, with a striking increase in San Salvador, Sonsonate, La Libertad, and Santa Ana, in particular (from Carcach 2008: 56). LAPOP AmericasBarometer data also reveal that the highest crime victimization rates are in the metropolitan region (41.9 percent) – compared to the paracentral region (28.6 percent), central region

---

[84] *La Prensa Gráfica* 5.10.2010 PNC: 10,074 menores han sido detenidos en los últimos 16 meses.

(26.1 percent), western region (21.3 percent), and eastern region (19.2 percent; reported in Córdova, Cruz, and Seligson 2013: 118).

In the newspaper violence database, general news articles about violence (versus articles about specific crimes) often highlighted the context and the role of gangs (and drug-related violence), as in 2005. In an evaluation of newspaper reporting, Bethany Park observed:

> Homicides were so closely associated with gangs in 2005 newspaper reporting that nearly every article reporting a homicide mentioned whether or not the victim or suspected perpetrator belonged to a gang. That is, even when neither the victim nor the suspected perpetrator was a member of a gang, that fact was noted. (Park, 2005 Newspaper Articles, General Violence Memo)[85]

Aguilar (2012) also reports that increasingly well-organized gangs are arguably responsible for a sizable and increasing proportion of homicides and extortion, with the PNC reporting in 2011 that gangs were responsible for some 26 percent of homicides.

Before delving further into gang-related violence, it is important to reiterate and underscore that *gangs are not responsible for all violence* and that *data on gang-related violence vary considerably*. We know that the violence is high, yet the precise percentage is debated. The PNC has reported that 70 percent of homicides in El Salvador are gang related, the media has suggested 30 percent, according to reporting by IHRC (2007: 30, 73), and the IML reports 8–13.5 percent, between 2003 and 2006 (although gang involvement was not known in 30–60 percent of cases; World Bank 2010, Volume 1: 15–16).[86] The truth is that we don't know precisely what percentage of violence can be attributed to gang violence –

---

[85] The newspaper violence database coded articles about specific homicides. Those articles did *not* reveal or confirm that gangs were the overwhelming actors in instigating or receiving violence.

[86] See World Bank (2010) *Crime and Violence in Central America*. Volume 1. Washington, DC. World Bank Sustainable Development Department and Poverty Reduction and Economic Management Unit, Latin America and the Caribbean Region (July). See in particular volume 1: 16, which reports motives for murder based on data from El Salvador's Instituto de Medicina Legal (IML). IML data identify the motive for murder in terms of common crime, gang crime, unknown, and other. Strikingly, "common crime" is identified as the motive for murder in 57.4% of cases in 2003 (a figure that drops precipitously to 33.7% in 2004, 23.3% in 2005, and 18.2% in 2006). Moreover, "unknown" motive claims 28.9% in 2003 (and then rises precipitously to 48.4% in 2004, 59% in 2005, and 59.1% in 2006). It is striking that while "common" crime motives decline 30%, "unknown" motives increase by 30%. These figures themselves reveal not only a challenge in attributing responsibility for the violence but, in turn, a serious problem with state capacity to monitor and evaluate this situation. According to this same report, gang crime is reported as 8% in 2003, 9.9% in 2004, 13.4% in 2005, and

especially given the uneven institutional capacity of the very institutions that are supposed to monitor this situation. Indeed, Aguilar cautions against the hype that attributes all increased violence to gangs, since local and transnational organized crime has played an increasingly important role, data are not always reliable, attribution is not always legally proven, and "traditional common delinquency" is also present (Aguilar 2012: 482–483).

What we can conclude is that gang-related violence has increased dramatically; that El Salvador's high homicide violence rates are significantly, albeit partially, a by-product of gangs; and that we should not attribute all violence to gangs. The question, then, is under what circumstances homicidal violence has been deployed. In theory and in practice, reports indicate the use of violence to establish intra-organizational obedience and loyalty, to induce payment of rents (extortion), and to establish control over new territorial geographies. I elaborate on each in turn (to highlight the range of violence in play, although this book emphasizes the causal impact of territorial violence in particular). After discussing gang violence in light of these three mechanisms leading to higher violence, we return to the role of organized crime in El Salvador.

Violence to Induce Intra-Organizational Obedience

Initiation rites for gangs have become more violent over time, with beatings and rape used to initiate members, according to IHRC (2007: 30–34). So too, gang members seeking to exit a gang have encountered death threats and violence. In this context, there seems to be a rise in intra-gang violence. Experts (Jeanette Aguilar, priests working in this area, etc.) have observed that there is an "increasing prevalence of intra-gang killings, sometimes relating to drug or extortion activities" and that "Intra-gang violence and purges also occur with growing frequency" with an "intensified ... system of internal obedience" (IHRC 2007: 33–34). As part of this phenomenon, it also seems that youth are being coerced to join gangs under penalty of death: "Today, if you're not part of the gang, they kill you; joining a gang is the only way of surviving in the environment. Before the gang was like your family; now you have to join or they kill you," reported a former Salvadoran gang member, 30 years old (IHRC

10.7% in 2006. "Other" is reported as 5.7% in 2003, 8% in 2004, 4.3% in 2005, and 12% in 2006.

2007: 76–77). This is one aspect of violence used to assert obedience within the gang.

Violence Deployed to Defend Extraction of Rents in Territorial Spaces

Violence is also used to defend the ability to extract rents in particular territorial spaces. Gangs have always been identified with certain territories. We see over time that the gangs have increasingly moved not just to dominate neighborhood streets but also to extract rents from stores and transport drivers (IHRC 2007; Farah 2011; newspaper violence database). The penalty for refusing to do so includes violence.

The general violence memos written for this book's newspaper database emphasize, for example, that in 2000, the departments of La Libertad and La Paz had particularly high rates of violent deaths.[87] Violence was often reported on bus routes such as the Pan-American Highway. Drivers were often subjected to extortion (charged along certain routes) and/or passengers were victims of robbery. These violent acts most commonly occurred on routes 304 (San Salvador–La Unión) and 306 (Santa Rosa de Lima–La Unión) and less frequently on route 301 (San Salvador–San Miguel).[88]

In the two subsequent coding years for the newspaper violence database (2005 and 2010), there was also a major trend of homicides in the transportation sector. The national police estimated that while one in five *transportistas* were victims of extortion, 116 transportation workers were killed in 2005 alone.[89] And in 2010, bus drivers or fare collectors constituted around 60 of the 924 cases coded in our newspaper violence database, with this sector alone making up 6.5 percent of newspaper-reported homicides.[90]

Extortion rings were reportedly often run by gang members, who forced transportation workers (drivers, fare collectors, and owners) to pay a regular fee whenever they passed through a gang's territory; by one estimate, the fees were $5 a day and up to $250 a month. Extortion and robbery reports noted various means of capturing this rent: in some cases, gang members stopped the bus; in others, they boarded as passengers; in yet others, they were themselves the fare

---

[87] *La Prensa Gráfica* 1.29.2000 La Libertad registra el mayor número de muertes violentas; 2.3.2000 Continúa ola de violencia en La Paz; 7.3.2000 54 homicidios ocurrieron durante primer semestre en La Paz.
[88] *La Prensa Gráfica* 7.5.2000 Vuelve ola de asaltos en Panamericana.
[89] *La Prensa Gráfica* 11.22.2005 PNC: 20% de los transportistas bajo extorsión.
[90] *La Prensa Gráfica* 2.9.2010 Rutas de buses en paro por amenazas de muerte.

collectors.[91] Gangs were also known to kill drivers and bus collectors who refused to pay extortion fees, leading many to report feeling particularly unsafe on a bus (a reported 70 percent of respondents), although also unsafe in their communities (31 percent) and homes (27 percent), according to a *La Prensa Gráfica* article in 2005.[92] As in Guatemala, bus drivers were also fearful and occasionally went on strike, especially following a violent incident.[93] There was an increase in reported bus burnings in 2010, although these did not lead to homicides in most cases (with the notable exception of fourteen people killed by suspected gang members in Mejicanos) and seemed targeted against bus owners (not drivers), in retaliation for unpaid extortion fees.[94]

In an example of the link between extortion and violence, the *Los Angeles Times* reported that transnational gangs initiated mass killings on two city buses in 2010; one bus was riddled with the bullets of automatic weapons, and the other was set on fire after having been doused with gasoline. "Police said that the violence was aimed at bus drivers who refused to pay 'protection money' to the gang members who control territory along the routes the buses plied" (Farah 2011: 6).[95] The government responded with a stricter anti-gang law that made association with a gang an act punishable with jail time (Farah 2011: 6).

Overall, therefore, extortion was a subject of much reporting in *La Prensa Gráfica*, among other newspapers (newspaper violence database – Memo on General Violence on El Salvador 2010). By 2010, coverage discussed the increasing role of imprisoned gang members in coordinating extensive extortion and criminal schemes.[96] Most prison-related

---

[91] See, for example, *La Prensa Gráfica* 2.20.2005 Protestan dueños de microbuses. For another example, see 2.7.2005 Soyapango – 177 asesinatos el año pasado.

[92] *La Prensa Gráfica* 5.4.2005 Miedo a la cotidianidad.

[93] See, for example, *La Prensa Gráfica* 2.1.2005 Demandan seguridad en ruta 38-F.

[94] See *La Prensa Gráfica* articles, including 1.12.2010 Queman microbús en carretera Troncal del Norte; 1.26.2010 Queman microbús en Ciudad Arce; 1.17.2010 A pesar de marcha siguen los atentados; 8.26.2010 Queman microbús de la ruta 46; 5.4.2010 Desconocidos incendian cuatro buses en Chalchuapa. Also see 6.26.2010 Once pandilleros cometieron masacre.

[95] Ribando Seelke (2011: 6) reports: "In 2009, gangs reportedly killed 146 Guatemalan bus drivers. In early September 2010, the MS-13 and 18th Street gangs in El Salvador jointly organized a three-day strike in response to new anti-gang legislation that paralyzed the country's transport system."

[96] See, for example, *La Prensa Gráfica* 1.9.2010 Ingresan a cárceles $8.4 millones por extorsiones; 1.18.2010 Extorsiones desde penales aumentan 600%; 3.18.2010

extortion rings were tied to Ciudad Barrios prison, although extortion was also noted as an issue at Quezaltepeque, Chalatenango, Cojutepeque, and San Francisco Gotera e Izalco prisons, as well as the maximum-security prison of Zacatecoluca.[97] Extortion was not just a petty act but was reported to be a highly lucrative one. An article reported that inmates were receiving $700,000 per month in extortion fees; the funds were partially used to pay off prison guards, although forty-three guards and sixteen to nineteen prison directors were reportedly fired in light of these illegal payments.[98] Reinforcing the role of inmates in the broader illicit economy, the subdirector of investigations of the PNC, Augusto Cotto Castaneda, released a report indicating that in 2009, 80 percent of extortions were ordered from inside a prison. The anti-extortion division of the police apparently had nearly 3,910 reports of extortion in 2009, and strikingly over 3,000 of them originated from a cell phone call inside a prison. This was a marked increase from a year earlier, when there were 1,717 reports of extortion, a third of which (537) were tied to cell phones operating inside a prison.[99] Ongoing newspaper coverage noted prison extortion schemes in 2010.[100] In one particularly chilling account, the gangs reportedly devised a way to get San Salvadoran vendors to conduct extortion business for them – apparently gaining access to all 12,000 cell phone numbers belonging to the vendors and calling a random number each day, demanding that the vendor collect the $3 daily extortion rent on behalf of the gang.[101]

Extortion does not necessarily result in homicidal violence; however, it does imply the threat of violence. Violence is deployed to demand obedience from those who are the object of the operation as well as to dominate those seeking to assert control over the extractive process itself. In this sense, violence is always a function of a relational dynamic. It is not implicit in illicit activity alone; it is based on efforts to dominate what is otherwise a conflictual and often

---

Comercio el más afectado por extorsión en 2010; 11.18.2010 Extorsiones no paran de salir de centros penales; 4.22.2010 Crímenes desde las prisiones "es la regla"; 5.16.2010 Vendedores se enfrentan a "lotería de extorsiones."

[97] *La Prensa Gráfica* 1.18.2010 Extorsiones desde penales aumentan 600%.
[98] *La Prensa Gráfica* 1.9.2010 Ingresan a cárceles $8.4 millones por extorsiones.
[99] *La Prensa Gráfica* 1.18.2010 Extorsiones desde penales aumentan 600%.
[100] *La Prensa Gráfica* 1.18.2010 Extorsiones desde penales aumentan 600%; 3.18.2010 Comercio el más afectado por extorsión en 2010; 11.18.2010 Extorsiones no paran de salir de centros penales; 4.22.2010 Crímenes desde las prisiones "es la regla."
[101] *La Prensa Gráfica* 5.16.2010 Vendedores se enfrentan a "lotería de extorsiones."

competitive process. Efforts to control territory, in particular, form a core part of this process – both for gangs and organized crime (as elaborated later): *"The breaking of alliances and territorial disputes both over turf and control of specific trafficking routes in this superstructure and substrata of criminal activity leads to enormous levels of violence, social decomposition and the erosion of positive state attributes."* (Farah 2011: 30; emphasis added).

Political Responses to Gangs
This chapter has argued that weak state capacity in the police, courts, and prisons created permissive conditions for the rise in illicit organizations. Politicians did respond, however – if ineffectively, arbitrarily, and punitively. Salvadoran elected officials responded to gang violence with a series of hardline measures, starting in early 2000, commonly referred to as *mano dura* policies. These punitive measures did little to curtail the violence. Indeed, experts have argued that they exacerbated the situation, leading to the greater professionalization and organization of gangs and a rising recourse to violence.

The government implemented two rounds of *mano dura* policies (2003 and 2004). First, President Francisco Flores and the legislature joined forces in October 2003 to pass a "Ley Anti-Maras" (anti-gang law), which was subsequently overturned by the supreme court in April 2004.[102] The latter found this law unconstitutional, with violations of equality before the law: arbitrary arrests based on association, appearance (tattoos), location, lack of documentation, disregard for the Salvadoran principle of injury, and problematic application to minors (IHRC 2007: 40). This was followed by an interim measure that sought to correct some of the constitutional problems but that many continued to find problematic (IHRC 2007: 41–42). The next president, Antonio Saca, hardened this approach by introducing *super mano dura* (super-heavy-handed) policies that combined a focus on crackdowns with reforms to the penal code, the penal process code, and juvenile law and social policies to focus on prevention and rehabilitation. While the former increased penalties, the latter remained underfunded, according to IHRC (2007: 43–44).[103] The

---

[102] See IHRC (2007); José Miguel Cruz (2011a); Alisha Holland (2013).
[103] For newspaper coverage of these various policies – including *super mano dura*, gun control reform, *mano amiga, plan protección a la vida*, the creation of a new division of police officers and district attorneys, División de Investigación de Homicidios

laws led to serious police crackdowns (although often the courts could not keep up and did not have evidence to convict those who had been picked up on the basis of the laws).[104] Alongside *super mano dura* policies, the government also militarized its response to the violence, with the military joining the police in urban anti-gang units in 2005 and rural patrols in 2004.[105]

The policies were rooted in a coercive response, betting that repression would solve the problem, according to Judge Aída Santos Mejía, who served in juvenile court. This set up an institutional confrontation between the justice system and the executive and the police, which in turn led to institutional weakening, she argued. What is missing from the government's policies was an emphasis on prevention and on ameliorating social conditions that gave rise to criminal violence.[106]

These two rounds of *mano dura* policies did not curtail violence levels. To the contrary, reports suggest that the state flouted civil rights (as mentioned, arresting suspects based on appearance and association). Moreover, state-initiated violence was also deployed in these years, with the Human Rights Ombudsman noting that the PNC was the actor most reported as having committed human rights abuses and the archbishop's human rights office investigating cases of killings by the police (IHRC 2007: 53).

(DIHO), the deployment of more police officer into rural areas, and the increased reliance on the military, see *La Prensa Gráfica* articles, including 12.9.2005 Pandillas quieren tomar negocio del secuestro, dice PNC; 5.4.2005 Heredamos de la guerra el irrespeto a la vida; 1.6.2005 El Ejecutivo apuesta por restringir control de armas; 2.3.2005 Presidente Saca adjudica aumento de homicidios a "violencia social"; 6.6.2005 Junio ha sido el mes más violento del año; 5.28.2005 El Mano Dura no redujo los homicidios; 7.2.2005 Lanzarán plan Municipios Libres de Armas; 1.20.2005 PNC sin acceso a datos sobre armas.pdf; 6.4.2005 Inauguran II fase de plan Mano Amiga; 01.25.2005 Pandilleros de la 18 aceptan la "Mano amiga" del gobierno; 2.7.2005 Lanzarán plan para capturar homicidas; 2.4.2005 Crímenes dependen más de violencia social que de pandillas: Saca; 2.21.2005 Gobernación insiste en que delincuencia ha disminuido; 8.15.2005 Crean división antihomicidios; 8.23.2005 En una semana, la PNC capturó 75 homicidas; 4.20.2005 Hoy instalan Policía rural; 5.4.2005 Usulután, homicidios y seguridad; 7.27.2005 Saca dice que policía rural redujo muertes; 1.4.2005 Cafetaleros piden más seguridad; 11.15.2005 Patrullas militares contra las maras.

[104] According to their own police records, the police arrested some 14,000 people suspected of being gang members; they released over 70 percent of them for lack of evidence (Pérez 2013: 219).

[105] See IHRC (2007: 54). Also reported in newspaper violence dataset; includes reports on the militarization of public security.

[106] Interview with Judge Aída Santos Mejía de Escobar, August 14, 2008.

While these repressive measures were announced as a crackdown on gangs, they arguably had the opposite effect. In the context of these laws and the subsequent crackdown, gangs and organized crime further professionalized their operations. Gangs were less likely to advertise their allegiance by dress and tattoos, and they increasingly operated with greater control, structure, and discretion – making them harder to track and control. Moreover, the imprisonment and segregation of gang members provided the impetus for creating more sophisticated and coordinated forms of coordination (IHRC 2007: 26–27, 43). Director of the Consejo Nacional de Seguridad Pública, Óscar Bonilla, observed that gangs evolved from a largely territorial/social group to a moneymaking enterprise.

Gangs daily confront more constraints to develop their recruitments policies, because the culture of graffiti, tattoos, music, and modes of dress are in decline. They are embracing [or drawing more on] arms and drugs ...

[The gang phenomenon] is transforming itself. The gangs are coordinating their operations in the region, and I don't even know if one can continue to call them gangs (pandillas) because if they are no longer tattooing themselves, if they are no longer dressing as gang members, and if they no longer dispute territory but drugs and arms markets, the solution to the problem must be something else ... In any event, the gangs have changed, they are no longer the same as before.[107]

Echoing the concern that gangs were becoming moneymaking enterprises, the PNC reportedly feared that kidnapping for profit would be the gangs' next step.[108] In short, the *mano dura* policies backfired. Not only did they fail to place limits on gangs and violence, but they arguably catalyzed the consolidation, professionalization, and diversification into other moneymaking enterprises – and an attendant rise in homicide numbers.[109] Interviewed in 2008, Juan Daniel Alemán

---

[107] *La Prensa Gráfica* 11.3.2005 Las pandillas han evolucionado: "Las pandillas tienen cada vez más limitaciones para desarrollar su política de reclutamiento, porque la cultura del grafito, del tatuaje, de su música y de su modo de vestir, está en caída. Se abocan cada vez más a las armas y a la droga ... [El fenómeno de las pandillas] se está transformando. Las pandillas están coordinando su modo de operar en la región, y no sé incluso si se les podrá seguir llamando pandillas, porque si ya no se tatúan, si ya no visten como pandilleros, y si ya no disputan territorio, sino mercados de droga y armas, el tratamiento del problema deberá ser otro ... En todo caso, los pandilleros han cambiado, ya no son los mismos de antes."

[108] *La Prensa Gráfica* 12.9.2005 Pandillas quieren tomar negocio del secuestro, dice PNC.

[109] IHRC (2007: 60); Dudley (2013: 12); interviews with Benita Lara (August 19, 2008), Marlon Carranza (August 22, 2008), Jorge Simán (August 8, 2008), Carlos Dada

stated boldly: "The *maras* are organized crime structures based on extortion and murder-for-hire, in alliance with drug trafficking."[110] Jaime Martínez Ventura, coordinator of the juvenile justice unit of the supreme court, also observed in 2008 that the state's response had forced the *maras* to evolve: whereas once they lived off of whatever money they could get from passersby (extortion, for example), *mano dura* policies forced a closer alliance, he claimed, with drug peddling and others forms of income.[111]

Although other interviewees, such as Marlon Carranza, were more cautious about lumping all gang members into one category – noting that while some who are better organized, with firm territorial control (as in Soyapango and Apopa), are likely involved in organized crime, others are more appropriately identified as being involved in more common juvenile delinquency.[112]

Violence continued – not only in the streets but also in the prisons.[113] With the increased enrollment of gang members in the prisons, a rise in prison violence occurred, including a prison massacre of thirty-one prisoners in August 2004 and another of twenty-one prisoners in January 2007 (IHRC 2007: 55–56).[114]

Moreover, extrajudicial killings, the reemergence of death squads, and social cleansing reportedly also increased in these years, with some experts arguing that *mano dura* polices were linked to, and ideologically supportive of, the adoption of these violent and illicit societal

---

(August 8, 2008), Aída Luz Santos Mejía de Escobar (August 14, 2008), and Jaime Martínez Ventura (August 21, 2008).

[110] "Las maras son estructuras de crímen organizado, basado en extorsión y sicariato, en alianza con el narcotráfico." Interview with Juan Daniel Alemán, August 27, 2008.

[111] Interview with Jaime Martínez Ventura, August 21, 2008.

[112] Interview with Marlon Carranza, August 22, 2008.

[113] In the interview with Marlon Carranza, August 22, 2008, he noted that the prisons played an important role in bringing together gang members and organized crime, creating extensive criminal networks. In fact, some researchers and PNC officials believe that operations are frequently run out of the prisons.

[114] The newspaper violence database revealed a rise in violence in and around the prisons. Not only were homicides reported in the prison, but prison guards were also targeted (often outside and around their homes). Finally, violence also seemed to spike in surrounding areas in what was presumed to be retaliatory measures. For examples of such reporting in *La Prensa Gráfica*, see 2.6.2005 Custodios, víctimas de pandillas; 2.21.2005 Revelan supuesto plan para matar a custodios; 3.11.2005 Asesinan custodio de penal de Sonsonate; 8.21.2005 Asesinan a director de centro penal de Sonsonate; 7.15.2005 Asesinan a custodio de penal de Ciudad Barrios; 8.24.2005 Escuela asediada por maras; 6.29.2005 Presidente amenazado de muerte por maras; 12.23.2005 Diez asesinatos en prisiones en 2005.

actions (IHRC 2007: 17–18). IHRC (2007: 18) observes that social cleansing was taking place with impunity; this suggests, at best, that the state has not had the capacity to redress these human rights abuses, and at worst, that the state has been complicit in them. While there is no hard evidence to suggest a state policy sanctioning these acts, "established human rights institutions in El Salvador have documented the involvement of PNC officials in extrajudicial killings in recent years" (IHRC 2007: 18). Moreover, "the Salvadoran state's failure to protect, investigate, and prosecute violence is especially pronounced in cases of possible extra-judicial killings linked to state actors" (IHRC 2007: 61).

Hence, the hard-line response to gangs further escalated the violence – not only as public officials and citizens responded violently to gangs, but also as gangs reorganized to avoid detection. By the end of 2011, the Salvadoran PNC estimated that there were some 9,000 members of the main gangs in prison, but some 27,000 were still on the streets (Farah and Lum 2013: 5). Efforts to control neighborhoods and transit routes remained fierce. Where competition or resistance peaked to control these routes, violence was often the response.

The 2012–2014 Gang Truce

The crackdown on gangs only increased the stakes to control particular territories and led to greater competition between the two main gangs (as well as with the state) to assert control over particular areas. A quite unexpected policy was negotiated in 2012 that moved away from this punitive approach toward a negotiated truce. If organizational territorial competition leads to heightened violence, as this book has argued, the efforts to manage that competition should lead to a decline in violence. Indeed, between 2012 and 2014, there was a short-lived gang truce during which time violence declined; after the truce was violated, violence resurged. As this section highlights, this policy experiment (forged after the first draft of the book was written) supports the plausibility of one of the book's central arguments.

In spring 2012, El Salvador's two main gangs, MS-13 and Barrio 18, struck a truce. At the time it was negotiated, the terms of the truce (both how it was brokered and what it included) remained somewhat shrouded in mystery. The role of the government was unclear – not least because Justice and Public Security Minister David Munguía Payés "denied that the government had negotiated with the gangs"[115] and "the gangs issued a joint statement on 23 March denying they had negotiated with the government."[116] That said, it seems that the process was mediated by Raúl Mijango (a former congressperson and former FMLN guerrilla fighter) and Bishop Fabio Colindres (a military chaplain) (Dudley 2013: 3, 19). It remains unclear how involved the government was in the process, especially since it distanced itself from the deal when it was first announced and later acknowledged that it "facilitated" the process (Dudley 2013: 3, 15–16).

While details remained clouded, and the normative debate raged, it appears that the truce agreed (a) that the gangs would lower their homicide rates and (b) that the government would transfer some thirty gang leaders from maximum-security prisons, increase visitation rights, and remove military officers from some prisons (Dudley 2013: 3, 19). According to Ribando Seelke (2014), moreover, "gang leaders pledged not to forcibly recruit children into their ranks or perpetrate violence against women, turned in small amounts of weapons, and offered to engage in broader negotiations. They did not agree to give up control of [sic] over their territories or stop extortions."

Following the truce, the Funes government created "peace zones" in fourteen municipalities (*municipios santuarios*), in which social and economic programs (not restricted to gang members) were to be advanced in the context of the gangs' promise to refrain from crime (Dudley 2013: 25).

Strikingly, homicide rates declined in the aftermath of the truce, although reporting of the exact numbers varies. Some estimate that the homicide rate was halved in the first hundred days after the truce was signed (Dudley 2013: 19). "Homicides in this country of six million people are down 32 percent in the first half of this year; kidnappings have fallen 50 percent; and extortion has declined nearly 10 percent, according to the Salvadoran security ministry, which attributes the drop largely to the truce."[117] Referencing Salvadoran government reports, Ribando Seelke (2014: 11) notes that daily homicide rates dropped from an estimated 14 per day to 5.5 per day. Although some question the extent

---

[115] "El Salvador: Did a Pact with the Gangs Lower the Murder Rates?" *LatinNews*: Latin American Security & Strategic Review. March 2012 (ISSN 1741-4204).
[116] "Why Are Homicides Plummeting." *LatinNews*. Latin American Weekly Report. March 29, 2012.
[117] Randal C. Archibold. "Gangs' Truce Buys El Salvador a Tenuous Peace." *New York Times*, August 27, 2012.

of the decline.[118] Farah and Lum (2013:26) caution that homicide rates are not reducible to gang violence: "Aguilar and others who have studied patterns of violence in El Salvador for decades also point out that research has consistently shown that gang-on-gang violence has usually represented only about 25–30 percent of the overall homicide rate in El Salvador. A slightly higher percentage was attributed to criminal networks, and the remainder to traditional types of violence."[119]

If we look back at Figure 6.1 (at the start of the chapter), which reports homicide rates from 1999 to 2015 based on IML data, the dramatic drop during the years of the truce is striking and dramatic. Violence did not cease (note that Figure 6.1's x-axis begins at 35 not 0), and gang-related crimes were still concentrated in the capital region: "The metropolitan area of San Salvador accounted for 31% of all homicides in 2013. Three other administrative zones accounted for just under 20% each; paracentral (Cabañas, La Paz, San Vicente), eastern (La Unión, San Miguel, Usulután) and western (Ahuachapán, Santa Ana, Sonsonate)."[120] But the dramatic and short-lived decline is notable.

The truce did not last, and violence peaked once again. The year 2014 witnessed a rise in homicide rates – because of a division within the Barrio 18 gang between the Revolucionarios and the Sureños, President Funes argued.[121] Moreover, the Funes government wavered in its approach to the gangs in the final days of its term, suspending certain elements of the truce.[122] The new president, Sánchez Cerén,

---

[118] See Aguilar (2012: 484–487), who ponders if other actors were also part of the truce, given the rate at which homicides reportedly declined.

[119] Farah and Lum (2013: 25–26) caution against blindly accepting the extent of the decline in homicides. Gang members reported to them that homicides have not necessarily dropped; rather, they have buried the bodies instead of leaving them visible. In turn, officials have noted a rise in disappearances: "The *Instituto de Medicina Legal*, the forensic investigative unit of the Supreme Court, has noted a sharp rise in the number of people who have disappeared since the truce went into effect. Hard data is not available, but it seems that some portion of the violence has simply been driven underground, with the bodies being disposed of out of public view. However, there remains a broad consensus that the homicide rate is far below pre-truce levels."

[120] *LatinNews*. "Central America: Military No Panacea in Northern Triangle." *Security & Strategic Review* (January 2014).

[121] *LatinNews*. "El Salvador: As Funes Steps Down, Violence Peaks Again." *Security & Strategic Review* (May 2014).

[122] *LatinNews*. "El Salvador: Government Sends Maras Mixed Messages." *Caribbean and Central America Regional Report* (May 2014). *LatinNews*. "El Salvador: Sánchez Cerén and the Gang 'Truce': Redefinition." Latin American Security &

announced (via his minister of justice and security, Benito Lara) that the truce was not part of their formal security strategy and pursued a more aggressive anti-gang approach – including depending actively on the police and the military (loosening constraints on the excessive use of force).[123] By 2015, the homicide rate had skyrocketed to unimaginable highs.

While it would be foolhardy to presume (a) that all violence is gang related and (b) that all of the declining violence is truce related, it is also imperative to draw lessons. Clearly, competition between the gangs (and with the state) has been a critical variable in explaining the violence that has taken place thus far.[124] And just as clear, the coordination between

---

Strategic Review (June 2014). In fact, overall during the Funes term, we find a range of initiatives that advanced both police and military initiatives, a "ley antipandilla," and social programs. See examples of reports regarding various government initiatives in *La Prensa Gráfica* 2010 articles, including 11.3.2010 Preparan plan de seguridad para la zafra 2010–2011; 3.28.2010 Policía dará seguridad al interior de buses; 4.6.2010 91 homicidios pese al plan Vacaciones Seguras; 4.7.2010 Abril ya suma 67 víctimas de la violencia; 10.8.2010 Queremos recuperar y profundizar la naturaleza de la PNC como una Policía civil; 6.3.2010 Las armas, el dolor de cabeza; 1.11.2010 Arzobispo pide al Gobierno desarme; 1.27.2010 Implementan veda de armas en varias zonas de Sonsonate; 3.17.2010 Impulsan veda de armas en municipio de Sonzacate; 12.22.2010 Inicia veda de armas en San Salvador; 8.2.2010 Proponen reducir importación de armamento; 6.23.2010 Gobierno presentará anteproyecto de ley para criminalizar pandillas en El Salvador; 7.7.2010 Fiscalía pedirá cambios a la ley antipandillas; 7.15.2010 Fiscalía objeta ley de proscripción de las pandillas; 9.2.2010 El Salvador prepara ley para rehabilitar y reinsertar ex pandilleros; 8.31.2010 Asamblea busca consenso sobre ley antipandillas; 9.16.2010 PNC y FGR se alistan para aplicar ley que prohibe pandillas en El Salvador; 9.18.2010 Magistrado señala que poco servirá nueva ley; 9.18.2010 Militares listos para aplicar la Ley Antipandillas; 9.17.2010 Nueva Ley Antipandillas sumarán delitos a pandilleros presos; 9.19.2010 Ley de Proscripción de Pandillas entra en vigor desde hoy; 5.17.2010 Cámaras vigilan en el centro de Sonsonate; 2.17.2010 El Salvador equipa observatorios de violencia municipal; 2.19.2010 El Salvador revelará nuevo plan de combate a la criminalidad; 2.25.2010 Afinan protocolo para fiscalizar las escuchas; 8.9.2010 Centro de escuchas podría no funcionar por falta de dinero; 12.22.2010 Homicidios se redujeron 9% en 2010, dice Seguridad; 9.2.2010 El Salvador prepara ley para rehabilitar y reinsertar ex pandilleros; 10.21.2010 Autoridades lanzan campaña para reducir la violencia en El Salvador; 10.29.2010 Reviven modelo de la Policía Comunitaria; 12.17.2010 Policía impulsa operativo ciudadano.

[123] *LatinNews*. "El Salvador: Sánchez Cerén and the Gang 'Truce': Redefinition." Latin American Security & Strategic Review (June 2014). Also see www.insightcrime.org/news-analysis/gangs-find-common-ground-in-el-salvador-crackdown.

[124] For news reporting on the Salvadoran truce, see "El Salvador: Did a Pact with the Gangs Lower the Murder Rates?" *LatinNews*: Latin American Security & Strategic Review. March 2012 (ISSN 1741-4204); "Gangs' Truce Buys El Salvador a Tenuous Peace." *New York Times*. August 27, 2012.

the core gangs and the state impacted the dramatic decline in homicide rates. When the truce unraveled (following a withdrawal of support by the Funes government for the truce mediators as well as a closing of space for prison leaders to communicate with street gang members), homicides and attacks on the police increased dramatically (rising to 9 a day by April, and 20–25 per day by late May 2014; see Ribando Seelke 2014: 12).[125]

One might then infer that another gang truce might be a way forward. In 2016, a hybrid situation emerged, consisting of a March 2016 nonaggression pact (between the two main gangs, including MS-13 and the two rival parts of Barrio 18) and an aggressive state crackdown. While the former would raise expectations of lowering inter-gang violence – especially since the agreement included a coordinating committee and prohibited both taking over rival gang territories and killing rival gang members – the latter might raise concerns about increasing state violence against suspected gang members.[126] In a context of organizational competition to secure control of areas that have been dominated by gangs, states are relying on violence to mark their territory.

In short, territorial *competition* has driven much of the violence associated with gang violence. Yet gangs are not the only armed illicit group in El Salvador – even if they have received the greatest hype from politicians and press alike. A similar competitive and violence pattern emerges when we analyze the equally obscure world of organized crime and drug trafficking.

Transnational Illicit Economy

El Salvador's high levels of violence are not attributable to gangs alone. Indeed, they also map onto the transnational illicit economy associated with organized crime. With the disruption of trade flows though the Caribbean, DTOs looked to Central America, as noted in Chapter 3. As part of the Central American isthmus, El Salvador forms part of the strategic geographic corridor for moving cocaine north from Colombia

---

[125] Also see www.insightcrime.org/news-analysis/gangs-find-common-ground-in-el-salva dor-crackdown.
[126] See reporting by *InSight Crime*, including www.insightcrime.org/news-analysis/gangs -find-common-ground-in-el-salvador-crackdown and www.insightcrime.org/news-briefs /el-salvador-extend-extraordinary-anti-gang-measures-2018.

to the United States – although Guatemala has been far more prominent in this regard than El Salvador. Juan Daniel Alemán, cofounder of FUSADES, stated that the greatest problem in El Salvador is narcotrafficking, even if the dimensions are not (yet) as severe as in Guatemala and Mexico.[127]

Drug seizure data and an examination of historical trafficking routes show that drug trafficking activity is far more prevalent in Guatemala than El Salvador. Guatemala has long been on the U.S. list of "Major Drug Transit" countries (along with Panama, Mexico, and the Dominican Republic) but El Salvador has never appeared on this list, being referred to simply as a "transit country."[128]

By 2013, El Salvador was placed for the third year running on the US list of major drug-producing or drug-transit countries (Ribando Seelke 2014: 19).[129] "With its relatively unguarded Pacific coast that has long been a haven for smugglers – particularly during the civil war of 1980–1992 – and a weak and corruptible police force and political structure, El Salvador offered several advantages. This led to the development of specialized drug transport networks led by *transportistas*, or smuggling specialists, who were often protected or escorted by gang members from MS-13" (Farah and Lum 2013: 14). El Salvador's insertion into the illicit drug economy, thus, has increased over time, even if it is not as significant in this regard as its northern triangle peers.[130]

---

[127] Interview with Juan Daniel Alemán, August 27, 2008.
[128] Moran (2009: 8–9), citing US Department of State, "Counternarcotics and Law Enforcement Country Program: El Salvador," June 30, 2005. www.state.gov/p/inl/rls/fs/48915.htm, accessed May 18, 2008.
[129] Strikingly, "Comalapa International Airport in El Salvador serves as one of two cooperative security locations (CSLs) for U.S. anti-drug forces in the hemisphere" (Ribando Seelke 2014: 20).
[130] The newspaper violence database includes articles that report on the rising drug trade and consumption, although in 2005 there were no substantive articles that *primarily* focused on this issue (whereas they did mention it when talking about other issues, such as drug-related *violence*; General Memo for 2005, newspaper violence database). For examples of articles reviewed for the newspaper violence database, 2000, see *La Prensa Gráfica* 3.3.2000 Departamento de Estado revela informe sobre narcoactividad en el país; 10.18.1999 Sonsonate y Ahuachapán, nuevo territorio de narcos; 8.19.2000 10 Toneladas de cocaína pasan por El Salvador cada año; 8.19.2000 San Salvador, el gran mercado (de droga). In the 8.19.2000 article, the reporter suggests that sea transport had surpassed land transport in that year, especially with the destruction of major parts of the Pan-American Highway following Hurricane Mitch in 1998.

Looking back to the start of the century, a 2000 US State Department report identified El Salvador as a major drug trafficking route, particularly along the Pan-American Highway and at Puerto de Acajutla.[131] Other reporting noted the importance of drug trafficking in El Salvador, both in Sonsonate (Puerto de Acajutla) and Ahuachapán (along the Guatemalan border).[132] In the context of lucrative transportation routes and illicit goods, there was reportedly an increased effort, particularly after 2008, to control territories in which smugglers (*transportistas*) would seek both to sell the drugs and extort further money from local business and services, especially bus owners (Farah 2012: 60) – an observation that also resonates with newspaper reports about bus drivers being held up, as noted in the newspaper violence database reporting (and discussed earlier in the section on gangs). Newspaper coverage in 2010 continued to report ongoing and rising concern about drug trafficking in El Salvador (see the newspaper violence database and the 2010 General Violence Report for El Salvador), including reports of "narcobarriles" – purportedly containing more money in total than the total confiscated from narcotraffickers in the previous ten years.[133] Reporting on the *narcobarriles* implicated a Guatemalan narcotrafficker and an El Salvadoran ex-secretary general of the Dirección General de Transportes, among others.[134] While it was rare for Salvadoran officials to comment in the press on these issues, sub-director of investigations Howard Cotto remarked at the time of the barrels' discovery: "The [drug trafficking] cartel does not necessarily have to be here, but what is certain is that our territory is being used for these types of operations."[135] There were reports of drug consumption, but they were overshadowed by these concerns about trafficking.[136]

---

[131] *La Prensa Gráfica* 3.3.2000 Departamento de Estado revela informe sobre narcoactividad en el país.
[132] *La Prensa Gráfica* 10.18.1999 Sonsonate y Ahuachapán, nuevo territorio de narcos.
[133] *La Prensa Gráfica* 9.5.2010 Otro barril con dinero en Zacatecoluca. Also see other articles in *La Prensa Gráfica*: 9.10.2010 Autoridades localizan un nuevo barril con dinero en Lourdes; 9.11.2010 Barril encontrado en Lourdes contenía $4.2 millones de dólares; 9.4.2010 $9.2 millones, dinero hallado bajo tierra en Zacatecoluca; 12.20.2010 "El Gordo" Paredes es dueño de narcobarriles.
[134] *La Prensa Gráfica* 12.20.2010 "El Gordo" Paredes es dueño de narcobarriles.
[135] *La Prensa Gráfica* 9.5.2010 Otro barril con dinero en Zacatecoluca: "No necesariamente el cartel tiene que estar aquí, pero lo que sí es cierto es que nuestro territorio se está usando para este tipo de operaciones."
[136] For newspaper reporting of drug consumption, especially in San Salvador's poor neighborhoods, see *La Prensa Gráfica* 8.19.2000 San Salvador, el gran mercado (de droga).

By the end of 2010, maritime and highway routes had become particularly important. Farah (2011: 19) notes that transit occurred via "go-fast" boats and semi-submersible and submersible crafts. Cocaine entered El Salvador, therefore, from the coast and then traveled by truck (hidden in other cargo) along two main highways: the Pan-American and the Littoral/Coastal Highway (Farah 2011: 21). See Figure 6.6 for the drug trafficking routes highlighted by UNODC (2012: 36). Similar patterns occurred, according to Farah (2011: 21), in Panama, Nicaragua, Costa Rica, and El Salvador.

With limited capacity to monitor these flows, high levels of corruption among those responsible for doing so, and a border with Guatemala, El Salvador is valuable territory for drug trafficking (more so, as I have argued, than Nicaragua and Costa Rica). Silva Ávalos (2014), in particular, highlights the corruption and complicity of the Salvadoran police in the smuggling of drugs and the protection of ringleaders, chronicling the activities of the three ringleaders (José Natividad Luna Pereira, aka Chepe Luna, in the east; Daniel Quezada in the west; and Juan María Medrana, aka Juan Colorado) who have operated in the context of police (and judicial) collusion. Thus, even if UNODC (2012: 11) rightly notes that El Salvador has been less important in the drug trade than Guatemala and Honduras, it has not been exempt: "today, El Salvador is a crucial part of a transnational 'pipeline' or series of overlapping, recombinant chains of actors and routes that transnational criminal organizations use to move illicit products" (Farah 2011: 3).

The illicit economy has reportedly included drugs, money laundering, human trafficking, weapons, vehicles, and kidnapping, among other things – drawing on the key clandestine networks that had been built up during the war (Farah 2011). At times these clandestine networks drew on the expertise of demobilized armed groups, which could help gain control over territory.[137] In this regard, territorial control and state

---

[137] Demobilized groups from the civil war days are reported to have also taken part in the illicit economy, according to a special commission (with representation from the Salvadoran government, the UN, and the human rights ombudsman), with some motivated by economic and/or political considerations (Farah 2011: 7). Farah reports that over time the political considerations declined as economic motivations took a lead; erstwhile ideological enemies sometimes collaborated in these efforts, and he conjectures that alongside the armed and intelligence skills of former armed military officers and combatants, they possessed a knowledge of controlling territory. Farah writes: "The skill of the cadre of highly trained and well-armed individuals with the ability to control physical space inside the country,

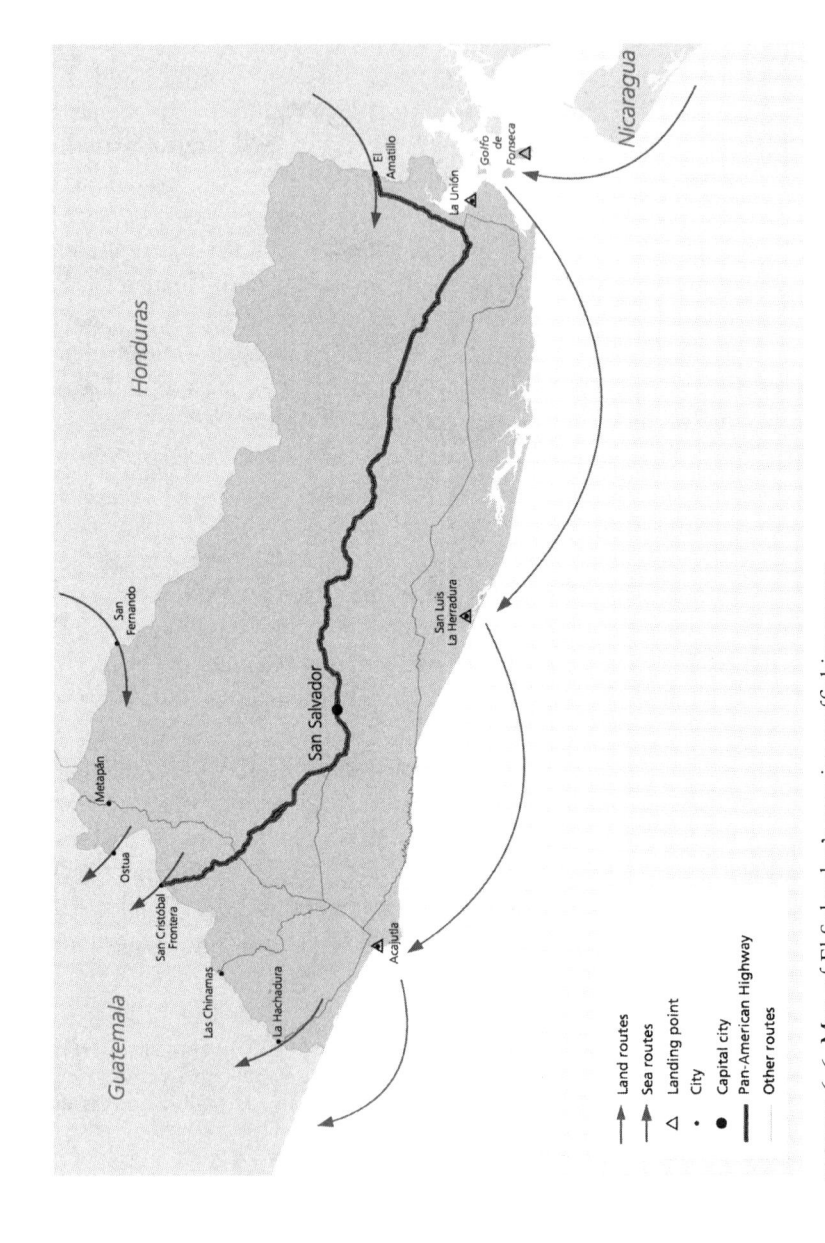

FIGURE 6.6 Map of El Salvador's cocaine trafficking routes
Source: UNODC 2012: 36

complicity have been key to the process, as the following quotes highlight so vividly.

[José Natividad Luna Pereira (aka Chepe Luna)] established himself as the most powerful smuggler in eastern El Salvador, *thanks to the territorial control* he exercised over the wetlands bordering the Gulf of Fonseca, his access to goods in Nicaragua and Honduras, and most importantly, his extensive network of collaborators he slowly built up within the state, especially the PNC, but also in the Attorney General's Office and the judicial system. A 2004 report prepared by the Finance Ministry said: "*The smuggling of all kinds of goods increased because police chiefs began receiving gifts from the powerful structures [...] in late 2003 and the first nine months of 2004; the police favored smugglers to the extent the merchandise owners who paid bribes went untouched.*"

Chepe Luna's strategy was the same as that of other smugglers on the continent who ultimately became drug traffickers; *territorial control*; access and management of a logistics transport network capable of moving goods safely and quickly; *and enough money to buy off the authorities and even bring them into the business*. (Silva Ávalos 2014: 10; emphasis added)[138]

The ability to control territory, in a region crisscrossed with traditional smuggling routes, is also one of the reasons the primary activity of the criminal groups in El Salvador revolves around transporting illicit goods. Producing no indigenous cocaine or heroin, El Salvador's geographic location is its value added contribution to the criminal pipeline structure traversing the

---

operate intelligence and counterintelligence groups and form alliance with powerful political and economic interest groups was a significant development. It is similar in some ways to the post-conflict developments in Guatemala and Nicaragua. In Guatemala, the military and its elite units have maintained a powerful web of political and intelligence alliances, and in Nicaragua both leaders of the Sandinista government and the Contra rebel intelligence structures have allied with drug trafficking groups to raise their operational capabilities" (Farah 2011: 9). He continues: "This phenomenon of the sophistication of former combatants entering the criminal world explains in part why El Salvador in particular and much of Central America more broadly emerged in the mid- and late 1990s, seemingly overnight, with sophisticated armed structures. Rather than spending years developing the capacities to form highly structured criminal enterprises, they simply adapted wartime structures and tactics to criminal activities" (Farah 2011: 9).

[138] The United States apparently knew about these routes and wanted the Saca government to capture its ringleader, José Natividad Luna Pereira (aka Chepe Luna). Chepe Luna was a cattle rancher who became renowned for his role in contraband, human trafficking, and later drugs (Silva Ávalos 2014: 9–10). Silva Ávalos (2014: 9–14) chronicles various instances where the Salvadoran authorities seem to participate in, tip off, or turn a blind eye toward his activities (with PNC officers even assuming leadership positions in intelligence despite ties to this figure). Chepe Luna was killed in Honduras in 2014.

region from Mexico to Colombia. Most of the organizations in El Salvador that participate in the drug trade are called *transportistas* because their primary role revolves around transportation and protection, while Mexican and Colombian groups are the managers and ultimate owners of the product. (Farah 2011: 9)[139]

Transportation groups, therefore, have become key to the transport of drugs throughout Central America, including El Salvador. Most notable is the role of the Perrones, who are commonly known as the *transportistas*. The Perrones, a powerful, consortia of smugglers, used their preexisting routes (previously used for dairy and undocumented workers) to move cocaine, a much more lucrative product (Farah 2011: 16–17; Silva Ávalos 2014: 9; and *InSight Crime* website).[140] In turn, they have developed an expertise in moving goods by land from the east to the west (reportedly goods offloaded from various kinds of water vessels, which they then transport by land to other Central American countries – often bound for the United States).[141]

As argued throughout this book, the presence of these groups alone is not enough to explain violence. It is the competition to control the territorial spaces that has catalyzed much higher levels of violence. Where longstanding trafficking organizations had hegemony over trafficking routes (or clear boundaries/collaborations), high levels of violence did not necessarily ensue; however, where they tried to expand their control (an example of competing) or defend it (from other organizations and/or the state), violence has spiked. UNODC observes a similar pattern of low violence where organized crime is not contested and increasing violence where competition ensues – as when the Perrones expanded its territorial control (UNODC 2012: 69).

[139] "*Transportistas*, or transporters in English, generally refers to home grown organized crime groups that have specialized in transporting or moving illegal goods and contraband within and amongst Central American countries" (Farah 2011: 9).

[140] The Perrones are a transportation group that apparently started off smuggling a range of goods (people and contraband, including staples like food and clothes) from Panama to Guatemala – with many members located at the border with Honduras. See a description of the organization on the *InSight Crime* website (www.insightcrime.org/groups-el-salvador/perrones), accessed on July 14, 2014.

[141] Farah (2011) and www.insightcrime.org/groups-el-salvador/perrones (accessed on July 14, 2014). Also see UNODC (2012: 26–27).

In El Salvador, for example, murder rates have traditionally been low along *el caminito*, the trafficking route used by the Texis cartel. They spiked, however, in areas where the Perrones were expanding, and a series of assassinations occurred following the arrest of the leader, Reynerio Flores in 2009. Some of the most peaceful places are spots the state no longer contests. (UNODC 2012: 69)

The trafficking organizations are not of a piece and have split into two groups: Los Perrones Orientales and Los Perrones Occidentales.[142] In both cases they move the product, control certain corridors, and are a conduit to bring the goods from one set of international actors to another. In this regard, they are part of a much longer international supply chain moving illicit drugs (and other products) northward.

The largest of these transportation groups in El Salvador is known as *Los Perrones Orientales*, operating in and around the eastern cities of San Miguel, Usulután and La Unión. This group takes custody of the cocaine that arrives on El Salvador's Pacific coast from Colombia and Ecuador, and is charged with protecting the product on a fleet of trucks that move westward toward Guatemala, or north to cross into Honduras. Once across the border, the drugs are turned over to Mexican or Guatemalan trafficking structures. (Farah 2011: 16)

The *Perrones Orientales*, in turn, are allied with an organization known as *Los Perrones Occidentales*, who operate around the city of Santa Ana and control corridors for transporting cocaine, weapons and human traffic by land into Guatemala. (Farah 2011: 16)

The Salvadoran *transportistas* are said to have close ties with Colombian and Mexican drug organizations, especially the Sinaloa drug trafficking group, as well as regional ties with Nicaragua and Guatemala (Farah 2011: 16). Also, they increasingly have ties with the Zetas in Mexico, according to reports.[143] Given their ability to move goods from the ocean to the highways, they are valuable to the transnational supply chain moving the drugs north.

The Perrones are able to operate in these spaces in no small part because of their alleged ties to the state, including "sophisticated intelligence networks through the police and other state officials"

---

[142] Farah (2011). Also see online summaries on *InSight Crime* (www.insightcrime.org/groups-el-salvador/perrones), accessed on July 14, 2014. *InSight Crime* also reports on other criminal groups, including the Texis. See www.insightcrime.org/groups-el-salvador/texis-cartel (accessed on July 14, 2014).

[143] *InSight Crime* (www.insightcrime.org/groups-el-salvador/perrones), accessed on July 14, 2014.

(Farah 2011: 16). Arrests have sometimes occurred, including those of senior police officials and politicians, with a confidential police report noting high levels of infiltration by the Perrones into local and national state institutions (e.g., "the senior levels of the police, the judicial system and the attorney general's anti-narcotics unit"), resulting in attending impunity for much of the illicit activity that was taking place (Farah 2011: 17–18). A study of the PNC and drug trafficking arrives at similar conclusions (Silva Ávalos 2014). State complicity and corruption have thus provided a permissive environment for these organizations, undermining official efforts to deter the illicit activity.

In the rare cases where drug kingpins are pursued, the void has been filled by others – both within the illicit economy and the formal organizations of the state. The Perrones have been able to regroup even after key members have been arrested. In turn, despite occasional sanctions of state authorities, complicity continues, with a reported increase in transport capacity, according to the head of the Salvadoran armed forces joint chiefs of staff (reporting on the eastern zone for 2012) as well as a US State Department report (reporting on the country as a whole for 2011; Silva Ávalos 2014: 23).

In 2012, both the head of the Armed Forces Joint Chiefs of Staff and the general director of the PNC, admitted that the drug traffickers of the eastern zone were regrouping and that their transport capacity had increased. A year earlier, despite the arrests of drug kingpins in El Salvador, a record number of up to 11 tons of cocaine transited through the country, according to a report by the U.S. State Department. (Silva Ávalos 2014: 23)

Indeed, if anything, Silva Ávalos (2014: 28) conjectures that state collusion and DTO penetration of the state became institutionalized during the period of 2004–2009 (during the Saca presidency) and remained apparent even in 2013 given the impunity of medium and high-ranking officials who were caught (Silva Ávalos 2014: 23).

Developing Ties between DTOs, Transportistas, and Gangs

The drug trafficking organizations and transportistas have over time arguably also had an impact on the evolution of gang activities, despite distinct origins and geographic operations. Historically, the gangs, *transportistas*, and DTOs developed independently, with the gangs largely located in the capital city and the Perrones/*transportistas* largely operating in the coastal cities (Santa Ana, San Miguel, Usulután, and La Unión). The gangs are not important players in transnational cocaine trafficking (UNODC 2012: 5). Indeed, organized crime organizations often saw gang members as "too undisciplined and unreliable" as well as "disposable" and "replaceable" (Farah and Lum 2013: 10).[144]

However, subsequent writings have questioned whether a closer relationship may have developed over time.[145] The crackdown in 1996 on Mexican crime (following an earlier 1990s crackdown on Caribbean routes) has led to debates about an increasing effort by Mexican DTOs to penetrate Central American countries, with attending pressures and opportunities for extant illicit groups (Farah 2012: 59 and Farah and Lum 2013: 13).[146] Gangs that previously might have had an ad hoc relationship, selling cocaine and crack that they had received for occasionally "guarding loads and arranging logistics," developed closer (albeit not institutionalized) ties after the 2006 Mexican crackdown led DTOs to search for other routes.[147] Confronted with the kingpin strategy targeting DTO leaders in Mexico, and the ensuing violence that resulted between DTOs and the state, there were increased incentives for Mexican DTOs to secure the drug routes passing through Central America in order to move illicit goods northward. In this context, Sinaloa and the Zetas reportedly increased their presence in the isthmus and their ties to Salvadoran illicit groups (Farah and Lum 2013: 13). Reportedly, gangs have increasingly helped protect these trafficking routes; paid in kind, they in turn have sold drugs in local

---

[144] For a quote about how DTOs use gang members: "While often viewed by TCO leadership as too undisciplined and unreliable to be partners in the cocaine trade, gang members are used most often as foot soldiers to protect the movement of cocaine by land, and of weapons and bulk cash shipments along specific routes controlled by regional *transportista* networks. Gang members are generally viewed as 'disposable' agents who are easily replaceable" (Farah and Lum 2013: 10).

[145] After highlighting that gangs and organized crime are distinct organizational phenomenon with distinct expressions, Aguilar also observed that organized crime has increasingly used gangs to pursue certain ends. Interview with Jeannette Aguilar, August 13, 2008.

[146] See articles in *La Prensa Gráfica*: 12.18.2010 No hay indicios de que Los Zetas estén en el país; 12.22.2010 FGR: Hay indicios de la presencia de Los Zetas en El Salvador.

[147] Quote from Farah and Lum (2013: 13); information also in Farah (2011).

markets (*narco menudeo*), generating turf battles and violence (Farah 2011: 13–15).

Moreover, reports indicate that gangs were occasionally hired by the Perrones (in eastern San Miguel) and el Cartel de Texis (in the eastern town of Texispeteque) to carry out violence for the *transportistas*, occasionally working with them when they wanted to transport goods through gang-controlled territories.[148] Farah and Lum (2013) have the most to say on this subject, although their report wavers between observing relatively undeveloped ties and a growing relationship – with some joint involvement in human trafficking, weapons procurement, and drug trafficking, as well as border extortions. Compared to Guatemala and Honduras, they suggest that Salvadoran gangs have gone the furthest in solidifying ties with organized crime, with occasional contacts in Guatemala and minimal ones in Honduras. While Salvadoran gangs have apparently largely worked with Salvadoran or regional organizations in drug trafficking (rather than Mexican DTOs), even that has apparently started to shift with some involvement with the Zetas (Farah and Lum 2013: 8–18, 29–30). Farah (2012: 62) writes that MS-13 has reportedly received training from the Zetas in Guatemala (el Petén) and parts of El Salvador (near the volcanoes outside of San Salvador), although it remains unclear how many are actually involved.

Drug Routes, Subnational Patterns, and Violence Revisited

The geography of the drug routes coincides with higher violence rates. Indeed, along these transportation routes (near coasts and borders on the western side of the country), violence has been particularly high. We cannot attribute violence to any one organization; but nor can we ignore the observation that increased use and increased competition to control these routes has coincided with high geographic violence – particularly in the west, including in places with low population density (UNODC 2012: 37 and Carcach 2008). What these observations suggest is that violence has been high along illegal routes – including those initially moving contraband and later moving illegal drugs. In this process, organized crime has come to play an increasingly important role.

---

[148] See Farah (2011: 18); Farah (2012: 59–60); *InSight Crime* website; Farah and Lum (2013: 7ff).

TABLE 6.1 *El Salvador's subnational per capita homicide rates (1999–2006)*

Department	1999	2000	2001	2002	2003	2004	2005	2006
Ahuachapán	37.7	29.1	27.9	24.6	29.4	29.9	32.7	31.2
Cabañas	53.3	37.9	54.0	42.7	38.6	28.2	54.2	47.6
Chalatenango	30.2	25.9	22.2	17.6	10.5	13.9	11.3	16.7
Cuscatlán	55.8	43.4	28.8	32.4	29.7	32.3	40	61.1
La Libertad	46.2	41.1	34.0	33.2	41.5	54	74.6	82.8
La Paz	43.7	63.2	47.3	43.6	42.6	36.1	62.6	54.7
La Unión	36.0	36.0	34.6	34.3	23.9	18.2	24.5	27.8
Morazán	24.9	25.9	18.9	16.5	12.5	11.3	14.5	15.0
San Miguel	33.5	35.0	45.3	32.8	24.9	28.9	42.5	47.8
San Salvador	36.8	42.3	38.1	35.0	39.2	52.9	68.7	65.2
San Vicente	37.7	52.1	23.9	33.3	25.2	33.7	38.6	28.9
Santa Ana	51.7	60.6	41.3	54.1	46.2	51.4	55.2	64.0
Sonsonate	54.4	56.0	47.7	51.1	54.2	70.3	77.6	62.5
Usulután	43.4	40.8	28.2	28.7	28.7	24.0	25.0	37.7

Source: Draws on the Organización Panamericana de la Salud, Unidad de Análisis de Salud y Estadísticas, Iniciativa Regional de Datos Básicos en Salud, Sistema de Información Técnica en Salud, Washington, DC, 2010, www.paho.org/Spanish/SHA/coredata/tabulator/newTabulator.htm.
Note: The raw data is from the Pan American Health Organization, Health Surveillance and Disease Management Area, Health Statistics and Analysis Unit, PAHO Regional Mortality Database. Rates based on World Population Prospects 2006, revised 2008.

There are also patterns of violence that are difficult to explain except in terms of the drug trade. The violence is particularly intense in the west of the country, especially along several transportation routes radiating from the coast and the borders. This concentration is suspicious, especially given that it affects some lightly populated areas with relatively low crime rates overall. (UNODC 2012: 37)

Breaking it down by departments and then cities, we gain a more granular understanding of the geographic concentration of the homicides taking place. The departments with the highest homicide rates in the 2000s are San Salvador, Sonsonate, La Libertad, and Santa Ana, all of which have rates that surpass the national average (and thus those of other departments in the country; see Table 6.1). Figure 6.7 illustrates these regional patterns for 2006 with a map including

FIGURE 6.7 El Salvador's subnational per capita homicide rates (2006)
Source: Draws on the Organización Panamericana de la Salud, Unidad de Análisis de Salud y Estadísticas, Iniciativa Regional de Datos Básicos en Salud, Sistema de Información Técnica en Salud, Washington, DC, 2010, www.paho.org/Spanish/SHA/coredata/tabulator/newTabulator.htm.
Note: The raw data is from the Pan American Health Organization, Health Surveillance and Disease Management Area, Health Statistics and Analysis Unit, PAHO Regional Mortality Database. Rates based on World Population Prospects 2006, revised 2008.

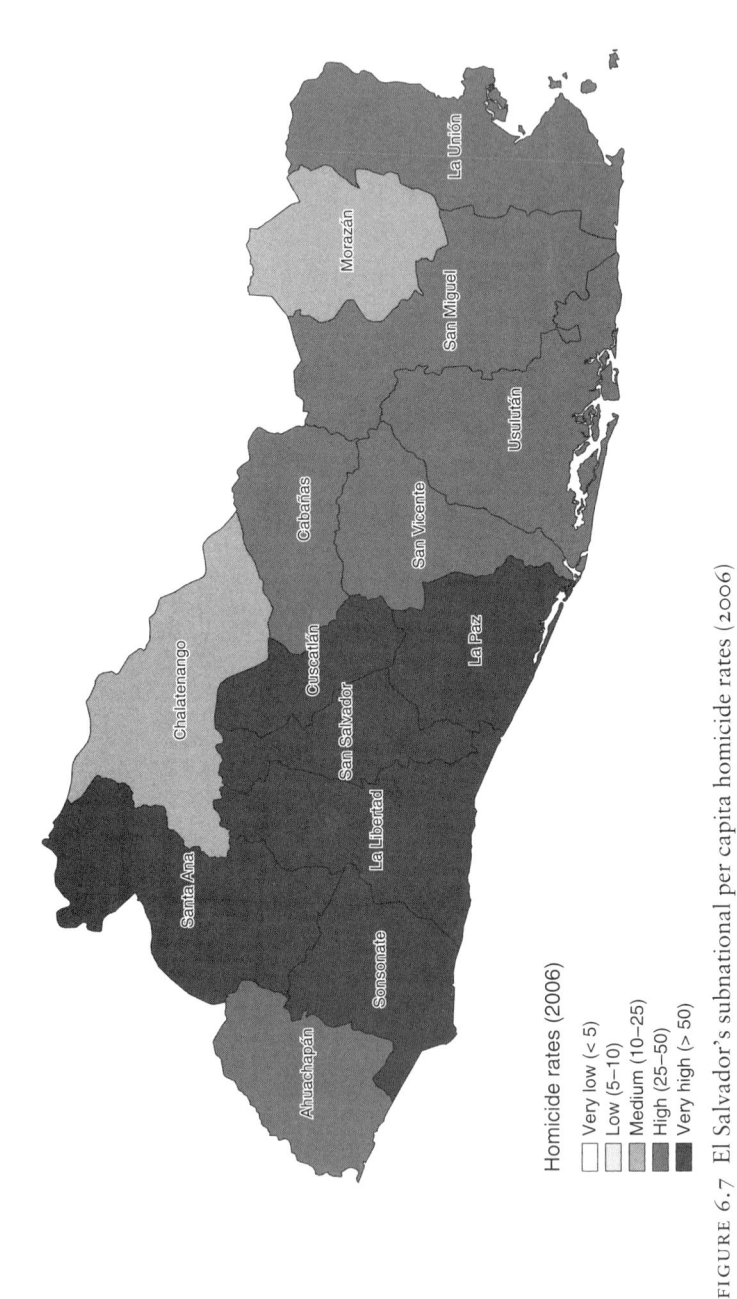

homicide rates by department (this map is one of several constructed for this book). In Table 6.1 and in the GIS maps developed for this book (including Figure 6.7), Sonsonate (among others) consistently shows a high homicide rate. Notably, Sonsonate includes the port, Azacutla, prominently highlighted in the aforementioned UNODC map for cocaine tracking. The Pacific coast, therefore, is not only where drug trafficking flows to a high degree but where violence is among the highest in the country (and region).

To gain a historical comparison, as noted earlier, Carcach analyzed regional homicide data reported in newspapers from 1965 to 1995 (admittedly incomplete and biased) and compared it with official data from the PNC, the IML, and the Salvadoran attorney general's office from 2002 to 2007; these data also suggest that violence is *considerably higher in the 2000s* than in it was in 1995 in almost all cases (the outlier here is Santa Ana, where the paper also reported very high numbers in 1995). It is precisely in the 2000s when we see the increasing role of *transportistas* smuggling illicit drugs and the rising competition to control these lucrative ports, territories, and borders, alongside the competition of gangs, particularly in the capital city of San Salvador and its environs. Table 6.2 provides a more extended historical overview of the period from 1965 to 2013.

The newspaper violence database (constructed for this book), which analyzed *La Prensa Gráfica* (2000, 2005, 2010), disproportionately reported on violence occurring in the two Salvadoran states with the highest homicide rates: San Salvador and Sonsonate. Given uneven coverage, however, the figures are not representative of officially reported data – for example, by El Salvador's forensic institute. See Appendix Tables 6.3, 6.4, and 6.5 for these data.

Moving from departmental to municipal data reinforces the point that homicide patterns are localized in nature and taking place in localities in which there is a significant competition between gangs or between organized crime groups over territorial control. Carcach emphasizes a geographic pattern to the violence that has emerged in the 2002–2007 period (in addition to being related to robbery rates, neighborhood effects, and informality).[149] Homicide has prevailed in the cities listed

---

[149] Carcach (2008) regresses various socioeconomic factors. Contrary to common wisdom, there was no statistically significant relationship found with either the percentage of female-headed households or the Gini coefficient and homicide rates.

TABLE 6.2 *Homicide rates in Salvadoran departments (1965–2013, rates per 100,000 population)*

Department	1965	1995	2000	2005	2010	2013
Ahuachapán	18.3	19.5	29.08	32.7	44.45	28.49
Cabañas	2.8	14.3	35.33	54.2	45.78	51.53
Chalatenango	8.9	6.1	25.94	11.3	41.37	26.37
Cuscatlán	13.3	17.1	38.43	40	48.6	57.82
La Libertad	19.3	20.8	41.78	74.6	80.41	31.43
La Paz	18.1	30.8	63.51	62.6	53.26	58.19
La Unión	4.6	4	33.91	24.5	44.53	45.58
Morazán	4.5	12.3	23.63	14.5	20.44	20.55
San Miguel	29.2	18.8	37.69	42.5	62.34	30.7
San Salvador	20.8	20.2	42.31	68.7	81.24	45.09
San Vicente	19.6	28.7	47.79	38.6	37.88	44.11
Santa Ana	22.6	52.1	60.41	55.2	159.28	31.46
Sonsonate	27.6	32.1	54.65	77.6	85.68	38.81
Usulután	21.8	19	39.31	25	38.1	48.36
Total	**18.5**	**22.7**	**43**	**55.5**	**64.8**	**39.9**

Table created by Daniela Barba-Sánchez for this project using Srata.
Sources: Data on homicide frequencies for years 1999, 2000, and 2010–2013 come from Fabio Molina Vaquerano (2002), *Estudio de mortalidad de El Salvador*. San Salvador: IML, p. 48, available at www.csj.gob.sv/comunicaciones/Estad%C3%ADsticas/IML/periodos/1999.html; Fabio Molina Vaquerano (2003), *Defunciones por homicidios y suicidios en El Salvador 2000*. San Salvador: IML, p. 182, available at www.csj.gob.sv/comunicaciones/Estad%C3%ADsticas/IML/periodos/2000.html; and IML homicide reports, various years, available at www.transparencia.oj.gob.sv/portal/transparencia.php?opcion=1&texto=homicidios&categoria=0.
Data on population by department for years 1999 and 2000 come from DIGESTYC, UNFPA, and Centro Latinoamericano de Demografía (1996), *Proyección de la población de El Salvador 1995–2025*. San Salvador, p. 144.
Data on population by department for years 2010–2013 come from IML reports, several years. Available at www.digestyc.gob.sv/index.php/temas/des/ehpm/publicaciones-ehpm.html.
Data on homicide rates for years 2001–2008 come from Fabio Molina Vaquerano (2009), Unidad de Estadísticas Forenses. Instituto de Medicina Legal (El Salvador). *Epidemiología de los homicidios en El Salvador período 2001–2008*, p. 113. Available at www.csj.gob.sv/comunicaciones/Estad%C3%ADsticas/IML/periodos/imagenes_IML/hasta_2009/ANUARIO_FINAL_HOMICIDIOS_%202001_2008.swf (accessed on September 17, 2015).
Data for 1965 come from Carcach (2008: 12).

later in this discussion. Based on municipal data, mapping, and the rate maps of Freeman-Tukey, in particular, he highlights that "these maps suggest that the geographic distribution of homicides in El Salvador during 2002–2007 is associated with the activities related with contraband, drug trafficking, illegal trafficking of merchandise, and gangs" (Carcach 2008: 90; my translation). These locations include "the northeastern part of the country, the northern side of the municipality of San Salvador, the southern side of the Department of Chalatenango, the north and eastern side of the municipality of San Martín, the northern side of the Department of San Miguel, the western side of the municipality of Usulután, and the northeastern corner of the country (along the Salvadoran and Honduran border)" (Carcach 2008: 89).

According to the police, 63 percent of murders committed in 2004 occurred in just twenty of El Salvador's 262 municipalities: Sonsonate, Quezaltepeque, Colón, Zacatecoluca, Ayutuxtepeque, San Juan Opico, Acajutla, Santa Ana, San Marcos, Soyapango, San Martín, San Salvador, Ahuachapán, Apopa, Ilopango, San Miguel, Ciudad Delgado, Santa Tecla, Mejicanos, and Chalchuapa.[150] San Salvador remained the most violent among them, although Sonsonate and La Libertad were identified as having similarly high levels of violence, according to official statistics and surveys.[151]

In the department of San Salvador, newspaper articles often focused on Soyapango's high violence. Notably, Soyapango has been described as a dividing line between territories controlled by the two main gangs (Mara Salvatrucha and Mara 18). Moreover, the police have had considerable problems controlling this area, not least because the same police force oversees not only Soyapango but also Ilopango and San

---

However, Carcach does report a statistically significant relationship between robbery rates and homicide rates, noting that a 1% increase in robbery rates was related to a 0.27% increase on homicide rates during the period 2002 and 2007 (at the 10% statistical significance level). Moreover, Carcach reports that history matters for homicide rates in later periods: a 1% increase in homicide rates in 1965 and 1995 correlates with an increase in homicide rates in the period 2002–2007 of 0.03% and 0.05%, respectively (at the 10% significance level). Additionally, he reports a neighborhood effect – with a 1% increase in homicide rates in cities correlating with a 0.07% increase in neighboring cities (at the 10% significance level) (Carcach 2008: 92–95).

[150] *La Prensa Gráfica* 5.27.2005 El Plan Mano Amiga iniciará en Sonsonate.
[151] For example, see *La Prensa Gráfica* 8.9.2005 Más joven, más frágil a violencia.

Martín (all violent municipalities), with a ratio of one police officer per 1,533 residents.[152]

Sonsonate, moreover, had the highest per capita homicide rate in 2004, averaging one murder per day.[153] These figures continued to rise in 2005, despite government efforts to address the violence – notably with the government's pilot program "Plan de Protección a la Vida."[154] At the end of 2005, the police estimated that gang disputes (*rencillas entre pandillas*) were responsible for more than 70 percent of the homicides (presumably an overestimate); in turn, the police noted that violence had spread from the city to the countryside: "The PNC has been able at least to control the assassinations in the center and commercial areas of the cabecera, but criminals have looked for other means of operating. The actions have extended to the rural zones, where they have thrown cadavers, taking advantage of the lack of police surveillance."[155]

La Libertad, which neighbors Sonsonate, was also the object of considerable reporting in the press, with particular attention focused on the three municipalities (Colón, Quezaltepeque, and San Juan Opico) that formed a so-called "triangle of death." One article declared: "The zone is infected with gangs, and the thousand and one paths for arriving to and leaving from the place have converted into a zone of constant robberies and the coming and going of drugs, according to the police."[156] Moreover, low police capacity was highlighted by both poor resources (patrolling 428,037 square kilometers of territory with only eleven vehicles) and low citizen trust in the police.[157] Newspaper reporting in 2010 continued to note high

---

[152] *La Prensa Gráfica* 2.7.2005 Soyapango: 177 asesinatos el año pasado.
[153] *La Prensa Gráfica* 1.1.2005 Sonsonate símbolo de la tragedia.
[154] *La Prensa Gráfica* 11.12.2005 Aumenta la cantidad de homicidios en Sonsonate.
[155] *La Prensa Gráfica* 12.14.2005 364 homicidios en 2005: "La PNC ha podido controlar al menos en la cabecera los asesinatos en el centro y los lugares comerciales, pero los criminales han buscado otra forma de operar. Las acciones se han extendido a la zona rural, donde son tirados los cadáveres aprovechando la falta continua de vigilancia policial."
[156] *La Prensa Gráfica* 2.7.2005 Lanzarán plan para capturar homicidas: "La zona está infectada de pandillas y los mil y un caminos para llegar y salir del lugar la han convertido en zona de constantes robos y trasiego de drogas, según la Policía."
[157] A policeman in Santa Tecla explained, "A pesar de que se nos dice que hay una gran cantidad de gente que observó los hechos delictivos, la mayoría es renuente a participar en la investigación, aun la misma familia de los fallecidos de entrada se niega a dar un

violence in many of these same departments in which drug trafficking had become prevalent – particularly Sonsonate.[158]

In short, weak state capacity has facilitated the growth of illicit actors (*transportistas* and gangs) who have become involved in the trade and transit of drugs. Taking advantage of prior smuggling routes, these actors have interacted with DTOs to help move goods north – at times drawing on gangs to participate in the process. This provides a homicidal ecology in which there are high profits, high stakes, and high risk. In those territorial zones where drugs transit, violence has been particularly high. The newspaper reports illustrate these dynamics, and the homicide rates in these departments and cities demarcate the severity of the issue.

CONCLUSION

El Salvador and Guatemala (along with Honduras) are countries with unimaginably high rates of homicide. These violence patterns are not self-contained, nor are the country units hermetically sealed (national boundaries notwithstanding). Hence, while Guatemala, El Salvador, and Honduras have exhibited the highest homicide rates in the Americas (and at times the highest in the world), their neighbors have also seen rises in homicides taking place – although at a much lower level. "According to the World Bank (2010: volume 2, p. 1), "murder rates have grown in all six [Central American] countries since 2003" (though rates have also swung up and down during this time).

With high rates, instability, and ballooning effects, one is left with important theoretical questions and gnawing policy concerns. If an optimist, one is left with the hope that rates can be contained, if not reversed. The implication of this work has been that lowering competition can reverse violence, but the mechanisms by which this would occur can be dramatically varied. Lowering homicides does not necessarily mean getting rid of the illicit economy. Scenario 1 is the democratic promise, where the democratic rule of law displaces

---

aporte mínimo acerca de probables pistas." See *La Prensa Gráfica* 2.20.2005 El triángulo del miedo y el silencio.

[158] *La Prensa Gráfica* 8.26.2010 Cifra de homicidios no baja en Sonsonate; 10.14.2010 IML reitera Sonsonate es el más violento; 10.11.2010 Autoridades de Sonsonate reportan 70 homicidios menos que en 2009; 12.10.2010 IML confirma reducción de 8% homicidios.

illicit actors, and the police and courts work together to systematically protect and defend civil liberties. Scenario 2 is the authoritarian threat, where coercive policies that restrict civil liberties at large are used to shut down illicit actors and close off avenues for independent action. Scenario 3 is an illicit actor cartel, whereby illicit actors agree on how to divide territories and associated spoils (often a situation that is hard to sustain, as the literature on cartels has amply explained). Scenario 4 is collusion (an extension of scenario 3, including a different subset of actors), whereby illicit actors collude with the state (democratic or authoritarian) to establish a monopoly of control over a relatively well-defined area. Each scenario can result in an observational equivalent of lower violence; however, the mechanism by which violence is contained is theoretically distinct and normatively consequential. As these four ideal-type scenarios suggest, we cannot infer from homicide data alone either the stability, directionality, or causes of these trends. And as noted in Chapter 1, all high-violence cases maintain highly unstable rates, raising questions about the durability of downward trends.

Since we do not yet have the empirical data to adjudicate among these four mechanisms, I have moved up the Sartorian ladder of abstraction to highlight what they all share: varied patterns of territorial competition (or lack thereof). The presence of illicit actors alone does not explain the violence; and nor does weak state capacity on its own. Rather, organizational territorial competition over lucrative turf drives the high homicide violence. Where competition is contained, as with the Salvadoran gang truce, violence has been significantly lowered; where competition is unleashed, the violent consequences have been made evident.

To explain when and why violence is low in seemingly auspicious environments for illicit activity and violence, we turn next to Nicaragua – a post-civil war case with geographic proximity to the United States, high levels of inequality, and noted patterns of political corruption, and yet comparatively low violence during the period studied for this book.

CHAPTER 6
Appendix

NEWSPAPER VIOLENCE DATABASE: SALVADORAN PATTERNS

The newspaper violence database coded articles from *La Prensa Gráfica* for three years: 2000, 2005, and 2010. We tallied reported homicides for all articles in these years and analyzed violence-related articles (many of which were cited in this chapter). The press reported only a fraction of officially recorded homicides, and it privileged reporting in some places more than others. As Tables 6.3 and 6.4 demonstrate, reported rates in El Salvador's *La Prensa Gráfica* are clearly a very *small* subset of the official numbers. Accordingly, the newspaper violence database was ultimately used to learn more about qualitative dynamics rather than quantitative patterns.

In addition to homicide rates, we coded for a range of other factors (see Table 6.5). In the end, this time-consuming process (conducted with the dogged support of many RAs, particularly Yanilda González and Bethany Park) was suggestive but inconclusive – given underreporting and bias in reporting and lack of reporter knowledge about the perpetrators and victims, among other issues. Nonetheless, the data are included here to give the reader a sense of what was being reported in the daily papers about homicides.

TABLE 6.3 *Percentage of homicides in El Salvador reported in* La Prensa Gráfica *(2000–2010, newspaper violence database)*

Overall	2000	2005	2010
Total coded events in newspaper	190	1,122	924
Total coded violent deaths in newspaper	252	1,296	1,175
Official number of violent deaths	2,616	3,738	4,005
Percent of officially reported violent deaths relative to those coded for newspaper violence dataset	9.6%	34.7%	29.3%

Note: Table 6.3 includes number of victims of violent deaths coded in homicide database over the number of official violent deaths ("Homicidios en Centroamérica," LPG Datos, accessed August 23, 2011, http://multimedia.laprensagrafica.com/pdf/2011/03/20110322-PDF-Informe-0311-Homicidios-en-Centroamerica.pdf). Data for El Salvador come from the Instituto de Medicina Legal.

TABLE 6.4 *Percentage of homicides reported in El Salvador by department in La Prensa Gráfica (2000–2010, newspaper violence database)*

Department	% of reported homicide events in 2000	% of reported homicide events in 2005	% of reported homicide events in 2010
Ahuachapán	6.80	3.60	5.80
Cabañas	4.20	1.30	0.90
Chalatenango	0.00	0.40	0.50
Cuscatlán	1.00	1.70	1.00
La Libertad	3.70	8.30	9.10
La Paz	21.50	6.00	8.30
La Unión	1.60	1.20	1.30
Morazán	1.60	0.80	0.60
San Miguel	4.70	9.40	10.10
San Salvador	28.30	42.78	29.90
San Vicente	3.10	1.40	2.80
Santa Ana	12.00	8.60	6.80
Sonsonate	6.80	12.60	16.30
Usulután	4.20	1.50	6.50
Unknown	0.00	0.40	0.00

Note: Table 6.4 includes number of victims of violent deaths coded in homicide database over the number of official violent deaths ("Homicidios en Centroamérica," LPG Datos, accessed August 23, 2011, http://multimedia.laprensagrafica.com/pdf/2011/03/20110322-PDF-Informe-0311-Homicidios-en-Centroamerica.pdf). Data for El Salvador come from the Instituto de Medicina Legal.

TABLE 6.5 *Homicide characteristics for El Salvador reported in newspaper violence database, La Prensa Gráfica (2000, 2010, 2015)*

Category	2000 (190 total coded events; 2,616 official homicide victims)			2005 (1,122 total coded events; 3,738 official homicide victims)			2010 (924 total coded events; 4,005 official homicide victims)		
	Number of events	Number of possible events	Percent of total homicide events reported (%)	Number of events	Number of possible events	Percent of total homicide events reported (%)	Number of events	Number of possible events	Percent of total homicide events reported (%)
Gang-related	18	11	9.5–15.3	308	22	27.5–28.4	212	0	22.9
Competition between gangs	3	4	1.6–3.7	35	12	3.1–3.7	56	8	6.1–6.8
Competition between gangs & state	0	0	0	2	0	0.2	1	0	0.1
Involving state agents	32	0	16.8	44	1	3.9–4.0	34	0	3.7
State agent victim	19	0	10	22	0	2.0	22	0	2.4
State agent perpetrator	16	0	8.4	7	0	0.6	10	2	1.1–1.3
Drug-related	0	1	0–0.5	18	5	1.6–2.0	13	5	1.4–1.9
Organized crime-related	2	4	1.1–3.2	1	1	0	1	0	0.1
Robbery-related	37	13	19.5–26.3	69	3	6.1–6.4	38	2	4.1–4.3
Defensive crimes	13	3	6.8–8.4	11	0	1.0	16	1	1.7–1.8
Crossfire victims	1	1	0.5–1.1	8	0	0.7	6	0	0.6

TABLE 6.5 (continued)

Category	2000 Number of events	2000 Number of possible events	2000 Percent of total homicide events reported (%)	2005 Number of events	2005 Number of possible events	2005 Percent of total homicide events reported (%)	2010 Number of events	2010 Number of possible events	2010 Percent of total homicide events reported (%)
Public transportation-related crimes (Crimes in which bus employees or passengers are victims)	1	0	0.5	51	0	4.5	69	0	7.5
Extortion-related crimes (Crimes in which extortion is stated as a likely or possible reason for violence)	0	0	0	12	5	1.1–1.5	18	6	1.9–2.6
Crimes against women	24	0	12.6	169	0	15.6	192	0	20.1
Crimes in which police moved beyond investigations to detain, prosecute, charge, or arrest	34	0	17.9	135	0	12.0	143	1	15.5

7

Circumscribing Violence in Post-Civil War Nicaragua

Nicaragua is a most unlikely case. Racked by a history of civil war, riddled with persistently high levels of inequality, burdened by a "weak" state, and situated in a "bad neighborhood" of high violence countries, Nicaragua stands out as a paradox. Contrary to most theoretical expectations, Nicaragua emerged from its civil war with much lower homicide rates than one might otherwise expect – in marked contrast to other high-violence cases in Central America (El Salvador, Guatemala, and Honduras, in particular).

Basic socioeconomic status indicators underscore the apparent paradox of Nicaragua's lower homicide rates relative to the rest of the region. Compared to the rest of Central America, Nicaragua entered the new millennia ranked last in terms of per capita income, urban unemployment, illiteracy, youth male urban unemployment, social spending, public housing, public education, average years of schooling (tied last with Honduras), and average years of schooling for males, according to ECLAC data reported by Rocha (2007: 18; see Figure 7.1). Multidimensional poverty rates reported both for incidence and intensity place Nicaragua at the highest or nearly highest spot compared to sixteen other Latin American countries measured in the middle and late 2000s – higher or comparable to the northern triangle countries of Honduras, Guatemala, and El Salvador (which had the lowest incidence of the four) – whether looking at national figures or disaggregating by urban and rural ones (ECLAC 2014: 81–82). Moreover, evaluations of present economic well-being and expectations for the future of offspring place Nicaragua at the bottom of an eighteen-country list based on the Latinobarometer 2011 database, followed by Honduras, Guatemala, and El Salvador; this holds both when looking at the sample as a whole and when looking at the data for (a) lower classes as well as for (b) upper or upper-middle classes (ECLAC 2014: 114–115). By 2012, education

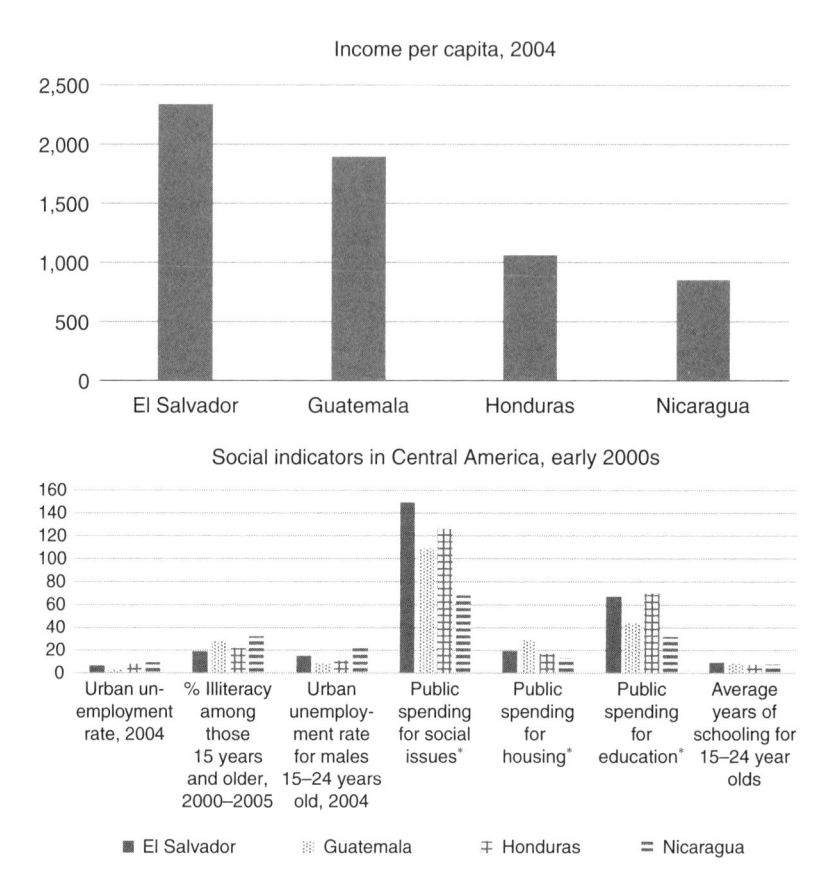

280 *Part III Divergent Trajectories: Three Post-Civil War Cases*

FIGURE 7.1 Social indicators in Central America (early 2000s)
Source: Rocha (2007: 18, table 4; based on CEPAL 2006 data).
*Per capita dollars in 2000.

profiles placed Nicaragua near the bottom of the heap as well: second lowest for completed primary education (for subset of people aged 15–19), completed secondary education (for subset of people aged 20–24), and completed tertiary education (for subset of people aged 25–29), with Guatemala ranking below Nicaragua and Honduras ranking slightly above (ECLAC 2014: 125).

Yet Nicaragua has exhibited lower violence than its post-civil war counterparts in the region. Indeed, the country not only reports much lower homicide rates than the rest of the region, but the overall pattern of concerns about crime (especially relative to unemployment) exhibited in Nicaragua is diametrically opposed to that found elsewhere. While only 1 percent of Nicaraguans identified crime as the most important issue

Circumscribing Violence in Post-Civil War Nicaragua 281

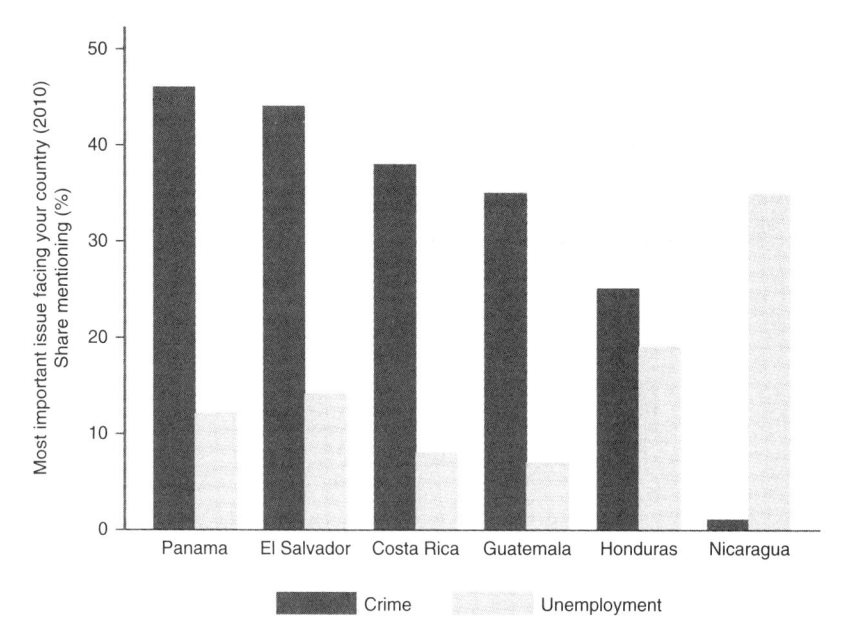

FIGURE 7.2 What is the most important issue facing your country in 2010?
Source: UNODC (2012: 15, based on Latinobarometer 2010 survey).

facing the country in 2010 (unemployment, by contrast, received a 35 percent response rate), all the other countries in the region ranked crime as the most important issue by far (relative to unemployment; see Figure 7.2). Although these perceptual figures do not correlate tightly with homicide rates (after all, the figure in Honduras is low relative to its high violence rates), the complete inverse response pattern in Nicaragua is indicative of Nicaragua's unique position.

This chapter addresses the seeming paradox of Nicaragua's comparatively lower homicide rates with attention to the country's comparatively strong state capacity in democratic policing, which has proven surprisingly effective at preventing the proliferation of gangs and organized crime that are so prevalent in its northern neighbors. The country's police have deterred the proliferation of transnational and local organized crime (although where these illicit organizations are present and are competing for territorial control, one finds homicide levels higher than in the rest of the country). Given these patterns, it is natural to ask why Nicaragua followed such a distinct trajectory.

To explain Nicaragua's distinct experience with post-civil war homicide rates, I develop a historical institutional argument about the bookends of the Sandinista Revolution, including revolutionary breaks and subsequent reform compromises. The 1979 Sandinista Revolution's regime change included the dismissal of the country's historically corrupt, abusive police and its replacement with an entirely new cadre of officers; in turn, a compromise for institutional reform following the Sandinista's 1999 electoral loss forged professionalization and organizational autonomy from the revolutionary party itself. This sequenced institutional break and then reform compromise included more than a change in formal rules and personnel; it was also predicated on – and behaviorally meaningful because it was built on – a new, dedicated cohort of officers who maintained a corporatist commitment to the institution and society. They entered the institution with a commitment to advance a new national project that included a more law-abiding, inclusive, and equitable policing model.[1] As this chapter highlights, the Nicaraguan police emerged with relatively clear role specification, relatively high homicide clearance rates, and relatively low imputed corruption rates – all tied to relatively high levels of trust in this institution. It is this more capable, dedicated, and relatively more visionary police that minimized opportunities for the growth of violent illicit organizations.

Based on original interviews, an original newspaper violence database, and a review of secondary literature, this chapter develops these arguments – first by delineating Nicaragua's unique state formation for the police and military and then discussing the more delimited types and geographies of violence that have emerged in the region (delimited relative to the high-violence cases in El Salvador, Honduras, and Guatemala). The chapter ends by revisiting the question of institutional reform.

FORGING A MORE CAPACIOUS SET OF LAW-AND-ORDER INSTITUTIONS

The Nicaraguan Police and State Formation

Nicaragua's contemporary police force has been lauded for its professionalism. It emerged as an "island of excellence" in what is generally seen as a state riddled with institutional weakness and partisan biases. Indeed,

---

[1] Author interview with Nicaraguan police chief Aminta Granera on March 7, 2007); *InSight Crime* (2012b) interview with Aminta Granera on July 9, 2012, www.insightcrime.org/nicaragua-a-paradise-lost/video-an-interview-with-nicaraguas-police-chief (accessed on June 27, 2013).

despite the fact that the Nicaraguan police force has been relatively small,[2] violence remains low and trust in the institution remains high. The Nicaraguan police has developed a reputation of higher trust relative to other police forces and relative to other Nicaraguan institutions. Moreover, the Nicaraguan police emerged with a distinct policing model that contrasts with its Guatemalan, Honduran, and Salvadoran counterparts. The Nicaraguan police have not only sustained a stronger corporatist commitment to uphold the rule of law, but moreover have adopted a more preventative role, in collaboration with community support. According to Nicaraguan Police Chief Aminta Granera,

> The police model here is preventive, proactive, deeply connected to the community. We are only 14,000 police in uniform but we work with 100,000 people who form an organized voluntary service with the police, to ensure their own safety. And this closeness with the community, the mutual respect [and] the public's confidence in their police, I think dates back to our origins.[3]

This record stands in marked contrast with other Central American cases that experienced longstanding civil wars and peace accords (including police reform) in the mid-1990s. Guatemala and El Salvador have highly corrupt police institutions that are widely noted for their inefficiency, incompetence, and corruption, as discussed in Chapters 5 and 6. This divergence across these three Central American police forces is striking

---

[2] Cordero, Gurdián, and López (2006: 176), writing in a different year, report a different absolute number (7,751 *unidades policiales*) but still note that Nicaragua's police force is significantly smaller than those of other Central American countries, with the exception of Belize: Belize 952; Guatemala 19,850; El Salvador 16,300; Honduras 10,725; Costa Rica 11,400; and Panama 14,806.

[3] Author interview with Nicaraguan police chief Aminta Granera on March 7, 2007; *InSight Crime* (2012b) interview with Aminta Granera on July 9, 2012, www.insightcrime.org/nicaragua-a-paradise-lost/video-an-interview-with-nicaraguas-police-chief (accessed on June 27, 2013). Aminta Granera was appointed as Nicaraguan police chief in 2006. In my interviews, she was anecdotally and universally referred to as an excellent leader. A common phrase was "tiene mística," taken to mean that she had a commitment to the institution that was independent of her class origins. While a member of the elite, she joined the Sandinista Revolution in the 1970s and held a number of high-level positions. According to Grigsby (2006b), her leadership roles during the Sandinista government include heading the chiefs of staff and the interior ministry's secretariat; she also led other police functions, including the national transit police and inspector general. Grigsby notes that there was some tension over who would assume the role as police chief, but Granera ultimately emerged victorious (following an internal scandal with the Managuan police chief that affected the competitor for this position). Her reputation for cracking down on police bribes of drivers, supporting flood victims, and standing up against corruption in general helped raise her profile. She resigned in April 2018, as this book was going to press, in the context of political protests against the regime.

when viewed historically. For much of the twentieth century, Nicaragua shared much with its northern Central American neighbors. The military played a disproportionate role in governing – either as an institution (as in Guatemala and El Salvador) or in support of the dictatorship (as in Nicaragua). The rise of Marxist insurgencies to overturn this military order (and the highly unequal and coercive societies that they governed) was shared by all. Yet only in one country did the insurgents win, leaving an institutional legacy that would subsequently prove consequential for limiting the geography and form of illicit organizations and economies in Central America. In Nicaragua, the Frente Sandinista de Liberación Nacional (FSLN/Sandinistas) overthrew the Somoza dictatorship in 1979 and initiated unprecedented revolutionary changes (initially forging a pluralist coalition with opposition forces, some of whom came to oppose the Sandinistas in later years). This radical divergence proved consequential for the evolution of the country's coercive institutions – including the police.

Indeed, the Sandinista Revolution's bookends (its founding in 1979 and its electoral loss in 1990) reconstructed and institutionalized the military and police by initially wiping clean the institutional foundations of the military and police and then subsequently negotiating its autonomy and further professionalization.[4] If the 1979 Sandinista Revolution destroyed the dictator's haphazard and brutal coercive institutions and replaced them with an entirely new revolutionary and visionary force, the 1990 election (in which the Sandinistas lost political power) forged a compromise among competing sides to institutionalize the Sandinista military and police as formally nonpartisan forces. The combined effect of these two events was the literal creation and consolidation of a new set of coercive state institutions – with a heretofore unseen level of commitment and capacity to uphold the democratic rule of law[5] – and the vesting of opposing sides in the state's coercive apparatus, both military and police.

The first section discusses the formation of Nicaragua's coercive state institutions in light of these two moments; I focus, in particular, on the police force (although references are inevitably also made to the military). After discussing these institutional developments, I analyze why this distinct institutional infrastructure has provided a less auspicious political

---

[4] The Sandinista Revolution introduced many changes. I focus here, however, solely on its impact on the state's coercive institutions.
[5] Cuadra (2005); interviews with Cuadra (March 9, 2007) and Granera (March 7, 2007), among others.

environment (or homicidal ecology) for the growth of gangs and the illicit drug trade (both of which have contributed to high levels of violence in the Central American region as a whole). The conclusion revisits these claims in light of events unfolding as this book goes to press.

Forging New Law-and-Order Institutions

The origins of Nicaragua's contemporary policing model date to the 1979 Sandinista Revolution. While most academics, policy makers, and revolutionaries were focused on the Sandinistas' redistributive ideological commitments and policies, arguably the Sandinistas' most enduring impact was on the country's coercive institutions (the military and police). The Sandinistas abolished the much-despised National Guard (both unprofessional and repressive).[6] As many of the people interviewed for this project stated, it is not simply that a new institution was forged with a new personnel and leadership; it is that those who occupied its ranks were formed in the anti-Somoza struggle and brought new values and commitments to this position – one with a social sensibility and obligation.[7] The origins and strength of Nicaragua's police dates back to these changes, as elaborated next.

Following the 1979 Nicaraguan Revolution that deposed the Somoza dictatorship, the Sandinistas built a new, coercive set of institutions (Grisby 2003; Ruhl 2003: 118; GTZ 2005; IEEPP 2007; Rocha 2007: 69). They forged two new institutions: the Ejército Popular Sandinista (the Sandinista popular army) and the Ministerio del Interior (MINT, the ministry of the interior), which included the Sandinista police (IEEPP 2007: 21). This separation of a civilian police force from the military was a striking institutional change, since there had been no separate police force prior to the Sandinista Revolution: "Between 1934 and 1979,

---

[6] Nicaragua did not have a professional military prior to 1927, when the National Guard was formed. Prior to that, the conservative and liberal parties relied on irregular armed forces. Soon thereafter, however, the National Guard became the "private army" of dictator Anastazio Somoza García and later his sons (Ruhl 2003: 118). Nicaragua also did not have a separate police institution prior to the 1979 revolution (Grigsby 2003). Hence, the National Guard fulfilled both internal order (policing) and external defense (military) functions (IEEPP 2007: 21). Its roles included those of transit police, border guards, spies, controllers of contraband, and antinarcotics agents (Rocha 2007: 69).

[7] Interview with General Joaquín Cuadra, Managua, Nicaragua, on March 9, 2007. In this interview, Cuadra highlighted an additional and related point: it is not simply that a new institution was forged; it is that those who occupied its ranks were formed in the anti-Somoza struggle and brought new values and commitments to this position (one with a social sensibility/obligation) – a point also raised by 2007 interviews with Police Chief Aminta Granera and Antonio Lacayo.

Nicaragua only had an army created by the United States, known as the National Guard (GN). Among other things, it assumed the policing responsibilities it inherited from the armed body created in 1926, which Conservative General Emiliano Chamorro and the US Marines called the Constabulary."[8] Otherwise stated, the National Guard had served both internal order (policing) and external defense (military) functions (IEEPP 2007: 21). Its roles included transit police, border guard, spying, contraband control, and anti-narcotics operations (Rochas 2007: 69).

The formation of a new police after the revolution, therefore, included a break between military and policing functions and required the forging of a new police that included a new organization, training, and orientations (Grigsby 2003; GTZ 2005: 16–17). Many Sandinista combatants and members of the Sandinista youth composed the new police force (Rocha 2007: 69) and fell under the auspices of the ministry of the interior, which in turn also oversaw state security, the penitentiary system, and the migration office.

In the early years of the Sandinista Revolution, the police were not highly regarded. While officers rotated through the various institutions, they looked askance at the police, which was viewed as inferior (Grigsby 2003). The police budget suffered as well, in the context of the ensuing civil war against the *contras* (IEEPP 2007: 21). Indeed, the return to civil war (this time with the "revolutionaries in power") and the emergence of a counter-revolutionary force made it hard for the new police to develop as originally planned, as it became subordinate to the other national issues that had to be addressed (GTZ 2005: 16–17).

Yet even if the police were valued less than the military, it experienced a parallel institutional overhaul, including new personnel and officers. Sandinista fighters (both trained in fighting, espousing revolutionary goals, and ostensibly committed to the "new Nicaragua") assumed leadership as well as rank-and-file positions. General Omar Hallesleuens, former head/military chief of the army (2005–2010) and later elected Nicaraguan vice-president in 2011, indicated that the officers not only had experience but also were well trained.[9]

In the 1980s, the Sandinista police and military were portrayed as revolutionary and popular institutions rather than institutions of domination. Without falling prey to revolutionary hagiography, it still remains commonly noted that police and military officers saw themselves as part

---

[8] Grigsby (2003), accessed on March 3, 2007, at www.envio.org.ni/utils/imprimir.
[9] Interview with Omar Halleslevens on March 13, 2007.

of a broader nationalist, socialist, and populist project. In contrast to its predecessor and those national security/repressive police in Central America's northern triangle, Nicaragua presented something unique. A study, coauthored by a former police chief and a former head of youth affairs in the police, observed that the initial police officers were young people inspired by a vision, a set of hopes, and feelings that they were in a position of lifetime commitment and importance – to create a revolution, including the police, with a social commitment (Cordero, Gurdián, and López 2006: 29–30). By 1988, the police were starting to pursue a process of institutionalization to minimize the explicit partisanship of the institution and its officers, according to GTZ's (2005: 17) study of the police's institutional modernization. Otherwise stated, the police were trying to modernize as a national force, not just a Sandinista one.

Even a prominent opposition leader, Antonio Lacayo, who opposed the Sandinista Revolution and subsequently assumed office as chief of staff during the post-Sandinista government of President Violeta Chamorro, distinguished the Sandinista coercive branches from its Central American neighbors. In this quote (talking about the armed forces, in particular) he stated,

The Nicaraguan armed forces were born with a revolutionary rupture and an enormous feeling of cohesion fully dedicated ... to the revolution ... [T]hey were born to begin something new, which was very attractive for the youth; this "mística" consolidated during the course of the struggle against the *contras* and imperialism. ... This [state institutional] body has a lot of mística. (Antonio Lacayo, March 10, 2007; translated by author)

In order to replace a repressive military institution with one committed to "the people," the Sandinistas created Comités de Defensa Sandinista, to defend the revolution from counterrevolutionary developments; in turn, the police also formed committees, as part of the Dirección General de la Seguridad del Estado (DGSE), according to First Police Commissioner Edwin Cordero, who was director general (police chief) of the national police from 2001 to 2006 (Cordero 2007 interview). Cordero indicated that these committees worked in the communities with women and men as well as children, and he believed that this helped maintain relatively low levels of crime-related violence – although Rocha (2007: 35) is less sanguine about the effectiveness of the committees in the majority of Managua's neighborhoods (doubting the role, capacity, and effectiveness of those taking part – both police and citizens).[10]

Viewed as a whole, the Sandinista period marked a profound *institutional break*, as the new Sandinista police (and military) had a new foundation, new personnel, and a new mission. They had mobilized to overthrow the dictator; they had mobilized to create a new, revolutionary military and police force. And when counterinsurgents (the *contra*, backed by the United States) mobilized a new civil war in the 1980s, they provided a line of defense. The new police officers brought, and were imbued with, a new *organizational structure and commitment* that drew on their revolutionary background and goals.

Compromising on Institutional Reform: Creating a More Autonomous and Nonpartisan Force

The 1990s ushered in new changes: a reinstitutionalization of the military and police, moving them from a partisan orientation to a national one. This process was negotiated among opposing forces, although the outcome was arguably unforeseen by all parties involved. This process of change began when the Sandinistas lost power in a highly polarized 1990 election, following a decade of revolutionary change to institutions, the economy, and society. This electoral loss marked the end of the Sandinista Revolution (and civil war with the *contras*) and the presumed dismantling of its programs and institutions. Unexpectedly, the political loss precipitated the consolidation of the very armed institutions (police and particularly military) that had allowed the Sandinistas to come to power by force. This turning point occurred through unanticipated negotiations between the outgoing and incoming forces. Opposing sides were implicated in the compromise and thus vested in the decision that resulted.

The victor of the 1990 presidential election, Violeta Chamorro, was backed by a wide-ranging opposition coalition (UNO, Unión Nacional Opositora) against the Sandinistas – although Chamorro had been part of the initial 1979 coalition that had joined forces with the FSLN against the

---

[10] In a coauthored book by Cordero, Gurdián, and López (2006: 37–38), Cordero notes that even in these years the police adopted the reactive approach shared by most police in the region – to respond to crime once it happened rather than act proactively. In contrast to other countries, however, he notes that the Nicaraguan police were providing all kinds of counseling and training services to youth in prisons.

outgoing dictator. As part of this transition process, her incoming team had to decide how to address the revolutionary institutions, policies, and personnel that it inherited from the Sandinista regime. The police and military, for example, were unambiguously Sandinista forces that had been formed by the revolution, just as its officers and rank and file were revolutionaries that had grown up within the Sandinista guerilla movement. The new Chamorro government and US officials wanted to dismiss Sandinista leaders, although the US did not necessarily distinguish at that point between the FSLN political leadership and the military (which they saw as one and the same, according to Antonio Lacayo in a 2007 interview).[11] For their part, the Sandinistas in this early period feared that the incoming government would undermine all Sandinista infrastructure and practice a politics of revenge, according to former police chief Cordero.[12] Both sides had the power of disruption, but neither side could force their hand.

In this highly polarized setting, the incoming administration *and* the military sought autonomy from their more radical political flanks. Committed to the army's survival, the military command had a choice between maintaining their historic loyalty to the Sandinistas or asserting a more autonomous role moving forward (Ruhl 2003: 120–121). In turn, incoming president Chamorro sought to gain autonomy from the *contra* (the counterinsurgent forces that had mobilized against the Sandinistas). This political context created an unexpected space for negotiations, according to Antonio Lacayo, who oversaw the 1990 transition as Chamorro's minister of the presidency/chief of staff (1990–1995). After Chamorro's election, he recalls that the Sandinista military was already exhibiting signs of autonomy (and institutionalization) from the Sandinista leadership. "It already had a sense of being a group and a pride in being professional, which others could not take away from them." According to Lacayo, many in the military upper ranks resented the Sandinista leadership for trying to make decisions, including

---

[11] See Vilas (1992) for a discussion of the family lineage of many Nicaraguan politicians during this period. Important families had members on both sides of the political divide. By way of example, Lacayo came from an elite family and married into the Chamorro family that was divided by Sandinista loyalties over time but was also first cousin of a key Sandinista general, later chief of the army, General Cuadra. This inter-elite cross-partisan set of networks was not unusual, according to Vilas, who outlines some of the ways in which elite families maintained key roles during and after the Sandinista period. Strikingly, the Ortegas (Daniel, who led the Sandinista government, and Humberto, who led the Sandinista military) were outside of these networks.

[12] Interview with Edwin Cordero on March 3, 2007.

operational decisions, for the army.[13] Lacayo observed that the military was trying to assert a professional autonomy from FSLN politics, and apparently the pragmatists predominated (Ruhl 2003: 120) – although in the heated political context of the time, that was far from clear to outside observers.

The fact that EPS (the Sandinista Popular Army) was led by pragmatists such as General Ortega and his second-in-command General Joaquín Cuadra, rather than by Marxist ideologues, also facilitated change in civil-military relations. General Ortega's principal goal was to ensure the army's survival as a guarantee against attempts by right-wing groups to take revenge upon those who had supported the Sandinista regime. He and his top subordinates quickly realized, however, that the only way to save the army would be to separate it from the Sandinista Front. The EPS found itself without external allies in a post-Cold War world dominated by the United States, and it was confronted by a strong anti-Sandinista majority inside Nicaragua. In this postrevolutionary political context, only a nonpartisan, national army could survive. Fortunately, General Ortega and the EPS high command, who had founded the army and led it successfully through the Contra War, had the legitimacy within the institution to demand disciplined acceptance of this fundamental change in political orientation. In a series of meetings, they convinced the officer corps to embrace the defense of democracy rather than revolution as its new historical mission. The gradual development of a corporate identity within the EPS facilitated this reorientation. With the Contra War over and no credible external threats on the horizon, the EPS leadership could also agree to a drastic reduction in the army's size and budget. (Ruhl 2003: 120–121)

Recalling the theoretical arguments made in Dankwart Rustow's classic (1970) article and the subsequent arguments in *Transition from Authoritarian Rule* (O'Donnell and Schmitter 1986), there was a division among the members of each side, creating the space and incentives for the less radical flanks from both the UNO coalition and the Sandinistas to forge a compromise. Out of these negotiations, recounted in Lacayo's (2005) autobiography, emerged a working agreement between Lacayo (from the incoming administration) and Humberto Ortega (from the Sandinista military and associated with the outgoing administration). While the agreement proved critically important for subsequent institutional developments, at the time it also drew criticism from both sides for the compromise that it struck.[14] The Sandinista

---

[13] "Ya tenía un sentido de grupo y un orgullo de ser profesional que no le quitan." Lacayo recounted that he learned of this decision only when former US president Carter arranged a meeting for the incoming government with Sandinista leaders – including Humberto Ortega, Joaquín Cuadra, and Jaime Wheelock (Lacayo 2007 interview).

[14] Those opposed to the Sandinistas strongly feared that this would provide the Sandinistas with a foothold for maintaining power. Those more supportive of the Sandinistas feared the incomplete process of demobilizing the *contras*. On both sides, although for different

military (the EPS) agreed to downsize by 85 percent, to become nonpartisan, to subordinate to civilian rule, and to agree to statutory and constitutional reforms that restricted its autonomy in exchange for the incoming administration's decision to keep the EPS and its military hierarchy as the only legal armed forces in Nicaragua (Ruhl 2003: 121, 134–135).

In exchange for Humberto Ortega's support of the UNO government and the constitution, Lacayo agreed that Ortega could maintain his leadership of the military (the only Sandinista who was allowed to keep such a high office); in turn, the government would not dismantle the Sandinista army.[15] Over the course of the next month, Lacayo and Ortega apparently worked together to forge an agreement in time for the FSLN to hand over power to the next elected president. This agreement laid the foundation for the further professionalization of the armed forces. The transition institutionalized the distinction between a military and civilian office: Humberto Ortega took office as *jefe del ejército* (as a military officer); the minister of defense was named as a civilian. In the ensuing years, the military forces shed some 60,000 soldiers, declining from 86,810 soldiers in 1990 to 15,250 in 1993 (Ruhl 2003: 121), 14,000 in 1995, and 12,187

---

reasons, initial writings about the Sandinista's loss of electoral power, the transition to the Chamorro government, and the end of the *contra* war were wary of the incomplete, inadequate, and contested nature of that process. Writings highlighted the "truncated" terms of the peace process, which resulted in ongoing conflict despite disarmament and demobilization – namely the initial remobilization of armed combatants and the political polarization that remained (see, for example, Spalding 1999). Ironically, these initial assessments saw the Nicaraguan case as more violent and incomplete than subsequent peace processes in El Salvador (which were more smoothly carried out and overseen by international forces, with more complete agendas (43). Spalding (49) says, "the contra war left a lingering legacy of rebellion and lawlessness that threatens to become an endemic feature in parts of the Nicaraguan countryside," although she ends her article by saying that levels of mobilization and polarization had declined somewhat by the mid-late 1990s. Even so, she finds that institutions are weak – including the police and judicial system – and that "elected officials still are pushing for more effective oversight of the military" (56). She also observes that crime rates increased significantly in this period of transition (51–52), a point also noted by Rodgers (2004 and 2006). Ironically perhaps, Nicaragua subsequently experienced lower homicide rates than the other countries located in Central America's northern triangle.

[15] Interview with Antonio Lacayo on March 10, 2007. According to Lacayo, Ortega had a pragmatic understanding that the Sandinista military would have to change their position and support the Violeta Chamorro government (although he indicated that he would not have supported the UNO coalition as a whole if they were the ones calling the shots); Ruhl (2003: 134–135) also identified Ortega as a pragmatist. For his part, Lacayo explained that while UNO had gained electoral office, it did not have effective power without military support: "What else could we do?" he said to me. "My personal philosophy was that we had won nothing; we have to begin to gain quotas of power through tactics that are a win-win situation."

in 2002 (Rocha 2011: 11).[16] In exchange, the incoming government facilitated the autonomy of the FSLN army, according to Lacayo (March 10, 2007 interview). In 2007, Lacayo was proud to say that there was respect for the Nicaraguan military, which was seen as professional and united. Citing the post-1990 military chiefs (Ortega, Cuadra, Carrion, and Halleslevens), he noted that they had abstained from politics at the time – unlike other Nicaraguan institutions (including the courts and national assembly, which he saw as corrupt and divided).[17]

The 1990 political transition was therefore a turning point for the military, a point also made by former chief of army (retired) General Moisés Omar Halleslevens (a longstanding member of the Sandinistas). He indicated that the military had to face new times and pursue three goals: professionalization, institutionalization, and modernization. "In Nicaragua, a soldier must fulfill all that is required of him by the laws, magna carta, constitution. The constitution orders that [the military] cannot make or become involved in politics; the military therefore did not speak of politics – so long as one was active in the military."[18] Halleslevens, citing a UCA (Universidad Centroamericana) survey conducted the year prior, observed that the armed forces were the most respected institution in the country and that the same survey identified him as the most respected official at that time. An internal survey, he continued, also indicated that those in the military saw themselves as very proud to be members of the military. After retiring from the military, he subsequently entered politics as vice-president in 2011.

While the actors interviewed for this book undoubtedly had personal reasons for highlighting this particular narrative, surveys and reports also highlight the military's autonomy and professionalism as well as generalized respect for the institution.[19] Some would

---

[16] Demobilized forces from the state and the *contras* were often granted land (as noted by Rocha 2011: 110–111), although this did not mean that demobilized soldiers felt fully integrated or cared for – as suggested by the remobilization of what was later referred to as the *revueltos* (discussed later in text).

[17] Interview with Lacayo on March 10, 2007.

[18] Interview with Halleslevens on March 13, 2007.

[19] Also see Ruhl (2003: 127–132) and Rocha (2011: 109–112). Assessing the Nicaraguan military in the 1990s, Ruhl (2003: 127–132) references work by Stepan and Fitch and finds that the Nicaraguan military has maintained relatively high prerogatives in institutional autonomy (coordination of the defense sector, role of the legislature, role of civilians in the defense sector, and role in military promotions) but that it has low prerogatives regarding civilian control over politics (vis-à-vis the constitution, executive, police, etc.) as well as the rule of law. Rocha, in turn, concludes that the Nicaraguan police and military emerged from the post-civil war period not only much smaller in size

argue that it is even more institutionalized and "democratic" than those who were subsequently elected to civilian office following the Chamorro administration. "Ironically, the formerly Marxist revolutionary armed forces seem to have become more committed to democratic principles and the rule of law than many of the nation's most important civilian politicians" (Ruhl 2003: 134).[20] They ended up partnering with the police at various points to combat *bandas delictivas*, as in 2000 in the RAAN (North Atlantic Autonomous Region, discussed later).[21]

The Nicaraguan police also began a process of increased professionalization and autonomy following the 1990 election (this process took several years), without maintaining continuity in Sandinista leadership, in contrast to developments in the military. Lacayo claimed in his 2007 interview that the head of the Sandinista police and former revolutionary leader, Tomás Borge, had to resign; however, prior to his forced resignation, Borge apparently filled the police with Sandinista members from the ministry of the interior, to which the police reported and belonged.[22] In this way, the institution lost its historically revolutionary leadership, sustained its revolutionary cadre, and took orders from a new set of leaders. To symbolize its national (versus Sandinista) orientation, its name was changed by executive decree to the "national police." To better specify its relationship to other law-and-order institutions, additional laws and decrees were passed. In 1992, Law 144 specified the police's relationship to the judiciary; 1992 also ushered in an executive decree, the Primera Ley Orgánica de la Policía Nacional, a 1995 constitutional reform that explicitly distinguished between police and military functions. Then in 1996, the country enacted and regulated Law 228, the "organic law" of the national police, subordinating the police to

---

but also more professional, less corrupt, and viewed as more legitimate than their Guatemalan, Salvadoran, and Honduran counterparts.

[20] Arnoldo Alemán and Daniel Ortega, from opposing sides of the political divide, have been charged with corruption and autocratic politics (Ruhl 2003: 134–135).

[21] *La Prensa* 6.4.2000 Ejército en ofensiva total.

[22] While the military also welcomed Sandinistas into its intelligence ranks, Antonio Lacayo claimed that the police had more of a problem, since it was in more contact with the population, costing it some of its democratic legitimacy. I include this information here, but I have no basis for evaluating this claim. According to Grisby (2003), during the transition, many feared the dissolution of much of the ministry of the interior, and thus many officials (including military officials) were transferred to the police force.

civilian power and further specifying its functions (GTZ 2005: 20; WOLA 2009: 6–7).[23]

With all these institutional changes, police leadership was still viewed critically, until the appointment of Police Chief Aminta Granera in 2006.[24] Prior to that point, many high-ranking Sandinista officials were dismissed. Cordero himself notes that many Sandinistas felt compelled to leave the police in the early 1990s because they did not want to work with the "enemy" (Cordero interview 2007). Indeed, writing in 2003, Grigsby reports that the police force only included 600 (out of 8,000 police officers) who had been guerillas. Recognizing the need for more police reform, Vice-President Lacayo sat down with the dismissed police chief,

---

[23] This extensive quote highlights how central these reforms were to the police's understanding of its identity, mission, and capacity. Grisby (2003) writes: "Franco Montealegre, who headed the Police between 1996 and 2001, would later stress the importance of that step: 'For the first time in the history of Nicaraguan public order, the police's organization, functioning and field of action is established. The foundations are laid [for the force] to acquire its own differentiated identity; the institution's civil nature is reaffirmed and it declares itself to have a non-party nature.' The establishment of that minimum institutional framework and minimum stability for National Police personnel was followed by a discussion of the legislation that would be politically approved in the National Assembly. Montealegre recalls this phase of police institutionalization as follows: 'In the constitutional reforms of 1995, the National Police functions and nature are spelled out at this highest level for the first time in the country's history, differentiating them from the Army's functions and nature. The climax came in September 1996, when after a long consensus-reaching process in a still highly polarized political context, we were able to get Law 228, the National Police Law, approved with a high level of consensus. Law 228 details and develops … the constitutional regulations regarding our institution and defines the police career and other important aspects. Its entry into force entailed the definition and definitive acceptance of the Police required by the state and society to guarantee the security of people and their belongings. It must be said that it was the National Police itself that succeeded in mobilizing public opinion and the main political and social actors, particularly in the final phase of designing, discussing and approving the law'" (Grigsby 2003; accessed March 6, 2007, at www.envio.org.ni/utils/imprimir).

[24] Police capacity and resources, or the lack thereof, was a frequent subject of reporting in 2000, including citizen complaints that the police were unresponsive (La Prensa 11.16.2000 Policía muestra falta de pericia). The director general of the national police emphasized lack of capacity, when noting insufficient budget and personnel (affected by low salaries) to meet security demands, even though crime reportedly increased by 2.5 percent between 1990 and 2000. "Dentro del Estudio de desarrollo de la Policía, se observa que la principal debilidad de la Policía es el área preventiva; vigilancia, presencia policial en las calles, para prevenir cualquier acción delictiva" (La Prensa 12.3.2000 La Policía es débil en el área preventiva). That said, the Nicaraguan police requires high school completion as the educational requirement for entry-level recruits and has a training program that lasts three years (La Prensa 12.11.2000 Hay vacantes en las academias militares y policiales).

René Vivas, and drafted an organizational law for the national police, which did not exist prior to that point (Grigsby 2003). The resulting Decree 45–92 forged a legal framework that outlined a clearer organizational hierarchy and subordination to civilian authority, with a clearer institutional policy. The police were arguably insulated from political interference and had a clearer organizational structure both within the agency and relative to the military (Grigsby 2003; WOLA 2009: 6–7).

Viewed together, the Sandinistas' loss of power forced a reinstitutionalization of the military and police, away from a partisan force to a national one – with a modified command structure (subordinated to civilian rule), modified legal framework, redefined mission, and restructured ties with the citizenry, including the creation of crime prevention committees (IEEPP 2007: 22, 30). In this regard, the period marked an important turning point for the military and police, as officers had to change their orientation of defending the revolution to operating autonomously from partisan/political affiliations (observed by General Cuadra in a 2007 interview with the author). Former police chief Cordero, in turn, commented in a 2007 interview that the 1980s police were seen as an organization of the revolution (and therefore were tied to a political agenda). With the 1990 transition, difficult though it was, the police formally stopped identifying itself as a Sandinista organization and developed into a national one – one that ultimately included officers of different political persuasions. Across both periods, there was a corporatist commitment, although the targets of that commitment changed.

At the time, the outcome seemed uncertain. There were doubts that the Sandinista military and the police leadership would exhibit a greater commitment to upholding their institutional loyalties than to their partisan origins, and few predicted that the police would come to be seen as one of the most respected and upright police forces in the Central American isthmus. Indeed, a 2005 incident highlighted uncertainties about whether the police would follow executive or legislative or judicial orders (when conflicts occurred across these branches).[25]

However, by the time I conducted interviews in the second half of the 2000s, interviews consistently underscored the police's professionalization. In fact, most interviews with former and current police and army chiefs highlighted a certain ideological commitment that recalls Weber's "Politics as a Vocation" (Weber 1946). Analyzing the police's successes

---

[25] See *La Prensa* 6.17.2005 Jueces quieren policía judicial; 6.24.2005 Jueces siguen en roce con Policía; 10.29.2005 A trámite Ley de la Policía Nacional.

(compared to Guatemala, El Salvador, and Honduras), former police chief Cordero highlighted, in particular, the quality of the police and those who join its forces; in this vein, he emphasized first the role of "ideology" – taken to mean that police officers still have a big sense of "responsabilidad social de vocación." He noted that even young recruits join with this "ideology," compared to other countries where young recruits saw the police as a *negocio*, or business. Where corruption or misconduct occurs in Nicaragua, there is a greater chance of the people involved being dismissed and held to account than in the northern Central American countries. Actors are indeed dismissed – both in the police and the courts. Cordero recounted a case where it was discovered that drug traffickers had bought off judges in Bluefield; this led to their dismissal (Cordero interview 2007).[26] Indeed, Police Chief Aminta Granera (2007) indicated that one of the challenges of the police is making sure that new recruits foster and maintain this kind of corporatist commitment – one initially forged as part of the revolutionary struggle – so that the police do not devolve into patterns found in the rest of the region. Where police officers renege, however, they are often dismissed.

Interviewees also recounted that while they were deeply committed to the Sandinistas, they were even more committed to making a new Nicaragua – even when split loyalties were in evidence, right after the transition. During the early 1990s, remobilization occurred among the *recontras* (former anti-Sandinista insurgency) and *recompas* (former Sandinistas who were often called *compañeros*, or *compas*) for a range of political, material, and ideological reasons (Spalding 1999: 44–46).[27] After initially trying to negotiate an end to the conflict,[28] the Chamorro

---

[26] The press reported on cases where police corruption was followed by sanctions. In the newspaper violence database (from 2000, 2005, and 2010) see, for example, *La Prensa* 2.10.2005 Castigo a 80 policías por vender nota roja; 10.24.2005 Depuración en la Policía; 9.27.2005 Policía llama a supervisar a jueces en RAAS; 12.30.2005 Acusan de estafa a jefe policial RAAS; 2.10.2005 Dan baja a 30 policías; 10.13.2010 Sacudida en Policía de Bluefields.

[27] According to retired General Cuadra (interview March 9, 2007), both sides rearmed and engaged in extortion, the *contras* felt betrayed, and the Sandinistas said that they wanted to rob to help the poor. For a summary of armed groups (*recontras* and *recompas*) that emerged in the 1990s, see United States Citizenship and Immigration Services: www.uscis.gov/portal/site/uscis/menuitem.5af9bb95919f35e66f614176543f6d1a/?vgnextoid=cc9153bc46d8d010VgnVCM10000048f3d6a1RCRD&vgnextchannel=d2d1e89390b5d010VgnVCM10000048f3d6a1RCRD (accessed on July 22, 2013).

[28] Spalding reports that the Violeta Chamorro government initially pursued three tactics to address this problem: "periodic general amnesties, weapons-buying campaigns, and new accords with specific groups" (Spalding 1999: 47).

Circumscribing Violence in Post-Civil War Nicaragua 297

government changed tactics in 1993 with a change in leadership and a move from negotiations to military responses (Spalding 1999: 48).[29] As a sign of its increased professionalism and move toward nonpartisanship, General Joaquín Cuadra Lacayo recounts that the military was asked to quash a protest in Estelí of *revueltos*, which included former *contras* and Sandinista *recompas*.[30] While it challenged former comrades to do so, they carried out their orders; the general recounts that this was a momentous decision that both reflected and consolidated a sense of professionalism, autonomy, capacity, and corporate commitment to the institution.[31] When comparing the Nicaraguan military to those of its Central American neighbors, Cuadra highlighted that although the Nicaraguan military gained increased legitimacy over time, the opposite

---

[29] The Chamorro government ultimately removed military chief Humberto Ortega (the longstanding Sandinista head of the military who had negotiated the 1990 transition with Lacayo) and replaced him with another Sandinista military officer, Joaquín Cuadra. In addition to making Cuadra (a member of the elite and related to both President Chamorro and Chief of Staff Lacayo) the next military chief, the government passed the new military code (Código Militar de Organización, Jurisdicción y Prevención Social Militar), which further placed the military under civilian control – as noted by Spalding (1999: 48) and Ruhl (2003: 122).

[30] Also see Ruhl (2003: 121), who recounts the role the military played in defending the Chamorro government from uprisings by *recontras* and *recompas* – also based on an interview with General Cuadra. Newspaper reporting in *La Prensa* in 2000 noted that the department of Estelí was seen as a site with many security problems. Crime in Estelí increased from a total of 339 crimes in 1990 to almost 3,000 in 2000. For other reports on increased crime in Estelí, see *La Prensa* 12.14.2000 Aumenta inseguridad en Estelí; 6.9.2000 Mientras, en Estelí el delito se ha disparado; 9.5.2000 Gran incremento delictivo reportan en Estelí.

[31] Interview with General Joaquín Cuadra, Managua, Nicaragua, on March 9, 2007, and Grigsby (2005). In the 2007 interview, Cuadra stated that this was a turning point – not only because the military had to turn against former Sandinista comrades, which was very difficult, but also because "it provided an enormous legitimacy," "it increased our legitimacy before the *whole* society," because the military was willing to maintain order even if it required them to fire on their former comrades. It demonstrated the military's capacity, autonomy, and seriousness of purpose. "Con esta gente no se juega," said the general. According to Cuadra, within the coming weeks, there was a significant disarmament in exchange for money; he estimates that some 15,000 were disarmed, although he also recognizes that some people kept arms. Grigsby (2005) reports that another former chief of the armed forces, General Carrión, emphasized the army's Sandinista roots and its professionalism in light of what happened at Estelí. "We don't' have any problem with our origins ... We have recognized that we come from Sandinismo, from a fight against a dictator. We're nonpartisan, apolitical, at the service of the people and have a national vision. We have clearly demonstrated our professionalism through the blood of our soldiers and fighting against former Sandinistas, in Estelí, for example."

was true for the others.[32] Social scientists might raise eyebrows about the endogeneity of this argument – they were loyal because they were loyal. Yet I was unable to unearth a deeper structural argument. Those who were willing to fight in the revolution and stayed within the military and police appear to have been more committed to the new Nicaragua than they were to partisan politics (which is not to say that they were devoid of partisan politics). In the context of a centralized command structure, prior revolutionary commitment merged with professional commitments to solidify a corporatist ethos.

The police experienced a parallel process by which the new police and military had to disentangle their loyalties to the Sandinistas, according to 2007 interviews with former and current police chiefs Cordero and Granera. In a context where former comrades took up arms (Sandinistas dismissed from office in the 1990s or *contras* not sufficiently rewarded for their service), the police and army had to respond accordingly. Yet if there was an underlying commitment to the institution above and beyond partisan ties, Rocha (2007: 68) observed that the top police jobs were still held by the forty remaining historic combatants serving in the police. In this regard, the institutions were still populated by revolutionary leaders, but their partisan origins were put to the test. Discussing primary goals for the police, Police Chief Granera maintained in her inaugural year of service that her primary goal was to focus on the institutionalization of the police (followed by anticorruption measures and increasing the standard of living of the police (Policía Nacional de Nicaragua 2006: 1) – a striking statement when the rest of the regions' police seemed so focused on cracking down on crime.

With all the changes since the revolution, the police maintained and reinforced a kind of Weberian loyalty to the institution – noteworthy given its apparent absence in other parts of the Nicaraguan state. Writing about all the changes that had ensued from 1979 to 2003, Grigsby (2003) highlights the corporatist commitment to the police as a national institution:

The intermediary and upper echelons of the National Police are essentially still patriotic, if not Sandinista from a party and ideological point of view, which is

---

[32] Comparing Nicaragua with its Central American neighbors, General Joaquín Cuadra argued that Honduras, for example, lacked all legitimacy, as it was a prostituted institution ("institución prostituida") that had been violated ("violada") by the *contras* and United States; with the end of the Cold War, the Honduran military was left with no clear enemy and therefore tried to seize power from others. Interview with Cuadra, Managua, Nicaragua, on March 9, 2007.

more than can be said for many other government institutions. They have a sense of dignity as an institution and honor as individuals and a relatively developed sense of national sovereignty. Although some of them have been polluted with other interests, the institution generally responds to the basic principles imprinted above its badge: Autonomy, Honor, Sovereignty.[33]

Creating New Social Ties in Local Communities

The bookends of the revolution, therefore, not only disbanded the dictatorship's often-brutal national guard but ultimately replaced it with an entirely new military and police force (new organizations, new personnel, new mission) that subsequently demonstrated greater professionalism and a move away from partisanship.[34] Yet the ability to pursue a law-and-order role – especially to contain crime – requires more than this. It requires a deterrent presence in the community. In this regard, the Nicaraguan police created a more socially embedded, proactive, and progressive role than its counterparts in Guatemala and El Salvador.

The police began to work in particular to establish new social ties through social prevention committees (*comités de prevención social del delito*).[35] Police Chiefs Cordero and Granera each noted that these new committees differed from the Sandinista committees of the prior decade.[36] These are community groups that were reported to number in the

---

[33] Grisby (2003), accessed March 6, 2007, at www.envio.org.ni/utils/imprimir.

[34] Kurtenbach (2013: 116) arrived at a similar conclusion. She noted how distinct (profound and professional) Nicaragua's security reform was relative to Guatemala and El Salvador: "Summarizing, Nicaragua's security sector reform was profound after the Sandinista victory in 1979. The old institution was abolished and replaced by the former insurgents. After the government change in 1990, the security sector was not only downsized but depoliticized and professionalized. In El Salvador and most of all in Guatemala, downsizing was mostly based on the termination of compulsory military service. The officer corps remained more or less unchanged and the reforms were subject to resistance by the traditional, military and economic elites" (Kurtenbach 2013: 116). Kurtenbach further argues that the terms to end civil war had an impact on the subsequent violence that unfolded. While I agree with her about the different state institutions providing a different environment, she does not explain how and why violence unfolds as it does in Guatemala and El Salvador (suggesting implicitly a continuity of violence). Although some violence has continued, I suggest that new patterns have also taken form – explaining the disproportionately high levels of violence that we see in these latter two countries (alongside Honduras, which did not have a comparable civil war).

[35] *La Prensa* reporting also noted the salutary effect of these committees on gang activity in Managua (although scant evidence was provided in this article). Communities have also organized other kinds of defense patrols. See 4.18.2005 Vigilancia comunitaria contra la delincuencia.

[36] Interviews with Granera on March 7, 2007, and Cordero on March 3, 2007.

thousands, according to Granera in our 2007 interview. With the idea that community involvement is critical and that solutions might differ by community, the committees gathered to identify *each* community's individual problems – including electricity, schools, alcohol, etc. This has provided an entry point for becoming involved in security issues and to work with at-risk youth. By way of example, Granera (2007 interview) discussed committees that focus on alcohol consumption while also organizing sports events in which police and gang members play alongside one another. In this same spirit, the police have worked with other NGOs, such as Nicaragua Nuestra and CEPREV, to address issues facing at-risk youth.[37] Cordero suggested that this entry into the community was key – not least because gang members in Nicaragua, he contended, maintain ties with their families (unlike the profile often provided for gangs in the northern triangle). He suggested that because gang members still sleep and eat at home, there are more opportunities for family and community to shape the process of reaching them. Talking about the military and police approach overall, Cuadra states: "Today, this relationship with the community forms the doctrinal pillar of Nicaraguan internal security, which makes the police more effective, despite being a small force with an extremely small budget" (Cuadra 2005).[38]

The police also adopted a preventative approach long before other post-civil war cases in the region considered doing so. While other countries were adopting zero-tolerance (*mano dura*) policies that violated civil liberties, the Nicaraguan police set out to sustain a community approach of incorporation, prevention, and rehabilitation. As a comparativist, I find that these claims notably distinguish Nicaragua from its neighbors, but I cannot unambiguously prove the causal impact of the decisions. That said, original field research did give voice to the following plausible narratives of actors who took part in the process. Police Chief Aminta

---

[37] Interviews with Clara Aviles of Nicaragua Nuestra on March 2, 2007, and Police Chief Aminta Granera on March 7, 2007.

[38] Examples of this kind of approach are also reported in the newspaper *La Prensa*, as compiled in the newspaper violence database for 2005 and 2010. See, for example, the following *La Prensa* articles for 2005: 6.19.2005 Ex pandilleros cuidarán fiestas patronales and 3.15.2005 Buscarán empleos a ex pandilleros; 6.20.2005 Presentan plan contra pandillas; 5.6.2005 País da cátedra sobre pandillas; 6.3.2005 Planifican la alianza anti-pandillas. For 2010, see: 10.4.2010 Marchan por su seguridad; 1.18.2010 Ciudadanos pasan lista de necesidades a la Policía; 2.16.2010 Jefes policiales a encerrona; 1.20.2010 Patrullando con la comunidad; 9.4.2010 Policía intenta combatir el crimen en Ciudad Sandino; 5.6.2010 Policía rechaza críticas sobre situación delictiva; 5.15.2010 Jóvenes en riesgo bajo la lupa.

Circumscribing Violence in Post-Civil War Nicaragua

Granera highlights these developments – whose temporal and substantive dimensions proved critical, according to her analysis.

> I would say that we had a sort of 10-year head start over other countries in Central America. I remember in the middle of 1985, we had the first meeting, the Nicaraguan police chiefs, where we were wondering what was going on in Honduras, because the first gangs in Honduras were appearing. We did not have them, and we said to ourselves, "Why don't we?" And we saw, well, young people at that time were involved in Nicaraguan literacy campaigns; vaccinations were going on; they were picking cotton, picking coffee; they were in the military. There was no room for Nicaraguan youth to engage in criminal activity or gangs.
>
> Ten years later, in the mid 1990s, we started getting our first gangs (we don't call them "maras"). And we met again, the same bosses, which is another advantage we have: the Nicaraguan National Police Command has continuity. We said, "How are we going to face up to this?" I remember in Honduras they were tackling it with zero tolerance, and for every gang member that they threw into prison, they would put a head, literally the head of a police officer or a person, in the park across from the presidential palace. And we said, if 10 years ago the reason why our young people were not in gangs was that they formed part of the state program, then the key word and the antidote for gangs is inclusion. And we are going to treat them with inclusion rather than repression. And we created a youth program section. We worked it the other way as well. Our intelligence agencies also penetrated them. We could tell whether they had links with foreign gangs. If they were armed or not. We could see if they were criminals, or they were just excluded from the labor market, cultural, student or even family life. We could see if they joined the gangs because they had no other reference point. We currently have 10,000 youths who have demobilized as part of the 100,000 people who voluntarily work with us. They have surrendered their weapons and are committed to the police.[39]

This preventative orientation was consistently stressed in interviews and original documents (including with Police Chiefs Cordero and Granera, 2007). In the same spirit, Hamyn Gurdián Alfaro, the division chief of youth affairs in Nicaragua's national police (Dirección de Asuntos Juveniles de la Policía Nacional), wrote of the preventative goals of the national police, creating a police station for women and children (Comisaría de la Mujer y la Niñez) in 1993 (Gurdián 2006: 24; also see Rocha 2011: 116).[40] Gurdián writes similarly in 2006 that in light of concerns about youth violence, the national police created the division of

---

[39] *InSight Crime* (2012b) interview with Nicaraguan police chief Aminta Granera on July 9, 2012. Written by Steven Dudley, www.insightcrime.org/nicaragua-a-paradise-lost/video-an-interview-with-nicaraguas-police-chief (accessed on June 27, 2013).

[40] Cordero (2007) interview indicated that the Dirección de Asuntos Juveniles was formed around 2000–2001.

youth affairs (Dirección de Asuntos Juveniles) to pursue the more proactive, preventative, and strategic set of responses (including community integration).[41] This community-based approach assumes an ecological model that has focused, critically, on prevention.

In 1997–1998, the police, moreover, started to adopt a more integral approach to youth in particular, responding not just punitively to past infractions but thinking more integrally about community approaches to youth and the special challenges that apply to them as subjects, not just objects, of the law (Cordero, Gurdián, and López 2006: 40–41). This proactive and integral approach coincided with special efforts to control and crack down on gang activity (although in ways that were quite different from the *mano dura* approaches adopted in the northern triangle). This included increased patrolling in Managua (Plan Pandillas Managua, 1999), which was deemed a success in controlling delinquent behavior and resulted in thirty youth being placed in prison (sixteen through judicial order; Cordero, Gurdián, and López 2006: 42–43). That said, in 2000, the Nicaraguan police adopted a more proactive and preventive approach toward gangs as well.[42] In 2001, they substituted anti-gang measures by doing the following: organizing house visits; working with the Comités de Prevencíon Social del Delito;[43] forming youth commissions; pursuing various efforts to talk to youth and incorporate them in various educational, cultural, civic, and community activities; changing methodologies; and working more closely with the community. These efforts were implemented throughout Managua, although in one district they pursued a different strategy (including a truce, armistice, and

---

[41] See Rocha (2007: 61–67) for a more critical discussion of these youth programs – including the creation of the Dirección de Asuntos Juveniles as part of the national police. He argues that the creation of these programs highlighted that Nicaraguan youth were no longer protagonists in the revolution but were now seen as problems.

[42] All the Central American countries have laws governing children and adolescents. They each have some kinds of youth programs that include components of the community approach – although the implementation is less clear. In Guatemala these programs include: Unidad de Prevención del Delito (UPREDE), which is responsible for Policía Tu Amigo, Programa de Prevencíon de Maras y Drogas, and the Policía Comunitaria. In El Salvador: Programa de Policía Comunitaria, Plan Eficacia Comunitaria, and Programa de Prevencíon de Drogas en Educación Media. In Honduras: División de Maras and Programa Comunidad Más Segura (Cordero, Gurdián, and López 2006: 182–183).

[43] Gurdián (2006: 28) notes that some 3,256 youth took part in the prior four years in a process of "participation, provision and even rehabilitation" ("participación, facilitación, e incluso con la rehabilitación"), although the exact nature and results of that participation was a bit vague.

social integration).[44] In describing this preventative model, Rocha (2011: 116–117) commented not only on the international funds that supported the efforts and the fortuitous creation of a whole array of youth-oriented institutions during the Alemán administration[45] (arguably to counter the widespread criticism following corruption of Hurricane Mitch international aid), but also on the practical opportunities that were afforded to the youth (in marked contrast to the repressive models being pursued in Guatemala, El Salvador, and Honduras). In Nicaragua, "young *pandilleros* could participate in social events and work on beaches as lifeguards, for example, and ongoing armistices included clearing the gang members' records to remove the stigma of labeling them as criminals, (Rocha 2011:116).

While other Central American countries were clumping youth groups together, the Nicaraguan police were trying to distinguish between at-risk youth and gangs (*pandillas*, not *maras*; Cordero, Gurdián, and López 2006: 50–52).[46] As of 2006, the Dirección de Asuntos Juveniles had created institutional structures in all of Managua's district police stations/delegations (Delegaciones Policiales Distritales) and in the country's regional departments – totaling some forty-one officials working on these issues throughout the country (Cordero, Gurdián, and López 2006: 77, chapter 4, esp. 141–142). The Dirección de Asuntos Juveniles was created during Police Chief Cordero's term and consisted of a multidisciplinary professional team of lawyers, anthropologists, sociologists, psychologists, and

---

[44] Cordero, Gurdián, and López (2006: 48, 50, 77, 79, chapter 3); Gurdián (2006: 25–28); Rocha (2007: 74); Rocha (2011: 115–117).

[45] The following youth-related codes, laws, and institutions were created during the Alemán administration: approval of the Code of Childhood and Adolescence (1998); the Law for the Promotion of the Integral Development of Nicaraguan Youth (2001); the National Plan for the Integral Development of Youth (2001); Special Ombudsman for the Child and Adolescent (2000); and the Secretary of Youth (2002) (Rocha 2011: 116). Rocha cautions, however, against painting too rosy a picture, given that lower-level officers did not initially comply – with early reports of beating detainees before setting them free and arbitrary seizures of youth. Yet he also concludes that the policy in this period, while not solely responsible for outcomes, has coincided with improved outcomes (declining gang-related homicides, injuries, and violations) between 2002 and 2007 (Rocha (2011: 118–119).

[46] As a symbolic indication of the different orientation of the Nicaraguan police versus those of other Central American countries, one can look at the names of police programs to address gangs (an astute observation made by Rocha 2007: 73). In Nicaraguan police operations, they have had an "ephemeral" name often tied to a holiday such as Christmas or Holy Week (Plan Belén en Navidad or Plan Playa en Semana Santa), while in the northern triangle, police operations have had a more ominous and repressive tone referring to sweeps, zero tolerance, and (super) heavy-handed policies (Plan Escoba, Plan Cero Tolerancia, Plan Mano Dura, and Plan Súper Mano Dura) (Rocha 2007: 73).

social workers focusing on the causes and conditions of, as well as solutions for, youth delinquency. The goal was to focus on the human rights of children, promote prevention, and engage with the community (Cordero, Gurdián, and López 2006: 139). Other observers remarked on this pattern.

Far from proposing an anti-gang (mara) law, as they have put in practice in Honduras and El Salvador, the police's official politics between 1999 and 2003 was: to form 123 Committees of Social Prevention throughout the country, provide scholarship to 445 youth who were formally gang members; and detain 921 youths tied to the gangs and diverse delinquent actions. From this number, 72 kids (muchachos) were placed under court custody (puestos a la orden de los juzgados). (Rocha 2007: 73–74)

Grigsby (2006b) also reports on the importance of this program:

One of the National Police's major sources of pride, and with good reason, is the juvenile delinquency prevention plan. The result is that gangs haven't taken over our streets as they have in the three Central American countries north of Nicaragua. A large part of the success of this plan is that dozens of police are fully dedicated to this work; they meet daily with parents and youth and are in close touch with social realities. A similar model needs to be applied to achieve a similar success in stopping common crime and drug dealing in the markets, neighborhoods and regions all over the country, and that can only happen with a large number of police officers. (Grigsby 2006b: downloaded March 6, 2007, from www.envio.org.ni/articulo/3348)

Thus, the police projected a civic-minded orientation lacking in other Central American police. Rather than focusing on punishment alone, it has advanced a prevention-oriented component.[47] Speaking at the closing session of the fourteenth meeting of police officers (Acto de Clausura de la XIV Reunión de Mandos Policiales), at the start of her term as police chief, Granera stated that part of their job was to disarticulate youth gangs and organized crime (especially drugs) – although this was only mentioned after noting the need for taking care of various institutions (banks, markets, bus routes, and schools), working with at-risk children and abused women, and controlling arms possession, etc.[48]

---

[47] Commenting on the same, Grigsby (2006a) notes the Nicaraguan police's Social Crime Prevention Committees (which include citizens/community leaders), formed in the early 2000s, and the Police-Community Policy, which was formed in 2002; some of this community outreach and collaboration includes reaching out to families with at-risk youth and supporting community events such as sports (Grigsby 2006a).

[48] Palabras de la Primera Comisionada Aminta Granera, Directora General de la Policía Nacional. March 2006. Acto de Clausura de la XVI Reunión de Mandos Policiales. Downloaded March 6, 2007, from www.presidencia.gov.ni/noticiaPolicial_210207.html.

If the Nicaraguan police was able to contain gang activity through its more holistic and preventative approach, it has assumed a more regulatory and punitive role vis-à-vis organized crime. In this case, a more capable and autonomous police force has become an obstacle to organized crime entry. As argued throughout this book, organized crime is a business. Part of the business model includes setting up shop in places that are the most propitious for organized crime. Nicaragua's police are more capable (relatively more trustworthy and effective) and have performed a more professional role than the Guatemalan, Salvadoran, and Honduran police forces. Accordingly, Nicaragua is a less attractive venue for the proliferation of transnationally integrated organized crime networks (even though its geographic location would make it an ideal transit point). There have been some organized crime forays – especially along the coast – including the Sinaloa Cartel along the Pacific and the Gulf Cartel along the Atlantic. But Nicaragua did not witness the same kind and level of proliferation of organized crime units at the start of the twenty-first century as did Guatemala and El Salvador – in no small part because the Nicaraguan police demonstrated greater commitment and capacity to control them. The police did not just seize drugs (the initial approach), but also penetrated the cells and destroyed them (in more recent years).[49] In these efforts, they have occasionally worked with the military – especially in rural areas, borders, and ports.[50] According to Moisés Omar Halleslevens (who at the time was the head of the army, 2005–2010, and prior to that chief of counterintelligence, 1980–1997), the military has supported the police largely through counterintelligence support,[51] including anti–drug trafficking operations. In one of these – in Managua, Rivas, and Chontales – officials interdicted nearly $40,000 worth of drugs (totaling 600 packages).[52] Thus the police (at times with the military) have

---

[49] *InSight Crime* (2012b) interview with Nicaraguan Police Chief Aminta Granera on July 9, 2012. Written by Steven Dudley www.insightcrime.org/nicaragua-a-paradise-lost/video-an-interview-with-nicaraguas-police-chief (accessed on June 27, 2013).
[50] For relevant articles in *La Prensa*, see: 4.29.2010 Policía y Ejército con plan de seguridad; 5.2.2010 Ejército fortalecerá planes en el campo; 10.28.2010 Arranca plan de seguridad; 11.4.2010 Ejército y Policía listos para cosecha cafetalera; 6.13.2010 Plan de Seguridad para Chontales; 8.10.2010 El Ejército apura plan contra el abigeato; 8.12.2010 Ejército con más presencia en Madriz; 10.5.2010 Ejército continúa en búsqueda de narcos y droga.
[51] Interview with Halleslevens on March 13, 2007.
[52] *La Prensa* 5.25.2010 Policía y Ejército golpean al narcotráfico.

taken a more proactive approach than that found in El Salvador and Guatemala.[53]

Of course, corruption can be found in any institution (and was arguably particularly manifest during the term of the first police chief and commissioner, Edwin Cordero),[54] the police are not uniformly capable across the territory,[55] and there are examples of drug trafficking corrupting the police.

It's an open secret that the tentacles of drug trafficking have penetrated middle and high levels of the National Police throughout the country. It's no longer just a problem for the Caribbean coast, where the most powerful Colombian mafia networks have settled. Drug money circulates generously between the small "retailers" in any neighborhood of any city in the country and those who run the extensive land, sea and air transport networks. This money often ends up in the pockets or bank account of some police chiefs. (Grigsby 2006b: downloaded March 6, 2007, from www.envio.org.ni/articulo/3348)

Yet even recognizing these blights on the police record, the way in which the police have dealt with these infractions (and how Nicaraguan citizens view the policy) differs from the approaches of their counterparts in the northern triangle.[56] There has been a more concerted and serious commitment to crack down on corruption where it occurs.[57] When Granera assumed office, the Nicaraguan police confronted these kinds of challenges – with concerns about corruption, decay, and drug trafficking influence happening at all ranks – by conducting a "cleaning" when Granera assumed office and letting go of several officers, including the drug chief.[58]

---

[53] In one botched job where the military accidentally fired on the police, one can see that the coordination was far from perfect. *La Prensa* 11.19.2010 Operación Halcón Negro continuará.

[54] Also see WOLA (2009: 25–26).

[55] Martínez (2016: 84–85, 87) notes, for example, that Rivas has high levels of police corruption and that, moreover, Police Chief Commissioner Aminta Granera has noted the challenges of police corruption and organized crime in Rivas. That said, Martínez also reports that other informants have noted that police corruption in Nicaragua is not as pervasive or systemic as in Honduras – with a few bad cases that the police have needed to address (Martínez 2016: 91).

[56] Grigsby 2006b: downloaded March 6, 2007, from www.envio.org.ni/articulo/3348.

[57] *La Prensa* reporting in 2000 includes various articles that talk about police corruption and infiltration. However, several of these articles also talk about the state effort to control corruption. See 6.2.2000 Narcos infiltran Policía; 6.3.2000 Narcos tejen red con ayuda de ex policías; 6.8.2000 Buscan más narcos infiltrados en policía; 6.13.2000 Policía reconoce infiltración de narcos; 7.29.2000 Condenan a nueve años de cárcel a ex jefe policial; 7.24.2000 Investigan apoyo de policías en atracos; 7.16.2000 Ordenan captura a comando policial; 8.13.2000 Bajas deshonrosas por corrupción y abuso policial; 8.17.2000 Policía caraceña expulsa a 44; 9.4.2000 Narcotraficantes infiltran sistemas de investigación.

[58] Interview with Granera on March 7, 2000; Grigsby 2006b.

During Granera's term, she kept the spotlight on prevention, internal corruption, and discipline – something that she had also done during the time when she led the national transit police. While one should be cautious of propaganda in police publications, it is notable that these issues are commonly published in the national police journal, *Visión Policía: Revista de la Policía Nacional* – as in the January 2007 (66th edition), which includes an article on the serious crackdown on corruption and abuses (among other infractions) and notes that investigations and sanctions occurred across ranks, with 11 percent of the police force affected. Moreover, there has reportedly been a steady increase in the seizure or confiscation (*incautación*) of cocaine: 2002 (2.2 TM), 2003 (1.11 TM), 2004 (6.27 TM), 2005 (7.31 KM), and 2006 (9.89 TM) (*Visión Policía* 2007: 13).

Placing Nicaragua's Police Capacity in Comparative Perspective

Nicaragua is clearly distinct from its neighbors in the Central American northern triangle. It also stands out in the region as a whole. In Latin America, in general, perceptions or belief of police involvement in crime are very high for the period 2004–2014 – including Venezuela, Bolivia, Guatemala, Mexico, Paraguay, Honduras, Peru, Argentina, Ecuador, and El Salvador. In comparison with sixteen other Latin American countries, only Chile ranks better than Nicaragua (see Figure 7.3 based on LAPOP surveys for 2004, 2006, 2008, 2010, 2012, and 2014).

A World Economic Forum ranking the reliability of police services across 144 cases showed that while Nicaragua was only ranked 94 worldwide, it was ranked 7 out of the fourteen Latin American cases (with a value closer to Colombia, Uruguay, and Brazil than to its violent neighbors of El Salvador and, certainly, Guatemala. See Table 7.1. And Latinobarometer surveys also highlight that the Nicaraguan police and perceptions of crime place Nicaragua in a much stronger position than all its Central American neighbors (see Table 7.2).

The Nicaraguan police have been able to achieve these outcomes even in the face of limited resources and material incentives (Grigsby 2006a; Cordero 2007 interview; Rodgers 2004: 117–118; Cruz 2012a; and UNODC 2007: 30).[59] Statistics indicate that Nicaragua is arguably

---

[59] José Miguel Cruz presentation at conference "Drug Wars in the Americas," at Brown University, Watson Institute and Center for Latin American Studies (April 12–13, 2012). Drawing on UNDP data and his own work, Cruz showed the limited fit between state

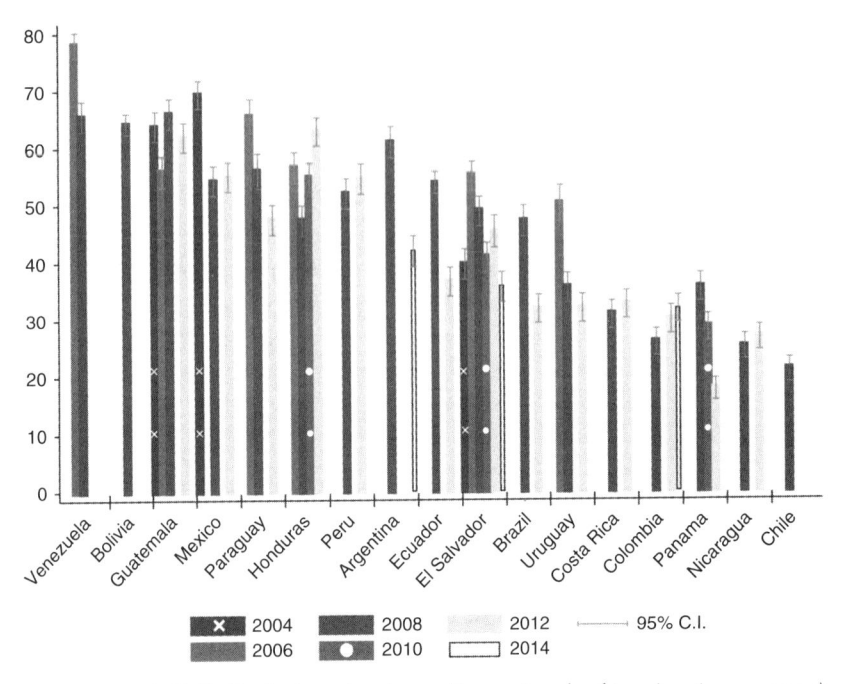

FIGURE 7.3 Belief in Latin America that police are involved in crime (2004–2014)
Source: LAPOP 2004–2012 Core Data. Specific country data for years 2010 and 2014.
Graph prepared by Daniela Barba-Sánchez using Stata.

the second-safest country in Central America, and it also has the lowest law enforcement capacity, at least in terms of raw numbers. But Nicaragua's police and prison system are regarded by some experts as the best in the

security infrastructure data (of numbers per capita, budgets, and wages from 2006 to 2008) and expected homicide rates. During the period of 2006–2008, Nicaragua did not have more police officers per 100,000; per capita numbers indicated that Honduras had 118, Guatemala had 152, Nicaragua had 155, Costa Rica had 277, and El Salvador had 300). Nicaragua's police officers received the lowest monthly wage in Central America ($150 in Nicaragua) compared to its counterparts in Guatemala ($470), El Salvador ($470), Honduras ($280), and Costa Rica ($584). Nicaragua also scored on the lowest end of public attorneys per 100,00 (with Guatemala at 1, Nicaragua at 2, Honduras at 3, El Salvador at 4, and Costa Rica at 6); lower end of judges per 100,000 (with Nicaragua and Guatemala at 6, Honduras at 9, El Salvador at 10, and Costa Rica at 17); and on the lower end of the average percentage of public spending on security in the national budget for 2006–2007 (with Nicaragua at 8.1 compared to Costa Rica at 7.7, Honduras at 8, Guatemala at 9.9, and El Salvador at 14.3). Viewed as a set, these numbers show a great deal of variation even among the high-violence cases of El Salvador, Guatemala, and Honduras.

TABLE 7.1 *Reliability of police services in Latin America (ranking of Latin American cases out of 144 cases studied worldwide)*

Country	Rank	Value
Chile	14	6.1
Costa Rica	46	4.8
Panama	52	4.7
Brazil	60	4.4
Uruguay	71	4.2
Colombia	74	4.2
Nicaragua	94	3.8
Ecuador	116	3.2
El Salvador	118	3.1
Bolivia	122	3.0
Honduras	125	3.0
Peru	128	3.0
Argentina	131	2.9
Mexico	134	2.8
Guatemala	137	2.6
Venezuela	142	2.1

Source: World Economic Forum (2013: 91, 111, 117, 137, 141, 143, 157, 161, 183, 191, 257, 277, 287, 291, 361, 363, 365).

region, suggesting that that there is more to government capacity than simply gross expenditure. When we compare the Nicaraguan police force to its Central American neighbors, the Nicaraguan police force is smaller per capita, has lower average salaries, and has a smaller per capita budget. IEEPP (2007: 25, 30), citing MHCP figures, notes that the budget in the early 2000s was a relatively stable percentage of the national budget, which increased somewhat in those years.[60] The police force's annual statistical report reveals that their numbers per 100,000 did increase steadily and nearly doubled since 2000, moving from 118 per 100,000 in 2000 to

[60] Interestingly, the budget apparently has been higher for human development (education and health expenditures) than for security (police and defense combined). While the former claims on average 19% of the budget (9% for education, 10% for health), the latter claims 4% of the budget (2% for the military and 2% for the police), when averaging the years 2000–2006, according to MHP figures. See IEEPP (2007: 26, 30).

TABLE 7.2 *Perceptions of Central American security and safety (2010)*

	Share approving of government security/crime policy in 2010	Share of people who feel safe in the country, 2010	Share of people who feel that the country is becoming less safe, in 2010
Nicaragua	58%	22%	36%
Costa Rica	47	10	61
El Salvador	48	4	57
Guatemala	22	4	77
Honduras	33	12	61
Panama	39	15	55

Source: UNODC (2012: 72, figures 68, 69, and 70; based on 2010 Latinobarometer surveys).

222 per 100,000 in 2014.[61] In this context, Nicaragua's police have gained international recognition for its comparative performance.

Statistics indicate that Nicaragua is arguably the second safest country in Central America and it also has the least law enforcement capacity, at least in terms of raw numbers. But Nicaragua's police and prisons system are regarded by some experts as the best in the region, suggesting there is more to government capacity than simply gross expenditure. (UNODC 2007: 30)

In short, Nicaraguan's police performance has exceeded police performance in El Salvador and Guatemala. Whether we look at perceptions, rankings, or homicide clearance rates, Nicaragua has stood out. The Nicaraguan police reportedly resolved 65–75 percent of reported homicides in 2009 and 2010 – a figure that is much higher than the paltry figures reported for El Salvador and Guatemala (as noted in Chapters 4 and 5) and reported by UNODC (2007: 31–32).[62] Looking at all cases of reported crime, the Nicaraguan police disclosed its institutional effectiveness by reporting the percentage of criminal cases solved by the police (see Figure 7.4).

[61] See Policía Nacional de Nicaragua. *Anuario Estadístico 2014*, figure 1.12, www.policia.gob.ni/cedoc/sector/estd/ae%202014.pdf (accessed on July 26, 2017).
[62] Policía Nacional de Nicaragua. *Anuario Estadístico 2010*, p. 58. Also see UNODC (2007: 31–32) for a comparison of homicide clearance rates in the Central American region. UNODC reports that they are high in Nicaragua (81 percent) and Costa Rica (82 percent), significantly lower in El Salvador (44 percent), and at a very low rate in Guatemala (7 percent, although the year prior it was higher, at 16 percent). However, this data should be read cautiously since UNODC 2007 figure 15 does not correspond with the data reported in the text.

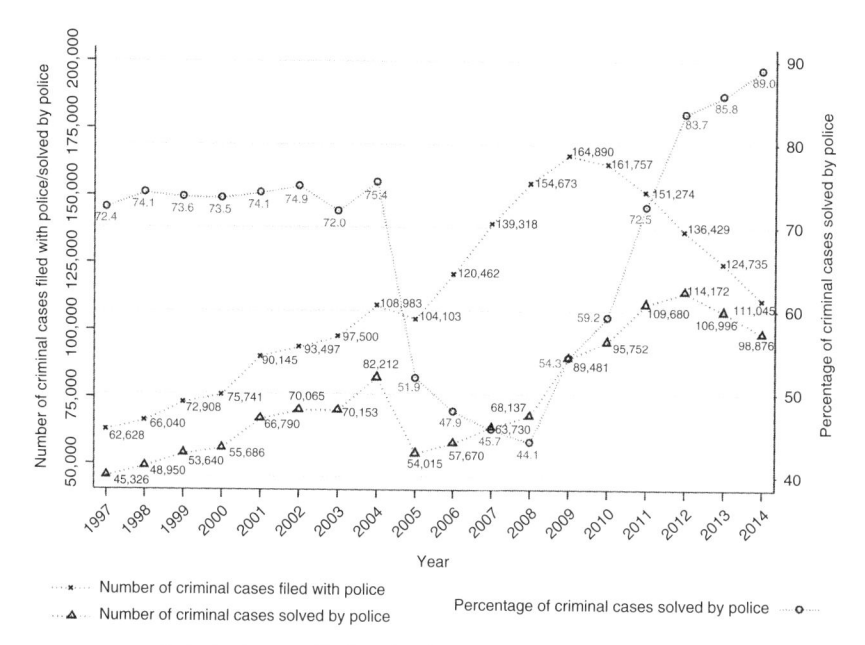

Circumscribing Violence in Post-Civil War Nicaragua 311

FIGURE 7.4 Criminal cases filed and solved by Nicaraguan police (1997–2014)
Source: Adapted from Policía Nacional de Nicaragua. *Anuario Estadístico 2014,* figure 1.12. www.policia.gob.ni/cedoc/sector/estd/ae%202014.pdf. Accessed on July 26, 2017.

These estimates provide a particularly powerful indication of the comparative capacity of Nicaragua's police and the comparatively more proactive role it plays in preventing the growth of gangs, the deterrent role it plays vis-à-vis illicit organized actors (gangs and organized crime) and associated illicit economic activities, and the accountability initiatives it has announced to hold its own officers to account where corruption has been manifest. Given this context, Nicaragua is less propitious ground for illicit organizations to operate with impunity and sustain illicit activity than are El Salvador and Guatemala.[63] Arguably, these features have enabled the Nicaraguan

---

[63] *La Prensa Gráfica* 8.23.1999 "El Salvador secuestrado" reports that kidnapping clearance rates are also very low in El Salvador. In the first semester of 1999, the Salvadoran national police received 89 reports of kidnapping (not including all the kidnappings that went unreported). The police made 61 arrests, 12 of these cases went to trial, and 7 people were convicted. "La relación entre las denuncias y las condenadas es de 12 a 1. Es decir, en el 89 por ciento de los casos investigados por la Policía no hay suficientes pruebas para procesar a los sospechosos, o las víctimas prefieren callar para evitar represalias."

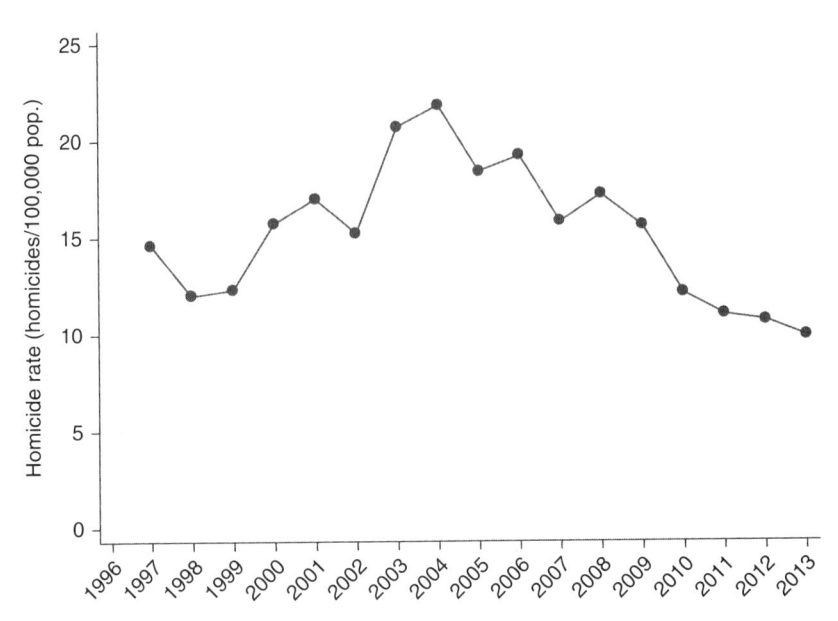

FIGURE 7.5 Homicide rates in Nicaragua (1997–2013, per 100,000)
Graph created by Daniela Barba-Sánchez using Stata.
Source: PAHO/WHO, 2016.

police to play a more effective role in policing and, in turn, to foreclose spaces for illicit activities, relative to its northern Central American neighbors.

VIOLENCE AND THE ILLICIT IN NICARAGUA

The second half of this chapter surveys the more limited role of gangs and organized crime in Nicaragua, the more delimited geographic spaces for organizational territorial competition, and the correspondingly lower homicide rates that Nicaragua has endured. Indeed, Nicaragua's homicide rates have been comparatively low, even while they have fluctuated over the period of 1995–2013 (see Figure 7.5, in addition to Latin America's comparative figures reported in Figures 1.1, 1.2, 1.3, and 1.4 in Chapter 1). The Appendix also includes Nicaragua's departmental homicide rates from 1998–2014 (see Table 7.5)

Over time, homicide rates grew least when political capacity (and political commitment to deploy it) was strongest – during the Sandinista Revolution and once again when Police Chief Granera assumed office. In both time periods, a corporatist commitment to the institution and a preventative

Circumscribing Violence in Post-Civil War Nicaragua 313

approach prevailed. Violent crime levels grew at a comparatively low rate in the 1980s – the period in which the Sandinista Revolution was in full swing – increasing at an annual rate of 2 percent in the 1980s, compared to an average of 10 percent per year from around 1990 to 2005, according to national police statistics reported by Rodgers (2006: 270). In the 1990s, crime rates did increase to an average of 10 percent annually, and violent crimes against persons (i.e., homicides, rapes, and assaults) increased 300 percent between 1990 and 2003 (Rodgers 2004: 116).[64] These are the years when the Sandinistas were no longer in power, the civil war was over, and the police and military were being reformed as more professional and nonpartisan forces. It is notable that while homicide rates increase in these years, they do so from a much lower baseline and increase at a lower rate than in the other post-civil war cases of El Salvador and Guatemala. "Absolute" homicide rates fluctuated between 10 and nearly 20 per 100,000 during the period of 1997–2011 (according to WHO data; see Figure 7.6). In the figure, one can see this upward trend until about 2004–2005, after which homicide rates decline again. This sustained and steady decline slightly predates, but also largely coincides with, Aminta Granera's term as police chief, starting in 2006. The Nicaraguan police report slightly different figures, although they also show that homicide rates stabilize and then decline during Granera's tenure (see Figure 7.5). Reporting a rate of 8 per 100,000 in 2014, Nicaragua moves from the intermediate to the low categorization of violence laid out in Table 1.1, at the start of this book – placing Nicaragua's among the lowest homicide rates in the region.

Thus, viewed comparatively, Nicaragua's rates fall far below the average of its Central American northern neighbors. The Nicaraguan national police has reported, moreover, that homicides are less likely to be committed with an *arma de fuego*, or firearm/gun; rather, the arm most commonly used is an *arma blanca*, or knife.[65] The limited use of military-grade weapons is consistent with what we found in the newspaper violence database constructed for this book, where we tracked daily violence reported in the Nicaraguan newspaper *La Prensa* for 2000, 2005, and 2010.[66] In the newspaper database for 2000 (June–December), no reported homicides used military-grade weapons (in contrast to El Salvador and Guatemala), and

---

[64] See Policía Nacional de Nicaragua (2006: 6–8) for a discussion of rape figures.
[65] See Policía Nacional de Nicaragua (2006: 10–11).
[66] The online newspaper archive for *La Prensa* is not complete for 2000 and begins in June. Thus, the 2000 data covers June–December. The 2005 and 2010 data, however, is inclusive of all months/days for those years.

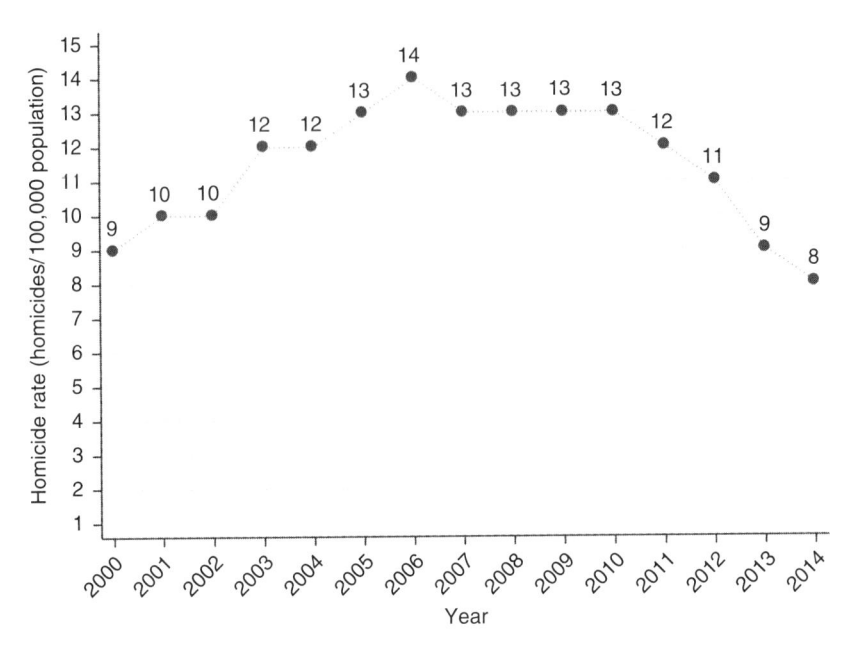

314 Part III Divergent Trajectories: Three Post-Civil War Cases

FIGURE 7.6 Nicaraguan police data on homicides (2000–2014, rates per 100,000)
Source: Based on Policía Nacional de Nicaragua. *Anuario Estadístico 2014*, figure 1.6. www.policia.gob.ni/cedoc/sector/estd/ae%202014.pdf. Accessed on July 26, 2017.

some 7.2 percent used automatic weapons (for a total of nine reported cases); the most common weapon reported was a knife/machete (36.8 percent), followed by a homemade shotgun (*escopeta hechiza*; 32 percent). In the newspaper database for 2010, no reported homicides used military-grade weapons, and only 2.2 percent of reported cases used an automatic weapon. Again, the most commonly reported weapon used was the *escopeta hechiza*, which was reported in 54.7 percent of the newspaper cases; a knife (or machete) was the next most commonly identified weapon used, in 25.1 percent of reported homicides (See Table 7.3).

We should not overdramatize Nicaragua's peaceful record. Rodgers (2006) in particular cautions against a rosy interpretation of Nicaragua's homicide rates given that the data undoubtedly underreport incidences. Yet even granting these underestimates (which are likely true of the region as a whole), there is no doubt that Nicaragua's homicide rates and trajectory follow a dramatically distinct path than those of its regional neighbors in the northern triangle. Comparative responses indicate,

TABLE 7.3 *Technologies of violence reported by press for homicides in Nicaragua (2000, 2005, 2010)*

Technology of violence	2000: Percent of total homicide events reported (%)	2005: Percent of total homicide events reported (%)	2010: Percent of total homicide events reported (%)
Automatic weapon	7.2	4.0	2.2
Human contact	8.0	6.5	8.9
Knife (machete)	36.8	30.4	25.1
Military-grade weapon	0	2.0	0
Homemade shotgun (*escopeta hechiza*)	32	45.0	54.7
Other	3.2[1]	6.5	2.2[2]
Stoning	0	1.3	0.6
Mutilation involved	4.8[3]	13.6	7.0[4]

Source: Newspaper violence database: compiled from the Nicaraguan newspaper *La Prensa*.
Note: 2000 data only covers June–December (the online archive begins in that month).

[1] "Other" technologies of violence included: choked with a wire (1), burned (1), explosion (1), beaten with mortar (1).
[2] "Other" technologies of violence included: wooden stake (1), ax (1), burning (1), beaten with mortar (1).
[3] Includes rape (5), decapitated (3).
[4] Includes rape (2), decapitated/dismembered (5), riddled with bullets/*acribillado* (4).

moreover, that Nicaragua's concerns about the rate of violence are among the lowest in the region. Figure 7.7 incorporates the Central American cases and the region's other high-violence cases (not including Colombia, which during the reported period was still experiencing a civil war). Clearly, Nicaragua remains an outlier and by the start of the 2000s exhibited the lowest relative concerns about crime – unlike the high concerns expressed in the rest of the region.

These comparative statistics about homicides (and attitudes toward crime) raise the natural question of why Nicaragua is such a regional anomaly. Previous chapters highlighted the role of gangs and organized crime in other countries – analyzing in particular why weak state capacity enabled them to flourish in Guatemala and El Salvador, as well as how territorial competition (within and between illicit organizations and with the state) has significantly increased violence levels in these countries. This

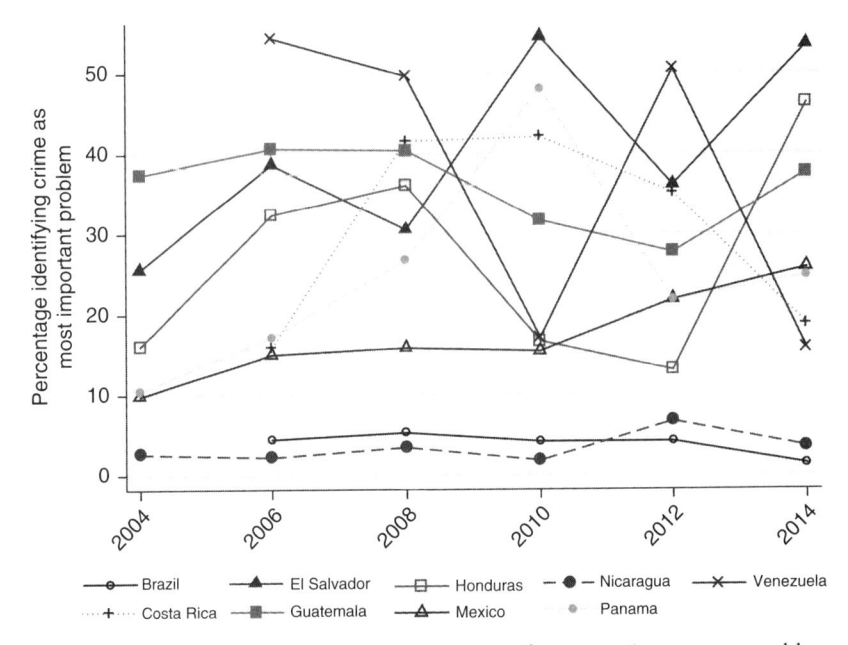

FIGURE 7.7 Percentage identifying crime as the most important problem (2004–2014, Central America and other high-violence cases in Latin America, excluding Colombia)
Table created for this project by Daniela Barba-Sánchez using Stata.
Note: Brazil's relatively low percentages are surprising. Its large country size might be obscuring the significant variation in concern by some regions relative to others. While all countries have subnational variation in homicide rates, only Brazil can claim such a large population and therefore a much larger denominator for calculating and averaging across these subnational outcomes.

chapter, by contrast, argues that Nicaragua's stronger state capacity and approach (within the police, in particular) has hindered the growth of these organizations beyond certain pockets. Violence does occur, especially when there is organizational competition to defend or acquire territorial bases of control. However, these pockets of competition are themselves more controlled and more bounded than in the low state/police capacity and high-complicity cases of El Salvador and Guatemala.

This final section discusses gangs and organized crime in Nicaragua, with some prior observations in mind: state institutions created an inauspicious context for the growth of an illicit sector and responded more forcefully to illicit activity where it did emerge. This discussion allows us to tackle one important reason why Nicaraguan *pandillas* do not transform into larger and more violent organizations (*maras*) as well as why organized crime (which exists but in smaller measure than in the rest of the region) does not develop a more significant presence in a country renowned for state corruption.

Gangs

Nicaraguan gangs date back to at least the 1970s, if not the 1940s (Rodgers 2006: 273, 283; Rocha 2011: 105). After a brief resurgence in the early 1980s, their presence declined during the Sandinista Revolution, arguably because of conscription and neighborhood vigilance activity associated with the Sandinista regime (Rodgers 2006: 283; Rocha 2011: 105; Rodgers and Rocha 2013: 50). The gangs reemerged in the 1990s (after the end of the civil war with the *contras*). Apparently, youth groups were particularly prevalent in Managua, and there was a rise in numbers during this time – although these groups did not evolve into the violent youth gangs that took form in Guatemala and El Salvador (Cordero, Gurdián, and López 2006: 24; see Figure 7.8). According to police statistics, they are predominantly located in one place – the department of Managua (see Table 7.4) – although Rodgers and Rocha (2013: 50) note that they became "a ubiquitous feature of poor urban neighbourhoods in all of the country's major cities."[67] In the 1990s, Nicaraguan gangs were arguably comparable to the Guatemalan gangs of a decade earlier insofar as they focused on "territorial control, a source of identity, primary socialization on the streets, and the quest for a 'family' in the gang" – characteristics that Rocha uses both to summarize Levenson's (1988) characterization of Guatemala's 1980s gangs and his own observations about Nicaragua's 1990s gangs (Rocha 2011: 106). In turn, they arguably defended neighborhoods from rival gangs as they yearned for social status, smoked marijuana, and engaged in petty assaults, among other things (Rocha 2011: 106).

Yet, if Nicaraguan gangs shared characteristics with early Guatemalan gangs, they did not follow the same trajectory. While Guatemalan gangs were largely absorbed by two violent organizations, Mara Salvatrucha and Calle 18 (although still with autonomy among the *clikas* that composed these *maras*), Nicaraguan gangs remained fragmented. Notably, as the number of gangs grew in the 1990s, by the early 2000s, the number of gang *members* had declined – suggesting an increasing fragmentation (rather than centralization) of these associations (Rodgers 2006: 273).

---

[67] Policía Nacional de Nicaragua. *Anuario Estadístico 2000*, p. 122.

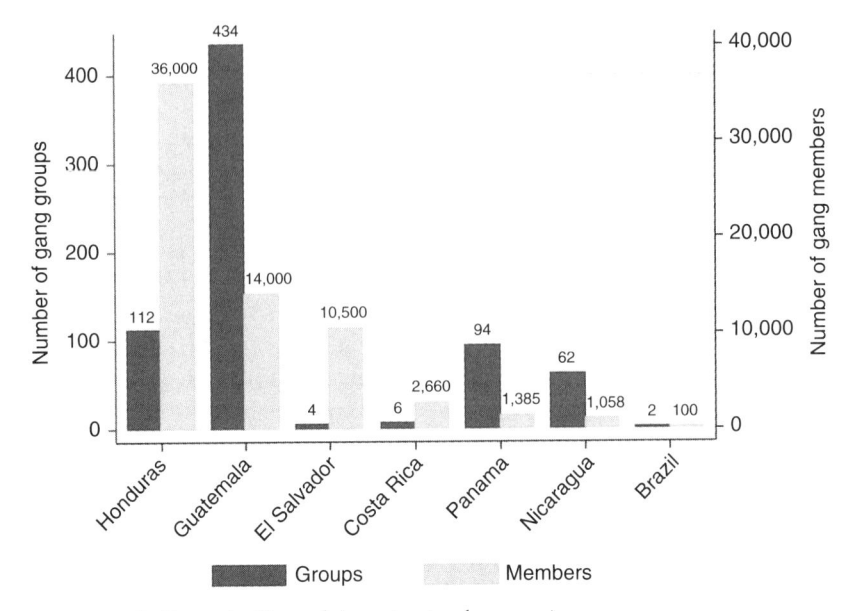

318   Part III Divergent Trajectories: Three Post-Civil War Cases

FIGURE 7.8 Gangs in Central America (early 2000s)
Source: Cordero, Gurdián, and López 2006: 179, drawing on a set of meetings of Central American and Caribbean police chiefs. Reported number of gangs and members reported, respectively: Belize, 2 and 100; Guatemala, 434 and 14,000; El Salvador, 4 and 10,500; Honduras, 112 and 36,000; Nicaragua, 62 and 1,058; Costa Rica, 6 and 2,660; and Panama, 94 and 1,385. The total for the region was reported as 920 gangs and 69,145 members.
Note: Rocha (2007: 16) arrives at similar numbers for Nicaraguan regional youth gangs for 2003, based on his own evaluation of police data – although he cites different numbers for 1999–2003 when referring to gang numbers in Managua (ranging from a low of 96 gangs in 2001 to a high of 118 gangs in 2002 – with an average of some 18 gang members per gang). In 2011 (107), Rocha reports higher figures based on police data, indicating 183 groups and 2,707 members.

Indeed, even though Nicaragua reportedly has among the lowest number of gang members in the region, proportionately it has had a very large number of gangs (reported as sixty-two in the early 2000s, according to Cordero et al. 2006: 179) – indicating that the average size of each gang is quite small.[68] As in Belize, Costa Rica, and Panama, Nicaraguan gangs are

---

[68] Based on reporting from a set of meetings of Central American police (Cordero, Gurdián, and López 2006: 179). Reported number of gangs: Belize (2), Guatemala (434), El Salvador (4), Honduras (112), Nicaragua (62), Costa Rica (6), and Panama (94). The total for the region was reported as 920 gangs and 69,145 members.

TABLE 7.4 *Comparative table of Nicaraguan gangs (*pandillas*)*

Departments	1999 # of gangs	1999 # of members	2000 # of gangs	2000 # of members	average age
Managua	80	1,992	85	1,689	14–30
Carazo	10	100			
Masaya	10	300	7	373	13–22
Madriz	5	55			
Jinotega	9	93	8	83	16–20
Matagalpa	8	180	1	11	13–20
Boaco	3	46			
Estelí	18	343	20	250	13–20
Granada	18	208	4	88	16–24
Chinandega	19	239	8	82	15–16
Rivas	3	50			
Nueva Segovia	4	59			
TOTAL	176	2965	133	2576	13–20

Source: Policía Nacional de Nicaragua. *Anuario Estadístico* 2000, p. 122. Translated by author (deleted 1999 average age column, since no figures were included).
NB: One needs to read these figures with great caution given competing data about gangs – a point also emphasized in all chapters in the edited volume by Bruneau, Dammert, and Skinner (2011) and repeated by Rocha (2011: 107). For example, Rocha (2011: 106–107) gives figures for 1995 (47 gangs with about 4,500 members throughout the country) and 1999 (100 gangs with about 8,250 in Managua, where he reports that 58 percent of gangs reside, although a later survey notes that this declines to 33 percent by 2003), citing other sources. By contrast, *Prensa Libre* reported in 2000 that the police indicated that there were 95 *pandillas* in the country, with 877 members and attributed to them activity such as "robbery with intimidation, assault and battery, possession of unregistered arms, drug consumption and sales, exposure of people to danger, habitual vagrancy, public disorder." (*La Prensa* 8.26.2000 Seguridad ciudadana empeora en Managua: "robos con intimidación, lesiones, tenencia ilegal de armas, tráfico y consumo de drogas, exposición de personas al peligro, vagancia habitual, alteraciones al orden público.")

much more localized, less violent, less armed, and less tied to organized crime than in Guatemala, Honduras, and El Salvador.[69] In the mid-2000s,

[69] See Cordero, Gurdián, and López (2006: 180–181), who single out the Gerber Boys and the Charly as examples of Nicaraguan gangs.

the largest gang presence in Nicaragua was reported in Managua, followed by Estelí (Rocha 2007: 16).[70]

Despite the proliferation of gangs, they are not commonly associated with the generation of high waves of violence in Nicaragua. Indeed, newspaper reports do not refer to Nicaraguan gangs as *maras* (highly violent and professional gangs), but rather as *pandillas* (traditionally used for youth gangs) or *grupos juveniles* (youth groups). In Nicaragua, "gangs" has largely referred to groups of boys and young men who gathered as peers – sometimes for social reasons but often to engage in (frequently petty) crimes such as robberies, fights, and vandalism.[71] National police reports generally do not single out gangs as the cause of the violence, and gang-related violence is rarely reported in the newspapers.[72] In 2005 and 2010, *La Prensa* did not focus a great deal of reporting on gangs in the country, although there were reports of Guatemalan gangs extorting Nicaraguan bus companies.[73] Police Chief Granera said that in her country, only 4.3 percent of homicides can be attributed to *grupos juveniles*.[74] By 2010, press reporting suggested a decline in gang membership, reportedly with some 10,000 demobilized youth and some forty-eight *pandillas* in the country.[75]

The rest of this section briefly delineates the broad characteristics associated with Nicaraguan gangs. The gangs are generally composed of

---

[70] For newspaper reporting on gangs see, for example, *La Prensa* reporting: 8.26.2000 Seguridad ciudadana empeora en Managua; 8.18.2000 Terror pandillero reina en calles chinandeganas; 7.12.2000 Aumentan las pandillas en Chinandega; 8.7. 2000 Fábrica de armas preocupa a Chinandega; 8.15.2000 Preocupa aumento de violencia juvenil; 8.8.2000 Pandilleros asolan Chinandega; 9.18.2000 Managua sitiada por pandillas; 8.19.2000 Cese al 'fuego' de pandillas en peligro; 11.18.2000 Inseguridad ciudadana el lado oscuro de Managua; 8.26.2000 Seguridad ciudadana empeora en Managua; 6.10.2000 Neutralizan las pandillas en Estelí; 6.18.2000 Grupos juveniles aumentan.

[71] Examples of gang disturbances and rival gangs facing off can be seen in *La Prensa* 3.14.2010 No aguantan a las pandillas, and 6.28.2010 Pobladores se quejan de pandillas en Granada.

[72] *La Prensa* reporting on gangs was limited, especially when compared to reporting in El Salvador. In 2005, for example, the few reports on gang violence largely portrayed them as a nuisance for communities, especially when gangs competed to acquire or defend territory. The violence, however, was often caused by lower-grade weapons, such as machetes and rocks (see *La Prensa* 1.4.2005 Pandilleros siembran el terror en Nueva Vida).

[73] *La Prensa* 1.9.2010 País denunciará ante Guatemala extorsión de mareros.

[74] *La Prensa* 5.7.2010 Policía tiene el reto de mantener credibilidad; also see 5.28.2010 Disminuye violencia de pandilleros.

[75] *La Prensa* 5.29.2010 Disminuye violencia de pandilleros, and 10.23.2010 Más jóvenes dejan filas de las pandillas.

youth, and thus they have experienced generational turnover during the course of the past few decades. Rodgers (2006: 283–284) observes that while the reemergence of the gangs (at the end of the civil war) might have been tied to demobilized Sandinista and *contra* fighters, they matured out of gangs by the mid-1990s; thus, the gangs of the late 1990s and 2000s were not direct outgrowths of the demobilization, post-civil war process. Rocha (2007: 59) makes a similar claim, noting that it is very unusual to find a gang member older than twenty-two and practically impossible to find someone older than thirty. Therefore, the newer gang members of the late 1990s and 2000s are decidedly of a post-civil war generation.

Unlike gangs in the northern triangle, Nicaraguan gangs have not adopted the highly structured and highly violent organizations associated with *maras* in El Salvador, Guatemala, and Honduras. The national police described Nicaraguan gangs in this way:

Las maras are considered a problem of national security in the countries of Honduras, El Salvador, and Guatemala, but not in our country, where youth groups don't have the same presence as in those countries. What's more, the youth groups often only get together for recreational activities. (Policía Nacional de Nicaragua 2006: 11)

The choice of words in this quote is telling. When describing northern triangle gangs, they are referred to as *maras* (violent youth gangs); however, when referring to Nicaragua, the police bulletin continues to refer to them as *grupos juveniles*, or youth groups (Policía Nacional de Nicaragua 2006: 11). In this quote, they are not even labeled as *pandillas*.

It would be an exaggeration, however, to look at Nicaraguan gangs as purely recreational. They have assumed a territorial role in which they engage in illicit activity but have also historically protected those who reside in the area. According to Rodger's ethnographic work in the mid-1990s, illicit activity coincided with a commitment to provide some level of protection to the community (also see Rocha 2011). Based on ethnographic work in one community, Rodgers argues: "A golden 'rule' of delinquency common to all groups, however, was not to prey on local neighbourhood inhabitants, but actively to protect them from outside thieves, robbers, and *pandilleros*" (Rodgers 2006: 275–277). Thus, even if gangs have been structurally tied to illicit activity and uncertainty, they have also structured and defended community members within this general system (also see Rodgers and Rocha 2013: 50). This form of community protection is illustrated in Rodger's interview with *don* Sergio from the period 1996–1997.

The pandilla looks after the neighborhood and screws others; it protects us and allows us to feel a bit safer, to live our lives a little bit more easily ... Gangs are not a good thing, and it's their fault that we have to live with all this insecurity, but that's a problem of *pandillerismo* in general, not of our gang here in the *barrio*. They protect us, help us – without them, things would be much worse for us. (Rodgers 2006: 277–278)

This territorial focus occasionally translates into territorial competition between gangs seeking to expand or defend their territory. In the name of protecting the neighborhood, fighting has sometimes broken out – although violence has been directed against other gang members and not community members. Apparently, gang fighting was highly ritualized – sequenced in a particular order, which might escalate to guns and mortar but never started out that way (Rodgers 2006: 276–277).[76]

To say that Nicaraguan gangs are not as violent as their Guatemalan, Salvadoran, and Honduran counterparts is not to say that they are immune to violence. With the proliferation of Nicaraguan gangs in the 1990s, they did take on more violent forms than in previous decades (Rodgers 2006: 273), becoming less solidary with their community and more "parochial, predatory, and feared organizations" (Rodgers and Rocha 2013: 50). Rodgers (2006) observed striking changes when returning in 2002 to the neighborhood (barrio Luis Fanor Hernández) where he had previously done ethnographic work. The gang was smaller, more

---

[76] While the number of newspaper-reported homicides is only a fraction of the total registered homicides, they do provide insight into how the public understands patterns and causes of violence. For example, in 2010 we coded 403 violent deaths; the official police record, however, recorded 479 homicides, 259 assassinations, and 47 parricides. In our coding, violent deaths include all these categories rather than separating them out. The newspaper violence database indicates that in 2000 (June–December), newspapers tied only 10 homicides to gangs, which were highly localized: 8 were reported in Managua, 1 was reported in RAAN, and 1 was unknown. In 2005, we coded 52 gang-related homicides; 46 (possibly 48) of these homicides occurred in Managua, with 1 or 0 gang-related homicides occurring in other departments. Based on our coding, nearly 35 percent of gang-related homicides were associated with competition between gangs. In 2010, the reported number declined to 34 (possibly 38), of which 32 (possibly 33) were reported in Managua (newspaper violence database). Of these 2010 events, 11 (or 33 percent) gang-related deaths were coded as competition between gang members. If we include the cases of ambiguous reporting (which might include as many as 16 cases of gang competition resulting in violence and as many as 38 cases of gang-related violence), then it is possible that as many as 42 percent of reported gang-related homicides were tied to competition between gangs (newspaper violence database). *If we take these newspaper reports at face value, it suggests that gang-related violence in Nicaragua is arguably more prevalent within the gang community than it is for their counterparts in the northern triangle, although we have little reason to find this conclusion compelling.*

unitary, and more violent. Notably, he ties the rise of a more violent organization to the penetration of the cocaine economy into the neighborhood (a point also noted by Rocha 2007, esp. pp. 35–38, and Rodgers and Rocha 2013: 50–51). In this case, cocaine was being sold (or its processed form, crack) in the neighborhood itself. *Pandilleros* became involved in selling the drug – to regular clients and to people on street corners. With the increasing sales and consumption, Rodger's noticed a change in *pandillero* behavior – less concerned about protecting the neighborhood and more concerned about profits, accumulation, and consumption patterns. In this context, *pandilleros* were willing to prey on neighbors whom they had previously protected (Rodgers 2006: 278–282). Rocha (2007: 31) also observes that gangs that started off as territorial youth groups started to exhibit changes from about 1999, with some becoming more concerned about smoking crack (*fumando "piedra"*) than defending territory (*lanzando piedras*, throwing stones). In this regard, some gangs have lost some of their organizational coherence as a group with a clear identity and commitment to defend their territory.[77] In the years 2005–2010, in fact, gangs were increasingly challenged (and at times surpassed) by drug-dealing groups, called *cartelitos*, which themselves fell victim to infighting. This lead some to move from drug dealing to drug trafficking – although

---

[77] Rocha (2007: 31). Rodgers (2006: 273, 287, 291) suggests that the gangs not only contribute to social disorder but are also a reflection of "ambient insecurity," serving in this context as "socially structuring institutions." Similarly, with the changing role of the state and politics, the gangs assumed, he argued, a kind of subpolitical role of structuring and ordering local-level dynamics. However, they transformed in the process from a collective form of expression (including violence) to one more reflective of individual economic concerns (with violence used toward that end). This recalls arguments by Levitt and Venkatesh (2000a and 2000b) about what happened to Chicago gangs once older generations were imprisoned and crack cocaine changed the dynamics among a younger generation of profit-oriented gang members. With this change in Nicaragua, the younger generation was more likely to deploy violence to pursue profit. Thus, the gangs assumed a more prominent role in generating insecurity in Nicaragua: "The most prominent actors within this panorama of insecurity are undoubtedly the *pandillas* that roam the streets of Nicaraguan cities, robbing, beating, and frequently killing. The 1999 *Ética y Transparencia* survey ... found that gangs were considered the most likely perpetrators of crime by over 50 percent of respondents, and over half of all those arrested in Nicaragua in 1997 were young males aged between 13 and 25 years old, which correspond to a typical *pandillero* age and gender profile, although obviously not all were gang members ... Indeed, gangs have largely come symbolically to epitomise crime in contemporary Nicaragua, with the words *pandilla* and *pandillerismo* often used interchangeably with 'criminality and 'delinquency'" (Rodgers 2006: 272).

apparently not without competition from Mexican and Colombian drug trafficking organizations (Rodgers and Rocha 2013: 51, 52).

Yet in Nicaragua this "violent" turn was kept in relative check (relative to the other cases in the Central American region), in part because of how state institutions responded to, and structured, the Nicaraguan gangs. As discussed earlier, the Nicaraguan police played a more systematic role – in this case not just criminalizing the behavior but also trying to play a preventative and restorative role, although this did not preclude arrests.[78] While Nicaraguan gangs did not disappear, the *pandillas* did not grow larger either, nor did they transform into *maras* (the highly violent and more centralized youth organizations so prevalent now in El Salvador, Guatemala, and Honduras) – although there has been fear of such development.[79] When confronted with the growth of gangs, police strategy was not solely repressive but also preventative: it sought to imprison leaders for illegal activity and promote disarmament, alongside citizen security measures and coordination with other sectors, including churches, NGOs, and schools, according to Rocha (2011: 115–116), who also observes that this preventative approach was sustained and even touted over time.

Variations in the police and its role in society play a critical role in this divergence, as argued throughout this book,[80] although it would be

[78] *La Prensa* reporting in 2000, for example, provides examples of this institutional response: Youth gangs (pandillas) were also targeted for special police activity. The police carried out Plan Pandilla in Tipitapa, where three people were killed and ten injured by alleged members of youth gangs. The plan led to the arrest of 86 young people and identified 8 youth gangs operating in the city in September, and 63 arrests in December (9.15.2000 Policía lanza S.O.S. contra pandillas; 12.16.2000 Plan Pandilla efectivo en Tipitapa). A different Plan Pandilla in Managua led to 117 arrests in two days, and would place officers undercover in buses, bus stops, and other locations to prevent robberies and arrest perpetrators (12.8.2000 Plan Pandilla deja 117 detenidos). The Plan Pandilla apparently also included a component of working with NGOs and state entities to design programs to reduce the number of youth gangs around the country (8.5.2000 Aún quedan 25 bandas rurales).

[79] *La Prensa* reports on such fears. See, for example: 4.20.2010 Ingreso de maras es un peligro real; 4.21.2010 Peligrosidad de pandillas en aumento; 5.16.2010 Preocupa incremento de armas; 5.5.2010 Pandillas se reorganizan en Estelí.

[80] *La Prensa* reported on an online poll in four Central American countries, which highlighted how distinct Nicaragua was relative to Guatemala, El Salvador, and Honduras. Whereas the latter three all identified the most serious problem as insecurity and delinquency, with an estimated 89% in Guatemala, 95% in El Salvador, and 77% in Honduras identifying crime and insecurity as a major problem, in Nicaragua the main problem identified was governmental corruption, with 41% identifying crime and insecurity as a major problem. In turn, trust in police also revealed a striking contrast, with 46.5% reported as trusting the police in Nicaragua compared to 0.04% in Guatemala, 22.9% in

erroneous to argue that it is the only cause.[81] A more cautious view is portrayed by Rodgers and Rocha (2013: 52ff), who note poor police performance, variability, partisanship, and corruption. Their cautionary note is important when characterizing Nicaragua on its own terms; however, the comparative point here is that the scale and depth of this corruption in Nicaragua is far below that experienced in Guatemala and El Salvador. There seems little doubt that Nicaragua's police record far surpasses that of its neighbors in the northern triangle.

Organized Crime: Drugs, Ports, and Borders

Organized crime and drug trafficking have been present in Nicaragua, but the footprint has been significantly smaller than in the territory of its northern triangle neighbors, and arguably there has been a more concerted state response of cracking down than in Guatemala and El Salvador. Police records reveal that interdiction of cocaine rose from 1990 to 2007, after which it saw a sharp decline (see Figure 7.9). Marijuana and especially crack and heroin have been interdicted at a much lower rate.[82] Interdiction is commonly cited to highlight drug trafficking flows, although it may arguably also measure state capacity. In 2010, the United States issued a report in which it placed Nicaragua on a "black list" of countries trafficking of drugs (as in the actual transport of drugs).[83] The UNODC (2012: 35) report, however, is arguably more cautious about the level of drugs moving through Nicaragua; drugs do pass through, but it happens on a considerably smaller scale than in contemporary Guatemala and Honduras. According to the UNODC *World Drug Reports* (WDRs), Nicaragua was responsible for 3 to 18 percent of Central American cocaine seizures between 1997 and 2005.[84]

El Salvador, and 17.3% in Honduras. Of course, this online reporting is unlikely to be representative, although it is consistent with the main themes developed in this book about how distinct these countries are when it comes to police capacity and perceptions of crime/insecurity. See *La Prensa* 4.14.2010 Istmo afectado por la inseguridad.

[81] NGOs also played a proactive role – working sometimes directly and other times indirectly to improve situations for youth and gang members, a point that was raised during fieldwork interviews and also noted by Rocha (2011: 114).

[82] Policía Nacional de Nicaragua. *Anuario Estadístico 2014*, figures 1.13 and 1.18: www.policia.gob.ni/cedoc/sector/estd/ae%202014.pdf (accessed on July 26, 2017). For different figures on seizures overall, also see UNODC (2008 and 2013).

[83] *La Prensa* 9.21.2010 Golpe de más de US$20 millones de narcotráfico.

[84] United Nations *World Drug Reports* (1997–2005). In 1997, 2.8 metric tons of cocaine were seized (about 8.7% of Central American seizures); in 1999, 0.8 metric tons of cocaine seized (about 5% of Central American seizures); in 2001, 2.7 metric tons of cocaine seized (about 16.7% of Central American seizures); in 2003, 1.1 metric tons of

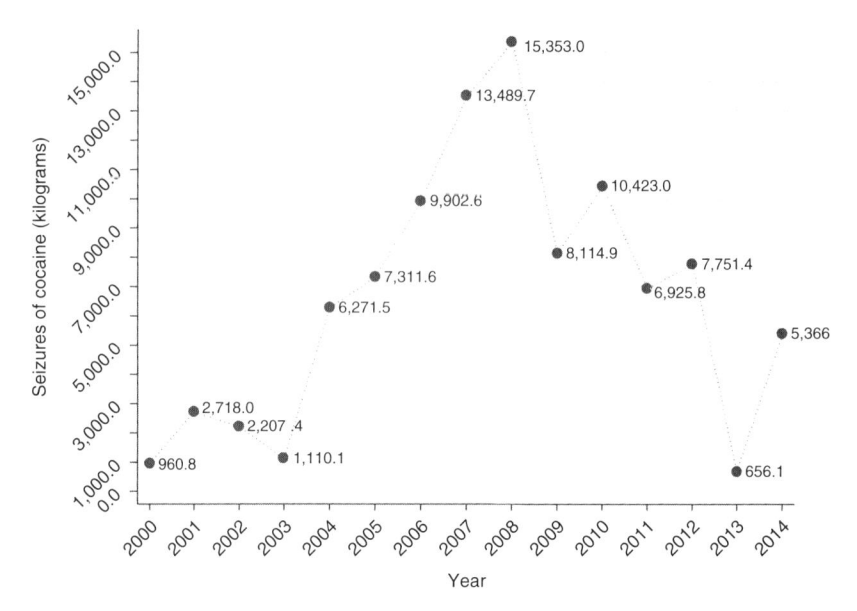

FIGURE 7.9 Interdiction of cocaine in Nicaragua, reported by Nicaraguan police
Source: Policía Nacional de Nicaragua. Anuario Estadístico 2014, figure 1.13. www.policia.gob.ni/cedoc/sector/estd/ae%202014.pdf. Accessed on July 26, 2017.

Nicaragua is thus a hub, but a comparatively minor one, in the transit of drugs, according to the UN WDRs. One can therefore leverage this lower overall level to ask where organized crime and drug transit is most relevant. Reporting shows that drug flows occur in geographically prime regions for trade and transit and in places where the state is weakest. The Caribbean coast is one such region.[85] The Caribbean coast of Nicaragua is known as a refueling point for go-fast boats carrying

cocaine seized (about 3% of Central American seizures); in 2005, 7 metric tons of cocaine seized (about 18% of Central American seizures). These numbers are difficult to interpret for two reasons. First, seizures can be a measure of drug levels and/or of state capacity to capture it. Second, these numbers fluctuate significantly based on single events (the capture – or not – of a single vehicle). Thus, it is difficult to assess in any given year if drug flows are increasing/decreasing; indeed, a drop in seizures from year to year may reflect the influence of state capacity in law enforcement, political will and policy, and/or the number/size of shipments going through the country in a given year. That said, we can infer with some degree of confidence that Nicaragua is *not* the most significant site of the trade and transit of drugs. We have cited cocaine here, but the same could be said for heroin, cannabis, and ecstasy (per World Development Reports).

[85] See Policía Nacional de Nicaragua. *Anuario Estadístico 2000*, p. 127; *InSight Crime* (2012b) and Sam Logan (2006).

cocaine, according to the WDR (2007); *La Prensa* in 2005, for example, also reports on the geographic concentration of drug trafficking on the Caribbean coast.[86] Investigative reporting by *InSight Crime* (2012b) and Logan (2006) have suggested the same. Notably, gangs have not seemed tied into this network (Cordero, Gurdián, and López 2006: 26–27). The 2000 police annual statistical report pictorializes the drug trafficking routes as seen in Figure 7.10, highlighting the centrality of locations on the Caribbean coast for the trade and transit of cocaine, as well as delineating the water and land routes for moving drugs north.

In the Caribbean region, Bluefields (a municipality in the RAAS region) is a particularly notorious port town, renowned for drug trafficking and insecurity,[87] although reports for RAAS (South Atlantic Autonomous Region) and RAAN highlight a broader reach for drug trafficking. According to *InSight Crime* (2012b), the city and coastal areas have been a particularly active site of organized crime. "There are no roads into Bluefields, the main city on Nicaragua's remote Caribbean coast, but the city and the surrounding region have nonetheless become a logistics and transportation hub of the international drug trade." While the number of police reported per 100,000 was the highest in RAAN and RAAS between 2006 and 2010, these numbers partially reflect low population density rather than the ability of the police to regulate this area as a whole. Strikingly, the number of police per 100,000 sq km is lowest in this region (two in RAAN, two in RAAS, two in Zelaya Central, and one in the Triángulo Minero), providing relatively little patrolling of the region and thus a weak state presence. 2010 police figures show that the police's ability to resolve homicides is particularly low in this region relative to the rest of the country.[88] The police report in 2010 states that their institution has

---

[86] *La Prensa* 2005 reporting, for example, includes: 8.28.2005 Bomba de tiempo en el Caribe; 3.12.2005 Nicaragua aún en ruta del narcotráfico; 4.17.2005 Nicaragua corredor de armas; 4.21.2005 Cocaína sigue brotando; 7.31.2005 Asoma gran red narco.

[87] Based on an evaluation of *La Prensa* reporting in 2000, 2005, and 2010, it was clear that Bluefields (RAAS) was an area besieged by crime (7.23.2000 Bluefields a merced de delincuentes). It was not the subject of frequent reporting in 2000, although it would be in subsequent years. See *La Prensa* 8.19.2005 Crece inseguridad en Bluefields. For later reporting, see 9.12.2010 Violencia se desata en Bluefields; 11.15.2010 Bluefields, blanco fácil del narcotráfico internacional; 11.6.2010 RAAS "permeada" por narcotráfico; 8.24.2010 Crece violencia en Bluefields.

[88] Policía Nacional de Nicaragua. *Anuario Estadístico* 2010, p. 41 (for police presence per 100,000); p. 105 includes the figures for homicide denunciations/resolution for RAAS (63.6% in 2009 and 47.1% in 2010). For comparative and regional data on criminal activity, see p. 88–111).

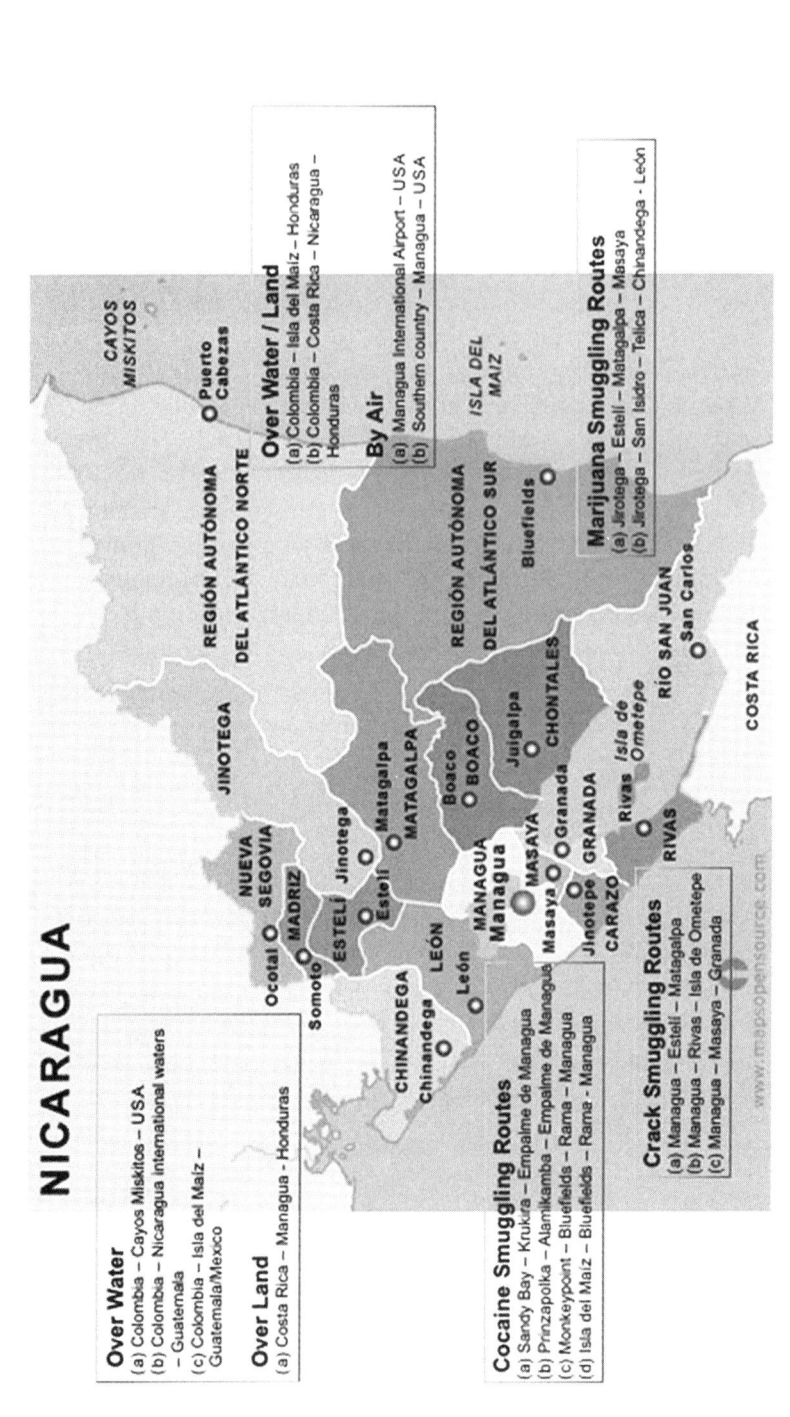

FIGURE 7.10 Trade trafficking routes in Nicaragua, according to Nicaraguan police
Sources: For drug trafficking routes: Policía Nacional de Nicaragua *Anuario Estadístico 2000*, p. 127. For Nicaraguan provinces map: www.mapsopensource.com/nicaragua-map.html (accessed on April 30, 2015).

been least effective in Managua (41 percent), RAAS (52.6 percent – with RAAS being precisely where the drug trade has been most consequential), and Carazo (53.6 percent) relative to the other sixteen departments (two of which scored 63–66 percent, ten of which scored between 70 and 77 percent, and four of which scored above 80 percent).[89] Interestingly, the overwhelming number of crimes (not restricted to homicides) have occurred in Managua and not RAAS.[90] The difficulty confronting the Nicaraguan police in the RAAS region is illustrated in a report that even the chief of police in Bluefields received a death threat, via an anonymous note (placed in his desk) warning him that his life was at risk if he did not stop persecuting drug traffickers ("narcos").[91] Noting weak state capacity, the prosecutor observed that there were only five prosecutors handling 3,500 cases.[92] The police reported a total of 2,733 crimes, of which the police resolved 1,559, or 48.1 percent.[93]

The Caribbean coastal region in general and Bluefields in particular thus provide a territorial space within which boats are refueled and repaired and drug shipments broken down for shipping in smaller amounts (*InSight Crime* 2012b).[94] Notably, according to the quote that follows, the local economy has become embedded in the drug trade.[95]

[89] Policía Nacional de Nicaragua. *Anuario Estadístico 2010*, p. 117.
[90] Policía Nacional de Nicaragua. *Anuario Estadístico 2010*, p. 117, figure 3.30: includes reporting of 2010 police effectiveness at the national level (59.2%) and subnational level (León 82.2%, Granada 81.2, Madriz 80.4%, Rivas 80%, Matagalpa 76.9%, Boaco 75.6%, Masaya 74.9%, RAAN 73%, Chinandega 72.7%, Jinotega 72.6%, Chontales 71.7%, Rio San Juan 71.1%, Las Minas 71.1%, Zelaya Central 70%, Nueva Segovia 66.2%, Estelí 63.4%, Carazo 53.6%, RAAS 52.6%, Managua 41%). While the methodology for these data is not made explicit, the figures follow pages of data regarding the ability to resolve various crimes, including homicides. The page following this figure includes the total number of crimes that were reported relative to those that were resolved in Managua.
[91] *La Prensa* 11.6.2010 RAAS "permeada" por narcotráfico.
[92] *La Prensa* 8.24.2010 Crece violencia en Bluefields.
[93] *La Prensa* 12.6.2010 Policía Nacional reprobó en la RAAS, según cifras.
[94] The newspaper violence database includes reports on drug trades and consumption in these areas – although the levels do not compare with discussions found in the Guatemalan newspapers. For 2000 reporting in *La Prensa*, see for example: 7.2.2000 Nicaragua, la ruta infectada del narcotráfico; 12.31.2000 Caen tres nicas con 248 kilos de cocaína en Guatemala; 6.10.2000 Carazo se ha convertido en paraíso para narcos; 6.13.2000 Barrio de Bluefields es el reino del crack; 12.14.2000 Droga diezma juventud de Sandy Bay; 12.26.2000 Drogas se toman pueblos de Carazo.
[95] *La Prensa* 9.2.2000 Bandas amenazan seguridad; 9.13.2000 Encuentran 200 kilos de coca; 12.15.2000 Actividad delictiva creció este año en la Ciudad de las Flores.

Many of the Nicaraguan traffickers started as fishermen of "white lobsters," the bales of cocaine shipments that wash up on the shores after traffickers are forced to offload them while being pursued by security forces. They established contact with traffickers when the latter came to buy back the loads. Locals insist they have been paid up to $500 a kilo for cocaine they found, a small fortune in these remote communities, whose only local employment opportunities, apart from drugs, come from fishing and logging.

"You need to understand that most of the local population in the RAAS, particularly in the more remote coastal communities, support the drug traffickers," said government prosecutor Suarez. "They provide employment, and when there are storms and hurricanes, it is the drug traffickers that help people rebuild, not the *government, which has little to no presence.*"

This was echoed by Captain Jose Castillo of the DNA, who said that, due to extreme poverty, "It is easy for drug traffickers to buy these communities." (*InSight Crime* 2012b; emphasis added)

Bluefields was thus used by drug traffickers to transport drugs from Colombia to markets due north. Given dire economic conditions in the region (official statistics put unemployment at 70 percent and poverty at 80 percent, according to one *La Prensa* article), many residents were amenable to working with the drug traffickers, including providing fuel as well as storing and transporting drugs.[96] Therefore more drugs circulate, with one Sandinista leader observing that as much as 40 percent of the municipality's economy is linked to drug trafficking. Even fishermen now go out to sea to search for packets of drugs left behind by drug traffickers, which fetch as much as $7,000 per kilo. Accordingly, the fishing town has fundamentally changed, especially since 2000.[97] Reports of drug-related killings and revenge were rare in the years analyzed for the newspaper violence database (2000, 2005, and 2010) constructed for this book,[98] although homicide rates in this subnational region are much higher than in the rest of the country (see the discussion that follows).

---

[96] Sandy Bay (RAAN), population 18,000, was also featured in a *La Prensa* report as a community besieged by drug trafficking. According to the article, the local Sandy Bay police station had been abandoned for two months (as of the September 2005 report) following a confrontation between police and local community members after the police carried out a search of the homes of alleged drug traffickers, where they seized $600,000 USD, drugs, jewelry, and guns. The article says a Sandy Bay councilmember and six local judges went to the police station in nearby Bilwi to ask the police to return to Sandy Bay. The officials said Sandy Bay had seen an increase in drug use and addiction, particularly crack. *La Prensa* 9.2.2005 Droga ha llevado la violencia a Sandy Bay.

[97] *La Prensa* 8.4.2005 Caribe nica convertido en tierra narco.

[98] *La Prensa* 9.6.2005 Narcos pagaron, sicarios mataron.

Circumscribing Violence in Post-Civil War Nicaragua 331

There have been some efforts to control the drug trade, although *InSight Crime* (2012b) reports that those have largely been unsuccessful. However, despite a rocky start to his tenure, former national police chief Edwin Cordero devised a comprehensive drug strategy by the time he left office (and prior to the start of Aminta Granera's term). Police access to weapons and vehicles increased more than twofold in 2001, and Cordero claimed that the national police had seized over 13,000 kg of cocaine between 2004 and 2005 (Logan 2006).[99] UN WDRs echo the idea that police enforcement improved. According to UN records, Nicaragua ranked second in Caribbean seizures and fourteenth in global seizures of cocaine. *La Prensa* reported on several successful police operations to control drug trafficking in 2009 and 2010.[100] In 2010, the army also engaged in drug interdictions on the coast (particularly in the RAAN).[101] The police and the military arrested four alleged drug traffickers near Cayos Miskitos (RAAN) following a shootout between the traffickers and the navy; the police and the military also seized 1,300 kg of cocaine.[102]

In this context of increased drug trafficking on the coast (with some noted state efforts to control it), this region has become among the most violent in the country – not because there is one dominant organization but because rival groups have emerged to contest control in the north and south autonomous regions (RAAN and RAAS):[103] "Disputes among rival groups over the theft of merchandise have turned the once bucolic region into one of the country's deadliest. In 2010, the latest year for which statistics are available, the murder rate in the RAAS was 40 per 100,000

---

[99] Grigsby (2006b) also notes that Cordero ended his term with reforms that improved living conditions for the police and ostensibly worked against corruption: he got back the Carlos Roberto Huembes Hospital for the police, initiated a modest housing plan, and increased salaries across all levels.

[100] See *La Prensa*, including 2.18.2010 Crece población narco en cárceles nicaragüenses; 1.17.2010 Nueva red narco desarticulada por Policía Nacional; 8.15.2010 Policía da golpe a célula narco.

[101] *La Prensa* reported on several cases where the army and police located planes carrying significant amounts of drugs or the navy captured speedboats also engaging in the transit of drugs. In the book's violence newspaper database, we identified several articles in 2010 about such incidents in Bismuna (RAAN), Wiwinack, Walpasiksa, and Wounta (RAAN). See, in particular, *La Prensa* 6.17.2010 Avioneta podría contener hasta 600 kilos de droga; 6.18.2010 Ejército ocupa narco avioneta en el Atlántico Norte; 6.18.2010 Ocho aeronaves recuperadas al crimen organizado; 9.21.2010 Golpe de más de US$20 millones de narcotráfico.

[102] *La Prensa* 11.21.2010 "Halcón Negro" golpea a narcos.

[103] Nicaragua's autonomous regions were formed during the Nicaraguan revolution when indigenous movements mobilized against the regime and demanded autonomy from it. See Charles Hale (1994).

compared to 17 per 100,000 for Managua."[104] This context has provided a homicidal ecology in which high profits, high risk, weak state capacity, and competition sometimes fuel violent control for territory prized for the trade and transit of drugs. In these places, subnational homicide rates are highest, and illicit crime and territorial competition are most in evidence. Some have expressed fear that the illicit economy, competition, and violence could spread. Outgoing commander of the Nicaraguan armed forces, General Omar Halleslevens, in a 2010 speech, warned of the threat of drug trafficking in Nicaragua (since the country is in a prime geographic location between Colombia's drug production and the North American market). Noting that drug trafficking was geographically delimited at that point, he emphasized the potential for it to spread to other parts of the country – especially because the army had fewer resources than those at the disposal of drug traffickers.[105]

Zooming out from Bluefields, in particular, we see that homicide rates are highest in the Caribbean coastal and border regions (although the absolute number of homicides is highest in the capital region of Managua). Violence levels per 100,000 are significantly higher in the four contiguous regions of RAAN, RAAS, Jinotega, and Matagalpa. Triángulo Minero and Zelaya Central, while reported separately and with very high rates, form part of the former, autonomous regions (see Figure 7.11). RAAS and RAAN border the coast and are territories that exhibited significant resistance during the Sandinista years, when they were arguably the least integrated regions of the country (Hale 1994). Jinotega is an important coffee-growing region that borders both RAAN and Honduras and has become central to the trade and transit of cocaine from the Andes to the United States. Matagalpa borders the two autonomous regions and Jinotega. The fact that such high rates exist within a county with relatively low or moderate homicide rates highlights how low the rates are in other parts of the country. In 2010, the national homicide rate was 13 per 100,000 inhabitants, but subnationally this rate varied from 1 percent in the department of Río San Juan to 40 percent in the RAAS.

[104] *InSight Crime*. 2012b. "Bluefields: Nicaragua's Cocaine Hub." Written by Jeremy McDermott July 8, 2012. Accessed online at www.insightcrime.org/nicaragua-a-paradise-lost/bluefields-nicaraguas-cocaine-hub on June 27, 2013.
[105] Examples of drug trafficking can be found in coastal communities (with weak state presence), as reported by *La Prensa* in 2010: 2.28.2010 La tragedia de Walpasiksa; 6.14.2010 Detienen a tres personas con presunto dinero narco; 8.7.2010 Detienen a tres mexicanos con más de US$200,000 en Tipitapa. Also see *La Prensa* 1.7.2010 Nicaragua puede ser víctima del narcotráfico.

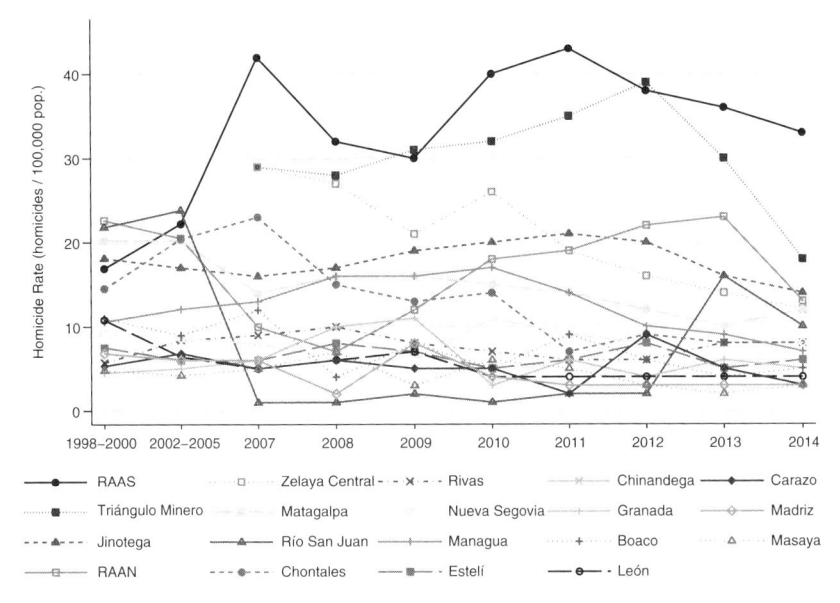

Circumscribing Violence in Post-Civil War Nicaragua 333

FIGURE 7.11 Homicide rates in Nicaraguan departments (1998–2014, rate per 100,000 population)
Graph created for this project by Daniela Barba-Sánchez using Stata (September 2017).
Sources: Data for 1998–2000 come from the *Anuario Estadístico de la Policía Nacional de Nicaragua*, 2000. Police statistics report *homicidios, asesinatos*, and *parricidios* separately.
Data for 2002–2005 come from UNDP report "Seguridad Ciudadana 1998–2010 Nicaragua: Riesgos, Retos, y Oportunidades," p. 85.
Data for 2007–2014 come from Policía Nacional de Nicaragua. *Anuario Estadístico 2014*, figure 1.20. www.policia.gob.ni/cedoc/sector/estd/ae%202014.pdf. Accessed on July 26, 2017.
Note: Homicide rates for RAAN and RAAS do not include Triángulo Minero and Zelaya Central, respectively, which are officially part of those regions but are reported separately by the police in its annual statistical report.

Recognizing this subnational variation (with the highest rates largely concentrated on the east coast, which has the country's lowest population density), Nicaragua's national rate remains relatively low – in no small part because of a more capable set of law-and-order institutions in the more densely populated areas. It is not that Nicaragua is perfect, but it is more capable relative to its neighbors. Latinobarometer public opinion data reveal that Nicaragua is the Central American country with the highest approval of government security and crime policy, the country with the highest perceptions of feeling safe, and the one with the lowest percentage indicating concern that the country is becoming less safe (in each case generating a more positive view than even Costa Rica). For the share of people who feel safe in the country, for example, Nicaragua's otherwise low rate of 22 percent is five times higher than the 4 percent reported for both El Salvador and Guatemala.[106] While these public opinion data tell us little about actual violence patterns, government political choices, and policy effectiveness, they strongly suggest that Nicaraguan citizens have had more confidence in their police than in other countries and that the police have generated an image of deterrence and order – at least until now. And in this context, Nicaragua's homicidal ecology has been relatively inauspicious for illicit actors, although with important exceptional geographies on the coast.

CODA

Institutions matter. This we know. I have argued here that we must take policing seriously if we are to understand the comparative politics of illicit economies and violence in the region. Institutions do not explain all violence, but they do provide the rules of the game. Where police forces are capable, autonomous, and nonpartisan, they have a greater chance of deterring crime and containing illicit activity. This is the story of Nicaragua – a story that highlights how revolutionary change and post-revolutionary compromise created and consolidated new institutions and an esprit de corps that made police officers more (rather than less) committed to the mission of maintaining democratic order. Violence has occurred; the end of this chapter highlights the territorial pockets in which organized crime acts to control trade and transit – places that provide a more propitious homicidal ecology. However, these territorial pockets are the proverbial exceptions that prove the rule. Indeed, a couple of 2010 polls revealed very high approval ratings at that time for the police chief and the police as an institution. The chief of the national police, Primera Comisionada Aminta Granera, was the most popular public official/figure among Nicaraguans;[107] 90.9 percent of Nicaraguans said they knew who she was, and 85.4 percent expressed a positive opinion of her. These figures surpassed even those for the president, with 91 percent of Nicaraguans saying they knew President Daniel Ortega but 52.6 percent

---

[106] Latinobarometer 2010 data, reported in UNODC (2012: 72).
[107] *La Prensa* 10.13.2010 Granera puntea simpatías entre nicas.

expressing a *negative* opinion of him.[108] Furthermore, a 2010 poll revealed improved public opinion of the police relative to the year before, with nearly 80 percent of Nicaraguans responding that that the country was just as safe (39.9 percent) or safer (38.3 percent) than the year before. Strikingly, independents gave the police the highest rating (49.8 percent saying they had a positive opinion of the police), pro-Sandinista respondents were less positive (only 36.8 percent of supporters of the Sandinista government were positive), and the opposition was quite negative (only 13.4 percent of "la oposición" saw the police favorably).[109] One conclusion is clear: in 2010, the Nicaraguan police chief headed an institution that commanded higher societal support and respect than other institutions in the country and certainly higher than other police forces in the region.

The historical argument about state formation and its legacy, however, is not deterministic. The revolution provided a radical breakpoint that forged a new institution that was further professionalized in 1990 (with buy-in from opposing sides) – a pathway *not* followed by Guatemala and El Salvador, where police and military reforms occurred on top of a preexisting institution that subverted reform agendas. Thus Nicaragua forged a new institution at this critical juncture. However, the lesson of this chapter is that reforms also took place in the aftermath of this critical change, allowing for smaller-level evolutions, especially when leaders had new visions and could rely on a largely professional force to carry it out. These more micro changes recall Thelen (2004), Mahoney and Thelen (2010), and Levitsky and Murillo's (2009) work on the possibility of smaller-level changes between critical junctures – ones that allow institutions to change within broader parameters. The Conclusion returns to these broader themes of state formation and state capacity – including the ability to forge nonpartisan institutions with a committed cadre of officers, as well as the preventative policies that have proven consequential in creating a less auspicious homicidal ecology (in contrast to the punitive stance adopted in El Salvador, Guatemala, and Honduras).

Recognizing that police capacity is not reducible to material resources, but rather is defined by the quality and orientation of its personnel, leads one to ponder if Nicaragua's police force will be able to sustain its institutional capacity and/or face new challenges to the autonomy and professionalization that were forged with the 1979 Sandinista Revolution and reforged in the aftermath of their 1990 electoral loss. In 2014, such challenges took place

---

[108] *La Prensa* 3.27.2010 Tres mujeres ostentan imagen más positiva.
[109] *La Prensa* 10.12.2010 Policía mejora imagen positiva entre los nicas.

when the FSLN did increasingly impinge on the autonomy of rule-of-law institutions, placing them under the control of the president. In January 2014, the Nicaraguan national assembly strengthened the hand of the president vis-à-vis the military, which gained an "internal security role."

> Reforms of the military code approved by Nicaragua's national assembly restore to the army the internal security role that had been removed in 1994 with a twist: using the military in this capacity is up to the President. They also give the President the power to keep the commander-in-chief of the army at his discretion and to appoint serving members of the military to unelected posts in the administration ... The most important amendment to the previous military code adds to the functions of the army that of "guaranteeing, according to what the President of the Republic should order, the security and protection of the nation's economic objectives and strategic resources, and the execution of plans contributing to security and peace in the national territory to foster progress and national economic development."[110]

Of greatest relevance to this book, and most concerning for the professional autonomy of law-and-order institutions, reports surfaced of increasing politicization of the police. (These included reports in *La Prensa* – owned by the Chamorro family and highly critical of the current Sandinista government, headed once again by Daniel Ortega – and criticism by various NGOs and human rights organizations.[111]) In particular, the jurisdiction of the police changed from the ministry of the interior to the presidency. On June 11, 2014, the Nicaraguan legislature approved a law for this change: "Dissident Sandinista legislator Víctor Hugo Tinoco noted that this was the first time the military and the police had been placed under the direct orders of the President since the Somoza dictatorship was overthrown in 1979."[112]

While a professional police force might remain in place, pressures coming directly from the president make it harder for society to view the police

---

[110] *LatinNews*. "Nicaragua: Re-Election Secured, Ortega Boosts the Army's Role." Latin American Security & Strategic Review (February 2014). Accessed online on July 11, 2014.

[111] *La Prensa* reporting in 2010 is filled with such concerns: 1.3.2010 Reforma policial sigue en secreto; 1.5.2010 Reforma abre ventana a cargos vitalicios; 5.3.2010 Policía se enfrenta "combo" de retos; 1.4.2010 Reforma policial debe ser debatida; 1.10.2010 Hijo de Ortega se casa con hija de candidato a jefe de Policía; 1.5.2010 Reforma abre ventana a cargos vitalicios; 2.2.2010 Seguridad en discusión; 1.2010 orteguistas hilan fino en la Policía Nacional; 3.26.2010 Ortega elimina unidad élite; 4.6.2010 Ortega "decapitó" unidad élite policial; 4.21.2010 Granera se declara incapaz; 4.23.2010 Maras orteguistas cercan a diputados; 7.9.2010 Chichigalpa y la UNEN, dos caras de la Policía; 7.13.2010 Policía parcializada en conflicto estudiantil; 4.26.2010 Policía bajo "bota" del orteguismo; 4.27.2010 Policía es "manoseada" por Ortega; 5.15.2010 Policía quedó mal ante organismos de DDHH; 7.3.2010 Policía pone en riesgo la paz.

[112] *LatinNews*. "Pointers: Nicaragua: President Takes Control of the Police." Latin American Security & Strategic Review. (June 2014). Accessed online on July 11, 2014.

as a national versus a partisan force. The contemporary police have stood out for creating a professional and autonomous force; indeed, their success in containing the illicit economy (and competition therein) has rested on this institutional framework. In the context of an increasingly politicized court system[113] (one suspected of infiltration by organized crime), we are left to wonder if the Nicaraguan police will be able to continue to resist the rising onslaught of partisan and corrupt pressures.

Indeed, as this book goes to press, Nicaragua's law-and-order institutions have been tested, and the outcome has been alarming. Political violence has unexpectedly mounted following an unanticipated wave of spring 2018 mobilizations against sitting President Daniel Ortega and his increasing use of authoritarian, corrupt, and violent measures. In response, Ortega turned to the police to repress the demonstrators, with current estimates of over 300 political deaths. Once widely-celebrated Police Chief Aminta Granera resigned in May 2018 under a dark political cloud. In this mobilizational moment of social protest and state violence, it remains an open question as to whether Nicaragua will emerge from this crisis with democratic, autonomous, and professional law-and-order institutions. The Sandinistas helped forge such institutions first when they toppled Somoza in 1979 and later after they lost elections in 1990. It is distressing to contemplate that these same law-and-order institutions have recently been repoliticized by the Sandinistas, with such detrimental consequences for human life and democratic practice. While this chapter has emphasized the positive role of the post-Somoza Nicaraguan police in circumscribing violence and minimizing homicidal ecologies, I unexpectedly close this chapter with unanswered questions about the future of Nicaraguan state institutions, democracy and the reemergence of troubling political violence.

---

[113] See *La Prensa* reporting for 2010: 2.18.2010 Crece población narco en cárceles nicaragüenses; 1.22.2010 Narcos libres con orden falsa; 1.26.2010 Indagaciones se amplían a otros penales; 2.24.2010 Declaran a tres culpables por narcoliberaciones; 2.26.2010 Apelan sentencia en caso de ex alcalde; 2.22.2010 Narcoliberaciones sacuden la PGR-RAAN; 7.3.2010 Poder Judicial a merced de crimen organizado; 6.2.2010 Ortega veta indulto a narco de Sinaloa; 8.24.2010 "Botín" de contrabando para la Policía; 12.22.2010 Más narcoliberaciones en Tribunal de Granada.

CHAPTER 7
Appendix

TABLE 7.5 *Homicide rates by Nicaraguan department (1998–2014)*

Department	1998–2000	2002–2005	2007	2008	2009	2010	2011	2012	2013	2014
RAAS	16.9	22.2	42	32	30	40	43	38	36	33
Triángulo Minero*			29	28	31	32	35	39	30	18
Jinotega	18.1	17	16	17	19	20	21	20	16	14
RAAN	22.6	20.5	10	7	12	18	19	22	23	13
Zelaya Central*			29	27	21	26	19	16	14	12
Matagalpa	20.2	20.2	14	16	16	15	14	12	10	12
Río San Juan	21.8	23.8	1	1	2	1	2	2	16	10
Chontales	14.5	20.4	23	15	13	14	7	9	8	8
Rivas	5.7	8.4	9	10	8	7	6	6	8	8
Nueva Segovia	9.3	8.6	8	6	6	11	9	8	5	8
Managua	10.6	12.1	13	16	16	17	14	10	9	7
Estelí	7.5	6	6	8	7	5	6	8	5	6
Chinandega	5.8	7.4	7	8	7	7	6	6	6	5
Granada	4.5	5	6	10	11	3	6	4	6	5
Boaco	11	9	12	4	8	5	9	6	4	5
León	10.8	6.4	5	6	7	4	4	4	4	4
Carazo	5.3	6.8	5	6	5	5	2	9	5	3
Madriz	6.8	6	6	2	8	4	3	3	3	3
Masaya	4.8	4.2	5	7	3	6	5	3	2	3
TOTAL	11.69		13	13	13	13	12	11	9	9

Sources: Data for 1998–2000 come from the *Anuario Estadístico de la Policía Nacional de Nicaragua*, 2000. Police statistics report *homicidios, asesinatos,* and *parricidios* separately. Data for 2002–2005 come from UNDP report "Seguridad Ciudadana 1998–2010 Nicaragua: Riesgos, Retos, y Oportunidades," p. 85. Data for 2007–2014 come from Policía Nacional de Nicaragua. *Anuario Estadístico 2014,* figure 1.20. www.policia.gob.ni/cedoc/sector/estd/ae%202014.pdf. Accessed on July 26, 2017.

* Homicide rates for RAAN and RAAS do not include Triángulo Minero and Zelaya Central, respectively, which are officially part of those regions but are reported separately by police in its annual statistical report.

PART IV

LOOKING BACKWARD AND FORWARD

8

Concluding with States

Violence has riddled Latin American democracy in the late twentieth and early twenty-first centuries. High homicide rates have literally diminished the practice and meaning of citizenship just as it has led many to question why the contemporary democratic period has been marred by the world's highest homicide rates. In 2012, over a third (36 percent) of intentional homicides in the world took place in the Americas (compared to 31 percent in Africa, 28 percent in Asia, 5 percent in Europe, and 0.3 percent in Oceania) (UNODC 2014b: 11). Central America (along with Southern Africa) has been marked with homicide rates at four times the global average; the average stood at 6.2 per 100,000, while there were over 24 per 100,000 in each subregion (UNODC 2014b: 12).[1] Confronting violence on a daily basis, many citizens are faced with untenable options: to stay in their home country, where the prospects of death are unfathomably high, or to migrate north, a path chosen by scores of undocumented children who have crossed the US borders in recent years.

This book set out to explain the causes and patterns of high homicide rates in the third wave of democracy in the Americas. Some might argue that democratization itself unleashed the violence that has taken place – as authoritarianism gave way to civilian rule and the freedoms that it allowed, as demobilized actors were unleashed in a polity and economy that had no home for them, or as electoral competition heated up and led to cyclical waves of violence. This was an alternative argument commonly posed during this project. However, the empirical evidence does not support it. Third wave democracies did not unleash high levels of violence everywhere, demobilized actors did not enter the illicit world everywhere and fight violently to defend it, and electoral cycles have not yet mapped

---

[1] Young males (15–29) in Central and South America are particularly affected; they are four times as likely to be killed than the global average for young males (UNODC 2014b: 14).

onto violence patterns throughout the region – although there is some evidence of this in recent work on Mexico. Otherwise stated, regime type and the transition between military and civilian rule have not been the cause (even if they were the backdrop). Rather, the varying capacity and complicity of law-and-order institutions were critical to the violence that followed. In particular, weak and corrupt public security forces (forged as part of a historic process of state formation) provided advantageous geographies for lucrative illicit political economies (some transnational, some local), which together forged homicidal ecologies in some parts of the region.[2] This book explored this argument theoretically, conceptually, and empirically.

The research thus moved beyond the study of formal democratic institutions to analyze the role of weak and corrupt states that (have failed to) protect citizens; the illicit organizations that have defined, carved out, and defended lucrative and illicit political economies; and the organizational competition (between illicit groups and often with the state) to control subnational territorial enclaves that serve as the geographic hub for the trade and transit of illicit goods, especially but not only illicit drugs. These three core factors have created homicidal ecologies – ones in which there is a high propensity for the use of violence to secure territorial control when challenged by other organizations, be they other illicit competitors and/or the state itself. The book laid out how these three factors interacted over time and across space. While the argument does not claim to explain specific incidences of homicide, it does provide strong analytic leverage to explain which countries and regions would be most violent and why. These factors combined to forge among the world's highest homicide rates in Guatemala and El Salvador, as discussed in Chapters 5 and 6; they also arguably shed light on soaring rates in Honduras, Mexico, Venezuela, and Brazil, as discussed later.

Strikingly, not all Latin American countries have suffered from exceedingly high homicide rates. Nicaragua was a telling contrast. Despite otherwise shared features (geography, inequality, dictatorships, civil war histories, etc.) with other high-violence cases in Central America, its homicide rates have been comparatively and significantly lower. It has been closer in this regard to Chile than to other civil war cases in the

---

[2] Cruz (2011b) makes a similar argument about the centrality of the state, although his analysis situates these states in the context of democratization, while I see these reforms as part of the end of civil wars (independent of, sometimes following, the formal process of democratization).

Americas. To explain why, this book developed the argument that the illicit political economy (and associated illicit and violent organizations) have been comparatively less developed in this country than in its northern neighbors, in significant part because the country entered the third wave of democracy with a more capable and professional state (particularly the coercive arm of the state), raising the costs for illicit organizations seeking to expand their presence in the national territory.

Viewed generally, law-and-order institutions (particularly the police) shape the incentives for illicit organizations deciding where to set up shop. Where the police are weak (and/or complicit), illicit organizations face decreased costs in developing and sustaining an illicit economy. By contrast, where the police are professional (including able to discipline their own cadre), illicit organizations face higher hurdles and therefore face incentives to search for more hospitable conditions. Thus, the type of law-and-order state fundamentally shapes which countries are seen as prime territory for organized crime and gangs; weak and corrupt states make certain countries particularly attractive for (transnational and local) organized crime. States are therefore pivotal, even if they do not shoulder all the responsibility or act in isolation. Thus, this book emphasized how states shape where illicit economies flourish and why.

This concluding chapter briefly restates the core argument of the book before delving further into some of the book's associated themes about how states, territories, and policy shape homicidal ecologies. In turn, the conclusion speaks to the empirical generalizability of the argument. While the book's findings were tied to the systematic analysis of three cases, the theoretical intuitions and argument have broader implications for analyzing and promoting public security and democratic order following brutal war and dictatorship. Thus, this conclusion aims to identify fruitful avenues for future research, while speaking to the policy implications for addressing homicidal violence in the region.

REVISITING STATES AND VIOLENCE

I have argued that states are pivotal to explaining which countries provide propitious grounds for illicit organizations and illicit political economic activity. While seemingly uncontroversial, the literature has largely neglected to theorize the state institutions that play a role in defining law and order in the third wave of democracy. Our analytic gaze has largely been on the military – both because our theories have privileged the role of war and state making and because militaries have dramatically too often subverted democracy and abused their own citizens through egregious human rights abuses – particularly in the Southern Cone and Central America but beyond as well. With the transition to democratic rule, militaries were supposed to return to the barracks and civilians were supposed to reassume the primary role of governing the polity. Accordingly, most studies of democratization focused on the military and efforts to strip them of prerogatives without precipitating a coup. A primary concern was to disempower the coercive institutions that had overseen state violence and to usher in a moment of democratic rule to uphold and respect human rights (O'Donnell and Schmitter 1986; Schmitter and Karl 1991; and Hunter 1997; among many others). The laser focus on the military was understandable but, in retrospect, shortsighted if we are interested in understanding law and order in democratic contexts.

It is the police (along with the courts), rather than the military, that are theoretically responsible for imposing, defending, and upholding order in civilian spaces. Far from being incidental, they are the bureaucratic face of the state in the streets (Lipsky 1980; Gonzalez 2014). And while our theories of the state have focused on the military as the coercive arm that monopolizes the legitimate use of force over a given territory, it is in fact the police that is supposed to do so on the home court and especially in democratic regimes. Yet until recently, the police have largely been overlooked in studies of democratization (or in democratic governance – including in the United States). This has been an oversight with significant political and theoretical consequences.

Variation in police capacity and orientation, this study found, has in fact been critical to an explanation of the politics of homicide. While the police force (alongside the courts and prisons) has often lacked such capacity (indeed been corrupt and complicit) in some contexts, it has been much more capable (even legitimate) in others. Weak and corrupt states have contributed to homicidal ecologies by providing propitious ground for the growth of illicit organizations; and where those organizations vie or compete for territorial control, violence is more likely to break out. Mexico, Guatemala, El Salvador, and Honduras all provide powerful examples of this violent competitive dynamic. The role of the police became particularly evident in the empirical analysis of higher- and lower-violence cases. The research revealed how difficult and consequential police reform is. A few additional observations are worth highlighting in this conclusion. I outline six general areas for further theoretical and empirical research into the police, order, and violence. This is followed in this first section by a discussion of how a focus on the state (and the police in particular) provides analytic leverage to explain varied homicidal ecologies in other cases.

Research Agendas on Policing Order and Violence

The comparative analysis in this book generates a research agenda for future work on policing order and violence. Indeed, to advance our understanding of democratic governance, violence, and order, we need more comparative theorizing and empirical analyses of the police. The police are a core part of the complex of institutions addressing law and order.[3] They should be integrated into our broader comparative studies of state formation and governance rather than it being presumed that they are solely of interest to scholars of criminal justice or public administration. Alongside the military and prison systems, the police constitute the coercive arm of the state and of the three constitutes the most proximate coercive institution interacting with citizens – shaping their quotidian experiences with order and violence (in the context of both democratic and authorian regimes) and shaping the incentives and constraints of actors on the ground. Therefore, additional comparative work is needed on the police as an institution.

First, more work needs to address *types of police*, including how, where, and why the police diverge along a critical set of dimensions: varying degrees of organizational capacity (territorial reach, professionalism, ability to meet the stated mandate, relationship to auxiliary state and partisan institutions), organizational practice (including [in]efficiency, corruption, and/or complicity), and legitimacy. This book has analyzed some of these dimensions (especially those focused on organizational capacity) and has argued that the capacity of law-and-order institutions (particularly the police) shapes incentives for illicit organizations to set up shop while also creating incentives for illicit actors to forge alliances with corrupt police officers, among other state officials. Thus, further comparative work would advance our understanding of order, discipline, and punishment. This focus on the types of police is relevant to our analysis of third wave democracies but is of equal importance to our understanding of more-established democracies, where the police diverge

---

[3] The pioneering work of scholars such as Chevigny (1995 and 2003b), Bailey and Dammert (2005), Ungar (2009 and 2011), and González (2014) has conveyed the practices and political uses (and abuses) of the police.

significantly and exhibit a wide range of behaviors – from the exemplary to the deplorable.

Second, the police have proven resistant to institutional change, and thus much can be gained by analyzing the *origins* of the divergent police forces that do exist. Historically corrupt and abusive institutions, including police forces, have been particularly difficult to reform – not least because their officers carry arms, the officers have a great deal of autonomy on the street, and they are able to extract obedience and "taxes" given their coercive resources and, at times, their ability to act with impunity. Where the police have been unprofessional, corrupt, weak, and/or abusive, they have often entered the democratic period with the same norms, institutions, and personnel in place as before. Analyzing these historical roots relative to contemporary reform efforts is key to assessing the police that exist today – their institutional organizations, practices, and norms. Indeed, if institutions are sticky, there is no reason to assume that democracy wipes the slate clean. Even concerted institutional effort to do so will face obstacles to reform unless there is a radical break. Therefore, the empirical analysis in this book suggests that most police are likely to maintain the institutions and associated practices and norms that they had prior to the transition – unless there is a radical reform or rupture to the personnel, institutions, and norms that existed previously, in which case there is the possibility (although not a certainty) that the new institution will chart out a new course. While reforms can make a difference at the margins, thoroughly weak, complicit, and/or corrupt forces do not reform so easily, particularly when the individual actors are embedded and incentivized to act in a range of corrupt and/or complicit ways.

Thus, *police reform* for the most extreme cases of police weakness, corruption, and complicity arguably requires clean breaks – with new institutions, a clear set of mandates (distinguishing between the police and the military, as well as the police and the district attorney's office), sanctioning mechanisms for rogue and corrupt agents, and arguably new personnel. Compromising on any of these listed changes increases the likelihood that old practices will persist. It is not simply (or primarily) budgets or size that drive the outcome. For a force committed to policing, one should be focusing on who is in office (new versus old personnel), sanctioning mechanisms, training, and mandates with defined role specification. Otherwise, it is likely that past practices will persist. Cruz (2011b) makes a similar argument about the legacies of state formation (although he theorizes these reforms as part of democratization) and emphasizes that corruption remains endemic in these institutions in much of Central America, a point also made in Part III of this book. The persistence of institutional weakness (what Cruz 2011b: 26 refers to as "authoritarian institutions") and individual corruption (by petty and high-ranking officers) is rampant. Examples abound: "In 2009 and 2010, the Salvadoran and Guatemalan top national police chiefs and antinarcotics deputies were accused of drug trafficking and covering up criminal investigations" (Cruz 2011b: 24). In these types of contexts, radical breaks are important to change the institutional landscape. But new personnel and institutional reform alone are not enough. One ideally aspires to change the orientation and norms that prevail in the institution, as noted next.

Third, because the police are a corporatist institution with a public responsibility, their performance assumes a collective commitment, a certain esprit de corps, to defend a public enterprise. Putting aside for the moment whether that esprit de corps is used for democratic or authoritarian ends, the police force's performance as an *organization* requires its staff to be committed to the ends in question (or sanctioned if they do not). Where the police lack such loyalty, the force becomes a particularly dangerous institution – especially since the state distributes arms to officered men and women (often for little pay) and sends them into the streets to regulate the interactions between and among citizens; such a context primes individuals to join the police for unclear motives and can encourage police officers to shirk their responsibilities and increase their susceptibility to outside influences (including bribes, external alliances, and influence peddling). This is precisely the kind of situation that can breed and reinforce low commitment and high corruption. By contrast, if an institution can draw on and foster a collective commitment/esprit de corps (one where individuals join for a collective cause and are sanctioned when they violate it), there is a greater chance that individual police officers will pursue the public project of defending and upholding public order. This kind of loyalty does not come easily, it is hard to sustain, and yet it is critical to the functioning of the police force as a capable and public-minded state institution.

While difficult to study, esprit de corps unexpectedly emerged as an important mechanism shaping political behavior. We need better analyses of where it comes from and how it is reproduced. The empirical analysis provides some clues for future work. Esprit de corps was most evident when it grew out of a shared nationalist project, a revolution, where nationals took up arms to fight for a different political order.

The Nicaraguan case illustrated this situation in dramatic form. It is not reducible to the classic Tilly argument about war making and state making (although this does resonate with the case). It is that nationalist insurgencies fighting for revolutionary ends forged public-minded security institutions with corporatist commitments – a point that parallels the comparative work by Bermeo (forthcoming) and Levitsky and Way (forthcoming). If the public security institution emerges with this corporatist orientation from revolution or war, it leaves an institutional and normative precedent that can persist in the aftermath of war – as younger police officers replicate the behavior of their superiors, either out of emulation, with self-interested hopes for promotion, or because of sanctions when they violate these norms. The new police can be primed, then, to socialize others through training, as police academies commit to instill that collective spirit if not to the country as a whole or to the institution, at least to the matriculating class.

Future work might therefore consider if there are other pathways to forging and sustaining this kind of corporatist spirit, which is in such low supply in Latin America. Chile and Costa Rica stand out in this regard for developing a more professional corporatist orientation, while other countries have been less likely to do so; these two countries experienced radical breaks in their coercive institutions, yet they did not experience the kind of nationalist socialist revolution that occurred in Nicaragua. Costa Rica experienced a break in its coercive institutions following its 1948 civil war that famously abolished its military (see Yashar 1997), while Chile's highly repressive secret police was replaced in 1997–1998 with a restructured and more restrained police force than during the prior Pinochet dictatorship (Policzer 2009). Nicaragua, Costa Rica, and Chile shed some light on the kinds of institutional breaks and personnel that can foster a professional police force with greater esprit de corps; more comparative analysis would enhance our understanding of this mechanism that moderates between institutions and behavior. A related project would analyze how path dependent those processes are alongside the mechanisms of reproduction (not just fostering esprit de corps but sanctioning those who violate it). As Nicaraguan police commissioner Aminta Granera noted in a 2007 interview, it is hard to know whether new generations of police officers will sustain the commitment upheld by those who fought in the revolutionary war.[4] In light of police repression against Nicaraguan protesters in 2018, this warning is ominous, indeed.

---

[4] Interview with Nicaraguan police commissioner Aminta Granera on March 7, 2007.

Fourth, the police force benefits from a certain institutional and non-partisan *independence* distinct from the kind of political or partisan embeddedness so often found in this institution. While no police force is entirely apolitical, the central question is, on balance, whether the police force is used and seen as an extension or tool of one side (a party, the military, a dictator, etc.) and whether it is able to develop some degree of organizational autonomy from political parties and partisan actors. A baseline of independence logically seems like a sine qua non for the ongoing professionalization and capacity building of the institution. We know that politicians are apt to use the police for political ends (Chevigny 2003a; Wilkinson 2004; González 2014), and we know that the line between military and police mandates are often blurred in Latin America (WOLA 2009). Being tied to a particular political project can compromise the capacity of the police, facilitate its political capture, decrease societal trust and the willingness to follow police orders, and increase opportunities for police officers to engage in actions that advance personal and/or partisan gain. Such unclear institutional boundaries and individual-level actions can compromise the institution and its capacity – especially if partisan behavior becomes an informal institution or norm, occurring repeatedly and creating generalized expectations.

Fifth, the weakness of the police in Latin America has coincided with the increased turn to *alternative forms of security* – a reflection of the contemporary and uneven provision (and distortions) of security in the region. Latin America has witnessed the growth of private security firms (only some of which are officially registered) and calls for community policing (much of which has been cosmetic) (Arias and Ungar 2009; Frühling 2012; González 2014). It has also coincided with explicitly illegal forms of security provision. Paramilitary and vigilante groups have persisted or emerged in Guatemala, El Salvador, and Honduras – at times with ties to the police itself (see Cruz 2011b: 22–24; Bateson: n.d.). They have been notorious in other cases as well – including in Colombia and Brazil, where vigilante groups were used for various ends (social cleansing, conservative agendas, corruption). Extrajudicial groups have been known to pursue justice denied or ignored by the official state system (lynching cases in Guatemala are one such example). The proliferation of private security firms and extrajudicial groups is an outgrowth of weak states, but weak states are further undermined by these alternative forms of order. Thus, there is an endogenous process that emerges as weak public security states give rise to societally generated demands for order, which in turn can further undermine the police as a legitimate and capable institution. Analyzing the parallel forms of security and their implications for order, democracy, and citizenship is an important area for further research.

Sixth, weak states not only invite and take part in illicit political economies; in practice they are also *endogenous* to it. In this regard, formal and informal institutions (and illicit and licit authority) are blurred in significant ways. Not only do formal states that are weak and corrupt provide inviting spaces in which illicit groups and economies can thrive, but these same groups and economies can continue to undermine the legal formalism that states are supposed to represent and advance. As van Schendel and Abraham (2005: 7) state, "Students of illicit practices need to begin by discarding the assumption that there is a clear line between illicitness and laws of states." This is because illicit actors operate not only where the state is weak (as with informal markets) but *also* where the state is complicit. In this sense, the range of gang activity, in particular, and organized crime, in general, is in part a product of the kind of state that is present, which in turns shapes whether illicit institutions compete, undermine, accommodate, and/or complement the state, as hypothesized by Helmke and Levitsky (2004). Hence, we need more attention to the distinctions between the formal, informal, and illicit but also to the relationship *among* them (as discussed in Part I of this book).

Policing Homicidal Ecologies in Post-Civil War Cases and Beyond

This book's observations and stated research agenda about the police, state formation, and homicidal ecologies grew inductively out of careful comparative empirical work analyzing the cases of Guatemala, El Salvador, and Nicaragua (Part III of this book). The three cases were defined by decades of repressive authoritarian rule, civil war, highly unequal societies, and police incompetence and subservience to the military, as well as a common geography. Yet when confronted with the end of their civil wars, they diverged. Nicaragua provided leverage, in particular, for analyzing a country that was able to reform and switch institutional paths – forging a capable police force and security apparatus that subsequently made homicidal ecologies less likely during the third wave of democracy. I briefly revisit this case and then consider how this book's argument travels to other cases.

Nicaragua emerged in the aftermath of civil war with a capable and increasingly esteemed police force (praised throughout the region, even by opposing political forces in Nicaragua). It was able to do so because it instituted a clean institutional break and drew on the revolutionary esprit de corps to forge a new police force. In 1979, after overthrowing the dictator, Nicaragua abolished the weak and much-despised National Guard and forged a completely new police force, composed of insurgent Sandinista fighters with a nationalist (and socialist) orientation. These previous guerilla fighters were ostensibly committed to creating the "new" Nicaragua, and many came to the institution with this ideological orientation. Contemporary debates about greed versus grievance resonate little in this context; the insurgent fight was largely ideological in orientation; it was not about seeking fortune, as the contemporary civil war literature is apt to presume. The police that emerged was a new institution with new personnel and a new mandate – although in its early years it was institutionally much weaker than other state agencies. Therefore, when the Sandinistas lost elections and power a decade later, the police (and military) were largely retained but refashioned to become a more apolitical force, drawing on a nationalist esprit de corps above all else, sustaining their revolutionary ties with local communities, and delimiting their ties to their revolutionary brethren. Nicaragua's police force (and military) sustained a capable set of institutions that distinguished them for many years from others parts of the Nicaraguan state (which has become known for its weak capacity, overall).

This institutional break and orientation long distinguished the Nicaraguan police from its counterparts in Guatemala and El Salvador, where civil war peace accords reformed the police but left in place many of its prior personnel (corrupt, abusive, and poorly trained), an unclear relationship with the military, and a tolerance for incompetence, corruption, and complicity (see Chapters 5–7 in this book; also see the excellent work by Cruz 2011b). These divergent states in Central America created different political environments within which illicit organizations and political economies persisted and subsequently flourished – not only in the 1990s but especially in the 2000s. Part III delineated how the illicit political economy grew in this context and how competition generated violence to control key spaces – especially in El Salvador and Guatemala. This concluding chapter shines a spotlight on how varied patterns of state formation (antecedent conditions) – including historical patterns and reforms versus revolution – have affected the public security apparatus that countries inherited following civil war (and during the third wave of democracy) and, in turn, the homicidal ecologies that emerged.

This analytic focus on police capacity and its ties to state formation has implications beyond the three post-civil war cases. The implication of this book is that countries that had weak and corrupt police forces during their military periods were likely to experience ongoing problems in the democratic period if there were not radical breaks (which was uncommon); problems also remained if the police became the institutional home for demobilized or decommissioned military officers from the prior authoritarian period. Where the police and military remained weak, corrupt, and/or complicit, they provided prime territory for the growth of an illicit economy – in particular sectors governed by urban gangs or drug trafficking organizations prone to competitive violence.

Honduras is a telling example of the pattern of weak state security forces alongside very high homicide rates in the contemporary period. Given its geographic and historical proximity to the three post-civil war cases discussed in Part III, Honduras is discussed next at some length, before the text turns more briefly to address other Latin American cases. Honduras has experienced among the highest homicide rates in the world. While it did not experience its own civil war,[5] it followed a twenty-first century homicidal trajectory similar to that of its Guatemalan and Salvadoran neighbors, in large part because of a historically corrupt police force that allowed for the growth of a significant illicit economy. As in the rest of the northern triangle, a historically corrupt and complicit state (including the military and police) was pivotal to the growth of this homicidal ecology. Honduras's weakly institutionalized state was the historical outcome of what Mahoney (2001) has referred to as aborted liberalism – creating the context for the growth of dictatorship and repression asserted over a fragmented territory.[6] With the transition to democratic rule, these institutions did not fundamentally change. Hondurans did not overhaul their coercive apparatus. The military continued to dominate the security apparatus and engaged in human rights abuses against its own population in the 1980s, and while the military was subordinated to civilians (the executive) in 1998, the military remained a powerful actor, as manifested by its subsequent role in Honduras's 2009 coup. It was moreover reported to have ties with drug trafficking or, at the very least, was incapable of regulating the territories dominated by

---

[5] Honduras did not experience its own late twentieth-century civil war, yet it did play a proxy role for US and Nicaraguan fighters engaged in the Salvadoran and Nicaraguan civil wars.

[6] Also see Gutiérrez Rivera (2013: 37–38).

organized crime (Ungar 2011: 150; Cruz 2011b: 12–13, 17–18; Gutiérrez Rivera 2013: 56–59).[7]

The initial round of democratization also left much of the Honduran police intact, even though 1993 reforms were announced that separated the police from the military, created a ministry of security (that included the police and prisons) and a ministry of defense, and in 1998 created an organic law governing the national police. However, these reforms did not constitute a clean break from the previous coercive institution, since personnel were carried over from the old to the new (composed of an investigative wing; a municipal police force; and a national, preventative police force). Moreover, the police structure suffered from a lack of accountability and coordination, and the unit was weakened by political favoritism and uses.[8] Efforts at holding military and police officers to account for human rights abuses were also minimal – although there were some successful efforts in 1998 (Cruz 2011b: 18). Indeed, police were connected to a dramatic rise in the extrajudicial killings of youth. While numbers varied between the higher estimates provided by the NGO Casa Alianza and the lower estimates offered by a government-formed special unit to investigate children's deaths, both noted police responsibility for some of the deaths. The more conservative government estimates of violent youth deaths and police responsibility are shockingly high – with the government special unit reporting that security officers were connected to 24 percent of the 967 violent deaths that occurred between 1998 and 2004; of these, there were only three convictions (Ungar 2011: 152–154). This record highlights the lack of serious reform and professionalization of the Honduran police forces.

In Honduras, the persistence of a highly corrupt and weak police force, operating with relative impunity and with continuing personnel, created propitious ground for the operation of illicit organizations taking advantage of a booming illicit political economy in the trade and transit of

---

[7] Some argue that the domestic instability and international condemnation (including reduction in foreign aid) following the coup provided an opportunity seized by drug traffickers in the north of the country. The state has since announced crackdowns on gangs in the cities and drug traffickers on the coast (using the police and military). Violence rates soared, however, after the coup, and some see these policies as cover for also targeting the opposition (Bosworth 2011: 86–90). Also see *InSight Crime*. "Honduras." December 6, 2016.

[8] Ungar (2011: chapter 4); Cruz (2011b: 18); Gutiérrez Rivera (2013: 91–94); www.insightcrime.org/honduras-organized-crime-news/honduras. Downloaded on August 11, 2017.

drugs.[9] In turn, the police were used as a political pawn in government efforts to pursue constitutionally questionable policies against its growing and increasingly violent urban gangs. Its police, weak and repressive during the authoritarian period, did not take on democratic policing and, moreover, remained unprofessional, corrupt, and complicit. Indeed, some claim that the Honduran police force is "one of the most corrupt police forces in the region," exhibiting incapacity, corruption, and complicity in street-level and organized criminal activities, including the trade in drugs.[10] This institutional environment made Honduras a welcome space for organized crime. And with the country's location between drug-producing and -consuming countries, it was also a strategic and lucrative draw. During the course of this book's research, gangs and members of organized crime were salient, competitive, and violent actors. Honduras's violence rates grew, and the country currently claims among the highest homicide rates in the world.[11] A kleptocratic operating system infused with criminal elements is how Chayes (2017) describes it.[12]

The parallels extend beyond the Central American isthmus. In this regard, Mexico is another telling case about police and violence. As this

[9] For contemporary reporting on organized crime in Honduras, see insightcrime.org/Honduras-organized-crime-news, which reports on Honduran DTOs (including the Cachiros, Valles, and Atlantic "cartels"), the presence of Mexican DTOs, and related news. The site's Honduras profile notes that an estimated 140–300 tons of cocaine transit through the country, with the increase starting in the early 2000s as Mexican DTOs maneuvered to increase their role in the transit of drugs. Also see Bosworth (2011), who reports on the presence of Mexican DTOs (Sinaloa, the Zetas, and the Gulf Cartel) in Honduras and the main trafficking routes in the country that are by land, air, and sea.

[10] www.insightcrime.org/honduras-organized-crime-news/honduras. Downloaded on August 11, 2017. As I conclude this book, there are some who raise hopes of successful efforts to crack down on corruption in the public security system. (See Tristan Clavel. "As Honduras Tackles Police Corruption, Security Indicators Improve." August 1, 2017. See also www.insightcrime.org/news-briefs/as-honduras-tackles-police-corruption-security-indicators-improve. Downloaded August 11, 2017.)

[11] For a discussion of violence in Honduras and its ties to organized crime and drugs, as well as gangs, see Bosworth (2011); Gutiérrez Rivera (2013); and reporting by *InSight Crime* reports (e.g., December 6, 2016), including www.insightcrime.org/honduras-organized-crime-news/honduras, www.insightcrime.org/honduras-organized-crime-news/atlantic-cartel, www.insightcrime.org/honduras-organized-crime-news/cachiros-profile, and www.insightcrime.org/honduras-organized-crime-news/lvalles (all downloaded on August 7, 2017).

[12] Honduras's homicide rates started to decline in 2017 (although they remain extraordinarily high). Some would argue that recent police reforms have contributed to the decrease, although it is too early to ascertain if homicide rates will continue to fall or if police reforms are the partial cause. See Ronna Rísque. "7 Keys to Understanding Honduras' Declining Homicide Rate." *InSight Crime*. www.insightcrime.org/news/analysis/7-keys-understanding-honduras-declining-homicide-rate/ (accessed on November 25, 2017).

now well-known case also illustrates, the police were not significantly reformed with the transition from one-party rule. The force underwent many reforms, but none that effectively wiped the slate clean, created new rules of accountability, or incorporated new personnel with a commitment to policing (see Davis 2017, Snyder and Durán-Martínez 2009, and Barba-Sánchez 2015). Indeed, we know that the police have historically been complicit in the illicit economy and before the politically mandated crackdown on Mexican DTOs, played a particularly weak role in regulating these sectors – often complicit and protective of DTOs (Snyder and Durán-Martínez 2009; Trejo and Ley 2017). In this way, Mexico also became both a prime geographic locale for the trade and transit of drugs and a politically attractive location for illicit actors that presumed that they could operate with relative impunity.

Brazil could arguably be viewed in a similar way – analyzing the historic origins of policing and the failure to radically reform the institutions and its personnel with the transition to democracy. While Brazil has undertaken innovative (if controversial) twenty-first-century experiments for creating elite forces to crack down on particular neighborhoods, these pilot projects remain exceptions rather than the rule (see Magaloni 2015 for a fascinating evaluation of these efforts in Rio de Janeiro). As Desmond Arias (2006a, 2006b, 2017) has highlighted in his work, the police have historically been either absent or complicit in the illicit world and violence that has unfolded in that country. Other examples abound in the region of weak and corrupt states that make their territories more propitious ground for the growth of illicit economies. The question for this book is not whether policing causes violence. Rather the question is if a weak and corrupt police force makes some places (versus others) more propitious for the growth of illicit economies and organizations.

Stronger (although far from perfect) police in Nicaragua, Costa Rica, and Chile have made these places less attractive as illicit venues than their neighbors. Strikingly, these three cases had either professional (if abusive) forces that were radically reformed during their military periods (Chile) and/or radical breaks following a civil war (Nicaragua and Costa Rica). In all three cases, a more professionalized, apolitical, and corporatist organization emerged, with an esprit de corps lacking for many of their neighbors. And in these cases, not coincidentally, corruption and violence have been lower and illicit economies have been more contained than for their neighbors. The three police forces in question are not above reproach, but compared to the rest of the region, they have developed a reputation for holding their police to account and for governing their territories with greater professional commitment and performance. In turn, illicit economies and homicidal ecologies are less significant (albeit not absent) in these cases than in Guatemala, El Salvador, Honduras, Mexico, and Brazil.

Viewed as a whole, the comparative historical legacies of weak and corrupt police are not limited to civil war countries, although these countries are the ones where the need and the evidence are most apparent. The research agenda coming out of this analysis suggests the need to theorize and analyze the varied types of police that countries inherited and how pivotally they shaped the spaces for illicit organizations and activity. Extremely corrupt and complicit state institutions are likely both to be resistant to reform and to persist if they are not subject to radical/thorough breaks in institutional design, personnel, and orientation. We can confidently infer that a radical break is needed to change behavior, because these institutions not only benefit actors with strong vested interests, but they also have sunk costs and (in)formal rules that entrench behaviors, patterns, and processes. While regime change arguably offers this opportunity, it is one that was largely missed with the third wave of democracy and one in which countries have faced difficulties – e.g., in professionalizing their police forces. Thus, contemporary public security is best analyzed as a historic process of state formation and the resulting police institutions that emerged – whether through neglect, vested interests, moderate reforms, and/or radical breaks. State formation and variations in state capacity/complicity are therefore key to explaining the police forces (and associated law-and-order institutions) responsible for creating (un)viable environments for the growth and persistence of illicit economies. Our theories of state formation would benefit from paying closer attention to the police tasked with sustaining order but also responsible for producing a range of restrictive and permissive homicidal ecologies.

In short, more scholarly attention needs to address whether and how the police overcome patterns that emerged under authoritarian rule – especially if the police have historically been weak, corrupt, abusive, "every man out for himself," and partisan. Turning such a police force around, particularly following civil wars, is no easy task. Where these reforms are most needed, they are arguably the most difficult to pass and to implement. In turn, the failure to do so leaves in place a state that provides welcome ground for illicit organizations and the growth of illicit political economies, all of which undergird the homicidal ecologies that have emerged in parts of Latin America.

TERRITORIES BIG AND SMALL: POLICING NATIONAL BOUNDARIES AND SUBNATIONAL ENCLAVES

Territory has been key to the book's argument about violence. States aim to control specific territories just as some illicit organizations seek to dominate certain subnational territorial enclaves. Territory is thus a core variable of interest since it is not just about location but is also a valued asset. It is critical to an explanation of contemporary violence, because different actors compete to dominate particularly lucrative territorial spaces. Territory, however, manifests in different ways. This conclusion offers the opportunity to revisit what is meant by territory, big and small, from the vantage point of different sets of actors and to restate territoriality's causal relevance to an explanation of homicidal violence in contemporary Latin America.

For state actors, territory has been about governing political geographies defined by national boundaries. The Weberian refrain is that the state should have legitimate monopoly over the use of force in a given territory. Tilly (1985, 1990) has reminded us that states are forged in war to defend/expand borders (in interaction with capitalists seeking to accumulate capital). Thus, we often take as given that the modern state should be able to assert its authority over its national geography. This book reminds us how far afield this assertion can be – even in the contemporary period. State capacity to govern territories has varied dramatically – particularly in the developing world. Mann (1984 and 1993), O'Donnell (1993), Herbst (2000), and Scott (2009) vividly underscore the unevenness of the state's geographic reach and the variation in the state's authority and legitimacy – whether talking about Mann's infrastructural and despotic power; O'Donnell's green, blue, and brown areas; Herbst's discussion of broadcasting power; or Scott's evocation of ungoverned areas such as Zomia. Territoriality, thus, is a variable for states; it is more than just staking out borders. It is about power – physically penetrating given areas, having the ability to govern, and compelling others to follow the rules.[13] The ability of states to do so varies not only based on the levels of development but also by coalitions and domain of action (see Centeno, Kohli, and Yashar 2017). Work on state formation, civil wars, and ethnic politics in Latin America reminds us of how difficult it is for states to assert

---

[13] Citing Robert Sack, Gutiérrez Rivera writes (2013: 27): "Sack defines territoriality as '[T]he attempt by an individual or group to affect, influence, or control people, phenomena, and relationships by delimiting and asserting control over a geographic area. This area will be called the *territory*' (1986, 19, italics original in text)."

control over territories – especially when there is a lack of domestic legitimacy and/or competing sources of power (see Centeno 2003, Yashar 2005, Soifer and Vom Hau 2008, Soifer 2015, Arjona 2016, Davis 2017, and Giraudy and Luna 2017).

States therefore aspire to control "big territory" – to manage national boundaries and regulate the subnational spaces, people, and practice contained therein. This is what one might refer to as the classical understanding of political geography – the one that coincides with internationally recognized state boundaries and aspirations. In the effort to defend national territories, states have classically used armies. In their effort to control internal territories, they have relied on civilian bureaucracies – including but not limited to the police. These are not simply functional state agencies but territorially bounded ones with territorial missions to regulate and order specific precincts. The interplay between national territorial boundaries and subnational territorial governance is at the heart of what modern states are supposed to do. This book has analyzed whether and how the state has been able to pursue public security and order at the subnational level, although one could look at other domains such as developmental and inclusionary challenges, as conceptualized in the opening and concluding chapters of Centeno, Kohli, and Yashar (2017).

Territories and boundaries, however, assume a different meaning when analyzed from the vantage point of the primarily illicit organizational actors operating in Latin America: transnational DTOs and the more localized youth gangs known as *maras*. Transnational DTOs seeking advantageous territory considered other issues, including which territories were most advantageous from the perspective of trade and transit routes. This entailed identifying geographic locations along a transnational route between production and consumption and then zeroing in to identify subnational territories that were least regulated – both by national states and in some cases by international forces (such as the US Drug Enforcement Agency. DEA). Territory from this perspective was less about "national" boundaries and more about territorial enclaves (along a supply chain) that would best serve to move goods north (to the United States) and sometimes east (to Europe). Locating territorial enclaves (or smaller territories), however, was more than simply identifying landing pads and ports. The enclaves also represented the ability to operate relatively freely within those spaces (at the very least to create the alliances to effectively operate in those spaces and to evade being caught). Thus, these territorial enclaves also included a degree of governance: with

DTOs competing to shape, take, or wrestle control from local authorities; to regulate those spaces; or to subvert, evade, and corrupt governing forces that would otherwise seek to constrain them. In Mexico, DTOs were able to do so directly in their home country, in particular regions (especially near the northern borders). In Central America, Mexico, and Colombia, DTOs did so in alliance with local *transportistas* and corrupt state officials and have been particularly prevalent in port towns and borders, along prime transportation routes. For these illicit actors, the goal (thus far) has not been to overthrow the national state as much as to coexist with it – beyond the reach of the national state and/or in complicit alliance with it – with the aim of making money (and probably also of securing status). In this regard, territorial control for DTOs has been a prerequisite for profit. Violence becomes a tool of the illicit political economy to stake out and defend specific spaces and to assert economic hegemony therein.

Urban gangs have not had the same transnational muscle or trade and transit goals of DTOs.[14] Their illicit political economy, and therefore economic livelihood, has often been much more localized. However, like DTOs, they have sought to control territorial enclaves. They have been rooted in particular spaces, seeking to dominate particular neighborhoods, to control particular transportation routes, and, when imprisoned, to control particular blocks of cells. These illicit actors are not lurking in the shadows and not trying to move stealthily from one illicit action to another. Unlike a bank robber, who strikes and moves on, gangs have actively developed an organizational identity rooted in particular spaces and the control of these. Thus, gangs have a clear territorial dimension; although given the scale of that control, it is often discursively minimized as turf. Turf is territory, although it is smaller in scale and arguably more open to competition. Yet similar dynamics appear in these "small territories." Like states and drug trafficking organizations, gangs have set out to dominate clearly defined spaces within which they assert their power, extract taxes, and use violence to defend their domain. As this book comes to a close, reports surfaced that highlight this very point, noting the ways in which Salvadoran gangs have created illicit alliances with local mayors.[15] Arias (2006a, 2006b, 2017) highlights, in fact, how gangs

---

[14] As discussed in Part III, some gangs do have a transnational presence, although their organizational control over events in Central America has arguably been overstated.
[15] See Tristan Clavel. "El Salvador Police Chief Warns of Gang Infiltration in Municipal Elections." *InSight Crime*, November 1, 2017. www.insightcrime.org/ne

along with other forms of criminal governance have depended on territorial control, often in alliance with political and state actors – as depicted in Rio de Janeiro, Brazil; Medellín, Colombia; and Kingston, Jamaica. Gangs clearly differ from the state and organized crime in that they draw on a different demographic – primarily on the young. They have developed a particular set of cultural practices peculiar to marginalized youth, and in Central America they are often scapegoated for all ills. Part III analyzed how youth gangs (*pandillas*) turned into violent gangs (*maras*) in Guatemala and El Salvador; they have become equally violent in Honduras. Yet youth gangs are not destined to evolve this way, as the Nicaraguan case highlighted. Youth gangs are defined by their control of territory, but they do not everywhere engage in high-stakes violence to dominate and defend it.

Space and territory thus are key to an explanation of violence, with licit and illicit organizations (states, DTOs, and gangs) seeking to control specific spaces, including with recourse to homicidal violence. This has some parallels with the older literature on state formation and (civil) wars, insofar as actors might use violence to defend and/or extend their turf and insofar as these actors might develop greater leverage to develop legitimacy among the population – not only through violence but also through the provision of order, protection, and services. The parallels are limited, however. The literature on state formation and civil war is about political claimants ultimately seeking to govern and rule across a wide swath of national territory in exchange for extraction and power. If democratic, they need to develop electoral legitimacy and backing to sustain their authority. The brilliant theoretical analyses about European state formation as criminality brought us vivid images of protection racketeering (Tilly 1985, 1990) and the stationary bandit (Olson 2000), which might lead one to suspect that DTOs and gangs are competing proto-states (paramilitary or otherwise). If one were to analyze the "long term" (as Tilly and Olson do), this might become true; yet this conclusion also miscasts the contemporary goals of DTOs and gangs, which do not (yet) include a commitment to gain political power and govern unilaterally as legitimate political authorities. These illicit organizations do not generally seek to overthrow the state; nor do they generally seek election. Rather, they seek to operate within and around extant states, taking advantage of weak and/or complicit states to carve out territorial enclaves within

ws/brief/el-salvador-police-chief-warns-gang-infiltration-municipal-elections/ (Accessed on November 25, 2017).

(and sometimes across) national territorial boundaries and buying off elected officials rather than running for office.[16] This creates complex and dynamic competition to control spaces within spaces (a dynamic of particular salience in countries with states that cannot assert primary territorial control – over ports, borders, roadways, and even urban neighborhoods). This is a strategic dynamic complicated further when the US DEA is involved. Where boundaries and alliances are clear and stable (even if illicit), then violence is experienced more as threat than as action. However, where territorial competition and uncertainty increase – with licit and illicit actors seeking to shift the status quo – violence has been a lethal weapon to establish territorial hegemony, leading to rising homicide rates (some quite gruesome and visible in nature, as analyzed by Durán-Martínez 2015).

In short, states seek to define and regulate territories. And mapmakers seek to capture that stated political reality. In practice, however, competition to control subnational territorial enclaves within and across these national borders can also be a defining feature of illicit political economies. Many illicit organizations often operate in the shadows and depend on the mobility and elusiveness of their cadre. What is striking about Latin America's contemporary illicit political economy rooted in DTOs and gangs, however, is that they are not operating in the shadows but are highly territorialized. They not only seek to capitalize on specific spaces but plant their flags in those spaces as well – creating homes, infrastructure, and networks, among other features. These might include legitimacy; they might not. But what they clearly include is a competitive drive to control those territories for profit. And with that economic incentive, they have often used violence to stake out their turf, to demand loyalty, to defend it, and to expand their boundaries. Economic competition rooted in specific territorial control has therefore motivated corrupt state officials, DTOs, and *maras* to use violence. It has at times also elicited a national state response to reassert control (see Lessing 2015 and 2017). Organizational territorial competition among illicit actors has thus contributed to a homicidal ecology of deadly proportions. In its wake, the state's weakness becomes endogenous to the illicit world that

---

[16] For a discussion of organized crime and gang efforts to corrupt elected officials, see three 2017 articles about Guatemala, Honduras, and El Salvador: www.insightcrime.org/investigations/electing-criminals-municipal-power-and-organized-crime-in-the-northern-triangle/ (accessed on November 25, 2017).

it initially helped foster. Those who most pay the price are the citizens who are caught in the crossfire.

POLICY IMPLICATIONS AND FUTURE RESEARCH

The scope and intensity of homicidal violence in the Americas has clearly raised serious policy questions. If weak state capacity supports the growth of illicit actors and illicit political economies in specific territories, what are the policy options in the third wave of democracy? If the democratic promise alone has proven incapable of preventing violence, what are the policy options to address the threat of violence in the region – recognizing that policy and law provide the putative parameters for what the police can and should do and the (dis)incentives for illicit actors when engaging in violent crime? This book did not emphasize policy as the primary cause of varied homicide levels across the region. However, policy could and did amplify trends that were already in place. Indeed, countries adopted a range of policy approaches – although not all of them are normatively or politically ideal choices for tackling violence related to drug trafficking and gangs.[17]

First, some cases engaged in *policy avoidance or equivocation*: that is to say, not articulating an explicit or clear policy toward the illicit political economy and the rule of law. No position (or contradictory policy) contributed to a permissive environment for the illicit world. It dovetails with the earlier argument about weak state capacity. Together, weak public security and weak policy indicate that the government has no intention of taking action and that even if it did, state actors might have incentives to continue collusive and corrupt practices that support (rather than undermine) the illicit economy. Almost by definition, this is the most favorable environment for the growth of illicit crime, in particular. If the state turns a blind eye, engages in half-hearted measures, and/or lends a helping hand, then organized crime has incentives to set up shop in these locations and to expand. This was often the context for organized crime in the northern triangle countries

---

[17] While worldwide the criminal businesses with the largest global retail value are reported in descending order of importance as counterfeiting, drug trafficking, illegal logging, human trafficking, and illegal mining, in Latin America the largest-value illicit sectors are drug trafficking, illegal logging, and illegal mining. See *Latin American Weekly Special Report – Crime and Security Trends and Solutions* (SR 2017–02: ISSN 1741–4474), p. 7 (reporting on report by Global Financial Integrity).

of El Salvador, Honduras, and Guatemala. Despite rhetoric to the contrary, policy positions and implementation overall were initially relatively absent, lax, or inconsistent. Whether this was because of weak capacity or complicity is an open question and probably an endogenous dynamic. The point is that no policy, or a half-hearted effort to implement policy, makes for good business for the illicit sector.

Second, some cases pursued a *punitive approach*. This aggressive, often repressive, and authoritarian policy approach includes both the *mano dura* policies targeting gangs in El Salvador, Guatemala, and Honduras and the kingpin strategies targeting DTO leaders in Mexico.[18] In these particular cases, the state has coercively targeted a particular population, the state cracked down on suspected criminals, reports surfaced of state abuses and increased discretionary powers, and the state's repressive approach led illicit organizations to regroup and use further violence (although the mechanisms across these cases varied somewhat). *Mano dura* targeted gangs. Of questionable constitutional legitimacy, it rounded up people based on gang membership (often using associational gatherings and visible markers such as tattoos), threw many of them into jails with overcrowded conditions, and in many cases, courts could not process the cases – many of which were subsequently dismissed for lack of evidence.

These policies have been roundly criticized for their questionable constitutional provisions and were ultimately overturned. But even had they operated within constitutional boundaries, the repressive strategy of rounding up and imprisoning gangs has had a negative spiraling effect. Scholars have noted that these policies made youth gangs even more hierarchical and organized and led many to use fewer visible markers to avoid state monitoring. Prison life exacerbated these trends, and the competition to control particular territories became even more intense. While based on a counterfactual, most would agree that *mano dura* policies did not work, at best, and exacerbated homicide trends, at worse. Homicide rates remained high and in some cases increased. Importantly, it is striking that in El Salvador, Guatemala, and Honduras *mano dura* policies targeted and vilified one particular illicit sector: *maras/* gangs. It did not target the heavy rollers involved in organized crime – often based outside the capital cities – even if these were responsible for many of the most egregious violations. Thus, *mano dura* policies scapegoated gangs as the source of all violence and yet coincided with

---

[18] For Guatemala and El Salvador, See Chapters 5 and 6. For discussions of *mano dura* in Honduras, see Bosworth (2011: 82) and Gutiérrez Rivera (2013: 8–11, 84–85, 113–114).

a lack of real policy positions toward the DTOs operating in the same countries.

Mexico's repressive strategy has also been roundly criticized for its negative impact – although it notably targeted a different sector (DTOs) and focused on leadership ranks (rather than on all associated members). Starting in 2006, the country cracked down on DTOs (rather than gangs). The kingpin strategy literally took out leaders of competing drug organizations. But scholars found that rather than diminishing and containing the violence, in the short term it exacerbated it.[19] Homicide rates increased dramatically in the wake of this violent and targeted approach. Rather than undermining the DTOs, in general, evidence suggests that this policy simply cleared the way for new illicit actors and organizations to fight to fill the vacuum – much as occurred in response to *mano dura*.

Viewed as a generalized approach, a violent and punitive policy can theoretically succeed if it wipes out the illicit organization, but in practice it has had negative short-term consequences. Its implementation has raised constitutional questions about human rights abuses and the disregard of civil liberties. Moreover, the policies have spawned organizational responses that can both strengthen violent capacities in the illicit organizations and generate violent competitive dynamics in their wake. This is the commonly agreed-on narrative for *mano dura* crackdowns against gangs in Guatemala, El Salvador, and Honduras; it is the emerging consensus in Mexico for the kingpin strategy. In all cases, violence spiked in the wake of these repressive policies – policies that might play well at the polls even if they do not produce the intended goals. This approach has, in practice, been based on the *authoritarian threat*, where coercive policies that restrict civil liberties at large are used to shut down illicit actors and close off avenues for independent action.

A third policy approach entails direct *negotiations* between organizations that are identified as parties to the violence; this requires not only an agreed-upon understanding between "opposing sides" but also the organizations' ability to dictate what their members do. This approach can assume both a formal agreement and informal arrangements. El Salvador provides a powerful example of a short-lived gang truce (brokered in 2012 between the gangs and some members of the state and civil society), during which time homicide rates plummeted. When the formal truce

---

[19] See 2015 *Journal of Conflict Resolution* special volume for a discussion of Mexico's kingpin strategy and its negative consequences, although Signoret (2016) questions whether the impact diminishes over time.

broke down, homicides skyrocketed once again, as discussed in Chapter 6. Efforts to revive a truce in 2016–2017 were under discussion (MS-13 and Barrio 18 were reported to have agreed to a unilateral truce in March 2016), but the Salvadoran government subsequently adopted a punitive approach in 2016, declaring a state of exception in the most violent municipalities, deploying more police and military, creating elite police units with greater powers to detain and search and seize, and announcing major prison reform.[20] Strikingly, there is speculation that the Salvadoran government has complemented these repressive measures with "clandestine pacts" with the gangs.[21] Although this is a confusing policy space, it is striking that homicide rates have not declined significantly when repressive policies were pursued; rather, the earlier negotiated gang truce had the most visible impact in containing violent competition and associated homicide rates.

In addition to formal truces, there are also examples of informal agreements of mutual toleration – perhaps with independent domains of governance and/or shared revenues. Such an approach combines turning a blind eye toward illicit actors, with likely collusion and complicity on the part of local powerbrokers; it might include the creation of illicit-actor cartels and/or state-DTO collusion. These informal agreements have arguably occurred across history (e.g., in Mexico during PRI rule and arguably in Colombia's response to the DTOs in the aftermath of the Medellín and Cali cartels, among other cases). They echo Gambetta's (1996) classic insight about the Italian mafia and state: that where the state and illicit actors have arrived at an agreement to contain competition, violence can be curtailed (at least in the short term). In this set of scenarios, the "policy" response (formal and informal) is not about undermining the illicit actors (or the illicit political economy) as much as

---

[20] See "El Salvador's Sánchez Cerén Ratchets Up Pressure on Gangs," in Caribbean & Central America Report, *LatinNews* (April 2016), and "El Salvador: Special Force Deployed to Combat Maras," in Caribbean & Central America Report, *LatinNews* (May 2016). Also see Héctor Silva Ávalos, "El Salvador Violence Rising Despite 'Extraordinary' Anti-Gang Measures. *InSight Crime*. October 3, 2017. Accessed on November 25, 2017. www.insightcrime.org/news/analysis/violence-el-salvador-rise-despite-extraordinary-anti-gang-measures/. In writing about the "extraordinary" measures approved in 2016 by the Salvadoran congress, Silva writes: "These measures included extended detention periods, the use of the army in public security activities, increased flexibility for the execution of searches and seizures, and the tightening of administrative measures in prisons.

[21] Héctor Silva Ávalos, "El Salvador Violence Rising Despite 'Extraordinary' Anti-Gang Measures." *InSight Crime*. October 3, 2017.

arriving at a modus vivendi to contain the violence that both sides can always threaten to unleash. While the short-term consequences can be salutary, the failure to address the underlying competitive drive to profit and control territories means that homicidal violence remains a tool at the actors' disposal, and other forms of violence might be in operation just below the surface.

A fourth policy approach – arguably the most democratic and sustainable – is a combination of *rule-of-law accountability and social prevention and rehabilitation*. This approach presumes that those who engage in criminal acts (within governing institutions as well as on the street) need to be held accountable through legal, constitutional measures. Rather than unleash the repressive policies outlined in the second approach, this fourth response pursues the rule of law: where crimes are committed, criminals should be held responsible (within constitutional limits), homicide clearance rates should be high, and court responses should be swift and constitutional. Moreover, governments should hold state agencies to account if they violate the law, replacing a history of impunity with accountability (including purging those who transgress the law), professionalizing law-and-order institutions, and creating the complementary institutions necessary to pursue these ends. Nicaragua went the furthest in this regard, among the cases studied in this book, although Guatemala has seen some notable advances with the creation of the joint UN-Guatemalan Commission (CICIG, Comisión Internacional Contra la Impunidad en Guatemala), designed, according to their stated mandate, as an independent body to support state agencies as they address crimes committed by illegal and clandestine security forces. CICIG works with the public prosecutor's office (MP), the national civil police (PNC), and other state institutions to investigate and disband such illegal forces.[22] While Guatemala has far to go, this institution has made some notable moves to contain corruption and high-level political and security-related crime. And notably, although not singlehandedly, with the increased visibility of these efforts, homicide levels have moved in a downward direction.

However, this rule-of-law approach has arguably been most successful where it has been combined with crime prevention, social policy, and rehabilitation, targeting those at risk of criminal behavior and finding alternatives for them. The commitment to effective rule of law combined

---

[22] See CICIG website, www.cicig.org/index.php?page=mandate (accessed on August 21, 2017).

with prevention was nominally noted by all cases discussed in Part III of this book but was only seriously pursued in Nicaragua. The Nicaraguan police made a concerted and sustained effort early on to crack down on illicit activity in drug trafficking, set out to hold the police to account, and reached out to at-risk urban youth with a preventative and rehabilitative approach, as discussed in Chapter 7. Being embedded in the community, engaged in social activities, and focused on prevention and access were some of the defining features of Nicaragua's police policy from the 1980s on. This policy has been praised by many, especially given that it has coexisted with comparatively low homicide rates that declined over the course of this study. The promise of addressing the root causes that lead youth to join and leave gangs motivates this approach. It is a community response that is often touted in other places. That said, there is still more to learn: We would benefit from policy analysis comparing Nicaragua's design and implementation relative to social programs in other countries. And while social prevention seems to have been effective, more attention to its terms and implementation is needed. This approach has policy and normative implications but also theoretical ones about how policy choices, institutional design, and implementation shape human behavior.

This fourth approach holds forth the democratic promise – where the democratic rule of law displaces illicit actors, the police and courts work together, and there is social policy to protect and defend civil liberties. Perhaps then it would be more precise to say that this is the social democratic promise – to use social policy alongside law and order to redress the underlying conditions that lead some people to join illicit organizations, engage in intense competition, and resort to violence. Even in El Salvador, where the gangs are commonly portrayed as among the most violent and intractable, a *mara* leader noted the importance of social policy: Carlos Lechuga Mojica, alias "El Viejo Lin," a Salvadoran leader from Barrio 18, indicated in an interview with *InSight Crime* that in the absence of addressing the underlying social problems, gangs will continue to recruit and engage in violence: "We believe that the problem here is social exclusion, discrimination, lack of education, lack of employment and unequal treatment by the law. We think that if you resolve these problems, the violence between gangs will end."[23] While this interview is far from representative, it is a powerful reminder that many of these illicit actors

---

[23] Stephen Dudley. "Barrio 18 Leader 'Viejo Lin' on El Salvador Gang Truce," *InSight Crime*, Friday, June 7, 2013, www.insightcrime.org/investigations/barrio-18-leader-viejo-lin-on-el-salvador-gang-truce (accessed on August 21, 2017).

are not only thriving in a context of weak states but also marginalized in a polity that has failed to provide basic and sustained social policies. Thus, law and order combined with social prevention and rehabilitation provides the democratic promise that has been so elusive in many parts of the region.

These various policy scenarios are *ideal types*. They are not all normatively appealing. In practice, they are not mutually exclusive. No country pursues one alone. No state is so homogeneous that its policy, implementation, and individual actions are entirely coherent. Policies can evolve over time; they can be incoherently rolled out based on state capacity and partisan preferences. Striking the right balance, therefore, is the ongoing task for criminal justice, especially since the national position is consequential for setting the tone that the police are supposed to follow, and the context within which illicit actors will try to maneuver. In general, the first two approaches (no policy or repression) have generated greater competition and violence for territorial control, while the latter two (truces and law and order combined with preventative social policy) seem to diminish incentives for doing so (at least in the short term). Arguably, it is only the fourth approach that is focused on long-term consequences, although its impact depends on how it is implemented and systematic studies are needed – all the more so as organizational actors hunker down to carve out their own territorial enclaves on the streets, in trade and transit routes, and in prisons. Ultimately, policy pronouncements mean little if they are not implemented across the territory, especially if competing organizational actors are vying to control the same territorial spaces. Thus, policy cannot determine the outcome absent thinking systematically about both state capacity and its reach across the territory.

CONCLUSION

The state remains aspirational in much of Latin America, if we consider the classic image of the Hobbesian or Weberian state that possesses the legitimate monopoly over the use of force in a given territory. In places like Guatemala, El Salvador, Honduras, Mexico, and Brazil, it is not a defining feature – particularly in those regions where subnational enclaves have been dominated by illicit organizations and there is violent competition to control those spaces. These are the places with homicidal ecologies that have given rise to high homicide rates during the third wave of democracy.

The intensity and horror of this violence affects the lived experiences of millions of citizens living in high-homicide regions: those living in places where the police do not protect them (and sometimes harm them); those obliged to live in neighborhoods and ride on public buses where gangs regularly extort with the threat of armed violence; those residing in borderlands where DTOs in alliance with *transportistas* and others are wielding weapons to assert their hegemony over lucrative spaces to produce and transport drugs. Most people do not elect to live in such circumstances. They are thrust into high-violence and high-risk contexts – hoping for life over death, yet uncertain if the police can or will protect them in the face of the violence in their streets. This is the travesty of citizenship in much of Latin America and the tragedy of state formation in the region: the failure of states to secure and defend public spaces. No citizen should have to endure such violence. Freedom from harm should not be aspirational; it should be a realized right.

In much of Latin America, and particularly in the northern triangle of Central America, therefore, citizens confront a practical and political challenge. To achieve citizenship in practice (not just in form), one needs a state that can provide the basic rights that states are supposed to provide. Meaningful citizenship requires the presence of a capable, accountable, and committed state. This includes the Marshallian courts, legislatures, and welfare states designed to protect civil, political, and social rights. But it also includes the Hobbesian/Weberian security institutions designed to provide order and freedom from violence. This is not a democratization issue alone. Rather, it is also a question of building up a state that can provide for security alongside civil, political, social rights; of building a state where the citizens can trust, at a minimum, that the police and military are protecting and providing for them instead of preying on them. Absent these kinds of states, citizenship is not just low (as O'Donnell 1993 noted), but it might also be foreclosed. Many Latin American states have largely failed to achieve this kind of state, exhibiting complicity (and at times incompetence) with the informal and illicit patterns that have emerged.

Citizens in the third wave of democracy therefore face a practical and political dilemma: how to promote citizen security without empowering the very forces (inside and outside the state) that have abused the rule of law in the past. The historic record shows how critically important and difficult it is to effect successful state reform (especially in the courts and security forces). Nicaragua offered one striking counterexample that included radical reforms and professionalization of the police and associated law-and-order institutions, accountability for violators both within the state and in the streets, preventative and rehabilitative policies that aim to address the causes and not just the consequences of criminality, and an esprit de corps committed to national governance and human dignity. It remains an open question whether the Nicaraguan police will be able to sustain this institutional capacity, commitment, and performance – especially given longstanding challenges and weaknesses in other parts of the state as well as unanticipated and alarming political violence as this book goes to press. So too it remains an open question whether there are other pathways to achieve a professional and legitimate police force. Given the stakes, it is essential to continue analyzing Latin America's law-and-order institutions, especially the circumstances under which they uphold democratic principles and protect citizens against violence and abuse. This is a theoretical call. It is also a normative imperative.

Bibliography

INTERVIEWS

Titles listed refer to their title at the time of the interview.

Guatemala City, Guatemala

Tani Adams, Centro de Investigaciones Regionales de Mesoamérica, August 5, 2005.

Gabriel Aguilera Peralta, Organization of American States (OAS), August 1, 2005, and July 28, 2006.

Maya Alarcón, Fundación Myrna Mack, August 3, 2006.

Anonymous, taxi driver, July 21, 2006.

Anonymous, US embassy source, August 4, 2006.

Clara Arenas, AVANCSO, August 3, 3005.

Bernardo Arévalo, War Torn Societies Project, August 4, 2010.

Lucrecia de Becker, Madres Angustiadas, July 2006.

Demetrio Cojti, Consultant at OAS, August 3, 2005.

Gabriela Contreras, FOSS and Asociación para el Estudio y Promoción de la Seguridad en Democracia (SEDEM), July 20, 2006.

Carlos Fernando González, Instancia de Monitoreo y Apoyo a la Seguridad Pública (IMASP), July 2006.

Celvin Galindo, former Fiscal Jefe de la Fiscalía and special prosecutor for organized crime, July 2006.

Víctor Gálvez, union leader of Frente de Resistencia y Lucha por los Recursos Naturales y los Derechos de los Pueblos (FRENA), July 2006.

Verónica Godoy, IMASP, July 2006.

Iduvina Hernández, director and cofounder, SEDEM, August 3, 2005, and July 2006.

Francisco Jiménez, Interpeace organization, August 1, 2006.
Claudia Paz y Paz, founder of Instituto de Estudios Comparados en Ciencias Penales de Guatemala (Institute for Comparative Criminal Studies of Guatemala, ICCPG), August 2, 2005.
René Poitevin, sociologist, August 1, 2005.
Luis Ramírez, ICCPG.
Héctor Rosada Granados, sociologist, August 4, 2005.
Claudia Samayoa, based at SEDEM, August 3, 2005, and July 2006.
Alex Segovia, Salvadoran economist, August 1, 2005.
Arturo Taracena, historian, August 5, 2005.
Karin Wagner, Asociación de Investigación y Estudios Sociales (ASIES), August 3, 2006.

San Salvador, El Salvador
(unless otherwise noted, all July and August 2008 interviews in San Salvador, El Salvador, were conducted by Vinay Jawahar for this project)

Jeanette Aguilar, director, Instituto Universitario de Opinión Pública, Universidad Centroamericana (UCA), August 13, 2008.
Juan Daniel Alemán, ex-president, Comisión de Estudios Legales, Fundación Salvadoreña para el Desarrollo Económico y Social (FUSADES), August 27, 2008.
Edgardo Amaya, formerly with Fundación de Estudios para la Aplicación del Derecho (FESPAD), Asesor del Despacho de la Procuraduría para la Defensa de los Derechos Humanos, August 15, 2008.
Katherine Andrade Eekhoff, August 8, 2005.
Anonymous, employee of USAID, August 2008.
Oscar Bonilla, president, Consejo Nacional de Seguridad Pública, August 20, 2008.
Carlos Briones, Facultad Latinoamericana de Ciencias Sociales (FLACSO), August 9, 2005.
Marlon Carranza, coordinator, Instituto Universitario de Opinión Pública, UCA, August 22, 2008.
Ricardo Córdova, FUNDAUNGO, August 9, 2005.
Benjamín Cuéllar, director, Instituto de Derechos Humanos de la UCA, August 27, 2008.
Carlos Dada, co-publisher of *El Faro*, August 8, 2008.
Héctor Dada, deputy of Cambio Democrático (CDU), August 9, 2005.

David Holliday, program officer, Open Society Institute (Washington, DC), July 30, 2008.
Benito Lara, deputy, Frente Farabundo Martí para la Liberación Nacional (FMLN) August 19, 2008.
Carlos López, coordinator, Centro de Monitoreo de la Violencia, August 11, 2008.
Aída Luz Santos Mejía de Escobar, judge, Juzgado Primero de Ejecución de Medidas al Menor de San Salvador, August 14, 2008.
David Morales, coordinator, Seguridad Ciudadana y Justicia Penal, Fundación de Estudios para la Aplicación de Derecho, August 26, 2008.
William Pleitez, United Nations Development Programme (UNDP), August 8, 2005.
Beat Rohr, UNDP resident coordinator and representative, August 8, 2005.
Roberto Rubio, FLACSO, August 9, 2005.
Jorge Simán, co-publisher of *El Faro*, August 8, 2008.

Managua, Nicaragua

Clara Avilés, Nicaragua Nuestra, March 2007.
Javiera Blanco, undersecretary of carabineros, Chilean Ministry of Defense, May 14, 2007. (Interview in Santiago, Chile about Nicaraguan and Chilean police)
Joaquín Cuadra, general, March 9, 2007.
Edwin Cordero, first commissioner and director general of the national police (2001–2006), March 3, 2007.
Ivette Espino, Centro de Prevención de la Violencia (CEPREV), March 7, 2007.
Aminta Granera, chief of the national police, March 7, 2007.
Moíses Omar Halleslevens, general, chief of counterintelligence, 1980–1997; chief of army, 2005–2010; vice-president, 2012–2017; interview March 13, 2007.
Antonio Lacayo, minister of the presidency/chief of staff, 1990–1995, March 10, 2007.
Claudia Paniagua, Fundación Nicaragua Nuestra, March 7, 2007.
José Luis Rocha, professor at Universidad Centroamericana, March 3, 2007.
Marvin Sotelo, March 7, 2007.

NEWSPAPER VIOLENCE DATABASE

Following are newspapers consulted for the newspaper violence database. Many are also cited in footnotes throughout this book.

Newspapers consulted for all violence-related articles:
- *La Prensa* (2000, 2005, 2010). Nicaragua.
- *La Prensa Gráfica* (2000, 2005, 2010). El Salvador.
- *Prensa Libre* (2000, 2005, 2010). Guatemala.

Memos concerning violence-related newspaper articles:
- Yanilda González wrote memos summarizing general articles for a given year and evaluating the database.
- Bethany Park wrote memos summarizing general articles for a - given year and evaluating the database.

Coding of violence-related newspaper articles:
- Coordinated by Yanilda González and Bethany Park.
- Coding by
  - Sergio Gálaz García
  - Yanilda González
  - Marcus Johnson
  - Nathalie Kitroeff
  - Bethany Park
  - Alexander Slaski

See Chapter 5 and 6 Appendices, which include descriptive statistics and a discussion of the newspaper violence database data for Guatemala and El Salvador, respectively.

BOOKS, ARTICLES, ORIGINAL DOCUMENTS

Aguilar, Jeannette. 2012. "Coyuntura actual de las pandillas. Cátedra de Realidad Nacional. Discurso." *IUDOP (Instituto Universitario de Opinión Pública). Revista de Estudios Centroamericanos (ECA)* 731 (67): 481–487.

2004. "La mano dura y las políticas de seguridad." *Estudios Centroamericanos (ECA)* 667: 439–449 (Elecciones y Medios de Comunicación: No. Monográfico 441–443).

Anderson, Elijah. 1999. *Code of the Street: Decency, Violence, and the Moral Life of the Inner City*. New York, NY: W.W. Norton.

Andreas, Peter. 2013. *Smuggler Nation: How Illicit Trade Made America*. Oxford: Oxford University Press.

2011. "Illicit Globalization: Myths, Misconceptions, and Historical Lessons." *Political Science Quarterly* 126 (3): 641–652.

2004. "Illicit International Political Economy: The Clandestine Side of Globalization." *Review of International Political Economy* 11 (3): 642–652.

Arana, Ana. "How Street Gangs Took Central America." *Foreign Affairs* 84 (3): 98–110.
Arendt, Hannah. 1969. "Reflections on Violence." *Journal of International Affairs* 23 (1): 1–35.
Arévalo de León, Bernardo. 2001. "Transición democrática y reconversión militar en Guatemala: limitaciones y retos de un proceso inconcluso." Unpublished paper.
Arias, Enrique Desmond. 2017. *Criminal Enterprises and Governance in Latin America and the Caribbean.* Cambridge: Cambridge University Press.
  2011. "State Power and Central American *Maras*: A Cross-National Comparison." In Thomas Bruneau, Lucía Dammert, and Elizabeth Skinner, eds., *Maras: Gang Violence and Security in Central America.* Austin, TX: University of Texas Press, pp. 123–136.
  2006a. "The Dynamics of Criminal Governance: Networks and Social Order in Rio de Janeiro." *Journal of Latin American Studies* 38: 293–325.
  2006b. *Drugs and Democracy in Rio de Janeiro: Trafficking, Social Networks, and Public Security.* Chapel Hill, NC: University of North Carolina Press.
Arias, Enrique Desmond and Daniel M. Goldstein. 2010. "Violent Pluralism: Understanding the New Democracies in Latin America." In Enrique Desmond Arias and Daniel M. Goldstein, eds., *Violent Democracies in Latin America.* Durham, NC: Duke University Press, pp. 1–34.
Arias, Enrique Desmond and Mark Ungar. 2009. "Community Policing and Policy Implementation: A Four City Study of Police Reform in Brazil and Honduras." *Comparative Politics* 41 (4): 409–430.
Arias Foundation. 2005. *Legislaciones centroamericanas: análisis comparativo.* San Jose: Fundación Arias para la Paz y el Progreso Humano.
Arjona, Ana. 2016. *Rebelocracy: Social Order in the Colombian Civil War.* Cambridge: Cambridge University Press.
Arnson, Cynthia J. and Adam Drolet. 2011. "The Administration of President Mauricio Funes: A One-Year Assessment." Washington, DC: Woodrow Wilson International Center for Scholars: Latin America.
Arriaga, Irma and Lorena Godoy. 2000. "Prevention or Repression? The False Dilemma of Citizen Security." *CEPAL Review* 70: 111–136.
Astorga, Luis. 1999. "Cocaine in Mexico." In Paul Gootenberg, ed., *Cocaine: Global Histories.* New York, NY: Routledge Press, pp. 183–191.
Auyero, Javier. 2007. *Routine Politics and Violence in Argentina.* Cambridge: Cambridge University Press.
  2006. "The Political Makings of the 2001 Lootings in Argentina." *Journal of Latin American Studies* 38: 241–265.
Bailey, John and Lucía Dammert, eds. 2005. *Public Security and Police Reform in the Americas.* Pittsburgh, PA: University of Pittsburgh Press.
Barba-Sánchez, Daniela. 2015. "Transitional Impunity after One-Part Rule." Paper 591 for Department of Politics, Princeton University.
Bates, Robert. 2001. *Prosperity & Violence: The Political Economy of Development.* New York, NY: Norton.
Bateson, Regina. n.d. "Security from Below." Book manuscript. Cambridge, MA, Massachusetts Institute of Technology.

Becker, Gary S. 1974. "Crime and Punishment: An Economic Approach." In Gary S. Becker and William M. Landes, eds., *Essays in the Economics of Crime and Punishment*. New York, NY: National Bureau of Economic Research, pp. 1–54.
Beittel, June S. 2017. "Mexico: Organized Crime and Drug Trafficking Organizations." *Congressional Research Service*. https://fas.org/sgp/crs/row/R41576.pdf, accessed June 16, 2017.
Benson, Peter, Edward F Fischer, and Kedron Thomas. 2008. "Resocializing Suffering Neoliberalism, Accusation, and the Sociopolitical Context of Guatemala's New Violence." *Latin American Perspectives* 35 (5): 38–58.
Berman, Sheri. 1997. "Civil Society and the Collapse of the Weimar Republic." *World Politics* 49 (3): 401–429.
Bermeo, Nancy. Forthcoming. "Democracy after War." Manuscript.
Bobea, Lilian 2010. "Organized Violence, Disorganized State." In Enrique Desmond Arias and Daniel M. Goldstein, eds., *Violent Democracies in Latin America*. Durham, NC: Duke University Press, pp. 161–200.
Bohm, R. M. 1982. "Radical Criminology: An Explication." *Criminology* 19: 565–589.
Booth, John A. and Walker, T. W. 1993. *Understanding Central America*. Boulder, CO: Westview.
Bosworth, James. 2011. "Honduras: Organized Crime Gained Amid Political Crisis." In Cynthia J. Arnson and Eric L. Olson, eds., *Organized Crime in Central America: The Northern Triangle*. Woodrow Wilson Center Reports on the Americas #29. Washington, DC: Woodrow Wilson Center Press, pp. 62–103.
Bourguignon, François. 1998. *"Crime as a Social Cost of Poverty and Inequality: A Review Focusing on Developing Countries."* Washington, DC: World Bank. Mimeographed.
Brands, Hal. 2010. "Crime, Violence and the Crisis in Guatemala: A Case Study in the Erosion of the State," Strategic Studies Institute.
Brenneman, Robert. 2011. *Homies and Hermanos: God and Gangs in Central America*. New York, NY: Oxford University Press.
Brinks, Daniel M. 2003. "Informal Institutions and the Rule of Law: The Judicial Response to State Killings in Buenos Aires and Sao Paulo in the 1990s." *Comparative Politics* 36 (2): 1–19.
Bruneau, Thomas. 2011. "Introduction." In Thomas Bruneau, Lucía Dammert, and Elizabeth Skinner, eds., *Maras: Gang Violence and Security in Central America*. Austin, TX: University of Texas Press, pp.1–19.
Bruneau, Thomas, Lucía Dammert, and Elizabeth Skinner, eds., 2011. *Maras: Gang Violence and Security in Central America*. Austin, TX: University of Texas Press.
Caldeira, Teresa P. R., 2000. *City of Walls: Crime, Segregation, and Citizenship in São Paulo*. Berkeley, CA: University of California.
Caldeira, Teresa P. R. and James Holston. 1999. "Democracy and Violence in Brazil." *Comparative Studies in Society and History* 41(4): 691–729.
Calderón, Gabriela, Gustavo Robles, Alberto Díaz-Cayeros, and Beatriz Magaloni. 2015. "The Beheading of Criminal Organizations and

the Dynamics of Violence in Mexico." *Journal of Conflict Resolution* December 59: 1455–1485.

Call, Charles T. 2007. "The Mugging of a Success Story: Justice and Security Sector Reform in El Salvador." In Charles T. Call, ed., *Constructing Justice and Security After the War*. Washington, DC: United States Institute of Peace.

2003. "Democratisation, War and State-Building: Constructing the Rule of Law in El Salvador." *Journal of Latin American Studies* 35 (4) (November), pp. 827–862.

2000. "Sustainable Development in Central America: The Challenges of Violence, Injustice and Insecurity." CA 2020: Working Paper #8, Hamburg: Institut für Iberoamerika-Kunde.

Call, Charles T. and William Stanley. 2001. "Protecting the People: Public Security Choices after the Civil Wars." *Global Governance* 7 (2) (April–June): 151–172.

Call, Chuck. 1998. *Police Reform, Human Rights and Democratization in Post-Conflict Settings: Lessons from El Salvador*. Inter-American Development Bank

Canache, Damarys and Michael E. Allison. 2005. "Perceptions of Political Corruption in Latin American Democracies." *Latin American Politics & Society* 47 (3): 91–111.

Carcach, Carlos Alberto. 2008. *El Salvador: Mapa de violencia y su referencia histórica*. San Salvador, El Salvador: Centro de Monitoreo y Evaluacíon de al Violencia desde la Perspectiva Ciudadana, with Open Society and Catholic Relief Services.

Carmack, Robert, ed. 1988. *Harvest of Violence: The Maya Indians and the Guatemalan Crisis*. Norman, OK: University of Oklahoma Press.

Centeno, Miguel. 2003. *Blood and Debt: War and the Nation-State in Latin America*. University Park, PA: Penn State University Press.

Centeno, Miguel and Alejandro Portes. 2006. "The Informal Economy in the Shadow of the State." In P. Fernández-Kelly and J. Shefner, eds., *Out of the Shadows: Political Action and the Informal Economy in Latin America*. University Park, PA: Pennsylvania State University Press, pp. 25–48.

Centeno, Miguel, Atul Kohli, and Deborah J. Yashar, eds., with Dinsha Mistree. 2017. *States in the Developing World*. Cambridge University Press.

Centro de Estudios Guatemala. Reported March 1, 2006. Printed online at http://c.net.gt/ceg/diario/2006/mar2006/dimso301.html.

Chambliss, William J. 1976. "The State and Criminal Law." In W. J. Chambliss and M. Mankoff, eds., *Whose Law? What Order?* New York, NY: Wiley.

Chandra, Kanchan. 2006. "What Is Ethnic Identity and Does It Matter?" *Annual Review of Political Science* 9, pp. 397–424.

2004. *Why Ethnic Parties Succeed: Patronage and Ethnic Headcounts in India*. Cambridge Studies in Comparative Politics. Cambridge: Cambridge University Press.

Chayes, Sarah. 2017. *When Corruption Is the Operating System: The Case of Honduras*. Washington, DC: Carnegie Endowment for International Peace.

Chevigny. Paul. 2003a. "The Populism of Fear: Policies of Crime in the Americas." *Punishment & Society* 5 (1): 177–196.
  2003b. "Control of Police Misconduct in the Americas." In Hugo Frühling and Joseph S. Tulchin, eds., *Crime and Violence in Latin America: Citizen Security, Democracy, and the State*. Baltimore, MD: Johns Hopkins University Press.
  1995 *Edge of the Knife: Police Violence in the Americas*. New York, NY: W.W. Norton.
Chinchilla Miranda, Laura. 2003. Chapter 2: "Public Security in Central America." In John Bailey., ed., *Public Security in the Americas: New Challenges in the South-North Dialog*. Occasional Paper series, Political Database of the Americas at Georgetown University, Center for Latin American Studies. http://pdba.georgetown.edu/Pubsecurity/ch2.pdf.
Cóbar, Amaya and Palmieri, G. F. 2000. "Debilidad institucional, impunidad y violencia." In *PNUD violencia en una sociedad en transición: ensayos*. San Salvador: PNUD, pp. 75–114.
Collier, Paul and Anke Hoeffler. 2004. "Greed and Grievance in Civil War." *Oxford Economic Papers* 56 (4): pp. 563–595.
Comaroff, Jean and John L. Comaroff. 2006a. "Figuring Crime: Quantifacts and the Production of the Un/Real." *Public Culture* 81 (1): 209–246.
Comaroff, Jean and John L. Comaroff, eds., 2006b. *Law and Disorder in the Postcolony*. Chicago, IL: University of Chicago Press.
Cordero Ardila, Edwin, Hamyn Gurdián Alfaro, and Carlos Emilio López Hurtado. 2006. *Alcanzando un sueño: modelo de prevención social de la policía*. Managua: Ediciones Cripto.
Córdova Macías, Ricardo, José Miguel Cruz, and Mitchell Seligson. 2013. *Cultura política de la democracia en El Salvador y en las Américas, 2012: hacia la igualdad de oportunidades*. San Salvador: FUNDAUNGO, Vanderbilt University, USAID.
Costa, Gino. 1999. *La Policía Nacional Civil de El Salvador (1990–1997)*. San Salvador: UCA Editores.
Cruz, Consuelo. 2005. *Political Culture and Institutional Development in Costa Rica and Nicaragua: World Making in the Tropics*. Cambridge: Cambridge University Press.
Cruz, José Miguel. 2012a. "Drug Wars in the Americas: Looking Back and Thinking Ahead." Presentation at Watson Institute Conference, Drug Wars in the Americas, Brown University, April 12–13.
  2012b. "The Transformation of Street Gangs in Central America." *ReVista: Harvard Review of Latin America* (Winter 2012). http://revista.drclas.harvard.edu/publications/revistaonline/winter-2012/transformation-street-gangs-central-america.
  2011a. "Government Responses and the Dark Side of Gang Suppression in Central America. In Thomas Bruneau, Lucía Dammert, and Elizabeth Skinner, eds., *Maras: Gang Violence and Security in Central America*. Austin, TX: University of Texas Press, pp. 137-157.

2011b. "Criminal Violence and Democratization in Central America: The Survival of the Violent State." *Latin American Politics and Society* 53 (4) (Winter): 1–33.
  2010. "Democratization under Assault: Criminal Violence in Post-Transition Central America." Vanderbilt University. PhD dissertation.
  1999. "Maras o pandillas juveniles: los mitos sobre su formación e integración." In O. Martínez Peñate (coord.) *El Salvador. Sociología general. Realidad nacional de fin de siglo y principio de milenio*. San Salvador: Editorial Nuevo Enfoque.
Cruz, José Miguel and María Beltrán. 2000. *Las armas de fuego en El Salvador: situación e impacto sobre la violencia*. San Salvador: UCA
Cuadra Lacayo, Joaquín. 2005. "General Joaquín Cuadra Lacayo: The Lessons of Nicaragua That Can Be Applied to Iraq and Afghanistan." Posted on History News Network, http://hnnn.us/roudup/entries/10663.html, accessed on March 6, 2007.
Cuevas, F. and G. Demombynes. 2009. "Drug Trafficking, Civil War, and Drivers of Crime in Central America." Unpublished paper.
Dammert, Lucía. 2014. *Fear and Crime in Latin America: Redefining State-Society Relations* (Routledge Studies in Latin American Politics). New York, NY: Routledge.
  2006. "From Public Security to Citizen Security in Chile." In John Bailey and Lucía Dammert, eds., *Public Security and Police Reform in the Americas*. Pittsburgh, PA: Pittsburgh University Press.
Davis, Diane. 2017. "Violence, Fragmented Sovereignty, and Declining State Capacity: Rethinking the Legacies of Developmental Statism in Mexico." In Miguel A. Centeno, Atul Kohli, and Deborah J. Yashar, eds., *States in the Developing World*. Cambridge: Cambridge University Press.
  2006a. "The Age of Insecurity: Violence and Social Disorder in the New Latin America." *Latin American Research Review* 41 (1) (February): 178–179.
  2006b. "Undermining the Rule of Law: Democratization and the Dark Side of Police Reform in Mexico." *Latin American Politics and Society* 48 (1): 55–86.
Davis, Diane and Anthony Pereira, eds. 2003. *Irregular Armed Forces and Their Role in Politics and State Formation*. Cambridge: Cambridge University Press.
Dell, Melissa. 2015. "Trafficking Networks and the Mexican Drug War." *American Economic Review* 105 (6): 1738–1779.
Demombynes, Gabriel. 2011. "Drug Trafficking and Violence in Central America and Beyond." World Development Report 2011 Background Papers. Washington, DC: © World Bank. https://openknowledge.worldbank.org/handle/10986/27333. License: CC BY 3.0 IGO.
  2009. "The Effect of Crime Victimization on Attitudes towards Criminal Justice in Latin America." Unpublished paper.
Demoscopía. 2007. *Maras y pandillas, comunidad y policía en Centroamérica. Hallazgos de un estudio integral*. Tegucigalpa: Swedish International Development Cooperation Agency (Sida) and Banco Centroamericano de Cooperación Económica.

Dilulio, John J.Jr. 1996. "Help Wanted: Economists, Crime and Public Policy." *Journal of Economic Perspectives* 10: 3–24.

Dirección General de Estadísticas y Censos del Ministerio de Economía (DIGESTYC, El Salvador). 1996. *Proyección de la población de El Salvador 1995–2025*. San Salvador: Ministerio de Economía.

Dodson, J. Michael and Donald W. Jackson. 1997. "Re-Inventing the Rule of Law: Human Rights in El Salvador." *Democratization* 4 (4): 110–134.

Dowdney, Luke. 2005. *Neither War nor Peace: International Comparisons of Children and Youth in Organised Armed Violence*. Brazil: COAV, Viva Rio, ISER, and IANSA.

"Drug Violence in Mexico." 2015. *Journal of Conflict Resolution* 59 (8) (Special Issue, December).

Dudley, Steve. 2013. "The El Salvador Gang Truce and the Church: What Was the Role of the Catholic Church?" CLALS Working Paper Series No. 1. Washington, DC: Center for Latin American and Latino Studies, American University, and *InSight Crime* (May 5, 2013).

2010. *Drug Trafficking Organizations in Central America: Transportistas, Mexican Cartels and Maras*. Woodrow Wilson International Center for Scholars.

Dunkerley, James. 1989. *Power in the Isthmus: A Political History of Modern Central America*. New York, NY: Verso.

Durán-Martínez, Angélica. 2018. *The Politics of Drug Violence: Criminals, Cops and Politicians in Colombia and Mexico*. Oxford: Oxford University Press.

2015. "To Kill and Tell? State Power, Criminal Competition, and Drug Violence." *Journal of Conflict Resolution* 59 (December): 1377–1402.

2013. "Criminals, Cops and Politicians: Dynamics of Drug Violence in Colombia and Mexico." Brown University. PhD dissertation.

Durkheim, Emile. 1950. *Suicide: A Study in Sociology*. Translated by George Simpson. New York, NY: Free Press.

1947. *The Division of Labor in Society*. Translated by George Simpson. New York, NY: Free Press.

Eaton, Kent. 2006a. "Decentralization's Non-Democratic Roots: Authoritarianism and Subnational Reform in South America." *Latin American Politics and Society* 48 (1): 1–26.

2006b. "The Downside of Decentralization: Armed Clientelism in Colombia." *Security Studies* 15 (4) 2006: 1–30.

ECLAC (Economic Commission for Latin America and the Caribbean). 2014. *Social Panorama of Latin America, 2014*. (LC/G.2635-P) Santiago: United Nations.

2005. *Social Panorama of Latin America, 2004*. Santiago: United Nations.

ECLAC Population Division. *Aglomerados metropolitanos y ciudades de 20 mil y más habitantes: población censada y tasas de crecimiento medio anual. Censos de 1950 a 2000*. Retrieved June 9, 2015, from www.cepal.org/celade/depualc/default_2011.asp.

Economist. Intelligence Unit. "El Salvador." April 14, 2014. Retrieved July 14, 2014 from http://country.eiu.com/el-salvador.

Elias, Norbert. 1939/1978. *The Civilising Process*. 2 vols. Translated by Edmund Jephcott. New York, NY: Urizen Books.
Fajnzylber, Pablo, Daniel Lederman, and Norman Loayza. 2002a. "Inequality and Violent Crime." *Journal of Law & Economics* 45 (1): 1–40.
  2002b. "What Causes Violent Crime?" *European Economic Review* 46 (7): 1323–1357.
  2000. "Crime and Victimization: An Economic Perspective." *Economía* (Fall): 219–302.
  1999. *Inequality and Violent Crime*. Washington, DC: World Bank.
Farah, Douglas. 2012. "Central American Gangs: Changing Nature and New Partners." *Journal of International Affairs* 66 (1) (Fall/Winter): 53–67.
  2011. "Organized Crime in El Salvador: The Homegrown and Transnational Dimensions." Woodrow Wilson Center for Scholars, Latin America Program, Working Paper Series on Organized Crime in El Salvador (February).
Farah, Douglas and Pamela Phillips Lum. 2013. Central American Gangs and Transnational Criminal Organizations: The Changing Relationships in a Time of Turmoil. Report (February 2013). Alexandria, VA: International Assessment and Strategy Center.
Farer, Tom, ed. 1999. *Transnational Crime in the Americas*. New York, NY: Routledge Press.
Fearon, James D. and David D. Laitin. 1996. "Explaining Interethnic Cooperation." *American Political Science Review* 90 (4) (December): 715–721.
Ferranti, David de, Guillermo E. Perry, Francisco Ferreira, and Michael Walton. 2004. *Inequality in Latin America and the Caribbean: Breaking with History?* Washington, DC: World Bank.
Fisman, Raymond and Edward Miguel. 2008. *Economic Gangsters: Corruption, Violence, and the Poverty of Nations*. Princeton University Press.
Frühling, Hugo. 2012. "A Realistic Look at Latin American Community Policing Programs." *Policing and Society* (special issue edited by Mark Ungar and Desmond Enrique Arias): 76–88.
  2009. "Recent Police Reform in Latin America." In Niels Uildriks, ed., *Policing Insecurity: Police Reform, Security, and Human Rights in Latin America*. Lanham, MD: Lexington Books, a division of Rowman Littlefield.
  2003. "Police Reform and the Process of Democratization." In Hugo Frühling and Joseph S. Tulchin, eds., with Heather A. Goldings. 2003. *Crime and Violence in Latin America: Citizen Security, Democracy and the State*. Washington, DC: Woodrow Wilson Press and Johns Hopkins Press.
Frühling, Hugo and Joseph S. Tulchin, eds., with Heather A. Goldings. 2003. *Crime and Violence in Latin America: Citizen Security, Democracy and the State*. Washington, DC: Woodrow Wilson Press and Johns Hopkins Press.
Gallie, W. B. "Essentially Contested Concepts." *Proceedings of the Aristotelian Society* 56 (New Series) (1955–1956): 167–198.
Gambetta, Diego. 1996. *The Sicilian Mafia: The Business of Protection*. Cambridge, MA: Harvard University Press.

Gartner R. 1990. The Victims of Homicide: A Temporal and Cross-National Comparison. *American Sociological Review* 55: 92–106.

Gavigan, Patrick. 2009. "Organized Crime, Illicit Power Structures and Guatemala's Threatened Peace Process." *International Peacekeeping* 16.

Gaviria, Alejandro. 2000. Response to Pablo Fajnzylber, Daniel Lederman, and Norman Loayza. "Crime and Victimization: An Economic Perspective." *Economía* (Fall 2000): 219–302.

Gay, Robert. 2010. "Toward Uncivil Society: Causes and Consequences of Violence in Rio de Janeiro." In Enrique Desmond Arias and Daniel M. Goldstein, eds., *Violent Democracies in Latin America*. Durham, NC: Duke University Press, pp. 201–225.

Giraudy, Agustina and Juan Pablo Luna. 2017. "Unpacking the State's Uneven Territorial Reach: Evidence from Latin America." In Miguel Centeno, Atul Kohli, and Deborah J. Yashar, eds., *States in the Developing World*. Cambridge: Cambridge University Press, pp. 93–120.

Glebbeek, Marie-Louise." 2001. "Police Reform and the Peace Process in Guatemala: The Fifth Promotion of the National Civilian Police." *Bulletin of Latin American Research* 20.

  2009. Post-War Violence and Police Reform in Guatemala." In Niels Uildriks, ed., *Policing Insecurity: Police Reform, Security, and Human Rights in Latin America*. Lanham, MD: Lexington Books (a division of Rowman Littlefield).

Glebbeek, Marie-Louise, W. Gonick, R. Muggah, and C. Waszink. 2003. *Balas perdidas: el impacto del mal uso de armas pequeñas en Centroamérica*. Geneva: Small Arms Survey and Norwegian Initiative on Small Arms Transfers.

González, Yanilda María. 2014. "State Building on the Ground: Police Reform and Participatory Security in Latin America." Princeton University. PhD dissertation.

Gootenberg, Paul. 2008. *Andean Cocaine: The Making of a Global Drug*. Chapel Hill, NC: University of North Caroline Press.

Green, Linda. 1995. "The Paradoxes of War and Its Aftermath: Mayan Widows and Rural Guatemala." *Cultural Survival* 19 (1) (Spring).

Grigsby, William. 2006a. "Nicaragua: Do We Have the Police We Deserve?" *Revista Envío* 301 (May).

  2006b. "Nicaragua: The New National Police Chief Faces Colossal Challenges." *Revista Envío* 301 (August).

  2005. "Hawks, Missiles, Pressure, Reasons and Resistance. *Revista Envío* 285 (April), accessed on March 6, 2007, at www.envio.org.ni/articulo/2869.

  2003. "Nicaragua: The National Police under Attack: The Clues behind the Crisis." *Revista Envío* 265 (August).

Grillo, Ioan. 2016. *Gangster Warlords: Drug Dollars, Killing Fields and the New Politics of Latin America*. London: Bloomsbury Circus.

GTZ. 2005. *Una historia que merece ser contada: modernización institucional con equidad de género en la Policía Nacional de Nicaragua, 1996–2005*. Managua: Proyecto de Promoción de Políticas de Género (with support from Policía Nacional de Nicaragua, Gobierno de Nicaragua INM, GTZ,

Ministerio Federal de Cooperación Económica y Desarrollo de Alemania, BMZ, Banco Interamericano de Desarollo).
Guerrero, Eduardo. 2012. "Mexico's Challenge: Lessons in the War against Organized Crime (2007–2011)." *ReVista: Harvard Review of Latin America* (Winter).
Gurdián Alfaro, Hamyn. 2006. "Juventud y violencia: la experiencia policial en Nicaragua." *Mirador de Seguridad: Revista del Instituto de Estudios Estratégicos y Políticas Públicas*. Issue: Una visión sobre las pandillas en Centroamérica (August–October): 19–28.
Gurr, Ted Robert. 1970. *Why Men Rebel*. Princeton, NJ: Princeton University Press.
Gutiérrez Rivera, Lira. 2013. *Territories of Violence: State, Marginal Youth, and Public Security in Honduras*. New York, NY: Palgrave Macmillan.
Hale, Charles. 1994. *Resistance and Contradiction: Miskitu Indians and the Nicaraguan State*. Stanford, CA: Stanford University Press.
Hall, Peter A. and Rosemary R. Taylor. 1996. "Political Science and the Three New Institutionalisms." *Political Studies* XLIV: 936–957.
Hanchard, Michael. 1998. *Orpheus and Power: The Movimento Negro of Rio de Janeiro and São Paulo, Brazil, 1945–1988*. Princeton, NJ: Princeton University Press.
Handy, Jim. 1984. *Gift of the Devil: A History of Guatemala*. Boston, MA: South End Press.
Helmke, Gretchen and Steven Levitsky. 2004. "Informal Institutions and Comparative Politics: A Research Agenda." *Perspectives on Politics* 2 (4): 725–740
Herbst, Jeffrey. 2000. *States and Power in Africa*. Princeton, NJ: Princeton University Press.
Hernández, S. 2005. "The Phenomenon of Criminal Youth Gangs in Central America and the Importance of Regional Cooperation." Paper given at the OAS meeting on Transnational Criminal Youth Gangs: Characteristics, Importance and Public Policies, Tapachula, Chiapas, Mexico, June 16 and 17, 2005.
Hobbes, Thomas. 1985. *Leviathan*. New York, NY: Penguin.
Holiday, David and William Stanley. 2000. "Under the Best of Circumstances: ONUSAL and the Challenges of Verification and Institution Building in El Salvador." In Tommie Sue Montgomery, ed., *Peacemaking and Democratization in the Western Hemisphere*. Boulder, CO: Lynne Rienner.
Holland, Alisha. 2016. "Forbearance." *American Political Science Review* 110 (2): 232–246.
  2013. Right on Crime? Conservative Party Politics and Mano Dura Policies in El Salvador." *Latin American Research Review* 48 (1): 44–68 (Spring).
Holston, James. 2008. *Insurgent Citizenship: Disjunctions of Democracy and Modernity in Brazil*. Princeton, NJ: Princeton University Press.
Human Rights Watch. 2017. *World Report 2017: Events of 2016*. https://www.hrw.org/sites/default/files/world_report_download/wr2017-web.pdf, accessed on July 7, 2017.

2007. *Human Rights Watch 2007 World Report*, Brazil country summary. New York, NY: Human Rights Watch. Retrieved June 10, 2007, from www.hrw.org/legacy/wr2k7/pdfs/brazil.pdf

Hume, Mo. 2007. "El Salvador Responds to Gangs." *Development in Practice* 16 (6) (November): 739–751.

2004. "Armed Violence and Poverty in El Salvador: A Mini Case Study for the Armed Violence and Poverty Initiative." Center for International Cooperation and Security, University of Bradford, UK.

Hunt, Flor. (2008, July 3) "Interview with Astor Escalanate Saravia." Innovations for Successful Societies, Oral History Program, Series: Policing, Interview No. M11. Princeton University Bobst Center for Peace and Justice. Downloaded from https://successfulsocieties.princeton.edu/interviews/astor-escalante-saravia.

(2008, July 2). "Interview with Knut Walter." Innovations for Successful Societies, Oral History Program, Series: Policing, Interview No. M1. Princeton University Bobst Center of Peace and Justice. Downloaded from https://successfulsocieties.princeton.edu/interviews/knut-walter.

Hunt, Flor and Wendy Hunter. 1997. *Eroding Military Influence in Brazil: Politicians against the State*. Chapel Hill, NC: University of North Carolina Press.

IEEPP (Instituto de Estudios Estratégicos y Políticas Públicas). 2007. *La gestión presupuestaria de la seguridad y sus políticas en Nicaragua*. Managua, Nicaragua.

InSight Crime. 2014a. "Perrones Cartel Profile." Retrieved July 14, 2014, from www.insightcrime.org/groups-el-salvador/perrones.

2014b. "Texis Cartel Profile." Retrieved July 14, 2014, from www.insightcrime.org/groups-el-salvador/texis-cartel.

2012a. Interview with Nicaraguan Police Chief Aminta Granera, July 9, 2012. Accessed online at www.insightcrime.org/nicaragua-a-paradise-lost/video-an-interview-with-nicaraguas-police-chief on June 27, 2013.

2012b. "Bluefields: Nicaragua's Cocaine Hub." Jeremy McDermott, Sunday, July 8, 2012, Accessed online at www.insightcrime.org/nicaragua-a-paradise-lost/bluefields-nicaraguas-cocaine-hub on June 27, 2013.

Instituto Brasileiro de Geografia e Estatística (IBGE). 2007. *Contagem da População 2007*. Rio de Janeiro: IBGE. Retrieved June 9, 2015, from www.ibge.gov.br/home/estatistica/populacao/contagem2007/contagem.pdf.

1996. *Contagem da População 1996, Contagem da População 2007*. Retrieved June 9, 2015, from www.ibge.gov.br/home/estatistica/populacao/contagem/default.shtm

Instituto de Derechos Humanos de la Universidad Centroamericana (IDHUCA). 2006. "Los derechos humanos en el 2005 (II)," *Proceso* (January 11, 2006).

Instituto de Medicina Legal, Unidad de Estadísticas Forenses. 2014. *Anuario Estadístico: defunciones por homicidios en El Salvador*. San Salvador.

2010. *Anuario Estadístico: defunciones por homicidios en El Salvador*. San Salvador.

2000. *Anuario Estadístico: defunciones por homicidios en El Salvador*. San Salvador.

Instituto de Medicina Legal and Fiscalía General de la República. 2002–2007. Estadísticas de homicidios de la Policía Nacional Civil. San Salvador.
Instituto Nacional de Estadística (Guatemala). 2003. *Características de la población y de los locales de habitación censados. Censos 2002. XI de Población y VI de Habitación.* INE, UNFPA. Retrieved June 9, 2015, from www.ine.gob.gt/sistema/uploads/2014/02/20/jZqeGe1H9WdUDngYXkW t3GIhUUQCukcg.pdf
  2001. Guatemala, proyecciones de población a nivel departamental y municipal por año calendario: período 2000–2005. Guatemala: INE.
  1991. Guatemala: población urbana y rural estimada por departamento y municipio, 1990–95. Publicaciones estadísticas temáticas, 2.11.4. Guatemala: INE.
  1989. Guatemala: población urbana y rural estimada por departamento y municipios, 1985–90. Publicaciones estadísticas temáticas, 2.11.4. Guatemala: INE.
Instituto Nacional de Estadística y Censo (Panama). 1990, 2000. *Censos nacionales de población y vivienda, 1990, 2000.* Retrieved June 9, 2015, from www.contraloria.gob.pa/inec/Redatam/censospma.htm
Instituto Nacional de Estadística y Censos (INEC, Costa Rica). 2008. Cálculo de población por provincia, cantón y distrito. Al 31 de diciembre de 2007. San José: INEC. Retrieved June 9, 2015, http://biblioteca.icap.ac.cr/BLIVI/UNP AN/CARPETA%20AGOSTO%202008/Calculo_de_poblacion_%20por_ %20provincia_INEC.pdf
Instituto Nacional de Estadísticas y Censos (INEC, Nicaragua). 2006. VIII Censo de Población y IV de Vivienda. Retrieved June 9, 2015, www.bio-nica.info /biblioteca/VIIICensodePoblacion.pdf
Instituto Nacional de Estadística y Geografía (INEGI, México). 2005. *II Conteo de población y vivienda 2005.* Retrieved June 9, 2015, from www.inegi.org .mx/inegi/default.aspx?s=est&c=10215.
Inter-American Development Bank. 2000. Report. Reprinted in Hugo Acero Velásquez. 2002. "Salud, violencia y seguridad." Ciudad y políticas públicas de seguridad y convivencia. www.suivd.gov.co/ciudad/MexicoMar zohacero.doc.
International Human Rights Clinic (IHRC). 2007. *No Place to Hide: Gang, State, and Clandestine Violence in El Salvador.* Cambridge, MA: Harvard Law School Human Rights Program (February).
International Monetary Fund (IMF). 2005. El Salvador: Report on the Observance of Standards and Codes – Fiscal Transparency Module. IMF Country Report No. 05/67 (February 2005), Washington, DC.
Jamal, Amaney. 2007. *Barriers to Democracy: The Other Side of Social Capital in Palestine and the Arab World.* Princeton, NJ: Princeton University Press.
Jonas, Susanne. 1991. *Battle for Guatemala: Rebels, Death Squads, and the U.S. Power.* Boulder, CO: Westview Press.
Kalyvas, Stathis. 2015. "How Civil Wars Help Explain Organized Crime – and How They Do Not." *Journal of Conflict Resolution* (December).
  2006. *The Logic of Violence in Civil War.* Cambridge: Cambridge University Press.

Karp, Aaron. 2008. Estimated firearms distribution in 27 Latin America and Caribbean countries 2007. Unpublished background data from Geneva: Small Arms Survey.

Kaufmann, Daniel, Aart Kraay, and Massimo Mastruzzi. 2010. "The Worldwide Governance Indicators: Methodology and Analytical Issues." World Bank Policy Research Working Paper No. 5430. Washington, DC: World Bank.

Keefer, Philip and Norman Loayza, eds. 2010. *Innocent Bystanders: Developing Countries and the War on Drugs*. World Bank e-Library. New York: NY: Palgrave Macmillan, World Bank.

Keefer, Philip, Norman V. Loayza, and Rodrigo R. Soares. 2008. "The Development Impact of the Illegality of Drug Trade." Policy Research Working Paper 4543 (February 2008). The World Bank Development Research Group Macroeconomics and Growth Team.

Kenney, Michael. 2007. *From Pablo to Osama: Trafficking and Terrorist Networks, Government Bureaucracies, and Competitive Adaptation*. University Park, PA: Penn State Press.

Kitroeff, Natalie J. 2011. "Touching the 'Untouchables': An Evaluation of the International Commission against Impunity in Guatemala." Senior thesis, Woodrow Wilson School, Princeton University.

Klein, Malcolm and Cheryl Lee Maxson. 2006. *Street Gang Patterns and Policies*. Oxford: Oxford University Press.

Koonings, Kees and Dirk Krujit, eds. 2004. *Armed Actors: Organised Violence and State Failure in Latin America*. London: Zed Press.

Krug, Etienne G., Linda L. Dahlberg, James A. Mercy, Anthony B. Zwi, and Rafael Lozano, eds. 2002. *World Report on Violence and Health*. Geneva: World Health Organization.

Kurtenbach, S. 2013. "The 'Happy Outcomes' May Not Come at All – Postwar Violence in Central America." *Civil Wars* 15 (1): 105–122.

Kurtz, Marcus J. and Andrew Schrank. 2007. "Growth and Governance: Models, Measures, and Mechanisms." *Journal of Politics* 69 (2).

Lacayo, Antonio. 2005. *La difícil transición nicaragüense en el gobierno con doña Violeta*. Managua: Fundación Uno.

LaFree, Gary. 1999. "A Summary and Review of Cross-National Comparative Studies of Homicide." In M. Dwayne Smith and Margaret A. Zahn, eds., *Homicide: A Sourcebook of Social Research*. Thousand Oaks, CA:Sage Publications.

LaFree, Gary and Andromachi Tseloni. 2006. "Democracy and Crime: A Multilevel Analysis of Homicide Trends in Forty-Four Countries, 1950–2000." *Annals, AAPSS* 605 (May): 26–49.

Latin American Public Opinion Project (LAPOP). AmericasBarometer, www.LapopSurveys.org.

LatinNews. www.latinnews.com/ (specific articles cited in text).

Leander, Ann. 2004. "Wars and the Un-making of States: Taking Tilly Seriously in the Contemporary World." In Stefano Guzzini and Dietrich Jung, eds., *Copenhagen Peace Research: Conceptual Innovations and Contemporary Security Analysis*. London: Routledge.

Lederman, Daniel, Norman Loayza, and Ana Maria Menéndez,. 2002. "Violent Crime: Does Social Capital Matter?" *Economic Development and Cultural Change* 50 (3): 509–539.

Lee, Rensselaer W., III. 1999. "Transnational Organized Crime: An Overview." In Tom Farer, ed., *Transnational Crime in the Americas*. New York, NY: Routledge Press, pp. 2–38.

Lessing, Benjamin. 2017. *Making Peace in Drug Wars: Crackdowns and Cartels in Latin America*. Cambridge: Cambridge University Press.

  2015. "Logics of Violence in Criminal War." *Journal of Conflict Resolution* 59 (December): 1486–1516.

Levenson, Deborah. 2005. *Hacer la juventud: jóvenes de tres generaciones de una familia trabajadora en la Ciudad de Guatemala*. Guatemala City: AVANCSO.

Levenson, Deborah T. 2013. *Adiós Niño: The Gangs of Guatemala City and the Politics of Death*. Durham, NC: Duke University Press.

  1988. *Por sí mismos: un estudio preliminar de las maras en la Ciudad de Guatemala*. Guatemala: AVANCSO.

Levitsky, Steven and Victoria Maria Murillo. 2009. "Variation in Institutional Strength." *Annual Review of Political Science* 12: 115–133.

Levitsky, Steven and Lucan Way. Forthcoming. *The Durability of Revolutionary Regimes*. Princeton: Princeton University Press.

Levitt, Steven. 2004. "Understanding Why Crime Fell in the 1990s: Four Factors That Explain the Decline and Six That Do Not." *Journal of Economic Perspectives* 18 (1): 163 (28 pages).

Levitt, Steven and Sudhir Venkatesh. 2000a. "'Are We a Family or a Business?' History and Disjuncture in the Urban American Street Gang." *Theory & Society* 29 (4).

  2000b. "An Economic Analysis of a Drug-Selling Gang's Finances." *Quarterly Journal of Economics* 115 (3).

Ley, Sandra, Shannan Mattiace, and Guillermo Trejo n.d. "Indigenous Resistance to Drug Violence in Mexico. Why Indigenous Mobilization and Ethnic Autonomy Institutions Deter Criminal Violence." Presented at "Unequal Security in the Americas," at Watson Institute, Brown University, April 29–30, 2016.

Lipset, Martin Seymour. 1959. "Some Social Requisites of Democracy: Economic Development and Political Legitimacy." *American Political Science Review* 53: 69–105.

Lipsky, Michael. 1980. *Street-Level Bureaucracy: Dilemmas of the Individual in Public Service*. New York, NY: Russell Sage Foundation.

Logan, Sam. 2006. "Nicaragua's Curse of the White Treasure." ISN Security Watch. September 27, 2006. Accessed on March 6, 207 at www.isn.ethz.ch/news/sw/details.cfm?id=16720.

López, Julie. 2012. "The Zetas' Bad Omen: From Mexico to Guatemala." *ReVista: Harvard Review of Latin America* (Winter).

LPG Datos, Opinión Pública e Investigación. 2011. "Homicidios en Centroamérica." *La Prensa Gráfica*. March 2011. Retrieved from http://multimedia.laprensagrafica.com/pdf/2011/03/20110322-PDF-Informe-0311-Homicidios-en-Centroamerica.pdf.

Magaloni, Beatriz, Edgar Franco, and Vanessa Melo. 2015. "Killing in the Slums: An Impact Evaluation of Police Reform in Rio de Janeiro." CDDRL Working Paper, Stanford University.

Mahoney, James. 2001. *The Legacies of Liberalism: Path Dependence and Political Regimes in Central America*. Baltimore, MD: Johns Hopkins University Press.

Mahoney, James and Kathleen Thelen. 2010. "A Theory of Gradual Institutional Change." In James Mahoney and Kathleen Thelen, eds., *Explaining Institutional Change: Ambiguity, Agency, and Power*. Cambridge: Cambridge University Press, pp. 1–37.

Maingot, Anthony P. 1999. "The Decentralization Imperative and Caribbean Criminal Enterprises." In Tom Farer, ed., *Transnational Crime in the Americas*. Abingdon: Taylor & Francis Ltd., pp. 143–170.

Mainwaring, Scott and Aníbal Pérez-Liñán. 2003. "Level of Development and Democracy: Latin American Exceptionalism, 1945–1996." *Comparative Political Studies* 36 (9): 1031–1067.

Mann, Michael. 1993. *The Sources of Social Power. Vol. II, The Rise of Classes and Nation-States, 1760–1914*. Cambridge: Cambridge University Press.

  1984. "The Autonomous Power of the State: Its Origins, Mechanisms, and Results." *European Journal of Sociology* 25 (2): 185–213.

Mansfield, Edward D. and Jack Snyder. 2002. "Democratic Transitions, Institutional Strength, and War." *International Organization* 56 (2): 297–337.

Manz, Beatriz. 1988. *Refugees of a Hidden War: The Aftermath of Counterinsurgency in Guatemala*. Albany, NY: State University of New York.

Mares, David R. 2006. *Drug Wars and Coffeehouses: The Political Economy of the International Drug Trade*. Washington, DC: CQ Press.

Martínez, Óscar. 2016. *A History of Violence: Living and Dying in Central America*. London: Verso.

Maurer, Noel. 2012. "Criminal Organizations and Enterprise." *ReVista: Harvard Review of Latin America* (Winter).

McAdam, Doug, Sidney Tarrow, and Charles Tilly. 2001. *Dynamics of Contention*. New York, NY: Cambridge University Press.

Mejía, Thelma. 2006. "Central America; Soaring Violent Crime Threatens Democracy." Inter-Service Press Service News Agency, October 14, 2006.

Méndez, Juan E., Guillermo O'Donnell, and Paulo Sérgio Pinheiro, eds. 1999. *The (Un)Rule of Law and the Underprivileged in Latin America*. South Bend, IN: University of Notre Dame Press.

Mendoza, Carlos. 2006. "Structural Causes and Diffusion Processes of Collective Violence: Understanding Lynch Mobs in Post-Conflict Guatemala." Paper prepared for Latin American Studies Association Meeting, March 15–18, 2006 (San Juan, Puerto Rico).

Meyer, Maureen, with contributions from Coletta Youngers and Dave Bewley-Taylor. 2007. "At a Crossroads: Drug Trafficking, Violence and the Mexican State." Briefing Paper 13, Washington Office in Latin America and the Beckley Foundation Drug Policy Programme.

Migdal, Joel S. 1988. *Strong Societies and Weak States: State-Society Relations and State Capabilities in the Third World.* Princeton, NJ: Princeton University Press.

Ministerio de Economía, Dirección General de Estadística y Censos (El Salvador). 2008. Censos VI de Población y V de Vivienda 2007. San Salvador: Ministerio de Economía. Available at www.censos.gob.sv/util/datos/Resultados%20VI%20Censo%20de%20Poblaci%C3%B3 n%20 V%20de%20Vivienda%202007.pdf

MINUGUA (United Nations Verification Mission in Guatemala). 1997. *La construcción de la paz en Guatemala.* Guatemala City: Editorial Serviprensa.

Moncada, Eduardo. 2009. "Toward Democratic Policing in Colombia? Institutional Accountability through Lateral Reform." *Comparative Politics* 41(4): 431–449.

Moran, Patrick J. 2009. "El Salvador and Guatemala: Security Sector Reform and Political Party System Effects on Organized Crime." Master of Science in National Security Affairs, Naval Postgraduate School (June).

Morris, Stephen D. 2006. "Corruption in Latin America." *The Latinamericanist* (Spring).

Moser, Caroline and Cathy McIlwaine. 2006. "Latin American Urban Violence as a Development Concern: Towards a Framework for Violence Reduction." *World Development* 34 (1).

  2004. *Encounters with Daily Violence in Latin America: Urban Poor Perceptions from Colombia and Guatemala.* New York, NY: Routledge.

Muggah, R. and C. Stevenson. 2008. "On the Edge: Considering the Causes and Consequences of Armed Violence in Central America." Background paper for World Bank Crime and Violence in Central America Economic and Sector Work Studies.

Naím, Moisés. 2005. *Illicit: How Smugglers, Traffickers, and Copycats are Hijacking the Global Economy.* New York, NY: Doubleday.

Naylor, R. T. 2009. "Violence and Illegal Economic Activity: A Deconstruction." *Crime, Law and Social Change* 52 (3): 231–242.

Neapolitan, Jerome L. 1997. *Cross-National Crime: A Research Review and Sourcebook.* Westport, CT: Greenwood Press.

Nield, Rachel. 2001. "Democratic Police Reforms in War-Torn Societies." *Conflict, Security and Development* 1 (1): 21–43.

Nobles, Melissa. 2000. *Shades of Citizenship: Race and the Census in Modern Politics.* Palo Alto, CA: Stanford University Press.

North, Douglass. 1990. *Institutions, Institutional Change, and Economic Performance: The Political Economy of Institutions and Decisions.* Cambridge: Cambridge University Press.

North, Douglass, John Wallis, and Barry Weingast. 2009. *Violence and Social Orders: A Conceptual Framework for Interpreting Recorded Human History*. Cambridge: Cambridge University Press.

O'Donnell, Guillermo A. 1993. "On the State, Democratization and Some Conceptual Problems: A Latin American View with Glances at Some Postcommunist Countries." *World Development* 21 (8): 1355–1369.

  1973. *Modernization and Bureaucratic-Authoritarianism: Studies in South American Politics*. Berkeley, CA: Institute of International Studies, University of California.

O'Donnell, Guillermo and Philippe C. Schmitter. 1986. *Transitions from Authoritarian Rule: Tentative Conclusions about Uncertain Democracies*. Baltimore, MD: Johns Hopkins University Press.

Olson, Mancur. 2000. *Power and Prosperity*. New York, NY: Basic Books.

O'Neill, Kevin Lewis and Kedron Thomas, eds. 2011. *Securing the City: Neoliberalism, Space, and Insecurity in Postwar Guatemala*. Durham, NC: Duke University Press.

Organización Panamericana de la Salud, Unidad de Análisis de Salud y Estadísticas, Iniciativa Regional de Datos Básicos en Salud. 2010. *Sistema de Información Técnica en Salud*. Washington, DC: Organización Panamericana de la Salud, www.paho.org/Spanish/SHA/coredata/tabulator/newTabulator.htm (visited in September 2012).

Organization of American States (OAS). 2013. *The Drug Problem in the Americas*. Washington, DC: OAS General Secretariat.

Osorio, Javier. 2015. "The Contagion of Drug Violence: Spatiotemporal Dynamics of the Mexican War on Drugs." *Journal of Conflict Resolution* 59 (December): 1403–1432.

Paige, Jeffery. 1998. *Coffee and Power: Revolution and the Rise of Democracy in Central America*. Cambridge, MA: Harvard University Press.

Pan American Health Organization, Health Surveillance and Disease Management Area, Health Statistics and Analysis Unit. 2010. *PAHO Regional Mortality Database*. Washington, DC.

Pan American Health Organization, Health Information and Analysis Unit. Regional Core Health Data Initiative. Washington DC, 2014. Available at www1.paho.org/English/SHA/coredata/tabulator/newTabulator.htm.

Pan American Health Organization and World Health Organization. Health Information Platform for the Americas (PLISA). Washington DC, 2016. Available at http://phip.paho.org/views/Pro_Reg_Fin_Nca_Pub_Anu_Tab_Ing_IBS_homicides/Table?:embed=yes&:comments=no&:display_count=no&:showVizHome=no. Last visited in September 2017.

Parra-Torrado, Mónica. 2014. "Youth Unemployment in the Caribbean." Working Paper, Caribbean Knowledge Series. Washington, DC: World Bank.

Peacock, Susan C. and Adriana Beltrán. 2003. *Hidden Powers in Post-Conflict Guatemala: Illegal Armed Groups and the Forces Behind Then*. Washington, DC: Washington Office on Latin America.

Peña, Uzziel and Tom Gibb. 2013. "El Salvador's Gang Truce: An Historic Opportunity." *NACLA Report on the Americas* 46 (2): 12–15. Retrieved from http://search.proquest.com/docview/1433385998?accountid=13314.

Pereira, Anthony. 2005. *Political (In)justice: Authoritarianism and the Rule of Law in Brazil, Chile, and Argentina.* Pittsburgh, PA: Pittsburgh University Press.

Pérez Orlando, J. 2013. "Gang Violence and Insecurity in Contemporary Central America." *Bulletin of Latin American Research* (March): 217–234.

2003–2004. "Democratic Legitimacy and Public Insecurity: Crime and Democracy in El Salvador and Guatemala." *Political Science Quarterly* 118 (4): 627–644.

Pierson, Paul. 2000. "Increasing Returns, Path Dependence, and the Study of Politics."*American Political Science Review* 94 (2): 251–267.

Pinheiro, Paulo Sérgio. 2007. "Youth, Violence, and Democracy." *Current History* 106 (697): 64–69.

Polanyi, Karl. 1944. *Great Transformation: The Political and Economic Origins of Our Times.* Boston, MA: Beacon Press.

Policía Nacional de Nicaragua. 2014. *Anuario Estadístico 2014.* www.policia.gob.ni/cedoc/sector/estd/ae%202014.pdf, accessed on July 26, 2017.

2006. *Boletín de actividad policial de circulación interna.* Año IX, No. 77 (November–December). Ministerio de Gobernación, Managua, Nicaragua.

Policzer, Pablo. 2009. *The Rise and Fall of Repression in Chile.* Notre Dame, IN: University of Notre Dame Press.

Popkin, Margaret. 2000. *Peace without Justice: Obstacles to Building the Rule of Law in El Salvador.* University Park, PA: Pennsylvania State University Press.

Portes, Alejandro and Manuel Castells. 1989. "World Underneath: The Origins, Dynamics, and Effects of the Informal Economy." In A. Portes, M. Castells, and L. Benton, eds., *The Informal Economy.* Baltimore, MD: Johns Hopkins University Press, pp. 11–37.

Portes, Alejandro and Kelly Hoffman. 2003. "Latin American Class Structures: Their Composition and Change During the Neoliberal Era." *Latin American Research Review* 38 (1): 41–82.

Portes, Alejandro and Bryan Roberts. 2005. "Free Market City." *Studies in Comparative and International Development* 40 (1): 43–82.

Przeworski, Adam, Michael E. Alvarez, José Antonio Cheibub, and Fernando Limongi. 2000. *Democracy and Development: Political Institutions and Well-Being in the World, 1950–1990.* Cambridge: Cambridge University Press.

Putnam, Robert D. 1993. *Making Democracy World: Civic Traditions in Modern Italy.* Princeton, NJ: Princeton University Press.

Putzel, James. 1997. "Accounting for the Dark Side of Social Capital." *Journal of International Development* 9 (7): 939–949.

Ranum. E. C. 2006. "Diagnóstico Nacional Guatemala." *Proyecto pandillas juveniles transnacionales en Centroamérica, México, y Estados Unidos.* Mexico City: Centro de Estudios y Programas Interamericanos (CEPI) del Instituto Tecnológico Autónomo de México.

Ranum, Elin Cecilie. 2011. "Street Gangs in Guatemala." In Thomas Bruneau, Lucía Dammert, and Elizabeth Skinner, eds., *Maras: Gang Violence and*

Security in Central America. Austin, TX: University of Texas Press, pp. 71–86.
Reno, William. 2002. "Mafiya Troubles, Warlord Crises." In Mark R. Beissinger and Crawford Young, eds., Beyond State Crisis: Postcolonial Africa and Post-Soviet Eurasia in Comparative Perspective. Washington, DC: Johns Hopkins University Press/Woodrow Wilson Center, pp. 105–127.
  2000. "Clandestine Economies, Violence, and States in Africa." Journal of International Affairs 53 (2): 433–459.
Reuter, P. and V. Greenfield. 2001. "Measuring Global Drug Markets: How Good Are the Numbers and Why Should We Care about Them?" World Economics 2 (4): 159–174.
Reuter, Peter. 2014. "Drug Markets and Organized Crime." In Letizia Paoli, ed., The Oxford Handbook of Organized Crime. Oxford: Oxford University Press, pp. 359–380.
  2009. "Systemic Violence in Drug Markets." Crime, Law, and Social Change 52 (3): 275–284.
  1985. The Organization of Illegal Markets: An Economic Analysis. Washington, DC: US Department of Justice: National Institute of Justice.
Reuter, Peter and John Roman. 2000. Response to Fajnzylber, Pablo, Daniel Lederman, and Norman Loayza. "Crime and Victimization: An Economic Perspective." Economía (Fall 2000): 219–302 (279–288).
Ribando Seelke, Clare. 2014. "El Salvador: Background and U.S. Relations." Congressional Research Service, prepared for Members and Committees of Congress, CRS 7-5700, R43616 (June 26).
  2011. Gangs in Central America. Congressional Research Service, 7–5700, RL34112.
Ribeiro, Eduardo, Doriam Borges, and Ignacio Cano. 2015. "Calidad de los datos de homicidio en América Latina." Prepared for Conference, September 7–9, 2015, "Conferencia sobre calidad de datos de homicidio en América Latina y el Caribe." Bogota, Colombia. Funded by Open Society Foundation. See http://conferenciahomicidiosbogota2015.org/.
Rocha, José Luis. 2011. "Street Gangs in Nicaragua." In Thomas Bruneau, Lucía Dammert, and Elizabeth Skinner, eds., Maras: Gang Violence and Security in Central America. Austin, TX: University of Texas Press, pp. 105–120.
  2007. Lanzando piedras, fumando "piedras": evolución de las pandillas en Nicaragua, 1997–2006. Cuaderno de Investigación No. 23, Colección Humanidades. Managua: Universidad Centroamericana (UCA).
Rodgers, Dennis. 2006. "Living in the Shadow of Death." Journal of Latin American Studies 38 (2): 267–292.
  2004. "'Disembedding' the City: Crime, Insecurity and Spatial Organization in Managua, Nicaragua." Environment & Urbanization 16 (2): 113–123.
Rodgers, Dennis and José Luis Rocha. 2013. "Turning Points: Gang Evolution in Nicaragua," Small Arms Survey 2013: Everyday Dangers. Cambridge: Cambridge University Press.

Ruhl, Mark J. 2005. "The Guatemala Military since the Peace Accords: The Fate of Reform under Arzú and Portillo." *Latin American Politics & Society* 47 (1): 55–85.
  2003. "Civil-Military Relations in Post-Sandinista Nicaragua." *Armed Forces and Society* 30 (Fall): 117–139.
Rustow, Dankwart. 1970. "Transitions to Democracy: Toward a Dynamic Model." *Comparative Politics* 2 (3): 337–363.
Sanford, Victoria 2008. "From Genocide to Femicide: Impunity and Human Rights in Twenty-First Century Guatemala." *Journal of Human Rights* 7 (2): 104–122.
Santacruz Giralt, María L., Alberto Concha-Eastman, and José Miguel Cruz. 2001. *Barrio adentro: la solidaridad violenta de las pandillas*. San Salvador: Instituto Universitario de Opinión Pública (IUDOP), Universidad Centroamericana José Simeón Cañas, Organización Panamericana de la Salud, and Homies Unidos de El Salvador.
Schirmer, Jennifer. 1999. *The Guatemalan Military Project: A Violence Called Democracy*. Philadelphia, PA: University of Pennsylvania Press.
Schmitter, Philippe C. and Terry Lynn Karl. 1991. "What Democracy Is ... and Is Not." *Journal of Democracy* 2 (3): 75–88.
Schneider, Friedrich, Andreas Buhn, and Claudio E. Montenegro. 2010. *Shadow Economies All over the World: New Estimates for 162 Countries from 1999–2007*. (Revised version). Washington, DC: World Bank Development Research Group, Poverty and Inequality Team, Europe and Central Asia Region, Human Development Economics Unit.
Scott, James C. 2009. *The Art of Not Being Governed: An Anarchist History of Upland Southeast Asia*. New Haven, CT: Yale University Press.
Seligson, Mitchell. 2006. "The Measurement and Impact of Corruption Victimization: Survey Evidence from Latin America." *World Development* 34 (3): 381–404.
Shirk, David and Joel Wallman. 2015. "Understanding Mexico's Drug Violence." *Journal of Conflict Resolution* 59 (December): 1348–1376.
Sieder, Rachel, ed., 2002. *Who Governs? Guatemala Five Years after the Peace Accords*. Cambridge, MA: Hemisphere Initiative.
Signoret, Patrick. 2016. "Do Kingpin Removals Cause Violence? Testing Mechanisms and Reassessing Evidence." Paper 591 for Department of Politics, Princeton University.
Silva Ávalos, Héctor. 2014. "Corruption in El Salvador: Politicians, Police and Transportistas." CLALS Working Paper Series, No. 4. Washington, DC: Center for Latin American and Latino Studies, American University, and *InSight Crime* (March).
Smith, Peter H. 2005. "The Political Economy of Drug Trafficking." Unpublished presentation, University of California at San Diego.
  1999. "Semi-Organized International Crime: Drug Trafficking in Mexico." In Tom Farer, ed., *Transnational Crime in the Americas*. New York, NY: Routledge.
Snodgrass Godoy, Angelina. 2006. *Popular Injustice: Violence, Community, and Law in Latin America*. Palo Alto, CA: Stanford University Press.

Snyder, Jack. 2000. *From Voting to Violence: Democratization and Nationalist Conflict*. New York, NY: W.W. Norton and Company.
Snyder, Richard and Angélica Durán-Martínez. 2009. "Does Illegality Breed Violence? Drug Trafficking and State-Sponsored Protection Rackets." *Crime, Law, and Social Change* 52 (September): 253–273.
Sohnen, Eleanor. 2012. *Paying for Crime: A Review of the Relationships between Insecurity and Development in Mexico and Central America*. Washington, DC: Migration Polity Institute.
Soifer, Hillel. 2015. *State Building in Latin America*. Cambridge: Cambridge University Press.
Soifer, Hillel and Matthias Vom Hau. 2008. "Unpacking the Strength of the State: The Utility of State Infrastructural Power." *Studies in Comparative International Development* 43 (3): 219–230.
Spalding, Rose J. 1999. "From Low-Intensity War to Low-Intensity Peace: The Nicaraguan Peace Process." In Cynthia J. Arnson, ed., *Comparative Peace Processes in Latin America*. Washington DC: Woodrow Wilson Center Press and Stanford: Stanford University Press, pp. 31–64.
Spence, Jack, David R. Dye, Paula Worthy, Carmen Rosa de León-Escribano, George Vickers, and Mike Lanchin. 1998. *Promise and Reality: Implementation of the Guatemalan Peace Accords*. Cambridge, MA: Hemisphere Initiatives.
Stanley, William. 2000. "Building New Police Forces in El Salvador and Guatemala: Learning and Counter-Learning." In Tor Tanke Holm and Espen Barth Eide, eds., *Peacebuilding and Police Reform*. Portland, OR: Fran Cass & Co. Ltd.
  1999. "Building New Police Forces in Guatemala and El Salvador: Learning and Counter-Learning." *International Peacekeeping* 6 (4): 113–134.
  1996. *The Protection Racket State: Elite Politics, Military Extortion, and Civil War in El Salvador*. Philadelphia, PA: Temple University Press.
Stanley, William and Mark Peceny. 2001. "Liberal Social Reconstruction and the Resolution of Civil Wars in Central America." *International Organization* 55 (1): 149–182.
Thelen, Kathleen. 2004. *How Institutions Evolve: The Political Economy of Skills in Germany, Britain, the United States, and Japan*. Cambridge: Cambridge University Press.
  1999. "Historical Institutionalism in Comparative Politics." *Annual Review of Political Science* 2: 369–404.
Thelen, Kathleen and Sven Steinmo. 1992. "Historical Institutionalism in Comparative Politics." In Sven Steinmo, Kathleen Thelen, and Frank Longstreth, eds., *Structuring Politics: Historical Institutionalism in Comparative Perspective*. Cambridge: Cambridge University Press, pp. 1–32.
Thoumi, Francisco E. 1999. "The Impact of the Illegal Drug Industry in Colombia." In Tom J. Farer, ed., *Transnational Crime in the Americas: In Inter-American Dialogue Book*. New York, NY: Routledge.
Tilly, Charles. 2003. *The Politics of Collective Violence*. Cambridge: Cambridge University Press.
  1990. *Coercion, Capital, and European States, 990–1990*. Oxford: Blackwell.

1985. "War Making and State Making as Organized Crime." In Theda Skocpol, Dietrich Rueschemeyer, and Peter B. Evans, eds., *Bringing the State Back In*. Cambridge: Cambridge University Press.
Transnational Institute (TNI). 1998–2010. Corruption Perception Index. Latin America.
Transparency International. 2007. Corruption Perception Index 2007. Retrieved June 10, 2015, from www.transparency.org/research/cpi/cpi_2007/0/.
Trejo, Guillermo and Sandra Ley. 2017. "Why Did Drug Cartels Go to War in Mexico? Subnational Party Alternation, the Breakdown of Criminal Protection, and the Onset of Large-Scale Violence." Comparative Political Studies. https://doi.org/10.1177/0010414017720703.
  2016. "Federalismo, drogas y violencia: por qué el conflicto partidista intergubernamental estimuló la violencia del narcotráfico en México / Federalism, drugs, and violence: Why intergovernmental partisan conflict stimulated inter-cartel violence in Mexico." *Política y Gobierno* 23 (1).
Tutela Legal del Arzobispado: Comisión Arquidiocesana de Justicia y Paz [Salvadoran archbishop's office]. 2007. La violencia homicida y otros patrones de grave afectación a los derechos humanos en El Salvador: Año 2006. San Salvador, Informe de las investigaciones y lucha contra la impunidad realizadas por Tutela Legal del Arzobispado.
Uildriks, Niels, ed. 2009. *Policing Insecurity: Police Reform, Security, and Human Rights in Latin America*. Lanham, MD: Lexington Books, a division of Rowman Littlefield.
UNDP (United Nations Development Programme). 2009. "International Human Development Indicators." Cited in Brenneman 2011.
  2007. *Informe estadístico de la violencia en Guatemala*. Guatemala City: Magna Terra Editores.
  2005. *Informe nacional de desarollo humano* (Guatemala).
Ungar, Mark. 2011. *Policing Democracy: Overcoming Obstacles to Citizen Security in Latin America*. Baltimore, MD: Johns Hopkins University Press.
  2009. "Police Reform, Security, and Human Rights in Latin America: An Introduction." In Niels Uildriks, eds., *Policing Insecurity: Police Reform, Security, and Human Rights in Latin America*. Lanham, MD: Lexington Books, a division of Rowman Littlefield.
  2003. "Prisons and Politics in Latin America." *Human Rights Quarterly* 25 (4).
UNICEF, Stop the Violence against Women and Girls. 1999. Reported in World Vision International 2002, *Faces of Violence in LA and the Caribbean*. Online report.
United Nations, Department of Economic and Social Affairs, Population Division. 2009. *World Population Prospects: The 2008 Revision*, Highlights, Working Paper No. ESA/P/WP.210.
  2007. *World Population Prospects: The 2006 Revision*, Highlights, Working Paper No. ESA/P/WP.202.
United States Senate. 2013. Statement of Senator Patrick Leahy on a Second Millennium Challenge Compact for El Salvador, September 12, 2013. Retrieved July 16, 2014, from www.leahy.senate.gov/press/statement-of-

senator-patrick-leahy-on-a-second-millennium-challenge-compact-for-el-salvador.

Universidad Centroamericana. 2004. *Maras y pandillas en Centroamérica*. Vols. I–III. Managua: Universidad Centroamericana.

Unnithan, N. P. and Whitt, H. P. 1992. "Inequality, Economic Development and Lethal Violence: A Cross-National Analysis of Suicide and Homicide." *International Journal of Comparative Sociology* 33: 182–196.

UNODC (United Nations Office on Drugs and Crime). 2014a. *World Drug Report 2014*. New York, NY: United Nations.

2014b. *Global Study on Homicide 2013: Trends, Context, Data*. New York, NY: United Nations.

2012. *Transnational Organized Crime in Central America and the Caribbean: A Threat Assessment*. Vienna: UNODC.

2011. Global Study on Homicide. Trends, Context, Data. New York, NY: United Nations.

2010. *World Drug Report 2010*. New York, NY: United Nations.

2008. *World Drug Report 2008*. New York, NY: United Nations.

2007. *Crime and Development in Central America: Caught in the Crossfire*. New York, NY: United Nations.

2006. *World Drug Report 2006*. New York, NY: United Nations.

n.d. *Statistics on Criminal Justice*. Retrieved July 24, 2014, from www.unodc.org/unodc/en/data-and-analysis/statistics/crime.html.

USAID. 2006. "Central America and Mexico Gang Assessment." Retrieved June 9, 2015, from http://pdf.usaid.gov/pdf_docs/pnadg834.pdf.

US Department of Homeland Security, Office of Immigration Statistics. 2011. *2010 Yearbook of Immigration Statistics*. Retrieved from www.dhs.gov/xlibrary/assets/statistics/yearbook/2010/oil_yb_2010.pdf.

US Department of State. 2005. "Counternarcotics and Law Enforcement Country Program: El Salvador, June 30, 2005, www.state.gov/p/inl/rls/fs/48915.htm, accessed May 18, 2008.

Van Cott, Donna Lee. 2005. *From Movements to Parties in Latin America: The Evolution of Ethnic Politics*. Cambridge: Cambridge University Press.

van Schendel, Willem and Itty Abraham, eds. 2005. *Illicit Flows and Criminal Things: States, Borders, and the Other Side of Globalization*. Bloomington, IN: Indiana University Press.

Varese, Federico. 2005. *The Russian Mafia: Private Protection in a New Market Economy*. New ed. Oxford: Oxford University Press.

Varshney, Ashutosh. 2002. *Ethnic Conflict and Civic Life: Hindus and Muslims in India*. New Haven, CT: Yale University Press.

Vilas, Carlos M. 1992. "Family Affairs: Class Lineage and Politics in Contemporary Nicaragua." *Journal of Latin American Studies* 24 (2): 309–341.

Visión Policía: Revista de la Policía Nacional. 2007. Año VII, Edición 66 (January). Managua.

Volkov, Vadim. 2002. *Violent Entrepreneurs: The Use of Force in the Making of Russian Capitalism*. Ithaca, NY: Cornell University Press.

Wacquant, Loïc. 2006. *Deadly Symbiosis: Race and the Rise of Neoliberal Penality*. Cambridge: Polity Press.
Walsh, John. 2009. *Lowering Expectations Supply Control and the Resilient Cocaine Market*. Washington, DC: Washington Office on Latin America.
Weber, Max. 1946. "Politics as a Vocation." In H. H. Gerth and C. Wright Mills, eds., *From Max Weber: Essays in Sociology*. New York, NY: Oxford University Press.
Weinstein, Jeremy M. 2007. *Inside Rebellion: The Politics of Insurgent Violence*. Cambridge: Cambridge University Press.
Wilkinson, Steven I. 2004. *Votes for Violence: Electoral Competition and Ethnic Riots in India*. Cambridge: Cambridge University Press.
Williams, Phil. 2009. "Illicit Markets, Weak States and Violence: Iraq and Mexico." *Crime, Law and Social Change* 52 (3): 323–336.
Wilson, Suzanne and Marta Zambrano. 1994. "Cocaine, Commodity Chains, and Drug Politics: A Transnational Approach." In Gary Gereffi and Miguel Korzeniewicz, eds., *Commodity Chains and Global Capitalism*. Westport, CT: Greenwood Press, pp. 297–315.
Withers, George, Lucila Santos, and Adam Isaacson. 2010. *Preach What You Practice: The Separation of Military and Police Roles in the Americas*. Washington, DC: Washington Office on Latin America.
WOLA (Washington Office on Latin America). 2009. *Serve and Protect? The Status of Police Reform in Central America*. Washington, DC: WOLA.
  2006. *Youth Gangs in Central America: Issues in Human Rights, Effective Policing, and Prevention*. A WOLA Special Report. Washington, DC: WOLA.
Wolf, Sonja. 2011. "Street Gangs of El Salvador." In Thomas Bruneau, Lucía Dammert, and Elizabeth Skinner, eds., *Maras: Gang Violence and Security in Central America*. University of Texas Press, pp. 43–69.
Woodward, Ralph Lee. 2008. "Guatemala: Year in Review." *Encyclopedia Britannica*. Retrieved August 8, 2013, from www.britannica.com/EBchecked/topic/1493276/Guatemala-Year-In-Review-2008?anchor=ref1014352.
  1999. *Central America, a Nation Divided*. 3rd edition. New York, NY: Oxford University Press, pp. 436.
Woolcock, Michael and Deepa Narayan. 2000. "Social Capital: Implications for Development Theory, Research, and Policy." *World Bank Research Observer* 15 (2).
World Bank. 2010. *Crime and Violence in Central America*. 2 vols. Washington, DC: World Bank Sustainable Development Department and Poverty Reduction and Economic Management Unit, Latin America and the Caribbean Region.
  2009. *World Bank Data Rule of Law Index*.
  2004. *World Development Report 2005: A Better Investment Climate for Everyone*. © World Bank, https://openknowledge.worldbank.org/handle/10986/5987 License: CC BY 3.0 IGO.
  1996. *World Bank Data Rule of Law Index*.
  n.d. *World Bank Country Data Report for El Salvador, 1996–2009*. Retrieved from www.govindicators.org.

World Economic Forum. 2013. *The Global Competitiveness Report, 2012–2013: Full Data Edition*. Klaus Schwab, ed. Geneva: World Economic Forum.

World Health Organization (WHO). 2002. *World Report on Violence and Health*. (Chapters 1–2 on Introduction and Youth Violence). Geneva: WHO.

Yashar, Deborah J. 2013. "Institutions and Citizenship: Reflections on the Illicit." In Mario Sznajder, Luis Roniger, and Carlos A. Forment, eds., *Shifting Frontiers of Citizenship: The Latin American Experience*. Leiden: Brill.

2011. "The Left and Citizenship in Latin America." In Steven Levitsky and Kenneth M. Roberts, eds., *The Resurgence of the Latin American Left*. Baltimore, MD: Johns Hopkins University Press.

2005. *Contesting Citizenship in Latin America: The Rise of Indigenous Movements and the Postliberal Challenge*. Cambridge Studies in Contentious Politics. Cambridge: Cambridge University Press.

1997. *Demanding Democracy: Reform and Reaction in Costa Rica and Guatemala, 1870s–1950s*. Stanford, CA: Stanford University Press.

Youngers, Coletta A. and Eileen Rosin, eds. 2005. *Drugs and Democracy in Latin America: The Impact of U.S. Policy*. Boulder, CO: Lynne Rienner Publishers.

Ziegler, Melissa and Rachel Nield. 2002. *From Peace to Governance: Police Reform and the International Community*. (A rapporteur's report based on a November 2001 conference sponsored by the Washington Office on Latin America and the Johns Hopkins Nitze School of Advanced International Studies). Washington, DC: WOLA.

Index

Acajutla, El Salvador, 258, 269, 271
accountability. *see also* impunity
  El Salvador, 213
  Guatemala, 156, 159, 163, 166, 176
  Honduras, 353
  Mexico, 355
  military, 166
  policy approaches, 366–367
  state capacity, 100, 102, 104, 108, 110–118
Africa
  drug markets, 75
  homicide rates, 341
  violence in, 146
Aguilar, Jeannette, 215, 228, 243, 244, 254, 265
Aguilera Peralta, Gabriel, 158
Ahuachapán, El Salvador, 258, 270, 271, 276
air transport, 89, 177, 182, 257, 306
Alarcón, Mayra, 171
Alemán, Arnoldo, 293
Alemán, Juan Daniel, 250, 257
Alta Verapaz, Guatemala, 178, 181, 182, 192
Amaya, Edgardo, 220, 228
AmericasBarometer, 226, 242
Amnesty International, 163
Andreas, Peter, 71
anti-gang approaches, 239, 246, 248, 249, 255, 256, 304
Antilles, 87
Apopa, El Salvador, 251, 271
Archibold, Randal C., 253
Argentina
  corruption, 140, 143
  drug trade and transit, 102
  homicide rates, 8, 12, 13, 22, 29
  inequality, 48, 49
  neoliberal reforms, 52
  non-homicide crime, 6
  police, 111, 136, 139, 307, 309
  political violence, 5
Arias, Enrique Desmond, 37, 52, 57, 70, 89, 97, 108, 136, 349, 355, 359
arms
  armed robbery, 6
  El Salvador, 216, 224, 266
  gangs, 93, 127
  Guatemala, 202–203, 207
  gun control, 30
  gun rates, 28, 30
  imports, 29
  in prisons, 198
  Nicaragua, 313
  post-civil war transition arguments for violence, 26, 27, 346
  technologies of violence, 202–203, 207, 315
  trafficking, 94, 173, 224, 235
Arnson, Cynthia J., 228
Arrivillaga Tánchez, Sergio (Lencho), 170
Asia
  drugs, 74, 78
  gang-related homicide rates, 123
  homicide rates, 5, 341
Asíes (think tank), 175
Astorga, Luis, 85
Attorney General's offices
  El Salvador, 214, 217, 219, 221, 230, 232, 261
  Guatemala, 167
  state capacity, 106, 109, 111
authoritarian regimes, 5, 34, 58, 146, 274, 341, 364

Bahia, Brazil, 14
Baja Verapaz, Guatemala, 178, 182
bandas, 189, 196
banks, 173
Barba-Sánchez, Daniela, 10, 16, 23, 40, 116, 209, 211, 270, 308, 316, 333, 355
Barrio 18/ Calle-18/ M-18
  El Salvador, 237, 239, 240, 246, 252, 254, 256, 271, 365, 367
  Guatemala, 172, 188, 189, 192, 194, 198
Bateson, Regina, 43, 349
Becker, Gary, 44, 53, 117, 222
Belize, 92, 283
Beltrán Leyva, 80, 86
Beltrán, Adriana, 166, 168, 170, 173, 174, 175,
Beltrán, María, 30, 209
Benson, Peter, 152
Berger, President Óscar, 150, 160, 166, 167
Berman, Sheri, 38
Bermeo, Nancy, 348
black markets, 69, 72
Bluefields, Nicaragua, 296, 327, 329, 330, 332
Bobea, Lilian, 53, 136
Bolivia
  cocaine production, 75
  corruption, 140, 143
  drug trade and transit, 77, 102
  ethnic diversity, 42
  homicide rates, 8, 22
  inequality, 48, 49
  non-homicide crime, 6
  police, 139, 307, 309
  rule of law, 134
Bonilla, Óscar, 250
border towns/ regions
  competition, 178–181
  conclusions on, 357–362
  El Salvador, 266, 271
  Guatemala, 167, 174, 178–181, 182, 183, 185, 207
  Honduras, 177
  Nicaragua, 305, 332
  organized crime, 181
  trade and transit, 89, 125
Borge, Tomás, 293
Borges, Doriam, 8
Bosworth, James, 354, 363
Brazil

citizen security, 349
corruption, 140, 143
drug trade and transit, 87, 89, 104, 129
extrajudicial action, 97
gangs, 91, 93, 96, 127, 190
homicide rates, 8, 12, 13, 14, 22, 29, 342
human rights, 130
inequality, 48, 49
non-homicide crime, 6
perceptions of security, 316
police, 111, 139, 307, 309, 355
political violence, 5
Brenneman, Robert, 47, 92
bribery, 117, 140, 170, 232, 261, 283, 347

Cabañas, El Salvador, 267, 270, 276
Caldeira, Teresa P.R., 96, 97
Calderón, Gabriela, 120, 125, 130
Cali cartel, 80, 81, 85, 104, 125, 365
Call, Charles T., 26, 33, 35, 212, 213, 215, 216, 217, 222, 230, 231, 232, 234, 235,

Calle-18/ M-18/ Barrio 18
  El Salvador, 237, 239, 240, 246, 252, 254, 256, 271, 365, 367
  Guatemala, 172, 188, 189, 192, 194, 198
  Revolucionarios, 254
cannabis/ marijuana, 74, 81, 85, 124, 177, 325
Cano, Ignacio, 8
car hijacks, 94
Carazo, Nicaragua, 329, 338
Carcach, Carlos Alberto, 209, 242, 266, 269, 271
Caribbean
  drug markets, 76
  drug trade and transit, 81, 86, 87, 102, 103, 104
  homicide rates, 82
  organized crime, 147
Caribbean crackdown, 83, 117, 156, 177, 237, 256, 265
Carranza, Marlon, 239, 251
Carrión Baralt, David, 292, 297
Cartel del Pacífico, 177, 178, 182, 185
cartels. *see* Drug Trafficking Organizations (DTOs)
Casa Alianza, 353
cascades of violence, 130
Castillo, Jose, 330

Centeno, Miguel, 56, 68, 108, 110, 156, 357–362
Central America. *see also specific countries*
  conviction rates, 113
  drug markets, 76
  drug trade and transit, 83, 87, 88, 102, 104, 129
  police, 111
Centro Latinoamericano de Demografía, 211, 270
CEPAL (Comisión Económica para América Latina y el Caribe), 280
CEPREV (Centro de Prevención de la Violencia), 300
Chalatenango, El Salvador, 209, 247, 267, 270, 271, 276
Chamales, Guatemala, 178, 182
Chamorro, President Violeta, 287, 288, 289, 296
Chandra, Kanchan, 43
Chayes (2017), 354
Chevigny, Paul, 97, 349
Chile
  corruption, 140, 143
  drug trade and transit, 102
  homicide rates, 8, 12, 13, 22, 29, 342
  inequality, 48, 49
  non-homicide crime, 6
  police, 109, 111, 136, 139, 307, 309, 348, 355
  political violence, 5
  rule of law, 106, 134
  state capacity, 133
Chiquimula, Guatemala, 30, 152, 170, 181, 192
Chontales, Nicaragua, 305, 338
CICIG (Comisión Internacional Contra la Impunidad en Guatemala), 162, 168, 200, 366
citizen rights, 96
citizen security, 97, 175, 181, 283, 299
citizenship, meaningful, 369
Ciudad Barrios prison, El Salvador, 238, 247
Ciudad Juarez, Mexico, 89
civil rights, 221, 300
civil societies, 36–38
civil war
  conclusions on, 356
  El Salvador, 208
  Guatemala, 152, 155, 187

Nicaragua, 279, 286, 288, 299
territorial competition, 121–122
theoretical debates, 35, 342, 348, 356
trade and transit, 83
clikas. *see* gangs
coast guards, 106
coastal areas. *see also* maritime routes; ports
  competition, 102, 178–181
  El Salvador, 257, 259, 265, 266, 269
  Guatemala, 178–181, 182
  Nicaragua, 305, 306, 326, 327–330
cocaine
  El Salvador, 259, 260, 262, 263, 265
  Guatemala, 176, 178, 181, 185, 191
  Honduras, 354
  Mexico, 85
  Nicaragua, 307, 325, 326, 327, 331
  organizational competition, 124
  production, 78
  trade and transit, 74–77, 83, 84, 88, 90, 98, 103, 105,
coercion
  conclusions on, 345
  El Salvador, 212, 244, 249, 274
  Guatemala, 165, 191, 193
  historical institutionalism, 56, 57
  Honduras, 352
  Nicaragua, 284,
  organizational territorial competition, 119
Colindres, Bishop Fabio, 253
collusion, 19, 199, 264, 274, 362, 365; *see also* complicity
Colombia
  cartels, 80, 81, 83, 85, 104, 124, 125
  citizen security, 349
  civil war, 5, 14, 77
  cocaine production, 75
  corruption, 140, 143
  drug trade and transit, 77, 80, 83, 85–86, 87, 102, 103, 177, 262, 263, 306, 330
  homicide rates, 6, 8, 13, 14, 22, 208
  inequality, 48, 49
  informal agreements of mutual toleration, 365
  non-homicide crime, 6
  opium production, 74
  police, 307, 309
Comaroff, Jean, 6
Comaroff, John L., 6

Comités de Defensa Sandinista, 287
community
  community justice in Guatemala, 175
  community policing strategies, 176, 283, 299–307, 349–350
  gangs, 92, 187
competition. *see also* organizational territorial competition
  drug trafficking, 78–81, 120, 185
  electoral competition, 120, 342, 361
  gangs, 96
  turf wars, 121, 127, 187, 192, 197, 241, 359
  uncertainty, 119–123
  with the state, 130
complicity. *see also* collusion; impunity
  Brazil, 355
  conclusions on, 344, 350, 356, 359, 360, 362, 365
  El Salvador, 223, 259, 261, 264, 359
  Guatemala, 166, 172, 184, 191, 196, 197
  historical institutionalism, 56
  Honduras, 354
  military, 166
  of state, 105, 108, 130, 135
  police, 114, 116, 118, 129, 137
  prisons, 172, 197
Concha-Eastman, Alberto, 126, 238, 239
contract enforcement, 124, 129
conviction rates, 112, 163, 168, 220, 221
cooperative security locations (CSLs), 257
Copán Ruinas/El Florido (CA-11), 185
Cordero Ardila, Edwin, 283, 287, 288, 289, 294, 295, 296, 298, 299, 301, 302, 303, 304, 306, 307, 317, 318, 319, 327, 331
Córdova Macías, Ricardo, 218, 224, 225, 243
corruption
  conclusions on, 344, 345, 346, 347, 355, 356, 361
  corruption indices, 140–144
  El Salvador, 140, 143, 212, 213, 214, 221, 222–224, 234, 259, 261, 264, 283
  Guatemala, 158, 166, 169, 184, 196, 200, 283, 366
  historical institutionalism, 57
  homicidal ecologies, 342
  Honduras, 140, 143, 306, 352, 353, 354
  illicit economies, 67, 70
  measurement of, 107
  Mexico, 86

  military, 156, 166
  Nicaragua, 140, 143, 282, 296, 306–307, 331, 337
  Panama, 143
  police, 137, 158, 160, 161, 217, 222–224
  prisons, 156, 162, 171–173, 192, 197, 198, 234
  state capacity, 105, 133–143
cost/benefit calculations of crime, 44, 119, 122, 125, 185
Costa Rica
  conviction rates, 112
  corruption, 140, 143
  drug trade and transit, 105, 259
  firearms rates, 30, 204
  gangs, 92
  homicide clearance rates, 112, 163, 310
  homicide rates, 6, 8, 12, 13, 22, 29
  inequality, 48, 49
  labor markets, 94
  non-homicide crime, 6
  perceptions of security, 310
  police, 139, 283, 307, 309, 348, 355
  rule of law, 106, 134, 137
  state capacity, 133
Costa, Gino, 215
Cotto Castaneda, Augusto, 247
Cotto, Howard, 258
counterinsurgency movements, 28, 166, 174, 229, 288, 289
counterintelligence, 305
coups, 105
courts and judicial system
  capacity, 105, 106, 109
  conclusions on, 344
  El Salvador, 229–233
  Guatemala, 156, 168–176, 181
  illicit institutions, 70
  Nicaragua, 292, 329, 337
  police working with, 170
  Supreme Courts, 214, 229, 230, 233, 248, 251
  trust in, 136
crackdowns
  Caribbean, 83, 117, 156, 177, 237, 256, 265
  Colombian cartels, 83, 104
  El Salvador, 233, 234, 237, 248, 250, 265
  Guatemala, 190, 200
  Mexican, 199, 265
  Nicaragua, 298, 307

Index 403

punitive policies, 353, 355, 363–364
state capacity, 130
criminal records, as data source, 8
criminalization of goods, 69
Cruz, José Miguel, 30, 35, 70, 93, 94, 97, 108, 209, 217, 228, 239, 248, 307, 342, 346, 347, 349, 351, 353,
Cuadra Lacayo, General Joaquín, 284, 290, 292, 295, 296, 297, 300,
Cuba
  homicide rates, 8, 12, 13, 22, 29
  rates of young people, 39
Cuevas, F., 185
Cuilapa, Guatemala, 32
Cumaraswamy, Param, 170
Cuscatlán, El Salvador, 267, 270, 276

Davis, Diane, 56, 355
de Rodríguez, Deysi, 219
death squads, 212, 236, 251
definition of homicide, 7, 8
deindustrialization, 57
Dell, Melissa, 120
demilitarization, 111, 216
democratic promise, 367–368
democratization
  conclusions on, 344, 346, 352, 356, 362
  El Salvador, 213, 235, 273
  Guatemala, 156, 176
  Honduras, 352, 353
  hope of lower violence, 146, 341, 343
  meaningful citizenship, 369
  Nicaragua, 284, 293
  policy approaches, 367–368
demographic variables, 38–43
Demombynes, Gabriel, 17, 185
Demoscopía, 95, 96, 127
deportation from US (gang members), 93, 188, 189, 237, 239
deterrence roles, 169
DIGESTYC (Dirección General de Estadística y Censos), 211, 270
Dominican Republic
  drug trade and transit, 86, 87, 257
  homicide rates, 13, 22, 29
  inequality, 48, 49
  neoliberal reforms, 53
  non-homicide crime, 6
  rule of law, 136
Dowdney, Luke, 127, 136
Drolet, Adam, 228

drug trade and transit. *see also* transportation routes
  Colombia, 77, 80, 83, 85–86, 87, 102, 103, 177, 262, 263, 306, 330
  conclusions on, 352
  Ecuador, 83, 87
  El Salvador, 77, 89, 216, 241, 251, 256–264, 266–273
  Guatemala, 77, 83, 86, 89, 105, 150, 156, 174, 175, 176–185, 191, 193, 257, 263
  Honduras, 352, 354,
  hubs, 181, 326, 327
  illicit economies, 69, 77–81
  Mexico, 77, 83, 85–88, 89, 102, 104, 129, 177, 178, 181, 257, 262, 263, 265, 359
  Nicaragua, 259, 263, 306, 307, 325–334, 367
  organizational territorial competition, 119–131, 358
  Panama, 98, 105, 257, 259
  state capacity, 101–108
  tripartate argument of book, 19
  Venezuela, 77, 87, 88, 102, 104, 129
  violence, 81–90
Drug Trafficking Organizations (DTOs). *see also* cartels; transportistas
  alliances, 182
  as part of illicit economies, 80, 81, 86
  Beltrán Leyva, 80, 86
  Cali cartel, 80, 81, 85, 104, 125, 365
  Cartel del Pacífico, 177, 178, 182, 185
  crackdowns, 355
  El Salvador, 213, 222, 256, 258, 263, 264–266
  Familia Michoacana, 80
  geographical motives, 103
  Guadalajara DTO, 86
  Guatemala, 170, 177, 178, 183
  Gulf Cartel, 80, 86, 177, 182, 305
  hegemony, 124, 125
  Honduras, 354
  illicit economies, 78
  Juarez/ Vicente Carillo Fuentes organization, 80, 86
  kingpin strategy, 364
  Lorenzanas, 178, 182, 184
  Los Perrones, 262, 263, 264, 265, 266
  Luciano cartel, 170
  Medellín cartel, 80, 81, 85, 104, 124, 125, 365
  Mendoza family, 181, 182, 184

Drug Trafficking Organizations (cont.)
  Mexican Gulf Cartel, 28
  Mexico, 177, 178, 181
  Nicaragua, 330
  organizational territorial competition, 119–131, 361
  Sinaloa cartel (Sinaloa Federation), 86, 124, 177, 181, 182, 263, 265, 305
  state capacity, 101
  strategic calculations, 106, 123–126
  territorial enclaves, 359
  Texis cartel, 263, 266
  Tijuana/Arellano Felix organization, 80, 86, 124
  trafficking routes, 72
  trafficking vehicles, 85
  transport, 103
  violence, 83, 86
  Zetas, 80, 86, 177, 178, 181–182, 185, 263, 265, 266
drug-related deaths, 77
drugs. *see also* cocaine
  background on rising drug trade, 74–81
  courts and judicial system, 170
  decriminalization, 71, 200
  drug consumption, 75, 77, 78, 80, 81, 87, 90, 128–129
  drug flows, 75, 83, 88, 183, 326
  gangs, 93, 95, 96, 98, 126, 127, 128, 192, 193
  heroin, 74, 75, 78, 85, 177, 325
  inequality, 51
  interdiction, 82, 83, 103, 305, 325, 326, 331
  international markets, 79
  local consumption rates, 258
  local markets, 266
  marijuana/ cannabis, 74, 81, 85, 124, 177, 325
  methamphetamine, 74, 81, 85, 124, 177
  production, 74, 78, 80, 81, 90, 128–129
  seizures of, 75, 81, 82, 103, 257, 307, 325, 331
  supply chains, 78, 102, 263, 358
Dudley, Steven, 238, 253, 301, 305, 367
Durán-Martínez, Angélica, 20, 101, 109, 119, 120, 125, 205, 355, 361

ECLAC (Economic Commission for Latin America and the Caribbean), 39, 41, 47, 51, 94, 279, 280

economic arguments for high violence rates, 44–58
economic reforms, 33
Ecuador
  corruption, 140, 143
  drug trade and transit, 83, 87
  ethnic diversity, 42
  homicide rates, 13, 22, 29
  inequality, 48, 49
  non-homicide crime, 6
  police, 139, 307, 309
  rule of law, 134
education levels, 279
efficaciousness, 110–118
El Boquerón prison, Guatemala, 172
El Pavón Prison, Guatemala, 162, 172
El Salvador
  citizen security, 349
  civil societies, 37
  conviction rates, 112, 163
  corruption, 140, 212, 213, 214, 221, 222–224, 234, 259, 261, 264, 283
  crime as barrier to investment in, 197
  deportation from US (gang members), 93
  drug trade and transit, 77, 89, 216, 241, 251, 256–264, 266–273
  extortion, 224, 240–241, 244, 245–248, 258, 266, 277
  extrajudicial action, 97
  gang truce, 212, 237, 239, 252–256, 364
  gang-on-gang violence, 126
  gangs, 91, 92, 93, 96, 97, 147, 188, 189, 190, 198
  gun rates, 30, 203, 204
  homicide clearance rates, 112, 114, 163, 219–222, 310
  homicide rates, 6, 8, 13, 14, 22, 208–209, 241, 244, 254, 267, 269, 270, 272, 275
  human rights, 146, 215, 221, 249, 252
  impunity, 213, 216, 219, 221, 228, 233, 252, 264,
  inequality, 47, 49
  kidnapping, 113
  law and order institutions, 212–235
  mano dura, 229, 234, 237, 248–252, 363
  military, 212, 215, 222, 224–227, 228, 249
  Newspaper Violence Database, 155, 217, 220, 223, 240, 243, 245, 246, 251, 257, 258, 269, 275

non-homicide crime, 6
organizational territorial competition, 237, 252, 255, 256, 259–264, 269, 274
organized crime, 215, 223, 228, 235, 250, 256–264, 265, 269, 277
peace process, 27, 208, 212, 213, 215, 216, 228, 230, 234, 351
perceptions of security, 114, 310
police, 109, 112, 139, 157, 159, 160, 212–229, 233, 236, 243, 249, 256, 257, 259, 261, 264, 271, 272, 277, 307, 309, 324, 351
political violence in 1960s/70s, 5
post-civil war transition arguments for violence, 26
poverty, 279
prisons, 216, 233–235, 251, 365
reason for comparative study on, 16
rule of law, 134, 213, 221, 229, 232, 233
subnational variation, 32, 209, 242–243, 245, 254, 266–273
violence rates, 150
weak state, 106, 118, 344
youth, 303
electoral competition, 120, 342, 361
electoral cycles, 43
electoral fraud, 67
embezzlement, 67
employment, 94, *see also* unemployment
endogeneity, 88, 101, 108, 147, 197, 228, 298, 350
Enterprise Surveys, 196
Escobar, Pablo, 121
Escuintla, Guatemala, 89, 155, 158, 170, 172, 183, 184, 192
espionage, 174, *see also* intelligence structures
Estelí, Nicaragua, 297, 338
ethnic cleavages, 42–43
ethnic violence, 35, 107, 130
EU Drug Market report, 87
Europe
    drug markets, 75, 76, 79, 87, 102
    gang-related homicide rates, 123
    homicide clearance rates, 112
    homicide rates, 5, 341
extortion
    El Salvador, 224, 240–241, 244, 245–248, 258, 266, 277
    gangs, 95, 128
    Guatemala, 193, 194, 196, 202

illicit economies, 73
    Nicaragua, 296
    of public transport drivers, 194, 196, 202, 240, 245–246
    prisons, 246–247
extraditions, 184, 200
extrajudicial action, 97, 114, 130, 137, 197, 236, 349, 353

Fajnzylber, Pablo, 36, 44, 45, 46, 51
Familia Michoacana, 80
Farah, Douglas, 231, 238, 239, 241, 245, 246, 252, 254, 257, 258, 259, 262, 263, 264, 265, 266,
Fearon, James D., 121, 130
femicide, 163, 204
fertility rates, 94
firearms. *see* arms
FMLN (Farabundo Martí de Liberación Nacional), 157, 212, 214, 215, 231, 235
fraud, 67
frontiers/ borders. *see* border towns/ regions
Frühling, Hugo, 109, 349
FSLN/Sandinistas (Frente Sandinista de Liberación Nacional), 284, 288, 290, 291, 336
Funes, President Mauricio, 214, 254, 256
FUSADES (the Salvadoran Foundation for Economic and Social Development), 219, 257

Galápagos, 85
Galindo, Celvin, 171
Gambetta, Diego, 20, 101, 119, 120, 134, 365
gangs. *see also* Calle-18/ M-18/ Barrio 18; Mara Salvatrucha (MS or MS-13); maras/ violent gangs
    alliances, 239, 262, 265
    bandas, 189, 196
    civil society, 36
    clikas, 189, 239, 240, 241
    conclusions on, 350, 352, 359
    deportation from US, 93, 188, 189, 237, 239
    destroyed families, 26
    drugs, 87, 93, 95, 96, 98, 126, 127, 128, 129, 192, 193, 251, 264–266

gangs (cont.)
  El Salvador, 213, 223, 227, 233, 234, 236, 237–256, 264–266, 271, 277, 359
  ex-military members, 27
  gang truce (El Salvador), 212, 237, 239, 252–256
  gang truces (Nicaragua), 302
  Guatemala, 91, 92, 93, 96, 128, 165, 172, 186–199
  hegemony, 96, 128, 194
  Honduras, 91, 92, 93, 96, 97, 147, 188, 189, 198, 301, 354, 360
  illicit economies, 72, 90–98
  inter-gang rivalry, 193, 197, 198, 331
  intra-organizational obedience, 244–245
  migration of, 189
  Nicaragua, 92, 300, 301, 302–304, 317–325, 327
  organizational territorial competition, 120, 126–129
  organized crime, 90, 96
  pandillas/ youth gangs, 90–98, 126, 187, 192, 193, 250, 303, 316, 360
  political nature of, 190
  prisons, 172, 190, 192, 197
  professionalization of, 94, 126, 250
  punitive policies (including war on drugs, kingpin strategy against DTOs and Mano Dura against gangs), 363
  rivalry and factions, 127
  rule of law, 135
  social democratic promise, 367
  socioeconomic conditions, 47
  state capacity, 101
  Sureños, 254
  territory, 359
  transnational gangs, 127, 246, 359
  United States, 188, 190, 237, 238
  urban gangs and territorial enclaves, 73
García, César, 197
Garrid Safie, Félix, 219
Gaviria, Alejandro, 45, 46, 51
Gay, Robert, 52, 53, 77, 127
GDP (Gross Domestic Product), 34, 45, 183
gender, 145
General Violence Report for El Salvador, 258
generalizability of the argument, 343
geography, 72, 73, 102, 358, *see also* territory
Gibb, Tom, 239, 240–241

Gini index, 34, 44, 46, 47, 48, 49, 51, 61
Giraudy, Agustina, 58
globalization, 53,
Godoy, Angelina Snodgrass, 154
González, Yanilda, 16, 17, 18, 116, 148, 157, 176, 275, 344, 349
Gootenberg, Paul, 71, 74
Granera, Aminta, 282, 283, 284, 294, 296, 298, 299, 300, 301, 304, 306, 312, 313, 334, 348
greed, 121
Grigsby, William, 283, 285, 286, 293, 294, 295, 297, 298, 304, 306, 307, 331
Grillo, Ioan, 86, 87, 96
Grupo Guatemalteco de Mujeres, 163
GTZ (German Organization for Technical Cooperation), 285, 286, 287, 294
Guadalajara DTO, 86
Guardián Alfaro, Hamyn, 283, 287, 288, 301, 302, 303, 317, 318, 319, 327
Guatemala
  accountability, 366
  cabecera (urban) violence, 202
  citizen security, 349
  conviction rates, 112, 163
  corruption, 140, 143, 158, 160, 161, 283
  crime as barrier to investment in, 197
  deportation from US (gang members), 93
  drug trade and transit, 77, 83, 86, 89, 105, 150, 156, 174, 175, 176–185, 191, 193, 257, 263
  education levels, 280
  ethnic diversity, 42
  extortion, 193, 194, 196, 202
  extrajudicial action, 97
  gang-on-gang violence, 126
  gangs, 91, 92, 93, 96, 128, 165, 172, 186–199
  gun rates, 30, 202–203
  homicide clearance rates, 112, 156, 163, 168, 171, 310
  homicide rates, 6, 8, 13, 14, 22, 150, 152, 154, 179, 366
  homicide rates (map), 31
  human rights, 146, 155, 157, 160, 165, 167, 169, 170, 173
  impunity, 159, 165, 168, 169, 174, 184, 192, 200
  inequality, 48, 49
  law and order institutions, 106, 155–176, 196

mano dura, 189, 363
military, 156, 164–167, 173, 184, 259
Newspaper Violence Database, 148, 155, 183, 192, 194–196, 201, 275
non-homicide crime, 6
organizational territorial competition, 178, 185, 195, 197, 199
organized crime, 147, 157, 169, 173, 174, 178, 181, 183, 184, 197, 199, 266
peace accords, 150, 156, 157, 158, 163, 164, 165, 168, 190, 351
perceptions of security, 310
police, 109, 112, 136, 139, 156–167, 170, 176, 182, 184, 188, 191, 283, 307, 309, 324, 351
political violence, 5, 149
poverty, 279
prisons, 156, 159, 162, 171–173, 192, 197
reason for comparative study on, 16
rule of law, 134, 169, 171, 175, 196
state capacity, 118, 155–176, 344
subnational variation, 30, 152, 178, 179, 181–185, 192, 201, 202
types of homicide, 203
urban violence, 202
violence patterns, 152–155
weak state, 118, 150, 155–176, 183, 186, 189, 192, 196, 197, 199, 344
youth, 302, 303
Guatemala City, 32, 152, 155, 167, 173, 182, 183, 186, 187, 191, 192, 194
Guatemalan Kaibiles, 28
Guerrero, Mexico, 86
guerrillas, 208, 216, 229, 294, 351
Gulf Cartel, 28, 80, 86, 177, 182, 305
gun control, 30
gun rates, 28, 30, 202–203, 207, 313
Gurr, Ted Robert, 47
Gutiérrez Rivera, Lira, 353, 354, 357, 363

Haiti
  homicide rates, 8, 22
  non-homicide crime, 6
Hale, Charles, 332
Halleslevens, General Moisés Omar, 286, 292, 305, 332
health records, as data source, 8
hegemony
  drug trafficking organizations (DTOs), 124, 125

gangs, 96, 128, 194
  state, 96
  territorial, 98, 119, 262, 361
  territorial enclaves, 19, 359
Helmke, Gretchen, 68, 70, 108, 350
Hemisphere Initiatives, 174
Herbst, Jeffrey, 357
Hernández, Iduvina, 156, 164
Hernández, S., 92
heroin, 74, 75, 78, 85, 177, 325
hidden powers, 174
historical institutionalism, 20, 25, 55–58, 281
hitmen, 94, 189
Hobbes, Thomas, 368, 369
Hoffman, Kelly, 53
Holland, Alisha, 97, 248
Holston, James, 96
homicide clearance rates
  Costa Rica, 112, 163, 310
  El Salvador, 112, 114, 163, 219–222, 310
  Guatemala, 112, 156, 163, 168, 171, 310
  Honduras, 353
  Nicaragua, 112, 163, 310, 327
  police capacity, 112–113
  policy approaches, 366
homicide rates
  Asia, 5
  civil war transitions, 29
  Colombia, 208
  El Salvador, 6, 8, 13, 14, 22, 208–209, 241, 244, 254, 267, 269, 270, 272, 275
  empirical trends of violence, 8–15
  Europe, 5
  Guatemala, 6, 8, 13, 14, 22, 31, 150, 152, 154, 179, 366
  Honduras, 352, 354
  Latin America, 5, 151, 341, 342
  Mexico, 8, 12, 13, 14, 22, 342
  national versus subnational variation, 14, 16
  Newspaper Violence Database, 201
  Nicaragua, 6, 13, 22, 29, 279, 312, 313, 314, 331, 332, 333, 338
  punitive policies, 363
  reason for focus on, 6
  stability of, 13
  types of homicide, 203
  urban versus rural, 202
Honduras
  citizen security, 349

Honduras (cont.)
  conviction rates, 163
  corruption, 140, 143, 306, 352, 353, 354
  coup, 105
  crime as barrier to investment in, 197
  deportation from US (gang members), 93
  drug trade and transit, 77, 105, 177, 185, 332
  education levels, 280
  gang-on-gang violence, 126
  gangs, 91, 92, 93, 96, 97, 147, 188, 189, 198, 301, 354, 360
  gun rates, 30, 203, 204
  homicide clearance rates, 353
  homicide rates, 6, 8, 13, 14, 16, 22, 29, 208, 342, 352, 354
  human rights, 353
  impunity, 353
  inequality, 48, 49
  lack of civil war, 146
  mano dura, 363
  military, 298, 352
  non-homicide crime, 6
  organized crime, 266, 354
  perceptions of security, 310
  police, 139, 159, 160, 283, 307, 309, 324, 352–354
  poverty, 279
  rule of law, 134
  violence rates, 150
  weak states, 106, 118, 344
  youth, 302, 303
Huehuetenango, Guatemala, 192
human rights
  civil war, 28
  El Salvador, 146, 215, 221, 249, 252
  Guatemala, 146, 155, 157, 160, 165, 167, 169, 170, 173
  Honduras, 353
  Nicaragua, 304, 336
  state and society, 130
Human Rights Ombudsman, 230, 249, 259
Human Rights Watch, 130
human trafficking, 199, 259, 266, 362
Hume, Mo, 30, 37, 204, 209, 220
Hunt, Flor, 217, 218
Hurricane Mitch, 257, 303

IDHUCA (Instituto de Derechos Humanos de la Universidad Centroamericana), 215, 241

IEEPP (Instituto de Estudios Estratégicos y Políticas Públicas), 285, 286, 295, 309
illicit activity. *see also* Chapter 3
illicit economies. *see also* drug trade and transit; gangs
  conclusions on, 343, 361, 362
  gangs, 90–98
  organizations, 25
  rising drug trade, 74–81
  state capacity, 101
illicit institutions, 70, 71
illicit spaces, 73
illicit, the. *see also* Chapter 3; drug trafficking organizations (DTOs); gangs; illicit economies; organized crime
  black markets, 69, 72
  claims about, 66
  conceptualizing, 66–72
Ilopango, El Salvador, 271–272
immorality, 70
import substitution, 57
impunity. *see also* military; police; state capacity
  conclusions on, 346
  El Salvador, 213, 216, 219, 221, 228, 233, 252, 264,
  Guatemala, 159, 165, 168, 169, 174, 184, 192, 200
  Honduras, 353
  institutional weakness, 110–118
  Nicaragua, 311
  social cleansing, 252
  versus accountability, 366
indigenous people, 175
indiscriminate violence, 122
individual-level crime, 117
inequality, 25, 33, 44–52, 61, *see also* poverty
informal economy, 68, 70, 94, 96
informal institutions, 68, 70, 71
informal markets, 57
informants, networks of, 27
infrastructural power, 58
infrastructure
  drug transit points, 73, 78, 88–90
  organizational territorial competition, 125, 135
  police, 218
  state capacity, 104

InSight Crime, 262, 263, 266, 301, 305, 327, 329, 331, 332, 367
Institute of Legal Medicine (IML) (El Salvador), 210, 211, 218, 220, 243, 254, 270
institutional breaks, 288
institutional weakness, 53, 347, *see also* weak states
institutions. *see* courts and judicial system; informal institutions; law and order institutions; military; police; state capacity
insurgents, 121, 284, 351
intelligence structures, 37, 165, 174, 263, 293, 301
InterAmerican Commission on Human Rights, 170
interdiction, 82, 83, 103, 305, 325, 326, 331
inter-gang rivalry, 193, 197, 198, 331, *see also* El Salvador; gangs; Guatemala; Honduras
intermediary organizations, 72
international aid, 159, 303, 353
International Commission of Jurists (Comisión Internacional de Juristas, CIJ), 169
International Human Rights Clinic (IHRC), 213, 216, 220, 221, 231, 237, 239, 240–241, 243, 244, 245, 248, 249, 251, 252
international law, 69
international monitoring, 103, 104
Itty, Abraham, 70, 350
IUDOP-based surveys, 126
Izabal, Guatemala, 30, 89, 152, 167, 171, 181, 189

Jamaica
  drug trade and transit, 87
  homicide rates, 6, 8, 13, 22, 29
  non-homicide crime, 6
Jamal, Amaney, 38
Jawahar, Vinay, 16, 18, 152
Jinotega, Nicaragua, 332, 338
Juarez/ Vicente Carillo Fuentes organization, 80, 86
judges, protection of, 170, 213
judiciary. *see* courts and judicial system
jurisdiction shopping, 101
Jutiapa, Guatemala, 30, 152
juvenile crime, 94

kaibiles, 183
Kalyvas, Stathis, 66, 101, 119, 121, 122,
Keefer, Philip, 69, 72, 78, 79, 80, 124
Kenney, Michael, 83, 86, 103
kidnapping, 6, 113, 150, 172, 235, 250, 259, 311
kingpin strategy, 130, 177, 264, 265, 363, 364
Kitroeff, Natalie J., 168, 173, 181
knife/ machete violence, 313
Knut, Walter, 218
Kohli, Atul, 56, 108, 110, 156, 358
Krug, E.G., 6
Kurtenbach, S., 299

La Libertad, El Salvador, 89, 209, 242–243, 245, 267, 270, 272, 276
La Paz, El Salvador, 209, 245, 254, 270, 276
La Unión, El Salvador, 245, 254, 263, 265, 267, 270, 276
labor markets, 19, 54, 94
Lacayo, Antonio, 285, 287, 289, 290, 291–292, 293, 294
Lafree, Gary, 33, 34
Laitin, David D., 130
LAPOP surveys (Latin American Public Opinion Project), 6, 16, 97, 116, 134, 136, 218, 224, 225, 226, 232, 242, 307
LatinNews, 254
Latinobarometer, 16, 97, 115, 133, 134, 136, 279, 281, 307, 310, 333
law and order institutions. *see also* courts and judicial system; police; prisons
  conceptualizing the illicit, 65
  conclusions on, 343, 345
  El Salvador, 212–235
  gangs in, 199
  Guatemala, 106, 155–176, 196
  Nicaragua, 282–312
  patterns of efficaciousness and impunity, 110–118
  professionalization of, 366
  state capacity, 100, 105, 109
  territorial reach, 117–118
  tripartate argument of book, 19
laws
  define the illicit, 68
  morality, 71
Leahy, Senator Patrick, 214
Lecasan, Rudio, 158
Lechuga Mojica, Carlos El Viejo Lin, 367

Lee III, Rensselaer W., 83, 86, 101
Leones, Los, 182, 184
Lessing, Benjamin, 120, 121, 125, 130, 361
Levenson, Deborah T., 91, 92, 172, 173, 186, 187, 188, 189, 190, 192, 194, 198
Levitsky, Steven, 68, 70, 108, 335, 348, 350
Levitt, Stephen, 54, 120
Ley, Sandra, 43, 120, 355
Lima, Byron, 173
Lipsky, Michael, 106, 157, 344
Littoral/Coastal Highway, 259
Logan, Sam, 327, 331
López, Carlos, 228
López, Julie, 177
Lorenzanas, 178, 182, 184
Los Perrones, 262, 263, 264, 265, 266
Luciano cartel, 170
Lum, Pamela Phillips, 238, 239, 252, 254, 257, 265, 266,
Luna Pereira, José Natividad aka Chepe Luna, 259, 261
Luna, Juan Pablo, 58
lynchings, 137, 152, 154, 349

M-18. *see* Calle-18/ M-18/ Barrio 18
mafia, 120, 134, 306, 365
Mahoney, James, 335, 352
Maingot (1999), 104
male violence, 145
malfeasance, 222–224
Managua, Nicaragua, 302, 305, 329, 332, 338
Mann, Michael, 117, 357
mano dura
  El Salvador, 229, 234, 237, 248–252, 363
  Guatemala, 189
  Honduras, 363
  Nicaragua (not in), 300
  punitive policies, 94, 97, 137, 363–364
  super mano dura, 94, 248
Mansfield, Edwards D., 33, 34
Mara Salvatrucha (MS or MS-13)
  El Salvador, 237, 238, 239, 240, 246, 252, 256, 266, 271
  Guatemala, 172, 188, 189, 192
  truce (2016), 365
maras/ violent gangs, 94, 95, 186–199, 316, 358, 360, 361, 363, *see also* Calle-18/ M-18/ Barrio 18; Mara Salvatrucha (MS or MS-13)

marijuana/ cannabis, 74, 81, 85, 124, 177, 325
maritime routes, 259, 262, 306, 326, 327–330
marketization reforms, 33, 34
Martínez Ventura, Jaime, 251
Martinez, H.E. Hugo, 228
Martínez, Luis, 223
Martínez, Óscar, 178, 181, 182, 183, 184, 306
Marxist insurgents, 284, 293
Matagalpa, Nicaragua, 332, 338
Maurer, Noel, 125
McIlwaine, Cathy, 36
Medellín cartel, 80, 81, 85, 104, 124, 125, 365
Medrana, Juan María aka Juan Colorado, 259
Mendoza (2016), 181
Mendoza family, 178, 181, 182, 184
Mendoza, Carlos, 154
methamphetamine, 74, 81, 85, 124, 177
Mexican crackdown, 199, 265
Mexican Gulf Cartel. *see* Gulf Cartel
Mexico
  conviction rates, 113
  corruption, 140, 143
  drug trade and transit, 77, 83, 85–88, 89, 102, 104, 129, 177, 178, 181, 257, 262, 263, 265, 359
  electoral competition, 120, 342
  ethnic diversity, 43
  gangs, 91
  historical institutionalism, 57,
  homicide rates, 8, 12, 13, 14, 22, 342
  human rights, 130
  inequality, 47, 48, 49
  informal agreements of mutual toleration, 365
  kingpin strategy, 130, 177, 264, 265, 363, 364
  neoliberal reforms, 52
  non-homicide crime, 6
  non-urban areas, 58
  opium production, 74
  organizational competition, 125
  organized crime, 80, 85, 147
  police, 109, 111, 136, 139, 307, 309, 354–355
  subnational variation, 89
  weak states, 344

Index

Meyer, Maureen, 85, 86
Michoacán, Mexico, 86
migration, 37, 93, 94, 145, 187, 189, 341
Miguel Insulza, José, 198
Mijango, Raúl, 253
military
   conclusions on, 343, 345
   demobilization and arms, 26
   demobilized groups, 259, 341, 352
   El Salvador, 212, 215, 222, 224–227, 228, 249
   Guatemala, 156, 164–167, 173, 184, 259
   Honduras, 298, 352
   illicit institutions, 70
   Nicaragua, 259, 284, 285, 286–287, 288, 289–293, 295, 305, 331, 332, 336
   police and the, 109, 111, 164–167, 184, 216, 222, 227, 228, 249, 286–287, 349
   post-civil war transition arguments for violence, 26
   state capacity, 109
millennium challenge compact, 214
MINUGUA (Misión de Naciones Unidas para Guatemala), 157, 158, 159, 167, 173
Molina Vaquerano, Fabio, 211, 270
money laundering, 150, 169, 214, 222, 235, 259
monopoly, territorial, 119, 125
Montealegre, Franco, 294
Morales, David, 227
Morales, Sergio, 169, 172
morality, 70
Moran, Patrick J., 147, 157, 166, 189, 215, 216, 222, 257
Morazán, El Salvador, 209, 267, 270, 276
Moreno Molina, Alfred, 174
Moser, Caroline, 36
Munguía Payés, David, 224, 227, 252
Murillo, Victoria Maria, 335
mutilation, levels of, 203
Myrna Mack Foundation, 171, 173

Naím, Moisés, 68, 70
Narayan, Deepa, 38
narco-barriles, 258
national boundaries, 357–362
National Drug Threat Assessment, 98
Naylor. R.T., 99,
negotiations, 364–366
neighborhood watches, 175

neoliberal reforms, 25, 52–54, 77, 187, 189
Newspaper Violence Database, 17, 148
   El Salvador, 155, 217, 220, 223, 240, 243, 245, 246, 251, 257, 258, 269, 275
   Guatemala, 148, 155, 183, 192, 194–196, 201, 275
Nicaragua
   accountability, 366
   civil societies, 37
   civil war, 28
   corruption, 140, 143, 282, 296, 306–307, 331, 337
   crime as barrier to investment in, 197
   democratization, 35
   deportation from US (gang members), 93
   drug trade and transit, 259, 263, 306, 307, 325–334, 367
   extortion, 296
   gangs, 92, 300, 301, 302–304, 317–325, 327
   gun rates, 30, 204
   homicide clearance rates, 112, 163, 310, 327
   homicide rates, 6, 13, 22, 29, 279, 312, 313, 314, 331, 332, 333, 338
   human rights, 336
   impunity, 311
   inequality, 47, 49
   knife/ machete violence, 202
   law and order institutions, 282–312
   mano dura, 300
   military, 259, 284, 285, 286–287, 288, 289–293, 295, 305, 331, 332, 336
   Newspaper Violence Database, 155, 313, 329, 330
   non-homicide crime, 6
   organizational territorial competition, 281, 315, 331
   organized crime, 305–306, 325–334, 337
   peace process, 27, 290
   perceptions of security, 114, 310
   police, 109, 112, 114, 136, 139, 160, 215, 216, 217, 281, 282–312, 327, 331, 334–337, 350–351, 370
   prisons, 302, 308
   rates of young people, 39
   reason for comparative study on, 16
   rule of law, 134, 283, 284, 333
   subnational variation, 305, 306, 327–330
   weak states, 279, 327, 332, 351
Nicaragua Nuestra, 300

nonaggression pacts, 256
non-homicide violence, 6
North, Douglas, 55
Nuevo Laredo, Mexico, 89
null hypothesis, 362–363

Obama administration, 75–76
O'Donnell, Guillermo, 117, 290, 344, 357, 369
Olson, Mancur, 125, 360
ONUSAL (United Nations Observer Group in El Salvador), 217, 219, 232
opium production, 74, 78
Organization of American States (OAS), 72, 79, 83, 87, 103, 170
organizational coherence, 108, 110, 111
organizational territorial competition.
  see also Chapter 4
  conclusions on, 342, 361
  El Salvador, 237, 252, 255, 256, 259–264, 269, 274
  Guatemala, 178, 185, 195, 197, 199
  in general, 119–131
  Nicaragua, 281, 315, 331
  organizational competition, 19, 65, 99, 101
organizations, focus on, 24, 25
organized crime. see also Drug Trafficking Organizations (DTOs); *specific organizations*
  as a business, 102
  background on rising drug trade, 74–81
  conclusions on, 350, 361
  courts/ judicial system, 169, 337
  drug trade and transit, 87
  El Salvador, 215, 223, 228, 235, 250, 256–264, 265, 269, 277
  gangs, 90, 96, 198
  Guatemala, 147, 157, 169, 173, 174, 178, 181, 183, 184, 197, 199, 266
  Honduras, 266, 354
  illicit economies, 72, 73
  infrastructure, 135
  Mexico, 80, 85, 147
  Nicaragua, 305–306, 325–334, 337
  organizational competition, 125
  punitive policies, 363
  state capacity, 102
Ortega Menaldo, General Luis Francisco, 165, 174
Ortega, Humberto, 290, 291–292, 297

Ortega, President Daniel, 290, 292, 293, 334, 336,
Osorio, Javier, 120, 125

PAHO (Pan-American Health Organization), 8, 9, 12, 23, 143, 150, 242, 267, 268, 312
Panama
  conviction rates, 112
  corruption, 140, 143
  drug trade and transit, 98, 105, 257, 259
  gangs, 92
  gun rates, 30, 204
  homicide rates, 6, 13, 22
  inequality, 48, 49
  non-homicide crime, 6
  perceptions of security, 310, 315
  police, 139, 283, 309
  rates of young people, 39
PanAmerican Highway, 245, 259
pandillas/ youth gangs, 90–98, 126, 186, 187, 190, 192, 193, 250, 303, 316, 360
Paraguay
  drug trade and transit, 102
  homicide rates, 13, 22
  inequality, 48, 49
  non-homicide crime, 6
  police, 307
  rule of law, 134
Paraiba, Brazil, 14
paramilitary groups, 349
parastatal groups, 73, 95, 118, 128
Park, Bethany, 17, 148, 243, 275
Parra-Torrado, Mónica, 41
Pasaco, Los, 172
peace accords
  conclusions on, 299
  El Salvador, 27, 208, 212, 213, 215, 216, 228, 230, 234, 351
  Guatemala, 150, 156, 157, 158, 163, 164, 165, 168, 190, 351
  Nicaragua, 27, 290
peace zones, 253
Peacock, Susan C., 166, 168, 170, 173, 174, 175,
Peña, Uzziel, 239, 240–241
perceptions of security, 97, 315, 316
Pereira, Anthony, 56
Pérez Molina, Otto, 200
Pérez Orlando, J., 249
Pérez Santos, Felipe, 183

permissive political environments for violence, 35
Perrones, Los, 262, 263, 264, 265, 266
Peru
  cocaine production, 75
  corruption, 140, 143
  drug trade and transit, 102
  drugs, 77
  ethnic diversity, 42
  homicide rates, 8, 12, 13, 22, 29
  non-homicide crime, 6
  police, 109, 139, 307, 309
Petén, Guatemala, 30, 89, 152, 161, 167, 171, 178, 181, 182, 183–184, 201, 202, 266
Pinheiro, Paulo Sergio, 97
Plan de Protección de la Vida, 272
Plan Escoba, 190
Platform for the Americas (PLISA), 9, 23
police. *see also* conviction rates; homicide clearance rates
  and illicit institutions, 70
  as factor of state capacity, 100
  brutality and criminality, 160
  capacity, 105, 106
  Chile, 109, 111, 136, 139, 307, 309, 348, 355
  community policing strategies, 37, 176, 283, 299–307, 349–350
  complicity, 114, 116, 118, 129, 137
  conclusions on, 19, 343, 344–362
  corruption, 137, 158, 160, 161, 217, 222–224
  democratization, 35
  efficaciousness, 111–112
  El Salvador, 109, 112, 139, 157, 159, 160, 212–229, 233, 236, 243, 249, 256, 257, 259, 261, 264, 271, 272, 277, 283, 307, 309, 324, 351
  esprit de corps/ corporatist ethos, 110, 216, 282, 283, 295, 296, 298, 312, 334, 347–348, 351, 355
  getting drawn into violence, 129
  Guatemala, 109, 112, 136, 139, 156–167, 170, 176, 182, 184, 188, 191, 283, 307, 309, 324
  historical institutionalism, 57, 58
  Honduras, 139, 159, 160, 283, 307, 309, 324, 352–354
  Mexico, 109, 111, 136, 139, 307, 309, 354–355
  military and the, 109, 111, 164–167, 184, 216, 222, 227, 228, 249, 286–287, 349
  national boundaries, 358
  Nicaragua, 109, 112, 114, 136, 139, 160, 215, 216, 217, 281, 282–312, 327, 331, 334–337, 350–351, 370
  Panama, 139, 283, 309
  perceptions of, 114–117, 136, 159, 196, 283, 294, 295, 307, 309, 324
  politicization of, 336, 349, 354
  post-civil war transition arguments for violence, 27
  professionalization of, 111, 160, 215, 228, 282, 284, 293–294, 295, 335, 343, 349, 355
  public opinion/ perceptions, 114, 136, 159, 196, 218, 283, 294, 295, 307, 309, 324
  reform, 282, 346, 348, 351, 353, 354, 355
  reliability of police services, 139
  resource shortages, 218
  role in homicidal ecologies, 334
  role specification, 111–112, 156
  state capacity, 109
  types of, 345
  voluntary police, 283
police archives (Guatemala), 155, 159
Policzer, Pablo, 348
political illicit activity, 67
political transition, as factor in higher violence, 24
political violence, 5, 26, 47, 58, 88, 146, 149, 222
Polyani, Karl, 68
Popkin, Margaret, 214, 215, 216, 217, 219, 229, 230, 231, 232, 235
popular (in)justice, 97
Portes, Alejandro, 52, 53, 68,
Portillo, President Alfonso, 160, 164, 165, 166, 169, 200
ports
  drug trade and transit, 89,
  El Salvador, 269
  Guatemala, 155, 181
  homicide rates, 88
  Nicaragua, 305
  organizational territorial competition, 125, 135, 178
post-civil war transition arguments for violence, 26
post-colonialism, 146

poverty, 25, 39, 90–91, 238, 249, 269, 279, 330
preemptive violence, 130
preventative policy measures, 200, 249, 300–304, 335, 367,
Primera Ley Orgánica de la Policía Nacional, 293
principal-agent argument, 122
prisons
  conclusions on, 344, 345
  corruption, 156, 162, 171–173, 192, 197, 198, 234
  El Salvador, 216, 233–235, 251
  extortion in, 246–247
  gangs, 172, 190, 192, 197
  Guatemala, 156, 159, 162, 171–173, 192, 197
  Nicaragua, 302, 308
  state capacity, 110
private security, 349–350
profit maximization motives, 69, 73, 74, 78–80, 95, 101, 119, 121, 185, 250, 332
prohibition (by law), 70, 83, 90
protection rackets, 96, 120, 246, 360
public opinion surveys, 15
public opinion/ perceptions
  corruption perceptions index, 140
  crime, 196, 307
  El Salvador, 213, 218, 224, 232
  extortion, 258
  most pressing issues, 281
  Nicaragua, 280, 292, 307, 333
  police, 114, 136, 159, 196, 218, 283, 294, 295, 307, 309, 324
  safety/ security, 27, 310, 334
  trust in institutions, 136, 159, 218, 224, 283, 324
public transport
  extortion of drivers of, 194, 196, 202, 240, 245–246
  homicides related to, 277
Puerto Barrios, Guatemala, 181
Puerto Rico
  drug trade and transit, 86
  homicide rates, 13, 22, 29
punitive policies, 363–364, *see also* anti-gang approaches; crackdowns; kingpin strategy; mano dura; war on drugs
purges, 161, 223, 228, 244
Putnam, Robert D., 38

Quezada, Daniel, 259
Quezaltepeque, 247, 271

RAAN region, Nicaragua, 293, 327, 331, 332, 338
RAAS region, Nicaragua, 327, 329, 330, 331, 332, 338
Ranum, Elin Cecile, 160, 186, 187, 188, 191, 192, 197
rape, 6, 244
redemptive violence, 130
Reguillo Cruz, Rossana, 190
Reich, Otto J., 168
relative deprivation theories, 47
Reno, William, 70
renta, 240
  rent-seeking behavior, 55, 95, 245–248, *see also* extortion
repertoires of violent acts, 33
reporting of violence, 7
research agenda for future work, 345–350, 362–368
research design, 15–18, 350
Reuter, Peter, 45, 46, 78, 79, 81, 99
revenge killings, 192, 330
revueltos, 292
Ribeiro, Eduardo, 8
Rio de Janeiro, Brazil, 14, 37, 89, 127, 136
Río San Juan, Nicaragua, 332, 338
Rivas, Nicaragua, 305, 306
roads
  competition, 178
  El Salvador, 259
  gang extortion, 245–246
  Guatemala, 195
  highway attacks, 195
  homicides on/near, 202, 207
robbery, 6, 46, 65
  El Salvador, 224, 235, 241, 245, 269, 272, 277
  Guatemala, 193, 204
Roberts, Bryan, 52
Rocha, José Luis, 30, 91, 92, 93, 204, 279, 280, 285, 286, 287, 292, 298, 301, 302, 303, 304, 325
Rodgers, Dennis, 290, 307, 313, 314
Roman, John, 45, 46
Ruhl, Mark J., 157, 164, 165, 166, 167, 168, 285, 289, 290, 291, 292, 293, 297

rule of law. *see also* law and order institutions
  El Salvador, 134, 213, 221, 229, 232, 233
  Guatemala, 134, 169, 171, 175, 196
  homicide rates, 109
  Nicaragua, 134, 283, 284, 333
  policy approaches, 366–367
  state capacity, 105, 133–143
rural areas, 58, 185, 189, 207, 272, 279, 305
Russia, 208
Rustow, Dankwart, 290

Saca, Antonio, 233, 248, 261, 264
Salvadoran Archbishop's Office, 221, 236, 249
San Marcos, Guatemala, 167, 170, 178, 271
San Martín, El Salvador, 271–272
San Miguel, El Salvador, 245, 254, 263, 265, 266, 267, 270, 271, 276
San Salvador, El Salvador, 37, 208, 209, 242–243, 245, 254, 267, 269, 270, 271, 276
San Vicente, El Salvador, 254, 267, 270, 276
Sánchez Cerén, President (El Salvador), 254–255
Sandinista Revolution, 284, 285, 286, 288, 295, 312, 331, 335, 347
Sandinistas, 37, 93, 259, 282, 293, 298, 335
Sandy Bay, Nicaragua, 330
Sanford, Victoria, 169
Santa Ana, El Salvador, 209, 242–243, 254, 265, 267, 269, 270, 271, 276
Santa Rosa, Guatemala, 30, 32, 152, 161, 192
Santacruz Giralt, María L., 126, 238, 239
Santos Mejía de Escobar, Aída Luz, 220, 228, 233, 249
São Paolo, Brazil, 14, 89
Schendel, W., 350
Schendel, Willem van, 70
Schmitter, Philippe, C., 290, 344
Schneider, Friedrich, 72
score settling, 124
Scott, James C., 357
security
  alternative forms of, 349–350
  citizen demands for, 97
  citizen security, 97, 175, 181, 283, 299
  community justice in Guatemala, 175
  El Salvador, 224
  gangs providing, 95, 128
  Guatemala, 166
  military and, 166, 336
  Nicaragua, 300
  perceptions of, 27, 310, 334
  private security in El Salvador, 218
  security gaps, 129
security institutions. *see also* courts and judicial system; police; prisons
  historical institutionalism, 57
  neoliberal reforms, 53
  permissive political environments for violence, 35
Seelke, Clare Ribando, 223, 227, 246, 253, 256, 257
Seligson, Mitchell, 140
Sieder, Rachel, 166, 168
Signoret, Patrick, 364
Silva Avalos, Héctor, 216, 222, 259, 261, 262, 264,
Simons, Paul E., 175
Sinaloa cartel (Sinaloa Federation), 80, 86, 124, 177, 181, 182, 263, 265, 305
Sinaloa, Mexico, 85, 86
slums, urban, 91
small-N comparative study methodology, 16, 47
Smith, Peter H., 124
smuggling, 78, 182, 257
Snodgrass Godoy, Angelina, 97, 154, 175
Snyder, Jack, 20, 33, 34, 101, 119, 120, 355
social capital, 36, 37,
social cleansing, 97, 129, 137, 236, 251, 349
social democratic promise, 367–368
social imaginary, 190
social indicators, 280
social justice, 187
social networks, 37
social norms, regarding illicit activity, 70
Social Panorama of Latin America, 51
social prevention and rehabilitation, 300, 302, 366–367
social prevention committees, 299
socioeconomic conditions (poverty), 25, 39, 90–91, 238, 249, 269, 279, 330
sociological arguments for high violence, 36–43
solidarity, 92
Somoza dictatorship (Nicaragua), 285
Sonsonate, El Salvador, 89, 209, 242–243, 254, 258, 267, 269, 270, 271, 272, 276
Sosa, Carlos Guillermo, 171

South Africa/ Swaziland, 6
Soyapango, El Salvador, 251, 271
Spalding, Rose J., 290, 296, 297,
Sperisen, Erwin, 161–162
Stanley, William, 215
state capacity, 100, 101–118, 133–143
　complicity, 105, 108, 130, 135
　conclusions on, 356
　efficaciousness, 101–118
　El Salvador, 106, 118, 344
　Guatemala, 118, 155–176, 344
　historical institutionalism, 56
　Nicaragua, 333, 343, 351
　organizational coherence, 108, 110, 111
　violence (conclusions), 343–345
　weakness, 19, 33, see also weak states
state institutions. see also courts and judicial system; military; police
　civil war transitions, 33
　democratization, 35
　historical institutionalism, 55–58
　tripartate argument of book, 19
　weakness, 65
state prohibition, 70, 71, 90
state regulation, 68, 70, 71, 97
state/ inter-state monitoring, 102, 104
strategic calculations, 106, 125
strategic warehousing, 89
street children, 97
submersible crafts, 259
subnational variation
　civil war transition arguments, 28, 30, 32
　cocaine production, 75
　conclusions on, 357–362
　drug transit points, 88
　El Salvador, 32, 209, 242–243, 245, 254, 266–273
　ethnic cleavages, 43
　Guatemala, 30, 152, 178, 179, 181–185, 192, 201, 202
　inequality-based comparisons, 47
　labor markets, 54
　neoliberal reforms, 53
　Nicaragua, 305, 306, 327–330
　state capacity, 58
　subnational spaces, 73, 78, 88, 104, 125
　subnational territorial enclaves, 73
super mano dura, 94, 248, see also mano dura
supply chains, 78, 102, 263, 358

Supreme Courts, 214, 229, 230, 233, 248, 251
Sureños, 254
surveillance, 174
Sznajder, Mario, 70, 97

Taylor, Charles, 190
technologies of violence, 202–203, 207, 315
territorial enclaves, 19, 65, 73, 98, 123, 191, 357 362
territorial organizational competition. see organizational territorial competition
territorial reach, 56, 109, 110, 117–118, 345
territoriality, 95, 100, 148, 357–362
territory
　conclusions on, 357–362
　gangs, 90–98, 192, 197, 245–248
　hegemony over, 19, 98, 119, 262, 359, 361
　illicit economies and, 72
　turf wars, 121, 127, 187, 192, 197, 241, 359
Texis cartel, 263, 266
Thelen, Kathleen, 335
Thoumi, Francisco E., 104, 364
Tijuana, Mexico, 89
Tijuana/Arellano Felix organization, 80, 86, 124
Tilly, Charles, 55, 66, 96, 101, 119, 120, 121, 125, 348, 357, 360
tolerance levels for risk and security, 33
tolerance levels for violence, 156
Torres, Óscar, 233
trade and transit. see drug trade and transit
transit points, 88–90, see also drug trade and transit
transit routes, 77–81, see also drug trade and transit
transit vehicles, 78
transnational criminal organizations, 239, 259, 358
transnational gangs, 127, 246, 359
transnational illicit economy, 18, 66, 256–264
transnational illicit trade, 77–81
Transparency International (TNI) surveys, 140, 143, 158
transportation routes
　El Salvador, 240, 258, 259, 266–273
　Guatemala, 195, 202
　national boundaries, 358

Index

Nicaragua, 306, 326, 327–330
transportistas, 245–246, 257, 262, 264–266, 269
Trejo, Guillermo, 120, 355
Triangle of Death, 272
Triángulo Minero, Nicaragua, 327, 332, 338
trust
  civil societies, 37
  El Salvador, 218, 224
  Guatemala, 159, 324
  law and order institutions, 136
  Nicaragua, 283, 324
Truth Commission, 231
Tseloni, Andreomachi, 33, 34
tumbadores, 182
turf wars, 121, 127, 187, 192, 197, 241, 359

UCA (Universidad Centroamericana), 292
UN Mission, Guatemala, 157
UNDP (United Nations Development Program), 9, 16, 143, 183, 202, 209, 231, 307, 333, 338
unemployment, 39, 45, 94, 279, 330
UNFPA (United Nations Population Fund), 211, 270
Ungar, Mark, 97, 349, 353,
United Nations (UN)
  in El Salvador, 234, 235
  ONUSAL (United Nations Observer Group in El Salvador), 217, 219, 232
  United Nations police force, 157
  World Crime Survey, 45
United States
  aid programs, 111
  Citizenship and Immigration Services, 296
  DEA (US Drug Enforcement Agency), 103, 174, 358, 361
  deportation of gang members, 93, 188, 189, 237, 239
  drug markets, 75, 76, 79, 85, 87, 102, 177, 332
  drug trade and transit, 82, 86, 103
  El Salvador and, 231, 261
  gangs, 188, 190, 237, 238
  homicide rates, 12, 13, 22, 29
  in Nicaragua, 286, 289
  migration to, 145
University of Central America (UCA), 36, 37

UNO (Unión Nacional Opositora - Nicaragua), 288, 291
UNODC (United Nations Office on Drugs and Crime)
  competition and drug trafficking, 185
  corruption, 158
  crime perceptions, 197
  drug trade and transit, 74, 75, 76, 77, 79, 81, 82, 83, 84, 86, 87, 88, 89, 176, 177, 178, 181, 182, 185, 259, 265, 266, 267, 325
  gangs, 91, 92, 98, 189, 194, 196
  homicide clearance rates, 112, 163, 168, 310
  homicide rates, 6, 7, 10, 13, 14, 145, 341
  illicit economies, 72
  lynchings data, 154
  most pressing issues, 281
  organizational competition, 123, 148
  organized crime, 28
  perceptions of security, 310
  police, 117, 163, 310
  state capacity, 103, 104, 109
  territoriality, 148
  use of criminal records, 8
  violence levels, 42, 149, 262
  World Drug Report, 75, 76, 79, 82, 83, 84, 98, 103, 196, 325, 326, 327, 331
urban gangs, 90–98, 186
urban illicit economies, 95
urban slums/ favelas, 91
urban violence, 202, 207
urban youth, 38
urbanization, 37, 57
URNG (Guatemala), 157
Uruguay
  corruption, 140, 143
  homicide rates, 8, 12, 13, 22, 29
  inequality, 48, 49
  non-homicide crime, 6
  police, 111, 136, 139, 307, 309
  rule of law, 134
  state capacity, 133
  strong rule of law institutions, 106
Usulután, El Salvador, 254, 263, 265, 267, 270, 271, 276

Varshney, Ashutosh, 38
Venezuela
  corruption, 140, 143

Venezuela (cont.)
  drug trade and transit, 77, 87, 88, 102, 104, 129
  gangs, 96
  homicide rates, 8, 12, 13, 14, 22, 29, 342
  inequality, 48, 49
  non-homicide crime, 6
  organized crime, 147
  police, 136, 139, 307, 309
  political violence (current day), 5
  rule of law, 134
Venkatesh, Sudhir, 120
victimization surveys, 15, 97, 224, 235
vigilante groups, 349
Vilas, Carlos M., 289
Villa Nueva, 194
violence. *see also* homicide rates; political violence
  rates of non-homicide violence, 6
  reason for focus on homicide, 8
Vitória, Brazil, 89
Volkov, Vadim, 120

Wagner, Karin, 175
war on drugs, 130
Way, Lucan, 348
weak states. *see also* complicity; corruption
  civil war transitions, 25
  conclusions on, 344, 362,
  drug trafficking, 103
  El Salvador, 212–235
  gangs, 94
  Guatemala, 118, 150, 155–176, 183, 186, 189, 192, 196, 197, 199, 344
  homicidal ecologies, 342
  Honduras, 352
  illicit economies, 65
  Nicaragua, 279, 327, 332
  state capacity, 104, 107, 110, 118, 133
Weber, Max, 295, 357, 368, 369
Weinstein, Jeremy M., 122

WHO (World Health Organization), 7, 8, 12, 13, 16, 23, 33, 38, 44, 47, 150, 152, 208, 312, 313
Wilkinson, Steven I., 43, 107, 349
Williams, Philip, 78, 89, 99
Withers, George, 111
witness protection, 169, 220
WOLA (Washington Office on Latin America), 111, 126, 158, 159, 164, 173, 294, 295, 349
Wolfson Index of Income Polarization, 51
women, crimes against, 277
women, killing of, 163, 204
Woodward, Ralph Lee, 174
Woolcock, Michael, 38
World Bank, 6, 17, 28, 29, 32, 72, 109, 133, 134, 135, 140, 142, 185, 192, 196, 203, 204, 208, 209, 232, 243, 273
World Drug Report, 75, 76, 79, 82, 83, 84, 98, 103, 196, 325, 326, 327, 331
World Economic Forum, 133, 139, 307
Worldwide Governance Indicators, 135, 142

Yashar, Deborah, 42, 56, 66, 72, 108, 110, 156, 348, 358
youth
  at-risk youth in Nicaragua, 300
  El Salvador, 303
  gangs, 90, 91, 93, 94, 360
  Guatemala, 302, 303
  homicide rates, 145, 241, 341
  Honduras, 302, 303, 353
  Nicaragua, 302–304
  pandillas/ youth gangs, 90–98, 126, 186, 187, 190, 192, 193, 250, 303, 316, 360
  percentages of, 38
  social investment in, 40

Zacapa, Guatemala, 30, 167, 171, 182
Zelaya Central, Nicaragua, 327, 332, 338
zero tolerance, 301, *see also* mano dura
Zetas, 80, 86, 177, 178, 181–182, 185, 263, 265, 266

Other Books in the Series (*continued from page ii*)

Leonardo R. Arriola, *Multi-Ethnic Coalitions in Africa: Business Financing of Opposition Election Campaigns*
Andy Baker, *The Market and the Masses in Latin America: Policy Reform and Consumption in Liberalizing Economies*
David Austen-Smith, Jeffry A. Frieden, Miriam A. Golden, Karl Ove Moene, and Adam Przeworski, eds., *Selected Works of Michael Wallerstein: The Political Economy of Inequality, Unions, and Social Democracy*
Laia Balcells, *Rivalry and Revenge: The Politics of Violence during Civil War*
Lisa Baldez, *Why Women Protest: Women's Movements in Chile*
Kate Baldwin, *The Paradox of Traditional Chiefs in Democratic Africa*
Stefano Bartolini, *The Political Mobilization of the European Left, 1860–1980: The Class Cleavage*
Robert Bates, *When Things Fell Apart: State Failure in Late-Century Africa*
Mark Beissinger, *Nationalist Mobilization and the Collapse of the Soviet State*
Pablo Beramendi, *The Political Geography of Inequality: Regions and Redistribution*
Nancy Bermeo, ed., *Unemployment in the New Europe*
Nancy Bermeo and Deborah J. Yashar, eds., *Parties, Movements, and Democracy in the Developing World*
Carles Boix, *Democracy and Redistribution*
Carles Boix, *Political Order and Inequality: Their Foundations and Their Consequences for Human Welfare*
Carles Boix, *Political Parties, Growth, and Equality: Conservative and Social Democratic Economic Strategies in the World Economy*
Catherine Boone, *Merchant Capital and the Roots of State Power in Senegal, 1930–1985*
Catherine Boone, *Political Topographies of the African State: Territorial Authority and Institutional Change*
Catherine Boone, *Property and Political Order in Africa: Land Rights and the Structure of Politics*
Michael Bratton and Nicolas van de Walle, *Democratic Experiments in Africa: Regime Transitions in Comparative Perspective*
Michael Bratton, Robert Mattes, and E. Gyimah-Boadi, *Public Opinion, Democracy, and Market Reform in Africa*
Valerie Bunce, *Leaving Socialism and Leaving the State: The End of Yugoslavia, the Soviet Union, and Czechoslovakia*
Daniele Caramani, *The Nationalization of Politics: The Formation of National Electorates and Party Systems in Europe*
John M. Carey, *Legislative Voting and Accountability*
Kanchan Chandra, *Why Ethnic Parties Succeed: Patronage and Ethnic Headcounts in India*
Eric C. C. Chang, Mark Andreas Kayser, Drew A. Linzer, and Ronald Rogowski, *Electoral Systems and the Balance of Consumer-Producer Power*
José Antonio Cheibub, *Presidentialism, Parliamentarism, and Democracy*
Ruth Berins Collier, *Paths toward Democracy: The Working Class and Elites in Western Europe and South America*

Daniel Corstange, *The Price of a Vote in the Middle East: Clientelism and Communal Politics in Lebanon and Yemen*
Pepper D. Culpepper, *Quiet Politics and Business Power: Corporate Control in Europe and Japan*
Sarah Zukerman Daly, *Organized Violence after Civil War: The Geography of Recruitment in Latin America*
Christian Davenport, *State Repression and the Domestic Democratic Peace*
Donatella della Porta, *Social Movements, Political Violence, and the State*
Alberto Diaz-Cayeros, *Federalism, Fiscal Authority, and Centralization in Latin America*
Alberto Diaz-Cayeros, Federico Estévez, and Beatriz Magaloni, *The Political Logic of Poverty Relief*
Jesse Driscoll, *Warlords and Coalition Politics in Post-Soviet States*
Thad Dunning, *Crude Democracy: Natural Resource Wealth and Political Regimes*
Gerald Easter, *Reconstructing the State: Personal Networks and Elite Identity*
Margarita Estevez-Abe, *Welfare and Capitalism in Postwar Japan: Party, Bureaucracy, and Business*
Henry Farrell, *The Political Economy of Trust: Institutions, Interests, and Inter-Firm Cooperation in Italy and Germany*
Karen E. Ferree, *Framing the Race in South Africa: The Political Origins of Racial Census Elections*
M. Steven Fish, *Democracy Derailed in Russia: The Failure of Open Politics*
Robert F. Franzese, *Macroeconomic Policies of Developed Democracies*
Roberto Franzosi, *The Puzzle of Strikes: Class and State Strategies in Postwar Italy*
Timothy Frye, *Building States and Markets after Communism: The Perils of Polarized Democracy*
Geoffrey Garrett, *Partisan Politics in the Global Economy*
Scott Gehlbach, *Representation through Taxation: Revenue, Politics, and Development in Postcommunist States*
Edward L. Gibson, *Boundary Control: Subnational Authoritarianism in Federal Democracies*
Jane R. Gingrich, *Making Markets in the Welfare State: The Politics of Varying Market Reforms*
Miriam Golden, *Heroic Defeats: The Politics of Job Loss*
Jeff Goodwin, *No Other Way Out: States and Revolutionary Movements*
Merilee Serrill Grindle, *Changing the State*
Anna Grzymala-Busse, *Rebuilding Leviathan: Party Competition and State Exploitation in Post-Communist Democracies*
Anna Grzymala-Busse, *Redeeming the Communist Past: The Regeneration of Communist Parties in East Central Europe*
Frances Hagopian, *Traditional Politics and Regime Change in Brazil*
Henry E. Hale, *The Foundations of Ethnic Politics: Separatism of States and Nations in Eurasia and the World*
Mark Hallerberg, Rolf Ranier Strauch, and Jürgen von Hagen, *Fiscal Governance in Europe*

Stephen E. Hanson, *Post-Imperial Democracies: Ideology and Party Formation in Third Republic France, Weimar Germany, and Post-Soviet Russia*
Michael Hechter, *Alien Rule*
Timothy Hellwig, *Globalization and Mass Politics: Retaining the Room to Maneuver*
Gretchen Helmke, *Courts under Constraints: Judges, Generals, and Presidents in Argentina*
Gretchen Helmke, *Institutions on the Edge: The Origins and Consequences of Inter Branch Crises in Latin America*
Yoshiko Herrera, *Imagined Economies: The Sources of Russian Regionalism*
Alisha C. Holland, *Forbearance as Redistribution: The Politics of Informal Welfare in Latin America*
J. Rogers Hollingsworth and Robert Boyer, eds., *Contemporary Capitalism: The Embeddedness of Institutions*
John D. Huber, *Exclusion by Elections: Inequality, Ethnic Identity, and Democracy*
John D. Huber and Charles R. Shipan, *Deliberate Discretion? The Institutional Foundations of Bureaucratic Autonomy*
Ellen Immergut, *Health Politics: Interests and Institutions in Western Europe*
Torben Iversen, *Capitalism, Democracy, and Welfare*
Torben Iversen, *Contested Economic Institutions*
Torben Iversen, Jonas Pontussen, and David Soskice, eds., *Unions, Employers, and Central Banks: Macroeconomic Coordination and Institutional Change in Social Market Economics*
Thomas Janoski and Alexander M. Hicks, eds., *The Comparative Political Economy of the Welfare State*
Joseph Jupille, *Procedural Politics: Issues, Influence, and Institutional Choice in the European Union*
Stathis Kalyvas, *The Logic of Violence in Civil War*
David C. Kang, *Crony Capitalism: Corruption and Capitalism in South Korea and the Philippines*
Stephen B. Kaplan, *Globalization and Austerity Politics in Latin America*
Junko Kato, *Regressive Taxation and the Welfare State*
Orit Kedar, *Voting for Policy, Not Parties: How Voters Compensate for Power Sharing*
Robert O. Keohane and Helen B. Milner, eds., *Internationalization and Domestic Politics*
Herbert Kitschelt, *The Transformation of European Social Democracy*
Herbert Kitschelt, Kirk A. Hawkins, Juan Pablo Luna, Guillermo Rosas, and Elizabeth J. Zechmeister, *Latin American Party Systems*
Herbert Kitschelt, Peter Lange, Gary Marks, and John D. Stephens, eds., *Continuity and Change in Contemporary Capitalism*
Herbert Kitschelt, Zdenka Mansfeldova, Radek Markowski, and Gabor Toka, *Post-Communist Party Systems*
David Knoke, Franz Urban Pappi, Jeffrey Broadbent, and Yutaka Tsujinaka, eds., *Comparing Policy Networks*
Ken Kollman, *Perils of Centralization: Lessons from Church, State, and Corporation*

Allan Kornberg and Harold D. Clarke, *Citizens and Community: Political Support in a Representative Democracy*
Amie Kreppel, *The European Parliament and the Supranational Party System*
David D. Laitin, *Language Repertoires and State Construction in Africa*
Fabrice E. Lehoucq and Ivan Molina, *Stuffing the Ballot Box: Fraud, Electoral Reform, and Democratization in Costa Rica*
Benjamin Lessing, *Making Peace in Drug Wars: Crackdowns and Cartels in Latin America*
Mark Irving Lichbach and Alan S. Zuckerman, eds., *Comparative Politics: Rationality, Culture, and Structure, Second Edition*
Evan Lieberman, *Race and Regionalism in the Politics of Taxation in Brazil and South Africa*
Richard M. Locke, *The Promise and Limits of Private Power: Promoting Labor Standards in a Global Economy*
Pauline Jones Luong, *Institutional Change and Political Continuity in Post-Soviet Central Asia*
Pauline Jones Luong and Erika Weinthal, *Oil Is Not a Curse: Ownership Structure and Institutions in Soviet Successor States*
Julia Lynch, *Age in the Welfare State: The Origins of Social Spending on Pensioners, Workers, and Children*
Lauren M. MacLean, *Informal Institutions and Citizenship in Rural Africa: Risk and Reciprocity in Ghana and Côte d'Ivoire*
Beatriz Magaloni, *Voting for Autocracy: Hegemonic Party Survival and Its Demise in Mexico*
James Mahoney, *Colonialism and Postcolonial Development: Spanish America in Comparative Perspective*
James Mahoney and Dietrich Rueschemeyer, eds., *Historical Analysis and the Social Sciences*
Scott Mainwaring and Matthew Soberg Shugart, eds., *Presidentialism and Democracy in Latin America*
Melanie Manion, *Information for Autocrats: Representation in Chinese Local Congresses*
Isabela Mares, *From Open Secrets to Secret Voting: Democratic Electoral Reforms and Voter Autonomy*
Isabela Mares, *The Politics of Social Risk: Business and Welfare State Development*
Isabela Mares, *Taxation, Wage Bargaining, and Unemployment*
Cathie Jo Martin and Duane Swank, *The Political Construction of Business Interests: Coordination, Growth, and Equality*
Anthony W. Marx, *Making Race, Making Nations: A Comparison of South Africa, the United States, and Brazil*
Doug McAdam, John McCarthy, and Mayer Zald, eds., *Comparative Perspectives on Social Movements*
Bonnie M. Meguid, *Party Competition between Unequals: Strategies and Electoral Fortunes in Western Europe*
Joel S. Migdal, *State in Society: Studying How States and Societies Constitute One Another*

Joel S. Migdal, Atul Kohli, and Vivienne Shue, eds., *State Power and Social Forces: Domination and Transformation in the Third World*
Scott Morgenstern and Benito Nacif, eds., *Legislative Politics in Latin America*
Kevin M. Morrison, *Nontaxation and Representation: The Fiscal Foundations of Political Stability*
Layna Mosley, *Global Capital and National Governments*
Layna Mosley, *Labor Rights and Multinational Production*
Wolfgang C. Müller and Kaare Strøm, *Policy, Office, or Votes?*
Maria Victoria Murillo, *Labor Unions, Partisan Coalitions, and Market Reforms in Latin America*
Maria Victoria Murillo, *Political Competition, Partisanship, and Policy Making in Latin American Public Utilities*
Monika Nalepa, *Skeletons in the Closet: Transitional Justice in Post-Communist Europe*
Ton Notermans, *Money, Markets, and the State: Social Democratic Economic Policies since 1918*
Aníbal Pérez-Liñán, *Presidential Impeachment and the New Political Instability in Latin America*
Roger D. Petersen, *Understanding Ethnic Violence: Fear, Hatred, and Resentment in 20th Century Eastern Europe*
Roger D. Petersen, *Western Intervention in the Balkans: The Strategic Use of Emotion in Conflict*
Simona Piattoni, ed., *Clientelism, Interests, and Democratic Representation*
Paul Pierson, *Dismantling the Welfare State? Reagan, Thatcher, and the Politics of Retrenchment*
Marino Regini, *Uncertain Boundaries: The Social and Political Construction of European Economies*
Kenneth M. Roberts, *Changing Course in Latin America: Party Systems in the Neoliberal Era*
Marc Howard Ross, *Cultural Contestation in Ethnic Conflict*
Ben Ross Schneider, *Hierarchical Capitalism in Latin America: Business, Labor, and the Challenges of Equitable Development*
Roger Schoenman, *Networks and Institutions in Europe's Emerging Markets*
Lyle Scruggs, *Sustaining Abundance: Environmental Performance in Industrial Democracies*
Jefferey M. Sellers, *Governing from Below: Urban Regions and the Global Economy*
Yossi Shain and Juan Linz, eds., *Interim Governments and Democratic Transitions*
Beverly Silver, *Forces of Labor: Workers' Movements and Globalization since 1870*
Prerna Singh, *How Solidarity Works for Welfare: Subnationalism and Social Development in India*
Theda Skocpol, *Social Revolutions in the Modern World*
Andy Baker, *The Market and the Masses in Latin America: Policy Reform and Consumption in Liberalizing Economies*
Austin Smith et al., *Selected Works of Michael Wallerstein*
Regina Smyth, *Candidate Strategies and Electoral Competition in the Russian Federation: Democracy without Foundation*

Richard Snyder, *Politics after Neoliberalism: Reregulation in Mexico*
David Stark and László Bruszt, *Postsocialist Pathways: Transforming Politics and Property in East Central Europe*
Sven Steinmo, *The Evolution of Modern States: Sweden, Japan, and the United States*
Sven Steinmo, Kathleen Thelen, and Frank Longstreth, eds., *Structuring Politics: Historical Institutionalism in Comparative Analysis*
Susan C. Stokes, *Mandates and Democracy: Neoliberalism by Surprise in Latin America*
Susan C. Stokes, ed., *Public Support for Market Reforms in New Democracies*
Susan C. Stokes, Thad Dunning, Marcelo Nazareno, and Valeria Brusco, *Brokers, Voters, and Clientelism: The Puzzle of Distributive Politics*
Milan W. Svolik, *The Politics of Authoritarian Rule*
Duane Swank, *Global Capital, Political Institutions, and Policy Change in Developed Welfare States*
Sidney Tarrow, *Power in Movement: Social Movements and Contentious Politics*
Sidney Tarrow, *Power in Movement: Social Movements and Contentious Politics, Revised and Updated Third Edition*
Tariq Thachil, *Elite Parties, Poor Voters: How Social Services Win Votes in India*
Kathleen Thelen, *How Institutions Evolve: The Political Economy of Skills in Germany, Britain, the United States, and Japan*
Kathleen Thelen, *Varieties of Liberalization and the New Politics of Social Solidarity*
Charles Tilly, *Trust and Rule*
Daniel Treisman, *The Architecture of Government: Rethinking Political Decentralization*
Guillermo Trejo, *Popular Movements in Autocracies: Religion, Repression, and Indigenous Collective Action in Mexico*
Rory Truex, *Making Autocracy Work: Representation and Responsiveness in Modern China*
Lily Lee Tsai, *Accountability without Democracy: How Solidary Groups Provide Public Goods in Rural China*
Joshua Tucker, *Regional Economic Voting: Russia, Poland, Hungary, Slovakia and the Czech Republic, 1990–1999*
Ashutosh Varshney, *Democracy, Development, and the Countryside*
Yuhua Wang, *Tying the Autocrat's Hand: The Rise of The Rule of Law in China*
Jeremy M. Weinstein, *Inside Rebellion: The Politics of Insurgent Violence*
Stephen I. Wilkinson, *Votes and Violence: Electoral Competition and Ethnic Riots in India*
Andreas Wimmer, *Waves of War: Nationalism, State Formation, and Ethnic Exclusion in the Modern World*
Jason Wittenberg, *Crucibles of Political Loyalty: Church Institutions and Electoral Continuity in Hungary*
Elisabeth J. Wood, *Forging Democracy from Below: Insurgent Transitions in South Africa and El Salvador*
Elisabeth J. Wood, *Insurgent Collective Action and Civil War in El Salvador*
Deborah Yashar, *Homicidal Ecologies: Illicit Economies and Complicit States in Latin America*
Daniel Ziblatt, *Conservative Parties and the Birth of Democracy*